# JOHN STUBBS

# Jonathan Swift

## *The Reluctant Rebel*

PENGUIN BOOKS

## PENGUIN BOOKS

UK | USA | Canada | Ireland | Australia
India | New Zealand | South Africa

Penguin Books is part of the Penguin Random House group of companies
whose addresses can be found at global.penguinrandomhouse.com.

First published by Viking 2016
Published in Penguin Books 2017

001

Typeset by Palimpsest Book Production Limited, Falkirk, Stirlingshire
Printed in Great Britain by Clays Ltd, St Ives plc

A CIP catalogue record for this book is available from the British Library

ISBN: 978–0–241–96289–3

www.greenpenguin.co.uk

MIX
Paper from
responsible sources
FSC® C018179

Penguin Random House is committed to a
sustainable future for our business, our readers
and our planet. This book is made from Forest
Stewardship Council® certified paper.

Only one Thing I know, that the cruel Oppressions of this Kingdom by England are not to be borne.

*– Swift, writing to Benjamin Motte, 25 May 1736*

# Contents

# Illustrations

# A Note on the Text

With a few exceptions, dates are given according to New Style, i.e. following a calendar in which the year begins on 1 January rather than on 'Lady Day' (25 March). Quotations from Swift, his contemporaries and earlier writers are selectively modernized: that is, in practice, I have minimized the frequent italics in eighteenth-century printed literature, and occasionally altered punctuation for the sake of intelligibility. At the same time I have tried to preserve the feel of an early edition of Swift as much as possible. This has involved retaining for the most part contemporary spellings and the convention of capitalizing the initial letters of key words in the text.

# Introduction

One midsummer night in Dublin, 1710, two students made their way from a tavern in the heart of the old city back to the enclosure of Trinity College. They were in breach of the college curfew and, quite 'contrary to the former course of their lives', as they protested later, had taken drink.[1] The two undergraduates, Graffon and Vinicome, fell into company with a dubious character they knew called Harvey. For a lark, he suggested they get up on to the statue of the late King, which stood proudly on the wide street in front of the college.

At this hour the hub was quiet if not deserted. The shops on Dame Street and the warehouses in the alleyways had long been shut up for the night. The elegant, modestly Baroque front of Trinity was darkened. Across College Green to the north, also in shadows, stood Chichester House, where the Irish Parliament usually sat. It was an old building in a state of poor repair – much, it might have been said, like the Parliaments it hosted. The Irish Lords and Commons had little power, and often little wish, to argue with orders from London. The record does not show whether the three hi-jinksers had an audience. They might have had a spectator or two in a passer-by, from one of the high-gabled houses at the rim of the green, or from a college window in Trinity's wide complex. In theory, a porter should have been standing on duty at the gate, looking out for those 'haunting the town'.[2] The tipsy students were dressed in the plain, dark, inexpensive coats and britches that formed the basic undergraduate uniform, and must have stashed their academic gowns somewhere before making their ascent. Their target on the spacious thoroughfare was in Roman dress: in a skin of cold lead, mounted on his charger, the life-sized statue of William III raised his sword and truncheon towards the sleeping city and the stars. It was quite a climb to join him on his tall pedestal. Ornamental lanterns, as well as a lengthy

Latin inscription, offered hand-and-toe-holds; yet from the bottom of the granite base to the laurel wreath that crowned him, William's monument was some thirty feet high.

This expensive tribute had been installed nine years before, and inaugurated with a long procession of the Lord Mayor, aldermen, sheriffs, masters, wardens and councillors, while the crowds enjoyed cakes and hogsheads of claret set up on scaffolds. Since then it had been vandalized quite regularly. Trinity students were for the most part to blame. Over the years the royal effigy had been smeared with muck and festooned ironically with green boughs or sometimes with hay. The college was regarded by some in the city as a nest of Jacobites, and no doubt some of the rogue scholars were indeed supporters of Queen Anne's exiled half-brother, James Francis Edward, the 'Pretender'. Many of those who insulted King William's memory, however, may have had no quarrel with his status as the official saviour of the Protestant nations of Great Britain and Ireland; the hero of the 'Glorious Revolution' who had rescued the kingdoms from popery and slavery. Members of Trinity were upset that the King had been offensively set presenting his back to the gates of the college.

It was eight years since King William's death: with an irony that may have pained the city fathers who paid so much for the statue, he had been thrown from his favourite steed. In this latest assault on his memorial, the offending trio went further than previous miscreants. Their timing was particularly malicious to those who treasured William's memory. The anniversary of his most famous victory, at the Battle of the Boyne in 1690, would follow in a matter of days. The mud with which the three assailants soaped the King's grey face might be quickly washed away. The sword and truncheon they stole from his hands, though, would be difficult to replace before the annual celebrations on 1 July.[3]

Predictably, when Dublin's citizens awoke, any sniggers were soon drowned out by the offended uproar. Somewhere, having slept off their wine or their ale, Vinicome, Graffon and Harvey were also coming to – and evidently soon panicking about their sinful trophies. Within days, the Irish Parliament had reacted stormily to this 'great indignity' and demanded retribution. Queen Anne's viceroy, Lord Wharton, offered £100 in reward for information leading to an arrest. The Corporation of the City matched his offer with one of their own. Meanwhile a new truncheon was made and in a solemn ceremony placed in King William's unfeeling yet still princely hand.

## 2

A Dublin cleric with a growing literary reputation, Jonathan Swift, was in London when hands were finally laid on the vandals. Swift had taken rooms with a kind-hearted, huge-limbed and quick-fisted Irish servant, and moved in with a few boxes of clothes and books. Ostensibly his business in England was to lobby for a grant of money to the lower clergy of Ireland's Anglican Church – a Church he served with staunch devotion. In November, as Vinicome and co. were coming to terms with expulsion from the University of Dublin, a fine of £100, six months in prison and the prospect of standing for a dangerous half-hour on College Green, holding a card inscribed with a record of their crime, Swift was enjoying a rapid promotion in secular affairs. He had been courted and recruited by the Queen's chief minister, Robert Harley, to serve her new ministry as one of its leading propagandists. His job would be to discredit comprehensively the record of the outgoing government. Within a few months, enjoying the company and admiration of some of the highest-placed figures in the Royal Court, he would establish himself as the foremost political writer of his day. He was now a man who seemed, in total contradistinction to the reprobates who had desecrated the late King's equestrian statue, the epitome of an insider, a voice of the establishment.

Success had not exactly come overnight. At the end of November, Swift would be forty-three. He was middle-sized and plump in the face, his hair already thinning at the front, but his domed forehead and somewhat stocky physique gave him an air of both authority and strength. He strictly observed all decorum of dress, encasing his throat in clerical bands as occasion demanded. He was fastidious about the state of his shirts, his black frock-coat and fashionable periwig. He kept one black clerical gown for best and another for his daily walks around the city and sometimes beyond. Any indecency met a cold stare from his large and startlingly bright blue eyes. There were, nevertheless, delicate tinges in this rather forbidding exterior: a scholarly slope to the shoulders, gentle bow lips and a long bridge to a nose that was almost elegant. A small cleft chin nestled in a band of fat. When he spoke, Swift's pronunciation was meticulous, but his voice was somewhat high-pitched. And a trailing cadence in his accent may have told a careful ear where he had been born and grown up: for he was, to his regret, an Irishman.[4]

He provoked admiration and resentment in equal measure: since for every friend he made among the current ministry and its supporters, an enemy was confirmed amid the opposition. He had a commanding, patriarchal air that, alternating with an engaging ease in conversation, allowed him to speak freely almost regardless of rank. He reported proudly, on one typical occasion, of having scolded a former lord lieutenant of Ireland 'like a dog'.[5] He tolerated no foul language. He rarely smiled – and, as he grew older, was never heard to laugh. Behind or within this deeply, indeed painstakingly orthodox personage, however, was a character who took extraordinary liberties with the conventions of his time. This was Swift's other, mercurial self – one with the character and temperament of an unstoppable practical joker and, in some ways, a rebel. For, although at times his writing stemmed from a sermon-like and utterly didactic drive, the form it took was often most unsuitable for the pulpit. The hoax was his hallmark in a writing career that would span five decades. He spoke and behaved in the manner of a cleric, but at moments one had the sense this was merely one of his personae, one of innumerable voices he could do. His closest women acquaintances knew him, at a friend's suggestion and his own bidding, as 'Presto'.[6]

Swift's masters in the ministry – tubby, cunning Robert Harley and his handsome young rival for power, Henry St John – knew about this alter ego, Presto, although they directed their approach to the conservative priest. Swift had made his name with a number of highly respectable political papers. In one of them, he lamented the partisanship that was deforming the country – even though it had defined British and Irish politics for as long as anyone could remember.

> How has this Spirit of Faction mingled it self with the Mass of the People, changed their Nature and Manners, and the very Genius of the Nation? Broke all Laws of Charity, Neighbourhood, Alliance and Hospitality; destroyed all Ties of Friendship, and divided Families against themselves? And no wonder it should be so, when in order to find out the Character of a Person; instead of enquiring whether he be a Man of Virtue, Honour, Piety, Wit or good Sense, or Learning; the modern Question is only, Whether he be a Whig or a Tory, under which Terms all good and ill Qualities are included.[7]

Both these terms were originally insults: the Tories were named after Irish outlaws, the Whigs after Scottish cattle-drivers. But, while Swift sincerely desired to be 'above party', he would find himself driven to side with the former. On one side you had the Whigs, who in general supported the

'Low' Dissenting creeds that shunned the Established Church: on the other side were Tories, who were on the whole High Anglicans. Swift was 'High Church' – and was grievously afraid that the Test Act would soon be repealed, thus ending the legal restrictions that prevented Nonconformists, 'fanatics', as he called them, as well as Catholics, from holding public office. The guarantees Harley offered on this point were vital in persuading Swift to lend his pen to the new administration, which was backed by a large new Tory majority in the House of Commons.

A hidebound character, then, this Swift – or 'Jonathan', as Harley and St John insisted on calling him at their regular meetings and sometimes agreeable suppers. Yet the truth was equally that Swift had been brought on board for the mayhem he was capable of creating; as a mud-slinger, indeed, of infinitely greater subtlety and power than the drunken amateurs of his old college in Dublin. Whereas minnows such as Vinicome, Graffon and their ilk might satisfy and gratify themselves with a little idle hooliganism, Swift would prove a spirited crusader in defacing living heroes of the British cause: his targets from the autumn of 1710 included not only the ousted Lord Treasurer, the Earl of Godolphin, a mainstay in administration since the days of Charles II, but also a man who had proven himself the finest general the kingdom had ever produced – the Duke of Marlborough. Both, along with many of their associates – such as the Marquess of Wharton, Lord Lieutenant of Ireland – would lose their swords and truncheons to the campaign Swift was about to unleash against them.

It was a campaign of wit. For Swift was not only the moderately well-known author of essays such as *The Sentiments of a Church-of-England Man*. It was an open secret that he was also the alarming mind behind a book that shocked all who weren't entirely confused by it. *A Tale of a Tub* made extravagant fun of heretics, atheists and charlatans, but it did so by means of parody. To a careless or untrained reader, it could easily appear the work of a dilettante or a maniac: and this many took it to be, at no little cost for Swift. As we shall see, the *Tale of a Tub* is wholeheartedly concerned with defending the Established Church in which Swift was ordained. Yet the book didn't seem so orthodox to a good number of influential readers who were actually on his side in the struggle over social and religious change. His *tour de force* was at odds with the public persona he presented. The Archbishop of York, the Queen's closest adviser on Church affairs, was convinced that *A Tale of a Tub* was blasphemous, and utterly inappropriate for a priest to have written. Both the Archbishop and the Queen, Swift learned soon enough, were resolved that he should not progress far in the Church. For the present, he would prove simply too useful to his friends in the ministry to abandon. On his side, he declined all payment for his services; though he expected a reward in the form of an ecclesiastical preferment at some time in the near future.

An apparent self-contradiction was therefore written deep both in Swift's character and in his situation. At one and the same moment he was a stern authoritarian and a daring cultural bandit. Managing as best he could the torsion these tendencies created would make up a large part of the business of his life. The overall direction, however, in which these twisting forces would lead him was towards the side of the outlaws – the 'Tories' in the literal sense of that borrowed Irish word – and the precise location for his assaults on central authority would be his home city of Dublin.

Already, in December 1710, Swift was confiding firmly sceptical views about the political entity that King William had helped to create. A literary crony had angered him with an article:

> Steele, the rogue, has done the impudentest thing in the world; he said something in a *Tatler* that we ought to use the word Great Britain in conversation, and not England, [phrases such] as *The finest lady in Great Britain, &c.*[8]

The offending party was Swift's friend Richard Steele, and his paper, the *Tatler*, was one of London's most popular publications. Steele, an ardent but somewhat unsubtle writer, was often assisted by a mutual friend, Joseph Addison; and Swift had made a number of celebrated contributions to the paper himself. But here Steele was printing sheer heresy for one of Swift's disposition. The 'Kingdom' of Great Britain had been created by an Act of Union between England and Scotland in 1707. The supposed 'sister kingdom' of Ireland had been purposefully left out of the Act; an exclusion that would soon allow the country to lose in all but name the status it acquired from one of the three equal and technically separate crowns the ruling monarch possessed. Swift was cynical about the Act; but he was more hostile still to the notion of people blurring their national identities. The matter was especially important to him, as a Protestant born in Ireland. So long as cultural and ethnic distinctions held, he could always say, on account of his ancestors, that he was not Irish but definitively English.

He co-signed a letter to the *Tatler* that Steele duly published; but the protest quoted above was written to his closest friend. Having established his digs in London that autumn, he wrote to her every day his work and health allowed. The result was a long epistolary journal, throwing unequalled light both on Swift's private life and on the political culture of his day. The softer side of Swift's personality was reserved for the correspondent he had left behind him in the Irish capital. She was a young woman he had first known as a child when he came to live in England in his early twenties. They were separated for some time when he returned to Ireland, but, on meeting her again some nine years before, he persuaded her to move to Dublin; and took steps to ensure she remained his constant satellite. Now, having taken charge of a ministry-funded paper, the *Examiner*, he missed and worried about her in equal measure. Only the day before his harangue on Steele and 'Great Britain', he had written:

> I was dreaming the most melancholy things in the world of poor Stella, and was grieving and crying all night – Pshoh, 'tis foolish: I'll rise and divert myself; so good morrow, and God of his infinite mercy keep and protect you.[9]

His *Journal to Stella*, as the letters bundled together became known, would be full of 'Pshohs' and other expostulations – outbursts of sympathy, concern, exasperation; throughout which Stella was Swift's beacon. 'Stella' was the pseudonym he gave Esther Johnson, whom he admired for her 'beauty and virtue' but more specifically for her turn of phrase, force of character and intolerance of fools. There was talk that, a few years later, after his return to Dublin, they were secretly married. The truth seems to be that they merely lived within walking distance, saw each other daily and shared the deepest thoughts either was capable of uttering. Swift could take, and shrug off, the jests and charges of impropriety in the knowledge that he had never once seen her in the morning, and never without another person present – usually Esther's chaperone, the well-meaning but simpler Mrs Rebecca Dingley. Swift extended these precautions by addressing his letters from London technically to them both – though for much of them he was preoccupied only with the younger, more intelligent of the two.

Swift published all but a few of his works anonymously, yet he still stood out, by means of an arresting presence as well as superior prose; a guarded but still very public, noticeable figure. He was unsmiling, while comic; ruthless in print, yet touchingly sincere and sensitive in his personal relationships. He was a keen walker and rider, and strong in body; and he was extremely delicate on the matter of his personal hygiene. His cleanliness was peculiar in an age when a bath was still a rare event for the majority of any class. Meanwhile, you might say what you liked against Dr Swift – if you dared; the rather fearsome figure in his black coat and wig. But you could not escape having your attention caught by Presto, the spirit of play in Swift's nature; or by his stories and asides at the club or in the drawing room; or by the hilarious touches in his many sorties into print. Those who knew him also knew there was, however, another facet to Swift, which, for all his seeming robustness and indeed belligerence, could render him helpless in the space of minutes. In the trinity of his nature, along with Father Swift and Presto, the joking Son, this third element was a marauding unholy ghost.

From about the age of twenty Swift suffered from an acute disorder of the inner ear, causing vertigo and periodical attacks of tinnitus and deafness. He tended to treat the aural problems as symptoms of a disorder distinct from his terrible dizziness and nausea, though, in fact, they were both attributes of a condition diagnosed much later as Menière's Disease.[10] As years passed, an attack might leave him prostrate for weeks. With the sad perspicuity of the invalid, he learned to spot the danger signals in his abdomen and temples, the throb in hearing and vision that might spread and confine him within hours to a wheeling bed. Remarkably, the strain of continuously watching an inner horizon did not warp or closet him as much as it might another person. He remained a vehemently public personality. Friends knew of his fits, and sympathized. When he was older, political allies had rooms made up in which he could convalesce when he visited their estates.

'Stella' was his chief comfort in a world that often exasperated him. He suffered terribly from his bouts of dizziness and deafness; and made little secret to friends of his disillusionment with life but for the presence and love of Esther Johnson, assumed by most to be his mistress. Across town, however, there was another woman, who complicated the comfortable arrangement. Esther Vanhomrigh (pronounced 'Vanummery'), styled by Swift 'Vanessa', after both her names, was an Irishwoman whose family had relocated to London after the death of her father. Unlike Stella, who was guarded and watchful in company, Vanessa was outspoken and impetuous. Swift met her in 1707, and from that time became a regular visitor at the Vanhomrighs' townhouse. Again, apparently unlike Stella, Vanessa began to press Swift for more than the slightly flirty, wordy if still heartfelt friendship he offered her. She would make the mistake of believing he might one day relax the limits of that friendship. Managing the tension between these two contrasting characters took up much of Swift's considerable will-power and emotional strength. Yet both were integral to a select group of friends – amid a vast acquaintance – who stimulated him in writing his best known work.

Outside his lodgings – which he took, over the years, at various addresses near Westminster or St James's Palace – was a city that had never quite grasped the import of Copernicus's discoveries. By many of its residents, London was viewed very much as the centre of the universe. It held more than a tenth of England's five million souls. This half a million was unevenly divided between the fine townhouses and prosperous shops in the City proper, running from the Tower to Temple Bar, and the hovels of weatherboard and scrap timber struck up in spare nooks and outlying scrublands. In tenements near the port, a family of ten or more might share a single cellar room with pigs and chickens. Pits of deprivation and disease lay open on or near even the most prosperous streets, sucking at the ankles of business, progress and power, and the carriage-wheels of the peers and merchant princes with incomes of tens of thousands a year. London's new architectural language was imperious yet ornate, the Baroque, Continentally inspired façades of Vanbrugh-style mansions blending uneasily with the narrow and crooked terraces that had survived the Great Fire. The shopfronts spoke of luxury, French lace and Dutch ornaments: but there was no real surplus. Every twig on the commons had its use for fuel. Barrow-men heaped up the sewage and butchers' leavings from the gutters almost nightly, to sell to market gardeners out of town. The ornate medieval halls in Westminster enshrined a modern wonder – the world's only limited, or 'constitutional', monarchy: yet a wrong turn quickly taught you the rules that much of London ran on. Alsatia, the bankside sprawl south-west of Fleet Street, in the grounds of old Whitefriars, had only just lost its legal status as a sanctuary for the town's worst cut-throats and pimps. This was the realm of desperate yet sometimes exuberant vice that Swift's friend John Gay would immortalize – off-bounds to the decent, but known to every citizen.

At the turn of the century, the city had awoken to financial revolution. The Grocers' Hall, an infinitely more respectable old building in the heart of the old City, contained the future in its vaults. Appropriately close to the site of a temple dedicated to Mithras, the Roman god of contracts, this was the home of England's first national bank. At large, the country still generally assumed that it could live only on what the land would yield, and what the rents would pay. Taking lessons from the Dutch, however, English financiers had realized that banks could lend the government all it needed, and more than it could foreseeably repay, if a mortgage were taken on the nation's taxes. The Bank of England was created in 1694 with a view to financing the state, offering lenders a very fair return on the money they contributed. Here was the realm of the 'moneyed' men, the 'stock-jobbers'; a class that was destroying, in Swift's view, the 'landed' society that made up the true heart of England. He would spend his life fighting them.

Although Swift instinctively opposed any group or subclass threatening the established order, his work betrayed counter-cultural leanings of his own. Theoretically the literature of the day embraced refinement, proportion and stable magnificence as its presiding 'Augustan' values. Licence was granted for a writer to tackle debased elements with their own lack of decorum, but from a superior stance. Swift's imagination exceeded that licence. He was irresistibly drawn to the more basic, brutal and visceral areas of human existence. In consequence an uneasy doubleness found its way into his oeuvre. While writing for the government in the years 1710–14, he deployed his mastery of the Parnassian vein; his journalism is written with perfect classical hauteur. He maintained this mode of address for the rest of his life in letters to his former masters and associates. Notwithstanding such restraint and gravitas, he could at moments throw aside the etiquette of polite style: in *A Tale of a Tub*, he had already described, with bravura, an inmate of Bedlam hurling stool at his attendants. As Swift aged, a political exile in his country of birth, he gave greater freedom to such visions. Until the power of speech and writing deserted him, he would never lose the gift of composing a charming note or epigram; yet dark and cruel poems would follow, depicting the condition of ageing, partially disabled prostitutes; there would be a voyeuristic verse-tour of a lady's dressing room, crowing over stains that were otherwise concealed; and, above all, there would be the Yahoos, the naked beshitten bipeds, biologically human, who lob their droppings at an understandably offended Gulliver.

Large numbers of Swift's readers down to modern times would never forgive Swift for appearing to savour the horridness and fetidity he discovered in life. He seemed, such critics reasoned, simply at odds with humanity, and as such merited expulsion from reasonable discourse. Swift was, nevertheless, both a brilliant practitioner of 'polite conversation' and the supreme English satirist of decorous platitudes. As for the horridness, more precisely, he loathed the pretensions with which men and women cloaked practices he considered foul.

He was discriminating, but no crank. He liked a great many of the city's entertainments. The elder statesman of the stage, Congreve, was a friend; Swift himself was a moderate frequenter of the theatre, though a critic of the rabble in the pit or the brightly coloured gallants chatting through the play. When older, he urged that there was no harm in a young clergyman going to the theatre unless something lewd or subversive were being staged, and provided he left his gown at home.[11] This was evidently Swift's own practice before he became a recognizable figure in town; and even then, in 1713 he would feel free to attend the dress rehearsal of *Cato*, a politically inflammatory tragedy. Clerical garb, meanwhile, was no bar to entering a coffee- or chocolate-house like any other respectable citizen. Will's for the literati and Truby's for the clergy were two of literally hundreds of coffee-houses across the old City and its neighbouring boroughs. White's was famously a den for aristocratic layabouts – 'noble cullies', as Swift called them – gamesters in gold-laced coats by day, and often highwaymen by night.[12] Some coffee-houses vanished after weeks or months, leaving no record; others became institutions of the eighteenth century. Each had its own specialty, its sources of a particular brand of news – such as, in time, shipping at Lloyd's – but all were open to any decently dressed man who could pay a penny to enter and his bill upon leaving: earls and tradesmen were seen bending an ear to the same listener, who might be drawn from any (non-labouring) class or calling. The coffee-houses displayed the osmosis that was possible, under certain conditions, between regulated social levels. The chocolate, coffee and tea being drunk, the tobacco smoked and, when the craze for snuff came in, the sneezes heard were signs of a booming international trade. Like Turkish or Indian silk on the backs of the wealthy, such international markers were by now almost taken for granted; as was England's right to stake a claim on all such bounty.

The Swift we remember and admire today despised all of this; or at least we suppose that he did. As Dublin's foremost citizen in his latter years, he cried out against indulgent imported goods purchased at the cost of Irish tradespeople. We identify him, too, with Gulliver's outcry against imperialism at the end of the *Travels*.

> Ships are sent with the first Opportunity; the Natives driven out or
> destroyed, their Princes tortured to discover their Gold; a free License
> given to all Acts of Inhumanity and Lust; the Earth reeking with the

Blood of its inhabitants: And this execrable Crew of Butchers employed
in so pious an Expedition, is a *modern Colony* sent to convert and
civilize an idolatrous and barbarous People.

A second later, Gulliver seems to moderate this explosion by insisting
that he is not, of course, referring to British activities. But Gulliver's
defence of his countrymen's 'Wisdom, Care, and Justice in planting Colonies' nevertheless sounds very sardonic indeed. After a loyal digression,
Gulliver then tartly observes that the distant lands he visited showed
little desire of being conquered.[13] But at other moments, Swift was a
great advocate of international trade and not unsympathetic to the colonial project. In old age he still felt that his greatest achievement was the
part he played defending the Tory-dominated ministry of 1710–14. This
was a government that secured for Britain the *asiento de negros*, the
licence granted by Spain to trade in human lives in the Americas. Swift
defended the Treaty of Utrecht, which awarded Britain these rights,
rather than the gain itself; yet the *asiento* arguably taints his legacy as it
blights that of his country.

His heart and mind were each divided. Though 'reason' – the attribute he valued above all – would always show him where injustice lay,
and throughout his life he would charge against it, the English were his
tribe, and the idea of belonging to them raised and soothed his spirits.
The book we call *Gulliver's Travels* was in many ways shaped as a
response to a state of confusion. It is defiantly English, but reveals painful misgivings about the English themselves. It expressed in comic form
Swift's horror at ugliness, his despair at human depravity; but also his
wonder and amusement at the way things change with perspective. It is
a fantasy written with inimitable literalness.

It began as a creative pastime. In 1721, near the beginning of a ten-
year pamphlet war in defence of Irish interests, Swift informed his close
friend Charles Ford, 'I am now writing a History of my Travells, which
will be a large Volume, and gives Account of Countryes hitherto
unknown; but they go on slowly for want of Health and Humor.'[14] By
the time Swift wrote these words he had been living in Dublin for five
years as the Dean of St Patrick's Cathedral – his prize for serving the
ministry, awarded shortly before the Tories were swept away by a Whig
resurgence. By the time he began recording 'his' travels, his fixed habits
and traits had only grown stronger. He was still an obsessive walker and
rider, stringent as ever about keeping clean and the saying of prayers, a
prodigious worker in his study and a keen socialite in the parlour. He

was still prey to losing his hearing and his balance. Old concerns for expense were turning into parsimony. He was as devoted as ever to Stella. And by this time, Vanessa had gone to her grave without ever really forgiving him.

The 'history', published another five years later in 1726, took a while before it became Gulliver's, and not (explicitly) Swift's. If the long work began as an allegorical account of Swift's own tribulations, they in turn nourished a fiction with a life of its own. The *Travels* contained a record of Swift's time, yet has remained a classic of every age that followed. Then, as now, much of the book's appeal stemmed from its vibrant humour. For a considerable section of Swift's readership, however, the fascination and controversy of *Gulliver* lay with the debate over the verdict Swift reached on his contemporaries, as much as with the imaginative power with which he passed judgement.

The *Travels* was recognized immediately as a work of genius. While Samuel Johnson scornfully suggested there was little more to the work than the big men and the little men – the Brobdingnagians and the Lilliputians – unwittingly he identified perhaps the most elementary pull Swift's book exerts on our imaginations.[15] Most humans know what it means to feel terribly small and vulnerable, from infant experience; and most, too, know the grandiosity of picturing oneself as a giant such as those that stalk above and around us in our childhood. Gulliver's humbling transition from one state to the other captures an essential doubt people may carry about their ultimate stature and status in the world, since no one can see his or her own body or merits objectively. The resulting dizziness was reported in the earliest responses to the *Travels*: 'in some,' an old acquaintance assured Swift, 'the imagination is struck with the apprehension of swelling into a Giant, or dwindling to a pigmee.'[16] Swift's implication, a startling one for a clergyman of his dogmatic stamp, is that no objective measure exists. The strapping six-footer of one country is an insect in another, and the same principle might apply to whole civilizations: the giant King of Brobdingnag tells Gulliver that the people of Europe, for all their pomp, sound to him like an appalling strain of vermin.

## 3

Such assaults on the complacency, corruption and putative enlightenment of his time still lay ahead when the three young Dubliners faced the consequences for stealing King William's sword and truncheon back in the second half of 1710. In the end, as it happened, the Lords Justices were slowly persuaded that Vinicome and Graffon would be sufficiently punished without, after all, having to suffer a pelting by the mob on College Green. By the time he wrote the *Travels*, Swift half expected an hour in the pillory himself for his troubles. At a crucial interval in 1725, he would admit his need of a printer brave enough to risk his ears: since the hangman might clip them, and then put the offender in the pillory for publishing seditious material.[17] As time passed, even though cushioned by his status in the Church, Swift grew ever more convinced of the need to risk such penalties in the broader interests of justice. By the 1730s he was a hero and talisman in Dublin, known commonly as 'the Patriot', while styling himself 'the king of the mob'. When Chief Minister Walpole considered charging Swift with sedition, he was informed that a substantial army would be needed to storm the grounds of St Patrick's and make the arrest.

The figure of King William on horseback suffered further indignities over the decades. The statue's finely moulded features were gradually lost through botched restorations – the face became almost indistinguishable beneath 'repeated coats of paint'.[18] Towards the end of his life, Swift was a battered monumental figure in his own right. Although still technically an adherent of the original Williamite revolution, he was by then at open war with those who took the subsequent remodelling of the state to unwarranted lengths. He was also unafraid to signal a barely veiled contempt for the hero of the Boyne: though as a keen rider and lover of horses, he would firmly have spared King William's mount from any insult.

But he was never any great respecter of reputations. He embodied a paradox, since his radicalism stemmed from, or at least thrived upon, an extremely authoritarian, conservative outlook: and this was a feature of Swift that never changed until he lost his voice. He had always disliked modern things and ideas. 'I think therefore I am,' Descartes had proposed; Swift was unmoved. Doing anything, surely, was proof that you are something. In the teeming streets of Swift's Dublin or London, there was too much evidence of people existing, and all too few signs of them thinking.[19] As for Hobbes's 'The Life of Man is Nasty, Brutish and Short', the lives of too many Swift knew were nasty, brutish yet too long by a score.[20] His scepticism about the alleged advances brought by science became more robust the older he grew: later Swift despised Isaac Newton for his politics and personal malevolence. He belittled the mathematician as a conjurer, a sundial-maker and an 'obscure mechanic'.[21] He had gentler but still indulgent feelings for a thinker who was his younger, more idealistic friend, and who suggested that the world we perceive is nothing but a thought in the mind of God.[22]

It merely irritated him when, from early on 30 November 1742, Swift's birthday and the feast-day of St Andrew, the crowds of Dublin lit bonfires in his honour. Bells were rung, guns fired. The provincial city's fiddlers and rope-dancers joined the general salute in their own fashion. Dublin Castle, the seat of the Lord Lieutenant and his administration, maintained a dignified, offended silence. In the benighted deanery by the cathedral of St Patrick, the dominant crag on the skyline of the city's southern quarter, Swift sat immune to it all, in spite of the fact that the revelry was for him, commemorating his birthday. He was seventy-five. A series of strokes had left him all but silent. He still wore the black clerical gown of his office, but neglected his periwig. He was shaved regularly, but a long white beard ran down his throat. He sat quietly for the most part, took strolls around the house, and here and there surprised his guardians with a sudden remark. The exact expression he sought would generally elude him; at which he would shrug his shoulders or wander off. He would leave his meat untouched for hours, circling the long table where he ate in strict solitude, as if checking that it no longer lived, before deigning to pick at it.

Outside, on that November night in 1742, the people of Dublin were applauding a rebel and a national hero. He was the scourge of the province's English rulers: the defender of Irish trade, the Irish poor; the 'Drapier' who had laid the government low in its attempt to debase the Irish coin. When his long-standing housekeeper crept into his chamber to tell him of the celebrations, he dismissed her without stirring, replying only, 'it is all folly, they had better let it alone.'[23]

In his lifetime and immediately afterwards, he was lauded by some as a man of 'such exalted virtues, and as an author, possessed of such uncommon talents . . . that his parallel is not to be found either in the history of ancient or modern times'.[24] Such praise was voiced, nevertheless, in awareness of another school of thought, which regarded him as a beast. In this view, he was something close to a sociopath, certainly a misanthrope, who had maintained that people were nothing more than the mindless yet capricious apish brutes Gulliver encounters in the land of the Houyhnhnms. These opposing judgements are equal tributes to his impact as a master of controversy. This book is about the course that made him the most notorious writer of his day, a giant personality in

Georgian Britain and Ireland, and a champion or 'avenger' – in his unusual and puzzling Latin word, a *vindicator* – of liberty.[25] The superb aptness of this epithet has never been fully appreciated for the way it captures both the fury and sardonic bleakness of Swift's vision. He was not one fighting to create or install liberty; for liberty was dead. He was, simply yet mordantly, the self-appointed nemesis of those who had murdered it.

The liberty Swift for which sought revenge was very much an early-modern, English concept, but his basic enemy was tyranny, and he bequeathed to later generations a vocabulary and an attitude to deploy against abuses of power. He spoke for all those who in more recent times have felt only disgust and dismay for their supposed representatives:

> Let them, when they once get in
> Sell the Nation for a Pin;
> While they sit a picking Straws
> Let them rave of making Laws;
> While they never hold their Tongue,
> Let them dabble in their Dung.[26]

Swift came to equate the government of his day with a systematic betrayal of its duty. Accordingly his writing sought revenge. In this respect his creativity reached its pinnacle with a nonpareil work of political horror: the *Modest Proposal* of 1729, in which a deranged yet icily rational social pragmatist suggests that the babies of Ireland's poor might be butchered for food. A source of despair for Swift was that he could have no vengeance for his own unhappiness, a misery largely corresponding to that expressed so copiously and humorously in the *Travels*: the distress, namely, of a man who never quite belonged where he found himself. The first and worst cause of this suffering, in Swift's mind, was the place where he was born, and where – despite his best efforts – he would live out his days.

# 1. Ireland and the Civil Wars

We are slaves already, and from my youth upwards.
— *Swift, letter of 1733*[1]

## I

He was a near-abandoned, half-orphaned child. Although a Dubliner by birth, he would always insist he was English. He had English backing on this point, for Ireland belonged, thought London, to England.

Swift was born on 30 November 1667 – 'in time to save his mother's credit', he is said to have remarked.[2] He never knew his father, who died in March or April that year. Not long after his birth, his nurse took him from a moderately affluent home to live with her and her husband in Whitehaven. He is reported to have denounced his homeland on rejoining his relatives at the age of four or five, old enough to have settled opinions.[3] 'Sometimes he would declare, that he was not born in Ireland at all; and seem to lament his condition, that he should be looked upon as a Native of that Country; and would insist, that he was stolen from England when a child, and brought over to Ireland in a band-box.' Swift's early life, in this account, belonged in a folktale. The story of the boy in a band-box counts as one of his earliest inventions. The circumstances of his departure and return, a relative noted, 'gave occasion to many ludicrous whims and extravagancies in the gaiety of his conversation'.[4] The image of this precocious child would be easier to make out if we knew whether he already smiled and laughed as rarely as he did in later adulthood. In any case, Swift seems to have discovered early on the power of simultaneously amusing and chastising: yet, when one looks back from the pages of Gulliver's *Travels* at the figure of the gifted young performer both chiding and entertaining his elders, there is a more than a faint suggestion of Gulliver put on show in Brobdingnag – dancing and gambolling for the casual delight of astronomically large leering faces, and driven to the point of fatal exhaustion by his captors.

The scene for such anecdotes was a parlour in a Dublin townhouse belonging to one of Swift's uncles. The room was wainscoted and candlelit, with hangings on the walls for insulation, and no doubt a sooty gilt-framed canvas or two lending a further touch of dignity. Stout beams spanned the ceiling; in some parts, such a home might well have been a timber-framed construction in the Tudor style, but the newer brick dwellings retained the same compact economy. An angled chimney breast gave the company their warmth and the room its heart; what natural light there was from the narrow road outside filtered in through an oblong wood-cased window. It was an affluent setting compared with what young Swift had known with his nurse's family in Whitehaven – a labourer's or craftsman's cottage, smoky and matted with rushes, perhaps adjoining a comfortless workshop. Returning to live with his relatives in Dublin, turning up at a smart and imposing terraced house that rose sheer from the street, most likely capped with a steep sloping brick gable, he moved to more luxurious though possibly less relaxed surroundings. A man of his uncle Godwin's station could afford a dwelling with a fine stone door case; behind it, a smallish hall led into two large chambers, back to back, with a kitchen to the rear, and a steep tight staircase leading to another two storeys and an attic for the cook and maid.[5] Inside, the bourgeois women wore gowns that made noise as they moved. They built their hair into complex arrangements, displayed their throats and sported modest jewellery. The men wore decent suits, velvet and satin rather than workers' wool or hemp, silk stockings under their boots and white wigs on their heads. The indigenous Irish workers the young boy saw in the town or who served the family in varying capacities differed mainly from the English labourers and domestics he had known in the unfamiliar language they spoke with each other, or the shawls and tunics worn by some of those coming in from the country-side on market days. There were glimpses, in the streets, of harrowing poverty; in the family living rooms, all was richer and self-consciously elevated. Yet when he reviewed his early life, coming to Dublin for Swift could only mean moving down in the world.

Given the circumstances, his opinion of Ireland from (it seems) a very young age is no surprise. Returning to Dublin involved losing the pro-tection of his nurse, and the calmer if no doubt humbler environment in which she took care of him. But this is by the by. Notwithstanding his difficult infancy, history alone made it likely for a boy of English roots in Ireland to resist being classed 'a Native of that Country'. The colonists clustered behind boundaries erected or imagined in the cause of protecting their Englishness as well as their estates. The 'Pale', literally denoting a fence, was the name the English had long ago given to the horseshoe of territory around Dublin they controlled directly. The border was symbolic, naturally, as well as physical, and had always been reinforced by steady hatred and revulsion towards the 'other side'. The English preferred to maximize the differences in custom and attire they discovered between themselves and the native Irish. Comments on the native Irish residing in Dublin were confined more to their manners, since they were gradually becoming more Anglicized in their dress. Out in the Pale – and beyond – a common garment for both men and women was a peasant mantle, which could be worn cowl-like by day and serve as a blanket at night. The mantle always seemed extremely odd to English observers, notwithstanding its versatility; it became a rarer sight, it seems, later in the century.[6]

As might be expected, in reality Irish dress was diverse. The better-off women wore red petticoats, which startled (and beguiled) conservative eyes. They sometimes bleached their hair. Irish gentlewomen traditionally also wore linen hoods or distinctive rolls of linen on their heads, which could be variously arranged to give complex social signals. Irishmen belonging to the class of *scológ* – smallholding gentleman farmers – might be found in a blue swallowtail coat, sturdily tailored, and a fur-lined cloak.[7] Men working outdoors wore rough canvas doublets that reminded one observer of a saddle pack; those lucky enough to possess one added a woollen overcoat or a rough cloak of goatskin in winter. Trousers were more like leggings, close-fitting, and worn low on the waist. Brogues, made from cattle hides, were 'single-soled, more rudely sewed than a shoe but more strong, sharp at the toe'. The men had frieze or fur caps with 'lappets' that buttoned under their chin if need required.[8]

It is breathtaking how contemptuously the English wrote about the Irish in the two centuries before Swift was born. They defined the indigenous people variously as inhuman, as lazy, as barbarous – in the language they spoke, their oddly non-proprietorial attitude to the land, in their dress, their customs and their eating habits. As such, the English planters found it easier to justify taking land from the 'wild Irish' and sometimes massacring them, while insisting all the time that their horror was genuine.

The wild and (as I may say) mere Irish, inhabiting many and large provinces, are barbarous and most filthy in their diet. They scum the seething pot with a handful of straw, and strain their milk taken from the cow through a like handful of straw, none of the cleanest, and so cleanse, or rather more defile, the pot and milk . . .

Many of these wild Irish eat no flesh, but that which dies of disease or otherwise of itself . . .

These wild Irish never set any candles upon tables. What do I speak of tables? since, indeed, they have no tables, but set their meat upon a bundle of grass, and use the same grass for napkins to wipe their hands . . .

. . . the women wash their hands in cows' dung, and so gently stroke their dugs, yea, put their hands into the cows' tail, and with their mouths blow into their tails that with this manner (as it were) of enchantment they may draw milk from them.[9]

Fynes Moryson, an English official, set down these rather Swiftian observations about the cleanliness of Irish people early in the seventeenth century. Moryson was typical of many settlers in being deeply struck by the Irish landscape and its fauna while critical of the natives' apparent 'natural sloth'.[10] Another writer encapsulated the colonial attitude to the land in a sexual conceit.

This Nymph of Ireland, is at all poynts like a yong wenche that hath the greene sicknes for want of occupying. She is very fayre of visage, and hath a smooth skinn of tender grasse. Indeed she is somewhat freckled (as the Irish are) some partes darker than other . . . Her breasts are round hillockes of milk-yeelding grasse . . . And betwixt her legs (for Ireland is full of havens), she hath an open harbour, but not much frequented.[11]

So: while the people of Ireland were unspeakable the country itself, in the unlovely simile above, was a young woman to be deflowered, willingly or not.

Such attitudes prohibited the children of English migrants to Ireland ever regarding or describing themselves as 'Irish'. To be Irish, in eyes east of Dublin, was to be despicable or (perhaps still worse) 'occupied'. As in most colonial contexts, the idea of a pure – the English said 'mere' – native population was a terrible simplification. Although overwhelmingly Catholic, Ireland had experienced ethnic mingling for centuries, most recently as Scandinavian, Anglo-Saxon and Anglo-Norman raiders and traders visited and settled. Yet the later newcomers were fixated with the idea of not belonging to the native majority. Even the descendants of Norman settlers, although still Catholic and with many 'mere' Irish relations, emphatically described themselves as 'Old English'. These Old English were a breed apart, nevertheless, from the much more recently established families of Tudor and Jacobean colonists, and they were viewed with suspicion from London. The morass of ill-feeling poisoned Swift's attitude to the island from very soon after his birth. His view of Ireland and the Irish remained typical, broadly speaking, of the colonial class until he died in 1745. When he rose to defend the interests of Ireland, he acted firstly on behalf of the Anglo-Irish enclave. Yet, while feeling the need to distinguish himself from the natives, he refused to condone an imperial project that lowered them to the status of a raw natural resource.

He saw no contradiction between abhorring the native Irish and opposing tyranny. Being thought of as Irish was a deep embarrassment to him. Writing to a younger friend, Swift declared it shameful that any 'man of worth' should have to call Ireland his homeland.[12] Counting as such a man, he explained to another, older and rather rascally friend, was possible only if one was spared the hated epithet 'Irish'. One of his great grievances was the following:

> That all persons born in Ireland are called and treated as Irishmen, although their fathers and grandfathers were born in England; and their predecessors having been conquerors of Ireland, it is humbly conceived they ought to be on as good a foot as any subjects of Britain, according to the practice of all other nations, and particularly of the Greeks and Romans.[13]

Here Swift echoes Anglo-Irish (or 'Old English') complaints that had been heard since the 1630s, and indeed before. His story does not present a Damascene moment at which he decisively renounces these essentially racist ideas: indeed he expressed them here at the very height of his activity as a 'great Irish Patriot'.[14] There were moments, however, when he did lean away from such thinking, and expanded his sympathies. His career provides moments of minute variation in a climate of hatred. Nevertheless, the idea of being treated as an Irishman would always appall him. The sight of a Catholic peasant family's dwelling would repel him as much as it did Fynes Moryson almost a hundred years earlier. But over the decades Swift noticed that the people living in such conditions – conditions brought about by hardship and want as much as by cultural predisposition – were sometimes Protestant, not Catholic; the children and grandchildren, sometimes, of people 'born in England'. The fault, he gradually saw, lay with colonialism. By his time Ireland had been occupied and redivided by waves of conquest and plantation it was difficult to count. On each occasion the 'New Invaders', Swift observed, treated their predecessors as 'mere' or 'perfect Irish', and drove them into the worst deprivations of body and mind.[15] He came to sense that 'Native', 'perfect', 'wild' or 'mere', among the other standard expressions for those who had their roots in Ireland, were relative terms. The typical situation of the 'wild' Irish family was an image of the predicament in which the 'English' observer's descendants might very well find themselves when the next generation of invaders swept in. The real 'savages' – the real Yahoos, in Swift's nomenclature – were to be found authorizing such attacks from Westminster. This is to anticipate and indeed generalize the thought and writing of Swift's final decades; but by that time Ireland had become the equivalent of a close relative whom he felt free to criticize but would defend robustly if others took the same liberty.

By the time Swift was old, Dublin's chattering classes had long been emulating their counterparts to the east. In 1732 Edmund Lloyd, 'a citizen of London', assured Anglo-Saxon readers that Ireland was thoroughly domesticated.

> As the People of Ireland take a Pleasure in imitating the English in their Way of living, their Manners and Customs, so they do in their manly Exercises, Sports, Recreations and Vices – [such] as Back-Sword, Cudgels, Boxing and Wrestling; Bull-baiting, Cock-fighting, Hunting, Coursing, Hawking, Setting, Fishing; Cards, Dice, Billiards, [gaming] Tables, Draughts, Balls, Plays, Consorts of Musick, Singing, Dancing, Women and Wine.[16]

By then, however, Swift had shunned the mainstream effort to minimize the foreignness of Ireland. He had grown openly peculiar, in ways that were idolized by many and tolerated by most; and those who disliked it, he felt, could lump it. By his final decade, Swift was stressing the corresponding singularity of Ireland: both he and his country were victims, outcasts, dignified in spite of their oppressors. The depression and famine he witnessed in the late 1720s stirred Swift to write his indignant *Modest Proposal* in the voice of a psychopath suggesting that poor Irish children could be farmed as livestock. He responded furiously to imperial aggression or condescension. Ireland was expected to function without an autonomous Parliament, without its own mint and even without grain.

> I know very well that our Ancestors, the Scythians, and their Posterity our Kinsmen the Tartars, lived upon the Blood and Milk, and raw Flesh of their Cattle, without one Grain of Corn; but I confess my self so degenerate, that I am not easy without Bread to my victuals.[17]

Here, dealing with a well-meaning but meddling outsider, Swift upended in one ironic sentence the lazy hostile prejudice of Ireland as a feral place, and tossed the stereotype back in the teeth of those who nurtured it. '*Our* ancestors' (that is, pointedly, Swift's Anglo-Irish readers' English forebears) were the Scythians and Tartars – watchwords for cruel inhumanity in the discourse of the time. The people of Ireland, seemingly all Irish people, were implicitly not the real savages. Such conditions as those imposed by civilized England could, though, drive anyone to barbarity.

On its side, the indigenous Gaelic civilization of Ireland harboured its own, much more justified hatreds of the colonizing forces. Irish outrage was founded on depredations and massacres stretching back to murderous incursions in the reign of Henry VIII and beyond. The lack of quarter shown in subsequent rebellions was wearily familiar long before Cromwell's notorious campaign in 1649–50. In the space of a summer month in 1569 Sir Humphrey Gilbert ordered his men to put all captives to the sword, including women and children, and put their heads on display in his camp as he moved through the country. Sir Charles Blount, Lord Mountjoy, was still more methodical upon assuming command of the English forces in Ireland in 1600. A tenuous quiet held until the unequalled bloodshed of the 1640s, culminating in the massacres perpetrated during Cromwell's reconquest. Yet, in between such scarlet spikes on Ireland's timeline, the 'mere' Irish were subjected to the continuous trauma of losing formerly common land to the new planters, and of legal degradations codified by alien statutes. Though much of Irish culture was lost amid violence and suppression, voices and images of protest have survived. Eoin Ó Gnímh summarized the experience as one in which the natives of the land became strangers and exiles within it, looking in from the outside on the warmth and plenty of their invaders.

We starve by the board,
And we thirst amid wassail –
For the guest is the lord,
And the host is the vassal.[18]

Irish literature and music perforated Swift's sphere frequently: he is known to have listened to Gaelic musicians and even translated verse from Irish.

In the balance against England, he would always repudiate Ireland. But England, like Ireland, meant many different things to Swift, and he would refer to them all by the same word. There was an England he adored and one he loathed. When he praised England, he was thinking of an old, archetypal, rural Albion. His vision of this good place was homogeneous and radiant. The England he hated, meanwhile, was multi-levelled. The topmost layer of dishonour had been laid in his life-time: it consisted of the muck that covered the land when the Hanover dynasty succeeded to the Crown in 1714, beginning a long period of Whig ascendancy. The political writing of Swift's early maturity, and his unparalleled *Journal to Stella*, record his struggle to prevent this disaster in the last years of Queen Anne. The failure of the Tories furnished him with heroes and demons to rue over for the rest of his years. However, before the catastrophe of 1714, England was far from untainted in Swift's mind. He carried sectarian resentments forged in the aftermath of the Jacobite and Williamite revolutions of the late 1680s; and irresistible grudges he had inherited and absorbed in childhood.

When Swift was young, all regions of Britain and Ireland carried the memory of a prolonged mid-century disaster. A decade and more of rebellion and civil war had left heavy traces, of which his grandparents all bore their share. With regard to the wars' legacy of guilt and revenge, however, it might be appropriate to begin with the side of his family he could barely accept as his own.

## 2

The village of Thornton's single road runs along a scarp some eight miles north-west of Leicester. The ground drops steeply behind the thirteenth-century church dedicated to St Peter, where James Ericke, a Cambridge graduate, was presented as vicar in 1627.[19] Inside, many of the fixtures of worship used by the little community he served may still be seen: the octagonal font by the doorway, with Tudor roses carved in the entablature; the sixteenth-century pews; stained glass, dating from the 1300s, in an east-facing window. In the chancel arch, a final suggestion also survives of the rood screen, a feature removed after Ericke's time, in the years of the Civil War. Such fittings, reflecting patronage and local social ties, were given immense sacred importance by the ecclesiastical policy of Charles I in the 1630s. Charles was a reserved, formal ruler, but had a lavish and discerning taste in art. With the aid of the Archbishop of Canterbury, William Laud, Charles set out to restore a respect for ceremony and ornament that had faded from England's Reformed Church, and that a large section of the flock condemned as 'Papistical'.

By name, Thornton evoked a stronghold protected by thick brambly hedges. The place still gives the impression that anyone holding the church's vantage point would be hard to root out if the village closed ranks behind them. A measure of the thoroughness of Charles and Archbishop Laud's campaign to enforce conformity in the Church is that even the Vicar of Thornton was checked for unorthodox practice. For Ericke was closer by conviction to the 'Puritan' side, also sneeringly labelled the 'Godly' or 'Precisian' wing of English Protestantism. Priests such as he and those he spoke for increasingly had more in common with the more austere and more autonomous Presbyterian 'Kirk' of Scotland, and they resented the King for stifling their faith. In contrast to the regulations of the official liturgy, these Nonconformist Protestants put greater stress on spontaneity from the pulpit and personal inspiration from the congregants.

In adulthood sixty years later, Swift looked unsympathetically upon their plight. Branding such people 'zealots', 'enthusiasts', 'fanatics', to give a few of the terms applied to specific kinds of the godly flock, from early on Swift was to be merciless in describing the emotional convulsions that resulted from their worship. They were, he felt, adorers of wind, and their preachers nothing but belchers of spiritual sedition – whose 'eructations' 'were received for sacred, the Sourer the better, and swallowed with infinite Consolation by their meager Devotees'.[20]

In May 1634, Ericke was summoned to London to appear before one of the institutions that brought some of the strongest Puritan objections: the Court of High Commission, which heard and ruled primarily on cases of canon law. Not infrequently in the past, parishioners would report fellow members of the laity for 'atheistical' behaviour or other improprieties. The court, presided over by bishops, other senior clergy and respected laymen, also had the basic function of maintaining clerical discipline. Churchmen leaning towards 'Popery' and 'Puritanism' were equally subject to indictment and punishment; but the latter, the Godly stock, so their brethren felt, had been treated much more stringently since Charles had married a Catholic princess of France, Henrietta Maria. Constitutionalists, moreover, strongly disapproved of the commission's standard procedural instrument: the *ex officio* oath that obliged those being examined to answer all questions put to them. A person refusing to answer was transferred promptly to the so-called Court of the Star Chamber, dreaded for its arbitrary powers of imprisonment and torture.

In an age when all religious activity was strictly monitored and licensed, Ericke was accused and evidently convicted of holding an illegal prayer meeting in his brother-in-law's house. In an example of the fair-mindedness that in practice the commission often displayed, he was granted a further trial period in which to prove that he could still carry out his ministry as the protocols demanded. When this ended, his assessors were still unsatisfied; so Ericke was deprived of his living, and the village of Thornton was left to await a new parson. Ericke and his wife, both apparently of Leicestershire stock, put county and country behind them. They made their way to a new life in Ireland, where paradoxically, despite the overwhelmingly Catholic population, Dissenters could expect greater freedom than was possible in England. There it was impossible to police the Protestant settlers of diverse Presbyterian and more heterodox persuasions with the same rigour London could exercise on distant Thornton. That said, Laud and his ally, Thomas Wentworth, Lord Deputy of Ireland, the other leading exponent of the policy of 'Thorough' in Church and State, had every intention of extending the crackdown.

When the Erickes emigrated, King Charles was still enjoying the 'peaceable part' of his reign, a period that Ericke's grandson, Jonathan Swift, would always regard as the highest point in English civilization – an apex from which it rapidly decayed. He and similar-minded Loyalists were to have some difficulty smoothing over Charles's own contribution to this sad falling off. No ruler could hope to keep everyone happy; but Charles pushed his personal agenda too far to keep his regime immune to circumstance. After a series of missions against Spain and France ended in catastrophe in the 1620s, Charles had pursued a conciliatory policy towards the great Catholic powers since 1629. Protestant nationalist suspicions at home were further aroused by his refusal to commit troops to the genocidal vortex on the Continent, where the Thirty Years War was well into its second decade. The King's decision to rule without calling a Parliament was not in itself enough to incite a rebellion; but it deprived him of a store of trust and goodwill when his government was beset by external crisis. His single greatest mistake was to try forcing his reform of the Church north of the border. In 1637 an adapted version of the English Book of Common Prayer was issued in Scotland, and the Kirk was required to follow the liturgy it prescribed. The result was a National Covenant defying the prayer-book, and then open revolt. Swift would allude to these Covenanters and Scots generally as dwellers in a 'Land of Darkness' (supported by some malicious wordplay in Greek) and the source of that lethal spiritual virus, 'inspiration'.[21] Two unsuccessful military campaigns, known painfully as 'The Bishops' Wars', obliged the King to seek funds from an unfriendly Parliament. By the summer of 1641, Scottish forces had occupied Newcastle; Charles's credibility had been further damaged by developments in foreign policy; while in Ireland, fatally for the King, a coalition of rebellious elements moved to exploit his weakness.

The Old Irish aristocracy had been driven to the point of ruin, especially in the north, by new waves of English and Scottish plantation from the second half of the previous century. With the decay of the native earldoms, the older social order they supported was also placed in jeopardy. James I had explicitly regarded the Catholic Irish as 'half subjects', excluded from public office and with no real say in Parliament. Vast expanses of land that, although unplanted, had formed their estates were either confiscated or mortgaged away by the Irish lords themselves. Every act of self-assertion was deemed treasonous, exposing the Gaelic families to further forfeiture. By 1641 it was now almost fifty years since their previous great campaign against the English and Scots, under the leadership of Hugh O'Neill, the Earl of Tyrone. O'Neill was the last of their number with a credible chance of unifying them and becoming their king: but after some inept and ineffectual responses from Elizabethan generals, notably the second Earl of Essex, the rebels were eventually laid low. Many of the Irish earls, along with large numbers of their followers, fled for the Continent. In romantic moments posterity likened these exiles to a skein of wild geese. They never flew back; but then, the winter they were fleeing never ended.

In 1641 a number of Irish lords and gentry saw their moment in the weakened King's predicament, and mustered arms and reinforcements from their exiled kinsmen. Their rising against the settlers began in

Ulster on 22 October, and within two days they controlled much of the
north. Planters were dispossessed and driven out; some were killed. A
plot was also laid in Dublin to seize the Castle and supposedly murder
the chief members of government. Yet from Dungannon the day after, a
proclamation by one of the rebel generals insisted they were not in arms
against either the King or his true subjects. The expression might be
termed the standard safety clause of early-modern rebellion: it would be
published many times over the next decade, even as thousands died in a
single day of fighting in or against armies commanded by Charles and
his generals. But until they reached the point of identifying the King as
the source of their problems, his enemies were often sincere in adding
this caveat. Sir Phelim O'Neill, after a relatively bloodless opening to the
insurgence, declared that he and his men were merely defending their
long-usurped interests. Their rebellion officially began on the day it
was defined as such, when the government in Dublin termed it 'a most
disloyal and detestable conspiracy intended by some evil-affected Irish
papists'.[22]

The declaration of a state of emergency, and the discriminatory
grudges it supported amid the growing panic in the Pale, placed the Irish
Papists who were not so 'evilly' disposed in a very awkward, not to say
perilous, position. An Irish Parliament was still in session, and the Catholics attending it protested their loyalty to the King and his deputies in
Ireland. A considerable dilemma confronted the Old English, the faction
mentioned earlier, those Catholic descendants of English colonists who
had settled in Ireland before the Reformation.

The Old English movement towards a 'Confederation' with the Old Irish
had little of political calculation about it. It was driven much more by the
sparsest of concerns for survival, as the peace between long-neighbouring
groups gave way with terrifying speed, and Protestant magnates began
indiscriminate attacks on Catholic estates and homesteads. In many cases,
reprisal for the northern uprising was a mere pretext for basic acquisitional
urges, with the distinction between soldier and civilian rendered a memory.
A particularly chilling directive from the Lords Justices in Dublin would
target and condone attacks specifically on Catholic women.[23] A great share
of the guilt for the rebellion belonged to these women, it was said, for stirring their husbands to arms. Such orders took the combatants and their
victims far beyond the normal conventions of warfare, and could only
darken the cycle of revenge. By the end of 1641, fighting and pillaging had
swept across Ireland, with the government's forces struggling to hold on to
Dublin itself.

The Puritan Erickes emphatically belonged to the class of most recent settlers who sought refuge in, or at least protection from, the island's Crown-held fortresses. The Erickes were also among those who, not only in Ireland but across all three kingdoms, were seized with terror and anger at news of massacre. The Papists were said to be slaughtering Protestants, spearing and burning their children in numbers that were simply impossible, yet which, from the latter months of 1641 and throughout the war, were given total credence by a public growing insatiable for vengeance. The Erickes' daughter Abigail was born in 1640. From the earliest age she was thus enveloped both by fear of real danger and by paranoid hatred fuelled on decades of territorial rivalry. Where exactly the family spent the war years has never been established. They could well have joined the numbers understandably leaving for safety with relatives in England or Scotland; but equally they might have stayed in the Irish capital, where Abigail met her husband twenty-odd years later. There their fate lay in the hands of two men who would successfully navigate all changes of regime over the next generation, and who would in time be good friends to the Swift brothers: James Butler, Earl of Ormond, who eventually led the King's armies against the rebels, and Sir John Temple, a privy councillor.

Ormond's family, although Protestant, had been settled in Ireland for generations, and so he was able to understand the rebels' anger if not support their actions. He was well qualified not only to fight them on home territory but also to negotiate with them. Temple, meanwhile, a product of a more recent colonial initiative, typified the subjugating attitude that despised the native Irish absolutely. Though born in Ireland, and educated at Trinity College, he had spent most of his time before the rebellion in England. His intransigency on national questions no doubt did much for his mental stamina in organizing a food supply for Dublin Castle as the rebels threatened the Pale; but it also closed his mind to all the human complexities of the situation, the validity of perspectives other than his own, and in his incendiary account of events, *The Irish Rebellion* (1646), it led him to perpetuate anecdotes and statistics he was well enough placed to know were exaggerated or entirely false. It is notable what a different mind his son Sir William, Swift's patron, would bring to such questions, both in his diplomacy and in his essays. Yet the agnostic son's position in life allowed him literary luxuries unavailable to his father. In Sir John's narrative, the Irish war involved a stark explosion of evil against just rule. He reported how the rebels, having taken control of the north, were simply incapable of restraining their lust for murder: 'then they could control themselves no longer, but in a most fierce, outrageous manner, furiously broke-out, acting, in all places of that Province, with most abominable cruelty, such horrid massacres and execrable murders as would make any Christian ear to tingle at the sad commemoration of them.'[24]

Sir John Temple collected accounts and depositions that had already reached sympathetic English ears in rougher form than his powerfully written, learned and rhetorically astute chronicle. An avid English and Scots public was quickly brought to the point of frenzy by apoplectic pamphlets such as James Cranford's *The Teares of Ireland* (1642), and countless more still less distinguished publications: these Temple summarized and codified. Such testimonies tended to multiply tenfold or more the deaths and casualties that surely did occur, as long-standing local scores were settled. Temple's rendering of events, *The Irish Rebellion*, thus unfolded a catalogue of burning, drowning and indiscriminate slashing, children being fed to swine, Protestants stripped naked and driven naked 'like hogs' to places of execution by rivers and in wildernesses. Irish children, claimed Temple, were trained to kill English children. The book certainly still has the power to move, through its combination of striking polemic and circumstantial detail. It is worth studying for both, since both aspects would have their effect on a still highly impressionable Jonathan Swift when he entered the household of Temple's son, Sir William. An alleged atrocity that may have found its way into Swift's imagination was the boiling alive of a twelve-year-old in a cauldron.[25] The book would be retrieved and reprinted at almost every crisis involving a 'Papist threat' well into the nineteenth century – when its editor claimed Temple's history was so 'faithful and exact' as to require no external confirmation.[26]

The authenticity of Temple's account was tainted when scholars questioned whether the colonial population really could have provided a thousand victims for a mass drowning at the single bridge of Portadown in County Down.[27] As many as a hundred, however, may well have been thrown to their deaths there. The official contemporary estimate of 150,000 Protestants murdered greatly exceeded the total size of the colonial population. Where Temple is, however, more credible, if some of the emotive detail is toned down, is in describing the refugee crisis that ensued as dispossessed planters escaped to Dublin. With nauseating speed, rebels closed in on the capital both from the north and the south; and while the garrisons of the Pale struggled with the military emergency, Temple and his fellow administrators were confronted with the problem of feeding and often clothing a population enlarged by 'the daily repair of multitudes of *English*, that came up in troops, stripped and miserably despoiled, out of the North'.

> Many persons of good rank and quality, covered-over with old rags, and some without any covering than a little twisted straw to hide their nakedness. Some reverend Ministers; and others, that had escaped with their lives, sorely wounded. Wives came, bitterly lamenting the murder of their husbands; mothers the death of their children barbarously destroyed before their faces; poor infants ready to perish, and pour-out their souls in their mothers' bosoms ... Thus was the town, within the compass of a few days after the breaking-out of this Rebellion, filled with these most lamentable spectacles of sorrow, which, in great numbers, wandered up and down, in all parts of the City, desolate, forsaken ...[28]

Somewhere amid this panic and want, or not far from it, we can place the 'reverend Minister' Ericke and his family – possibly missing the comparatively quiet quarrels of Thornton. In William King's chilling words, 'those that escaped got away with such circumstances, that the memory of what they had suffered was as ill as death.'[29] Such memories, in one form or another, were carried by Swift's mother, Abigail; in her pulse and nerves, perhaps, rather than in distinct images she could consciously recall. They have a bearing on her actions in the winter of 1667/8, when she either turned a blind eye to her baby being taken from her Dublin home, or even actively conspired in his removal. Allowing for a moment that the mid-century history of Ireland, in particular the terrors of 1641, had some bearing on Abigail's outlook, it should also change our view of Swift's 'abduction'. In this light, his journey with his nurse to England re-enacted an earlier flight, an evacuation. When he was born, it might just be that the spirit of a crisis long before took over Abigail Swift; and, in an Irish emergency in those times, you took what you could carry and got the children to safety.

## 3

It was a rebellion, wrote Sir John Temple of the Irish rising in 1641–2, 'so *execrable* in itself, so odious to God and the whole world, that no age, no kingdom, no people, can parallel the horrid cruelties, the abominable murders, that have been, without number, as well as without mercy, committed upon the British inhabitants throughout the land'.[30] The fear and humiliation suffered by the planters, Temple makes clear, was the most unbearable thing of all. From Dublin Castle, the Lords Justices therefore called for reinforcements.

English troops were dispatched to Dublin; 10,000 more from Scotland descended on County Antrim to the north; in Westminster an 'Adventurers' Act' was passed to raise money for a still greater invasion. While some in the colonial establishment, such as Ormond, had hopes of restoring the previous balance, fragile though it had been, the initiative now lay with those demanding a more drastic solution. The bait of rebel property to be shared out in victory, some two and a half million acres of it, proved irresistible both to the public and to Parliament. Much doubt, however, surrounded the question of whether King Charles might be trusted with a force of the magnitude required. First, his military record was less than inspiring; and second, some held reasonable suspicions as to what he would do with such an army when it had finished its job in Ireland.

The Protestant interest in Ireland had to wait more than a decade for the Catholic rebellion of 1641 to be completely extinguished. It would take longer still to redress the dishonour they felt they had suffered at 'savage' native hands. To complicate matters, the Protestants were divided in themselves, between supporters of the King (whose entourage in fact included many Catholics) and comrades of Parliament and the Scottish Covenant. The worst suspicions the latter group held of the King were confirmed by the intermittent truces his forces agreed with the rebel Catholic Irish 'Confederates'. The Royalists were led by Ormond, by 1644 a marquess and lord lieutenant, who, although he claimed to prefer English rebels to Irish ones, was perpetually compromised, in the eyes of the godly, by circumstance and his own divergent inclinations. While frequently condemning their actions, he could never entirely lose his view of the Catholic Irish gentry as his neighbours, fellow subjects and indeed members of the same species. During the King's last months, Ormond found himself at the head of a desperate and, in hindsight, unworkable coalition made up of his remaining Cavaliers, Confederates defying a papal threat of excommunication, and former Parliamentarians appalled by the prospects of a republican revolution.

Thus for a long time 'true' Protestants had to console themselves with the occasional capture and vivisection of a rebel commander such as Lord Maguire, harried at his final prayers by the Sheriff and a Puritan minister before being hanged, drawn and quartered at Tyburn in 1645. They could breathe easier when Ormond's gathering of reprobates was defeated at the Battle of Rathmines in August 1649, but comprehensive relief would come for them only in the shape of Oliver Cromwell. He and his New Model Army arrived in the late summer of 1649, and set about performing the unflinching conquest that Sir John Temple had awaited for many years. The earlier Lord Lieutenant, Thomas Wentworth, had declared himself 'thorough'; but he seemed lenient and slapdash beside Cromwell. Combining reserves of fanatic energy with systematic patience, Cromwell thrived by a preternatural gift for judging the moment, commitment to detail and an all but unwavering conviction that he was doing God's work. This unity of purpose and conviction deprived King Charles of his right to rule and indeed to live, in Cromwell's mind; it also progressively narrowed his once permissive thoughts on freedom of conscience. Cromwell in the end had little compunction about suppressing the Nonconformists he had at one point defended in his ranks. Papists he viewed as damnable by definition. In reaching a fervent sense of the proper political order, and seeing no other person but himself qualified or elected by God to uphold it, he, in fact, became a mirror image of Charles in his own kind of absolutism.

The series of engagements and sieges Cromwell oversaw from September 1649 destroyed the Irish Confederacy. It also gave the Old Irish – the 'natives' who were presently uprooted from their homes in the fertile eastern and midland counties – a counterpart to the Protestants' incendiary horror stories of the 1641 rising. Cromwell's conduct at the sieges of Drogheda and Wexford would confirm him for ever as both a monster and object of horrified fascination for Irish nationalism. Yet, even when his orders were brutal and merciless, they still followed protocols that were largely accepted in his day. Whatever his views at prayer, in the field Cromwell thought like a soldier: although Papist rebels such as Sir Phelim O'Neill would have their own account to settle with the almighty, they were entitled to quarter. They surrendered this right, however, if they declined to exercise it when offered, and thus obliged an opposing general to risk and sacrifice lives in giving battle or storming a town. In permitting the bloodshed that ensued when walls were breached, some historians have argued that Cromwell was acting as a conventional seventeenth-century general rather than as a sectarian fanatic. His prosecution of the Irish war put Anglo-Irish families such as Swift's in a paradoxical, not to say deeply hypocritical, position. They abhorred

Cromwell for the judicial murder of Charles, but condoned the events at Drogheda in autumn 1649.

The caveats that put Cromwell's military principles in context, like the empirical factors that reduce the number of Protestants actually killed in 1641, do not in any way diminish the insensate horror of the butchery itself, nor its impact on the communities involved. A measure of the ferocity at Drogheda, for example, is that distressed and repentant accounts of the massacre later began appearing even from veterans of Cromwell's army. On his return in 1650, the brother of the English antiquary Anthony à Wood told his mesmerized relatives of how the assailants picked up children and carried them as shields, 'to keep themselves from being shot or brain'd' as they fought the last resistance coming from the city's main church. Thomas Wood still could not or would not admit the stain the massacre left on him personally; he shared Cromwell's belief that the beleaguered Papists deserved the death they had met. After all of the combatants in the church had been slaughtered to a man, Cromwell's troopers descended to the crypt, where 'the flower and choicest' of Drogheda's female population were hiding. When a young woman pleaded with him for her life, Wood tried to help her escape over the city walls – perhaps for a price. She was run through on the parapet by one of his comrades, who saw what he was attempting. Seeing there was no hope for her, rather than leaving her to die of her wound, Thomas threw her over. His mercy forgotten, or in any case rendered pointless, Thomas took care to relieve the dying woman of her money and jewels before pushing her over the battlements.[31]

None of Swift's immediate family seem to have been directly involved in the military campaign that swept on from Drogheda, and that Cromwell left in the hands of his son-in-law Henry Ireton in 1650. An English minister of James Ericke's complexion might have been expected to justify the Cromwellian operations on religious grounds from the pulpit; but there is no evidence as to whether the former Vicar of Thornton followed the official doctrinal outlook of the new Commonwealth. In this exceptional period, individuals of a seemingly set persuasion frequently defied expectations. Contradictory currents of conscience, loyalty to family or patrons, or the force of personal experience very often caused people to change tack. Ericke's private convictions, for instance, might have taken him further towards the now ostracized and suppressed elements of dissent, such as the Levellers, which unreservedly condemned the slaughter in Ireland. Had he done so, the greater the subsequent cause for scandal would have been among the Swifts, his young daughter's in-laws. Conceivably, Ericke belonged to the sizeable group within the Presbyterian side that felt Parliament had gone too far in executing the King. Supposing that Abigail respected her father's politics, her alliance to a fervently Royalist family suggests that the Erickes may not have been out-and-out Cromwellians. But Ericke would still have belonged to a broad consensus of English and Scots Protestants who, other differences aside, saw Cromwell's conquest as a just retribution on the Irish.

The grim work of subduing rebel-held towns and cities such as Limerick, Galway and Duncannon was complete by 1652. A further spell of skirmishing, dying out in exhaustion, famine and plague, ended in 1653. By then the task of driving all and any suspected of involvement in the rebel Confederacy off their land – 'to hell or Connaught' – had gained momentum. It was largely accomplished by the time Cromwell died, in 1658; and it was not reversed when the monarchy was restored and the younger Charles was obliged to satisfy a further clamour for reward and restitution.

It is impossible to say how deeply Abigail Ericke shared the religious attitudes for which her father had been thrown out of Thornton thirty years earlier, since nothing is known exactly of his fate beyond his emigration to Ireland. Swift himself never mentioned even that; in his brief memorial, he preferred to prune the branches of the maternal family tree.

> Mrs Abigail Erich of Leicester-shire descended from the most antient family of Ericks, who derive their Lineage from Erick the Forester, a great Commander, who raised an army to oppose the Invasion of William the Conqueror, by whom he was vanquished, but afterwards employed to command that Prince's forces, and in his old age retired to his house in Leicester-shire where his family hath continued ever since, but declining every age, and are now in the condition of very private Gentlemen.[32]

Here Swift was repeating what he had heard as a child, and reinforcing it to preserve continuity and propriety in his beginnings. Nothing too personal should be read into this against Abigail herself. Swift pays no greater attention to his father or uncles than to her. Yet there is no gentleman more 'very private' in Swift's story than James, his maternal grandfather, who is not mentioned at all.

# 4

To follow the experiences of the paternal side of Swift's family, it is necessary to trace the course of the Civil War in England. And this means
first going back to late 1641, as Parliament mobilized its adventurers to
assault the rebels in Ireland.

Politically, by Christmas 1641 Charles I was all but disabled. He had
lost his two chief councillors: Wentworth was tried by Parliament, convicted, and lowered his head to the block with striking and disdainful
calm earlier in May that year, while Laud was shut up in the Tower for
the long wait before his own inevitable execution in 1645. Attempts to
bring the shattered English army to London by groups of 'Cavaliers' – a
term previously reserved for dandies and dubious gallants, but now
scornfully bestowed by pro-Parliament protesters on the officers who
made up a self-appointed royal bodyguard – only deepened widespread
distrust of the King. Other ministers had fled. Charles himself meanwhile was forced to give up key powers to Parliament. It was, however,
Parliament that overplayed its hand: the concessions it forced from
Charles involved a drastic shift in the balance of constitutional power,
leaving the monarch little more than the figurehead of state. With Scotland and Ireland still torn wide open, a conservative backswing occurred
in England as the nation recalled that Charles, for all his faults, was still
its lawful sovereign. In the spring and summer of 1642 he regained
support and sympathy, and mustered an army. Charles, rather than
Parliament, formally began the English Civil War by raising his standard
at Nottingham that year in August.

The English Civil War has always been taught as a clash of Cavaliers
and Roundheads; the former being insouciant and dashing, the latter
puritanical and intransigent. Yet one should really bear in mind that
Charles and his most committed supporters were every bit as fanatical
as any of their enemies in Parliament. Charles could not concede that the
cause of a monarch anointed by God could ever be lost. This was a doctrine fundamental to the Lutheran 'magisterial' Reformation rather than
the later, more volatile Reformed creed the Puritan divines preached
from Edinburgh or Westminster. It reasoned that, while the Church of
Rome may have lost all claim to be either holy or apostolic, the princes
of Europe still held power by divine right. For what basis, Charles asked,
did the political order have without him? For generations to come, those
who cherished his memory asked the same question; and those who

sought to innovate the constitution struggled to make their answers heard. Some of the strongest ideological commitment to the King's position came from within the ranks of his clergy. This was unsurprising since, just as the Church supported the monarch's divinely justified claim, so the God-given ruler validated the true Church he commanded. 'No bishops, no king,' Charles's father had intoned long before; and the reverse could in theory be equally true. For if there were no king, people might found whatever Church they please. It was a lesson England's bishops learned soon enough, when they were abolished by the freely careering Parliament. Grudges bred grudges in return, and satisfying them demanded ever more barbarous remedies. Nonconformists had long resented their treatment under Laud's primacy in the 1630s; now the suppression of episcopacy fomented militancy and vengeful desires among those who supported its old form under Charles. As good an example as any of the passion of clerical Royalism can be found in the experiences of the Reverend Thomas Swift, the Vicar of Goodrich and Rector of Bridstow, Herefordshire. As his more celebrated descendant observed, Reverend Swift undertook and suffered more for his prince 'than any person of his condition in England'.[33]

Beyond memory, the village of Goodrich occupied a strategic point on the River Wye, among the low hills of southern Herefordshire. Watching over it is an ancient stronghold, of which the existing form was begun in the twelfth century. Its defining features are a fine square keep and massive blast marks on its outer walls. Over the centuries, Goodrich Castle was a seat of the Earls of Pembroke, Shrewsbury and Kent, but throughout successive eras retained its original purpose of commanding the ford below and controlling communications with nearby Symonds Yat in the Wye Valley. It remained a key fortress in the region during the English Civil War. If the story is true, it is almost certainly here that Thomas Swift, by then in his sixties, set out one day in wartime from his little estate near the village below. He was wearing a waistcoat packed with gold. While other local bases changed hands frequently, Goodrich Castle was held almost throughout the war by the Royalist Sir Henry Lingen. Reverend Swift, so his sympathizers claimed, was on friendly terms with the Governor – who, on receiving the priest and no doubt pouring him a glass, asked him for a donation to the Royalist war chest. At this, the tale continues, Reverend Swift took off his coat, and held it out to his host. The Governor politely declined the gift, taking the garment as both a show of loyalty and a modest plea of poverty, 'observing it to be worth little'. 'Then take my waistcoat,' answered his guest. Presumably with some effort, he removed and held it out, insisting the Governor take it. Sir Henry was startled by its weight. When the Governor ordered a servant to rip open the lining, 300 'broad pieces of gold' spilled out. Reverend Swift had raised this extraordinary sum by mortgaging his lands in Goodrich, leaving his wife and dozen children with all but nothing.

Reverend Swift himself had designed the house he and his family occupied in the valley below. It was still standing when his grandson, the Dean of a distant cathedral, wrote a short tribute to him. In its style, the house suggested the amateur architect was 'somewhat whimsical and singular, and very much a Projector'. But, as the writer reflected, colourfulness along with clericalism ran in the family: Thomas Swift's father, William, the Rector of St Andrew's, Canterbury, and a prebendary at the cathedral, had been a 'person somewhat fantastic'. As the Civil War progressed, in the course of which the strange little house at Goodrich was raided some thirty-six times (though 'some say above 50'), the parson devoted his singularity of mind to defending the world of his ancestors. His father, who was born in 1566 and died in 1624, had been a preacher of modest distinction. Thomas's grandfather, also Thomas, who was born in 1535, in the opening stages of the English Reformation, had occupied the same rectory in Canterbury through the later Tudor struggles of the Church until his death in 1592. A house and glebe were small sacrifices, to the Vicar of Goodrich, for the sake of an order both personal and divine.

Although the Swifts' most celebrated descendant would outdo them all in whimsy and eccentricity, not even the Dean could rival one wartime stratagem he attributed to his grandfather Thomas. It exhibited something of the ruthlessness that the satirist was forced to confine to his writing. Looking to the river flowing close by Goodrich, and 'having a head mechanically turned', Thomas Swift manufactured a set of iron barbs consisting of three prongs hammered to stick out at angles – one of which, however the implement rested, would always point upwards. These he took under the cover of darkness and rowed out into the ford below Goodrich Castle. Zeal and the inherited concern his grandson would also display for physical fitness evidently gave the ageing churchman little difficulty shifting the heavy, unwieldy metal spiders. The next day, in Swift's family legend, when a rebel cavalry division attempted to cross the ford, some 200 of their men were thrown and either trampled by their wounded horses or were themselves impaled on the spikes the vicar had dropped into the water. For Jonathan Swift, 'mechanical' was rarely a complimentary term in defining intelligence; but the Dean also showed a grasp of engineering detail in devising and describing the contraptions observed by Gulliver on his travels, and indeed gave Gulliver himself a talent for such things. He clearly considered the country parson's 'engine' (as it would have been called) a fine stroke of practical wit. The device displayed, moreover, sound knowledge of classical history: for Reverend Swift was surely inspired by the stakes the ancient Britons used to hinder Caesar's crossing of the Thames.[34] Regardless of how real or how deadly in truth his 'engines' were, his grandson thought their use was entirely justified.

Royalist apocrypha also record that Swift's paternal grandmother, Elizabeth, née Dryden, was another versatile character. Her resourcefulness, it seems, was both more credible and more sympathetic than that of her husband, the Vicar. A book Swift knew and recommended, *Mercurius rusticus*, a compendium of heroics performed by supporters of the King, tells how she spent most of the war – like many women on either side of the conflict – doing her best to keep a roof over her family's heads. Her task was a heavy one, since she was in the end the mother of fourteen children. In October 1642, on hearing that their home was likely to be plundered the next day, she took action that may well have displeased her husband: she went immediately to the nearby Parliamentarian commander, the Earl of Stamford, and pleaded that her home be spared. 'According to his good disposition', the Royalist account goes on (with heavy sarcasm), the Earl sneeringly threw her written petition back at her, and swore with ugly oaths that she could count on a visit from his men. He did not, however, count on his supplicant's presence of mind. Abandoning her first (rather optimistic) plan, Mrs Swift immediately hurried back to Goodrich, where she managed to clear the house of almost everything of value by the following dawn.[35] She could not be so vigilant against the many future raids by Parliamentarian troops, although Reverend Swift seemingly took steps to fortify the house. In December of the same year, soldiers under the command of one Captain Kirle were unable to force the Swifts' front door and gained entry only by sawing through bars that had been set in the window. Enraged by the delay, they picked the house and its occupants bare. It was a good thing that by this time Reverend Swift had presumably given away his waistcoat. The Swifts' children, including no doubt Godwin and his younger brother Jonathan, were swung about and dashed against the walls when they held on to their clothes and bed linen. The raiders had no mercy either on the humblest or the youngest in the household: 'They took away all his Servants cloaths, and made so clean work with one, that they left him not a Shirt to cover his Nakedness. There was one of the Children, an Infant lying in the Cradle, they rob'd that, and left not the little poor Soul a rag to defend it from the cold.'[36] When the maid begged the men to leave a little pap for the baby's gruel, they took even that. They went so far as to tell the village miller that if he baked another loaf for the Royalist brood, 'they would grind him in his own mill.'[37]

Many of such details are doubtless both generic and added here for extra effect; but they also reflect the suffering reported by civilians on either side in the war. If Captain Kirle's horsemen and dragoons did not take the Swifts' last crumbs, the pantry was clearly often empty. The story of Elizabeth Swift is one of hundreds that say much about how goodwill and patience in divided communities – and English societies at large – were all but exhausted by the conflict. Her entry in the partisan literature describes how Elizabeth economized and negotiated, dealing with the nitty-gritty matters that kept her family in house and home. Her husband seems to have gone into hiding: he ended the war in prison in Wales. Back in the village of Goodrich, when plunderers stole the family's horses, Elizabeth traded to retrieve them. They were stolen again almost immediately, as she probably knew in her heart they would be. Perhaps most remarkably of all, she kept her older sons from being caught up in the fighting itself, either as conscripts or as volunteers inspired by their father's politics. Godwin, the eldest, would have been almost twenty and highly eligible for active service when Charles made his last call to arms. Most English families finished the war with a martyr or more who fell in the field or were jailed for one or other cause. More still emerged with experience of hardship, grinding worry and trauma.

It would be hard to say whether the Swifts were made safer or placed in greater danger by the Royalist fortress above them, which held on stubbornly for almost four years. The King's garrison weathered frequent attacks and undermining operations on the castle's thick medieval walls. Then, in 1646, Parliamentary forces rolled up a giant mortar that, it is said, was developed especially for the capture of Goodrich. The huge gun, nicknamed 'Roaring Meg', discharged a 200-pound shell and left a gaping hole in the castle's southern side. The fall of Goodrich joined a wave of more celebrated victories for the Parliamentary Roundheads, reorganized into the New Model Army and inspired by the command of Sir Thomas (later Lord) Fairfax and his already infamous deputy, Cromwell. By the end of 1646 Charles's Cavaliers had been crushed; and, despite one last push in 1648, later termed the 'Second'

English Civil War, what largely remained for Parliament was a clean-up operation. This culminated in the trial and execution of the King, addressed by his captors as 'Charles Stuart', in January 1649, and left a delicate alliance of victors in a constitutional void. From this vacuum, however, a radical and at first exciting constitutional experiment took shape: a short-lived republic known as the 'English Commonwealth'.

The reform of King Charles's Church and State was put in motion, wherever possible, long before his death at Whitehall. In the purging of 'delinquent' clergymen, one as militant as Thomas Swift could not expect to escape notice. The ageing diehard evidently had no wish to, either, wanting nothing to do with a decapitated 'new model' Church. In 1646 he was deprived of both his livings. He seems to have received his verdict of 'ejectment' *in absentia*, and may, in fact, have been on the run for some time. During the war years he is last reported as being incarcerated in another former Royalist base, Raglan Castle in Monmouthshire.[38] Since Wales provided Charles with one of the last refuges where he could deny the reality of his impending defeat, Reverend Swift may have journeyed to join the royal entourage there. In theory, since Charles stayed a few days at Hereford during the mournful summer following the defeat at Naseby in June 1645, the Vicar possibly even travelled with the King's party to Monmouthshire. Charles rested at Raglan Castle, the seat of the Marquess of Worcester, through much of July. There his retinue enjoyed 'sports and entertainments' and peaceful church services as in former times, living for a while as if the war itself had been a mere interlude.[39]

Yet in time Raglan also caved in, and the King's retreat became a prison for followers such as Thomas Swift. It may even have been easier for him there than at large, where the post-war kingdom was being redrawn. Many years later, his grandson brushed off the minister who replaced Reverend Swift at Goodrich as 'a fanatical saint' – one whose beliefs were closer to those of James Ericke.[40]

Royalists would refer to the next decade merely as an 'interregnum', a space between reigns. In this, technically speaking, they were somewhat inconsistent, since they also held that Charles's son and namesake, a loping, dark-haired and conspicuously sensuous teenager, succeeded him the moment the headsman brought down his axe. For Jonathan Swift, who appointed himself the bearer of the principles of his grandfather Thomas, the Civil War epoch left a manifold legacy of wounds to resent. He inherited, that is, all the hatred of the rebels and timeservers to Church and State; but he also developed more personal, less consistent grudges of which he may have been only partly conscious. He made much of a dubious connection to an old Yorkshire family led by a great Loyalist and patriot whom he dubbed 'Cavaliero Swift'. The relationship was genealogical fantasy, but it shows where and with what Swift felt he belonged.[41]

In May 1660 the new – or renewed – King returned from his 'low and wandering Condition' in Continental exile. Charles II's garments were almost threadbare: Parliament, on inviting him to take up the throne, was obliged to buy him a bed and provide for a new crown and sceptre. The cloth of silver and gold lace he wore on his entry into London was specially ordered for the occasion, since the trappings of majesty used by his father had been lost or broken up or pawned in the decades of war and republican rule. The Commonwealth, despite early successes and the potential that John Milton, sore-hearted as well as blind, still saw in it, had divided England into 'cantons' and decayed into a dreary and deeply unpopular dictatorship. The death of Cromwell took away not only its head but its backbone. In a matter of months Charles found that 'multitudes of his Loyal Subjects [who] had not, until this time, openly owned his Majestie but had lived at home with the hazard of their lives & fortunes, under the oppression of Barbarous Tyrants' were now avowing their loyalty and stood ready to welcome him back.[42] A relatively small retinue had stayed with the thirty-year-old exile in his years of vagrancy, and perhaps that was just as well so far as the new regime was concerned. The fewer who had seen Charles's Court in its uncertainty and need, the better.

Nowhere in the three kingdoms was the detente more delicate than in Dublin. Ormond, soon made a duke, and reinstated as the Lord Lieutenant, was remembered for surrendering the city to Parliament rather than to the Confederacy in 1647; but also for then taking command of the Irish rebels, for his part in the ongoing carnage and for fleeing the country towards the end of 1650. Working relationships between the Duke and the Lords Justices, many of whom were also veterans, would take time to restore. And, just as the restored monarchy had its memorabilia of a martyred king, individual families had mementos of the heroes who had suffered for his sake. The households of the Swift brothers held precious heirlooms from a line deprived of its birthright – including a chalice used by their father the parson, and his priestly vestments. Portraits of their grandparents, the Reverend Mr and Mrs William Swift, hung as sacred images in Godwin's home. Their grandmother was said to have had an habitually sour expression, and their grandfather, as mentioned earlier, had become something of an eccentric by the time he died; but their portraits and other effects were passed down the generations with all due solemnity.[43] As the Swifts' grandchildren grew up in Dublin, the veneration bestowed on such relics was all the greater since they were symbols of a way of life that had been dislodged, damaged or destroyed. It was, in fact, the fragility history had exposed in these family treasures that made their inheritors attach all the more power and significance to them. The same principle was true of the larger, institutional remnants salvaged from the shattered older order.

The family 24-year-old Abigail Ericke joined by marriage in 1664 was beginning to prosper, protected by a sense of long-delayed and well-earned victory. It is hard to assess the Swifts' real difficulties in material if not emotional terms in the 1650s. Thomas had died in 1658, the same year as Cromwell, too early to regain his benefices or temporal possessions. As a boy, his grandson heard a story in which Charles II vowed that he would have honoured the Reverend Swift's long record of service if the aged and combative priest had lived into the Restoration. The younger Jonathan Swift also heard, though, that his grandmother would often say, 'More of your Lining and less of your dining' – less silverware and more actual food on the plate.[44] The matriarch's expression summed up many years of shrinking expectations. Given the fate of others like him, Reverend Swift's death probably spared him further painful disappointment. The restored King may have known his name; but then Charles knew the names of so many worthy followers. He could not help them all.

Times had no doubt been hard for the recalcitrant Swifts. Yet, despite undoubted poverty in comparison with their former condition, Thomas and Elizabeth were able to have their sons educated: Godwin and his brothers, regardless of the Restoration, had set out on a reasonably safe professional path by the latter days of the Commonwealth.

One at a time, from the late 1650s to the early 1660s, three of Thomas and Elizabeth's sons found footholds in Ireland. Their third boy, Jonathan, gained a place at the King's Inns in Dublin in 1660. Their fourth, William, was working as a solicitor in the city by the end of the year. The eldest brother, Godwin, having begun practice in London, was called to the Irish Bar in 1663. There was too little land to satisfy everyone the new King was honour bound to pay off; but there were more than enough lawsuits to benefit the three young attorneys. Uncle Godwin was 'an ill pleader' yet 'dexterous in the subtil parts of the Law'; possibly a little too dexterous, his nephew thought. Jonathan the elder was also making respectable progress in the city's legal fellowships when, in 1664, he was made a 'steward of the house' at King's Inns. He apparently felt his prospects allowed him to marry, as he did so the same year. By then he was surely well advanced in establishing a 'reputation for integrity with a tolerable good understanding'.[45]

Getting on in Ireland, as the Swift brothers did – by widening their legal practice and, before long, by acquiring property in the country – called for additional toughness in those seeking to prosper. All the defining traits and hardships of the time that were present across the Continent were to be found in Dublin and around the Pale. Men carried blades openly in public, and the glint of armour was no strange sight. Women belonged to a virtually separate species, irrational and manipulative to the complacent male mind, and prized by men ultimately for their ability, when basic desires had been satisfied, to produce heirs who might acquire further holdings. Towns carried the memory of pestilence; the fields and roads, like most of Europe, had recently hosted soldiers in their tens of thousands, in campaigns when any settlement crossed by troops might reasonably expect its homes and crops to end the day as ash. Toil and horsemanship, candlelight, sore eyes and dirty utensils, inns, mud-tracks, duels, infant coffins and inexplicable, remorseless and untreatable pain were among the standard imagined properties associated with that era. Making one's way in Ireland, moreover, took extra thickness of skin. One had to close one's eyes and harden the heart to the evidence of mass persecution that littered the countryside, often in the form of abandoned houses and herdless pastures. Through the 1650s Catholics had been driven in thousands from their fertile holdings in the north and midlands into the barrenness of Connaught in the west. Transportation to a life of slavery in distant plantations was a regular experience for those running foul of blatantly corrupt courts. Impressment on to English ships was a common fate, meanwhile, for Irish mariners who took their chances at sea. Much of the Irish 'protest literature' to have survived from this period expresses sympathy with the families of Old English descent who were transplanted westwards: solidarity the Old English, protesting their Anglicism to the last, tended not to reciprocate towards their fellow Catholics. A poem in Irish written in or around 1658 described the miseries commonly experienced by indigenous Catholic people: it is known by a title that, roughly translated, means 'Alas, alas for the day of my death'. In one place the speaker echoes, strikingly, the English terms of abuse and legal procedure used so frequently against his people; and, as if in the counter-motions of a tide, he sees new colonists roll in as entire native communities ebb out. He observes the sherifal courts at work:

Should a judgement ever go our way, in one of these litigations, then a bribe will immediately change the judge's mind. One man waits for 'execution' of sentence; another cannot pay the bumped-up fees the court demands. When I think of English, all I hear is 'Transport! Transplant! Shoot him! Kill him! Strip him – tear him. A Tory: hack him, hang him, rebel! A rogue, a thief; a priest, a papist.' And so we leave, willingly or not, in our thousands, for exile in Spain; while they, in their hundreds, arrive at every harbour in Ireland.[46]

Among these incomers, from the late 1650s on, were Godwin Swift and his brothers; and their professional lives immediately involved them in the very processes that brought such despair to the Munster poet just quoted. Those 'mere' Irish (and Old English) who tried to fight for their property received no more reparation under the Restored Monarchy than they had clemency under Cromwell's Commonwealth. To be Irish was to be regarded as 'A Tory' – meaning *tóraidhe*, an outlaw and a fugitive. The Gaelic Brehon Laws – one of the oldest legal cultures in Europe – had been all but crushed, and with them Irish expectations of a fair hearing. However much a good Protestant may have doubted the humanity of Papists, he would need an especially watertight heart not to be moved by the cries for clemency raised not only in verse but orally and immediately in Ireland's townlands. When such a catastrophe is experienced only through paperwork, its claim on basic sympathies is inevitably diluted. In this context it is notable that Swift's foremost health problem throughout adult life was a disorder of the ear, and that the single great injustice he refused to fight openly in his homeland was the treatment of the native Irish; both, to stretch a point, hint at a desire not to listen – to the complaints of an enemy, and the promptings of conscience.

## 5

What effect did the family saga have on the very young Swift? It would be unsurprising if the Erickes and Swifts were somewhat straitlaced, unsmiling people, and passed their sombreness on to their celebrated offspring; although a fore-glimpse of Swift's latent zaniness can also surely be seen in the idiosyncrasies and ardour of his paternal grandfather, the redoubtable Reverend Swift of Goodrich. The larger question of family influence can be brought into focus by considering how

Abigail's son might have turned out had the status the grandfathers held in his eyes been reversed – had Swift, that is, been brought up to venerate James Ericke as well as (or even instead of) Thomas Swift. If this had been the case, the story of the Dissenting minister might well have produced in Swift one of the leading literary voices of the English Nonconformist tradition. In consequence, Swift's brief record of his family history would pass down to us the adventures and fate of a Puritan. As it happened, Swift *would* achieve his greatest literary fame for writing the adventures of a Nonconformist: Gulliver belongs to Dissenting rather than Anglican stock. There is surely a buried identification with the figure of the disenfranchised castaway in Swift's creation of Gulliver, and this subtext radiates appealingly towards the fate of Swift's half-known maternal grandfather. But Swift gave his character a Dissenting background for manifestly satirical purposes: it emphasizes, for one thing, the disguise he lent a protagonist whom the fiction's earliest readers identified as his own alter ego. Gulliver may be the heir of Bunyan's Pilgrim, and he may appeal to the Christianity of pirates; but he is remarkably *un*-Godly and indeed quite materialist in his everyday thinking. He has Puritan Crusoe's practicality but much less of the earlier adventurer's fatalistic piety.

Viewed somewhat formulaically, the Swifts' fervent Royalism, plus an understandable tendency to count the pennies, had their outcome in Swift's own passionate conservatism and something of a fixation with financial detail. One of his recurring satirical devices was to expose a corrupt position by totting up its cost in the most literal-minded way imaginable, to devastating comic and moral effect. His Royalist background and fascination with currency and expense are best exhibited in a short piece for the *Tatler* that Swift himself does not seem to have written, but that he inspired with the over-generous gift of a 'hint' he later regretted. The idea was for a history of the seventeenth century in miniature, told through the adventures of a 'splendid shilling'. The coin is minted from silver carried to England by Sir Francis Drake and put through myriad transactions before gaining novelty value as a minor antiquity. The shilling speaks of its shame during the Civil Wars when used to levy soldiers for Parliament; only to lie 'undiscovered and useless' during Cromwell's rule. In a typically Swiftian reversal, the shilling misses its retirement shortly after being found and squandered by a hard-up Cavalier.[47]

The shaping influence of the Civil War period on Swift is really too great and diverse for a single example to capture. The epoch needs to be read into every chapter of Swift's biography. The wars left the institutions Swift claimed to love vulnerable to further irresistible change; they also disfigured his parents' childhood, and dislodged his paternal family from the place where they belonged. Most heinously of all, they indirectly caused Swift himself to be born in Ireland, and made him the product of a union of 'High' and 'Low' religious backgrounds. They led him to idolize his origins, but to dislike his home country. The wars could even be held responsible for Swift's hatred for change and indeed the movement of time itself, which he would always regard as shifting in the direction of irrevocable decay. The outcome in Swift's writing was irreconcilable fury at all subverters of the constitution; a mixture of despair and disdain towards a rebel homeland; and, most enduringly, the final aversion felt by Gulliver for a Britain rife with the Yahoos that, in Swift's later mind, the mid-century rebellions had created.

# 2. Upbringing

Like as the arrows in the hand of the giant: even so are the young children.

– 'The Thanksgiving of Women after Child-birth'[1]

I

Swift regarded childhood as a time of chastisement and mortification. He felt humbled by his upbringing, and later criticized almost all those concerned with it.[2] Being a child, for him, entailed having one's wishes and pleasures systematically crushed – and rightly too, in his later opinion. His public career makes sense only when one understands the two desires he managed to harness together: an urge to dole out punishment and an irresistible delight in making mischief. In his first book, he would speak of satirists treating the general public as they would a little boy they had the duty of caning. Swift gladly took up the birch in this profession, but refused to kiss it when occasion seemed to demand. One of his lifelong traits, of refusing to accept blame, surely stemmed from a connection in his mind between criticism and helplessness. To be criticized, let alone satirized, meant being shamed; it meant feeling like a boy again.

The sense of victimhood was compounded by his Irishness. Hating Ireland, however, did not equate with liking England, since he resented England for abandoning him to Ireland. Emotionally as well as physically, his life passed going back and forth between the two islands, a prisoner of the Irish Sea.

The Liffey leaves her source just twelve miles south of Dublin, then winds a course of seventy miles or so through the hills before dividing the city between her two banks and running into the sea. For generations, her waywardness transmitted itself as far as the opposite shore, as sea traffic leaving Wales for Ireland invariably fell into a wending and frustrating path on its journey westwards. First-timers cursed the journey that enfolded them in its redirections. A party finding they had missed the packet from Chester would trail through the dispiriting countryside of Anglesey, to waylay a smaller boat in hope of making a crossing from Holyhead. But, even if they were lucky, on setting sail they might still not sink the shore for another twelve hours or longer. During such spells experienced passengers would resign themselves to their fate and fish for gurnards in the upper depths. It was not a voyage assisting dispatch.

The trip brought sea-sickness, frequent storms and, till the second half of the seventeenth century, often chase from pirates or French privateers. Ships from England and beyond ideally needed a safe and efficient harbour to offload their goods and collect raw Irish produce. Instead, when they had raised the mountains backing Dublin Bay – the travel-book commonplace spoke of Naples minus Vesuvius – they met 'a vile barred haven', offering no shelter, and impeding most ships of more than 400 tonnes. As Sir William Brereton put it earlier in the century, 'the harbour is very naked, plain.'[3] The blustery bay would often force them into moorings a good march from the city itself, frequently by the hill of Howth on its northern side. Sometimes the winds would scatter them altogether. And then, instead of the navigable waterway that merchants needed to pursue their interests inland, they encountered the Liffey, flowing heedless of their priorities on her winding route, and rising two fathoms at high tide.

Travellers of means who disembarked on the spit of land at Ringsend committed their effects to one or more of a band of permanently ready waiting porters, and took a coach along the Liffey into town. Going west towards the centre, they passed Trinity College in its spacious grounds, and came up to the sinking walls of the medieval city. They entered through one of the eastern portals, Isolde's Tower or the stout Dame Gate, and passed into an old if not ancient, overcrowded settlement.

This was where Vikings of the eighth or ninth century had first fortified their camp, on a south-bank ridge commanding the estuary. Initially it had served as a loading point for the loot the Norsemen plundered from monasteries inland, and the Irish they captured and enslaved on their raids. Gradually it became one of outlying Europe's more important centres of trade and craft. In Norman times a rough square of stone walls boxed in the town; a fortress was added and first one cathedral, then another, outside the battlements. St Patrick's stood on an island created by a wide fork in a river that flowed on into the Liffey. By the time Swift's relatives reached Dublin, the last of the thatched medieval buildings had been replaced by tiled terraced houses of two or three storeys. Rough plaster may have covered stone and brick, but the crooked streets were unpaved; and the irregular, improvised layout of narrow tangling streets preserved the character of the Middle Ages. Swift has always been taken as fixating on the dirt and faeces in his birthplace; but ignoring the muck took considerable powers of denial. The streets were open sewers, through which pigs and other household animals trotted freely. As in London, hawks frequently descended to the thoroughfares to pick off a rat or unattended rabbit, or simply scavenge in the waste. By the 1600s, custom had led residents to tip their rubbish and their privies through holes bored long ago in the increasingly vestigial city walls. A complaint of 1489 spoke of how 'dung-heaps, swine, hog-sties, and other nuisances in the streets, lanes and suburbs of Dublin infect the air and produce mortality, fevers and pestilence.' One historian reports how little had changed by 1661, when official protests were lodged again at identical problems. The 'sturdy beggars', unfortunates for whom Swift would have very little sympathy, had been a drifting feature of Dublin's street corners for as long as records existed.[4]

One traveller observed convincingly that he had difficulty distinguishing the 'figure' of the original Dublin, 'because the walls are [so] covered with houses that one cannot well surround it'.[5] The governing classes clung as much as possible to this old city, making the best of it – even though the original site resisted the imperial, classical air they gradually sought to impose on their capital. The old town would not surrender its historical character. Outside the walls north of the Liffey, the colonists and other blow-ins had a clean sheet, more or less, to build or dream of building on; but here in this first quarter they had the antiquated, tumbling structures of an earlier Ireland, convents and abbeys, to work around and convert. For all its vulnerability to modern warfare, the seat of colonial power itself, the Castle, was more stubborn than anything else. Occupying the south-east corner of the fortifications, the Lord Lieutenant's residence lay behind a dry moat, drawbridge and portcullis, and an uncertain wall, sitting in a perennial state of decay, awaiting the next rebellion to break down the latest incumbent's sprinkling of superficial improvements. A stone rood hundreds of years old, the market cross, a vital urban landmark, place of congress and anchor for devotion, proved much more durable than a cage rigged up in the corn market, during Cromwell's time, to punish idle boys and women.[6]

The middle of the old town, and its heart, was taken up by the first of Dublin's two cathedrals, Christ Church. Standing on higher ground, this was the administration's place of worship and the religious venue for state occasions. However, it dinned throughout the week with social, commercial and litigious life. Tradesmen had long taken over the cloisters of the old sanctified grounds and set up shops there. The fine if weathered abbey house standing beside the cathedral now sheltered the law courts. From Christ Church, old Dublin spilled out in all directions, and the cathedral stood in the middle of the perplexing network of medieval lanes (lost beneath the dual-carriageway system that now isolates the cathedral near Wood Quay). Close by was the Tholsel, an ancient double-fronted pile serving as Dublin's exchange, rather small for the crowds who pressed through its arcades, and where the civil dignitaries marched by in their gowns on their way to hear service on Sundays. Statues of two kings, Charles the martyr and his reigning son, watched down from plinths on top of the arches.[7]

Wealthy and more rarefied neighbourhoods were found in the southern district, within and beyond the walls, sticking near to the Castle for safety. Strolling or looking towards them, in the direction of the Wicklow Mountains, one contemplated an urban horizon dominated by the tower of Dublin's other cathedral. Christ Church might try to look down on the cathedral church of St Patrick's, but its steeple still seemed lower than the merlons of its sister church and rival. St Patrick's had been built in a somewhat odd location, a shallow basin, with the nearby river seeping underground and frequently flooding neighbouring houses. It was said that ordinary graves became troughs as soon as they were dug; and it was common to see corpses lowered into water.[8] For several generations, nevertheless, the chapter of a normally affluent cathedral had grown accustomed to making the best of testing situations. Unlike Christ Church, during the Reformation St Patrick's had for periods lost its official existence.

An official or a dignitary returning to the capital would usually head westwards, inland and usually south, then, on disembarking, towards his house or lodgings, or to make an appearance at the Castle. Swift's relatives had houses in this quarter; by the time he was middle aged, the outlying south-western district where St Patrick's towered, in the 'liberties' beyond the old city proper, would decline into one of the poorer parts of town.[9] In the early 1660s the streets closer to the Castle within the walls offered a natural location for citizens seeking to achieve distinction. This was the district where Swift's first home was located, in a quiet side street.

Towards the centre and beyond, north and westwards, Dublin offered numerous niches for business, diversion and comfort. A new theatre down by the southern quays – which were soon in development too, to better serve the Jacobean Customs House – had just opened. The play-house opened into a lane cramped enough to make one think of London's Blackfriars. Continuing inland, however, and leaving the old city at the north-western gate-tower – going beneath a fine Elizabethan clock and through Ostman's Gate – the northern half of the city unfurled in front of you. Across a narrow thirteenth-century bridge lay the Inns of Court, where the Swift brothers became established members, and beyond them a more heterogeneous, soon rather affluent outer metropolis on the north side of the Liffey. The Inns took up a handsome complex that fronted the river in a well-situated row: in the cloister within, along with offices and lodgings supporting the collegiate and club-like environ-ment, was a large hall where 'judges and the other men of law' dined at commons during the legal term. Not far away was a large bowling green, which one visitor said was the single thing in which Dublin equalled or exceeded London.[10] Towards Oxmantown, where the Liffey often over-flowed, you soon reached open grassland. A Frenchman visiting in 1666, having fought a young coxcomb at Holyhead for a slur against his nation, was well satisfied with the inn he found himself here, the bowl-ing green and adjacent diversions. Soldiers came here to exercise and drill in the nearby fields, although in time the Lord Lieutenant's garrison were obliged to transfer their manoeuvres southside, to Stephen's Green, for the plain beside Oxmantown was soon cluttered with houses and new streets.[11]

Dublin offered a shocking surge of activity to a small child carried or led through its streets. Vast draymen collected and deposited their loads from tightly packed shops, horses clopped everywhere, wagons and bar-rows bumped over cobbles and dredged through mud, great barges lined the quays. The ubiquity of squalor, loudness and rudeness in Swift's writing, and his frequent weariness with all three, owes much to his lifelong exposure to big-city conditions. Dublin's noise and sprawl had more than enough power to bewilder a young boy re-exposed to them suddenly, as Swift was, when he was brought back from Whitehaven at the age of about three. Later Swift was divided, as on so many other subjects, with regard to the city's tumult. His chronically erratic hearing sensitized him to roars and rushes of sound and action; yet he grew, in his way, to love the street cries as a source of amusement. It pleased him to point out the literal absurdity of vendors yelling 'Herrings, herrings alive here': for was it not proverbial that nothing was deader than a her-ring? But when he urged that Dublin's hawkers should improve their elocution, he did so through his pompously 'progressive' mock-persona.

> And therefore until our Law-makers may think it proper to interpose so far as to make those Traders pronounce their Words in such Terms, that a plain Christian Hearer may comprehend what is cried, I would advise all new Comers to look out at their Garret Windows, and there see whether the Thing that is cried be Tripes, or Flummery, Buttermilk or Cowheels.[12]

Accompanying this exhortation is a sketch that gives us the pokey upper-floor windows of the townhouses, the tenants peering down from them to the clumps of hats and bonnets moving below, and the wares piled up on the criers' carts, destined for one pantry and table or another. Dublin changed a great deal in Swift's lifetime, as any city may in nearly eighty years, but, with the necessary adjustments of fashion and construction, some things remained constant. The sights of his eighth decade reincar-nated, in part, those of his boyhood, and innovations made him testy. Even while burlesquing the manners of city footmen, as an old man he instinctively sided with them against foppish (and vaguely seditious) interlopers who had begun appearing – 'lewd, idle, and disorderly Per-sons . . . daily seen in the Walks of this City, habited sometimes in Green Coats, and sometimes laced, with long Oaken Cudgels in their Hands, and without Swords . . . pretending and giving themselves out to be true genuine Irish Footmen'.[13] He named these interlopers after their toupees, a new kind of periwig then coming into fashion among men of question-able character; but there had always been such types to be met with, in the Restoration's height of vanity and violence as much as the dark days of Hanover loutishness.

Another lasting aspect of the sense of Dublin Swift gives us is his disapproval of the wider civilization it embodied. His criticism of the scrappiness and harshness of the society surrounding him suggests that he had trouble accepting it earlier in life. There was no escaping, he later concluded, 'the Barbarity of those *Northern* Nations from whom we are descended'. Dublin, the former Viking outpost, was as blighted by that heritage as anywhere in England: 'the same Defect of Heat which gives a Fierceness to our Natures, may contribute to the Roughness of our Language, which bears some Analogy to the harsh Fruit of colder Coun-tries.'[14] The rude cries of the street vendors around Christ Church and the quays were in truth little rougher, he implied, than the supposed verbal refinement he met with indoors. The strategy adopted by the adult Swift urged active intervention: if he was stranded among such barbarians, then he could at least offer 'proposals' for taming and refining them a little. His real quarrel here, it might be noticed, lay with England and the English in Ireland; his own language, and his own people, transplanted into another land. Yet he never swerved from the position he adopted, according to his relative Deane Swift, at the age of four or five, of refusing to accept that he belonged where he found himself. 'Ireland', even when it was English, would always be shorthand for where he was obliged to live; 'England', except when he was actually there, for where he wanted to be.

Swift's fastidiousness in this area always sits oddly with the experience of his parents' generation. His paternal uncles were eager and satisfied colonists. Whatever nostalgia they felt for England, their desire for promotion and affluence were unhindered by it. His parents also had every reason to be pleased with their prospects. They made their home in Hoey's Court, close to Dublin Castle and just within the southern city wall, reached via Werburgh Street, a bustling thoroughfare. Hoey's Court was a relatively peaceful alleyway, running roughly south-east towards the Castle's western wall, insulated from the clatter of coaches and wagons by the fact that one could enter it only by foot or sedan chair. Jonathan's brothers, Godwin and William, lived in streets close by.[15] Just under two years after they married, in May 1666, the Swifts' first child was born, their daughter Jane. A year later, Abigail was pregnant again. She was also a widow; Jonathan had died in March or April. When the child Abigail was carrying was an old man, he told a young female friend that he had lost his father to the most banal of causes. The young lawyer had been away on work, 'and returning from the circuit, he unfortunately brought home the itch with him, which he had got by lying in some foul bed on the road. Somebody advised him to use Mercury to cure it, which prescription cost him his life in a few days after his return.'[16] 'The itch' was syphilis, and the mercury cure was administered through an infusion or a sweat-bath, which could derange the patients it did not poison outright: Jonathan Swift the elder seems to have fallen into the second category, and may have been spared the further suffering the treatment brought, in which the quicksilver corroded the lining of the mouth and often destroyed the whole nose. Facial prosthetics covering these injuries were a fairly common sight in European cities. They were taken, with cruel comedy, as marks of sexual promiscuity, which was more generally assumed to be the usual cause of syphilis. Swift, though, if his thoughts are reported accurately, laid no charge of infidelity against his father. In the version given here, Jonathan Senior was killed by infected bedding. This supposed cause of death may in turn have contributed to Swift's very open horror at dirty linen.

Much depended, though, on how Abigail took the story of a 'foul bed' and whether indeed this was the story her dying husband gave her. If it complicated her feelings towards her unborn child, and possibly her daughter too, such a response is surely understandable, alongside grief and possibly sheer stupefaction at the direction life had taken. Pregnant, she was to be left to cope with a little daughter as well as her new baby. The glimpses we get of her later in life suggest that she sometimes managed difficult situations through humour, as her son would. Abigail had grown up during a period in which as much as a fifth of the population of Ireland had died from the direct consequences of war; what she made of the nervous peace of Restoration is a matter for conjecture, but hardship and distress must have been familiar to her.

Her husband, it seems, was killed by grubby sheets. Now dirt would test her own powers of survival. As her lying-in drew near, the lack of pain control in delivery was arguably the least of her problems. The air and every surface teemed with pathogens untreatable from lack of antibiotics and basic hygiene. Had Swift possessed present-day knowledge of infectious diseases, microbiology would surely have made his fear of uncleanliness still worse. In parturition his mother faced the trial of the midwife's finger, as it searched her womb for a weak spot to tear the epidermis with a sharpened nail or thimble, and so speed up the birth. Afterwards, there was the exhaustion that can follow the ordeal in the best of circumstances, the plunge of spirits felt by so many mothers, and the unknowable light experience cast on the infant she was given to hold, before the nurses and neighbours, her 'gossips', took it from her hands.

About a month after her delivery, custom required Abigail to go to the doorway or vestibule of her local church, 'decently apparelled', and then kneel before a priest. In church he would then intone the words from the prayer-book for the postnatal 'Churching' of women, a compulsory ceremony of cleansing as much as of thanksgiving: 'Forasmuch as it hath pleased Almighty God of his goodness to give you safe deliverance, and hath preserved you in the great danger of childbirth, you shall therefore give hearty thanks unto God.'[17]

## 2

It is difficult merely imagining Swift, the Doctor and Dean, the terror of ministers and magnates, as a baby: the image is almost absurd. Picturing it means endowing him with a vulnerability, a physical and emotional need he cancelled altogether from his adult personality. But then, what should we expect? At an early stage in his career, Swift ridiculed the idea of understanding writers through biography. This was the sort of approach recommended by idiotic 'moderns'. 'I hold fit to lay down this general maxim,' argues one of his early personae:

> Whatever Reader desires to have a thorow Comprehension of an Author's Thoughts, cannot take a better Method, than by putting himself into the Circumstances and Postures of Life, that the Writer was in, upon every important Passage, as it flow'd from his Pen; For this will introduce a Parity and strict Correspondence of Ideas between the Reader and the Author.[18]

Because Swift's crackpot expert extolled the above idea, Swift must be taken as meaning it was risible. It rendered writing entirely circumstantial, contingent on disappearing moments and vanishing impressions. That was not how letters should be: Swift adhered to the belief that literature weathered history, unmarked by incidentals. It imparted universal truths from one epoch to another. That was why the 'ancients' had lasted.

Yet it is surely important to know that Swift was old and angry, and troubled by lapses of memory, when he wrote the short account of his family and his early life with which his biographers must always begin. The brief note he made on his parents in around 1738 is highly unsympathetic – but also separated from the loss it describes by a distance of seventy years. Swift made the memorial still more impersonal by writing of himself as 'he', not 'I'. Cloaked in the third person, he distances himself from his humble beginnings.

> This marriage was on both sides very indiscreet, for his wife brought Mr Swift her husband little or no fortune, and his death happening so suddenly before he could make a sufficient establishment for his family: And his son (not then born) hath often been heard to say that he felt the consequences of that marriage not only through the whole course of his education, but during the greatest part of his life.[19]

The elderly Swift writing here blames the marriage, but at the same time makes it plain that the event with deeper consequences for his future was the loss of his father – 'his death happening so suddenly'. If the elder Jonathan had not died so young, Swift manifestly implies that he *could* have made 'a sufficient establishment for his family'. Jonathan and Abigail Swift were by no means unique – in their own age or any – for starting married life with little money. Jonathan Sr's relatively secure professional prospects really gave them every justification in marrying. But their son could not excuse them, and transferred his grief and anger from his father's death to the marriage it ended so abruptly. Instead of coming to terms with the loss of his father, Swift set himself the task of accepting that his parents had married and forced the world upon him. Swift calls his parents' marriage 'indiscreet', though they were neither especially young nor poor by contemporary standards. Both were twenty-four years old and Jonathan was already a steady earner. The elderly man's reproach sounds like something he heard seventy years earlier in the households of his uncles – who were left the obligation of supporting him.

Swift's Christian name was a sign of affinity with his paternal family. A widow falling back on her parents or relatives for support might equally have been expected to name the boy after her own father; but Abigail Swift seemingly had nobody of her own left in Ireland. The christening was not, though, a simple patriarchal matter. It reflected the enduring influence of the late Mrs Elizabeth Swift, née Dryden, Swift's grandmother. Swift's father, Jonathan, was named after one of her brothers. Elizabeth's second son, Dryden, carried her maiden surname. The eldest Swift brother, Godwin, was christened in memory of another of Elizabeth's brothers, who had died in infancy. The name Godwin had in fact belonged to other older relatives on Elizabeth's side of the family. The most famous offspring of this maternal line, which stretched back to a family based in Canons Ashby, Northamptonshire, was John Dryden, a distant cousin of Swift, who, in 1667, was close to establishing himself as England's leading poet and professional writer.[20]

These were the family associations on which Swift put the greatest emphasis. To posterity at least, they crowd out his maternal line, with his grandmother Elizabeth's relations in effect taking the symbolic place of his mother's. Yet this was the family Abigail needed to help bring up her children, let her keep what she could of the serenity and security of the house in Hoey's Court and, quite possibly, retain her own social status. Her son later recorded that she had brought a humble dowry to her marriage. Her 'very private' relatives in Leicestershire probably could not have saved her from having to 'go into service', the perennial nightmare of impoverished gentlewomen. Such women could and did face a long drop: Hannah Wolley, the prolific author of a book designed to help those who were 'forced to serve, whose parents and friends have been impoverished by the Late Calamities, viz the Late wars, Plague and Fire [in London]', pointed out 'what mean places they are forced to be in because they want accomplishment for better'.[21] The dead man's brothers stepped in to ensure that his widow and children did not lose their place in society. In manhood nevertheless Swift remained extremely sensitive on the question of his social standing, and his sister made him furious by marrying 'beneath her'. The prospect of social demotion was a very real one for Abigail, without the help of her in-laws. It would surely be wrong, though, to assume that Swift inherited from his mother the class anxieties he later exhibited: these might stem rather from resentment on his part at her lot in life, since she could easily have been accustomed to thrift and housework from her childhood.

As was customary for a child of gentry, the baby Jonathan was put in the care of a wet nurse. Later eighteenth-century writings, notably in heartfelt essays by Sir Richard Steele, Swift's contemporary, compatriot and sometime friend, lamented the corrupting influence and outright neglect or abuse of children that resulted. An earlier and broader-minded reflection on the subject by the French essayist Montaigne had found it sad and strange that such nurses frequently treated their foster-infants much more kindly than their own; proof, for Montaigne, of the arbitrary and habit-led nature of human attachment. The foster-mothers of Ireland apparently resembled those observed by the great Renaissance Frenchman. An English traveller commented in 1680 on how 'Irish nurses are very tender and good to the children of others of higher degree than their own, this begets a relation and kindred without end, and they become followers of their foster brothers and sisters.'[22]

The stereotype itself here is, as ever, suspect. In the soft-hearted Irish nurse, this writer probably wished to show how deeply the conquered people had accepted their colonial masters. Still, it has been suggested that Swift's nurse displayed attachment of this kind. Swift is explicit, though, in saying that his nurse was English (with or without Irish roots). Instead of lavishing care on him, she subjected him to the rigours of a difficult journey, undertaken for the sake of her own affairs. He claimed that he was about a year old when he was abducted:

for his Nurse, who was a woman of Whitehaven, being under an absolute necessity of seeing one of her relations, who was then extremely
sick, and from whom she expected a Legacy; and being at the same
time extremely fond of the infant, she stole him on shipboard unknown
to his Mother and Uncle, and carryed him with her to Whitehaven,
where he continued for almost ~~two~~ three years. For when the matter
was discovered, His Mother sent orders by all means not to hazard a
second voyage, till he could be better able to bear it.[23]

Many paragraphs in Swift's brief autobiographical note are questionable.
The above is one such passage. The reasons Swift gives for his abduction,
and then his stay in Whitehaven being so prolonged, are tersely factual
but also evasive. His nurse feasibly might have 'stole him on shipboard'
without being detected, since she may have been keeping the baby in her
own home. It could well have been days, conceivably weeks, before Abigail learned that Jonathan was gone. Did the Swifts spend nearly three
years of heart-stricken searching to track down the nurse and the baby?
Seemingly not; Swift strongly implies that most of his absence from
Dublin was subsequent to 'the matter' being discovered. The story as
Swift tells it indicates that if he did indeed disappear, his mother and
relatives responded largely with indifference: unless, that is, they simply
allowed his nurse to take him away with her to Whitehaven. There is no
devoted carer on either side, in Swift's account here. His nurse travels
on business; his family lets her keep him. A more plausible reason for
the nurse taking him away is that Abigail Swift's small household was
broken up to save expenses.

Throughout his private 'history' Swift never stints on recording oddi-
ties or failings among his relatives, or conduct that he felt did him
personal wrong; but neither does he write a bad word about his mother
– aside from saying that she was poor and her background obscure. He
had perhaps internalized the role of dutiful son too strongly to complain. Nor did he criticize the nurse, understanding instead the care she
took of her legacy. However, in another version of the unusual 'event',
both women are drawn very differently. The elderly Swift told his story
to Laetitia Pilkington, a visitor and admirer whose youth and mild flirti-
ness cheered him when she and her husband came to dine. Her account
is considerably more emotional:

He was given to an Irish Woman to nurse, whose Husband being in
England and writing to her to come to him; as she could not bear the

Thought of parting with the child, she very fairly took him with her, unknown to his Mother or any of his relations, who could learn no tidings of him or her for three years; at the end of which time she returned to Ireland, and restored the Child to his mother, from whom she easily obtained a pardon, both on account of the Joy she conceived at seeing her only Son again, when she had in a manner lost all hope of it, as also that it was plain the nurse had no other Motive for stealing him but pure Affection . . .[24]

This breathless sentence belongs not only to a quite different person, but another cultural epoch, the coming age of 'sentiment'. Pilkington was not above changing some details in recalling her conversations with Swift to suit her own views of the matters they discussed. It does seem likely that, consciously or not, she has decided to put the two women in a better light; but one cannot rule out Swift altering some emphases in the tale for the sake of his listener. Here the nurse takes ship to England for love – or marital duty at least – rather than an inheritance, and Abigail lives for three whole years without her little boy only because she has no idea where he is. Her forgiveness of the nurse's offence in her gladness at the child's return suggests a moment in the final act of a Shakespearean comedy.

In all, it reads like an anecdote that changed every time someone told it – and not only when Swift recounted it or someone repeated him but also, many years before, on each occasion Swift himself heard it as a child. Was it three years he was away, or just two? He was always imprecise with dates and times. In one telling, Abigail seems positively cold; in another she is a yearning mother, moved to forgiveness by the 'pure Affection' of her surrogate. In both versions here, though, his mother 'forgave' the kidnapper when she discovered what had happened, while the infant's paternal uncles are distant and more or less irrelevant.

The subtext would seem to involve Abigail acquiescing, after some appropriate alarm, to her son living away from her. In Swift's version, she allowed him to remain with his nurse at Whitehaven; in Pilkington's, she had no wish to punish the kidnapper when her young child was returned. Swift's 'kidnapping', that is, might say more about his mother's state of mind, in the grip of depression or anxiety, than the surrogate affections his nurse was supposedly unable to control; or it might simply have been the result of an arrangement the family regarded as entirely practical.

Despite rumours to the contrary during and just after his lifetime, when his relationship with Stella and Vanessa attracted much conjecture, there is no evidence that Swift himself ever had children. Indeed, his comments on procreation suggest that the shock of becoming a parent might well have sent him, in his father's footsteps, to an early grave. He had little direct contact with young children in later adulthood and he rarely alludes to a child's experiences in his work. It would be several more generations, in any case, before the shift to a more Romantic view that saw childhood as a topic meriting exploration in itself. But it is worth recalling that when he does mention babies, even metaphorically, he rarely fails to introduce a note of horror. The obvious example is the chilling suggestion at the heart of his *Modest Proposal*. This famous pamphlet confronted his contemporaries with one of the few last acts of cruelty to the young that was beyond their limits. The gruesomeness is already there, however, in Swift's earliest mature work, the *Tale of a Tub*. At one point he speaks of the standard fate met by 'children of the mind' (books) at the hands of Time:

> Unhappy Infants, many of them barbarously destroyed, before they have so much as learnt their Mother-Tongue to beg for Pity. Some he stifles in their Cradles, others he frights into Convulsions, whereof they suddenly die; Some he flays alive, others he tears Limb from Limb. Great numbers are offered to Moloch [a demon], and the rest tainted by his Breath, die of a languishing Consumption.[25]

Although comically applied, the language here is distinctly evocative of the terrible catalogue of child-murders in Sir John Temple's account of the Irish rebellion of '41. Infancy for Swift connoted nightmare, and he attacked any incipient sentimentality about the nursing of babies: Gulliver, notoriously, is disgusted by the sight of a Brobdingnagian woman breast-feeding – shortly after the child has almost bitten off his head.[26]

It was the cradle and the nursery specifically that seem to have irked Swift. To say that he was entirely devoid of parental urges would be to misrepresent him. His vocation as priest, and frequently his contact with younger writers, allowed him to develop a nurturing side, and his eventual attitude to Ireland is sardonically, disappointedly yet still adherently paternalistic. Moreover, the ambiguous history of his relationship with Esther Johnson shows him assuming the role of guardian from the outset. He made an entirely voluntary contribution to her education and upbringing; although, by the age of eight or nine, she was old enough for him to treat her as a miniature adult.

As for Whitehaven, it was just the sort of outpost that Swift tended to hate. Had it been an Irish rather than an English town, the mere idea of it would have been insufferable. Instead, although he never described the place or preserved the name of his devoted nurse, he remained unshakably fond of his foster-home. In his seventies, he would still react with pleasure on hearing of visiting merchants from Whitehaven.[27] The northwestern harbour town, just by St Bees Head, had not yet grown into the major port for coal and other merchandise it would become in the next hundred years. The area did, however, furnish a few modest veins of deeply English local mythology, with its abandoned copper mines ten miles or so to the north-west in the Newlands Valley. The rocks also held gold, it was said; yet nobody would take on the venture, since Queen Elizabeth had claimed all the precious ore for the Crown, and discouraged prospectors. The resulting situation belonged in a satire by Swift: it held the ingredients of greed, stubbornness and lack of vision that so frequently drew comment from him. Locals lived and laboured with a fortune on their doorsteps, or so they imagined, in the untapped seams. But since no single magnate could bag the entire lot for himself, none were willing to organize themselves for the sake of a more modest, but still substantial, share of the gold. The Queen in fact licensed a group of German prospectors to develop the mines.[28]

In Whitehaven he was still too young, presumably, to develop his early habit of roaming the countryside; but at about three years old he was evidently deemed strong enough for the 'hazard' of the Irish crossing. To some extent, the experts confirmed the reservations he claimed his mother had about his making the journey. 'Our mariners observe the sailing into Ireland to be more dangerous,' observed one earlier traveller, 'not only because many tides meeting makes the sea apt to swell upon any storm, but especially because they ever find the coast of Ireland covered with mists, whereas the coast of England is commonly clear and to be seen far off.'[29] As so often, more than a little pro-English bias probably triumphs here over geography, but the remark may still reflect a common presumption.

Notwithstanding the physical barrier, real or imaginary, between him and his mother, the very young Swift returned safely in or around 1670. If his own and his relatives' memories are to be trusted, the little boy aboard ship was already an observant child with a receptive memory, who was soon to develop firm views. Notably if not exceptionally, he could read, and the miracles and injunctions of scripture were familiar to him. His nurse – who presumably escorted him back – had taught him to spell, and by three 'he could read any chapter in the Bible.'[30] He was already well acquainted, then, with the literary surroundings that provided his profession; now he was transplanted back to where the greatest part of his life would be spent. Even so young, he was not pleased.

# 3

There may have been no armies in the field, but the civil wars were still being fought out in courts of law and palace antechambers when Swift was born. They were being reviewed and relived, too, beside countless hearths across the kingdoms of Charles II. As with the ideological side of any political and cultural conflict, the minds of the young provided a fresh battleground. Swift, with his paternal family of ardent Royalists, as well as the undercurrents of Puritan blood in his veins from his mother's side, was indoctrinated from an early age.

Swift's upbringing followed a pattern that the Lilliputians adopt as a system. Gulliver extols their nation's approach to nurturing the young. 'Parents are the last of all others to be trusted with the Education of their own Children.' They are barred from looking after their offspring, because babies, the Lilliputians reason, are made simply as a side-effect of sex. 'Men and women are joined together like other Animals, by the Motives of Concupiscence.' In their 'Love-Encounters', bed-mates do not reflect on the well-being of the creatures they might conceive. For this reason, Lilliputian children are brought up 'in Publick Nurseries' and are relieved of bearing any obligation to their parents. Swift here adapted the philosophy of Sir Thomas More's earlier fiction of an alternative society, *Utopia*; but it may be that this Lilliputian custom expresses the way he came to terms with his own birth. Conception was an impersonal matter so far as the infant was concerned, so no harm was meant if the parents abandoned the child to foster-care. Here it may be that Swift tacitly addressed his mother's remoteness if not outright negligence. In Lilliput, if only as a thought-experiment, he floated the notion that children were in no way indebted to their parents.[31]

Gulliver sometimes thinks like a child but is wary of children. When the Brobdingnagian farmer who discovers him brings him home to his table, his ten-year-old son grabs the voyager and almost kills him. Gulliver is no longer in Lilliput, but he feels Lilliputian. He is saved, however: the father gives his boy a clout on the ear that, says Gulliver, 'would have felled an *European* troop of Horse to the Earth'. Although terrified, Gulliver has presence of mind to think tactically: 'being afraid the Boy might owe me a Spight; and well remembering how mischievous all Children among us naturally are to Sparrows, Rabbits, young Kittens, and Puppy-Dogs; I fell on my Knees, and pointing to the Boy, made my master to understand, as well as I could, that I desired his Son might be pardoned.'[32] From the young, from anyone in their natural state, Swift expected cruelty. In front of adults, Swift frequently implies, children felt surrounded as if by Brobdingnagians; and their experience was one of ongoing punishment and humiliation. In the *Tale of a Tub*, his persona mentions how 'I have observ'd some Satyrists to use the Publick much at the rate that Pedants do a naughty Boy ready Hors'd for Discipline: First expostulate the Case, then plead the Necessity of the Rod, from great Provocations, and conclude every Period with a Lash.'[33] The speaker goes on to say that such pedagogues are wasting their energies: nothing is more 'callous and insensible' than the world's posterior. Underlying that is an understandable reluctance to remain among those 'horsed for discipline'. If the general public's position is that of a young boy awaiting the birch, Swift's preferred option would always be to stand among those holding the rod, intoning the old line that 'this will hurt me much more than it hurts you.' Implicitly, being a writer offered a way out for Swift of feeling like, or counting as, a powerless child.

Leaving aside the young Swift's subjective view, the city of Dublin during these years was, superficially, almost optimistic and enlivened in comparison with the sunken English capital. It was expanding, physically and demographically. During Swift's Whitehaven years, meanwhile, London was recovering from pestilence and inferno. The Great Plague had devoured the population; the Great Fire took unrecorded numbers, and consumed the old City for ever. Two leading writers caught the moment in contrasting idioms. Appearing soon afterwards, the first edition of Milton's *Paradise Lost* in 1667, the year of Swift's birth, spelled out a timeless predicament felt all the more acutely at that traumatic juncture. God's judgement was irrevocable. A burning sword barred the way back to Eden: the only way forward was through hard labour, on heavy soil. John Dryden, that 'near relation' of the Swift brothers on their mother's side, had composed a celebrated poetic almanac for the preceding year of wonders, the 'Annus Mirabilis'. He pictured the ghosts of traitors howling down from their heads impaled on London Bridge, to revel in the mayhem as buildings caved in. At the same time, the living behaved like phantoms, haunting the 'yet warm ashes' of their vanished homes, 'As murdered men walk where they did expire'.[34] Dryden looked for sources of hope; but it is the devastation in the poem that sticks in the mind. The two disasters justifiably seemed biblical in proportion. Along with embarrassment in a naval war against the Dutch, they left the English jaded and disoriented, and the Restoration honeymoon a distant memory.

Charles II, who had long lost his novelty as a ruler, had looked to Dublin as a source of reserve strength. Earlier in the 1660s the Duke of Ormond, the inveterate survivor, now the King's viceroy, had made efforts to boost building work and trade in Dublin and beyond. The Irish economy gave some cause for optimism. In this respect the favourable contrast with London was superficial. While Ormond's programmes served only the interests of the colonizing minority, the benefits they brought were offset by legislation from London, which put a leash on any expansive or independent competitive movement from Ireland. The Navigation Act of 1660 prevented Irish goods from being exported directly and sold in colonial markets; and from 1663 Irish cattle-breeders were prohibited from exporting their livestock into England. Ormond protested, but the ban was extended in time to cover mutton, lamb and dairy produce. A slow stranglehold was thus put upon the very progress government in London ostensibly encouraged. In the meantime, nothing was done to address the despair and bitterness created by the great dispossessions. Consequently, the underlying dread of rebellion and Papism was unabated. In retrospect, the 1660s and '70s could mislead observers in the same way as the '20s and '30s, tricking them into seeing the period as one of peace and even reconciliation. Instead the grounds for resentment were as strong as ever; with a corresponding and conscious anxiety among those who operated the repressive machinery. There were reasons even for a prospering Godwin Swift to feel quite ill at ease.

The situation in Ireland brought an added layer of tension to Swift's boyhood. The 'usual' privations of the period, meanwhile – that is to say, the conditions Swift would have endured even if he had grown up in the English shires – were in no way relaxed. A gentleman of his uncle the attorney's standing ran his household on lines that did not allow much contact between him at its head and children or servants. Although Swift was fatherless, other boys of his class saw comparatively little more of their parents. Manuals on the bringing up of children stressed the need for emotional remoteness in order to preserve one's paternal authority. The emphasis placed on the child's part, moreover, lay with silence and near-invisibility in the domestic regime. Swift had a playmate in his sister Jane, a year his elder; but there is little evidence of warmth or intimacy between them, and it is entirely possible they were 'shared out' between separate uncles.

The time available at home for 'sports and pastimes' may have been strictly limited, in any event. There was no conception then of childhood as a period of life meriting or requiring special treatment. Children were expected to behave much as diminutive grown-ups. That they could not, in most cases, merely reinforced the need for intensified discipline and instruction. Girls were set to learning the essentials of housekeeping, skills on which Jane Swift would eventually depend; boys, to whom the liberal arts and sciences were normally confined, were trained up in languages and sometimes more advanced mathematics. The higher placed, or more ambitious, the family, the more demanding studies tended to be. Books for children – or, more commonly, for use *on* children – were never childish. Tales and rhymes were all to be improving, or were to be avoided at all cost. John Bunyan, author of one of the most reprinted English books of all time, had to take especial pains to justify the fictitious vehicle of *The Pilgrim's Progress* against a scepticism that he himself shared. A long-standing compromise was the device of the fable, one that Swift would draw on in *A Tale of a Tub*. Many still had their doubts even about that, but since one of their most admired historical figures had taught with parables, so too, reckoned some, might his followers.

In Swift's case, the suspicions educators and social thinkers held towards 'fiction' are especially important: by turning raconteur and fabulist, notwithstanding his conformity in so many respects, he rejected a major tenet of the standard upbringing. A historian of the children's book points out that, for two unbroken centuries, the authorities felt that stories for the sake of stories were a bad idea. Hugh Rhodes, in his sixteenth-century *Book of Nurture*, urged parents to keep children 'from reading of feigned fables, vain fantasies, and wanton stories, and songs of love, which bring much mischief to youth'. In the 1740s the Earl of Chesterfield was still typical in declaring that 'The reading of Romance is a most frivolous occupation, and time really thrown away.'[35] The aptitude for narration, the knack for a turn of phrase that Swift seemingly displayed so early in speculating on his birth, his passage to Ireland in a band-box, and surely other topics besides, thus had to find other sources of inspiration and satisfaction than the purely imaginary. The obvious direction lay in the scripture he could already (he claimed) read fluently, and in a genre stemming from it: the 'conduct' literature expounding on morality and manners. It was a field to which he would contribute a great deal – though frequently with the aim of showing humans as incorrigible.

One particular vein of writing for the guardians of small children should also be touched on here, although Swift's exposure to it is a matter of debate. This was the genre of 'good godly books' derived from Puritan teaching. These works had many precursors but came into renewed vogue during Cromwell's Commonwealth. They addressed the passionate, highly individualized spirituality that had by then become almost mainstream, and also took in a perennial concern of parents: the high infant mortality rate. Under the old Catholic faith, and indeed in the form the Established Church had reached by the middle of the century, baptism in infancy was deemed enough to save a dying child from damnation. But Puritans had never been so sure; indeed, those who postponed baptism till adulthood had no security on this point whatsoever. It was therefore necessary to bring a child to embrace Christ entirely as early as possible; and this was where books such as James Janeway's *A Token for Children* or Thomas White's *A Little Book for Little Children* made themselves useful. Often using devices we might call 'child-friendly', pictures and rhymes, they invoked young children to adore their Saviour, know him entirely, forgo all sinful pleasures and preoccupations, and meditate obsessively on death. The number of editions and imitations these works passed through gave them an almost general cultural presence. A passage such as the following, from *Spiritual Counsel; or, A Father's Advice to His Children*, may be considered representative:

> Be much . . . in the Contemplation of the four last things, Heaven, Hell, Death and Judgement. Place yourselves frequently on your death beds, in your Coffins, and in your Graves. Act over frequently in your Minds, the Solemnity of your own Funerals; and entertain your Imaginations with all the lively scenes of Mortality.[36]

The eldest child of the author, John Norris, was barely four when these words were written, apparently for his benefit. They were published in 1694, and Norris was roughly Swift's contemporary. Obviously, then, the point is not that the paragraph itself could have had any direct bearing on Swift as a child; but rather that Swift would have done very well to have grown up at this time and have escaped thought of the kind being transmitted here. For Norris's *Spiritual Counsel* merely elaborates upon the imperatives delivered by an earlier generation, faithfully passing on their substance. Janeway's bestselling *Token for Children* had pictured ideal children scorning the sinful frivolity of a spinning top, and instead gazing serenely on a body in a coffin, or trying out their own for size. The effect of such thought could be as directly sobering as one might imagine but also subliminal. In Swift's 'ludicrous' childish idea that he was carried from England in a 'band-box' there is more than a faint connotation of a premature death, an infant coffin in which he was 'buried' in Irish soil.

In any case, these are enduring images and injunctions not only from Swift's childhood but also from his mother's. Her puritanically tinged background makes it possible, even probable, that Swift too was exposed to this harsh formative ethos, at least when he was returned to Ireland.

There are two obvious objections to suggesting that 'godly books' had some influence on Swift as a child. First, as we have seen, the outlook of his paternal family was determined by the mores of the Established 'Anglican' Church. Second, Swift exhibits no 'godly book' tendencies in his own writing; unlike John Norris, he spent the mid-1690s working on the much more exuberant *Tale of a Tub* rather than on a work of mordant spiritual counsel. Yet the first objection is weakened by recognizing that, as we shall see from Swift's schooling, the Anglican Church was not as immune to the values and fixations of Puritan teaching as its leaders preferred to think; indeed, by the early 1700s High Anglicans were commonly called 'godly'. The second objection holds only at a superficial level. For Swift comes across as someone whose breaks from study in early years have been properly devoted to coffin-gazing rather than to spinning tops.

There is a morbidly deadpan aspect to Swift, an attitude distant emotionally from all the scenes of life and diversion he surveys. Suppressing for a moment the obvious differences first of genre and then of individual talent, the attitude of the *Tale of a Tub* is not so far removed at all from Norris's *Spiritual Counsel*. The creative mind behind the *Tale*, indeed, has absorbed all such counsel and more, and, beneath the brilliant scathing play, looks on human existence as an empty parade of paper, a waste of wind, a carnival of clothes – in which mere garments, indeed, are more substantial than people, 'in Reality the most refined Species of Animals'.[37] All is vanity. Of the two, the *Tale* is much the more comfortless work, since it finds precious little consolation in the grave.

Even without the severe consolations of Janeway or White, there were fewer more austere places than a seventeenth-century nursery, few stories darker than the ones told at bedtime. Contrary to the usual view of

Swift's infancy, his years with the devoted nurse in Whitehaven – if her attachment was truly the cause of his stay there – may even have exposed him to more affection than was customary at the time. Back in Dublin, the anecdotal evidence suggests he seized attention when it was offered; but that in childhood, as in maturity and old age, he frequently found something wanting in his audience. As for the relations he entertained with his speeches, he would later consistently express dissatisfaction with the care most of them took of him. Still, the Swifts of Dublin set about providing him with the best education the island could offer. At the age of six, having been reunited with his mother for three years, he was again packed, metaphorically, into his band-box.

# 4

Almost twenty years after the rebellion of the late 1590s and early 1600s, an English observer commented with regretful fancy on the wreckage still scattered over the Irish countryside. The scene across the island resembled the latter end of a feast, this onlooker claimed. Crumbling homesteads, churches and fortifications were strewn everywhere. The ruined castle he saw in one direction seemed 'like the remainder of a venison pasty'; in another, an abbey lay 'like the carcass of a goose broken up'.[38] He did not remark on who or what such a banquet might have fed; but a generation later similar leftovers were to be seen again. Serving another course for war to eat up would be the work of further decades. The reconstruction process was still under way when Swift was sent from Dublin as a boarder, aged about six, to Kilkenny, some eighty miles to the south. There the thirteenth-century Cathedral of St Canice offered him one of his earliest and most powerful statements on the consequences both of rebellion and of Puritan fanaticism: it stood roofless and windowless, its once rich interior plundered, overshadowing the old school building at the western end of the churchyard.

A special example had been made of Kilkenny, for in 1642 the Irish Confederates had adopted the city as the seat of their breakaway government. Cromwell's forces had thus carefully ransacked St Canice's, carrying off the cathedral bells and internal ornaments. By the time Swift arrived, control of the state having revolved once more, Kilkenny lay at the heart of plans to impose the Restored Anglican regime on the island. The Duke of Ormond's castle overlooked the River Nore from a high point three quarters of a mile to the south of the cathedral. The

Duke himself adopted much the same supervisorial air towards his family demesne and the territory beyond, beginning with the town of Kilkenny below. He and his advisers regarded the school, which he set about accommodating in a larger building on the eastern bank of the river, as a nursery for future churchmen and administrators.

The surrounding county of Kilkenny was always singled out by travellers. Where the English in general found Ireland uneven, mountainous, soft, watery, woody, and open to winds and floods of rain, Kilkenny proved an exception.[39] Flowers and fruits they saw rarely elsewhere in the country grew abundantly there, and they approved of the town itself, a city by royal charter since Jacobean times. Earlier in the century, a visitor described it as 'an inland towne scituate in a pleasant valley, and upon a fresh ryver. It is praysed for the wholsom ayer, and delightfull orchards and gardens, which are somewhat rare in Ireland. The houses are of grey marble fayrely builte, the fronts of theyr houses are supported (most of them) with pillars, or arches under which there is an open pavement to walke on.'[40] Much of this architecture had obviously suffered in the Civil Wars, and by the 1670s no doubt seemed rather outdated and provincial; to an early eighteenth century eye it all looked 'but ordinary'.[41] The roads leading to the town were in a very poor state: in 1676 the Mayor ordered parish officers to rally all the men they could to turn out with 'shovels, spades, mattocks and other necessary instruments' and make some basic repairs.[42] Yet sightseers were still urged to go to the castle, the family seat of the Butlers for centuries, and having been newly restored by Ormond it was now 'rich on every side with marble, and ornamented with many things so curious, that those who have seen it say that it surpasses many palaces of Italy'.[43]

Surrounded by these prospects, Swift joined another poor relation at Kilkenny. For a further quasi-orphan had been foisted upon the Swifts of Dublin. This older boy was the son of one of Swift's uncles who remained in England, the namesake of the beloved patriarch, Thomas. The boy Thomas, like Jonathan, was fatherless. But on his mother's side he had been exposed to a very different set of family associates. He was the grandson of one of the leading if less celebrated cavaliers, who also happened to be one of the century's most impressive survivors. Sir William Davenant, London's dominant theatrical manager until his death in 1667, had been successively poet laureate, master of ordnance in the King's northern army, a spy, a gun-runner and a pirate. He had settled finally on introducing opera to the English theatre.

Davenant represented the other side – the polar extreme – of Royalism to that of the Reverend Thomas Swift of Goodrich. He was deemed (somewhat unfairly) a 'cavalier' in the sense the word had carried until the outbreak of war – a gamester, a prodigal and a bit of a dandy; or a 'gallant', as polite circles put it, usually mixed up in duels, intrigue or pandering. This was his character in all eyes but the Queen's, who, in fact, set high standards on such matters; and his profile was marred quite literally by an early dose of syphilis. The mercury steam-bath or infusion prescribed in such cases only exacerbated the disease's attack on the sensitive tissues of the mouth and nose. The tip and septum of Davenant's nose were corroded away; a later portrait, used for the frontispiece to his collected *Works*, shows him with a disturbing apse in his face. Although he was undeterred by it, the injury became the cruel toast of wits for another thirty years.

The disfigurement remained a common enough sight in Swift's time. Swift himself would cast a highly elaborated slur on the private morals of 'fanatics' in 'The Mechanical Operation of the Spirit' by alluding to 'the *Snuffling* of Men, who have lost their Noses by lewd Courses'. A syphilitic 'saint' of Banbury finds that his voice resembles the drone of a bag-pipe, a sound highly attractive to '*British* Ears'.[44] The nasal defect proves a great help in swaying brethren; so much so that no doctrine sounds orthodox to these believers unless delivered through blocked or damaged nostrils. In short, Swift would turn the defining feature of William Davenant, a politically orthodox if personally disreputable Royalist connection, into a hallmark of more or less everything Davenant had opposed. But Davenant's relatives had no cause to be offended by the passage. Rather the opposite is true: Swift was suggesting Puritans had equal need of facemasks or artificial noses, and implied that a declared rake such as this poet and showman was at least innocent of the fanatics' hypocrisy.

In time, friendship with Cousin Thomas acquainted Swift with a dimension to the Royalist story that the Swifts' preferred version excluded: namely, its more avant-garde 'Cavalier' aspect. In the early-to-mid 1670s at Kilkenny, this slightly older relative provided a humbler but more substantial link to what Swift called his home. Sometimes the association between them may well have taken the form of the headlocks and affectionate drubbings that remain the prerogative of elder siblings and close-placed cousins; and whether he welcomed it or not at the time there is no saying.

However Swift felt about it while he was there, with the Duke's fortress watching over him from one side of town, and the skeletal cathedral from the other, historically he was in select company. Kilkenny was the academy the Old English gentry had preferred for their sons for almost a century. The school had repaid their trust and patronage by producing generations of distinguished men of letters and public life. The complexion of its illustrious alumni, nonetheless, like the term 'Old English' itself, was ambiguous – and by no means exclusively Protestant. Star pupils had included Peter Lombard, a historian and Catholic archbishop of Armagh, and Luke Wadding, a Franciscan Irish patriot. The school's Protestant heritage, moreover, was also less than orthodox. When the Duke of Ormond's ancestor Piers Butler, eighth Earl of Ormond, founded the school, he chose for his headmaster a man who had been ejected from his living, the deanery of Waterford, for Nonconformity. Despite this black mark on his record, the gifted irregular in question, Peter White, had proved inspirational: all agreed that after he died the school went into decline, in the 1590s.

The blend of Papist scholars and unorthodox Protestants in its past made the school at Kilkenny unequalled in the colonial sphere of Irish society; and, although the Duke of Ormond sought to recapture this tradition, it did not really suit his present purposes. Kilkenny's school was to instil the doctrine of a Church reconstituted on the narrowest of principles shortly after the Restoration. These principles were expressed in a number of Acts that together came to be known as 'the Clarendon Code' – somewhat inaccurately and unfairly, since King Charles's ill-fated chancellor, the first Earl of Clarendon, was far from enthusiastic about the legislation's stringency. Then, crucially, the Test Act of 1673 demanded that all candidates for public office took an Oath of Supremacy and Allegiance to Crown and Church, specifically renouncing the Roman Catholic doctrine of transubstantiation. In England, Wales and Scotland, where Nonconformists and Papists were excluded from ecclesiastical office and public responsibility, the legislation was patently oppressive; but in Ireland, where the re-established Church encompassed a tiny minority, it was also only some way short of absurd. As a result of Ormond's efforts, the teaching at Kilkenny followed strictly doctrinaire lines. Along with his family's Anglican legacy, it formed another decisive stage in Swift's passage to a life in religious orders – much of which he would spend fighting injustice, but much too in rigidly defending repressive legislation such as the Test Act.

Some measure of the phase of development Ormond's programme reached during Swift's years at the school can be taken by trying to establish where the school was based in the city during that time. Pupils in the era of Peter White learned and slept in the house by the cathedral.

But in the 1660s Ormond evidently decided to relocate the school to a larger property. Thus one 'Mr Badge', the Duke's tenant in a well-sized house with gardens on the other side of the town, was asked to vacate the premises, and alterations were set in hand. Exactly when this occurred is somewhat unclear. The gateway in front of what became the school bears the date 1684, the year in which new official statutes were drawn up. By that time, however, the Duke's mission for his college had long been in progress; and, as subsequent pupils observed, work renovating and extending the buildings continued for decades afterwards.[45] Conceivably if not conclusively, Swift could have been among the first residents in Ormond's 'new' school at Kilkenny – as he was certainly one of the first to experience the educational programme it pursued.

The establishment consisted of two converted houses, one of which faced the street in the quarter known as St John's Town. It was fronted by two archways, leading into a quadrangle, and an imposing double flight of stairs took you directly up to the main classroom on the first floor. On the western side of its central courtyard was a second building, slightly newer, for 'domestic' purposes. The school itself was a venerable square four-storey structure, built in a style that already seemed out of date. In an earlier age it would have been an imposing mansion, having Gothic windows with separately leaded diamond-shaped panes, with projecting gables that discomfited passers-by in wet weather. One old boy of a later time described it as 'a gray reverend pile . . . having partly a monastic physiognomy, and partly that of a dwelling-house'.

The plan for renovating the property, at no little cost, shows that it was well adapted to its new function, and that it preserved the traditional layout of an older grammar school. Learning, living and sleeping all took place, that is, on different levels of a single staircase, on the model of a large home. The kitchens and a large dining hall were on the ground floor; teaching took place on the first floor, in a room measuring some twenty by sixty feet, with large heavy-timber-framed windows looking eastwards on to a mill-race; dormitories for the boys and rooms for the master and ushers occupied the second floor; and garrets for servants were on the third. In all, there was space for a school of around sixty boys, aged between six and fifteen. The old school by the cathedral was considerably smaller, but was run on similar lines: a single master supervising a household of pupils, aided in teaching by assistants who may have included one or two of the older poorer students, and who were to be screened with extreme care to exclude all 'insufficient or scandalous' characters.[46]

The plans for the new building give an idea of how Swift's school community was organized. Besides more space for teaching and accommodation, for sports and recreation, there was a fine park, the 'pigeon-house meadow' to the rear of the houses.[47] Such additional features aside, the new school retained much of the intimacy, no doubt unwelcome at times, of the original institution over by the cathedral.

The demands the curriculum placed on the very young children sent to grammar school surely added to the distress many felt at living away from home. Many of his fellow boarders, like him, had already experienced separation from their families. They were all expected to be able to read and write, and by six, the age at which Swift joined the school, to know the basic Latin declensions: this gave them the grounding for the immense course in 'grammar' to follow, a curriculum which in essentials by the late 1700s had long been largely standardized across England and Ireland. Although their pupils frequently disappointed, early-modern educationalists were indignant when handed an illiterate boy for schooling. One early leading theorist spoke for many in protesting, 'It is an extreme vexation that we must be toiled with such little petties, in teaching such matters whereof we can get no profit, nor take any delight in our labours.'[48] The lament among teachers has changed little over the ages; but a seventeenth-century master in truth set his standards rather high.

On entering the school, little 'petties' such as Swift would be spared any serious reading in Latin in the first form. Instead, work would begin on allowing them to comprehend and compose increasingly advanced sentences, and to use 'the Latin tongue with ease and delight'. Each boy was responsible for his own equipment and was to provide himself with pen, ink, paper (made into an exercise book), ruler, plummet and a pen-knife for maintaining his nib. He was to be able to make his own pen, choosing a quill 'of the best and strongest of the wing', harder so that it cleaved more cleanly. He was to see that his ink was neither too thick nor too thin, and that his paper was smooth enough to write on.

The second form usually introduced some simple reading, often from Aesop but sometimes the more challenging *Distichs of Cato*; Mantuan might follow in the third year.[49] Throughout, memory was the key faculty, driven hard from the first lesson in the very early hours of the morning, as the masters drilled their charges in storing and retrieving endless morphological and syntactical forms, adapting 'sententiae' and reproducing longer textual excerpts. A boy at Kilkenny would already have worked two hours or more before getting his breakfast, and the pauses for play and refreshment in the remainder of the day were few and short. The teaching was infused from the beginning with a rigidly Christian, and in particular Anglican, focus, and the schoolday traditionally closed with prayers and readings from scripture. At all moments the mind was discouraged from resting; and when it did, except at night, the body was kept busy. A sound beating would be administered as required. It sounds exhausting and brutal, physically and intellectually, and so it was. Swift is often quoted as recalling his schooldays fondly; but, as he explained to his friend Charles Ford, he was perfectly aware how his mind tricked him.

> Men are never more mistaken, than when they reflect upon past things, and from what they retain in their Memory, compare them with the present. Because, when we reflect on what is past, our Memoryes lead us onely to the pleasant side, but in present things our Minds are chiefly taken up with reflecting on what we dislike in our Condition. So I formerly used to envy my own Happiness when I was a Schoolboy, the delicious Holidays, the Saterday afternoon [free, along with Thursday afternoons], and the charming Custards in a blind Alley; I never considered the Confinement ten hours' a day, to nouns and Verbs, the terror of the Rod, the bloddy Noses, and broken Shins.[50]

The older Swift grew, the less often his memory would grant him even such short delusory trips 'to the pleasant side' of a former period. As an older man, his thoughts on education became very stern indeed. Bruises and fractures, he decided, were character-building. A late essay proposed that the British aristocracy were rapidly becoming unfit to govern precisely because methods of teaching and correcting were becoming so lax among the upper classes. It pleased him to hear of a young lord brought up properly in the classical languages, and 'well whipped when he deserved it'.[51]

When he spoke of school or childhood in his later years, he linked the recollection to a present argumentative purpose: more often than not to complain of negligence in his guardians. He associated his early years, too, with a lifelong sense of expectations cruelly flattened. Another apparent reference to Kilkenny, again often quoted, has been thought to put him on a bank of the River Nore or a nearby stream: 'I remember when I was a little boy, I felt a great fish at the end of my line which I drew up almost on the ground, but it dropt in, and the disappointment vexeth me to this very day, and I believe it was the type of all my future disappointments.' Thus the miniature Swift falls into the pattern the rest of his life would follow: he was writing in 1729, and calling to mind how he was always cheated of a good benefice in England. A veil of stoicism wafts thinly over a mass of resentment. 'I never wake without finding life a more insignificant thing than it was the day before: which is one great advantage I get by living in this country, where there is nothing I shall be sorry to lose.'[52] Boyhood, the ageing Swift was eager to assert, taught him everything he knew about crushed aspirations and life's general cruelty. Yet such lessons could have meant something only if Swift had been ardent and trusting in his hopes as a boy.

## 5

And life, as sessions for prayer and catechism insisted at regular intervals during normal schooldays, and all but incessantly every Sunday, was far from meaningless: the fate of the immortal soul and the future of the Christian Commonwealth were at stake. An influential primer the master at Kilkenny is likely to have used, *The Whole Duty of Man*, urged its readers to take up their duty to love, hope and fear God, and to labour. However long they took to sink in, such obligations were assumed seriously and unstintingly by Swift. He would have more trouble, in years to come, with the part impelling the faithful to enjoy God's love and blessings. 'It must likewise bring you to a sense and abhorrence of your baseness, and ingratitude, that have thus offended so good and gracious a God, that have made such unworthy and unkind returns to those tender and rich Mercies of his.'[53] Here Swift recoiled: he was proud, rather than grateful. While still at Kilkenny, even when the custards lost their charm, he could not have known that his great fish had eluded him for ever. In later years, although the school produced in him an exemplary faithful Churchman in most doctrinal respects, he would never shake off the sense that he had been hard done by.

The vacations were short, allowing only brief stays in Dublin. Tradition has it that his mother and sister migrated back to England shortly after he started school, settling with relatives in Leicester. The move would have made sense from both families' perspectives, if the Dublin Swifts felt less than obliged to support their dead brother's widow. The report is unsubstantiated, though; it stems from a nineteenth-century supposition, which seems to have unconsciously met some need to accentuate Swift the child as being rootless and uncared for. Victorians demanded something to explain the great oddity that, in their eyes, he became, and to extenuate Thackeray's vision of him as a misanthropic monster. In fact, the picture we have makes more sense if Abigail stayed on in Dublin. Her daughter remained closely connected to the city;[54] and Swift himself inherited the drier part of his wit from her – a mutual trait that appears to have furnished a channel of communication. Yet Abigail did not need to go as far as Leicester for her son to feel abandoned. Emotional distance would be quite sufficient, as indeed would her in-laws crowding her out from Jonathan's upbringing. To Swift, the chief party responsible for looking after him so poorly was always Uncle Godwin. Swift would be incapable of attributing unhappiness to a lack of basic affection; instead he spoke in terms he understood, and blamed inadequate schooling. 'He gave me the education of a dog,' he complained, in an apocryphal exchange at a public dinner. 'Then you have not the gratitude of a dog!' cried the Archdeacon, who, it was said, had questioned Swift about his childhood.[55]

The dogs at Kilkenny were really very well-read. In the later forms, the active intellectual work became more demanding and the reading more extensive and interesting. The fourth form of the standard curriculum brought Ovid's *Metamorphoses*, elements of Virgil and a taste of Greek; the fifth form introduced the favourite Latin comedies, some of the more sanitary satires, translations from Greek theatre and Caesar's commentaries.[56] The Greek testament might be ventured on; the most apt in their form were even taught rudiments of Hebrew. The set compositions for boys in the last three years reflected their likely future professions. On hearing an English sermon, they would be required to digest and comment upon its formal stages of text, division and exposition, and digest it into a set of chief headings. They might then be asked to render in Latin what they recalled of the sermon for discussion in class the following day. The skills drummed into them over previous years would also be turned to the art of letter-writing – vital to all prospective secretaries, men of affairs and indeed ordinary parsons. Even the slowest creature, then, emerging from a school of much lower standing than the one at Kilkenny would have a memory and facility for composition more or less inconceivable today. How long such powers lasted in all cases was another question, but a boy who cultivated both his 'natural parts' and his training was ready for a life's work with words – in the service of The Word.

Later on, Swift considered himself a poor student, and even reproached his guardians for not doing more to make him study. If his schoolboy mischief amounted to no more than a tale of his carving his name on his seat in the classroom, then he surely exaggerated the scale of his misdemeanours. A clause in the school statutes, which were formally drawn up a few years after Swift left, but most likely codified long-standing custom, directed that 'The master shall make diligent inquiry after such as shall break, cut, deface or any way abuse the desks, forms, walls and windows of the school . . . and shall always inflict open and exemplary punishment on all such offenders.'[57] Attitudes to graffiti change: later, an antiquary would record a very earnest search for the bit of timber the young Swift had supposedly defaced, which an old boy of the college had saved from the rubbish-heap during refurbishments.[58]

The master himself was expected to take good care of the facilities. The later statutes mention in particular his responsibility for the trees in the meadow. His chief care, though, was obviously the education, intellectual and moral, of his threescore pupils. The statutes were absolutely clear on the academic and political credentials required. Masters were to hold at least an M.A., be 'of good life and reputation, well skilled in humanity and grammar learning; loyal and orthodox'.[59] The need to put these requirements on a statutory footing is noteworthy, since two formidable and nakedly ambitious clerics presided over the school during Swift's time there. Both were alumni of Westminster School and Trinity, Cambridge, a college from which the churchmen tended towards the deeper shades of Reformed doctrine. The first, a Welshman named Edward Jones, took up the post at Kilkenny in 1670. He had been Ormond's private chaplain, and rose higher in the Church over the next decade. He left Kilkenny in 1680, two years before Swift finished school, and was made Bishop of Cloyne. On returning to England, and being promoted to the see of St Asaph, he pursued a career of rapidly mounting scandal. Bishop Jones was presently accused and convicted of giving benefices to paying candidates he knew were guilty 'of crimes and excesses', of siphoning off ecclesiastical revenues to his loving wife, and making free personal use of the incomes from livings to which he had appointed no vicar.[60]

The later Swift would always revere the institution of the Church above the sometimes substandard individuals who were supposed to serve it. One cannot repeat too often that he venerated episcopacy, but had a poor view of most bishops. If Edward Jones began manifesting his mature tendencies while still master at Kilkenny, Swift's critical attitude to his fellow clerics may have begun early. He had less time to observe Jones's relatively blameless successor, Henry Ryder, who did his best to combine his job as master with other preferments, but soon departed for a prebend in Dublin at St Patrick's Cathedral. Given their concentration on furthering their careers, the masters may have delegated much of the actual teaching to their younger assistants, the school ushers. But, just as the grammar-school curriculum and criteria had changed little for a century, the approach of a successful teacher in the classroom was much the same as that which Peter White, the first master at Kilkenny, had adopted to the 'proper imps' with whom he was entrusted in the late 1500s. Headstrong boys needed bridling; dull boys needed 'spurring'; delicate boys needed 'rewardes': finally, 'by interlacing study with recreation, sorrow with mirth, payne with pleasure, sowernesse with sweetnesse, roughnesse with myldnesse, he had . . . good successe in schooling his pupils.'[61]

The pupils' free Thursday and Saturday afternoons could relieve the monotony and frequent harshness of the week; speech days at Kilkenny might be enlivened by the great Duke's gift of 'a fat buck' for the evening feast.[62] And crucially, tedious, exhausting and punishing though it must have been, the school environment gave a space for verbal dexterity. It supported the twin paths of development on which Swift found refuge, literature and piety, and it trained up the immense capacity for work that he later combined with whimsy and imagination. The school's unyielding regime perhaps also helped him see the advantages of invisibility, or of adopting a persona.

Here and there, his writing offers glimpses of the sort of fun children got up to at the time. One of the most cryptic passages in *A Tale of a Tub* mentions how boys would light farthing candles in 'the Skull of an Ass' at nightfall, '*to the Terror of His Majesty's Liege Subjects*'.[63] Could Swift have been a boy who manufactured such a death's-head? Or was he rather the unsuspecting passer-by, startled by the donkey's glowing mouth and eye-sockets? The future revealed something of both in him.

# 3. Abuses of Learning and Religion

> But Swift? His mind had had a different schooling, and pos-
> sessed a very different logical power. He was not bred up in a
> tipsy guardroom, and did not learn to reason in a Covent Gar-
> den tavern. He could conduct an argument from beginning to
> end; he could see forward with a fatal clearness.
>
> – W. M. Thackeray[1]

## I

In many respects the venerable university syllabus at the relatively new college in Dublin, and the daily regime of prayer and religious observance there, merely continued the moulding of mind and instinct boys had experienced at schools such as Kilkenny. Nevertheless Trinity College exposed Swift for the first time to a trend of thought that lay outside the doctrinal curriculum: the great fascination with science for its own sake that had seized hold of Europe.

'Natural Philosophy' societies, inspired by the academies of London and Paris, had sprung up in many major towns. They were found everywhere: one of Swift's early personae sent his compliments to the 'Iroquois virtuosi' and the 'Literati of Tobinambou'.[2] The mission of such societies was to pursue pure knowledge. Quite a large number of men associated with Trinity in Dublin embraced this sometimes recondite culture of measurement and experimentation. At a chilly ceremony in January 1686, one of Swift's tutors stood up to give a speech in praise of the new scientific approach to the Creation. St George Ashe's daily work consisted of teaching a number of the boys and young men their Latin authors, yet he was also a passionate amateur scientist. Swift was extremely fond of the orator, an ordained priest and a young fellow of the college; and their lifelong friendship was strong enough to withstand

Swift's scepticism towards the 'New Learning' that Ashe extolled as an almost sacred force.

Swift's teacher was one of the leading lights in the Dublin Philosophical Society, first founded on an informal basis in the 1650s, and later modelled more closely on the Royal Society. Unfortunately his researches had already been subject to undergraduate jokes he clearly resented. A mathematician of some ability, Ashe had attempted squaring the circle, like Descartes and Hobbes before him. He also reported to fellow members on such subjects as an Irish girl he had encountered 'who has several horns growing on her body' and the oddly located penis of a hermaphroditic horse.[3] Addressing Ormond's successor as lord lieutenant, the second Earl of Clarendon, Ashe spoke of his pleasure at seeing that such endeavours were beginning to get the respect and patronage they deserved. Through the support of King Charles, and the Earl's father, the great historian of the Civil Wars and lord chancellor to Charles, natural philosophy 'was admitted into our palaces and our courts, began to keep the best company, to refine its fashion and appearance, and to become the employment of the rich and the great'.[4]

To Ashe, this 'employment' was pure avocation. When he and the former Provost of Trinity, Narcissus Marsh, used the Siberian winter of 1683/4 to observe the effects of freezing on eggs and urine, they did so with no other object but learning itself. The same might be said of contemporary college fellows such as Dr Allen Mullen, who pumped and injected stray dogs with liquids of varying toxicity, or the virtuoso who held that 'the parts of water are generally agreed to be oblong.'[5] Yet some members developed their science from less abstract motives. One great shaper of the society, William Molyneux – whose breadth of mind was reflected early on in his translation of Descartes's *Meditations* – and later his younger brother Thomas, became engineers of note. The Molyneux brothers were concerned as much with application as with observation and pure theory. Another, slightly earlier illuminatus of international renown, Sir William Petty, worked with the celebrated Robert Boyle on a new method for surveying land. They employed it in measuring up the property confiscated from Roman Catholics in the Cromwellian conquest.

St George Ashe's innocence in such realms can be gauged from his spiritual ecstasies on the subject of air – no doubt inspired by Boyle's experiments: 'like an anima mundi it permeates all.' Natural philosophy, Ashe declared, was nothing more than 'a learned romance' without detailed 'experiment and demonstration'. Above all, however, his researches fed back into the religious pleasure he took in what he had no doubt at all was God's handiwork. It was this spiritual reward, the glimpse of the divine in specks of data, which Swift missed when incorporating such inquiries into his fiction and polemic. Irvin Ehrenpreis noted how Ashe's rhapsodies on air resonate 'curiously' in one of the great venomous set-pieces of the *Tale of a Tub*: the disquisition on 'Aeolism' which establishes that Nonconformist Christians were nothing but worshippers of vapour.[6] Other luminaries of the society, fellows or close associates of Trinity, discovered and invented things that also prefigure Swiftian passages. Reports to the Dublin Society from his time, surveyed by Ehrenpreis, feature chemical, astronomical and linguistic investigations that now call to mind some of those Gulliver witnesses at the crazy Academy of Lagado. Poor Ashe's attempts to observe eclipses were frustrated by the fickle Irish skies. But the search itself, for him, was sufficient. Those of his school, students of the divine in the natural, had something of the purism of Descartes, who notably declined overtures to turn his work to battlements or ballistics.

The point of Swift's eventual satire on such efforts, notwithstanding his great affection for Ashe (though less for some of his colleagues), seems to lie with a conviction of its essential pointlessness. Since he missed the insights to God's artistry, or the joy of pure data, the endeavour for Swift was all to no purpose. One might expect Swift to have passed over the matter for being harmless: for when a philosopher did have a civil or military goal in mind, there was seemingly much greater cause for misgiving. Ehrenpreis noted how Sir William Petty was preoccupied in the early 1680s with building model carriages and a fleet of ships, with absolute realism on Lilliputian proportions, with the very definite aim of influencing full-scale lethal versions.[7] Something of a biographical mystery has existed as to why Swift should have devoted more satirical energy to the school of Ashe rather than to technologists such as Petty. The religiose pretensions made on behalf of empirical knowledge seem to have displeased him more than its harmful applications.

Engines of war were mere signs of humanity's inescapable destructive streak. Claims that science could see through the very fabric of things, however, displayed fatal presumption. Swift in effect rejected the rising view that even theories that seemed absurd in the sight of Reason should be considered tenable if enough evidence could be mustered or contrived to support them; for him, this was a short step away from the 'free-thinking' encouraged among 'fanatics' and 'visionaries'. In consequence, scientists in Swift's writing are generally shrunken characters, shrivelled to the dimensions of the minutiae in which they see grand schemes and definitive answers. In a striking passage from 'Mechanical Operation of the Spirit', Swift suggested scientific investigation was shrivelling the seat of Reason itself, as the human mind comes to resemble a carcass teeming with worms:

> For, it is the Opinion of Choice *Virtuosi*, that the Brain is only a Crowd of little Animals, but with Teeth and Claws extremely sharp, and therefore, cling together in the Contexture we behold ... like Bees in perpendicular swarm upon a Tree, or like a Carrion corrupted into Vermin, still preserving the shape of the Mother Animal.[8]

The paragraph, in fact, makes highly informed use of just the sort of observation the Dublin Society accepted and debated eagerly, but does so to the end of denigrating their broader purpose. A distaste for bodily things, for the physical detail obsessing those virtuosi also emerges: Swift implies that putting matter under the microscope should only make one appreciate its pettiness still more. Thus St George Ashe and other members of the Dublin Philosophical Society stood in need of correction.

Characteristically, later in the same passage, Swift exposes the absurdity of the 'Philosophical' method by raising the stakes in what it claims to explain. The learned spoof-author continues by asserting:

> That all invention is formed by the Morsure [bite] of two or more of these Animals, upon certain capillary Nerves, which proceed from thence, whereof three Branches spread into the Tongue, and two into the right Hand.[9]

The criticism Swift thus raises via this philosopher protests that human creativity *cannot* be reduced to the nibbling of these minute cephalic creatures. At the same time, typically of Swift, the effect of their 'Morsure' is rendered very credibly with some fine mock-anatomy. Their biting on the brain is also a very good metaphor for the headache so often required when we self-consciously think things through, and turn thought (via those 'capillary Nerves') into speech or writing. It possibly even opens a window on the exertions demanded of the young Swift at his studies. But the passage uses its irony to challenge the idea that human thought could ever be explained in such blunt empirical terms. It is an example of how the mature Swift belongs in the older realm of

Renaissance scepticism, in which the logical systems of the Middle Ages had lost their currency, but where the 'new philosophy', as John Donne famously had it, merely 'puts all in doubt'. The passage's oblique appeal to spiritual causes hints at Swift's seriousness as a minister, and also his reluctance to tamper with the foundations of his faith.

This is most likely not a position we can attribute to the young student, to whom his masters' scientific hobbies perhaps still seemed just a bit silly. Paying homage to Clarendon in early 1686, Ashe was probably speaking in the society's rooms at the Crow's Nest in Dame Street, a thoroughfare lined with 'mercers, booksellers, jewellers and other shop-keepers'.[10] There the virtuosi had set up a laboratory and were in the process of planting a garden for the botanists of their society. The presence of the Lord Lieutenant may well, however, have demanded a larger venue, in the college itself.

Trinity was to be found by travelling along Dame Street to the east of the old city, and across College (then called Hoggin's) Green. An antiquated gate-house marking a territorial divide had been demolished in the generation before Swift wandered here as a college man. When Swift studied at Trinity, the front of the college – a quiet façade behind a small lawned outer court – was very different to the more high-powered one we know today, completed in 1759, with the 'colossal order' of its imposing entrance giving way to a startling inner expanse. The front Swift knew had Baroque touches on its outer wings, and a central gateway rose through two emphatically punctuated storeys to a steeply pitched roof and a small domed bell-tower. The standard histories imply this foremost part of the college was a rather makeshift affair; but an illustration made in 1728 shows a pleasant blend of plainness and elaboration, with smart flat arches above the windows and stylish downward-rolling scrolls below the pediments at either end of the front. These outer flourishes do, admittedly, contribute to an awkward tension of vertical effects that arguably undermines the confidence of the structure: the tall chimneys on either side of the bell-tower, shooting up above the central pilasters and entablatures, in consequence seem a little jerky. But in the 1728 drawing, at least, the assembly looks a very dapper if more than faintly self-conscious piece of work. It was apparently completed in or around 1685. Behind it one found a large square made up of brick student houses, each a couple of storeys. In Swift's day this 'old front square', something of a building site, led through to the real heart of the college, the Elizabethan quadrangle, which one entered via the lodge that occupied the base of an ancient monastic steeple. A gatehouse stood at the nearest corner of the quadrangle, at the north-west. Running further along the same side was a roughly continuous block that held the college hall and kitchens, the library in an upper gallery and the adjacent new chapel, completed in 1683. This was apparently 'as mean a structure as you can conceive; destitute of monumental decoration within; it is no better than a Welsh church without'.[11] East and west were more houses for students, in the old timbered style; a legendary pump, the college omphalos, took pride of place amid the cobbles, and more comfortable lodgings for the fellows were situated on the southern side. There the Provost received his guests. On stepping through the parlours into the delightful fellows' gardens stretching southwards at the back, one Frenchman observed the poor life of a vine on which the fruit would never ripen, for want of heat, despite its being nailed to a chimney in plain view of the midday sun.[12]

In the Provost's garden, visitors encountered an impressive vista that unfolded on all sides around the path before them. The bay to the east, the Wicklow Mountains, the city, roughly to the west, the Liffey to the north – all lay in plain view. For at that time (from which none of the buildings survive), Trinity occupied Dublin's outermost fringe. It was a good run from the historic safety of the Castle; as the fellows had been uncomfortably aware for the century since the college was founded, it was now virtually the city's first line of defence.

The regime for college students was one to which the grammar-school boys were well used, though the hours spent in class were less severe. The day began before six, when Morning Prayer was sung in the chapel, followed immediately by the day's first lecture, with further services at ten and four. The most important days of the week academically were Mondays, Wednesdays and Fridays during term-time, when students engaged in public debates on a subject from their stage of the course. They faced oral exams in the hall, conducted by graduates and junior fellows, at the start of each term. From day to day, they could leave the college grounds only for two hours at a time at strictly set times, between two and four in the afternoon, and seven and nine in the evening. Still, 'town-haunters' (as the college record defined them) often proved uncontainable: in Swift's time, as long before and afterwards, there were 'many instances of public admonition and expulsion of Students for frequenting taverns, for engaging in unseemly riots in the streets, for being drunk and wounding citizens, for playing cards and gambling in houses in the city'.[13]

Despite the warm words Ashe spoke in defence of modern science, and the dedication shared by so many of his colleagues, this still young university was a bastion of ancient and medieval learning. In all vital points, the undergraduate curriculum merely continued the intensive training of grammar school, with some diversions into music, theology and mathematics, and almost everywhere, as for centuries, and in spite of Continental reformers, one still encountered Aristotle; 'Aristotle that hath an oare in every water, and medleth with all things', as Montaigne summed up both the prevalence of the venerated philosopher – and the annoyance that many teachers and writers felt towards his lingering shade.[14]

The degree course was four years long, with lectures dominated by Aristotelian logic and philosophy, and the tutorials – given each day, in Swift's case, by Ashe – by classical literature. Logic took up most of the first and second years, Aristotle's *Physics* was the main text for the third, with progression into metaphysics in the fourth.[15] The resulting qualification was still that required for the priesthood of the later Middle Ages, for which this 'scholastic' syllabus was developed in the first place.

The basic skill the college syllabus fostered, as at grammar school, was the art of disputation. Students were required to debate publicly, using syllogisms, every other day from Monday to Friday. Swift's formal education essentially involved the gathering of what were called 'topics' – a word Swift used frequently, in reference to a method that became second nature to him. A 'topic' was a 'subject', in the current sense, but it was also a point or argument that could be stored for use when talking *about* a given subject. At its Greek root the word meant a 'place', and this had been adapted to denote a mental storage point (sometimes preserved for reference in a notebook) from which material for arguments could be taken. In itself, a topic merely yielded ideas for use in defending or rebutting a given proposition. Some topics were specific to one subject; others could be used in discussing one or even many subjects, and were thus *loci communes*, or 'commonplaces'.

Throughout the sixteenth and seventeenth centuries educationalists had seen the useful element the Aristotelian logical texts – the *Organon* – contained, and had tried to distil it. The charismatic Provost, Marsh, composed a popular guide on such principles, the *Institutiones logicae*, which may in effect have been the college textbook. As R. S. Crane noticed on studying the manual, it contained a number of test propositions with tantalizing bearing on Swift's future works – including 'no horse is a rational creature' (*nullus equus est rationale*). The statement is at one level flatly contradicted by the race of Houyhnhnms Gulliver so much reveres; at another, it is supported by the readiness of Swift's speaking horses to commit genocide upon the Yahoos.[16] Marsh, an uncompromising churchman who fasted two and a half days in every seven, was nevertheless fonder now of his research on endocrinology and oriental languages; thus even leading pedagogues tacitly accepted that the old course was something students simply needed to get through. Swift's examiners were fairly forgiving, it seems, of his occasional poor displays in verbal tests.

Yet, by many scholars and teachers, the larger apparatus of scholastic interpretation was by now widely seen as mouldering Medievalism, a rubbish-heap that smelled, moreover, of downright popery. So when Ashe welcomed the Lord Lieutenant on behalf of Dublin's scientific brethren, he was fairly conventional in slighting the old learning that was still, officially, his own stock-in-trade. He lamented how knowledge had been 'heretofore condemn'd to melancholy retirements, kept as a minor under the tuition of ambitious and arrogant guardians, buried in cloysters, or the more dark obscurity of affected jargon and unintelligible cant'.[17] The fate of learning, as he declared quite conventionally, was monkish; it was also a fate still similar to that of many of the less prestigious boys in Trinity College, the fatherless Swift among them.

Common though they were by 1686 – for St George Ashe, despite his many pastoral virtues, was no innovator – such words still threw stones at the college's ministering spirit of learning. Up in the library above the hall, hard by the spire of a plundered monastery, sat the now somewhat mildewed book collection of the late Archbishop James Ussher, the Primate of All Ireland and one of the best-read men of his day. Ussher is remembered for calculating the date on which God created the earth, and is regularly sniggered at in popular histories of science. But the figure he produced was nonetheless valid in terms of the sources available to him: he reached the summit of what medieval scholasticism and Renaissance humanism could offer. His precious books, dumped by order of Cromwell in a damp room in Dublin Castle, but then brought back to Trinity during the Restoration, were still objects of pride for many of Trinity's more traditional fellows. Nevertheless there was no denying that most of these volumes embodied an order of teaching that was dying, and that endured both yawns and mockery. Swift was among those who, despite mixed feelings, found it obsolete.

The *new* learning was not immune from derision either, as Ashe was perfectly aware: by certain 'railleurs', he accepted, 'we are told . . . that our time is spent in vulgar experiments, in empty useless speculations.'

He countered such jeers, strikingly, in the language of the old curriculum: 'They should reflect that all things are capable of abuse from the same topicks by which they may be comended.'[18] One of the standard exercises a student might get in termly examinations would require him to give twenty-four syllogisms supporting a 'wrong' answer to a question – and twelve in defence of a 'right' answer.[19]

The unconscious paradox of the old pedagogical system is that it trained people who belonged to a very dogmatic society in a highly relativistic mode of thinking. The syllogism was widely accepted as the highest Aristotelian standard of proof; yet freshmen and sophisters were expected to deploy it skilfully in defending obvious falsehoods. Much can be said on the effect of this training on Swift. He can be found railing against its influence on a great many pages; but he also absorbed it and used it for his own purposes. In such ambivalence he was by no means unique. Although the drill of argumentation was essentially designed to develop a purely technical aptitude in developing sentences, the monotony and rigour of the exercises produced remarkable suppleness of mind in many of the brighter pupils. Generations of boys stretching back to antiquity were expected to see, and to argue for, both sides of a question – *in utramque partem*, as the phrase went. Such instruction encouraged the educated to see that most issues, however simple they seemed on first thought, proved to have multiple shades and dimensions. Simultaneously, practice in seeing 'both sides' of a question also inured the mind to the compromises many were obliged to make – often, to save their necks – in shifting their standpoint on divisive issues.

Swift's response to this paradoxical doctrine also involved contradiction. He can be seen taking the techniques of composition it nurtured to dizzying extremes. Instead of arguing 'on both sides' in his own voice, he tended to shift or distort a fictitious persona to articulate different, jarring positions. Perhaps the most notable example in his oeuvre is the passage at the end of the *Travels* when Gulliver denounces British imperialism at one moment, and then immediately extols the British for their 'Wisdom, Care and Justice in planting Colonies'.[20] The upshot of this literary strategy is a protest, often missed behind the sheer cleverness on display, against the ethos of modern inquiry. He takes a rather antiquated method of balancing and counterpointing different expectations against one another. In doing so he resists the rising demand of his age for a single demonstrable truth in answer to a philosophical or scientific problem. The effect of Swift's method was to place him beyond hope of such solutions ever holding. His scorn for scholastic pride in sophistry is thus equalled by his view of the satisfaction moderns could take in their 'philosophical' 'mechanical' discoveries. The most striking paradox of all, meanwhile, is that Swift's views about the widest questions of the relationship of State and Church, the rights of the individual and the nature of God could be as dogmatic as they were.

While disdaining both schools, of new and old learning, he could, however, ally himself with the classical. A distinction needs to be drawn between the arid logic books handed down from the Middle Ages and their forebears in antiquity, and the great corpus of poetry, drama, philosophy and history of Ancient Greece and Rome. The fact was, admittedly, that much of the latter had been shaped by the argumentative principles that were still being pounded into boys and some girls of Swift's generation; but it was also true that the 'classics' transcended those rules. A way for Swift of overcoming the rift between the Moderns and the Ancients – a divide he dramatized as a pitched 'Battle of the Books' – was to admire more recent authors who displayed classical virtues, in whatever genre. One such writer was the French aristocrat François de La Rochefoucauld (1613–80). In Swift's time, as now, La Rochefoucauld was best known for his *Maximes*, a book of crisp, realist statements about the ways of the world: he was the unwilling regent of the undeceived, and Swift later declared that 'I found my whole character in him.'[21] Certainly La Rochefoucauld left a mark on Swift's taste for pithiness, his confirmed tendency to compress a problem into an unanswerable apophthegm; and his fondness for constructing maxims of his own, though frequently in the guise of various champions of absurdity. Conversely, Swift was adept at unpicking the weak thread in principles that seemed axiomatic to others. In a late essay 'Maxims Controlled in Ireland', he would demonstrate how a number of supposed constants in political philosophy did not work at all in the Irish context – chiefly because Ireland was deprived of 'natural rights common to the rest of mankind who have entered into civil society'. He observed instead how one often found 'innumerable errors, committed by crude and short thinkers, who reason upon general topics, without the least allowance for the most important circumstances, which quite alter the nature of the case'.[22] Such a sentence might be taken to support the experimental approach to reality, but Swift was not above inconsistency on such questions. Some general principles might be subject to tests in varying 'circumstances', while others were sacred and exempt. There could be no tampering, for Swift, with the role of the Established Church, even in a society he could see was changing. His requirement otherwise of any

developed person was a stock of relevant – classical – learning combined
with practical, flexible thinking.

As an old man, Swift took a sorry view of his undergraduate career.
He blamed others for his failure to excel in college. Nothing, he declared,
could compensate him for 'the ill Treatment of his nearest Relations'.
Poor care from home, he said, left him 'so discouraged and sunk in his
Spirits, that he too much neglected his Academical Studyes, for some
parts of which he had no great relish by Nature, and turned himself to
reading History and Poetry'. In retrospect, he styled himself a well-read
dunce:

> So that when the time came for taking his degree of Batchelor, although
> he had lived with great Regularity and due Observance of the Statutes,
> he was stopped of his Degree, for Dullness and Insufficiency, and at last
> hardly admitted [i.e. to his B.A.] in a manner little to his Credit, which
> is called in that College, *Speciali gratiâ* ['by special grace'], [which] as I
> am told, stands upon record in their College Registry.[23]

He filed his education, in other words, among his other humiliating
ordeals. In truth, he had not done half so badly as he remembered. Neither was admission to degree by special grace either so unusual or so
onerous. It has been established that Swift was, on the whole, a competent and even above average student, though not the wonder of the
Schools he might have later wished to be.[24] He evidently disliked admitting that his gift, so far as textbooks were concerned, was for elaborately
spoofing their inadequacies.

His reading in 'History and Poetry' is in evidence throughout his
works, however. Classical modes guided his own verse even when he
subverted them. Surprising echoes also make themselves heard, as in his
chastening allusion to John Donne's famous 'To His Mistress Going to
Bed' in his own 'A Beautiful Young Nymph Going to Bed'. Quite a frequent tactic in Swift's prose, meanwhile, is using a brilliantly chosen and
succinctly delivered historical comparison. Swift always profits from the
disparities that trail along with the point or points the subjects being
compared have in common. Here, in 1725, he refines tenderness towards
his ailing friend Dr John Arbuthnot with a piece of scholarly comedy on
the eternal subject of falls at the finishing post:

> O, if the World had but a dozen Arbuthnots in it I would burn my
> Travells; but, however, he is not without Fault. There is a passage in

Bede highly commending the Piety and learning of the Irish in that Age, where after abundance of praises he overthrows them all by lamenting that, Alas, they kept Easter at a wrong time of the Year. So our Doctor has every Quality and virtue that can make a man amiable or useful, but alas he hath a sort of Slouch in his Walk.[25]

Combining memories of such 'passages' quickly and exactly with present phenomena was one of the chief skills of a wit (and surely is still); and it was in this respect that Swift really did take after his name.

## 2

For a 'dull and insufficient' 21-year-old, the literary fruits of his studies were still some way ahead. His recollections of his student years rankle with a sense of neglect. By this time his uncle Godwin had eight children to support from four marriages, and a growing brood of grandchildren. The attorney had also passed his zenith in more senses than one by the time Swift gained his B.A. He had invested heavily in a projected ironworks that failed spectacularly; and in or around the volatile year of 1688 he suffered a heavy stroke that deprived him of speech and, seemingly, of memory.[26] While record exists, meanwhile, of Swift's uncle William being positively considerate and helpful – in assisting Abigail Swift, and arranging paperwork from the university authorities for Swift himself[27] – overall Swift was evidently less than impressed by many of those charged with his care and education. His poor displays in examinations suggest not only that he failed to apply himself as he might have, but also that his masters' erudition had neither impressed nor enthused him. Over subsequent decades, he indulged himself with discreet character assassinations in the privacy of his notebooks. The great Narcissus Marsh, for example, the Provost of Trinity and eventually Primate of All Ireland, he brushed off as an intellectual miser: 'His disposition to study is the very same with that of an usurer to hoard up money, or of a vicious young fellow to a wench: nothing but avarice and evil concupiscence, to which his constitution has fortunately given a more innocent turn.'[28]

The character sketch of Marsh was written afterwards; but it hints that Swift was at least incipiently a rebel as his time at Trinity wore on.

The college elders, meanwhile, took a stern view of a 'vicious young fellow' when they found him. They also defined viciousness itself in broad terms. Students were disciplined for 'indecent conversation' with women and 'unseasonable walking' in the town after dark. The most regular offence was rowdiness, usually in or nearby city taverns during the night-time. Occasionally, nevertheless, a special example had to be made – as with the case of one John Jones, who made a little too free in his mockery of certain senior members of the college at an end-of-year entertainment in the heady atmosphere of July 1688: along with perfectly acceptable digs at new Catholic fellows, he made fun of the Philosophical Society's beloved scientific researches. Some time before, a student called Spencer had committed a graver crime. For wounding a college porter Spencer was deprived of his scholarship, which was diverted to compensate his victim, and commanded to make a public apology, on his knees, in the main hall. Punishments at Trinity varied, from the whippings and beatings that were standard teaching aids, to fines, confinement and expulsion (a frequent penalty for libels or scurrilous writings against 'persons of honour'). To pay for his satirical performance, Jones the japer had to reapply for admission to his degree and lost his scholarship privileges for a month. Later the same year – the year poor Uncle Godwin suffered his stroke and the whole fabric of the state seemed ready to tear – Swift himself got into trouble for similar misbehaviour.[29]

But such transgressions, and the varieties of viciousness they typified, were a routine part of collegiate existence. Swift would eventually cut loose by cultivating a way of seeing and speaking that found and exploited unpredictable, unstable connections and analogies – as in his comparison of the venerable Marsh to a visitor of prostitutes – and at the same time disguised its disregard for convention.

The old curriculum of logic and rhetoric cautioned students on what to avoid in their compositions. Swift's future work would incorporate a mode of thought and expression that classical and Renaissance rhetoricians had admired but also criticized. Since Aristotle, the theory of argument had directed speakers to move from more general, broadly acceptable ideas to more specialized and challenging content. A rhetorical manner the early moderns called 'farfetched', however, roundly disregarded this simple-to-complex principle.[30] Farfetched expression involved 'jumping over' – or *transuming*, in rhetorical jargon – more obvious ideas or words and using a deliberately unusual or unlikely expression. It represented things by means of things to which they were only slightly and tenuously related (often by means of a pun); attributing an event, for example, to a very distant and obviously irrelevant cause. One of Swift's favourite writers, Rabelais, experimented constantly with farfetched propositions. At one point Rabelais asserts, for example, that all the geographical discoveries of the fifteenth to mid-sixteenth centuries were indebted ultimately to hemp, from which the sails of every pioneering vessel were made. Without hemp, the great explorers would thus have got nowhere.

A kindred principle of misdirection and misattribution is integral to Swift's first major work, *A Tale of a Tub*. It is there even in the book's title, the floating tub being the decoy mariners would use to distract a whale from attacking the main ship.[31] Farfetched logic underlies many of the 'abuses of learning' Swift demonstrates in the *Tale*'s extravagant digressions. The joke is, admittedly, sometimes a little dry. In ancient times, Scythians claimed that the skies over the northern continent were filled with falling feathers; picking up on this in Herodotus, Swift's lecturing persona interprets this storm of quills as a profusion of pens, and concludes that the world even in those distant days was packed with aspiring writers.[32] The *ad absurdum* slant was a tangent Swift simultaneously criticized and exploited. In his haughty 'Apology' for the work, he discovered such reasoning, with the added ingredients of aggression and cynicism, in a critic's misplaced hostility: 'A Man who receives a Buffet in the Dark may be allowed to be vexed; but it is an odd kind of Revenge to go to Cuffs in broad day with the first he meets with, and lay the last Nights Injury at his Door.'[33] In general, as here, Swift sided with the classical view of the farfetched. Farfetched thinking in his works is usually a sign that the character or persona doing the thinking is misinformed, gullible or even deranged. Farfetched ideas Gulliver encounters on his travels include the Lilliputians' theories on egg-breaking and some of the conclusions they draw about the contents of his pockets. The efforts Gulliver sees in the Academy of Lagado to derive sunlight from cucumbers or reconstitute food from stool indicate a typically farfetched naivety about remote causes. Later still, Swift's best-known 'projector' would 'overleap' or transume more obvious approaches to child poverty with his *Modest Proposal* that the babies of the poor should be sold as food. In all these cases, farfetched thinking is botched thinking, either practically or ethically. Yet, as pieces of rhetoric, or as imitations of pieces of rhetoric, such inventions were nevertheless highly effective. The very memorable farfetched extreme in these examples helps us notice the less obvious degrees of absurdity, madness or barbarism we might easily accept as normal or rational. Swift's use of the farfetched, in fact, partly illustrates a broader dilemma that emerges in his writing.

Put very bluntly, this was a dilemma as to whether it was appropriate to write as he would, in the decade and a bit after he left Trinity, when he started work on *Tale of a Tub*. Was it acceptable to pursue moral themes through irony, aggressive comic allegory and farfetched, absurd and alien lines of argument? When he published a robust defence with an authorized edition of the *Tale* in 1709, Swift answered these questions with a brusque affirmative. The need he felt to address those questions at all nevertheless points to some anxiety, at least in earlier years, about whether his answer was the right one. Such anxiety, if he did feel it, stemmed from an essential tension in his work and personality. On one side, he was drawn with priestly seriousness to address 'abuses' of learning and religion, and later of social and political management. On another, every page of his work reveals his fascination with, and mastery of, the secular culture of wit.

Swift committed no personal testimony to paper during his student years, nor does any reliable description survive that was made of him at the time. There is probably now a computer program that might rejuvenate the portraits we have of Swift in middle age, and provide a fairly reliable image of a round-faced, blue-eyed, faintly stocky young man, patrolling Trinity's precincts in his gown; but any extensive ideas about his personality during this period rest on conjecture. Consequently there is no way of being sure if an urge towards literary invention began to clash with a settled and somewhat morose moral purpose while he was still sleeping on his straw bed in college lodgings. His earliest poems are surprising for rigorously avoiding irony, or not even contemplating its possibilities. Yet his earliest surviving letters give ample testimony that the life of a wit and a poet clearly attracted Swift from early on.

To be clear on why there was a contradiction between wit and moral respectability, something should be said about the culture of wit and its trendsetters in the 1670s and 1680s. In the memories of most, the period was marked out as decadent. The leading poets of Charles II's Court were glamorous, unconventional and, at least in legend, depraved. Such figures included George Villiers, second Duke of Buckingham, and Sir Charles Sedley; although the most flamboyant and best-known remains John Wilmot, second Earl of Rochester. He was described by his confessor, Gilbert Burnet – a historian Swift came thoroughly to dislike:

Wilmot, earl of Rochester, was naturally modest, till the court corrupted him. His wit had in it a peculiar brightness, to which none could ever arrive. He gave himself up to all sorts of extravagance, and to the wildest frolics that a wanton wit could devise. He would have gone about the streets as a beggar, and made love as a porter. He set up stage as an Italian mountebank. He was for some years always drunk, and was ever doing some mischief.[34]

The unlikeness between prudish, careful, insecure Swift and the extrovert Rochester is too obvious to pursue at length; yet they arguably shared an interest in disguise, and Swift's imagination in this respect proved much more elaborate than Rochester's. In print Swift posed as quacks of every kind, from astrologer to social engineer, and adopted the voices of lords and labourers alike. He abhorred the sexual promiscuity in which Rochester exalted, but his poetry especially came to display an oddly similar fixation with lust as a great (and troubling) universal, in the young and old, healthy and afflicted. The imaginative paths Swift felt inclined to follow had been disreputable since the degenerate heyday of the Restoration, if not before. As such, Swift's early work, notably *A Tale of a Tub*, tries to draw an assiduous line between the activities of the lurid beasts of the Restoration Court and his own literary agenda. The 'Apology' Swift added to the *Tale* in 1709 insists that the book was intended only for 'Men of Wit and Taste';[35] but since, by his own definition, such men should have a preternatural ability to discern his true intentions and their moral rectitude, the very need for such a defence is questionable. In fact, to respectable readers and many of his fellow 'Church-of-England Men', Swift's endeavour in the *Tale* looked dubious at least. The 'Apology' repeated the common allegation that Swift's second cousin twice removed, John Dryden, the sometime laureate, had lived in 'all manner of vice';[36] Burnet had also described Dryden as 'a monster of immodesty and of impurity of all sorts'.[37] Swift was anxious indeed to distinguish himself from such characters; but the pursuit he shared with them was tainting.

While decrying the traditional corruptions, Swift would speak proudly, in later years, of his knowledge of royal courts and his skills as a courtier. Literary success was inextricable from the prestige and patronage the Court could bestow. The Court had drawn earlier religious poets, notably George Herbert and John Milton, who both resisted its temptations – although as a Commonwealth official Milton had effectively served in Cromwell's unofficial court. But for an undergraduate in Dublin, whose

family connections and presumably his aspirations as well lay in England, a young Swift was likely to invest all the more magic in the regal
entourage. His near-abandoned status, as a fatherless son dependent on
his uncles, made the compensations offered by the Court all the more
potent. That attraction would always be complicated by the scandal surrounding the royal brothers, Charles and James, but for Swift the problem
could be at least partly resolved by following his grandfather's loyalties
and idolizing the Court of Charles I, the martyr king. Attaching one's
hopes to the Court historically involved a compromise for the individual
wishing to remain morally independent. But its lures were hard to resist:
only there could one win the fight for the attention and favour of observers who really mattered. If a Rochester could give in to glamour and
influence, so might a Swift – and more excusably, since his material need
of the benefits approval at Court might supply was all the greater. Even if
he decided on the priesthood, the young Swift knew that the Court
monopolized all substantial preferment in the Church.

Symbolically, the focus of any aspiring writer in English would always
lie at Court; and for an Irishman conditioned to despise Irishness, English geography and architecture added to this magnetism. The Court was
to be found in or near London, whether in the red-brick cliff of Richmond Palace on the Thames, topped with bulbous domes like a set of
coronets there for the taking; in the sprawl of Whitehall; or behind the
sombre front St James's presented to a capital that, despite the injuries
of plague and fire, was growing to be more or less unrivalled by any in
Europe. Swift was a child of two cities: the one to which he was confined
and another he had only imagined. By the 1680s London was resurgent.
New terraced streets of mansions were stacked in place. Bourses and
exchanges flourished; a magnificent white presence began taking shape
on the earth cleared of the ruins of the old St Paul's. London still offered,
in the meantime, many of its perennial sights and wonders, and Londoners still took huge pride and pleasure in describing them. The Tower still
stood guard beside the river's 'Noble Stream', and London Bridge, turreted and portcullised, was 'a single continuous street, well replenished
with large and stately Houses on both sides, and Situate upon twenty
stately Arches, whereof each one is made of curious Free-stone, every
one of them being threescore foot in height, and twenty Foot distant
from each other'.[38] Greater efforts, meanwhile, were slowly being made
to celebrate, or at least appreciate, Dublin. Visitors wrote complimentary accounts of the city. Yet, while they preserved and celebrated their
past in a resilient, elegiac oral culture, the native Catholic majority of the

island felt alienated from their supposed capital – as they did, it seems, from most of the country's larger towns. Meanwhile the ruling mixture of Protestants as yet felt little attachment, speaking generally, to the historic 'longhport' of Dublin. It was, with little exaggeration, a strategically vital yet still unwanted, unloved conurbation; its early-medieval past went largely unstudied until the twentieth century.[39] The neglect it suffered, in symbolic terms, would of course be instrumental to Joyce's decision to put his home city at the centre of his creative life. In Swift's time, Dublin received hardly anything of the care and delight that was found in the measuring of London's arches and pillars: as yet there was precious little done by way of copying and deciphering the inscriptions on its antiquities, or sizing up and prizing each stone in its bulwarks. It was a largely uncelebrated metropolis.

Given his circumstances, Swift had every reason to concentrate his energies on the idea of making a name in the distant English capital, or in the culture it both contained and represented. He might hope for a life of quiet prosperity as a colonial official in the Irish Church or State; but the appointments that made such a life possible were very frequently made from England. For that reason London, or what London stood for, was the place to make a splash, if that was what one wished to do; and the city's gleam, for all Swift's determined cynicism, drew out a side of him that would always be at odds with the deportment required of a dependable man of business or spiritual affairs. This was a side that wanted to entertain, win admiration and indeed take the stages and presses by storm. Dublin could do only so much, by sad contrast, to satisfy such desires. It was spreading, certainly, but its core remained a town clinging to a small rise in the land, packed behind crumbling walls above the Liffey to one side and, to the other, the Poddle – the partly subterranean river that still regularly rose through the walls of the houses built outside the original enclosure. The meeting of those two rivers created the 'black pool' from which Dublin – *linn dubh* – took its name. A name associated with sodden murkiness would seem apt to a person who felt stuck there; who was unimpressed by the grey minimalism of the two cathedrals' façades, the tumbledown Medievalism of the Castle, the uselessness of the original walls. Even those walls lacked the dignity of London's Roman ruins. Swift's unkind sketches of college fellows, or the worthy Narcissus Marsh, communicate a despairing grudge against the surrounding environment. The city cramped Swift's movements at Trinity, even as his reading spread far beyond the college curriculum, in space and time.

Another thing, for Swift, was the people. Again, the scorn and derision in which the 'mere', 'wild', or 'native' Irish were held by English expatriates can hardly be over-emphasized. And, as Irish-Irish citizens of Dublin tried to cultivate English manners, habits and dress, a further caricature began to develop. It was first caught in James Farewell's burlesque *The Irish Hudibras*, in which the stage Irish dialect was defined for another century or more of walk-on rogues and buffoons. Here, at a mock-heroic funeral, Farewell describes a typical gathering.

> Some for their pastime count their Beads,
> Some scratch their Breech, some louse their Heads;
> Some sit and chat, some laugh, some weep;
> Some sing Cronans [songs], and some do sleep;
> Some pray, and with their prayers mix curses;
> Some Vermin pick, and some pick Purses . . .[40]

Such well-captured liveliness might naturally have been translated into an English setting: and as for vermin, they roamed all but as freely in great houses as they did in humble cottages. Yet, in Ireland, the English view painted the entire native populace with the broadest of derogatory brushes, daubing them exclusively as the rowdy comic braggarts or simpletons typified by Farewell, his predecessors and his literary heirs. The 'higher' realms of Gaelic culture were entirely abnegated. One side-effect of this stereotyping for Swift was that there could be no larger native audience to whom he could appeal, since his own cultural background entirely rejected their authority or sophistication as judges. In his early stages as a writer, he could look only to the minority of English extraction, and recent extraction at that: and through them to the distant 'mainland' readership. Dublin, let alone Ireland, was not a place he showed any inclination to praise or in which to seek fame, since it inevitably felt parochial. Decades would pass before he saw and half admitted that it deserved better.

## 3

'We labour under two mighty Evils,' a Lilliputian courtier tells Gulliver; 'a violent Faction at home, and the Danger of an Invasion by a most potent Enemy from abroad.' By the time Gulliver gains royal confidence, the crisis has already lasted seventy moons. The faction is made up of those in Lilliput who wear high heels on their shoes. The courtier admits that high heels 'are most agreeable to our ancient Constitution', but now they pose a danger to the state. The Emperor only permits those on the low-heel side to join his government.[41]

Here is Swift's bitter spoof of the great running division in British politics and society. By the 1670s, Parliament was split openly between what we still call political parties but that were closer in fact to warring bands. The Tories, once traditionally closer to the Court, supported the 'High' Anglican Church in which Swift was being brought up, while the Whigs derived their support mainly from the 'Low' Nonconformist churches. Their respective heel sizes were obvious, but Swift's relationship to the parties was more complex than this paragraph in the *Travels* might suggest. By the time he created Gulliver, he had been committed to the Tory cause for decades. But there was a long earlier period, which he preferred to ignore or recast, when he too had worn somewhat shorter heels.

Across Europe, equivalents of Lilliput's historical struggles continued, both within and between nations. The hostile state of Blefuscu is to Lilliput what France was to the Atlantic kingdoms. But, whereas the politicians of Lilliput resist the very notion of a power exponentially greater than their own, that was not the case among those in Stuart England with any grip on reality. Louis XIV's victories across the Continent were benighting Protestant countries with the terror of Papism. By 1682, the year Swift progressed to university, Louis had humbled Spain, the Low Countries, Denmark and Prussia, and made England his mere puppet: for four years from 1670, King Charles's foreign policy had been dictated by secret French deposits in the Exchequer. Louis had also seemingly triumphed on the parallel domestic fronts that challenged any monarch aspiring to absolute power: Parliaments and ministers, on one side, and a fickle aristocracy on the other. Rival organs of state had been neutered in the 1660s, and the peers tamed. Louis both indulged and entrammelled his noble subjects by keeping them close in his evolving architectural fantasy at Versailles. Internally, Louis sought to snub out his kingdom's tendency to splinter into warring factions; in foreign affairs, he was preoccupied with undoing once and for all the confinement France had suffered for the past two centuries, encircled as it was by the ascendant powers of Spain and the Holy Roman Empire. Only a brief peace at the end of the seventeenth century would interrupt Louis's almost continuous war-mongering in Europe. Swift passed an early verdict on such regal audacity: 'The very same Principle that influences a

Bully to break the Windows of a Whore who has jilted him stirs up a Great Prince to raise mighty Armies, and dream nothing but Sieges, Battles and Victories.'[42]

England meanwhile was a demesne of fervid conspiracy. As most would later come to admit, however privately, the wider plots most feared existed largely in a realm of the imagination; yet the consequences were real enough. In the early years of the Restoration, the greatest threat supposedly came from 'fanatical' ex-revolutionaries. As time passed, as their good-humoured, clear-sighted, yet lascivious and by times downright brutal monarch failed to produce an heir, and as King Louis spread his pinions ever wider in Europe, English Protestants re-directed their suspicions to the Catholics in their midst. Pre-eminent among these, as Charles aged, was his brother James – similar in his build and dark features, though more introvert, and with something of Charles's knack for judging character; willing to use underhand means if absolutely required; popular as both a soldier and first lord of the admiralty; but feared, and in places loathed, for publicly admitting that he had converted to Rome.

People saw and heard treason everywhere. These tendencies were exploited by one astoundingly villainous personality. Titus Oates, a loping, limping, shrill-voiced, foul-mouthed son of a Baptist, with the thickest neck and sharpest chin of any man alive, returned from mad-dening his fellow priests and Jesuit sponsors across Europe in the late 1670s to spread poisonous word of a Popish plot. His interrogators, including the King himself, doubted and in some cases saw straight through him; but the public, and their leaders in the House of Com-mons, believed every word. Sceptics, such as the JP who first took Oates's testimony, and who was subsequently found lying stomach-down on his sword at the foot of Primrose Hill, tended to meet unpleasant ends – fates that usually corroborated, however, Oates's incredible fabrications. Soon a cell of Popish plotters was found in every major town, and high-placed figures were exposed as their leaders. The Catholic Queen's devoted secretary, dignitaries across the three kingdoms and later even the Queen herself were made suspects. According to Oates and his believers, the common aim of these conspirators, coordinated by a Jesuit network of impossible sophistication, was to take the life of Charles and ensure the accession of James, if he agreed to their demands. Some thirty-five people were executed on Oates's evidence before the nation snapped out of its paranoid trance.

Oates's adventures in perjury made him guilty of one of the lowest crimes in Lilliput, where accusers are routinely put to death if they are shown to be malicious. Gulliver notes approvingly that the Lilliputians see fraud as a worse offence than theft: 'For they alledge, that Care and Vigilance, with a very common understanding, may preserve a Man's Goods from Thieves; but Honesty hath no Fence against superior Cunning.'[43] In the case of this particular fraudster, men and women were blinded by hatred and fear more than by honest simplicity of mind. Oates was believed because the country was all too ready to take his word; and his stories – some manufactured for revenge, others in a spirit of pure fevered invention – suited the ends of a larger political organization. The main flanks of Whigs and Tories were very roughly speaking the descendants of Roundheads and Royalists. They would remain fixed parts of British society for many generations. In the 1690s Swift described the Tory–Whig division as one embedded in the biology of the nation. He joked of how the original Roundheads, 'in the age of our Fathers', moulded their skulls into spherical shape through the close-cropped haircuts common to apprentices and the tight-fitting caps favoured by Dissenting preachers. By Swift's time this 'operation of art' had become a naturally occurring phenomenon, like the elongated skulls found in certain Asian cultures, 'so that a *Round-head* has been ever since as familiar a Sight among Us, as a *Long-head* among the Scythians'.[44]

With the fault-line between Roundhead and Cavalier all but genetically engrained, a campaign to exclude James from the succession led to violent tremors across the kingdoms in the late 1670s. The dispute was almost synchronous with Oates's explosive allegations. As a consequence it seemed that the demands of Parliament would drive Charles into financial dependence on France. In the worst imagined scenario, an all-out rebellion against him seemed likely. Memories of the wars resurfaced; mid-century tracts and histories reappeared in the presses. Yet, to anyone opening their eyes from Cartesian meditation, and adapting his experimental approach to the circumstances at hand, it was evident that the real threat of conspiracy came not from the frightened English Catholic minority, but from the very quarter that was set on condemning them. And so it proved in 1683, when a group of Whig magnates and discontented officers supporting the King's illegitimate son, the Duke of Monmouth, thought of kidnapping Charles and James on their way to the races at Newgate. The Rye House Plot provided the King and his Tory supporters with the excuse they needed to uproot Whig networks all over the country. The greater threat in truth had passed two years previously, when the Earl of Shaftesbury, the Whigs' charismatic, philosophically disposed but politically merciless leader, took England to the brink of civil war during a volatile Parliament convened in Oxford. Having tee-tered and steadied himself, largely by accepting another secret pension from Louis, Charles had adopted his father's provocative strategy of governing without summoning Parliament. He passed the remainder of his reign in the pay of France.

The abortive Whig revolution, the Rye House Plot and the eventual exposure of Oates as a fraud all came to pass when Swift was in his teens, as he became more conscious of the public world, and presumably more fascinated by the human machinery that drove it. Soon after he enrolled at Trinity in 1682, he studied history far more avidly than the formal syllabus. The principals of the Whig and Popish intrigues were as absorbing as anyone Swift could encounter in Livy or Tacitus. Closer to home, Ireland had its share of victims and plotters. The perfectly inno-cent Primate of All Ireland, Oliver Plunket, was sent to his death by Oates's malign fantasy. By the time a former lord lieutenant of the king-dom, Arthur Capel, Earl of Essex, spoke up for Plunket, albeit weakly and too late, he himself had been drawn into a web of actual conspiracy. Although as lord lieutenant he dealt humanely and pragmatically with Catholics – relatively speaking – on returning to England Essex succumbed to the pandemic anti-Papist terror. He was implicated as a supporter of Monmouth and the Rye House plotters, and soon after his arrest was found in the Tower with his throat cut. The knife that killed him was driven with such force that it cut into the vertebrae; but Essex's death was accepted as a rebel senator's suicide. It rankled less than the execu-tion of two other high-born dissidents, Lord William Russell and Algernon Sidney, who would not renounce the right they claimed to overthrow a tyrannical ruler.

Swift was still at Trinity when the British struggle entered its next major phase. The college records show that Swift was guilty of the peccadilloes many of his fellow students committed. He skipped lectures – especially in mathematics – and missed chapel services, and incurred the usual fines of a penny or two per absence. He and his schoolmate Francis Stratford, subsequently a great merchant and speculator in stocks, exchanged the role of pace-setter in minor misdemeanours; during certain periods Swift's fines were heavier, at other times Stratford edged out in front. His cousin Thomas, meanwhile, was generally more diligent. Yet, in his later years at Trinity, Swift's disciplinary record shows a shift towards genuine recalci-trance. In March 1687 he and his cousin Thomas were disciplined, along with four others, for neglecting their duties and spending too much time

in the city, probably after curfew. He was charged with more serious misconduct in the autumn of the following year, near the climax of a
particularly stressful period both for the college and for the kingdom. On
his birthday in 1688 Swift was sanctioned – as one of a half-dozen offenders – for inciting 'tumults' in college and insulting a junior dean. The
college records identify Swift as one of two ringleaders who were publicly
admonished, and commanded to beg pardon, on bended knees, of the fellow they had insulted. As a measure of how gravely the fellows regarded
the incident, this was the same sentence given earlier to Spencer, the student who had physically injured a college porter.[45] Swift's crime of
insolence, moreover, suggests that he had already developed critical views
such as those discussed above, recorded many years later, of 'miserly' and
'vicious' Narcissus Marsh.

Although the fellows treated such breaches of decorum very seriously,
the college would not have been the same without them. In a manner of
speaking, moderate tumults were even expected. The entertainments
held in cloistered academic institutions, in propertied households and
even in the Royal Court always allowed for an element of misrule. The
same element was an acknowledged part of the communities these col-
leges, estates and the Court contained. In the masques, pageants and
other theatricals held on feast-days and special occasions, the forces of
impudence were given the chance to make fun of or even subordinate
the authorities that normally controlled them. The trick was not to over-
step the line, as John Jones did in the satirical sketch that put his college
place at risk. The point behind the custom was twofold: it let out unex-
pressed tensions in heavily regulated conditions; but it also demonstrated
the greater power the establishment held over the agents seemingly
undermining it. The opposites could not exist apart; they defined each
other. The disparity between the two was then always restored by an
effective piece of theatre. The single satirical libel uttered at a college
*tripos* (the event starring John Jones in 1688) was hopelessly overwhelmed
by the weeks upon weeks of sombre lecturing that filled the college year
in class and chapel. The same principle was seen more grandly in the
masques performed at the Royal Court and in some palatial homes. The
chaotic figures given their liberty in the antemasque performed before
nobles and royals were soundly cancelled out by the lavish and usually
longer display of order that followed in the masque proper. By insulting
the junior Dean and making trouble, Swift threw his hat in with the
masters of misrule; that strong flip-side of his personality, the side of the
joker, the hater of cant, the renegade, would always belong with them.

Yet he fell back in with the established order afterwards, and the imbalance of power was preserved when he dropped contritely to his knees before the assembled college.

A problem arose when the hierarchy itself was no longer what conformists felt it should be. Beyond Trinity's courtyards, in roughly the span between Swift's two greatest indiscretions as a student, the country passed through another of those periods when the lords of misrule seemed to have discarded the tacit agreement and broken their bonds altogether. For many months something much bloodier, and still more familiar in Ireland, had got loose in the land again.

The causes of the new troubles were as old as the Reformation. There was no surprise in their reawakening, since everyone agreed they had only been resting. The shock, as ever, came in the precise manifestation of events. A huge crisis was made inevitable by circumstances that might have been if not avoided, then at least handled differently. The origin of the subsequent catastrophe, in this sense, was the death of Charles II in 1685. He suffered a stroke, just when his political position seemed more or less secure: the secret agreement with France supported his finances, while his enemies at home were either banished or immobilized. Still only in his mid-fifties, without the patient care of his doctors the King might have been expected to survive. Hot glasses were placed on his flesh to draw out malignant humours; further remedies contributed to his suffering. When Charles's ordeal ended, power passed to his brother. James was an established and respected admiral, but his religion invited distrust. Before Charles was buried, he promised the dead King's councillors that he would respect the Protestant settlement. Almost immediately, however, Mass was said publicly at Court, and James set the repeal of the Test Act – excluding Catholics from holding office – as his major goal. He squandered early advantages, notably a Parliament willing to give him every backing if he maintained the status quo, and the alarmed support he gained when Monmouth rebelled. The Monmouth revolt gave James the chance to bolster his army with Catholics, many brought over from Ireland. A year into his reign, Papists were rising not only in the military but also in government and the Privy Council itself, reinforced by a remarkable number of high-ranking conversions. Moreover, the new Lord Lieutenant of Ireland, Richard Talbot, Earl of Tyrconnell, was the leader of a staunchly Catholic Anglo-Norman dynasty.

James had initially tried to ally Roman interests with the 'High' wing of the Established Church. His reasoning was in many ways sound:

some High Anglicans had more in common with Papists, in their attitudes to scripture and liturgy, than they did with the various shades of Nonconformists. James was disconcerted and then angered when the Church hierarchy defied this line of reasoning, resisted his overtures and then roundly opposed his policies. Why they did so is crucial not only to Swift's position, broadly speaking, as a priest, but also to the 'revolutionary' establishment that eventually swept James from power and took over the succession. The High Church cherished religious ceremony and ornament in a fashion that would always seem popish to Dissenters; but it had also learned the cost of splitting the Protestant nation. James therefore turned back to the Nonconformists for popular support in repealing the Test. These dissidents, though, were far from unanimously keen on aiding and abetting a new Roman Catholic ascendancy. James's two Declarations of Indulgence, suspending penal laws against Nonconformity, only alienated him further from the Established Church, the wider public and the networks of local officials on whom government depended. When seven bishops – including William Sancroft, the mild and elderly Archbishop of Canterbury – submitted a modest petition against a royal order that the second declaration be read out in every church in the country, James over-reacted. He charged the bishops – celebrated in posterity as 'The Seven' – with seditious libel, and had them imprisoned. In doing so, the King managed to outrage the shadows of Civil War partisans on both sides. Rebel passions stirred at the figure of a high-handed king as he bypassed Parliament, like his father and brother, and dispatched members of the Commonwealth to the Tower. Loyalist sensitivities, meanwhile, were pained by the memory of William Laud, Charles I's Archbishop of Canterbury, being incarcerated on a similarly brusque command. By the time James was facing down the Seven in the early summer of 1688, he had come to typify almost every wrong of the past two generations.

Inciting conflict at the summits of the state, James was also creating great resentment lower down. For every Catholic he promoted, at whatever level, be it a modest local sinecure or the lord lieutenancy of an entire county, he dislodged a Protestant. In Ireland, as in the 1640s, the grievances were all the stronger because the lines of opposition were the more pronounced. Few months had passed, when he took office in 1687, before Irish Protestants were wholly convinced that Tyrconnell and his Catholic peers were bent on revolution – revolution in the sense it carried most often at that time: not of something explosively new, but of something lurchingly familiar, turning the fixed order back in time and upside down. The dials in Dublin revolved back to 1641. Key posts were transferred to Papists, property rights laid open to dispute. At Trinity, the fellows were forced to accept Catholics into their society – and meanwhile maintain order. They were obliged to sanction the undergraduates who met the change with insolence and sometimes misdemeanours. In July 1688 the fellows ordered that the college walls be raised three feet higher: the better to keep students in and indistinct miscreants out. Understandably, some lost their nerve. A number of Swift's tutors and classmates had already followed the example of many in Dublin and beyond, and fled the country. As finances dwindled, the college struggled to keep going on shortening supplies.

In the summer that year the political situation in Westminster and Whitehall also reached its crisis. The Seven Bishops had been acquitted of libelling the King. Their status as symbols of resistance was guaranteed in any case, but their victory in court deprived James of the initiative. As surviving presences in public life, they were living monuments of James's defeat: some of the Seven were still firmly ensconced in their sees when Swift reached his height of influence in government circles more than twenty years later. He noted with disapproving sadness how one, William Lloyd, deranged from excessive meditation on the Apocalypse, arrived one day at Court to prophesize in the royal presence. It made Swift wince to hear his friend, the Lord Treasurer, enter the debate and turn the Bishop's own studies of Revelation against him; 'which made the old Fool very quarrelsom; he is near ninety years old.'[46] Yet such was the veneration Lloyd could still command in 1712 that Queen Anne was more than willing to see him by special appointment.

Indignation against James turned into alarm, however, with a personally joyful and triumphal yet politically traumatic event on 10 June 1688. James's second wife, Mary of Modena, gave birth to a healthy son. Whatever his enemies might have had against James, the law of succession trumped all, and a line of Catholic heirs stretched, potentially, as far ahead as the crack of doom. James's little son shook the order of things so deeply that a quiet club of politicians, including several unlikely allies, decided his claims should be curtailed. But instead of countering the monarch head on, in the all too familiar fashion of the last forty years, they steered around him.

To date, James and Mary's children had all died; and while the couple remained childless, most assumed that the Crown would pass to the King's nephew and son-in-law, William of Orange. Mary of Modena, a lonely Italian princess to whom England and the English were on the whole distasteful, endangered this calculation once again when her pregnancy was announced towards the end of 1687. Given the changes being made in the state, certain policy-makers could not rely on the odds on her miscarrying, or being delivered of another ailing infant. A month or so before James's son was born, Prince William was already consulting on how he might take power. In England, the healthy baby, James Frances Edward, was widely dismissed as a changeling. A story was floated of a child being smuggled in a warming-pan into Mary's bedchamber, and her stillborn infant carried out. Bishop Burnet was one of many who had his doubts about the delivery. He knew how the labyrinthine interior of St James's Palace lent itself to the intrigue – there were antechambers and hidden passages to facilitate the switch: 'No cries were heard from the child: nor was it showed to those in the room. It was pretended, more air was necessary. The under dresser went out with the child, or somewhat else, in her arms to a dressing room, to which there was a door near the queen's bed: but there was another entry to it from other apartments.'[47]

A multitude of rumours (and downright libels) on the heir, however, merely testified to the power of the event, and the impotency of James's hostile subjects. Yet the select group of statesmen and churchmen mentioned above decided that another option was possible. In response to the history of the past fifty years, traditionalists had equipped themselves with a defence for radical measures when other options seemed exhausted. Their argument was sustained by the paradox that the spirit of the constitution could sometimes be amended only by actions that, from the outside, seemed to take drastic liberties with it. With this principle in mind, acting on a prompt from William himself, seven dignitaries signed a tightly worded letter inviting him to come to their country's 'relief', and promising to attend him when he landed.

It was a well-chosen approach: William's character favoured precision and secrecy. History would make him a totemic, yet still hugely divisive and emotive figure. In 1712, when some lines in his honour were cancelled from a performance of Nicholas Rowe's *Tamerlane* in Dublin, Williamite Loyalists stormed the stage: this punch-up in a somewhat seedily located theatre in Smock Alley, ten years after his death, may have been one of the smaller confrontations fought over William, but was typical in the fervour displayed.[48] In person, however, the energy he provoked in others was quietened by his own reticence and irritability. He disliked fuss and preferred to withdraw from it. 'He was apt to be peevish,' observed Burnet: 'It put him under a necessity of being much in his closet, and of being silent and reserved, which, agreeing so well with his natural disposition, made him go off from what all his friends had advised, and he had promised them he would set about, of being more open and communicative.'[49] Notwithstanding this tendency, William demanded all pains be taken in any major endeavour. In 1688 his planning was boosted when fortune provided the 'Protestant Wind' that took him to the south-west English coast.

William, despite the many years he would spend there, always viewed England from an offshore perspective. In 1672 he had vowed that he would die in 'the last ditch' defending the Dutch Republic from French troops. His marriage to King James's daughter Mary in 1677 took place with a mind to cementing an alliance with the Stuart monarchy. Charles's secret agreements with Louis all but neutered that policy in the short term; but the match still gave William a powerful claim on the Crown and England's Protestants some cherished insurance. William did not reciprocate the fervour with which, notwithstanding the distant and lawyerly tone of his invitation to invade, he was widely regarded. His passions were dedicated to a wider struggle. For him, England and the other Atlantic Crowns were first and foremost much needed chess-pieces in the fight against Louis XIV: figuratively and literally, the British and Irish kingdoms gave him his queen. As he put his fleet together in the summer of 1688, he was not set on resolving an internal Anglo-Saxon conflict for its own sake, but on an act of mass impressment: England's staunch Protestants were to be recruited for his larger war.

To a number of those who welcomed him, there was nothing wrong with that. Lord John Churchill, for one, would make his name in European history by taking William's campaign against Louis to new levels. 'He was a man of a noble and graceful appearance, bred up in the court with no literature [i.e. little book-learning]: but he had a solid and clear understanding, with a constant presence of mind.'[50] As Duke of Marlborough, and the Captain-General of the Allied Armies fighting Louis, Churchill would eventually become one of Swift's most illustrious targets. Churchill and his wife Sarah (née Jenyns) were among the closest friends of James's daughter Anne: they and the Princess were absolutely committed to the Protestant cause. The man who drafted the formal invitation, Henry Sidney, commander of English regiments in Holland, could also identify with William's perspective. He and Edward Russell gave the document a rebel flavour. Russell's cousin Lord William and Henry's brother Algernon had been executed for asserting that subjects had the right to resist their monarchs. From others in the group who signed the document, celebrated for generations as another 'Immortal Seven', greater hesitancy might have been expected. They included the long-retired minister Thomas Osborne, Earl of Danby, later Duke of Leeds, who had been maimed by the original exclusion crisis but was respected for engineering the match between William and Mary; Baron Lumley, a general seen recently in action against Monmouth, but a new convert to Protestantism; and Henry Compton, Bishop of London. Months of secret correspondence now gave way to open preparations for a military land-ing. James took fright and began offering to reverse his more extreme policies. In August he ordered that elections be held for a new Parlia-ment: it would be summoned in November, and would guarantee nothing more than the most basic civil liberty for Catholics. They would be excluded from the Commons, and the primacy of the Church of England would be reaffirmed. James abolished his Ecclesiastical Court of Com-mission, and reinstated ousted office-holders – notably the fellows of Magdalen College, Oxford. By the autumn, however, his government had disintegrated to the point that he could not master the protocol required even to make far-reaching concessions. The delicate local procedures on which elections depended proved impossible. William was mustering his forces, and by the end of October was at sea. After a setback in storm, in early November 200 troop-carriers sailed in plain view past Dover. William landed at Torbay on a key anniversary in the English Protestant calendar: whether one followed the Gregorian reckoning, and recorded it as the 15th, or the Julian, as the 5th, the Dutchman had been brought ashore by the same will of providence that had thwarted the Gunpowder Plot on the same day eighty-three years earlier.

## 4

From the moment he touched English soil, William struck the pose of one restoring order. He was there, his banners claimed, to uphold 'the liber-ties of England and the Protestant religion'. Narrowly, though, he avoided being cast as what, in fact, he was: an invader. The King's failure to give battle at Salisbury worked entirely to William's advantage: he moved still closer to London in the guise of a peacekeeper. The risk of its coming to open war in England diminished, though, as the days went by. Tories and Whigs alike deserted James; and he, seeing the game was lost, got his son and wife to safety in France. He soon tried to follow them, but even flight went upsettingly wrong for him at the first attempt. Late in the evening of 11 December, a local Catholic gentleman among the King's small party was recognized as James waited to board ship at Faversham in Kent. The locals at the harbour mistook the King for a Jesuit priest, and stripped him on the dock for any Papist treasure he might have been carrying. James's false beard offered little protection from any relatively shrewd eye that knew the monarch's face. Sure enough, a mortifying recognition scene took place soon afterwards at a nearby tavern, during which James showed that he could still at least act the part of a prince: he reclaimed his breeches, but let the locals keep his gold.

James's return to Whitehall interrupted an ongoing riot. Fickle crowds welcomed him, but Dutch advance guards had taken up posts in and about the royal palace. Not much longer had passed before he received word from William, whose forces stood a short ride outside London, that his presence would be a source of disorder – and not a little awkwardness. James was not long in realizing the soldiers had unofficial orders to turn a blind eye if he left. William did not want a lawful monarch on his hands. Incognito again, the abashed King's second escape was successful, and he made it to France a day or so before Christmas, as the mob now prepared to greet the newcomer. To fill a grateful void, William entered the capital.

The glory got and the damage done to personal reputations during this takeover were still powder-stained topics when Swift reached middle age and his polemical prime. They remained so long after his death. The mood across the land that autumn of 1688 also persisted in memory. For the children of the tradesmen and apprentices who put orange bands in their hats and sent up huzzas for William in the streets, it was a period of relief and exhilaration. William, they felt, guaranteed their entire way of life. Among those who saw themselves in party terms, the Whigs could feel this thrill more or less single-mindedly: they had always maintained, tacitly and not, that subjects were entitled to overthrow a tyrant. For Tories the flight of James brought greater ambivalence; as did the figure of Danby, the champion of Charles II's prerogative, mustering northern rebels at York. It was a perplexing time – though also sickeningly familiar to English Catholics who wanted nothing more than a quiet life. To all concerned, though, it echoed with an infectious, insolent soundtrack. There was one piece of music that no one could rid from their minds, even those who hated it. Thomas Wharton originally wrote his song 'Lilliburlero' as a satire against Lord Talbot, Earl of Tyrconnell, on his being made lord lieutenant of Ireland. Although the eponymous refrain involves a muddled piece of Gaelic that might have many meanings, the gist of the lyric is clear. Two 'Teagues' (an insulting term for Irish Catholics) anticipate the new Governor's arrival:

> Oh by my soul it is a Talbot
> Lilliburlero bullen a la;
> And he will cut every Englishman's throat
> Lilliburlero bullen a la . . .

The song was revived in the autumn of 1688 and became a revolutionary (or counter-revolutionary) anthem. It united the Williamite camps and was heard to demoralizing effect in James's fragmenting ranks. Wharton claimed that it sang James out of three kingdoms. A successful jockey and racehorse owner, with a name as a libertine, Wharton the lyricist was given to immodest claims, and a certain brazenness with respect to his own misdemeanours. He was previously best known as a braggish prodigal who had desecrated a parish church one night with a group of drunken friends. A long career in politics stretched ahead of him; and 'Lilliburlero' undeniably captured the mood of the moment. The lyrics contain a jibe against Irish Catholic prophecy, but the song had a clairvoyant aspect of its own – a semi-conscious foresight as to where the suspended war between James and William would eventually be fought. Despite its contempt for most things connected with natives of Ireland, it also owed its sensational effect to the catchy tune, an old Irish jig, to which it was set. The melody, it seems, had been heard on the march back in the Civil Wars, and perhaps before; it raised inherited memories in the blood.

For Swift's generation, the English events of November 1688 were an initiation. They experienced for themselves fears of the nature their parents had gone through as the state split apart in 1641. The settlement that installed William and Mary as monarchs, albeit by the will of an assembly that, strictly, was no legal Parliament, offered an antidote to the constitutional emergency. Afterwards, an old constant of history quickly emerged: as soon as a greater enemy was repelled, sleeping divisions resurfaced in the alliance that had opposed it. A key sticking point was of course the Church of England. The new King was a Dutch Calvinist, and no admirer of Anglican ritual or doctrine. Hardliners within the Church found an Oath of Allegiance irreconcilable with the old doctrine of divine rule: these 'Nonjurors' left or were driven from their offices, and bothered the consciences of a great many who remained. A larger section of the conservative wing of the Church, meanwhile, was completely opposed to a new movement to include, or 'comprehend', the more moderate sections of the Dissenting community. It was actually a High Churchman, Daniel Finch, Earl of Nottingham, who advanced a pragmatic solution to the problem. In February 1689 he placed two ecclesiastical reforms before the House of Lords. One was a Comprehension Bill, whereby the majority of Dissenting Protestant worshippers might join the Church of England. The other was a Toleration Bill, which legislated for the predicted minority of Dissenters who refused all connection with the Established Church. If made law, the bill would grant these Nonconformists freedom of worship. The plan had broad moderate backing, but attracted steady opposition from the more extreme 'high-flying' Tory Anglicans. The scheme was destroyed, however, not by them but by the King. Two days after the bills had their second reading William made his own wishes clear by exhorting Parliament to abolish the old Test and Corporation Acts. His bullishness broke the tenuous consensus. The Anglican moderates were afraid to make the concessions the Comprehension Bill demanded of them, and joined the extremists. In consequence, only the bill for a Toleration became law.[51]

How much this argument mattered is plain when you keep in mind that at this time the Church claimed it held a monopoly on worship; it vied for equal authority with secular government; and its rituals and administration were still intricately interwoven with those of the State. The issue at the centre of the ferocious ensuing controversy thus had enormous implications. The schism within the Church had long existed, but now each side acquired a new set of martyrs and persecutors. The division also became institutional. William appointed only bishops who favoured toleration of the Dissenters; overwhelmingly these were Whig. The lower ranks of the Church, meanwhile, 'the inferior clergy' – to which Swift would soon enough belong – developed a strong collective grudge against their diocesan masters, and an aversion to reform. The overwhelming majority of these priests remained dependent on the 'lower' tithes brought in from their parishes; as such, they had a closer tie to the 'landed' class that was predominantly Tory in colour. Admittedly Nottingham's Comprehension Bill might not have ended this split. It surely would, however, have gradually dissolved or at least softened Anglican prejudices against all but the most extreme Dissenters. The Earl, who presently became a secretary of state to the King, was called 'Dismal' Finch by his enemies for his unusual olive complexion. Swift came to loathe Nottingham, especially when, twenty years after his pragmatic bid to heal the Church, Dismal sided with the Whigs in their bid to keep Britain at war with France. Yet the Comprehension scheme advanced by Nottingham might well have saved Swift much subsequent heartache. As it was, his fear and suspicion of Dissenters would never disappear; and he would be torn between his loyalties to the Williamite revolution and the High Church – however much he, like other Tories, insisted there was no contradiction between them.

For those of Swift's generation in Ireland, the solution was more ragged still. As James's English government unravelled entirely, his administration in Ireland intensified its work. After William's landfall, Tyrconnell swiftly dispatched troops to Protestant-dominated Ulster, where support for the challenger was greatest. For their part, Ulster Protestants barricaded themselves in a number of key positions, notably Enniskillen and Derry. Early in 1689, with nowhere else to base his authority or make his stand, James arrived in Dublin with the support of French troops and officials. He found himself the figurehead, and perhaps little more than the puppet, of a government that had gained its own momentum over the past two years. With James now present to legitimize its reforms, the 'Patriot Parliament' in 1689 tore up the colonial establishment of Ireland. It was decided that legislation passed in Dublin no longer required approval from England before it came into force. A ruling that Irish people would henceforth pay their tithes to the priest of the church where they worshipped spelled the end for the Anglican Church in Ireland. Most radical, though, was the Act of Attainder, which repealed the post-war redistribution of property in Ireland. The Cromwellian and Restoration settlements were swept away, and a judicial process of revenge was set in motion. Thousands of estate-holders were dispossessed; and those who were resident fled for their lives, guilty by default of a capital offence.

Where was the real revolution? The Bishop of London had met William of Orange with a banner saying 'We are not prepared to change the laws of England.' Such English revolutionaries thus claimed that nothing essential had changed. It was Ireland that was revolving, and lurching with the motion. Long-restrained Irish hands itched for retribution, and since their urges were sanctioned, up to a point, by Tyrconnell's urgent need for troops to replace those James had transferred earlier to England, they took up arms with licence from Dublin. They seized on 'half-pikes': and brigades made up of civilian irregulars were named after these weapons. The Protestant response was either to raise barricades, as at Enniskillen and Derry, or to evacuate.

Trinity College was one of many institutions where a siege mentality was developing – notwithstanding the growing numbers of Catholics who had already been received behind the walls. As the crisis worsened, provisions ran low and the fare in hall became increasingly spartan. With no money coming in from the rents on the foundation's considerable properties, the refectory could give students and fellows only a single bare meal a day. As a boy, Swift remarked that he was fond of 'stuffing' when opportunity arose – as perhaps it rarely did. But much later, he found that when invited to great banquets he could rarely manage more than one dish. As a boarder, he grew used to living with hollow legs. Hungry periods such as the emergency of 1688–9 gave him a 'sad vulgar appetite' of which he became defensively proud.[52] Yet, although he might have tightened his waistband further, the land was now unsafe for the Anglo-Irish. The coming months were violent and terrifying for Protestants who had left it too late to leave – or indeed had nowhere to go. Cattle were killed in the fields, farms raided, and families molested or murdered. Aboard the hopelessly overburdened outbound ships, scared faces and tattered coats became a common sight among the passengers. Propaganda added its usual zeroes to the real numbers of those dead or dispossessed, but the cycles of neighbourly atrocity and reprisal were not to be denied. Dublin, where Protestants had been disarmed by decree, was emptying of its former ruling citizens. In February 1689, a lump sum of Trinity College money – albeit only £200 – was physically sent to England as an emergency fund for fellows scrambling there for refuge. Some of the college plate was pawned to help balance the books.[53] Before the end of January, two months short of the seven-month period of residency he needed to obtain his Master's degree from Trinity, Swift had quit the kingdom.

The journey was never merely a matter of catching a ferry – or a 'packet,' as the mailships were called in those days; but in the early months of 1689, before escape for Protestants became all but impossible, there was a further terrible crush and panic to negotiate in getting a place aboard ship. Swift, a gentleman in name, belonging to a well-connected family, was presumably guaranteed his crossing, but he couldn't avoid the press and alarm of 'meaner people', as described by his future superior, the Reverend William King.

'Tis to be considered that it was no easy thing to get away; the freight of ships and licenses were at very high rates, and sometimes not to be purchased at all. Many of the country people could not get to the sea ports; they had little money, their riches were in their stocks; and these being plundered, they were not able to raise so much money as would transport them and their families, and they generally came too late to the ports. A strict embargo being laid on all ships before they could get to the sea-side; many of the citizens of Dublin and other sea-ports got off, but were forced to leave their shops and concerns behind . . .[54]

In the light of difficulties faced by some, Swift's flight (along with his cousin Thomas) was not the most heroic; but nonetheless it took no little determination. He was an object of sympathy, and possibly some respect, when he reached England – for the first time on definite record since being taken there by his nurse.

# 4. The Temples and the Tub

What mortal change does in thy face appear,
Lost youth, she cryed, since first I met thee here!
                        – 'Occasioned by Sir W— T—'s Late Illness'[1]

## I

Swift was twenty-one when he fled Ireland. Some years before, his mother had moved to live with family in Leicestershire, and he stayed some time with these relatives on arriving in England. Not long passed in 1689, however, before another family connection proved valuable: Sir William Temple, a retired diplomat, agreed to employ him as his secretary. Sir William's father, Sir John, had ardently propagandized (and heavily exaggerated) the atrocities committed by Irish Catholics in the great rebellion of 1641. He recovered his high office after the Civil Wars, and in his eminence became a friend and patron of Swift's uncle Godwin. The Temples had exerted a strong territorial presence within Dublin since the beginning of the century. Their mansion and gardens dominated St Andrew's Parish on the south side of the Liffey, and the area soon became known as Temple Bar. Then, as now, the Temple Bar was a lively quarter – adjoined by the long row of taverns and coffee-houses on Essex Street, running eastwards parallel to the river. The Temples' dignity was only slightly tinctured by the southerly alley that led towards Dame Street and the precincts of the original city. Dirty Lane, where the 'pit of Crow-street Theatre' broke a monotony of stables and warehouses, was renamed Temple Lane early in the eighteenth century.[2]

Swift's new master was a distinguished writer, a former confidant of Charles II and an elder statesman much respected by the new King. For years, however, he had given himself to a studiously retired existence at his estate Moor Park, near Farnham, Surrey, cultivating his garden and nurturing prose reflections with the same genial care. Describing Temple, William Makepeace Thackeray found it impossible to fight his instinct for a lovingly plumped-up caricature; but he was closer to the manners of the late Stuart Court than we can be, and those who sample Temple's essays and lectures will find much to bear out what the novelist describes:

> Temple's style is the perfection of practiced and easy good-breeding. If he does not penetrate very deeply into a subject, he professes a very gentlemanly acquaintance with it; if he makes rather a parade of Latin, it was the custom of his day, as it was the custom for a gentleman to envelop his head in a periwig and his hands in lace ruffles. If he wears buckles and square-toed shoes, he steps in them with a consummate grace, and you never hear their creak, or find them treading upon any lady's train or any rival's heel in the Court Crowd. When that grows too hot or too agitated for him, he politely leaves it.

Thackeray's imagining of Temple as encountered by Swift, from a feasible construction of sources, is meanwhile simply too good to ignore.

> Gulielmus Temple, Baronettus. One sees him in his retreat: between his study-chair and his tulip-beds, clipping his apricots and pruning his essays – the statesman, the ambassador no more; but the philosopher, the Epicurean, the fine gentleman and courtier at Saint James's as at Shene [Sheen, one of Temple's estates]; where, in place of kings and fair ladies, he pays his court to the Ciceronian majesty; or walks a minuet with the Epic Muse; or dallies by the south wall with the ruddy nymph of gardens.[3]

Thackeray did greater justice to Temple's self-conscious refinement than the 'darkness' that so appalled him in Swift, perhaps because the Baronet's character was closer to his own. At the same time, while he identified a streak of moroseness and melancholy that Temple and his new secretary had in common, he overlooked the complex example this new patron would set Swift – of how to work, how to move in society, and how to negotiate the fierce divisions and alliances that made historical disputes matters of present emergency. Swift's response to this example was complicated in turn, and evolved jaggedly over the next two decades.

William Temple first set out into the world in 1648. He was twenty, with connections. In young portraits he is vaguely terrier-like, wide-faced and sharp-nosed, wearing a thin moustache that he seems to have kept in later life; his face capped and bordered with a thick head of long, dark curling hair. He had spent much of his boyhood at Penshurst, the country home of the celebrated Sidneys, with whom his dignified Leicestershire family enjoyed a historic and almost mythological link. His grandfather, an earlier Sir William, was a staunch friend and comrade to Philip Sidney, the soldier-poet and favourite of Queen Elizabeth. They shared literary interests and an ideal of the courtier's life. When Sidney died of his wounds at Zutphen, it was said, he lay in this elder Temple's arms.

In 1641 this hero's son, Sir John, was made the Master of the Rolls in Ireland, a lucrative position he lost in the course of the war and regained in 1653. When the younger William embarked on his travels in 1648, the family was richer in renown than ready money. Yet the tour was still seen as necessary to round off a gentleman's education, and was all the more advisable given the wrecked state of the British kingdoms: throughout a life both adventurous and withdrawn, Temple would prize his freedom of mind above all his material assets. On his way to France during the last days of the English Civil War he visited an uncle on the Isle of Wight, where the King was still a prisoner at Carisbrooke Castle. Political motives may have influenced the detour. Temple's father, an MP, having sided with Parliament for most of the war, supported the move to make peace with Charles. The King rarely forgot a name and never a face, and the elder Temple may have wished for his son to be seen. Yet a more momentous event for William on the island was entirely personal.

Although his forces had been crushed across all three kingdoms, in 1647–8 Charles would accept neither defeat nor the loss of his monarchy. To his mind, there was no way his crown could simply be knocked off his head: it was as immovable, almost regardless of his person, as the fortified rings of stone that surrounded him up at Carisbrooke. There in a nutshell was what infuriated the soldiers and officers, with Cromwell as their chief, of an army that had reduced Charles to nothing in the field. The generous peace the Parliament had granted him in no way reflected the advantage it possessed on the ground. The eventual solution, for the army radicals, would be to take off Charles's head and crown at one go; but for now he still passed days playing bowls on the castle green, walking and riding on the downs of Wight, and occasionally giving an audience to local and visiting gentry in a townhouse or inn in Newport. Temple's uncle, Sir John Dingley, was among many of the propertied islanders dispirited by the state of things – by billeting troops and in time taking orders from the tradesmen and Dissenters who in Parliament's name had taken positions of authority across the land. Such squires and former JPs by now largely saw the need to make do for the sake of peace. Less experienced, hotter-headed Royalists, especially ones just passing through, were unconvinced of the need to compromise.

The royal prisoner at Carisbrooke now rivalled the celebrated market at Newport – 'Nippert' to the locals, tucked inland on the Medina estuary – as Wight's main attraction.

> I chanced to be in Newport town
> 'Twas on a market day –
> An over-right t' 'Rose an' Crown'
> I met a sargeant gay –

On one visit to Newport during his stay on the island, Temple witnessed a frightening brush with the law. By then he had also had an encounter that at least challenged the old saw that the island had never produced 'any extraordinary fayr handsome woman, nor a man of supereminent gifts in wit or wisdome'.[4] The person concerned may not have been a native of Wight, but Temple at least first saw her there; and for him she combined both sets of 'supereminent' qualities.

That day, another young man lingered by a window in the inn where King Charles had just held court, and scratched an inflammatory graffito in the glass. His target was the King's gaoler, and the parliamentary Governor on Wight, Colonel Robert Hammond, and his text was taken from the Book of Esther (7:10): 'So they hanged Haman on the gallows he had prepared for Mordecai.' The verse rounds off a tale of betrayal: Mordecai, having saved King Ahasuerus (Xerxes I) from assassination, thwarts another scheme by treacherous Haman, in whose name the echo of 'Hammond' is obvious. On finishing his inscription, and no doubt congratulating himself on its aptness, the young partisan's nerves caught up with him: in his hurry to rejoin the departing entourage he was noticed, and so was his crime. The crowd returned and the culprit was detained, and Hammond – sorely troubled anyway with his royal burden – was clearly prepared to make an example. The Bible-quoting vandal was identified as the son of the Royalist Governor of Guernsey; and he was saved at the last moment when his sister, dark-haired and crisp-mannered, stood forward and declared the writing on the windows was hers. Those who knew her could declare the wit of the epigram was more typical of her than of any of her brothers. In any case, the assembly had just enough leniency and humour left to spare the 21-year-old gentlewoman from the harsh penalty the male offender would have faced, and both were allowed to leave.

Dorothy Osborne and her brother – probably Robin – soon sailed to join their father, Sir Peter, at St Malo. A deputy was holding the fort for Osborne on Guernsey: the island was by then one of the few Cavalier outposts still defying Parliament, and was eventually the very last to surrender. Departing from Wight, the siblings were joined by Temple, handsome, curly-haired, cool-mannered but impressionable. He seems already to have fallen for Dorothy before her brave display at Newport. Potentially, he had some slight influence to exert on Sir Robert 'Hamon' Hammond if the matter truly turned ugly, for the Governor was his older cousin. His father, meanwhile, although favourable to the peace treaty with Charles, was no friend to the Royalist camp: Sir John was a fierce opponent in particular of the King's Irish general, the Marquess of Ormond. Although Temple's sister and earliest biographer carefully ignored this aspect of the relationship, it is one among countless instances of how family links both spanned the opposing factions of the Civil War, and might sometimes have prevented a complete breakdown of society beyond the battlefield. Such cross-overs were found on the Osborne family tree itself, among Dorothy's brothers and more distantly: she was related to Sir John Danvers, who would put his name on King Charles's death warrant.

Temple had no wish to upset his father with his choice of a wife, but would think of no one else but Dorothy. She was equally steadfast, and the pair waited six years for marriage to be possible. It might be said Temple's status spared him the sort of pragmatic calculation Swift later felt was so vital in deciding whether to marry. In Temple's case, his higher social position only raised the stakes and strengthened expectations: his cherished freedom was narrow in this one sphere. The pressure on him to increase his family's estates was immense, while the constraints on Dorothy were far worse: women were commonly deprived of all choice in the question of a husband. Both came from families rich in prestigious blood ties and dignified roots, but less well supplied, after the Civil Wars, with land and funds. William and Dorothy were singular for their time and class in finding a way to make love their priority when it went against their parents' hopes.

St Malo provided a peculiar background for their courtship. The walled harbour city, jutting out from the Brittany coast, was historically both an outcrop and a refuge. Defiantly speaking a language quite unlike French, and closer still to Welsh (it was said) than Breton, the inhabitants became notorious for sheltering pirates, homeless Cavaliers and a 'garrison' of English-bred dogs they released at nightfall to eat up stray vermin.[5] Nevertheless, the English exiles gathered there in 1648 had been in less accommodating places. Temple recalled the incident on Wight by taking a diamond and inscribing an epigram to Dorothy on a window in the Osbornes' house. By this time his father had heard of the courtship, and a letter soon came ordering him to proceed on his travels. Osborne herself was soon grounded back in England, as Temple explored the Continent, but in some respects those distinctive people at the fringe of France provided a fitting temporary base for one of the most individual voices of her time. The writings of Sir William Temple are eloquent, lively, thoughtful and rewarding; whereas the letters Dorothy wrote to him during the years of their courtship have another quality altogether of tone and perception: 'I never saw anything more extraordinary,' was the verdict of Martha, Lady Giffard, Temple's sister. Osborne herself disliked superlatives, and her prose works in every colour in the spectrum besides purple. 'I find I want Courage to marry where I doe not like,' she said, simply and characteristically, in reassuring Temple. One day after dreaming Temple's mother had written to her, sending her rings, she laughed it off by observing: ''Tis as likely your Mother should send mee letters as that I should make a Journy to see poore People hanged, or that your teeth should drop out at this Age.'[6]

## 2

Via Paris, where he witnessed the first outbreaks of the *fronde* against the child-king Louis and his chief minister, Mazarin, Temple began an exploration of the northern provinces. His travels in France surely fixed in his mind the supreme need of nations for diplomacy. Swift, addressing Temple in Pindarics, understood his patron's reasoning. Even if he was over-optimistic about its results, the greatest trophy of peace-work was a clear conscience.

> Only the Laurel got by Peace,
>> No thunder e'er can blast,
>> Th' Artillery of the Skies
>> Shoots to the Earth and dies;
> Forever green and flourishing 'twill last,
> Nor dipt in Blood, nor Widow's Tears, nor Orphan's Cries.[7]

A solution for internal military conflicts would nevertheless elude Temple as it had so many others. The Thirty Years War, recently brought to an end by the peace of Westphalia, had left France weak-centred. Rival nobles made extravagant claims and demanded lost privileges, and led regiments of veterans against one another and the Crown's makeshift forces.

While many Englishmen joined the French quarrel as mercenaries, Temple, although hardy enough for the long rides and frequent voyages stretching ahead of him, deemed himself physically 'unfit' for military service.[8] One of his undisputed gifts, though, was an ability to learn languages as easily as others get a tan. Observing and absorbing life around him all the time, he passed spare hours by translating French romances. Selecting from a vast literature, he adapted his material as he saw fit. The 'Madame' he addresses in these short tales is the generic female reader of early-modern fiction (for men's men, while writing such literature, dismissed it as idle amusement), but Temple's listener, 'my lady', is also clearly Dorothy herself. The stories are codicils to their correspondence. Unpublished till long after the couple died, the tales develop reserved but unmissable symmetries between the personalities and predicaments in the narrative, and those of the writer and his first reader. The women who emerge positively are fiercely single-minded in matters of love, as Temple perhaps suggested Dorothy was and should be. He was generally sketchy with characterization, but took greater care with one heroine: 'By the diligence and fondness of her parents all accomplishments of art and breeding were added to those shee had receiv'd from nature . . . her spring was so forward that at fourteen years old the discours of her bewty her witt and other perfections was the common entertainment of all companies thereabouts.'[9]

This Fleuria was the ideal Dorothy both fulfilled and exceeded. She was well known and widely courted, and knowing so was agony for Temple. With this in mind one can see why he is so complimentary of Fleuria for brutally torturing and murdering the suitor who kills her true love. He sympathizes with husbands who marry young women whose hearts have been plighted to others; but suggests they should have known better. He identifies with sincerely devoted parties, but rewards them with nothing in the end but tragedy. The young romance-writing Temple, in short, was palpably distempered by facts of life taken more coolly by Dorothy; and from which she did her best in her letters to salvage their friendship.

Despite his free-thinking tendencies, Temple could never have broken altogether from the boundaries of his class. Like Swift, he was brought up largely at school and college, and his background was a similar mixture of High Church and Puritan. His master at Penshurst, Henry Hammond, was a champion of Anglican principles. His tutor at Emmanuel College, Cambridge, Ralph Cudworth, was a Platonist and theoretician of the priesthood of the individual soul. The combination, over time, produced a true diplomat's solution: rather than torturing himself in reconciling conflicting doctrines, Temple decided that no one Christian Church could be everything to all. The reasoning individual should rather look for the limited good to be offered by each branch of Christianity. In resolving the question to his own satisfaction, Temple hoped to avoid the choice over religion that had carried such grievous political consequences in the reign of Charles I. Other sources of division were harder for him to fix, one being his father's wartime allegiances. By 1653 Sir John was back in Ireland assisting the Commonwealth regime redistribute land captured in Cromwell's conquest. The role he subsequently played in adjudicating claims for land, while receiving vast Irish properties himself, is pretty much indicative of the legal standards the process involved. An ashy thumbprint soiled the deeds to the Temples' newly enlarged Irish holdings; but that was unlikely to have bothered the Osbornes. The family's rebel past was harder to stomach. For his part, Sir John looked unkindly on the Osbornes' tribe of impoverished Royalists.

Nevertheless, William and Dorothy's perseverance paid off. Their relatives, although disgruntled, accepted the engagement. Sir Peter Osborne remained staunchly opposed to it, but assisted them by dying; while the Temples' position was eased by Sir John regaining his place as the Master of the Rolls in Ireland and still more by his share of the Cromwellian spoils. The wedding took place in Holborn on 25 December 1654. Dorothy in particular had escaped several forceful attempts to push her down the aisle towards other grooms. Even now, when she was allowed her choice, she was lucky to be alive to take it. Just a week before the first date set for the service, she had fallen 'desperately ill'. The doctors had given no hope until the raging fever broke, and the sores of smallpox broke out. The damaged face behind her veil on Christmas Day had survived, up to then, more or less everything its time and society could throw at it; but the Temples agreed that their sorrows only truly began with the loss of their children.

The following years were taken up with what became a typical move for Temple: retirement, at first with friends in England and then on an

Irish estate in County Carlow. He cultivated the literary and bucolic-minded gentleman's love of *otium* – private peace, which might be disrupted only by the call of duty. While Temple himself has always been regarded as the decision-maker in this respect, Dorothy's influence can also be seen. 'One may be happy to a good degree I thinke,' she wrote, 'in a faithfull friend, a Moderate fortune and a retired life: farther than this I know not how to wish.'[10] Before their controversial marriage, she frequently expressed a desire to retreat from the eye of the world.

Some claimed, however, that sadness along with the pressure of survival drove Temple into public life. By 1660, when the Restoration drew all members of their class scurrying to protect their assets and stake claims to more, he and Dorothy had buried five infants. On emerging from reclusion, Temple quickly and persistently made his name in the necessary high places – first in Ireland, with the Lord Lieutenant, and not long afterwards with Lord Arlington, then a secretary of state, and then soon with the King himself. In 1665, on his first secret mission abroad, he was entrusted with purchasing the cooperation of the Prince-Bishop of Münster against the Dutch. For much of the time this involved playing a role that suited him well: a gentleman of leisure, pursuing a private matter in Brussels – Temple's favourite of all the cities he had visited. As a reward, he was made a baronet and given the residency at Brussels; he was presented with further assignments, and thus pulled from his withdrawn existence into high-profile activity for the history books.

The household Swift entered in the spring or early summer of 1689 was that of a legend: albeit, by then, a faintly rusting legend who claimed to be out of touch with modern trends. Temple was on good personal terms nevertheless with the Prince of Orange: he had known him in his younger days, and would retain his personal trust when the Stadtholder was crowned William III. One mini-legend had it that while visiting Temple the King taught Swift to cut asparagus in the Dutch manner.[11] Yet Temple had, genuinely it seems, almost no idea of the Prince's invasion plan until the Dutch forces were ashore – having committed himself to another indefinite retirement some years earlier. Previously, Temple had put his wit, tact and naivety at Charles II's service for two decades. His goal had always been to steer Charles away from war with the United Provinces, where he enjoyed excellent contacts and where his gifts were highly regarded. His attitude towards the Dutch made him popular at home; made him, also, the ideal dupe and frontman for a policy that Charles would always betray. He was a diplomatic Ariel who shaped not only the Triple Alliance of 1668 with Sweden and the United Provinces, arranging a deal in just five days, having endured thirty hours of thunderstorm en route to The Hague, but also William of Orange's marriage to Princess Mary: both of which should have ensured a lasting peace with Holland were it not for King Charles's obligations to France, the power the Triple Alliance had been created to oppose. When he was dispatched on a third formal peace mission, this time to Nijmegen in 1678–9, Temple's professed 'distast to all thoughts of public imploy-ments' was turning chronic. On at least two occasions he stepped out of the costly dance that might have led to his purchasing the post of secre-tary of state. The position was, in fact, beyond his limited means, and he had been hurt too many times to desire closer involvement in govern-ment: notably by his sometime friend Arlington. Yet he remained a figure of great if slightly indefinite informal influence. At the height of the Pop-ish Plot crisis, Temple had advised Charles to stop balancing party interests and simply to banish from his table all except men he could personally trust. Charles did so, and a few days later Temple found him-self a privy councillor.

The post Temple offered Swift in 1689, although technically that of a servant, thus put the young refugee potentially in contact with any major courtier in England or Ireland. The most potent figures for the present, however, were the three formidable persons who had dominated the family's Surrey estates since they moved to the county in 1665: Temple himself, his wife, Dorothy, and sister Martha. The last, Lady Giffard, had lived constantly with the Temples since being widowed early and abruptly by Sir Thomas Giffard in 1662. After barely a fortnight as a married woman, Martha buried her husband and went to live with her brother. A fine miniature attributed to Caspar Netscher shows a young Lady Giffard, somewhat small-featured and with curling chestnut hair, dressed in low-cut lace and a brown sash of satin, looking out with her head tilted and a disenchanted, unimpressed and almost sardonic expres-sion that seems to say 'Well, what now?'[12] A touch of disappointment in their bearing made brother and sister a harmonious pair if their pictures hung together: another study of Sir William, by the same Dutch artist, finds him looking overworked, with an elbow on his table, slumped in his chair, loose-robed and satin-cuffed, his head resting on his left hand and a state paper clutched limply in the right. A rich hanging of French gold-and-blue brocade drapes partly over him; a misty landscape lies behind. The melancholy on show is thus a touch studied; yet by the time Swift arrived the other chief presence in the family home at Moor Park, and at their older residence at Sheen, near Richmond-upon-Thames, was undoubtedly bereavement. The Temples still lived with their children slipping away. A beloved fourteen-year-old daughter had died of small-pox in 1679, at which Temple had felt his life turn incurably sour.

The freshest wound, though, had been made the very April of the year Swift arrived. It is not clear whether Swift was already resident when Temple's eldest son John filled his pockets with stones and jumped from a boat by London Bridge. A later family tradition suggested an illness had clouded his mind. In a note, John Temple said he felt only love for his family and friends, but that life had for a long time been a burden. His only regret was the pain his death would cause those dear to him.[13] His father's affliction was possibly worsened by a nagging sense of responsibility. John had been delighted by the Prince of Orange's arrival; and, while Temple had with difficulty prevented him from riding off to join William's camp, he was soon keen for him to gain a place in the new ruler's government. Throughout the crisis, father and son were living together: Sir William and Dorothy had left the house at Sheen to John when he married, but they had moved back on a temporary basis during the emergency of 1688, since their old home offered greater safety. Sir William's affection for John comes across in the opening of the dedication to his *Memoirs*, 'To My Son', that he penned in 1683.

> I do not remember ever to have refused any thing you have desired of me; which I take to be a greater compliment to you than to myself; since for a young man to make none but reasonable desires, is yet more extraordinary than for an old man to think them so.[14]

Surely because of his regard for Temple, Prince William pressed an office upon John for which he had no experience and, as he protested himself, little aptitude, especially at such a moment. John was made a secretary of war, and the frailty of his judgement was almost immediately exposed when he petitioned the King on behalf of a military prisoner from James's Irish forces. The captive, Brigadier-General Richard Hamilton, gave his word that he would convince Tyrconnell to relent. Instead, on gaining his freedom in an exchange of prisoners, he simply returned to active duty.

The error, pardonable as it might have been even at the time, seems to have made John look on suicide as an act of honour. In his parting note, however, he denied that he felt burdened by any bad act, and was confi-dent of release rather than punishment. The letter suggests, overall, that

John Temple had inherited and developed his parents' independent cast of mind. Their melancholic tendencies might also have filtered through: in their letters, both quite frequently suggest they held on to life lightly. Each expected the other to care for his or her self for their partner's sake, since neither would for their own. In a family where such reasoning prevailed, as soon as one was convinced that remaining alive was no longer in the interest of those one loved, there was precious little reason to persist with the trouble of living.

The grieving man Swift served in these early months was not quite, then, the exuberant character preserved for us in a sketch written by his sister. In other times, Temple looked for the humorous side of any situation, and was typically easy and familiar with all people, 'from the greatest Princes to the meanest servants'. Although very fond of fine wines, he would rarely go beyond a third glass with dinner. The traveller in him died hard: he was happy with the simplest meal and a dry bed. He was now a year or so past sixty. He eschewed physicians; but his health was not the best. Evidently a wiry man with great nervous energy, he had been slowed in his fifties by gout, which depressed him, and had suffered with 'rheums' in his eyes and teeth since his early forties.[15] Despite many attempts, it is impossible to conjecture what sort of welcome, if any, given the formal nature of their arrangement, he might have extended to Swift. Bereavement may have reduced him to near-silence; while over time it may, as some have suggested, left him open to forming a loco-parental relationship with his secretary. A lot obviously depended on Swift, and whether he was interested in the role of a son.

## 3

Today, the house at Moor Park does not much resemble the Carolean mansion Swift lived in with the Temples. It was altered extensively, inside and out, during the century after he left, and these days presents a bleached Regency façade. But it orients the land about it, despite recent development, much as it has done since the early 1600s: it is still approached along a leafy carriageway, from the road leading to the nearby village. The River Wey defines the pasture, wood and ponds that made up the old estate, and a twelfth-century abbey (much extended) offers a further boundary to the south. A local legend surrounded a cavern in the nearby Wey Valley. There a medicinal spring was discovered by the monks: and a white witch made her home in the cliff-side grotto, known afterwards as Mother Ludwell's Cavern. A poem among Temple's papers, written by the baronet or quite possibly by his secretary, celebrated both the place and the legend. Here the poet found his Helicon: the dews, the meadow-floods, the woodlands and the birdcall made his muse quite at home. This is also the scene that should be pictured in the background to the writing Swift did at Moor Park.[16]

The poem about Mother Ludwell has sometimes been taken as the work of Temple himself: but it reads like one of the first tries at verse that Swift claimed he had burned, and more still like an attempt by a precocious child. The manuscript of the poem is in a distinctly immature hand. The script bears some resemblance to Swift's; but the writing belongs to a much younger copyist, or one very unused to holding a pen. The poem's modern editor, in a rare moment of fancy, suggested the lines might have been written out, if not actually composed, by the very young girl who became Swift's protégée during the 1690s.[17] Esther Johnson was eight years old when he, in his twenty-second year, arrived at the Temple household: long afterwards he forgetfully claimed she was six. She was the eldest child of Temple's housekeeper, Bridget. Her late father, Edward, had been Temple's steward, and, in time, her mother would marry the current holder of that post, Ralph Mose.[18] Besides Esther, there was another, older presence below stairs who would feature constantly if more quietly in Swift's future: Rebecca Dingley, with whom Esther later grew fast friends, served Lady Giffard as waiting woman.

These were Swift's equals in the house, however much he felt his true place was above stairs. The depth of the relationship with Esther, however, would set her apart from any class: 'she had little to boast of her birth,' he admitted, but her excellent moral and intellectual qualities made all comments of that nature meaningless, as they did all remarks about their friendship. Her beauty, in time, also attracted attention, though as a child Swift thought her 'sickly' until she reached her mid-teens. He never reflected on how and why she first caught his notice as a child. Not long passed, though, before he involved himself in her upbringing: '[I] had some share in her education, by directing what books she should read, and perpetually instructing her in the principles of honour and virtue; from which she never swerved in any one action or moment of her life.'[19]

Like Glumdalclitch, the nine-year-old who becomes Gulliver's 'little Nurse' in Brobdingnag, Esther was 'a Child of towardly Parts for her Age'.[20] Gulliver's relationship with this girl is also in some respects a direct and affectionate inversion of Swift's with Esther: in the *Travels* it is the little girl who schools the narrator in the Brobdingnagian language.

The testimonial Swift wrote of Esther's life and character mentions her weak constitution as a child; and from that it is all too easy to picture a weak and pallid, dispirited youngster. But he also paid tribute to her pluckiness, cool wit and powers of observation, and a self-assurance similar to his in her moral judgement; and there is no reason to assume those qualities were not at least taking root in her character when she was very young. They are also traits Swift may have helped her to develop. 'Never was any of her sex born with better gifts of the mind,' he declared, 'or more improved them by reading and conversation.' As a tutor, he found her memory only slightly deficient. He acknowledged that their association would always seem to have 'a secret history', but in his moving paean he tried to settle the record and put Esther's name above all hint of scandal.[21] In those terms, her 'honour and virtue' were paramount. But his actual correspondence, in the daily journal he wrote to her from London in 1710–13, shows that their closeness was founded on other attributes besides mutual moral excellence. He delighted above all in her wit and their affinity of temperament: and it was surely that mental and expressive quickness, however undeveloped, that first struck him in the eight-year-old Esther. She possibly reminded him of his own precocious efforts to capture attention and affection, half orphaned and in a similarly awkward position, in the houses of his uncles. Never a father, never a husband, Swift fixed on Esther some of the energies those roles would have demanded.

For those who might doubt the sincerity of Swift's conduct *in loco parentis*, it seems that he was frequently called on to look after other youngsters associated with the Temples, and went about fulfilling that trust in his own idiosyncratic style. He did not allow child-minding duties to interfere with the call of what he felt were higher principles if necessary. One story from a few years later illustrates the compelling and dynamic sort of guardian he was. A grand-nephew of Sir William Temple remembered how Swift, escorting him to London as a school-boy, had stood up to a rude and drunken boatman.[22] It was at Hammersmith, two or three years before the end of the seventeenth century, and the boy's name was William Flower. They had taken the river from Mortlake near Richmond-upon-Thames, and the captain of the skiff had treated them roughly. So, on disembarking at the edge of Hammersmith's scattering of small dwellings and the odd larger house, amid modest-sized crofts, Swift refused to pay the fare. At this the skipper railed and threatened, and a mob of river-workers and poorer travellers gathered to support him. The presence of a fop or two in red-heeled shoes, shaking an amber-topped cane, may not be ruled out, but the coats surrounding Swift, it seems, were as plain as his own, though of a ruder cloth and cut. The boots clumping impatiently at his words were fastened by laces at the back rather than buckles at the front. Cotton caps framed angry female faces; aprons pocketed tough raw hands. The men kept their heads covered, apparently, regardless of his priesthood – for by then he was ordained – and any pretensions Swift might have had to gentle status: his frock-coat and periwig seemed no defence against a gang in slops and woollens with justice on their side. A tense debate ensued, with some forceful speech-making by Swift. Young William Flower expected the people to strip him of his black clerical gown and fling him in the water. Instead, they relented, and the stern young priest and his charge continued on their way.

At Moor Park, while Swift relished the respect, responsibility and initiation Temple gave him, his post as servant highlighted the very incidental place that he held in the world. He had grown up in institutions where it was easy for a bright if disaffected pupil to feel his studies and his peers were beneath him. Leaving the shelter of Trinity, such a defence mechanism came under greater pressure. At Moor Park he was exposed to his social insignificance – a standard adult experience made much stronger by being so close to the centre of national power. The estate was in some ways much like the floating island of Laputa in the *Travels*. Although technically living aloof and in retirement, Temple could steer his kingdom as close as he wished to the greatest figures in the land, and hoist them into his presence whenever they called. Nonetheless, at a more independent-minded age Swift reacted fiercely against any awe he may have felt at two of the family's highest placed associates. One of Sir William's closest friends was Henry Sidney, the brother of the executed republican, Algernon. He was in his early fifties when Swift first met him, handsomely greyed and long-faced, with a firm chin, distinguished cheekbones and a dead-straight, prominent nose. In portraits from about this time he glares under grey and tufting eyebrows, framed by an enormous periwig, as if he has heard some impertinence from across the room. He was a rake, a self-styled soldier, and essentially a man of pleasure with little gift for the business or administration with which he was sometimes entrusted; yet Henry, a favourite of the King, soon elevated to the peerage as Earl of Romney, had indirectly brought about the 'Glorious Revolution', since he was apparently the first to tell Prince

William that he would be welcomed in England as a replacement for James II.

Meanwhile Elizabeth Seymour (née Percy), Duchess of Somerset, was best friends with Temple's sister, Lady Giffard. The Duchess acquired power and security while still very young, but at an advanced stage in terms of life-experience. By the time Swift knew her she had already survived two unspeakable marriages – having been farmed out by her relatives, for the sake of profit, title and property, as little more than a child-bride. A superb portrait of her as a young woman by Peter Lely tells something of the soft enigma she would later armour and conceal. Her brow and forehead are ghostly against her partly shadowed throat and breast, the dark rich folds of her gown and the suggestive corner in which she sits pointing indecisively beyond the frame. Later pictures show her face-on, emphasizing her red hair almost as crudely as Swift eventually would. Elizabeth, a daughter of the eleventh Duke of Northumberland and a cousin of the Penshurst Sidneys, gave the lie to the notion that the poor and nameless of that time had a monopoly on misery. She saved herself from effective sexual slavery through a command of intrigue and parsimony in matters of conscience. Rumour implicated her in the murder of her second husband; and also had it that Temple, at Lady Giffard's urging, had helped her escape. Less than half a year later she was married again, this time to the Duke of Somerset, a man much in Henry Sidney's mould.

Sidney and the Duchess, both of whom Swift later castigated, were just two of Temple's glittering circle. An exact head-count of all the illustrious personages passing through Moor Park, it has always been implied (especially by Lady Giffard), would be all but impossible. The King himself, Swift later claimed, visited Temple at home 'and took his advice in affairs of greatest consequence'.[23] We should not imagine the King as a regular house-guest at Temple's estates at Sheen or Moor Park; but he did seek the old ambassador's counsel on one important matter, in which Temple famously relied on Swift's developing skills.

Swift was not joining one of the wealthiest households in the country – not at all – but Moor Park at least put him within sight of comparative luxury. Fashions in furniture had moved towards sparser styles, and, even if upholstered, the high-backed and often narrow seats that served as armchairs were not always a guarantee of comfort. Restoration preferences swung back towards the more lavish. Dorothy and William had taste if not all the funds they needed to indulge it. By the 1680s a home such as theirs might be expected to contain the older, squarer chests and ball-footed cabinets of their parents' and grandparents' generations – those heavy, dark pieces rippling with dense floral carvings and oak figurines – alongside newer, lacquered and stained acquisitions, displaying incredible blends of maple, elm and cherry and, perhaps, given the Temples' links to the Low Countries, something of the period's wonderful Dutch marquetry.

It is notable, however, how scant the signs are of such treasures in Swift's writing. Plainness and bareness predominate in the backgrounds of his fictions: the regal interiors Gulliver visits, for example, are never described at length. Imaginatively, he gravitated towards the scene below stairs, which is where he began with the Temples. In a very late work, his *Directions to Servants*, he would write with unthinking intimacy about the stations at which a butler, cook, footman or chambermaid performed their duties. By the time he came to write the *Directions*, he had collected a lifetime's stock of hints as to how those in service could win favour, save strength and do their jobs better. A moist palm was better for pressing salt down in its salt-cellar; when draining off a hogshead, a finger put down the neck of the bottle was the only way to be sure it was full – 'for Feeling hath no fellow'.[24] Swift would always interest himself more in the practicalities of work than in the inventions of leisure, just as the basic arithmetic of trade involved him more than the astronomy of high finance. He was perhaps pragmatic by nature; in any case his place at Moor Park compelled his interest in the direction of functional detail. One byproduct of that interest would be the distinctive literal-mindedness Swift makes so convincing in Gulliver.

Sir William Temple provided him with a refuge; and was well satisfied, it seems, with his side of the bargain. As soon as 1690 Swift's employer described him approvingly in a letter of recommendation. The reference also gives a pleasant outline of Swift's daily routine at Moor Park. In the letter, Temple explains how Swift's college career was cut short by the Irish 'calamities' and then:

> Since that time he has lived in my house, read to me, writ for me, and kept all my accounts as far as my small occasions required. He has latine and greeke, some French, writes a very good and current hand, is very honest and diligent, and has good friends though they have for the present lost their fortunes in Ireland . . .[25]

Temple was writing here on Swift's behalf to Sir Robert Southwell, who was accompanying King William as a secretary of state on the mission to subdue the Jacobites in Ireland. Southwell was a born civil servant: mild-mannered, conciliatory, methodical, he was one of many lesser known officials who had worked and waited patiently through the excesses and crises of the Stuart brothers' reigns. He was a fellow of the Royal Society and a friend – from foreign travel and diplomatic service – of grandees abroad. He had something of Pepys's eye for detail and skill as a networker, without the naval secretary's fleshly vigour. Southwell came from a family of Munster planters and thus sided firmly with the Protestant and Presbyterian side of the question, but showed a rare equanimity and willingness to compromise amid the ferocity of the Jacobite war.

The idea of Swift going into the combat zone might strike some as incongruous; but, if one story of a royal visit is true, the King was not being whimsical in offering Swift a commission in the cavalry.[26] Swift was a dedicated rider and walker all his life: well into his sixties, he is described as running up and down the deanery stairs to keep himself in shape and shake off the spleen. An early biography by his younger cousin Deane Swift – the grandson of his uncle Godwin – has been discounted as largely fanciful, but in describing the writer's fitness it is backed up by other sources: 'When Swift was a young man he was prodigiously fond of rambling . . . upon his own feet he ran like a buck from one place to another. Gates, styles, and quicksets, he no more valued than if they had been so many straws. His constitution was strong, and his limbs were active.'[27] Bouts of illness periodically robbed him of this strength; when well, he was more than able to join a march.

On this trip, however, he was only to be a belated witness. Southwell did nothing materially for Swift. Neither did Ireland. The consensus puts his arrival soon after the catastrophic Battle of the Boyne on 1 July (Old Style calendar), when James abandoned his own cause and fled his kingdoms for ever. The engagement took place on the banks of the river a short way outside Drogheda, a city that, until the Irish revolution, had recovered somewhat after the trauma of the Cromwellian massacre. Both the ousted King and his newly crowned rival commanded their troops in person. James's army, poorly drilled and equipped, lacking in discipline and motivation, assembled on the southern banks of the Boyne. William's tactic, put simply, was to march at them across the river, and, after a glancing clash, his men put James's running. John Stevens, a loquacious Jacobite, and more a man of letters than the sword, described how he was almost trampled over in the rush to escape: 'I thought the calamity had not been so general till viewing the hills about us I perceived them covered with soldiers of several regiments, all scattered like sheep flying before the wolf, but so thick they seemed to cover the sides and tops of the hills.' The retreat could hardly be equalled in scale, but Stevens saw it matched in intensity a few days later, when he and some comrades were deprived of their horses by Tyrconnell.[28] The fallen Lord Lieutenant of Ireland was following his defeated master James, and their flight was little more dignified than the mass desertion Stevens witnessed on the hills beyond the water. The signal difference was that the native soldiers pouring south and eastwards were left to fight for their homes and herds. They pursued James in conscience, even if he left them to shift for themselves.

Summoning his Pindarics at a later date to celebrate the victory, Swift depicted William as a 'Bold Romantick Knight' whose personal leadership had all but single-handedly secured success. William's coat bore powder stains from a bullet that had grazed his shoulder while he reconnoitred the field the day before the battle. The image of his figure on a white horse became a much bloodied standard-banner in its own right in the violent history of Ulster. Swift could at this time frankly admire such a man. However, notwithstanding Swift's respect for romantic boldness and feats of arms in the right cause, one should bear in mind a remark in the *Tale of a Tub* about the knights of old, howsoever bold and romantic they might have been. Such heroes were wont to be 'a greater nuisance to Mankind, than any of those Monsters they subdued'.[29]

William's 'fond enemy', meanwhile, was a shadow of the soldier and sailor he had proven himself in earlier decades – and to his credit, James knew it. He was more than any of the clashing stock roles in which he was sometimes depicted: more than just a Restoration rogue, a tyrant, a pietist or a libertarian, he formed a pattern for other complex characters of the time – such as the poet Rochester – through an improbable fusion of all these things and more. At his nadir, he took his defeat as a sign of God emptying him of his power. A few lines from Swift's ode for William form one of the best epigrams on James's fall, since they reflect the deposed King's view of his own situation. They also show the young writer's growing proficiency, particularly in linking abstract sentiments to commonplace objects – here, a guttering flame.

> His scrap of Life is but a Heap of Miseries,
>   The Remanant of a falling Snuff,
>     Which hardly wants another puff,
>   And needs must *stink* when e'er it dies.[30]

Back near Dublin in the days following the battle, a few tattered stand-ards were set up in the fields around Kilmainham for the remainders of James's force to regroup around; but those who did so, including Ste-vens, scattered immediately when scouts reported the Williamites on a steady march south. The road from Drogheda to Dublin was a good one, and the country between the two cities rich and fertile, but Wil-liam's troops found most of the buildings in Drogheda 'ready to fall to the ground', the land to the south picked clean of crops and livestock, and Dublin all but starved of supplies and stripped of all the fleeing government could carry.[31] Exhausted from entertaining one garrison, the capital opened its bruised arms for the next. Civilians had suffered from a winter of bullying and debauchery; but even the usual profiteers in such conditions had had a lean time of it. A desperate shortage of coin had forced James to pay his Court and soldiers, and they their hosts and tradesmen, in brass. Only the French among the Jacobites got proper gold and silver, and they soon took it home. The strain on trade and the sense of disgrace worsened what would be one of Swift's key later grievances: the draining of gold and silver reserves and the resulting debasement of coinage. Money, in Swift's traditional view, was trash if the metal in a coin was worth less than the value it was stamped with.

He left no explicit record of what he saw on this journey. Powerful impressions are offered, though, by those who voiced the bias, drives and anxieties of his Anglo-Irish caste. In *The Irish Hudibras* James Farewell worked up a derogatory sketch of an Irish gentleman who might have served as an officer in James's army, and who could call on the loyalties of kinsmen and tenants to swell the ranks. He is found at home in a larger sort of hut, 'fenc'd with a wood, / Trench'd with a moat, and pav'd with Mud':

> His Glibbs [hair] hung down like Tails of Rats,
> His Goggles flam'd like Eyes of Cats:
> Where there was neither Crisp nor Curl,
> The very But-end of a Churl:
> His Mantle made of Blew Scar-leet,
> Which reach'd almost unto his Feet,
> He with a Wattle Twist had ty'd,
> With Knot from Shoulder unto Side:
> About his well-set Legs he drew
> Stockins, a pair of *Mazareen-Blue*,
> Turn'd in-side out, a shift in need,
> To stop the Holes on t'other sheed [side];[32]

The portrait of this glaring warrior is obviously painted to match the savage characteristics the writer and his reader assumed they would find in such a person. Down to the mockery of his Irish name, these lines are an exercise in prejudice. Nevertheless, they contain, albeit accidentally, precious touches of historical value. The mantle is the much commented on and long-scorned uniform of the 'wild' Irish; yet its manufacture from scarlet, an expensive woollen fabric (dyed in this case blue), is an unmissable indicator of the wearer's social status and former affluence – not to mention the craft of the weavers who produced it. Although Mac-Murreartagh's flaming, 'goggling' eyes produce the comically piratical look expected of such a character, nevertheless his desperation and 'wildness', even in this derisive genre, are a testimony to the fate of his class. He belongs to the native Irish gentry who were wrecked for good by the Williamite conquest that followed the defeat on the Boyne, and sent either westwards, reduced to extreme poverty, or, as implicitly in the present case, forced to turn outlaw. The figure in these verses is that of a bandit, a 'Tory' in the original sense. As with, essentially, the entirety of his hateful poem, Farewell's study here is also a tribute to the lingering danger such men and their followers posed. Although in theory the territory was conquered, a nocturnal raid or a hold-up on the road could not be ruled out by a returning English native such as Swift in the early 1690s.

Why was Swift really there? Aside from the danger, there could hardly be a worse moment to think of academic or clerical advancement in Ireland, with the old Anglican settlement on its knees: the nature of the Church or university that would emerge from the revolution was anyone's guess. William's victory at the Boyne brought Dublin's few remaining Protestant civilians out of the woodwork, and many thousands more returned with suits for restitution and revenge. It was little wonder that Swift's voice was then unheard, even with Temple's letter in his pocket among the wretched brass half-crowns. His whereabouts during this visit are uncertain: many houses in the city had served as billets, while the precarious state of the country made a stay at one of his uncles' estates most unlikely. The safest option may well have been to retake lodgings at Trinity, where Swift inquired about a fellowship (to no effect). His own slight reminiscence of this journey suggests, although perhaps misleadingly, he needed a peaceful berth. Significantly, he associated his return with the onset of the medical condition that would blight his entire life. Recalling this period from the 1720s, Swift claimed that he had gone to Ireland in 1690 'by advice of Physicians, who weakly imagined that his native air might be of some use to recover his Health'.[33] The mention of his illness adds to the sense of hardship and hazard the journey appears to have involved. As such, it is more realistic to see him travelling in spite of health problems than because of them; and, regardless of his later cynicism on such subjects, from loyalty to his 'native air'. He seems to have felt impelled to return to Ireland, that is, precisely *because* the Anglican constitution was so damaged and now in jeopardy from Dissenting influences expecting bounty from the conquering Dutchman. As soon as it became practical to do so, despite poor health and a comfortable position in England, he rallied to the place and cause he identified as his own. As it happened, he was denied the chance to help rebuild the fellowship at Trinity, or take another posting in the recovering bureaucracy: but he was eager to serve.

He remained in Ireland as the war continued. It ended with the humbling of the Jacobite cause, the native Irish and the Old (Catholic) English. There were admittedly some families in the Old Catholic gentry and nobility who escaped or at least weathered the defeat. The Barnewalls of Trimleston Castle in County Meath – near parishes Swift would later serve as vicar – held on to their land and their title, and their dynasty survived: one Lord Trimleston became a celebrated 'personality', philanthropist and amateur physician in the eighteenth century. A large eagle chained up at the castle's front door, nervously fed by the servants and preying on incautious hounds, was a living symbol of the peer's enduring aristocratic status.[34] Yet the consequences for most Catholics were grim, certainly for those who had taken up arms for James. The terms of the final peace and ensuing settlement were not as harsh as they might have been, but still bad enough to make clear which 'revolution', Tyrconnell's or William's, had won.

# 4

The first time we really hear Swift in his own voice, he is trying to clear his name of having treated a woman badly. The letter in which he does this, aged twenty-four, is both terse and expansive: it is written to a friend in the Midlands, the husband of a female cousin on his mother's side. The recipient, a clergyman, knew the woman in Leicestershire, and had told Swift that her family and friends had evidently expected a proposal. Swift claimed to be surprised. He counted a 'cold temper & unconfin'd humour' as much greater defects in his personality than any

tendency to flirt. He was sure, though, that the lady herself was in no
real doubts on the matter.

His business in Leicester was to visit his mother and relatives: he
made his first documented trip there on leaving Ireland in the midst of
the revolution. He returned in the autumn or not long into the winter in
1691, en route to Moor Park, on disembarking from his unsuccessful
journey back to Ireland. The stay near or with his mother was long
enough for the romance, such as it was, to develop between him and a
neighbour's daughter. In his letter to the Reverend John Kendall, Swift
stated firmly that he had no thoughts of marrying: as a student, a walk
of just half a mile beyond the sanctuary of Trinity College had always
been enough to suffocate any such notion. He would defer the question
entirely until he had got a decent position and income: he added, 'even
then ... I am so hard to please that I suppose I shall put it off to the
other world.'

Swift accepted that his pickiness was more of a problem than the
financial difficulties that made a match imprudent. The latter might be
removed with time; the former, the high and unreal demands he would
make of any wife, might only become all the stronger. He also admitted
he was very jealous by nature. He said that he would require a 'mathematical Demonstration' that any prospective partner's reputation and
character were entirely beyond reproach. This would be all but impossible, since people were in general a 'lying sort of Beast (and I think in
Leicester above all parts that I ever was in)'. His relationship with the
woman in question was also far from singular, he claimed: he had treated
as many as twenty other women exactly the same way. This was simply
the first time he had attracted notice – for which the news-starved gossips of Leicestershire (a 'parcel of wretched fools') were evidently much
to blame. He seriously intended to enter the Church, and he was perfectly willing to leave such moderate gallantries at the porch. Yet he did
not rule out the idea of marrying altogether, and so refused to renounce
social contact with women. He would need to retain 'so general a Conversation with that sex' as to be able to discern and judge potential
spouses. By his mid-twenties Swift believed that he had seen every error
made likely by love, and he was desperate to avoid them:

Among all the young gentlemen that I have known to have Ruined
their selves by marrying (which I assure you is a great number) I have
made this general Rule: that they are either young, raw & ignorant
Scholars, who for want of knowing company, believe every silk petti-

coat includes an angel, or else they have been a sort of honest young men, who perhaps are too literal in rather marrying than burning, & entail misery on themselves & posterity by an over acting sort of modesty.[35]

The Church taught that matrimony prevents fornication, but Swift maintained here that lovers of the latter sort were taking this directive too literally in surrendering themselves to a lifetime's misery. Behind these recent cases of folly also lay the formative example of his parents' marriage – the one above all he was determined not to follow. Even if a spouse met his exacting conditions, Swift would always look at the possible deficit: the expense of spirit and the material loss. His childhood, with the emotional deprivations he interpreted as a financial and physical lack, was an irresistible deterrent. The pain that stemmed from the loss of his father, and the neglect his mother appears to have shown him, really had nothing to do with material want; but he preferred to think that it did. Poverty, after all, was something one could at least try to fight. The idea of an impoverished home, 'a thousand Household thoughts', he insisted, would always drive away all ideas of marriage. Additionally, unlike the men who, as he put it, would rather marry than burn with frustrated carnal wishes, 'I am naturaly temperate, and never engaged in the contrary, which usually produces those effects.' Countless young priests, intent on their vows, have surely believed that chastity would not pose for them the problem it presented to others. Yet Swift bore out his claim by years of the closest love for a similarly minded woman; a relationship in whichhe claimed that sex, whatever people thought, played little or no part at all.[36]

By this time he was writing, and was describing his work as something that might take over his life. 'There is something in me,' Swift told Kendall, 'which must be employ'd, & when I am alone, turns all, for want of practice, into speculation and thought.' By the time he wrote defending his conduct with women in February 1692, he had been back at Moor Park seven weeks: during which time, 'I have writt, & burnt & writt again, upon almost all manner of subjects, more perhaps than any man in England.'[37] The sentence summons up an image of all the dedicated scribblers, seasoned and epicene, setting down their thoughts across the country at that moment; and of Swift, somewhere amid them, searching for the stamp in the language that would set his 'speculations' apart.

He would be some time finding it. The earliest work that truly reflects Swift's thinking and reading on 'all manner of subjects' would be the unclassifiable *Tale of a Tub*. His first efforts he burned, or so he claimed. The next wave consisted of ventures in verse in which imitation vied with the struggle for an individual view, and belied the feverish preparation that went into writing them. These early attempts took the form of lengthy odes written in the earnest, copious style of Abraham Cowley, a poet Swift would admire, somewhat guiltily, into middle age. 'I find when I writ what pleases me I am Cowley to myself,' he told his cousin, while admitting, 'I have the same pretence the Baboon had to praise her children.'[38] His affection for the love poems of Cowley's volume *The Mistress* does rather undercut the aloof and urbane attitude to women Swift airs in his letter to Kendall on the fools of Leicestershire. But Cowley's manner, ever since his standing was confirmed in the 1650s, had long ago worked its way into the literary climate. Poets who avoided satire (for which Cowley had no talent) found it hard not to sound like him. Cowley himself had been a prodigy, completing an accomplished romance by the age of ten. He served the exiled Stuarts as royal secretary and agent before slipping into nervous retirement in England in 1654. Like many who made their peace with the Commonwealth, he lived with a lingering charge of collusion, not least from his own conscience, and died a few months before Swift's birth in 1667.

Swift's chief model was the verse-form Cowley presented as Pindaric, in reality a loose, wandering and, in some hands, versatile stanza. The other main ingredient in Cowley's widely imitated odes was his characteristic and still touching sincerity, a bearing that struck a perfect chord with Swift in lines he wrote for King William:

> Sure there's some Wondrous Joy in *Doing Good*;
> Immortal Joy, that suffers no Allay from Fears,
>   Nor dreads the Tyranny of Years,
> By none but its Possessors to be understood.[39]

While its subject is ostensibly William's feats in the field, the poem is full of excitement about the writer's own future in the realm being liberated by his hero. The 'good' William has done is taken as self-evident; much greater suspense, and the main psychological pull of the poem, comes from the question mark surrounding the purpose the poet would serve: surely some great achievement was waiting for such passion and inspiration? This was the literary mode, and very much the vein, in which Swift also began praising the publishers of a journal of genteel if recondite learning, the *Athenian Gazette*, while he was still in Ireland in 1691.

There, he declared, 'I heard only a loose talk of your Society, and believed the design to be only some new Folly just suitable to the Age, which God knows, I little expected ever to produce any thing extraordinary.'[40]

Swift attributed great things to the Athenian Society, largely because he needed a theme that would do him justice, even as he acknowledged himself 'a young and (almost) Virgin-muse'. The extravagance of his claims and the undoubted force of his poem's Miltonic opening stanza clearly impressed the editors of the *Gazette* (later the *Mercury*): the ode was Swift's first published work. It invokes a 'great unknown', a source of all things in which the poet puts his trust, decrying empiricists who would reduce all life and learning to 'a Crowd of Atoms' (l. 127). Proteus, the metamorphic sea deity ('this surly, slippery God') makes a memorable appearance (stanza 8), and the poem hints at preoccupations that would prove deeper and enduring for Swift: the uncertainty of fame, the dubious nature of women and the slow but sure decay of civilization. Overall, even more than in the 'Ode to King William', the poet emerges as a young knight in search of his quest, worried if he will find his subject, but sure that he has all the ardour in the world to devote to it.

This fervent attitude brought technical difficulties in another ode, this time for William Sancroft, the embattled outgoing Archbishop of Canterbury. These problems, in fact, make it the most interesting poem, historically, of this early group. Born in 1617, and settling easily on the life of an ecclesiastic and academic, Sancroft adopted the Jacobean and Carolean creed that kings ruled by divine right. It formed the touchstone of his Royalism, and later guided him as primate. While Sancroft had led the bishops who opposed the liberties James was taking with the Church, his view of the Stuarts as God's anointed – for better or worse – remained the same. This meant that in conscience he could never accept William as king, and so found himself at the head of a body of 'Nonjuring' clergymen who refused to swear allegiance to the Prince of Orange. Swift was reportedly asked to write the panegyric for Sancroft in 1689 by another Nonjuror, the Bishop of Ely. He may have attempted to do so as the drama of Sancroft's last months at Lambeth Palace played themselves out, until his final retirement in June 1691, or have held off till the Archbishop's fate was decided. In May the following year, Swift reported that the poem in its present form had been torturing him for five months.[41] He had assembled nine long stanzas, and either split them into shorter sections or ground out another three before giving up.

The struggling ode suffered for its forthrightness in a political situation that, as Swift knew all too well, was fluid and ambiguous. Admitting so was difficult, yet Swift's feelings on the issues he faced in the poem were divided. On one side, he was loyal to the Glorious Revolution; on the other he admired Sancroft's motives. A personal tribute to Sancroft's piety and integrity would not have been taxing; no one of principle, however strongly they supported the Williamite settlement, could have denied it. So, as with the odes to William and the Athenian Society, Swift opened with the highest and most general of claims with regard to his subject and his own relationship to it. Sancroft, again in Miltonic periods, is made by Swift the direct and exclusive 'image' of God's truth on earth. By a logic infinitely simpler than the ode's baroque syntax, anything opposing Sancroft is considered at best erroneous and at worst ungodly. But this made the next bit difficult. The job of reconciling admiration for a principled man with happiness at William's victory was simply impossible. The stanzas expounding Sancroft's saintliness had too much bulk and momentum for nimble reverses: the 'turns' on which Pindarics technically depended. Moreover, they betrayed the issues that would increasingly nag Swift about the position he was contemplating in the Church. Could the revolutionary settlement really protect the institution Swift's grandfather had served and whose sacred qualities Sancroft exemplified?

> Necessity, thou tyrant conscience of the great,
> Say, why the Church is still led blindfold by the State?
> Why should the first be ruin'd and laid waste,
> To mend dilapidations in the last?[42]

The get-out here for Swift, if anyone asked, was that William was bound by necessity and thus not personally culpable for wrongs done to the Church. Swift was also careful to add that William's influence and charisma had by no means cancelled the sins of the nation – and it was these which had dilapidated the Church. Yet the dolour of the second couplet quoted above returned a troubling hint to the man who wrote these lines: they suggested namely that he should think about Nonjurism even before he took the cloth. Sancroft's example was a hard one to follow.

The 'Ode to Dr William Sancroft' cried out, in short, for the approach Swift would quite soon strike upon: of allowing 'truth' in his writing to assume more complex, and often paradoxically deceitful, forms. He complained insouciantly to his cousin Thomas that 'I cannot write anything easy to be understood though it were but in praise of an old Shoe.'[43] The method he discovered in the *Tale of a Tub* would allow him to make his earnest points in negative, through varying shades of irony. Sancroft put him close to exhausting the plaintive sincerity he had borrowed from Cowley. But he would use it to invoke one further subject.

In thought and personality Sir William Temple suited the Cowleyan attitude all but perfectly. In his politics, which he based upon the unfashionable principles of honesty and straightforwardness, he reflected both Cowley's courtly openness and his latent naivety. He also shared the poet's classicism and preference for peace. During this period, Swift declared that he too shared those values, and indeed all that Temple stood for. So much so, he told his cousin Thomas, that praising Temple amounted to no more than praising himself: 'I never read his writings but I prefer him to all others at present in England, Which I suppose is all but a piece of self love, and the likeness of humors makes one fond of them as if they were ones own.'[44]

The strength of such identification has led some to find the origins of a renewed Oedipal struggle in Swift's relationship with Temple. They are no doubt largely right, but if the diagnosis is indeed correct, the positive side of that formative stage should not be overlooked. Swift welcomed the support and detailed interest Temple gave him and his endeavours: later in the same letter he frets about having omitted some lines of the original in a translation from Virgil he was doing, which Temple promptly demanded he retrieve. It was perhaps the first time he had experienced such attention from anyone but St George Ashe. By May 1692 he was working for a Master's degree from Oxford, with Temple's blessing, and 'getting up' his Latin and Greek ready for the examination. In the letter to his cousin that month Swift sounds like a boy – somewhat anxious, but still happy and hopeful. 'I confess a person's happiness is a thing not to be slighted so much as the world thinks,' he wrote. He was not above suggesting to Thomas that he had already been introduced at Court – a statement the record suggests was a fib.

Swift instructed Cousin Thomas nevertheless that he should take some care about his future plans. Other friends, meanwhile, were finding their way, and resettling in Ireland now the reign of James appeared safely over – at least for the moment. Dr Ashe, it seemed, had been appointed the King's new provost at Trinity in Dublin: or at least so Swift had gathered from a French newspaper printed in Holland (he rather vaunted his reading of the international press). The news was spoiled slightly by the 'blockhead' writer misreading the 'St' in Ashe's Christian name and reporting him as 'George Chevalier'. Swift bridled: and his superior attitude towards the mistake over his friend's name

revealed gathering confidence that he would soon be making his own.[45]
Later in the year he was in Oxford, having matriculated at Hart Hall
(now Hertford College) – where John Donne had studied in the 1580s
– to take his M.A. Not long before or afterwards, writing in verse to Sir
William, Swift was less than complimentary about the academic community, having said what a mistake it was to look for Learning's 'troubled
Ghost' up among the dreaming spires, or to 'Confine her Walks to Col-
leges and Schools':

> Her Priests, her Train and Followers show
> As if they were all Spectres too;
> They purchase Knowledge at the Expence
> Of common Breeding, common Sense,
> And at once grow Scholars and Fools;
> Affect ill-manner'd Pedantry,
> Rudeness, Ill-nature, Incivility,
> And sick with Dregs of Knowledge grown,
> Which greedily they swallow down,
> Still cast it up and nauseate Company.[46]

Not exactly diplomatic words to recite at high table; but here was Swift's
grudge at Trinity, Dublin, speaking, not his experience at Oxford. He
was thrilled by the month or so he spent keeping term, before taking his
Master's degree. 'I was never more satisfied than in the behaviour of the
University of Oxford to me,' he reported. 'I had all the civilities I could
wish for, and so many favours, that I am ashamed to have been more
obliged in a few weeks to strangers, than ever I was in seven years to
Dublin College.' His uncle William arranged for Trinity to supply a
statement to support his candidature for the Oxford degree; and there
was no sign of any sniffiness at his gaining his Bachelor's scroll *speciali
gratiâ* ('by special grace'). The term seems to have been unfamiliar at
Oxford, but evidently meant less in 1692 than Swift later felt it did.

That summer, his sister visited him at Moor Park – travelling from
Leicester. As autumn came on, tasks for Temple confined him to the
library; and Sir William was demurring on his earlier enthusiasm for
Swift's future plans, which included taking orders. The baronet sensed
his secretary might want to fly the nest. In a letter to his uncle William,
a prospering Dublin attorney, Swift thanked him for sending over the
testimonium from Trinity – and lingered on the bleaker side of his exist-

ence. He would later always be reluctant to admit he was content when communicating to those he felt owed him a debt of guilt and sympathy. He implied (a bit rudely) that he was only writing, in any case, because his sister Jane had prompted him, and he was most likely mistaken if he thought that Uncle William, clever enough to make his fortune as a barrister, might miss the point.

> My sister told me, you was pleased (when she was here) to wonder, I did so seldom write to you . . . [I am] one who has always been but too troublesome to you: besides I knew your aversion to impertinence, and God Knows so very private a life as mine can furnish a letter with little else: for I often am two or three months without seeing any body besides the family; and now my sister is gone, I am likely to be more solitary than before.

People writing to their former guardians may often insist they are leading a quiet, housebound existence. One of the chief points of interest in the letter to William Swift is the relationship it shows Swift had, as a young man, with Jane – whom he later repudiated. If they were closer than is sometimes thought, his hurt at her marrying against his wishes makes more sense. How 'solitary' he really felt after she left is a matter for conjecture. In any case, the isolation and dejection mentioned here did not mean, probably, that the heady feelings about Temple and his prospects in his letter earlier that year to Thomas had evaporated altogether; they may instead have voiced the anti-climax and uncertainty that were mixed up with hope and growing confidence. 'I suppose he believes I shall leave him,' was Swift's explanation for Sir William being 'less forward' than before in advancing him. Swift's letter to his uncle shows Temple had reason to be worried.[47]

# 5

Swift's inevitable ode to Temple is a work of filial admiration, but written by a son who considers himself a grown-up. Temple is addressed as a guardian of virtue, more than truth, and is thus (unlike Sancroft) not quite so cosmically patriarchal. One might expect the great man his secretary addresses to make Swift, the novice and almost-virgin poet of the other odes, seem very paltry. Instead the opposite is the case: Temple's standing, if anything, invests Swift with poise and dignity. The exclamatory tone of the other Pindarics is not here – Swift's register is elevated, but measured. He speaks as a younger moralist, the junior of two conversing on equal terms; and the basic course of the poem is not one of breathless invocation but rather a dialogue. Two high-minded individuals, one at a later and greater stage of life, go through topics on which they agree entirely – matters of learning, politics, public duty and the relief of retreat.

Only in the final stanza does Swift feel obliged to nod to the difference of rank, saying, 'Then (Sir,) accept this worthless Verse.'[48] The parenthesis around 'Sir' is pointed here: the hierarchy is almost incidental (indeed the epithet was a perfectly common piece of courtesy, between friends). When placed back alongside earlier fine examples of English panegyric – the genre to which the poem technically belongs, that is – the ode to Temple does not fare badly at all. The work of an apprentice, it compares favourably with mature poems by Jonson, Davenant or indeed Cowley. The secret of the mode was a relaxed yet entirely decorous voice, a confident balance of ease and formality. The controlled tenor of Swift's poem thus tempers his comment on its worthlessness. His final complaint about his muse, the one gift of nature his 'niggard stars' allowed him, is that she has been debauched by praise – presumably from Temple.

His muse came in for much harsher and indeed shocking treatment in a poem written probably in 1693. That year Temple fell victim to a long spell of poor health, and his condition seems to have shocked Swift into an awareness of how precariously placed in life he was. Without Temple, he was nowhere. The poem he wrote after Temple recovered, this time abandoning Pindarics for heroic couplets, vents some of the strain and frustration he felt at his lot in life. It would have been curmudgeonly to blame Temple either for these feelings or for the situation that provoked them: and it would be wronging Swift to say that he did blame Temple. Swift was perfectly plain, later in life, in saying those emotions went much further back than his appointment as secretary. Instead, Moor Park allowed him to experience and express them, from a secure position that he was all too aware would not last.

It also needs remembering that Swift's health had been unsteady for some time now. 'I got my Giddyness by eating a hundred golden pippins at a time,' he said much later, 'at Richmond [i.e. the property at Sheen].'[49] The cause Swift found for his illness bears the marks of one of the Temples' great enthusiasms, and also one of Dorothy's cherished medical theories. The couple were devoted gardeners, and Temple indeed a noted theorist on both the practical and the aesthetic sides of horticulture. French guests, he claimed, had once said his grapes were as good as any to be had this side of Fontainebleau.[50] The gardens at Sheen and Moor Park benefited from and embodied this passion: one that, nevertheless, coincided with Dorothy's conviction that eating too much fruit was extremely unhealthy. As early as their furtive courting days, she had repeatedly warned Temple against over-indulging himself, while being sorely tempted by dishes of cherries. The now manifest dietary benefits of fruit were unknown; and a general medical injunction was given particular force in the Temples' home. Swift shared their love of fresh fruit, but never gave over thinking it was bad for him. The backgrounds of master, lady and secretary all had their Puritan tinge: and in this instance a bias against pleasure won out in all three.

Swift's poem 'Occasioned by Sir William Temple's Late Illness and Recovery' opens with a fine, almost Proustian paragraph on the power things have of returning the viewer to an earlier state and time. Swift is revisiting a rural scene he had, in fact, never left since his return from Ireland: a whispering stream on the estate where the muse, he fancies, first appeared to him. She promptly materializes once again, and is upset by the changes etched in his face by concern for Temple. For purposes of domestic diplomacy, the poet's sallow features are compared with those of 'Dorothea' and 'Dorinda' (Temple's sister, Lady Giffard). The two women are templates in dutiful suffering. Dorothy, 'peaceful, wise and great', bears her great trouble with an undisturbed countenance. The 'watery footsteps' of grief, on the other hand, are never absent from Lady Giffard's eyes. Their admirable presences, however, are a distraction from the key relationship of the poem, and the brutal volte that defines it. The panegyric vignette done, the poet turns viciously back to his muse, only to spurn her:

> Malignant goddess! bane to my repose,
> Thou universal cause of all my woes.

The following eighty-odd lines should cause anyone inclined to dismiss Swift's early output to look carefully again. The passage is a stunning work of self-examination and reproach carried out in iconographical terms; and, for all its (rather studied) classical gestures, it is altogether singular in the alarming way Swift bullies his unfortunate naiad. He pours vitriolic abuse over a woman who, he declares in the same breath, does not exist, granting her being only to denounce her as a cliché:

> Say, whence it comes that thou art grown of late
> A poor amusement for my scorn and hate;
> The malice thou inspir'st I never fail
> On thee to wreak the tribute when I rail;
> Fools common-place thou art, their weak ensconcing fort,
> Th' appeal of dullness in the last resort.

Every word of which, as the poet knows only too well, merely rebounds on him: he is an outraged Narcissus pounding his face in the water. But this is far from being a senseless splurge of feeling. The supremely well-orated rant takes time to offer a memorable epigram on how differently time passes according to one's emotional state.

> Time o'er the happy takes so swift a flight,
> And treads so soft, so easy, and so light,
> That we, the wretched, creeping far behind,
> Can scarce th' impression of his foot-steps find.

But the main drive of the poem is undoubtedly towards a break-up beyond all hope of reconciliation. Especially remarkable, given the suspicions Swift had already voiced about women, is that he steers largely clear of standard misogynistic charges against the muse. She is 'a painted name, / A walking vapor, like thy sister Fame' (ll. 101–2); but her greatest crime is that she has led young men, albeit mainly the 'dregs of youth' (l. 105), to nourish vain hopes and waste their time. The poem is iconoclastic in literary terms: it turns the vocabulary used so often to berate Fortune or Fame against the feminine presence that always nurtures a poet, the muse. It is a strike, if anything, against a maternal figure rather than a symbolic father.

At the same time as he casts the muse out, it is clear that, without Temple, she is all Swift has left. She also constitutes an obsession now inseparable from his nature, 'a fatal bent of mind' (l. 131), and so, while plucking this Minerva from his skull, he simultaneously tears into his brain. At the end, though, he expels her for good:

> I here renounce thy visionary pow'r;
> And since thy essence on my breath depends,
> Thus with a puff the whole delusion ends.

With this last gasp, he also announced the sort of writer he would be in the future: one working from his own wit, insights and predispositions

– foremost among which, he realized, was his 'scorn of fools, by fools mistook for pride' (l. 134).[51]

In Swift's earliest surviving work from Moor Park, then, he subsumes himself in fictitious machinery and casts it off. The presence of Temple, whatever later issues Swift might have with it, seems genuinely support-ive. Swift for his part had self-knowledge enough not to blame his master for problems Temple had not caused and could not make vanish.

# 6

After securing his hold on his three new kingdoms by sheer force of arms in Ireland, King William had returned to his original grand project: war against King Louis of France. By 1693 this was not going well. A disas-trous defeat at Beachy Head capped a number of setbacks and surrenders. The King, in time-honoured fashion, was fast losing the early hopes placed in him, and, although he astutely supported the principle of a strong assembly, he was growing frustrated with Parliament. Long-last-ing Parliaments had become familiar during the later Stuart reigns, and Charles II had proved adept at stacking the Commons with men the Court could rely on. The Whigs, while backing William firmly, were determined to stop him using such a strategy. In a bid to preserve their independence, they resurrected an old outlawed statute from the days of the Long Parliament, before the English Civil War. This became the Tri-ennial Act of 1694, which bound the monarch to hold elections – and, in William's view, waste an expensively maintained majority – every three years.

Lords and Commons combined to pass the bill at a point of extreme political and military strain, and, for the first time since the revolution, King and Parliament fell into deadlock. Firm resistance to the bill was advised by William's most trusted friend and counsellor, Hans Willem Bentinck, a fellow Dutchman, whom he had made Earl of Portland. Wil-liam, however, asked for a more expert if still sympathetic opinion from Temple, and sent Portland to Moor Park to speak with him. Portland's chief fear, which William reportedly shared, was that a Triennial Act would make the King a slave to Parliament. Charles I, they claimed, had given up all effective power by signing the first Triennial Act before the war. Temple, taking the question with typical good faith, corrected what he took as a sincere misapprehension. The Triennial Act of 1641 had not, he observed, prevented Charles I from dissolving Parliament as he pleased: that power had been taken out of Charles's hands by another, rightly reviled (in his view) Act, which there was no serious thought of reviving. Portland went away, vaguely displeased, and the King's position stayed as it was.

Temple clearly thought that his simple point of historical fact had not got through – and so explained the matter at more length, in writing. He then entrusted Swift, now in his mid-twenties and 'well versed in English history', to hand over the memorandum and give an oral account of its contents. Swift took the mission to heart and seems to have shared Temple's characteristic belief that the whole dispute arose from a fairly simple misunderstanding. The mistake, in fact, may rather have been Temple's rather than the King's: he failed to see that William was asking him to codify his stance on historical grounds, not correct it. Swift, however, faithfully journeyed to Kensington to dispel the King's doubts.

In 1693 King William and Queen Mary were still enlarging and enhancing their house and its parklands. They had bought their 'palace' from Daniel Finch, the dark-featured Earl of Nottingham. Nottingham, in fact, had been at best a tepid supporter of the Williamite revolution, and had proposed that William serve as regent rather than taking the Crown. But he took the royal couple's offer on his Kensington property, and the joint-sovereigns energetically set up home there. The palace was a work in progress when Swift was admitted to the state apartments, with Wren's dramatic extensions still incomplete. The great gallery would stand for many years as a half-drawn architectural cartoon. Swift's terse account of his visit, though written long afterwards, suggests that he found things not as he thought they should be, if pretty much what he had expected. The display of expenditure, the Queen's multitude of pets, the priceless art and ceramics – these were standard incidentals; the shock lay with first exposure to the posturing and wretched supplication that went with life at Court. All the more painful was the truth that Swift would have to join the mob of suitors if he hoped for greater fortune: a prospect from which a career in the Church did not screen him at all. He would not get far by emulating Temple's practised loftiness.

At Kensington, the King gave Swift's speech a brief hearing; Portland listened at more length. Neither, it seems, took much notice of Temple's written briefing. That, Swift claimed much later, was their hard luck: by blocking the Triennial Act, William only put himself at the mercy of the Whigs. He was consequently obliged to pacify them with 'Power and Employments', when the Act might have allowed him to flush them out by refreshing Parliament every few years. As it happened, a generation would pass before a Parliament outlived three years. Yet, if Swift disagreed with royal policy on this question, that was nothing compared with the dismay he felt at seeing the seat of regal business. 'It was the first time that Mr Swift had ever any converse with Courts,' he recalled, in his usual autobiographical third person; 'and he told his friends it was the first incident that cured him of vanity.'[52]

However he resisted that vice, his ego smarted sorely. The early glow of privilege with Temple was losing lustre. Swift felt he deserved greater chances, and he swallowed hard when they fell to others. At that time, none of his contemporaries had enjoyed swifter or higher success than his school- and college-mate William Congreve. In some ways they were similar men: both were critics of society, and both stood out by their wit. But, where Swift's was deadly, of that 'cold temper' he saw in himself, and often defensive, Congreve's was gregarious. He had a lightness Swift lacked, and charmed where Swift would daunt and impress. Although probably no more athletic than his peer, and surely not the horseman Swift was, there was something more of the jock about Congreve: with a run-up, he claimed he could jump twenty-one feet.

*The Old Bachelor*, Congreve's first play, delighted the audiences at the Drury Lane Theatre from its first appearance in March 1693. Dryden, the Poet Laureate (and Swift's distant relation), had read the work in manuscript and confessed himself astounded. The only hitch in the play's passage to production had been the attempt by Congreve, who had a faultless ear but on stage a wooden tongue, to read it himself to the Drury Lane company. As the actors listening clapped hands to their faces in despair and whispered mockingly, one of them took the manuscript from the writer to show him how it was done. When the professional took over, they were surprised to find themselves listening to a masterpiece of comedy. At the age of barely twenty-three – he was two years Swift's junior – he had already written what punters and critics alike were calling a classic of the English theatre. He had done so, too, with very little of the drudgery and servility that made up Swift's average working day. Swift had known him, though, since boyhood, and must have long viewed him as a boy of the lower forms.

Congreve was triumphant in a medium Swift knew and to some extent enjoyed. The main theatre in Dublin was to be found down a narrow lane near the quays south of the Liffey. It was described rather sniffily by John Dunton in the late 1690s:

Having got my ticket, I made a shift to crowd into the pit. I found the
Dublin Play-house to be a place very contrary to its owners; for they on
their outsides make the best show: but this is very ordinary in its outward appearance, but looks much better on the inside, with its stage,
pit, boxes, two galleries, lattices and music-loft; though I must confess
that even these, like other false beauties, receive a lustre from their
lamps and candles.

The 'Smock Alley Theatre', as it was always known, allowed the Dublin
public to keep roughly up to date with recent developments on the London stage, enjoy some exciting debuts of their own, and also watch
classics of the English repertoire. On the visit he described above, Dunton dressed as a Londoner, 'in my best clothes and powdered wig', and
evidently blended in with Dublin beaux in similar attire. He was willing
to concede some of the actors performing were the equals of their peers
in London; and the fashionable throng in the audience had no less 'vanity and foppery' than one might see in Drury Lane.[53] The theatre was a
social focal point, a source of excitement and discussion. Swift had no
thought, it seems, of writing for the stage himself; yet by this time he was
aware of what Congreve's achievement constituted in wider society.

A poem in honour of Congreve preserves Swift's view of what he
sampled further on his trips to London in these years. At one unspoken
level, celebrating Congreve in verse might well have grated; but, at
another, which Swift possibly found still harder to acknowledge, he
knew that Congreve might give his beached career a much needed shove.
So far as the pangs of envy were concerned, the task was made easier by
a dip Congreve suffered at the end of 1693. The town did not like his
new comedy The Double Dealer. The work bit too deep, offending fashionable male and female viewers alike. A few authorities, including
Dryden, thought it better than Congreve's debut, but the critical majority found it too satirical and a tad cumbersome. 'The women thinke he
has exposed their Bitchery too much,' reflected Dryden.[54] Congreve had
possibly struck when the iron was just too hot; but he had also shaped
his second work according to theories of theatre that had little appeal
for the pit. He was hurt, and berated his judges in a dedication to the
play on its publication. He would recover wonderfully with another hit,
Love for Love in 1695; but the early months of 1694 were difficult for
him.

This was roughly when Swift decided to offer consolation. His lines
'To Mr Congreve' were evidently drafted in November 1693. In this

poem Swift is still the friend and servant of the muse: indeed, he is indignant against a number of witlings who have given her offence, and still more so at the knot of young fops he finds trying to defile her. They lure her, a poor 'country virgin', with their 'lewd and fashionable prate'. At one point, the poet chides himself for spending 'the muse's hour' on mangling Congreve's critics rather than praising the playwright, but the former task clearly suits him better: the mortifying ritual of exalting the younger schoolboy is shelved for the much more satisfying opportunity of laying into his brainless bullies. The poem becomes, in short, an occasion for Swift to catalogue much of what he found to despise in the capital. He redirects his professional and social envy by exposing the typical 'expert' critic as a provincial greenhorn:

> Last year, a lad hence by his parents sent
> With other cattle to the city went;
> Where having cast his coat, and well pursu'd
> The methods most in fashion to be lewd,
> Return'd a finished spark this summer down,
> Stock'd with the freshest gibberish of the town . . .[55]

The illiterate drawl and scrawl of city beaux would be a recurrent target for Swift; the detail of the coat is a faint premonition of a central motif in *A Tale of a Tub*. He continues by disparaging the 'whores and fops' who make up the majority of Congreve's audience. The callow fellow going up to the town nevertheless mirrors something of the writer bent on mauling him. How easily might Swift himself be distinguished from the 'other cattle' journeying from the provinces, perhaps making a nervous introduction himself at Court and then passing a first evening at the theatre? Swift's fury is that of the perennial scholar against those who, lacking all substance, could *seem* both elegant and intelligent. His poem, meanwhile, is not quite able to bring Congreve on to his team: his college-mate had after all spent most of the previous year as the darling of these smart-coated hordes. One tactic Swift accordingly tries out is sympathy for Congreve's predicament as 'the fashionable wit', his name bandied about on the lips of London's coxcombs. 'Troth I could pity you,' he tells the younger man; but only risks suggesting that he covets the attention he comforts Congreve for enduring.[56]

Swift's cousin Thomas, a man of similar age and hopes, read the verses to Congreve. Wisely, he suggested Swift withhold them until Congreve's next play. Thomas evidently sensed, and rightly, that another

coup might not be long coming, and would make his relative's outrage
redundant. Swift reacted sharply to this advice; but never sent the
poem.[57]

# 7

It was many years, and quite a few books, before Swift equalled Congreve – though when he did, he rapidly exceeded him in influence.
Meanwhile a career for Swift as a literary professional, much less a
writer for the stage, was always out of the question. Instead he inched
along a path he had chosen some time before: he would take orders as
an Anglican priest, and seek a benefice in Ireland. He had taken his M.A.
at Oxford in 1692 to further his chances of advancement; later he supplemented this with a doctorate from Trinity, Dublin. In 1694 he revealed
that he intended to take the cloth, but did so in a tricky fashion, only
after asking if Temple would help him get another job. Temple offered
him a position worth about £100 a year in an office his family had long
controlled, the Master of the Rolls in Ireland. But Swift immediately
turned this down, and revealed his real plan of entering the Church. His
cousin Thomas, who had recently been ordained and was set on marrying his sweetheart with little in the way of supporting her, stood ready to
replace him as secretary. But Temple did not take the news well: 'he was
extream angry I left,' Swift reported from his mother's home in Leicestershire, where 'every Body judged I did best to leave him.'[58] He sailed to
Ireland late in the spring of 1694, hoping family connections would help
him to gain a living there – for he could not take orders unless he was
assured of a benefice. A niche was found for him, but later in the year he
needed to swallow his pride and ask yet another favour of Temple. A
strong character reference was needed, and at the shortest notice. Mag-
nanimously Temple dispatched one, seemingly by return of post.

Benefices might well have been easier to pick up in Ireland, or so one
might have thought, but the move in 1694 reflects a realistic sense in
Swift that his connections and best chance of a career lay over the water.
Quite possibly, as with his trip four years before, he may even have been
guided by a wish to serve in his country of origin, a patriotism he disguised as best he could in layers of defensive cynicism. In any case, Swift
was ordained priest in Dublin on 13 January 1695. Two weeks later, he
was presented to his living, the prebend of Kilroot in the diocese of
Down and Connor. Some doubt still exists as to which high-placed

friend acted as patron on this occasion. Assistance from the Temple family's widespread Irish network seems likely, however. From the stance of ambition, the favour was not so considerable. The parish lay far to the north, on the northern shore of Belfast Lough, in territory largely hostile to the Established Church in which Swift was now a minister. He moved into what had recently been a theatre of war, where only a handful of churches were in decent repair, and the one at Kilroot was little more than a roofless heap of stones. As was often the case, Swift's cure covered two other parishes besides Kilroot, in the villages of Templecorran and Ballynure, the homes of a few hundred Ulster and Scottish Presbyterians with a scattering of Anglicans.

His place in the north also put the labouring natives of Ireland before his eyes once more. Since the revolutionary war the territory lay theoretically under the military control of the Ulster Scots, but memories were still fresh of the bands of rapparees, outlaws and guerrilla fighters dispersed by the Williamite army but still in arms for the Jacobite cause; and still in need, too, for the indigenous people, hard set in the north since the plantation began a century and more ago, were struggling for subsistence. The shores of Connaught were far from being the only scene of incredible hardship in Ireland. 'It's a wonder to see how some of those creatures live,' one (far from sympathetic) English observer recorded. 'I my self have seen them scratching like Hens amongst the Cindars for victuals.' Such unfortunates offered prayers for the smallest handouts. Yet the same writer, an older minister in Swift's Church, was in no doubts about how the native population should be treated in defeat: 'as to the Irish, they are naturally a fawning flattering People, they'll down upon their Knees to you at every turn; but they are very rude, false, and of no courage . . . So that as Slaves, there's no way to deal with them but to whip them into good manners.'[59] The landowner Sir Henry Piers, a more even-handed, though still far from unbiased eyewitness, noted that the lower class of farmers known as 'scullogues' tended to be 'very crafty and subtile in all manner of bargaining, full of equivocations and mental reservations'. Yet Piers implicitly understood that this was a reasonable attitude among an oppressed people, and was no different to the bearing of those in similar straits in other countries. He criticized, in particular, the harshness of the landowners to their tenants. He observed that the Irish gentry were more concerned with establishing their pedigrees, of whatever hue, and proving their antiquity than in learning how to do anything useful. Piers himself was preoccupied with the natural philosophical angle – speculating on why a droplet of water should be drawn into a sphere, and tagging his territory with Augustan epigrams – than in making any larger political argument. Writing of the midland county of Westmeath in the 1680s, however, he recognized the seeds of catastrophe in Irish farming practices, particularly in the tendencies of overstocking and then over-dividing the land.[60] Sir William Petty, in his *Political Anatomy of Ireland*, said the Irish were not to be blamed for what the English took savagely as laziness. Since they were without incentive, branded idle and shiftless by the occupiers, he declared that they could only slump in a state of passive hostility.

Living conditions varied, even within a given class or region. Around Belfast, and in Ulster generally, the Catholic gentry – whether 'native', Anglo-Norman or Old English in complexion – had been more or less driven out. The big houses of the area were thus almost all held now by Protestant landlords. These larger dwellings were by no means always comfortable or even bearably warm. An Irish manor house might realistically be a converted old fortress, typically a small-windowed pile with a square keep, or something incorporating the remnants of a castle into recent extensions. Some still dated, at the core, from Viking times – 'square strong buildings of stone, with a small door and stone stairs, and windows like spike holes purposely for strength'.[61] The homes of tenant labourers, meanwhile, could be well-built, chimneyed houses; or they could be more or less improvised cabins such as those described by one Richard Head in the 1670s. Sometimes their very basic materials served almost as camouflage in a landscape that was largely without hedges or fencing.

> The cots are generally built on the side of a hill, not to be discerned till you just come upon them. The cottage is usually raised three feet from the eaves to the ground on one side, and the other side hath a rock for a wall to save charges . . . The hearth is placed in the middle of the house and their [the cottagers'] fuel is made of earth and cow-dung dried in the sun. The smoke goes through no particular place, but breaks through every part between the rods and the wattles of which they make their doors, sides and roof of the house, which commonly is no bigger than an overgrown pigstye.

The English observer has the usual innate bias; in suggesting the two are roughly equivalent in size, he trusts his readers will infer that the labourers' house shares the other key properties of a pigsty. But Head's eye was more sympathetic than that of others visiting the country. He recorded the cottagers' joke that 'they have the quickest architects in the world, because they can build a house in a day.'[62] The Jacobite John Stevens, exploring the country after his experience as a soldier at the Boyne, reported that even 'the better sort of cabins' offered very limited simple comforts.

> There is commonly one flock [sheepskin] bed, seldom more, feathers being too costly; this serves the man and his wife, the rest all lie on straw, some with one sheet and blanket, others only their clothes and blanket to cover them. The cabins seldom have any floor but the earth, or rarely so much as a loft, some have windows, others none. They say it is of late years that chimneys are used, yet the house is never free from smoke.[63]

Swift never distinguished between the diverse forms of rural workers' dwellings he encountered on his travels. As his story moves on, one should always refer back to these images as horrific epitomes for him. The peasant cabin became his stock idea of near-total deprivation, one he often attributed to moral or essential failings in the occupant. Yet his view of these conditions was far from monochrome. By the late 1720s he would point out that Anglo-Scottish Protestants were living as 'mere' Irish. In warmer months, when he established himself in his parishes in Meath, he would prove willing to live rough himself, in a cabin he built for himself in the townland of Laracor. The notion of being confined to such circumstances he nevertheless found utterly repellent.

To Swift, the common Irish people would always seem foreign and incorrigible, the women in their loose-bodied woollen dresses, sometimes covering their heads only with hoods, the men in their brogues and coarse suits of frieze. Their rough diet of potatoes in the summer months, sour eggs and butter, oatcakes and watercress, seemed foul and indigestible to newcomers. But, however scathing he was of their country habits, Swift still belonged on the whole with the Anglo-Irish observers who could not help regarding the natives as human beings, however alien. It may be that his time in the north in the mid-1690s furnished one often-quoted description in an appendix to the *Tale of a Tub*. Swift noticed how:

> it is usual for a Knot of Irish, Men and Women, to abstract themselves from Matter, bind up all their Senses, grow visionary and spiritual, by

Influence of a short Pipe of Tobacco; handed round the Company; each
preserving the Smoak in his Mouth, till it comes his Turn to take in
fresh: At the same Time, there is a Consort of a continued gentle Hum,
repeated and renewed by Instinct . . .[64]

Swift compared this mild practice with the forced spiritual narcoses of
British Dissenters. Tellingly, his intent is to criticize the 'fanatics' who in
their form of worship resemble Irish people having a smoke, and not the
Irish themselves.

All was far from well, meanwhile, in more empowered sections of
the population. While commentators such as the Reverend George
Story would always see the indigenous Irish as slaves, members of the
ruling Protestant class once again felt like the inhabitants of a subordinate state. Even Story took care to refer to Ireland as a 'kingdom', equal
in status if not in wealth and power with the fraternal Crown of
England. But Westminster for decades had grown more confident in
acting upon the commonly held view that Ireland was nothing other
than a colony. A key point of contention was whether English statutes
had the force of law in Ireland. This indeed was the presumption behind
the raft of legislation the English Parliament had issued to cripple Irish
trade since the 1660s. The legality of each Act was questionable: Westminster clearly had the right to ban imports of Irish beef, however
regrettable their wish to do so. But could they rule that Irish ships
returning from the colonies must harbour in English ports – and thus
pay English duties – before proceeding home? In all such cases, the Irish
Parliament was obliged to confirm the statute to give it legal force. In
the aftermath of the Glorious Revolution, the Anglo-Irish themselves
were now, it was said, beginning to accept direct rule from the legislature in London. One noted thinker on this question, William Molyneux,
suggested that the problem stemmed from the surge of emigration during Tyrconnell's supremacy in Dublin. Protestants fleeing the Catholic
'tyranny' sought protection and redress in London for lost Irish properties and interests. King William's defeat of James then reinforced the
English view of Ireland as a conquered state. Consequently, the exiles
returning to Dublin were able to do so thanks to English help; their
acceptance of which, Molyneux reasoned, was taken as a 'sign of our
submission and absolute acquiescence in the jurisdiction of the Parliaments of England over this kingdom'. Yet, in law and natural justice,
nothing could be further from the truth. 'If a man, who has no jurisdiction over me, command me to do a thing that is pleasing to me, and I

do it; it will not hence follow, that thereby he obtains an authority over me, and ever hereafter I must obey him of duty . . .' This line brought Molyneux to what was surely the crux of all political argument in Swift's lifetime:

If it be said, this allows subjects to obey only whilst 'tis convenient for them, I pray it may be considered whether men obey longer, unless they be forced to it; and whether they will not free themselves from this *force* as soon as they can. 'Tis impossible to hinder men from desiring to *free* themselves from *uneasiness*, 'tis a principal of nature, and cannot be eradicated.[65]

Such, in effect, had been the lessons of the great Civil Wars. Since then, Thomas Hobbes had proposed that subjects owed absolute obedience to their ruler only for as long as he could protect their interests. More recently, John Locke (a friend of Molyneux) had proposed that people could be governed only by their own consent.

The discontent behind Molyneux's argument – not published till 1698 – took up a proportion of the talk at tables in the region where Swift now based himself. It mingled, naturally, with the chatter over cards Swift affected to dislike, the word games at which he excelled, and the discourse on pet topics of natural philosophy he bore with patience and perhaps occasional interest. In the environs of Belfast, nevertheless, the predominant sense for his fellow Anglicans was one of remoteness and isolation, and suspended aggression from Presbyterian neighbours. The landscape about the lough was mountainous and boggy, enclosing passes it was fascinating but still quite dangerous to explore. Local legend has it that Swift lived in a round house in Kilroot itself, but the thatched cottage in question (now destroyed) seems to have dated from after his lifetime. In fact, there was almost certainly no habitable 'manse' – a house serving as rectory or vicarage – for Swift in any of the parishes. He probably took lodgings at Carrickfergus, a harbour town with a stout castle overlooking the fishing boats, which had been William of Orange's landing place in June 1690.

Here, then, was the reward for Swift's willpower and integrity. He was not without company at Carrickfergus. He made friends among the local Anglican gentry, led by the Earl of Donegal and his family, the Chichesters. The doors of Joymount Palace, their Jacobean mansion on the outskirts of the town, were open to him. Swift was capable of froideur, but was an innately sociable being; and, as he had insisted to John

Kendall in 1692, felt he had a perfect right to converse with people of both sexes. He was soon on good terms with local amateur scientists, and became involved with a local gentlewoman. His taste for the outdoors was nourished by the rough-backed majesty of the country. But, by his own account, not many months had passed before he grew weary of the consciousness of distance, the evenings that could not be filled, the dire lack of promise in his surroundings. He lacked the resignation with which Gulliver could accept his various places of exile. In April 1696 Temple offered him his former post back. Another winter on the Ulster coast evidently seemed unthinkable; Swift quickly accepted.

He left one emotional casualty behind. After the unnamed lady in Leicestershire, Swift was romantically implicated with three other women. The first of these was the only one Swift asked to marry him. Her name was Jane Waring, and he met her during his windswept and depressing year at Kilroot. Her relatives lived originally at Waring, a little town dominated by their big house and named after their family, just under a day's ride to the south-west of Carrickfergus. But when Swift knew them, Widow Waring and her daughter Jane were likely to have been living in nearby Belfast. Jane's father, also a clergyman, had died, young, three years before she met Swift in the course of 1695. The family's connection to the Church, and their place in the region's sprinkling of Anglican gentry, drew Swift and Jane together. She was twenty-one, and he twenty-eight. To match Swift's dizziness and hearing problems, her health was also troubled. As demi-orphans, they were roughly equal: her pain at bereavement was fresher, but the marks of his loss probably went deeper. Not long passed before he expressed serious intentions towards her. Jane was unique in Swift's life for the proposal he made to her, but also for being addressed by him in the closest he would come to conventional romantic terms.

His letters to Waring reveal him as an uncomfortable suitor. He used the language of a love-letter awkwardly and artificially. As if to make the task easier by placing her as a persona of his own making, he Latinized her name – a humorous poeticism he would use with Stella and Vanessa, and also, incidentally, in naming the disfigured and morally suspect female characters of a deliberately provocative late group of poems. As an ageing man, he extended this mock-dignification to a set of younger women writers as well as a number of elderly disabled female beggars in the vicinity of St Patrick's. Near the very beginning of this tradition, Jane Waring became 'Varina' when he urged her to become his wife, a suit he made to her in irksomely general terms: 'Impatience is the most inseparable quality of a lover, and indeed of every person who is in pursuit of a design whereon he conceives his greatest happiness or misery to depend.' Varina was resisting this impatience – which in all fairness was rather moderate on Swift's part. He assured her he had no intention of marrying until he was making a decent living and she was satisfied with it, but even so, she stopped short of consenting. It may have been that Jane's attitudes and temperament were too close to her suitor's: an unwell woman, she stalled at the prospect of childbirth, housekeeping and bringing up a family in a land that was basically hostile. In person and in writing, Swift demanded her consent brusquely rather than seductively: a make-or-break letter of April 1696 contains many withering sentences against Jane personally ('Varina's life is daily wasting') and women in general. But he also gives the impression that he felt they had a real chance of happiness. In one paragraph he relaxes, and shows the sort of thing they talked about, and which made him an attractive and lively companion. He uses a bit of news to reassure her about his character and ambitions:

> Two strangers, a poet and a beggar, went to cuffs yesterday in this town, which minded me to curse heartily both employments. However, I am glad to see those two trades fall out, because I always heard they had been constant cronies: but what was best of all, the poet got the better, and kicked the gentleman beggar out of doors. This was of great comfort to me [Swift being a poet], till I heard the victor himself was a most abominable bad rhymer, and as mere a vagabond beggar as the other, which is a very great offence to me, for starving is much too honourable for a blockhead.

Swift comes across much better describing a brawl in an Irish town than in lofty declarations. But he was writing to Jane here with real urgency, and, in fact, delivered an ultimatum: by now Sir William Temple had asked him to return to Moor Park, on a better footing than before. Swift took his leave of Jane with a solemn protest: 'by all that can be witness to an oath, that if I leave this kingdom before you are mine, I will endure the utmost indignities of fortune rather than ever return again.'[66] He left, unbetrothed, and soon cooled towards her. Jane, however, reconsidered, and over subsequent years let him know that she would welcome his former attentions. She recalled the ardour of protestations such as these.

> Surely, Varina, you have but a very mean opinion of the joys that accompany a true, honourable, unlimited love . . . Is it possible you can

be yet insensible to the prospect of a rapture and delight so innocent and so exalted? Trust me, Varina, Heaven has given us nothing else worth the loss of a thought.[67]

Swift's sentiments to Jane Waring have traditionally been dismissed as shallow and conventional; but that point is dispelled if one looks at how Swift sets up careful limiting safety devices throughout the letter to pull his language back from bathos. He uses a variety of tones with recognizable literary settings, and his reader could clearly follow (and perhaps enjoy) the contrast between them. He is far from cloying. Irony, harangue, the more than faintly sardonic Latinate apostrophe, frame and offset the earnest appeal to emotion in the sentences above. He clearly means to be taken seriously when he speaks of the 'rapture and delight' in marriage that make sacrifices worthwhile. And this adds another dimension to the time limit Swift puts on his offer of marriage to Waring. In speaking like this, even with the stylistic sheaths he took care to use, he exposed himself to hurt. Whenever Swift went so far to brave rejection, there was invariably a painful episode further down the road. His gallantry with Waring possibly put him off formal courtship for ever. Yet a lesser known side of his nature would sometimes make him ardent and profuse in affairs of the heart.

# 8

Swift was away from Moor Park for almost exactly two years, departing in May 1694 to be ordained in Dublin, and returning gratefully in the late spring of 1696. Resuming life with the Temples was evidently a relief after the far-flung and Presbyterian-infested territory by the shores of Belfast Lough. The family he rejoined, though, had shrunk in his absence, both in number and in vividness. Dorothy had died in February 1695. Her husband was so familiar with bereavement that he took the blow stoically. He had, after all, spent most of his early adult life preparing himself to lose her – to another suitor, to smallpox, to complications in pregnancy. Although a visitor had described him as 'healthy and gay' the previous summer, his gout and rheumatism were getting worse. He did not expect too many years in which to mourn. His sister, Lady Giffard, who had a long life still ahead, mentioned in her letters his digestive troubles, the pain caused by stiff joints and a lame knee.[68]

Swift took on a wider range of duties than before. Besides still being Temple's letter-writer and courier, his role was now that of family minder.

He kept the account-books, managed expenses, escorted younger relatives to town; and, perhaps most onerously, was entrusted with Temple's literary legacy. He was to edit and see through the press the large volumes of Temple's collected works, and the task would take longer than the time the ailing essayist had left. Temple had always had his moods, but in these last years, understandably, he was morose for seasons rather than short spells. Swift's days were brightened by a child who had grown up while he was away. Esther Johnson was still living at Moor Park, and Swift resumed his old role as her tutor. Writing to her for her thirty-fourth birthday, he reassured her she had lost none of the beauty that struck him 'Since first I saw Thee at sixteen / The brightest Virgin of the Green'.[69] She was fifteen when he returned from Ireland; he was twenty-eight. His teenage pupil cheered for him the stricken house. Yet Lady Giffard noticed that he was visibly glad when Temple sent him on some errand to London. He carried the Baronet's compliments to the King and associates at Court, and enjoyed some of the pleasures he condemned others for taking to excess, in the theatres and chocolate-houses.

Swift was assisting Temple to edit his collected works for the press, but he had also begun work on a book of his own, one unlike anything he or anyone else had yet attempted. He was seemingly grateful to be back in the fold at Moor Park. Yet, so far as the world was concerned, writing could exist only where it fought to be heard, in the element of relentless agitation that buzzed just a few dozen miles beyond the estate, as near as Kilroot was to Carrick. London was alive with an endless swarm of pamphleteering, disputation, doggerel, from comparably tiny people; some of which, nevertheless, stung the giants of the day and moved them. The most distant news, a pirate's actions in the East Indies, could release a cloud of argument, and, if it touched upon a home concern, become a storm. Equally, it could melt to nothing and be succeeded instantly by fresh news, fresh questions, and another build-up of wit and opinion. Mastering that perverse and changeable weather would be the chief task of Swift's political life.

In his *Tale of a Tub*, Swift dwelt ironically upon the problem of how anything could last in such circumstances. Assuming the voice of a 'modern', he denied that the age had produced no writers of learning and worth; the problem was rather that there were too many of them, all 'hurryed so hastily off the Scene, that they escape our Memory, and delude our Sight'. How could the world contain them all, indeed, and all their productions, those 'immense Bales of paper'?[70] Addressing His Royal Highness Prince Posterity, with a light cough into his fist, Swift directed his noble auditor where to look for the vanishing books. Their pages would be found lining bakers' ovens, heaped ready for use in the city's latrines, or pasted up to cover the indecencies occurring behind brothel windows.

Such was the end, he had every reason to suspect, that his own efforts would meet. Yet a powerful sense of the transience of letters, not to mention the disposable, combustible, mortifyingly absorbent nature of paper, was never enough to put Swift off writing. The activity became not only his métier but a necessity, as essential to his equilibrium as a daily ride or walk. He possessed a restless yet rigorously structured personality that, in modern times, has been attributed by some to Asperger's syndrome. Whether or not such a diagnosis holds, writing had become for Swift not only a retreat but also a means of holding a still point amid his fits of dizziness, and staving off an existential vertigo that oppressed him even more.[71]

Notwithstanding doubts and duties, his intellectual life remained voraciously active. During 1696–7, as he assembled the work that would become *A Tale*, amid his other secretarial and personal reading he made his way three times (he claimed) through *De rerum natura*, the discursive, anti-religious epic of the Roman poet Lucretius. The poem sets out to justify the materialist and atheist view of the universe developed by Epicurus – a thinker much admired for a time by Temple – arguing that all physical behaviour is governed by the movement of variously shaped atoms. Such a vision was in itself abhorrent to Swift, and in *A Tale* he placed Lucretius along with Epicurus in a band of lunatic philosophers. Quotations from Lucretius occur frequently in *A Tale*, and the poet seems to serve as a stand-by authority for Swift's eccentric narrator. Yet Swift's attitude to insanity, in *A Tale* and elsewhere, is always ambivalent, and so his relationship with Lucretius is far from straightforwardly critical. Lucretius's sustained assaults on metaphysics and spiritualism manifestly had their attractions, given Swift's contempt for evangelical free-thinking.[72] Moreover, one passage may have acted secretly on his imagination over a number of decades. Here Lucretius seems to suggest something of the paradoxes of scale that are so essential to the first two books of Gulliver, as he reflects on the way the customary size of the things that surround us, and indeed of our own bodies, limits our capacity to comprehend greater phenomena:

'But the raging fire of Etna,' you will say, 'is extraordinarily great.' Doubtless, I answer; and a river, which has been seen by any person, appears extraordinarily great to him who has never before seen a greater; and a man or a tree possibly appears large to the eyes of some animals; and everyone imagines every thing of every sort, which is the greatest that he has seen, to be extremely large, although all things that he beholds together with the heaven and the earth and the ocean, are nothing in comparison with the entire sum of the entire whole.[73]

Lilliputians live very much in the state of denial described here until Gulliver lands in their midst, a state that Gulliver shares until his own shocking arrival in Brobdingnag. Conversely, he is oblivious to how gigantic he must seem to a small animal before he encounters the host of little people who tie him up on their shore. The passage above, if it counts as one of many hints Swift found in books, folklore and life for the big and small worlds of Lilliput and Brobdingnag, may have stuck in his mind for its quite un-Lucretian implications. Lucretius is encouraging us to see that the same rules must govern all similar physical entities, regardless of their dimensions; but a more Swiftian point might also be inferred, namely that the 'entire whole' of the Creation is unknowable to mortal minds, and that there are more things in heaven and earth than are dreamed of in anyone's philosophy.

# 9

For nearly two centuries, European history had been twisted by the struggle between the old Roman Church and the proliferating shades of Reformed belief. Through an allegory in Lilliput, Swift would reduce the dispute to one over which end of a boiled egg should be chipped off with knife or spoon. 'Many hundred large Volumes have been published upon this Controversy: but the Books of the *Big-Endians* have been long forbidden, and the whole Party rendered incapable by Law of holding Employments.'[74] The literature of Reformation controversy was a thousandfold vaster again. Swift was well read in the major works on both sides: and, although he supported the Test Acts preventing Catholics from holding public office, he could admire, for example, the prose style of Robert Persons, the Elizabethan Jesuit and adroit polemicist.[75] At exactly the point he discovered his mature style, Swift's response to Europe's religious nightmare was not to contribute a work of his own on some theological crux, but instead to make fun of the long-winded war itself. The result, drafted in the mid-to-late 1690s,[76] was an eccentric, relentless, superlative performance: *A Tale of a Tub*.

The *Tale* is ostensibly just that, a sort of fairy-story: each of three brothers, Peter, Martin and Jack, receives a coat of the highest quality from their father. On his deathbed, the old man tells them that the coats possess two magical properties: 'they will last you fresh and sound as long as you live' and 'they will grow in the same proportion with your Bodies, lengthning and widening of themselves, so as to be always fit.' The three boys, who are triplets, set out from home on their adventures, in the course of which they meet 'a reasonable Quantity of Gyants' and slay 'certain Dragons'. When they enter a big city, however, they go the usual way of errant sons: 'They Drank, and Fought, and Whor'd, and Slept, and Swore, and took Snuff.' They go through the full round, in fact, of venial and mortal urban sins:

> They went to new Plays on the first Night, haunted the Chocolate-Houses, beat the Watch, lay on Bulks [shop-stalls], and got Claps; they bilkt Hackney-Coachmen, ran in Debt with Shop-keepers, and lay with their Wives: They kill'd Bayliffs, kick'd Fidlers down Stairs ... They talk'd of the Drawing-Room and never came there, Dined with Lords they never saw; Whisper'd a Dutchess, and spoke never a Word; exposed the Scrawls of their Laundress for Billets-doux of Quality; came ever just from Court and were never seen in it.[77]

In short, Swift places the trio in the rogue's gallery of London, as viewed both from his own trips to town and through the prism of Restoration comedy. Not long passes before two of the brothers wish to change their coats according to differing notions of fashion. Peter makes ludicrous additions to the fabric; Jack, meanwhile, strips his bare of all its tasteful ornament. Only Martin tries to preserve the original design. They fall out, and dispute their father's will, a document that Jack and Peter chop and change as their needs require. And so Swift unfolds his allegory of the three main branches of Western Christianity, with Peter representing the Church of Rome, Jack the Puritan and Calvinist front of Dissenting Churches, and Martin the original spirit of the Reformation, Martin Luther – embodied in the Anglican Church in which Swift himself was ordained.

In his choice of a hero called Martin, Swift was aiming at orthodoxy. Yet a sizeable number among the High Church intellectuals he was in many ways trying to impress would have disagreed with his argument here on point of doctrine. In 1687, at the height of James's contest with the clerical establishment, Francis Atterbury of Christ Church, Oxford,

had countered the idea advanced by some Catholic writers that Anglican
and Lutheran theologies were identical: he had done so, moreover, by
mingling merciless wit with acute scholarship, in a work that was widely
admired.[78] Atterbury defended Luther as a biblical scholar but aimed to
broaden the space 'High' Anglicans put between the Church of England
and the Germanic Reformed Churches, the latter taking the works of
Luther almost as gospel. The moral precedence Swift gives his Martin, in
the *Tale of a Tub*, shows him to be slightly out of step with such thinking, even though by the time he wrote the *Tale* he had made personal
contact with a number of leading Oxford clerics. Swift surely knew
Atterbury's pamphlet, and sought in his way to equal and excel such
works by Oxford men. He was highly gratified long afterwards, at the
height of his English political career, to report that Atterbury and friends
regarded him as a 'Christchurch man'.[79] Yet he would never quite belong
among them. His wilder and greater book, the *Tale*, despite his best
intentions, lacked the doctrinal proprieties and social graces of an Atterbury. In its stylistic audacities, even in its efforts to defend tradition, it
marked the start of a career of not quite fitting in.

The sharpest points of the satire are reserved for Jack, the figure of
Calvin; in comparison, Peter is given a relatively easy time of it. The comedy's pecking order thus reflects Swift's conviction that the Nonconformist
Protestant sects posed a much greater threat than England's and Ireland's
addled minority of Catholics – which was more abashed than ever following the defeat of James II. Yet the *Tale* is more comprehensive than a run
of jokes against Catholic superstition and Dissenting quackery. In a dazzling intellectual and linguistic display it lays bare the argumentative
strategies of all competing parties in the great religious dispute. Swift uses
his own superabundant verbal resources to ridicule the verbosity of the
fighting priests, and, in doing so, exposes the worldly ambition, the territorial calculations of a William or a James, that conflicting theories
covered up. The *Tale* is full of absurd propositions that demonstrate how
logic can be twisted, and highlight the nonsense that people are brought
to believe: 'Words are but wind,' runs one example, 'and Learning is nothing but Words; Ergo, Learning is nothing but Wind.'[80]

The story of the three brothers, meanwhile, is merely one strand in a
book of detours and entanglements that at one point digresses to praise
the art of digression itself. The tale proper stalls for subsidiary essays,
apologies, rebuttals and pseudo-scientific hypotheses – the greatest (if
bluntest) of which discusses how it is possible to operate the soul like a
piece of physical equipment. Another work, 'The Battle of the Books',

was appended to the *Tale* on publication. In this the scrambled battle-lines are drawn more clearly as ancient and modern works fight for control of St James's Library. Swift's quarrel throughout this extraordinary literary package was with modernity itself, and with the crimes committed against tradition in the name of progress – or 'tolerance', in the vocabulary of the Dissenters. The overall argument was extremely conservative, but the method was extremely novel. Samuel Johnson would only admit he knew no other work like it, and refused for that reason to believe it was Swift's: 'there is in it such a vigour of mind, such a swarm of thoughts, so much of nature, and art, and life.'[81]

There was also a great deal that could land a young priest in trouble with his superiors. Swift pokes merciless fun at two rather solemn (but nonetheless brilliantly learned) clerical scholars who had pointed out an error made by Temple; and higher authorities in the Church were also upset, when the *Tale* reached the press, by what they took as an outright satire on religion. Some years later, Swift would counter by claiming that the book was a work of youth and had been published without his knowledge or consent. In his 'Apology', though, he contested the point at stake:

Why should any Clergymen of our Church be angry to see the Follies of Fanaticism and Superstition exposed, tho' in the most ridiculous Manner? since that is perhaps the most probable way to cure them, or at least to hinder them from farther spreading. Besides, tho' it was not intended for their [i.e. Anglican clergymen's] Perusal, it [the *Tale*] rail-lies against nothing but what they preach against. It contains nothing to provoke them by the least Scurillity upon their Persons and Functions. It Celebrates the Church of England as the most perfect of all others in Discipline and Doctrine . . .[82]

Swift is guilty of rhetoric himself here: surely he could see that one of his offences was not taking the rival clergy seriously, and thus trivializing the distinctions both sides found weighty. One sect in the *Tale* believes that the universe is 'a large Suit of Cloaths, which invests every Thing': and from this, 'what is Man himself but a *Micro-Coat*, or rather a compleat Suit of Cloaths with all its Trimmings?' The heresy goes to the heart of the *Tale*'s main allegory: people are not only caught up in fights over trappings, they are nothing but walking garments, hollow within. In a typical development, Swift's idiot-speaker proposes that clothes are actually the most refined beings in the universe. More dangerously, he suggests that the robes of high office are nothing more than special arrangements of cloth – there is no deeper substance. 'If certain Ermins and Furs be placed in a certain Position, we stile them a *Judge*, and so, an apt Conjunction of Lawn and black Sattin we intitle a *Bishop*.'[83] One can see how this might have offended bishops: a 'fanatic' critic of the Established Church could not have scored a better hit against them. And so it was not quite true when he said the books contained nothing scurrilous against his fellow Anglicans. More precisely, none of the satire was directed against High Church members of the *lower* Anglican clergy.

As a phrase, 'A Tale of a Tub' meant an idle story, mere nonsense, and part of the offence Swift caused can be understood from his title alone. That a work identifying itself as codswallop should then address religious subjects was blatantly provocative. More specifically, the 'tub' of this tale's title is of the kind a Dissenting preacher would use as a makeshift pulpit; it is also the cock-boat or smaller vessel that whalers would lower overboard as a subterfuge for their prey to attack.[84] In its marine sense, the tub was one of Swift's many satirical decoys. As a portable pulpit, meanwhile, the tub is latently his preaching stand as much as any fanatic's. As he implied when he later defended the work, his purpose was sacred, and, in fact, had the potential to unify the righteous in all the sects. Had its arguments been stated more baldly, no Puritan could have objected to the book's scorn for the pandemic sins of vanity, hypocrisy and idle pleasure. Where Swift parted company with his Nonconformist readers, and went on to make merciless fun of them, was their preference for 'inspiration' over ecclesiastical tradition. In many ways an astounding exercise in overkill, the *Tale* is at war with all the superfluities of Swift's age, its excesses of violence, lust, conceit and frivolity, setting about them with its own surplus of exciting, unnerving creativity. It is pessimistic yet exuberant, embracing madness as an essential feature of humanity, indeed an antidote to Philistinism, and anticipating Gulliver's final view of a debased civilization.

Inevitably, such work put Swift at odds with many influences he had originally tried to emulate; and, understandably, some time would pass before he quite knew what to do with it. It would be many years before he felt free of Temple's spirit, but the break began with the prose exercises that in time made up *A Tale of a Tub*. The aim and content of the work supported Temple's position with regard to the classics; but in method and execution the book went against his entire outlook.

Swift's early Pindarics place him within an artistic culture of 'Augustan' writing. The Augustan mode followed Continental models, but was overwhelmingly English in its manner and orientation. As the name implies, those writers who were subsequently dubbed Augustans saw themselves as followers of the ancient Roman poet Virgil, writing for the Court of latter-day Caesar Augustuses. No less than Virgil, many of them had compelling doubts as to the real virtue of the royalty and nobility they wrote for, doubts that they communicated frequently through undertones and subtexts. For really the Augustans – among whom we count major names such as Dryden and Pope – were celebrating an image and an ideal. This ideal was at once political, artistic and spiritual; it was engrained in the literary language of the age, and it was one that Swift, despite some rather strained early efforts, simply could not share.

The supreme principle for the Augustans, to simplify a great deal of individual thought, was an idea of divinely instituted order. They saw this order as existing not above and beyond nature, but rather as being the true state of nature, nature with a capital N. The task of art, of architecture, of literature, of governance was both to reflect this balance and harmony and to bring it out of the disorder that disguised it, but that was merely superficial. The true state of things was objectively beautiful and coherent; it just needed unlocking, by a training of perception, the construction of beautiful buildings, the running of the state upon lines of decency and decorum. Even wilderness, when properly seen, and when employed for example as an element in a well-planned garden, was an agent of this Augustan ideal form. At the centre of it all, even though the universe was no longer generally thought to revolve about the earth, was the order implanted in 'Man'. When order inside and out was neglected, the social consequences could not be surprising: in nasty, turbulent conditions people would be turbulent and nasty. In 1664, two years before the Great Fire of London administered purgative reforms, the diarist John Evelyn complained how 'It is from the Asymmetry of our Buildings, want of Decorum and Proportion in our Houses, that the Irregularity of our Humours and Affections may be shrewdly discerned.'[85]

This link, so plain to the Augustans, adhered to a strong tradition of Renaissance Neoplatonism, and was in many ways surely a reaction against the immense violence and upheaval of the mid-seventeenth century. Swift was the most important writer of the day both to disbelieve it and reject it, in a body of verse that played merciless havoc with the precious codes and forms of Augustan artistic practice, even as he drew copiously on classical models and sources. This is not to say there was no common ground between him and the few living writers, such as

Pope, whom he thoroughly respected, and whose own unvoiced despair at the Augustan project is felt through the remoteness of his classical goals. The plight of Pope, struggling with physical disability and cruel emotional wounds, is the most affecting of all the poets abandoned by Virgil; his *Dunciad*, a despairing census of British ignorance and corruption, illustrates how sorely his Neoclassical tenets were tested. The careful lucidity of Swift's prose, meanwhile, indeed its frequent grandeur, epitomizes and transcends the classical mores of clarity, elegance and decorum that the Augustans upheld.[86] But the idea that such principles pervaded Nature, that they constituted, indeed, the true reality we might inhabit every day, simply could not move him. Instead it made him write almost obsessively about dirt and shit, as a breathless insistence that the contrary was true. And that is a large part of his lasting appeal to a more modern readership that accepts decay, mess and sometimes downright chaos as all but unavoidable – and in some cases a source of vibrancy and excitement.

This is not to say, either, that Swift would not have preferred the Augustan vision to be true. He very clearly would. His ideal woman – perhaps his ideal person – Stella, met Augustan standards of propriety, even though she shared his scepticism. A hugely charged part of his personality can be glimpsed in his praise for her restraint and cleanliness. But Stella by definition was an exception: she was miraculous. His view of the reality of women in general can be seen in the host of poems represented by 'The Lady's Dressing Room', which looks for its subject amid a sordid pandemonium of greasy cosmetic bottles, linen, combs and a stinking chamber pot. The attack is misogynistic, certainly, but not simply: it is also a blow against the pretensions and deceptions that women were expected to maintain in denial of what Swift describes. He had no more fondness for the biological requirements of men, or the tricks they used to disguise them, either.

Augustanism, in short, worked from the mistaken premise that humans are Brobdingnagian, giant in stature, unequalled by any living thing. Swift struck early against such ideas with his *Tale of a Tub*, in its simultaneous great subtlety and systematic indelicacy. By aping Modernity and the Moderns, the *Tale* exalts the Ancients. But, whereas for the true Augustan Virgil and Horace are living if elevated guides, for Swift they and their example are lost to us and unreachable. In 'The Battle of the Books' the Ancients and their champions are obviously greater than the Moderns; but the outcome of the war between them, though unstated, is bleakly obvious.

Part of Swift's purpose in the *Tale* was to defend Temple against two champions of the new learning. The Reverend William Wotton was a theologian with a genius for languages, great enthusiasm for trends in scientific research, but also a slowly growing reputation for drinking and wild living. He was a fellow of the Royal Society and much admired. In 1694 he compared the strengths and weaknesses of classical and contemporary approaches to knowledge in *Reflections upon Ancient and Modern Learning*, siding with an evidence-based method. Wotton's book contested a work of Temple's, *An Essay on Ancient and Modern Learning*, which adopted the more time-honoured stance towards the classics as founts of wisdom. A second edition of Wotton's *Reflections* appeared in 1697, and included Richard Bentley's exposure of a false classic in his *Dissertation upon the Epistles of Phalaris*. Phalaris was a tyrant of Sicily to whom a collection of essayistic letters had long been attributed. In the *Dissertation*, Bentley proved the epistles were fakes, and also responded to barbs from Charles Boyle, an undergraduate nephew of the famous chemist, in his recent edition of the *Epistles*. Bentley, a gruff-mannered cleric and meticulous philologist, had mustered irrefutable evidence. He presented it in academically dense yet at moments poised and highly sardonic periods. Readers held their breath: 'we expect impatiently some reply to his dissertation at the end of Wottons book,' wrote a young John Arbuthnot, physician and wit, and later Swift's staunch friend.[87] Such expectations were gratified by the efforts of Francis Atterbury, Boyle's tutor at Christ Church. Seeing that Bentley's case was irrefutable, in fact, Atterbury fought it with satire. Indeed with Swiftian verve he managed to suggest that Bentley's methods undermined the provenance of scripture; and, since this was obviously the work of some atheist, the Reverend Dr Bentley couldn't possibly have written it.[88]

The sting for Swift's master was that he had used the fake *Epistles* in his *Essay* to support his assertion that 'the oldest Books we have are still in their kind the best.' He went further: 'I think the Epistles of *Phalaris* to have more grace, more spirit, more force of wit and genius, than any others I have seen, either ancient or modern.' As Temple saw it, the argument in favour of Moderns over Ancients was that modern writers have the advantage of both ancient and contemporary knowledge, 'which is commonly illustrated by the similitude of a dwarf's standing upon a giant's shoulders, and seeing more or farther than he'.[89] But that, as Temple shrewdly observed, took it for granted that ancient knowledge had really been preserved entire, not to mention properly understood. He felt it was presumptuous to believe so implicitly; and so he continued preferring the company of classical giants. In *Gulliver*, the towering population of Brobdingnag inescapably allude back to this preference; as do the minuscule Moderns of Lilliput.

This was not the sort of argument to sway an analyst like Bentley; but, in any case, Temple deemed it beneath his dignity to answer such a 'Mean, Dull, Unmannerly Pedant'.[90] However, as Swift commented, it was generally felt that Temple had been 'roughly used by the two Reverend gentlemen' – a wry phrase that summons to mind the image of Bentley and Wotton mugging Sir William in a dark alley.[91] If Temple himself refused to fight back, Charles Boyle and a number of other rather crude wits from Christ Church leaped gleefully to the task; and, in essence, their defence of Temple, Phalaris and Boyle rested on little more than their view of Bentley as a dry and humourless fellow. The hostility was open to all, and ran deep. In his allegory of the engagement, 'The Battle of the Books', Swift imagined Bentley and Wotton skewered on Boyle's spear like a brace of woodcocks on the spit.[92]

## I O

As other writers weighed in, Swift contributed to the argument by ignoring Wotton and Bentley's subtle detail and methodical approach, not to mention their blatant mastery of ancient letters and history. Yet his answer distinguished itself from the gallant mud-throwing of Boyle and company. Swift's response to Wotton and Bentley, parodying their academic style in places, was to set forth the sort of mind he felt their teaching would produce. This was an intellect in which the culture of the West was rotting away. The result of 'modern learning' would be to relieve readers and students of the need to *learn* anything; memory would be almost unnecessary, since the idea of anything that might be of long-standing value would have been eroded to nothing. The narrator of the *Tale* is comfortable with this prospect: it constitutes progress. Yet, in a way that became typical of Swift, this 'character' is still complex. 'He' is also fragmented. The critics who have argued that the *Tale* is told by a gang or even a multitude of voices, displacing one another from the podium, have much to support their case. What unites these voices, or the shards of a single split personality, is an air of complacent erudition. However faulty or ludicrous the thinking, the self-assurance never wavers. So the narrator is not simply hostile towards the Ancients;

instead he is condescending, supported by a safety cushion of ignorance. He defends 'a certain author named Homer', for example, against critics who point out the Greek's lack of up-to-date knowledge. They are right, of course: Homer might know about the circulation of the blood but his understanding of tea leaves much to be desired. But how could they expect this poet to match the 'wonderful Acquirements' since his death, especially those of the last three years?[93]

A Tale of a Tub derides Modernity by taking on the voice of a committed Modern. It does so in a way that was unsettling for its early readers. Wotton actually wrote the first key to the work, annotating it in the scholarly fashion he used on ancient texts; it was published with the Tale in a pirate edition. But, while he may have pinpointed Swift's allusions, the tone of the Tale perplexed him when it did not simply offend. Something was active in this writing that eluded his and Bentley's forensic methods – the rationale behind an extravaganza in absurdity. Truth itself had fallen by the wayside long ago: in the ninth section of the Tale, 'A Digression on Madness', the cheerful Modern declares that the thoughts in Imagination are as true as those in Memory, and indeed superior, since the former is the 'Womb of Things' and the latter merely their grave.[94]

It is perhaps most disorienting of all that much of what is said in the Tale is still piercingly lucid. A powerful example of undeniable insight would be the closing paragraphs of the preface, where the presiding Modern observes that works paying compliments are always very stale: we have heard all the old flattery before. Satire, on the other hand, will always touch on something new: 'all the Virtues that have been ever in Mankind, are to be counted upon a few Fingers, but his Follies and Vices are innumerable, and Time adds daily to the Heap.'[95] The idea is Platonic, but here, surely, we hear Swift himself, or at least a statement with which he would agree. Such moments indicate that rather than viewing the Tale as a series of speeches by alternating and clashing voices, we should perhaps rather listen to it as a monologue continually slipping between degrees of perception and unreason. The switch can come literally in the space of a few lines; as when, at the end of the preface, Swift's speaker remembers that he has no talent or taste for satire, and indeed is 'entirely satisfied with the whole present Procedure of human Things'.[96]

Part of Swift's point is that an expert blending so many contradictions will necessarily be possessed by Legion; here and there a voice speaking sense will be heard. The resulting 'polyphonic' effect is a result of artistic intent, perhaps working intuitively and semi-consciously rather than by explicit design. At the same time, the lack of consistency must be due in part to the fact that Swift worked on the *Tale* in chunks and bouts of writing. He claimed moral and artistic coherence for his tale, not homogeneity. Some years after finishing it, he said that some writing must be done for one's own diversion. *A Tale of a Tub* supplied that need; however much he imagined a time when the wits of Christ Church, or a readership he later idealized as 'Men of Tast',[97] might give it their seal of approval, through the later 1690s it must have come together in pieces – bursts of composition that he could share only with a few trusted readers at most. One confidant and critic at some point appears to have been his 'little Parson-cousin' Thomas, whom in 1710 Swift suspected of passing on the manuscript – and accused of claiming a share of the authorship.[98] Swift acknowledged, moreover, that the *Tale* carried traces of youthful extravagance, recalling the 'unconfin'd humour' he had admitted possessing as early as 1692.[99] Writing of himself in the third person, he said: 'He was then a young Gentleman much in the World, and wrote to the Tast of those who were like himself; therefore in order to allure them, he gave a Liberty to his Pen, which might not suit with maturer Years, or graver Characters.'[100] By 'much in the World' Swift was far from suggesting that he had been leading the life of the three brothers in his story, who set out on a long, sustained spree on reaching London.

Swift's conduct at chocolate-houses and theatres was of course (one assumes) unimpeachable. The world that he spent, or wished he had spent, much time in was the world of Congreve and his admirers, the senior intellectuals who visited Moor Park, and fledgling associates of his own. He was writing for them, trying to 'allure'; *A Tale of a Tub* was thus a performance, teeming with voices and characters, an entertainment, not a tract.

Enjoying the liberty Swift gave his pen, the book splits into speeches and set-pieces, even within its numerous sections; as indeed does *Gulliver's Travels*.[101] But the apparent glitches also serve the overall purpose of the satire. With every slippage from a coherent to a mad or ignorant chain of thought, the reader has to stop, try to recover the whole, give up and move on. In the digression mentioned above, the one on madness, the writer remarks that happiness is possible only when people are in a state of delusion. The Modern himself therefore thinks that self-deception is highly advisable. Yet the ironist behind the persona, Swift, loads the comment with another implication. If our goal is to see things as they really are, then we must pursue it at the cost of happiness. Read as such, the passage says a lot about Swift's outlook; in one example of desirable delusion, it also gives a valuable clue to his approach to writing. Just as imagination is now superior to memory, the Modern declares, so fiction is preferable to truth, since it can produce greater wonders than reality. For that very reason, a Swiftian fiction, one that stops us duping ourselves, will not run altogether smoothly. Instead it will frequently sabotage its illusion of reality and bring us up short, force us to reread, check, reconsider: and this is precisely what *A Tale of a Tub* does throughout.

Swift had risen to the challenge and defended his ailing master: but he upheld the order embodied by the classics by showing that the world, far from the Augustan vision of things, was spinning close to insanity, and that lunacy was sometimes better than what called itself propriety. The ageing diplomat was of course no stranger to duplicity and malice, but the trust he displayed throughout his career in people's better nature was a sign of his basic attitude to life. He believed that, however bad things seemed, the universe would always permit and support an appeal to reason. Swift – with his family's harsher memories of Civil War, his glimpse of revolutionary upheaval, his experience in the hostile territory around Kilroot – had a darker vision, and in the *Tale* it began to seep out. It took shape, Swift claimed, with the full force of a young man's vivacity, with 'his Invention at the Height, and his Reading fresh in his Head'.[102] Since Swift saw, nevertheless, how it might offend those of 'graver Characters', the book would not be published for some years and would appear anonymously. It was not a work of which Temple, ever the diplomat, to whom satire was distasteful, could ever approve. Accordingly it shows Swift parting company from his mentor.

Physically, the actual separation came early in 1699. Swift kept a record of Temple's decline from the previous July, up to his death on 27 January. 'He died at one o clock in the morning and with him all that was great and good among men.'[103] Swift's comment is similar in feeling to the private note he made a decade later when he learned that his mother had died; and indeed the much more extensive memorial he immediately began when news was brought to him of Esther Johnson's death in 1728. He reached for his quill as a prop.

Many accounts of their relationship regard Temple as Swift's symbolic father: one much disputed and still compelling book, Denis Johnston's *In Search of Swift* (1959), suggests that Jonathan and Esther were Temple's natural children. The theory folds in a void of evidence, but it provides a fascinating and insightful way of viewing the familial bonds and dependences that formed in these years at Moor Park. Certainly Swift, though later prone to sardonic and resentful asides, spoke of Temple in the tones and overstatements of a dutiful son.

He was a person of the greatest wisdom, justice, liberality, politeness, eloquence, of his age and nation; the truest lover of his country, and one that deserved more from it by his eminent public services, than any man before or since: besides his great deserving of the commonwealth of learning; having been universally esteemed the most accomplished writer of his time.[104]

Yet if Swift sounded a more than filial note towards his master, Temple did not exactly reciprocate. He left Swift £100, the moral burden of preparing his writings for posterity, and little to go on with in the way of future appointments. Swift had resigned his northern Irish living early in 1698, expecting greater things. When these failed to transpire, he still hoped Temple's friend the Earl of Romney might put in a word for him for a prebend of Canterbury or Westminster. No such help was forthcoming, or was beyond the power of the Earl, whom Swift later declared 'a vitious illiterate old rake without any sense of Truth or Honour'.[105] He vented some of his spite for the Earl in a verse-libel called 'The Problem'. Romney's dedicated philandering aside, the poem links two of Swift's key aversions – courtship and bodily odour.

> Love's Fire, it seems, like inward Heat,
> Works in my Lord by Stool and Sweat,
> Which brings a Stink from ev'ry Pore,
> And from behind, and from before;
> Yet, what is wonderful to tell it,
> None but the Fav'rite Nymph can smell it.[106]

Regardless of these faults there was little Romney, despite his sometime closeness to the King, was now really capable of influencing. He had an unresounding record as an Irish lord deputy in 1692–3. Notably, in the meantime, none of the other grandees in the Temples' circle cared to intervene. The Duke and Duchess of Somerset were silent, although, even had Swift's relations with them been better, this was probably a lucky escape. Some years later Joseph Addison, Swift's future great friend, was sought out in no uncertain terms by the Duke – known as 'The Proud' – as a tutor and companion for his son; only to be dismissed and snubbed for using a phrase suggesting insufficient humility when he replied to the Duke's offer.[107] Yet Romney, for all Swift's resentment, did try to help. He introduced Swift to Charles, second Earl of Berkeley. Later in 1699, Berkeley was made a lord justice of Ireland – technically, a lord deputy and, in effect, a co-governor. Power would be shared with Berkeley's fellow lords justices, the Earl of Galway and the Earl of Jersey. Packing his trunks and moving out from Moor Park for good, Swift joined Berkeley's household as a private chaplain.

It was less than he had dreamed of, much less, but it was something. He had little time to dwell on his choice, since Berkeley's papers came through with a lack of stately slowness. Swift therefore made his good-byes and sailed for Ireland with the Earl that summer, with Temple's ghost and the unsorted influences of the last decade trailing not far in his wake.

# 5. Recovering Esther

Drive all objections from your Mind,
Else you relapse to Human Kind.
— 'On Stella, Visiting Me in My Sickness' (1727)[1]

## I

Swift's relationship with his new patron was soured almost instantly by an interloping upstart. The Earl's family, with Swift in tow, sailed from Bristol in mid-August 1699. The route upset Swift's personal custom: he was unable to visit his mother in Leicester on his way to Chester or Holyhead.[2] With his hopes of better things deflated, Bristol, England's second greatest port, for all its effort and industry, offered no comfort to a stranger who was feeling redundant and ill-used. Spread across lowlands and steep hills, the lopsided city was not yet paved and festooned with the profits of slavery, but Trade was paramount. The roads were smoothed by the sleds horses dragged, until they died from the work, up and down the difficult hills, back and forth from the port. Also disturbing was the strength of dissent in Bristol, the Low Churches so commonly preferred by the rising business interest. More's the pity, a sound churchman might reflect, on viewing the city's stables and the Nonconformists' meeting-houses, that no way existed of switching the occupants.

Waiting for him, Dublin was much as he had left it, although the Provost of Trinity had recently been killed by a brickbat thrown during a punch-up.[3] Yet Swift's contempt for his home city, and for the island as a whole, had only deepened. A little more than three years previously, he had told Jane Waring that he would rather 'endure the utmost indignities of fortune' than return to Ireland;[4] and so, in his own mind, he had – though further indignities still lay ahead. Jane Waring herself, as an integral part of the oath he had taken never to come back, was to re-enter his life during this next sojourn, with hurtful consequences for her. As he prepared to depart, Swift behaved as if he faced the blackest and deepest of whirlpools. He had completed his editorial and translating work on the first two volumes of Temple's letters, and left them ready with the printer as he set off for Ireland. Although dated 1700, they seem to have appeared the previous year.[5] In a morose yet rather sensational passage that he deleted from his published preface, he reflected on the loss the world would suffer if the collection were lost at sea in manuscript with him. More than once, he said, he had nearly drowned in the crossing. Having tempted fate so often, he implied, the Irish Sea had a claim on him.[6]

The real source of his gloom was the familiar sense of degradation. Here he was, his colossal talents still unseen, taking his place as a mere domestic chaplain, a 'Levite', as the wits of Congreve's theatre styled such persons. But there was no choice but to press on. Berkeley's party landed in Waterford and made its way towards Dublin. Resting at Kilkenny, the new Lord Justice was given a ceremonious welcome. The town met Swift with a glimpse of his schooldays – memories of a fish that got away, cakes in the alley and hard blows to the shins for grammatical slips or words out of turn. His past held no equivalents to the tributes that greeted his new master. If some of the respect Kilkenny paid Berkeley rubbed off on him, Swift's sense of dignity in his new position was precarious. It evaporated all but entirely when a glib opportunist met the family's carriage in the outskirts of Dublin.

Berkeley was rotund, prone to gout and, so far as might be expected, well-meaning. His orders to assume his new post had been peremptory; he had received them with the easy if slightly fatigued compliance of a diplomat. He had mobilized his household quickly – and this obliged anyone looking for employment or patronage to move equally fast. Arthur Bushe, the man doffing his hat and making the lowest of bows before Berkeley on the approach to Dublin, proved sufficiently nimble. Bushe held a small sinecure in the Irish Customs, and had been in London for much of the year tugging sleeves and scraping the floor at Court in hopes of a promotion. No gift had yet materialized when Bushe heard of Berkeley's appointment. He rushed to be in Dublin before the Lord Justice arrived, and, on introducing himself, was smooth-tongued enough for it to occur to the Earl that he should give the suitor a ride into town. Family members, one or two privy councillors and a tight-lipped chaplain made room for him, and by the time the Berkeleys reached the capital Arthur Bushe regarded himself as a member of the retinue.

Bushe ingratiated himself so far as to make Berkeley appoint him his private secretary. In doing so, he elbowed Swift out of a position he had previously combined with his role as chaplain. In the rush to get ready, Berkeley had lacked the time to bring his staff up to a full complement. Swift, used to handling correspondence and much wider responsibilities for Temple, took on familiar secretarial duties. Yet Berkeley, though doubtless glad of Swift's help, never promised him the job on a permanent basis. Confident of his abilities, Swift clearly assumed no such promise was necessary. He despised the arts of flattery and self-promotion Bushe practised so diligently, but his need of them was just as great. Berkeley may even have thought he was doing Swift a favour by freeing him of the secretarial workload. He didn't expect to be a lord justice for ever; he judged that Bushe, a friend of an old schoolmaster of Swift's at Kilkenny, clearly knew the lie of the land and would do until the time came to move on. Swift, on the other hand, entrusted with the cure of the family's souls, might expect to be retained. Berkeley apparently pointed out by way of excuse that he assumed that Swift would be seeking promotion within the Church; and so a secretaryship, essentially a bureaucratic or political appointment, would be of no use to him in the longer term. These arguments, offered too late, failed to satisfy. Swift added the grudge to others that crackled within him for decades. Having a low opinion of Berkeley's guile, he was convinced that Bushe – whose career made only the tiniest of subsequent advances – had persuaded the Earl 'that the post of secretary was not proper for a clergyman'.[7] The worst insult for Swift was that he must fight for such crumbs at all.

Bushe, said Swift, quickly made himself as necessary as an enema to Lord Berkeley's daily movements. In a lively poem he pictured the pair of them, Bushe tilting his head to receive mysterious directions, then twitching his lordship's sleeve for an urgent conference on the price of hay and oats.[8] Both, Swift decided, were blunderers and thus deserved each other. A contemporary described Berkeley at about this time as 'a Gentleman of Learning, Parts, and a Lover of the Constitution of his Country; a short fat Man, fifty years old'. Swift owned a copy of the book of *Characters* in which these words appeared, and took a prim pleasure in maligning a good number of those portrayed. Under the entry on Berkeley he added, 'Intolerable lazy & Indolent & somewhat Covetous'.[9]

His early biographer, Thomas Sheridan the younger, wrote that Swift, 'whatever mastery he had gained over the greater passions, had no command of his temper. He was of a very irritable make, prone to sudden starts of passion, in which his expressions of course were not very guarded.' Sheridan only knew Swift as the elderly Dean, in a position of authority, when he cared little whether he offended subordinates or superiors. He assumed that Swift had been as equally prone to outbursts at a time when he had more to fear. The final insult in this account was when Bushe's influence with Berkeley deprived Swift of a Church appointment. Swift smouldered at Bushe taking his place as Berkeley's secretary; but he exploded, wrote Sheridan, on learning that his rival had cheated him out of a preferment in his chosen sphere. 'God confound you both for a couple of scoundrels!' Swift roared, apocryphally, and turned his heel both on the Lord Justice and on his secretary. The story is usually dismissed, and it certainly smacks of hero worship when Sheridan voices his belief that 'Lord Berkeley was too conscious of the ill treatment he had given him, and too fearful of the resentment of an exasperated genius, not to endeavour to pacify him.' Malleable though he was, Berkeley could hardly have been so feeble; and the insult, if Swift had really blurted it out, would have meant his instant dismissal. The tale is nevertheless a good example of how a younger generation liked to mythologize the early exploits of the man they knew as a septuagenarian legend. It is also valuable for capturing Swift's real emotion at this time – a feeling that lingered poisonously for thirty years. Sheridan uses the example of Swift's petulance and insubordination to explain why this genius made so little progress as a courtier. That lack of progress might be better accounted for by the means with which Swift *did* seek his revenge, in the satire on his master mentioned above – 'which placed the Governor and his new-made Secretary in a most ridiculous point of light, and which was every where handed about to their no small mortification'.[10] Yet Berkeley either never saw or heard about the poem; or, if he did, he took the joke with incredible good humour, for Swift's association with the Earl's household lasted another ten years.

At this time Swift was certainly an 'exasperated genius' but one utterly unable to vent his frustrations in the high-handed way Sheridan describes. His satire on Berkeley and his human clyster, Bushe, could not be published openly; he could only smirk behind his master's back. The dependent situation Swift still endured as a man in his thirties influenced his manner of proceeding anonymously, for the most part, as a writer. It must also have some bearing on the liberties he took, perhaps by way of compensation, as an older celebrity.

To Swift, Berkeley had failed damningly as both employer and patron. The idea that a priest might not be a secretary was nonsense, Swift could

snort, since Berkeley knew full well he had served Temple in that capacity. He hoped to promote his secular career, and honour his obligation
to Temple, when he published two volumes of the diplomat's letters in
November 1699. Yet, if Berkeley was preserving Swift's energies for the
Church, he was doing nothing to boost them. This became plain (at least
to Swift) when, in January 1700, the death of an elderly priest after a
long illness opened the field for his vacated benefices. The race that
would normally have ensued for such a post would have been slow,
restrained yet fierce, like one in which running or any movement of the
arms is forbidden, yet biting is technically allowed. Instead on this occasion the competition was remarkably sedate, and stands out in
ecclesiastical history for the strangely discrepant reaction of one aspiring clergyman. Swift hoped and assumed he was in the line-up, all the
more so because he believed that Berkeley, as lord justice, had the power
to allot the newly available living; and all the more again because he felt
that Berkeley owed him compensation.

Coote Ormsby, the deceased, had been the Dean of Derry. The deanery
was a high-profile position that brought an ample income, but in one of
the island's politically most sensitive dioceses. Derry was sacrosanct in
Anglo-Protestant geography for its part in resisting popery, under lengthy
siege in 1689. The current Bishop, soon to be translated to the archbish-
opric of Dublin, was William King, and King needed a dedicated and
proven servant of the Church as his deputy. Ormsby, who had been
around sixty when he was made dean, had for many years satisfied this
requirement, but things had slipped as he aged. Bishop King, meanwhile,
was a proven champion who expected those he appointed to learn from
his example. In 1688, as the just-appointed Dean of St Patrick's, Dublin,
he had remained in Ireland during Tyrconnell's ascendancy. As other
Protestants, including his own archbishop, left the country in flocks, King
stayed at his post and defied the Jacobite government. Throughout this
time he fed intelligence to the Williamite camp in England. In July 1689
he was imprisoned in Dublin Castle, and remained there until the city
was captured by William's army after the Battle of the Boyne. The account
he published later of this period opened with a concise defence of why
orthodox Anglicans – such as Swift – were entitled to oppose James without breaking the doctrine of 'Passive Obedience' for which a number of
clergymen refused to swear allegiance to King William.

> It is granted by some of the highest assertors of passive obedience, that
> if a king design to root out a people, or destroy one main part of his

subjects in favour of another whom he loves better, that they may prevent it even by opposing him with force; and that he is to be judged in
such a case to have abdicated the government to those whom he designs
to destroy contrary to justice and the laws.

On the extreme Tory and High Church side of the political spectrum,
clerics would always face the question of why they weren't Nonjurors.
The position taken by Swift, an old-school Royalist but also a supporter
of the Williamite revolution (despite later doubts), is broadly spelled out
here by King.

As for those Protestants who fled (as Swift did) in 1689, King was
entirely forgiving. The Catholic natives had taken over the state on a
military footing. There was nothing normal Protestants, lay or clerical,
could do for the kingdom: 'to what purpose,' he wrote, 'should they stay
in a place where they certainly knew that all they had would be taken
from them, and their lives exposed to the fury of their enemies?' Suicide
was a sin, and history didn't help: 'the memory of the cruel usage and
difficult times those met with who staid in Ireland in 1641, did frighten
and terrifie all that reflected on them.' He recommended Sir John Temple's lurid 'history' of that earlier period to everyone who had forgotten
its horrors – authentic in nature, if not on the scale Temple and others
reported at the time. Conversely, King didn't uniformly praise all those
Protestants who remained. He commended highly those who tried to
relieve a bad situation by remaining in office, trying to work with Tyrconnell's government, while helping the quite large numbers of
Protestants turned out of their homes – so that 'not one was lost or
starved for want of meat or clothes, that we could hear of.'[11] Yet many,
he conceded, stayed simply because they couldn't get away, because they
lacked means to survive in England if they could, and not a few because
they hoped to profit from the troubles. The only ones he roundly condemned were those who changed their religion in order to get ahead.

2

It has sometimes been implied that Swift may have been overlooked for
the deanery of Derry for a lack of courage in the midst of the revolution.
King's grasp of the hard choices circumstances presented in 1689 suggested that, in his eyes, Swift was blameless in principle. Realistically,
moreover, Swift didn't figure in King's eyes at all. He had been ordained

for only six years, and had only just returned to Ireland. Irvin Ehren-preis's study of the relevant papers established that such a junior man as Swift could never have been in the running for Derry, and that it was King – not Berkeley or either of his fellow lords justices – who had the decisive say in the matter. Yet Swift, writing his autobiographical note decades later, was positive that he had been the natural candidate, and that his usurper Bushe and useless master had cheated him again: 'things were so ordered that the Secretary having received a Bribe, the Deanry was disposed of to another, and Mr Swift was put off with some other Church-livings not worth above a third part of that rich Deanry, and at this present time, not a sixth.'[12] In Sheridan's account – enriched no doubt by Swift's animated retelling as well as his own love of a lively tale – it is Bushe himself who blabs about the offering of a bribe: he is so candid as to tell Swift the deanery is his if he will equal the thousand a rival bidder has laid down. There was enough fuel in that corrupt pro-posal to keep a lifetime of moral indignation burning away. As it happened, Swift's outrage was as groundless as the sense he had of his chances. King had presented the Lords Justices with a list of three names, of which he strongly preferred that of one Dr John Bolton, the Vicar of Ratoath and Laracor. Bolton, however, turned down the deanery, despite the offer of an increased salary. Neither he nor King's second choice, Dr Edward Synge, Vicar of Christ Church, Cork, was overly ambitious or adventurous. Bolton preferred his comfortable livings near Dublin; Synge didn't wish to leave his mother alone in the south. Third on King's list was a more junior clergyman, but one still much more experienced than Swift: Dr John Stearne, the Rector of Trim, who would in time be Swift's long-standing colleague at St Patrick's and predecessor as dean. Stearne's presence on the shortlist was a measure both of how far Swift had to go and of how much further ahead were Synge and Bolton. After Synge refused, Archbishop Marsh of Dublin (the same Narcissus Marsh who was the Provost of Trinity in Swift's time) approached Bolton with an offer he couldn't refuse.[13] And so the deanery was settled – without Swift's name being mentioned and all but certainly without his calling Lord Justice Berkeley a 'scoundrel'.

To get as full a sense as possible of Swift's lasting sense of the incident, however, we still need the story of his shrieking out 'God confound you . . .!' to the cowering Earl and his half-witted underling. Sheridan's account might not be strictly true; but it preserves the more fantastic version Swift either spread, later on, or encouraged, as well as the inflated view Swift had of himself at this time – and that enlarged as the decades passed. In addition, the story offers a very clear gauge of his capacity to resent. The shout and walkout, the action of a moment, embody his strongest wish; while really all he could do was to bear a grudge and write a poem, one he could always deny was his. The account he gave in his private biographical memorandum, written long after Berkeley died, shows how assiduously he could nurse hurt feelings. When set alongside the evidence of his ongoing relations with the Lord Justice, his family and other persons involved in the affair, Swift's libel on Berkeley, Bushe and Bolton, in fact, suggests that they were not even the true objects of his outrage. Such figures, after all, were hardly worthy enemies of the 'exasperated genius' whose lordly master begs him to stay even after the worst of insults. Swift's real bitterness was still at Fate, Fortune or Life itself; or whatever power had made him fatherless and fortuneless, and had put him through long years of apprenticeship for Temple with no due reward. 'The Excuse' he claims Berkeley gave him for denying him Derry 'was his being too young, although he were then 30 years old'. Thirty such miserable years, in Swift's view, were surely worth a deanery, especially one at that northern extremity he had experienced in the mid-1690s. His rancorous note on the matter overlooked the facts that Dean Bolton was a dozen years his senior, had held his doctorate for eight years and had been in orders for more than twenty. But John Bolton, as Swift felt the manuscript of *A Tale of a Tub* entitled him to say – *he* was no Jonathan Swift.

As their chaplain, Swift looked after the Earl of Berkeley's family in their private devotions, directing them in prayers, saying services at home. During Berkeley's short spell as a lord justice, the family stayed in the King's House in Chapelizod, to the west of the old city, a mansion surrounded by meadows and woods, just over the river from the southern edge of the Phoenix Park, the vast royal hunting ground. In a note of July 1700 Swift refers to the 'lodge' in Chapelizod as the Berkeleys' base.[14] With its abundant fruit trees and a carefully tended vegetable garden, the King's House had a great deal in keeping with Moor Park, both in location – close to the metropolis, but certainly not of it – and in character. King William brought his Court there after the Battle of the Boyne. Dublin Castle, the official residence of the Lord Deputies or Lieutenants of Ireland, or their stand-ins the Lords Justices, and a landmark of Swift's childhood, was in a poor state of repair that allowed for, at best, only temporary residence. The roof of the Governor's apartments leaked, and the occasional improvements made throughout the seventeenth century had all been more or less destroyed by fire in 1684. There was a domestic legend nevertheless that in 1699 Swift himself almost burned the Castle down completely, 'and the lord Berkeley in the midst of it', one night as they slept there in neighbouring rooms. On nodding off with a book, Swift knocked his candle on to the bed, and was luckily woken by a small burn before the flames spread over his quilt and curtains. 'He took care to have the damages repaired,' his relative Deane Swift assures us; 'and by throwing away some guineas in hush-money, the accident was never made known in the castle.'[15]

By King William's time, the Crown's chief representatives in Ireland tended to operate partly from England in any case, and preferred more salubrious lodgings when they visited Dublin. Berkeley's fellow members of the commission of three governors were conspicuous absentees. One, Henri de Massue, was a Huguenot expatriate, with the French title of Marquis de Ruvigny, who had escaped Louis XIV's removal of tolerance for his Protestant subjects. He was made Earl of Galway for his services to King William, and remained a brave and effective servant in the next dozen years of war against France. The other in the trio of lords justices was Edward Villiers, Earl of Jersey, son of a family with a notorious history over the past hundred years, and brother to King William's mistress, Elizabeth. He was good-looking, well-tailored, quick-witted and Tory, whereas Galway was forthright, tongue-tied in English, largely unselfish and a solid Whig. The Earl of Berkeley, by contrast with both, was unglamorous and dependable, plain-dealing, the triumvirate's pen-pusher. He was probably one of the last Lords Justices who accepted the rather battered lodge in Chapelizod.[16]

Swift could muster little by way of gratitude when, in the wake of Bolton's final appointment as the Dean of Derry, the subsequent gradual shuffle of lesser clerics, like penguins closing ranks on an ice-cap, brought him an eventual reward. In February 1700 he gained the two parishes of Laracor and Rathbeggan and the rectory of Agher near Trim in County Meath. He had to petition to be allowed to hold these livings together. They gave him an income of £230, and he made good friends in Trim. His first breakthrough in the higher structure of the Church came later in the same year, when he joined the canons of St Patrick's Cathedral by becoming prebendary for Dunlavin. The canons were the clergymen who performed duties connected to a cathedral; at the head of their company, or chapter, was the Dean, a cathedral's most senior priest bar the Bishop, and often superseding the Bishop himself in matters directly concerning the cathedral. Certain benefices in the diocese, known as prebends, brought a place in the chapter of canons. As prebendary for

Kilroot in the diocese of Down and Connor, Swift had gained a stall in the Cathedral of Connor. A place in Dublin's cathedral, however, brought much greater hopes of influence and income, and kept him close to the seat of power and preferment. He was a long way still below the heights of St Patrick's deanery, a post reputedly worth £1,000 a year, or any of the major Irish bishoprics, which were all bestowed from London; but his foot was finally on a ladder that mattered.

Indeed his prebendary's stall and his livings a half-day's ride from the capital made him one of the wealthier priests in Dublin, and better off by far than the majority of clerics on the island. Thirty-five miles to the north-west of Dublin, Trim was a pleasant town situated on the River Boyne, with Ireland's largest Norman castle watching over it. Swift made no great show of enthusiasm about his gains. He coolly waited until June before going in person to Laracor in 1700, although red tape and duties for Berkeley may have caused the delay.[17] In all older accounts, he reacted to his new livings with the classic horror of the urbanite, and the dismay of an ardent priest at the poor state of his church. One nineteenth-century biographer sums up these testimonies, and gives a fine miniature of the scene that greeted Swift.

> The tradition of his surprise and indignation at his first sight of the church at Laracor may be accepted without question. A couple of miles from Trim, in a dull farming country at the northern extremity of East Meath, with a few huts around it, a parsonage-house too dilapidated for decent residence, and a glebe of one acre, rose the old, plain barn-like structure with its low belfry, in manifest neglect and decay.[18]

In a broader view Swift's response to his new livings displayed his life-long tendency to swipe with one hand at what he clutched, tightly and jealously, with the other. He was now, in external terms, worthy of being the descendant of his grandfather Thomas of Goodrich. He was the Vicar of a parish by no means lucrative or prominent, but a fair enough prospect, given the impoverished state of most Irish livings. More personally and importantly, he had reached one of the basic stations he expected in life, and drawn equal, in material terms if not in mystique, with his exemplary ancestor. The talk of deaneries and state appointments came with ambitions that became realistic, and thus the source of real disappointments, only in later years. He could speak disparagingly of Laracor, but – as so often with Ireland itself – as something no outsider had the right to deride. With almost exultant, self-justifying selfishness, he held on to the parishes he gained in 1700 for the rest of his life.

Laracor, of all his parishes, became his retreat and source of restoration. He would write nostalgically about it from London, and bear out his rhapsodies by putting a large amount of money and energy into his glebe when he returned. He put his land in order, planted trees and hedges, and took pride in a canal that formed an 'island' on his property. He enjoyed the river walk and fished pike and trout.[19] In time, a newly built small house met his needs during the warmer months. Beyond this base, he established close links with fellow clerics and major families in the area, even in the disturbingly Presbyterian townland of nearby Summerhill.[20] The congregation in his little church was rarely more than underwhelming; numbering perhaps fifteen, 'most of them gentle, and all simple'.[21] Trim offered Swift his main social base, and a place to stay, during much of the time he was 'resident' in his parishes. Anthony Raymond, the long-standing rector there (from 1705), was a keen and distinguished scholar of the Irish language, and in a few years he became one of the many steady, quiet friends Swift made among his parochial colleagues. He would observe Raymond's 'building itch' and from London ask about the extensions and improvements his neighbour and sometime host was making on his estate.[22]

Laracor itself features on few modern roadmaps. The site of Swift's parish is to be found on the corner of a junction a few miles south of Trim. The very small church of St Peter's that stands there now replaced whatever was left of Swift's church in the mid-nineteenth century. It was deconsecrated in 1981 and is now a private home. The first graves in the shady miniature churchyard are no more than 200 years old. Yet two vast beeches sheltering the stones were perhaps seen by Swift when they were saplings or very young trees. Although he never read prayers in the Victorian chapel, it is most likely similar in scale to the one that held his dozen or so parishioners on an average Sunday. The building he used was possibly even simpler than a drawing from the early 1850s, made shortly before it was demolished, might suggest: a small porch and tiny annex look like additions to the original chapel.[23] Tidy shuttered windows made the place seem homely; and the plainest of tables, which can still be seen in St Patrick's Cathedral, served for the preparation of Holy Communion. The semicircular shape of the Communion table indicates that it could be placed against a wall, and brought into the body of the church as required. How centrally it was placed in the nave was in itself an indicator of doctrinal persuasions. The more 'puritanical', Dissenting

Reformed traditions directed that the 'Lord's Table' should be in the midst of the congregation. As a High Church celebrant, Swift almost certainly kept his table close to the east end, 'altar-wise', maintaining the formality of a chancel. Fierce conflict could ensue over individual policy on this question, a hangover from the days of Charles I, but, since Swift's parishioners were often entirely absent and were timid when they attended, he seems to have faced little opposition on such matters.

A side road runs past the gate of the present converted church's garden, down a briary lane lined with sycamores. On the far side is a field occupied by a number of smart new houses; back on the church's side, inside the hedge, a few cattle graze, the spiritual successors of the cows Swift sometimes had to have driven off his little island; and somewhere near here, within the rough space of an acre, must be the place where he had his makeshift manse constructed. It was little more than a cabin, too cold for winter and the worst summer weather, but dry if not cosy, and by 1710 he had grown to like the sanctuary it offered. At the end of the side road, one comes to an old bridge that crosses the Knightsbrook River. The river, little more than a stream, is presumably the one that once was his canal, in which Swift found 'great beauty.'[24] It has silted up and narrowed, and there are bits of machinery just below the surface by the crossing. The clutter calls to mind Swift's anxiety about the bottom of the current being 'fine and clear'. When it flooded, his fish escaped over a close-lying hollybank or the path. He was often angry about the slackness of his agent, Isaiah Parvisol, in such matters, not to mention the more complex business his parish property sometimes involved.[25] There is no sign of the willows he admired; perhaps a survivor or two is further up or down stream, but they are probably long gone. Beyond the bridge, the way fades out now amid the fields beyond the bridge. It clearly once ran parallel to the modern R158, and thus on to Trim. It was the road that Swift knew and used on his way to visit Raymond and his wife, or to perform the Eucharist at Laracor when he stayed in warmer quarters – in the town, or on one of the wealthy estates in the area.

A single car creates more noise than was probably ever heard here in a single burst – except in wartime – when Swift lived here, but the landscape is inevitably less busy, in a way less peopled, than it was then. There are no traces of the labourers' homes from that time, although here and there small thatched cabins, most uninhabited, and all most likely built much later, offer hints for comparison. The current fences between the fields were non-existent then; Swift knew an unbroken, unenclosed landscape. The markers of the Church's presence in the locus of Laracor are also deceptive. The tall spires seen in outlying parishes are the work of the century and a half after Swift's death. Notwithstanding, the district is worth knowing. There is no memorial or mention of Gulliver here, just low hills Swift would have recognized, a patch of land he loved and tended.

## 3

In Swift's eyes, his new benefices offered a drop of solace in a desert of mortification. In the words of his petition to be allowed to hold them both, he said they were 'but a comfortable support'.[26] Since Temple's final illness he had progressively seen his worldly expectations diminish. There had been major setbacks, such as the lack of any alternative but returning to Ireland, followed by small yet infuriating slights and obstacles – Bushe and Bolton above all – to be recorded with cold resentment. These shameful incidents were compounded, late in 1699, by a family event Swift came to regard as a disaster. In December his 33-year-old sister Jane married a tradesman. The groom, Joseph Fenton, worked in the leather trade, apparently in the basic preparation and subsequent finishing and colouring of skins. He lived not far from William Swift, the uncle with whom Jane had been living for some time on Bride Street in Dublin. She had never been married, but was Fenton's second wife, and became stepmother to his three young children. To be fair, her brother may have given Fenton a chance to prove himself worthy of the family connection. It is usually assumed that the tanner and currier of hides singed a tender point in Swift's flesh from the moment the engagement was announced, but all of Swift's pungent remarks on the subject of his brother-in-law date from later decades.[27] That said, indignant outrage from the very outset still seems true to Swift's character. While he was fighting to retain their place among the gentry, Jane was giving in to loneliness and the discoloured hands of her new husband.

Of the pronounced subsequent dislike he developed for Fenton there is no doubt whatsoever. It was little short of loathing; and seems to have been fed if not founded on reasons of character as much as class prejudice. Fenton was a 'dunce', Swift declared years later, 'and with respect to him she loses little by her deafness.' (The remark has the additional interest of showing that Jane, like Swift, was poor of hearing, and suggesting the affliction was genetic.) He raged against Fenton and his brood, who lacked 'either worth or honor', long into old age; he even appears to have been unaware whether Jane had a child or not.[28] He refused to support his sister ('Mrs Fenton', as he coldly called her) until after Fenton died, when he began paying her an income. His main charge against her conduct was that it had 'disobliged' him.[29] Yet the marriage was clearly not altogether harmonious. Jane in the end followed a path something like that of Swift's nurse, leaving her husband in one country to seek work in another. Twelve years after they married, she moved away from Fenton to become a lady's maid to Temple's surviving sister, Lady Giffard. Perhaps the strongest mark against the Dublin tanner is that Swift's mother, when putting some money in trust for Jane, bound the sum on terms that prohibited Fenton from ever seeing a penny of it. Whether he deserved such precautions for treating Jane poorly, or was simply the victim of snobbery from the Swifts, the record is too sketchy to tell – mainly because from the time she was married Swift had as little to do with his sister as possible.

The initial shock and disgust connected with the Fenton affair was still in the background when, as the wet Irish winter receded in 1700, matrimony became an issue once more for Swift himself. Jane Waring, the infirm young woman to whom he had proposed (by means of something like an ultimatum) in his last days in Kilroot in 1696, now pressed him to revive his offer. This was by no means a bolt from the blue; they had remained in touch since Swift returned from Ulster to Moor Park. Swift seems to have been the less diligent correspondent of the two, and clearly regarded the marriage question as closed. Waring, they had established between them, was too poorly to take the strains of married life on the modest footing they seemed likely to be able to afford; and Swift was pessimistic about his prospects. Yet in 1700 he was prodded not only by Waring's mother but also by his uncle Adam, who owned land near the family home. It was time, both suggested, Swift make his intentions clear. He did so in excoriating terms.

Before considering how he responded to Jane Waring now, we should remind ourselves of how he had addressed her in 1696. In courting her, he had employed his characteristic blend of wit and imperative, putting her in a situation where she could have him or lose him by a certain date. Yet he had also exalted love and matrimony: 'Heaven has given us nothing else worth the loss of a thought,' he had insisted. He would always retain the idea he expressed at this time that love 'is a peculiar part of nature which art debauches, but cannot improve' – which was why since leaving Kilroot he had strenuously avoided the language of gallantry and seduction and indeed would ridicule the abuse of it by others. He never again laid himself open to anyone like this:

> To resist the violence of our inclinations in the beginning, is a strain of self-denial that may have some pretences to set up for a virtue; but when they are grounded at first upon reason, when they have taken firm root and grown up to a height, 'tis folly – folly as well as injustice, to withstand their dictates; for this passion has a property peculiar to itself, to be most commendable in its extremes, and 'tis as possible to err in the excess of piety as of love.[30]

Swift's original wooing of Jane, in short, shows him taking the part of lover seriously, and by no means viewing it entirely as a mere 'part'. As in his early odes, he was attempting the earnest mode in a spirit of real sincerity, a vein of feeling he subsequently buried as deep as he could – while remaining quite convinced that those depths were plain to all who knew him well. In fact the earlier letters to Waring already exhibit a touch of this guardedness and in these, unlike the Pindarics, he controlled the fervent register by blending it with humour, irony and invective.

When Jane Waring tried to stir those feelings four years later, Swift rejected her. He had read her last letter many times, he claimed, writing in May, and always put it down exasperated. Once, he admitted, he had hoped to take her from the 'company and place' in which she lived; but her reluctance to be rescued from 'such a sink' had slowly convinced him that she was actually indifferent to him. No, there was no other woman on his mind, he assured her; but now he was incapable of rescuing her in any case. He had no home to offer her: he would either have to build a house at Laracor, a project for which at present he lacked all necessary funds, or rent one in Trim, where there was hardly one to be found. Government business with Berkeley, in the meantime, detained him from even visiting Belfast. He went on to disable her inquiry with a cruel checklist of questions.

> I desire, therefore, you will let me know if your health be otherwise than it was when you told me the doctors advised you against marriage, as what would certainly hazard your life. Are they or you grown of another opinion in this particular? Are you in a condition to manage domestic affairs, with an income of less (perhaps) than three hundred pounds a year?

Here was revenge for the excuses Waring had made for turning him down at the first time of asking. Swift wondered if she would let him mould her to a shape and reduce her wishes to a size that suited him:

> Will you be ready to engage in those methods I shall direct for the improvement of your mind, so as to make us entertaining company for each other, without being miserable when we are neither visiting nor visited? Can you bend your love and esteem and indifference to others the same way as I do mine? Shall I have so much power in your heart, or you so much government of your passions, as to grow in good humour upon my approach . . . Shall the place wherever your husband is thrown be more welcome than courts or cities without him? In short, these are some of the necessary methods to please men who, like me, are deep-read in the world; and to a person thus made, I should be proud in giving all due returns toward making her happy.

The peroration is grim indeed. Swift dropped all pretension to Jane plighting her troth. He demanded instead that she swear an Oath of Allegiance, and promised in return to treat her as he would Dissenters or Papists: with principled intolerance. The rhetoric is redeemed only by the fact that he is, of course, spelling out an impossibility: for these are, he is saying, terms no self-respecting person could accept. He is telling Jane Waring to run as far and as soon as she can. Part of the near-evil mastery of this letter – which appalled nineteenth-century gallants such as Thackeray – is that in the same breath with which his requirements become ever vaster, Swift claims to be asking less and less of his prospective bride. A final hurtful touch is that the contract, on his part, is entirely generic, a standard nuptial agreement he would ask any woman to sign.

> These are the questions I have always resolved to propose to her with whom I meant to pass my life; and whenever you can heartily answer them in the affirmative, I shall be blessed to have you in my arms, without regarding whether your person be beautiful, or your fortune large. Cleanliness in the first, and competency in the other, is all I look for.[31]

'Withering' is a quality commonly accorded to Swift's manner; but does this have any rival? By the end of the letter he has whittled any future wife as small as a Lilliputian puppet; and, while insisting this is a one-size-fits-all offer, nothing personal against Jane Waring, he makes it clear that in join-ing him at the altar she must diminish herself to become this clean and competent doll. He annihilates all prospect of marriage; all sense, too, that his earlier proposal had carried with it any compliment.

Yet this heart-blasting letter should nevertheless be read in the light of those earlier, faintly haranguing but still fond addresses. Only then does Swift's subsequent rejection, and indeed much of his emotional com-plexion, become clear. For the key factor in his treatment of Jane Waring, as so often in his subsequent behaviour towards others, was his dread-fully delicate sense of honour and pride. He was cruel to Jane because, he felt, she had treated him cruelly and unreasonably. He had laid him-self bare, years before, in talk of 'rapture and delight' that seems incongruous to us now because of the writer he became – not because of the somewhat more conventional and distinctly vulnerable younger per-son he was at the time. She had spurned his offer to take her to a place he considered better for them both. She had humiliated him; and, oper-ating on a principle that became his second nature, he tried to humble her. To us, the imbalance between her (quite understandable) earlier affront and his moment of payback seems hugely disproportionate. It does not to Swift: in his eyes, Jane is a coquette. He is equalizing the scales, administering hurt on a par with the wound he was dealt.

Swift's cold severance from Jane is additionally important because he is talking all about himself. He, after all, is the despot, he is the Blue-beard past all reason, demanding that the woman let him shape her every thought and mood; and, ultimately, the diminutive, neutered, unprepossessing bridegroom who asks only for 'cleanliness' and 'compe-tency' is no one else but Swift. All he does is spell out the scale to which his partner must crush herself if she is to be at one with him. Perhaps the oddest thing of all about this letter, one of the sharpest put-downs surely ever written, is that Swift is doing Jane Waring a favour, and tells her so. His overall message, despite the paralysing sting in its tale, is 'flee'.

The letter says a great deal about Swift's rigorously guarded lack of self-esteem, security and hope in the early summer of 1700. It also casts light on his subsequent decision (despite legends and rumours to the con-trary) never to marry. The role of wife was one he would enforce on no woman he loved. The resolve in this letter reflects on the future of his relationship with Esther Johnson, in particular his determination to place her under his wilful protection. Retrospectively, it also takes its energy and bearing from a set of resolutions Swift penned in a famous private document about a year earlier.

When I Come to be Old, 1699

Not to marry a young Woman.

Not to keep young Company unless they realy desire it.

Not to be peevish or morose, or suspicious.

Not to scorn present Ways, or Wits, or Fashions, or Men, or War, &c.

Not to be fond of Children, or let them come near me hardly.

Not to tell the same Story over & over to the same People.

Not to be covetous.

Not to neglect decency, or cleenlyness, for fear of falling into Nastyness.[32]

Whether he kept those self-imposed rules in old age is obviously debatable. The relevance of this memorandum to an older self, with regard to his bitter parting from Jane Waring in 1700, is that Swift had in many respects become the elderly man he envisaged here. He was already the self-isolated, self-limiting person these sentences spelled out, committing himself to a regime of exact virtue. And, in becoming that person, he was not only safeguarding himself from degeneration, but protecting himself from suffering hurt in future. He knew himself better now than he had done in 1696; or he knew better, at least, what he wanted to be. He would no longer play the lover; he would no longer write earnest odes. He had discovered the dynamic crucial to the creative life that lay ahead: instead of suffering further shame he would castigate the pride of others who better deserved such pain. An armoury of mutable styles, already fully developed in the as yet unpublished *Tale of a Tub*, would guard his moral and emotional integrity. In the spring of 1700 he tested out some of his weaponry on an unfortunate, ailing target, Jane Waring, his sometime 'Varina'. Seven years his junior, she predeceased him, at the age of forty-six, by a quarter of a century in 1720.[33] The final implication of her correspondence with Swift is that she might not have lived so long had they married.

# 4

No marrying a young woman, no young company unless they wished him near; no uncleanliness, no being a bore by repeating the same story to the same listeners – in 1700, having broken with Jane Waring and accepted, seemingly, existence in Ireland for the present, Swift was still just thirty-three but well on the way to keeping in advance many of his resolutions for old age. Others on his list of vows, arguably, would always prove to be beyond him. He would not prove as immune to flattery as he wished; he would not forgo boasting of former feats; and he would find it hard not to give advice even when it wasn't desired. Above all, he could not resist scorning 'present Ways, or Wits, or Fashions, or Men, or War'. Indeed he came to feel admonishing the items on this list was nothing less than his duty. A bent of character of which he was quite unconscious, meanwhile, was a tendency to love and hate things simultaneously, to grow attached to what he once despised and vice versa, and forget the opposite was ever true. He both coveted and despaired of greater rewards from his Church, but grew to love his first vicarage jealously, and something similar guided him in prolonging his connection with the Berkeleys.

As their chaplain, he was more than the secretary he had been to the Temples. For all the disdain his notebooks held for the Earl, he liked too much being part of the family, and the comforts they shared with him when he returned to them on lengthy visits. He grew genuinely fond, in the meantime, of the Earl's daughter, Lady Elizabeth – Lady Betty, to Swift – who became a firm friend. At the time Swift joined the family, the Berkeleys' nineteen-year-old son James was just at the threshold of a distinguished naval career. He would be made a captain, celebrated for personal bravery, by his early twenties, and promoted to flag rank at the age of twenty-eight. Swift found him a 'rake' and disliked his choice of wife, Louisa Lennox, daughter of the Duke of Richmond, whom he dismissed as an ill-natured and covetous 'chit'.[34] His disapproval stemmed no doubt from a concern for the family, his esteem for Lady Betty, and also the affectionate tolerance he developed for her mother the Countess, to whom reading an improving book in the evenings was one of his daily tasks.

A good deal of Swift's tartness towards the Berkeleys, as with so many, protected tenderness from sentimentality or scorn. The handful of verses and prose cameos inspired by the family reveal how much he liked a home, and having the freedom to dish out little mockeries as an accepted member of the household. These impromptus also reflect his uncertain status, and in some cases the irony he felt able to express in that regard. One excellent poem, dating from around 1701, is written in the voice of Mrs Frances Harris, Lady Betty's maid, and catches her distress on having lost her nest-egg of savings. This means, she protests, that she will have no dowry to attract and make a husband of the Earl's chaplain – Swift himself. The joke is sympathetic because Swift's impersonation of the waiting woman is so uncannily realistic – with every phrase exuding the fullest knowledge of what it meant to be 'below stairs'. The poem is a 'petition' for compensation from Lord Berkeley. Mrs Harris swears:

> That I went to warm my self in Lady *Betty*'s Chamber, because I was cold,
> And I had in a Purse, seven Pound, four Shillings and six Pence, besides
>      Farthings, in Money, and Gold;
> So because I had been buying things for my *Lady* last Night,
> I was resolved to tell my Money, to see if it was right;
> Now you must know, because my Trunk has a very bad Lock,
> Therefore all the Money I have, which, *God* knows, is a very small Stock,
> I keep in a Pocket ty'd about my Middle, next my Smock.
> So when I went to put up my Purse, as *God* would have it, my Smock was unript,
> And instead of Putting it into my Pocket, down it slipt:
> Then the Bell rung, and I went down to put my *Lady* to Bed,
> And, *God* knows, I thought my Money was as safe as my Maidenhead . . .[35]

The Victorian biographer Henry Craik commented at length on the 'petition': his words are worth quoting, since they show that rightful esteem for Swift's craftsmanship as a verse-maker is no purely modern discovery. Craik presents a fine Hogarthian sketch of the parlour environment flickering in candlelight in which so much of Swift's existence passed. It was by no means all hardship:

> No contrast could be greater than that between the strained and stilted style of the Pindarics and the skill with which Swift, by his literary instinct, fastens our interest on a subject trivial in itself. But the right note once struck, Swift preserves it to the end in all his lighter poems. Above the servants' hall, the drawing-room too was depicted: the earl dealing round the cards and overdoing, in his fussy nervousness, the part of a careworn politician: her ladyship holding the stakes, and dropping to sleep over her cards and her snuff: poor Biddy Floyd, the companion, wisely cautious of her pence, and indulging in the mildest gambling with much timidity. 'Parson Swift' was the chartered satirist: his ribaldry condoned, perhaps because it could not be resisted.[36]

Some time was still to pass before such poems took on a life of their own in print, becoming the delight of readers in clubs and coffee-houses. His verse-impersonation of Mrs Harris was an entertainment in an older social mode, for the minor court of the Berkeleys' household, and it

tacitly indicates Swift's almost bardic role in the establishment, a role
that exceeded the stipulated position of a secretary or chaplain, bound
though it was by a decorum of its own.

The backdrop of these and other poems connected with the Berkeleys, a number of which Swift wrote in collaboration with Lady Betty,
was not, however, Dublin Castle or the mansion in Chapelizod. A political sea change in 1700 brought the appointment of a new lord lieutenant
of Ireland, the Earl of Rochester, in December; although Rochester's
concern for a fitting reception in Dublin – and also to be sure that greater
honours might not come his way in London – delayed the Earl of Berkeley's departure until April 1701. Swift, retained as family chaplain on a
more casual footing, sailed with his outgoing master, and for years to
come would regularly reside with the Earl at his London townhouse and
ancestral home in Gloucester, Berkeley Castle.

Steep-walled and turreted, with a motte-and-bailey fortress still insinu-
ating its character through the circular keep and the later, more domestic
extensions, the castle harboured almost every species of English ghost –
and the parables they offered. Great breaches in the outer walls held a
permanent lesson on the Civil War, the last stand of a Royalist fortress
and surrender to Parliament's Colonel Thomas Rainsborough. Edward
II, cheated of power by his wife Isabella, still groaned in his dungeon –
preserved to the present day – on the autumn anniversary of his murder
there in 1327. The castle might be said to enshrine examples supporting
Swift's view of British history as a cycle of human errors and occasional
grand betrayals. Yet he returned there gratefully enough, year on year;
and in the occasional verses he wrote on one stay with the family he
preferred to describe the typical scene at a game of cards. These poems
date, it seems, from August 1702 – when Swift didn't omit to mention
either his own lack of skill as a player or the doctorate of divinity he had
paid for from Trinity earlier in the year.

> *My Lord* to find out who must deal
>             Delivers Cards about,
> But the first Knave does seldom fail
>             To find the *Doctor* out . . .

> My *Lady* tho' she is no Player
>             Some bungling Partner takes,
> And wedg'd in Corner of a Chair
>             Takes Snuff, and holds the Stakes.

The Earl and Countess of Berkeley are shown at something of a loss; Mrs Harris, as ever rueing her luck; another lady-in-waiting, Mrs Weston, hoping to supply a silk lining for a new gown with her winnings; and, thanks to a deft addition by Lady Betty, a welcome miniature of the sometime chaplain himself, scattering half-appreciated witticisms to the company.

> With these is Parson *Swift*,
>     Not knowing how to spend his Time,
> Does make a wretched Shift,
>     To deafen 'em with Puns and Rhime.[37]

Though he couldn't have known it, Swift's spell as Berkeley's chaplain in Dublin brought to a close what we might call the passive period of his life, the first formative thirty-odd years. During this period he had suffered a great deal of what he felt was humiliation; soon his turn would come to begin administering it. His return with Berkeley to England in 1701 marked the beginning of the long and incredibly productive period in which he was soon acknowledged to excel at shaming the proud, the vicious and the unwitting.

# 5

Swift might have been leaving for England in April 1701, but his fortunes were still tied up in Ireland. He could not afford to ignore the appointment of the Earl of Rochester as the new Lord Lieutenant. While accompanying Berkeley home, it would soon be necessary to switch retinues, and continue the wearying campaign for preferment. Simultaneously, despite his frequent statements to the contrary, he could not escape his emotional ties to Ireland or an interest in the country's grievances.

Like Swift's, the mood in Protestant Ireland during his spell as a lord justice's chaplain was offended and tetchy, and covered by a veil of duty. The Wool Act of 1699 was the latest piece of legislation disabling Irish trade, prohibiting the export of another important national product. Severe limitations were placed on the movement of raw wool, in a measure that also afflicted the American colonies. As was often the case with such laws, a side-effect was innovation by the injured party, as Irish fullers and weavers in time were impelled to improve their wares in other forms of cloth. Such benefits, though, were generally unforeseen and would always be slow in coming. The Protestants of Ireland were still so shaken by Tyrconnell's rule that it was widely felt they should accept whatever constrictions London cared to place on them. Their Parliament had yielded its right to issue money bills, and stood by helplessly as shackles were placed on Irish trade. Nevertheless a body of respectful demurral was growing. The year 1698 saw the publication of an extremely well-researched and astutely argued tract on the question of Irish autonomy, William Molyneux's *The Case of Ireland's being Bound by Acts of Parliament in England, Stated.* A hawk-nosed progressive in matters of science and philosophy, the friend and judicious admirer of John Locke, experimenter in dioptrics and translator of Galileo in his spare time, Molyneux addressed the Irish predicament with the same keenness he applied to astronomy or the weather. His scientific publications brought praise from Halley and Leibniz, and invited rivalry from other natural philosophers; but none created the stir that greeted *The Case of Ireland.*

Molyneux is a writer against whom Swift's politics can be gauged. Ostensibly the two men belonged to the same ruling Anglo-Irish class, but Molyneux, more materially secure, could confront opinion from London much more openly than Swift did in the first half of his life. Molyneux was a member of the Irish House of Commons and believed in reasserting the chamber's lost powers. Indeed, he was quite prepared to remove Westminster altogether from the equation of Irish politics. The case he defined on behalf of Ireland's right to self-governance turned on a single point: the English Parliament had no right whatsoever to legislate directly for the Irish. Ireland, Molyneux reminded his readers, was a sovereign kingdom, which had originally made a free gift of the Crown to Henry II in return for his protection. Henry then bestowed his Crowns separately on his two sons, making Richard heir to England and giving Ireland directly to John. The two kingdoms might still have had different monarchs down to the present time, as Scotland and England did until the death of Queen Elizabeth, had Richard not died without children. Ireland was thus ruled by its own sovereign, even though he or she resided in England. Bills accepted by the Irish Parliament could become law only when approved by the English Privy Council; but those privy councillors represented the monarch in doing so, not the English Parliament in which most of them also sat. A similar principle extended to the judiciary: on Irish questions the King's Bench would always apply Irish law wherever it differed from the English. Thus, concluded Molyneux, Westminster had no foundation in law when it placed direct limits on Irish trade.

From this distance, Molyneux's very radical argument seems all the more adroit because it is at one and the same time very conservative. It offers no disloyalty or even any milder offence to the monarch; rather it calls for closer ties between the sovereign and his kingdom. When read carefully, Molyneux's book isn't really disrespectful to the English Parliament either. As a true student of Locke, he admires parliamentary procedure and is very clear in saying that the ideal solution would be to allow direct representation for Ireland at Westminster. Only in relation to Ireland, he suggested, was the English Parliament despotic. So, far from being a tearaway secessionist, Molyneux was in truth a strict unionist. The majority of English MPs were nevertheless displeased, unsurprisingly, by the mere idea of restricting their power, and apparently ordered the public hangman to burn the work.[38] It was answered in the press by several further books over the next few years, although Molyneux lived to read none of them. He suffered from weak kidneys, and died of renal illness in October 1698, a month after returning from a visit to Locke at Oates in Essex.

Molyneux's political thought met more unexpected coolness in other quarters. Notwithstanding the general sheepish sense among Protestant Irish that, having liberated them from Papist tyranny, the English could dictate whatever terms they please, *The Case of Ireland* went against an idea now sacred to Protestants across the land. Molyneux gave unacceptable power to the royal prerogative; he put clear air beneath the monarchy in its ascendance over Parliament. In arguing thus he crossed the 'Revolution principles' the majority of Protestants in Ireland, Anglican or Presbyterian, would back to the bitter end. As it happened, Swift himself would shortly be arguing against allowing assemblies too much freedom or authority, but his thinking and Molyneux's were as yet only superficially similar. The constant thread in Swift's early politics is a belief that a balanced constitution of lords, commons and sovereign works best, although the Whiggish faith he may once have had in parliamentary rule dwindled the more he saw what Whigs were ready to do with such power. The High Church party also suspected Molyneux of being a 'free-thinker' in more than science: they remembered him defending the work of John Toland, a progressive yet esoteric thinker we shall hear more of later, against indictment in Dublin. He could thus be marked out safely as one who would not only investigate nature, but tamper with God's order. Rather than encouraging such tendencies, many Anglican traditionalists could live with paying extra duty on their wine and a drop in exports, for now.

The incoming Lord Lieutenant, Laurence Hyde, Earl of Rochester, should have been highly agreeable to the stalwarts of the Anglican Church in Ireland. Middle-sized and hot-tempered with a regal bearing, he was the acknowledged leader of the English 'Church Party' and the Tories' chief. He was an old-school Royalist, now in his late fifties. Uncle to the Queen, second son of her grandfather Edward Hyde, Earl of Clarendon and Lord Chancellor, he had opposed the installation of William of Orange as king. He was a diehard legitimist who stood for the true succession, notwithstanding the sins of his brother-in-law King James, and was generally suspected of being a Jacobite. It was a time that prized long genealogies but demanded short memories: Rochester was not to be reminded of how his father, a commoner by birth, had called for his sister to be put on trial when he heard that she was carrying James's child in 1660. The Hydes, although they bore now the two earldoms of Rochester and Clarendon, were really quite recent entrants to the highest circles of Court society. With all the shrillness of the parvenu, Rochester demanded royal treatment from all, including his nieces and William, and cursed like a boatman when he didn't get it. Swarthy, handsome, well-built, the new Lord Lieutenant insisted on a fabulous welcome by the citizens of Dublin – on the scale that greeted Swift, quite spontaneously, some two decades later. But, while his High Church principles stood him in fairly good stead with Irish Anglicans, none but the most suspect could countenance him for questioning William and the Glorious Revolution. To outright Whigs and Presbyterians, the new Lord Lieutenant was a target for open hatred.

Rochester was only appointed lord lieutenant as a concession to the unbending Tories. As rewards for their help during the revolution and Williamite wars, the King had granted titles and huge estates to Whigs and numbers of his international followers. Henri de Massue de Ruvigny, the Huguenot Earl of Galway, had for example received an enormous portion of the lands confiscated from supporters of King James. As they found their way again in the later 1690s, the Tories pushed successfully for such grants to be 'resumed' and the lands placed in commission for sale or redistribution. The Whig trinity of lords justices were dislodged in order for the Tory Rochester to oversee this humiliating process in person.

The 'resumption' reflected a loss of personal power for King William. His war with France had ended, for the time being, with the Treaty of Ryswick (modern Rijswijk) in 1697. The treaty reset the diplomatic clock to 1679 by declaring that all towns captured since the Treaty of Nijmegen should be returned, with one or two controversial exceptions. Yet all but the blithest could see that Ryswick provided little but a breathing space. Diplomatic efforts of the next few years would all involve delaying or if possible averting the next war between Louis's and William's allies. The great question of the day was the fate of Spain. Charles II, the mentally and physically disabled ruler of the Spanish and their vast empire, and a leading victim of the Habsburgs' ill-placed confidence in marrying cousins to cousins, was dying; and there was a chance his Crown could pass to France. Louis resisted temptation and signed the First Partition Treaty, a diplomatic masterwork on the part of William, whereby the French waived the right of their candidate, Louis's grandson Philip, in favour of a compromise embodied in Prince Joseph Ferdinand of Bavaria. The riches of Spain, leaving Spain herself aghast, were therefore to be divided. The fragile arrangement collapsed when Joseph Ferdinand died, but again Louis and William chiselled out an agreement that seemed viable. In the Second Partition Treaty of 1699 France even accepted the Habsburgs' first choice for Spain, the younger son of the Holy Roman Emperor, Leopold, as the future King of Spain. Louis's conceding such a prize to the heir of his single greatest imperial rival, a claimant who would reunite the Spanish and Austrian wings of the Habsburg dynasty, should have alerted his enemies that he was merely playing for time. France still needed rest from an impoverishing war.

On paper and to some extent in reality, the Partition Treaties were extremely fine diplomatic achievements. Yet they were terribly unpopular across Europe. The Spanish were appalled that their empire was to be split; the Austrian Habsburgs turned up their noses at the benefits the treaties brought, and looked for heaven to unite the Crowns; and the English mercantile class were upset with William for giving up Naples and Sicily to Louis. These precious bases, reasoned the English, handed control of the Mediterranean to France, and placed the 'Levant trade' in jeopardy. The Tories, nicely judging the move in public opinion, used Whig principles against the embattled King. William had negotiated the Partition Treaties without consulting his ministers or Parliament, and his lord chancellor, Somers, had seemingly taken some liberties with the paperwork.

# 6

When Swift returned to London in the spring of 1701, the Partition Treaties were nothing but scraps of parchment in any case. Louis had torn them up the previous November, when King Charles died, having bequeathed the Spanish monarchy with all but his last gasp to France. The Spanish Royal Court, with strong backing on the streets of Madrid, felt the Bourbon claimant, Philip, had a greater chance than Austria of defending their far-flung possessions. Louis stood up for his grandson, and accepted Charles's will. In February 1701, dispelling all English and Dutch expectations that their ships might still be allowed to trade in Spanish territory, the French King made it clear that whatever had been Spain's was now, in fact, his. French troops occupied the Spanish Netherlands and took up stations just across the Channel at Ostend and Nieuwpoort. The English needed to accept, as William already knew, that they would have to fight France again; but for now the Parliament at Westminster concentrated on settling old party scores.

There was a savage campaign to impeach the ousted Chancellor, Lord Somers, along with three other lords accused of abusing office. The campaign was led by the bluffest Tory in the Commons, Sir Edward Seymour, with help from John 'Jack' Grobham Howe, but not at the head of an undivided party – or a party organized, in truth, on anything like contemporary lines. Somewhat nefariously, the Earl of Rochester stood above the fray but ready to aid and certainly to benefit from Seymour's and Howe's campaigns, and also to disown them should that be necessary. More conciliatory views were held by two younger influential Tories whose lives would link up closely with Swift's: Robert Harley, the Speaker, and a former Presbyterian, and Henry St John, twenty-two years old yet already attracting notice as one of the best orators in the House. Harley and St John offered reserved support for King William's initiative against France.

In key ports of call, London in early summer 1701 was much what it was when Swift had last passed through, the realm of casual vice, slack religion and religious money-making described by one of Congreve's rakes:

Oh, Prayers will be said in empty Churches, at the usual Hours. Yet you will see such Zealous Faces behind Counters, as if Religion were to be sold in every Shop. Oh things will go methodically in the City, the Clocks will strike Twelve at Noon, and the Horn'd Herd Buz in the Exchange at Two. Wives and Husbands will drive distinct Trades, and Care and Pleasure separately Occupy the Family. Coffee-Houses will be full of Smoak and Stratagem. And the cropt [short-haired; 'round-headed'] Prentice, that sweeps his Master's Shop in the morning, may, ten to one, dirty his Sheets before Night.[39]

The layout and architectural character of London were nevertheless in flux, as they had been since the year Swift was born. The post-inferno rebuild of the city had long since gathered momentum. Before the Great Fire, the streets were 'narrow, and the houses all built of timber, lath and plaster', in Defoe's words, 'or as they were very properly called, paper-work'. The compressed feeling of the old streets gave rise to the well-known images of people leaning out of upstairs windows and shaking hands across the divide, or leaping over it from one roof to another in order to escape a fire or an unwelcome visit below. Swift the young and middle-aged man is not to be pictured against this essentially medieval urban background. New, better-spaced houses of stone were climbing into view; yet, in Defoe's assessment, the city was more tightly packed and densely populated than before. For, although a lot of land was now set aside 'to enlarge the streets', the lost London was diffused by larger expanses between clusters of buildings:

> The old houses stood severally upon more ground, were much larger upon the flat, and in many more places, gardens and large yards about them, all which, in the new buildings are, at least, contracted, and the ground generally built up into other houses, so that notwithstanding all the ground given up for beautifying the streets, yet there are many more houses built than stood before upon the same ground.

By 1724, a couple of years before Swift's final stay in London, there were an estimated 4,000 more houses standing on the same area than in 1666. Even in the outer districts of the growing city, Defoe reported, people were following the course suggested by the fire – 'pulling down great old buildings, which took up large tracts of ground in some of the well inhabited places' and putting up several houses or even whole new streets in the clearing.[40] The London experiences of Swift's maturity – his associations with Addison and the Whig wits in the early 1700s, his years of near-eminence in 1710–14, and even his controversial visits, long delayed, in the mid-1720s – should therefore be imagined with the last signs of a more higgledy-piggledy, organic conurbation disappearing, and the arguably more mappable contours of 'eighteenth-century London' taking shape and wearing in around him. The great riverside palaces backing on to The Strand, the thoroughfare running roughly eastwards from the open ground that is now Trafalgar Square, were falling into disuse, being demolished or unrecognizably refurbished and renewed. The process was symbolic for nostalgic conservatives who looked to the past, since those structures had housed the aristocracy of England's golden age, the years of Elizabeth to the pre-war reign of Charles I. The decisive loss had come as early as 1698, when the Palace of Whitehall, one of the largest in Europe, an irregular, rather low-lying mass of accumulating mansions, cloisters, gardens and courtyards, overlooked by the surviving Banqueting Hall, caught fire for one last time and in the space of a night was reduced to a few walls, chimneys and a single water-gate.

By the kind of paradox that had so attracted the Elizabethans, the mutable Thames was conceivably the most constant feature – barring the stern ochre-faced Tower, perhaps – in the city it curved through and around. Its nobility offered comfort to one almanac-writer of the previous generation:

> To proceed, this Gallant River kindly floweth, and filleth all her Channels twice in 24 hours: and this Ebbing & flowing continueth on for the space of 70 miles within the main Land: the Tide being always highest at *London*, when the Moon doth exactly touch the North-east, and South-west Points, of which one is visible above the Earth, the other under the Earth.[41]

Swift looked for similar regularity in his surroundings and acquaintance, but this gushing register would always be foreign to him. Notably, even if they impressed him as a younger man, his public and private writing would never swell the chorus of voices glorifying the capital's natural attributes and civic structures. His weak point would always be, despite his scepticism, the confluence of power, tradition and mere gossip at the Royal Court; but he showed no inclination to rhapsodize, like Defoe, over supposed wonders of London such as the Royal Exchange. The bourse of red brick first built by Thomas Gresham and opened in 1571 had been claimed by the Great Fire. Now an imposing arch opened on to Cornhill, supporting a three-storey tower above the portico, and flanked by Corinthian columns, with statues of Gresham, Elizabeth, the Stuart monarchs and allegorical figures positioned in niches across the whole front. A brass grasshopper, the weathervane, hovered above the clock-tower. The bourse within, said Defoe, 'is the greatest and finest of its kind in the world . . . the beauty of which answers for itself'.[42] Swift left no similar descriptions of a city that manifestly fascinated him. He was not a writer to linger much on magnificence. He rather admired practical, economical, orderly work and applied ingenuity, and what he

later called an 'infusion of the Alderman'.[43] The dome of the new St
Paul's Cathedral, which was still being built in 1701, on which Defoe
and other contemporaries would hurl superlatives, would be used by
Swift to give a measure of the size of the palace oven in Brobdingnag.[44]
But, even though the invention of Lilliput lay many years ahead, his
satirically tinged outlook already flickered with the latent, possibly
unwanted sense that works of hands that seemed majestic to conventional eyes might appear much humbler from an alternative viewpoint.

Familiar sights (and sounds, and stenches) thus assailed Swift, amid a
city in physical transition; yet the air was more charged than it had been
since the tense days of 1689. Living in the Berkeleys' townhouse, Swift
heard Whig fulminations against the Tories at their strongest – and
against Jack Howe in particular. Although (to his lasting rage) Howe
had gained no formal place in the Tory-slanted ministry the King
accepted in 1700, he was at the vanguard in attacking William and his
Whig supporters. He was best known, and still reviled, as a would-be
rake who had claimed to share a mistress with Charles II. The Duchess
of Richmond proved Howe a liar in 1678, and he slunk away from
Court. Later, he had supported the revolution whose Dutch champion
he now denounced, and taken up posts he soon lost because of his roving hands and presumptuous manners. Now in his mid-forties, he was
the talk of the town again for having stirred up the mob and stretched
parliamentary privilege to its limit. Speaking in the chamber in March,
he had compared the King to a robber in a gang that had rifled the house
of an invalid. For many years Howe set the bench-mark of public insolence towards the Crown – about which the Whigs, for all their
revolutionary values, were really as prudish as the Highest Tories. A king
who defended their principles, as William did and the first two Georges
would, was as sacred to them as any a Jacobite claimed was God's own
anointed.

Swift's level in society and spiritual calling disqualified him from taking any direct role in the quarrel; but he was stirred to make a
contribution. He demurred, however, from doing so at the peak of the
crisis. In the meantime he had other, personal priorities. Before the year
warmed and stately families left town for their country estates, he
renewed close contact with the young woman who had enchanted him
on his return to Moor Park in 1696. Swift's bearing towards Esther
Johnson was always that of the tutor and mentor to the child he had
taught and encouraged as a very young man; and this would be the attitude he stuck to, for better or worse, with any younger lady he found

pleasant in the future. Esther and her mother, still in the service of Martha, Lady Giffard, Temple's devoted sister, now spent the cooler half of the year at a house on Dover Street, the aristocratic avenue off Piccadilly's cluster of bowling greens and meeting-places. Traditional entertainments had been challenged, though, by Henry Winstanley's 'Mathematical Water Theatre', a local landmark for the windmill on its roof. The shows inside involved fountains, sparklers and mechanical wonders; spectators emerged dazzled and often quite soaked. The area had once been dominated by Clarendon House, an extensive Neoclassical mansion built against public uproar by Rochester's father, allegedly on the proceeds of the sale of Dunkirk to Louis XIV. Lady Giffard's refinements thus found their home on a site of past controversy, one already half forgotten as subsequent possessors, Sir Thomas Bond and Christopher Monck, the second Duke of Albemarle, lent their names to close-lying streets. The avenues were not canyon-like, as they are today; the feel of the district was more spacious, since the present Georgian façades had not yet blocked off the views of the commons once commanded by Clarendon's vast home. In the summer Lady Giffard exchanged her fashionable address for the more traditional comforts of Sheen, where a nephew of Sir William had inherited his baronetcy and the gardens he had planted with Dorothy.

This was the life that Swift, on taking up all his old authority with Esther, urged her to leave as quickly as she could. He carried additional status in relation to the family – in his own eyes at least – since he was, as the title page of the volume spelled out, the published editor of Sir William's early correspondence and miscellanea. This power lent him strength, if he needed more, to prise Esther from the family.

She was twenty years old, dark-haired and attractive: 'and was looked upon', wrote Swift years later, 'as one of the most beautiful, graceful, and agreeable young women in London – only a little too fat'. He would bother her often to lose flesh and gain strength through exercise.[45] Swift urged his young friend to leave England, and live near him in Ireland. Though the move might look like, in his word, a 'frolic' – a romantic and indecent escapade – respectability would be ensured in form and substance by her making her new home with an older fellow member of Lady Giffard's household. Rebecca Dingley was Lady Giffard's first cousin, yet belonged to a hard-up branch of the family; fussy, impractical yet well-meaning, entering her mid-thirties, she was eager to make the most of her limited funds and was easily won over when Swift suggested she live as chaperone to Esther. For the arguments Swift presented in favour of his plan were strictly financial. He did none of the fervent protesting and cajoling he had inflicted on Jane Waring in the mid-1690s, even if his feelings for Esther more than matched such avowals.

In much of his writing to and about her, Swift added a further precaution to indicate that his motives towards her were pure. While paying tribute to her beauty – 'the brightest Virgin of the Green' – he often addressed and described her as if she were a man; as if, indeed, while possessing every desirable masculine attribute, she was above all sex. He testified repeatedly to her courage – and she was brave, after all, in leaving her small but relatively secure circle of protectors in England to settle under his exclusive care in Dublin. 'She thinks that Nature ne'er design'd / Courage to Man alone confin'd,' he claimed in one late poem. Elsewhere in the same poem, he suggested that at birth she had been divinely equipped to leave her chastity unquestionable.

> *Pallas*, observing *Stella*'s Wit
> Was more than for her Sex was fit,
> And that her Beauty, soon or late,
> Might breed Confusion in the State,
> In high concern for human Kind,
> Fixt *Honour* in her Infant Mind.[46]

Pallas had played her part; but so had Swift, in cultivating and later publicizing this virtue, which had the benefit of freeing Esther from desiring marriage.

The mystery will always be to what extent Esther herself wanted the unusual life on which she now embarked, and how much Swift might have controlled her contrary wishes. If, as he more or less insisted, they were kindred creatures, equally uninterested in a more accustomed form of partnership, then he helped her to an existence that, as a wife and mother, or some richer lady's follower, would otherwise have been impossible. If their desires were not, however, identical, she would need to follow a still firmer course of self-adaptation. It is impossible, and perhaps all the harder what with all the speculating Swiftians have done on the subject, to know what his deepest motives might have been. In Swift's lifetime and ever since, some would always assume he was bringing Esther back to Dublin as his mistress, a few among them conceding that he might have had an eye to a future secret marriage. The marriage theory does seem, though, to belong with the one that she was really his sister or half-sister. Others have seen him unconsciously trying to remake and re-enact his unhappy early circumstances, making substitutes of the two women for his sister and mother. In doing so, he would be satisfying a need he could never have expressed, to compensate for early deprivations through his female companions. That Esther served as surrogate mother, sister and daughter is the interpretation fancied most by Irvin Ehrenpreis, who offered it purely as a theory, largely in line with the Freudian constructions of the past century. The only definite points the evidence yields is that Swift was very determined indeed to have his friend near him in Dublin and that he was prepared to put their relationship on a footing that, despite the precaution of installing Mrs Dingley, would always seem unconventional.

If in fact he wished to marry Esther, something blocked him from taking that step; if he wanted to be close to her but not as her husband, he was quite prepared to face the shame, disapproval or ribaldry they attracted rather than enter into a fake marriage or risk the pains and conflicts of a real one. The proposal he made public, meanwhile, was based on sound housekeeping. Sir William Temple had bequeathed to Esther the lease on lands worth £1,000 a year; Lady Giffard managed another £500 on her behalf. Yet the interest in Ireland offered an incomparable rate of 10 per cent, and the cost of living was half what it was in England. Rebecca Dingley's slender annuity of £14 would also go much further in Dublin. To settle the deal, Swift offered to supplement the couple's income by £50 a year from his own pocket, acknowledging his responsibility for them as he did so. The accounts wouldn't lie: in budgetary terms there could be no dilemma, especially when there was no conflict either between the interests of companionship and those of balancing the books. Swift reasoned in the way he would often use to great satirical and rhetorical effect, compressing and concentrating nebulous and ambiguous issues into the hard language of pennies, shillings and pounds. However, he couldn't avoid suspicions that he had other motives. To minimize rumours, with the decision made, Esther and Rebecca were to reach Ireland some weeks ahead of him, in the summer of 1701, and establish their lodgings independently.

As the two women prepared to leave, Swift meanwhile was working intensely on a short book setting out his view of the political crisis. His pamphlet offered its comments by means of historical example – a common strategy that, if any treasonous or libellous content were detected, always allowed authors to claim they had been misunderstood. *A Discourse of the Contests and Dissensions between the Nobles and the Commons in Athens and Rome* was the first published display of Swift's deftness at giving an extreme position the air of studious moderation. His historical framework allowed him to address the most contemporary of matters with the attitude of one concerned only for eternal things. He took care to strike a much higher-minded tone than that found in most other polemics on the impeachment of Somers and the other four lords. The writings of Charles Davenant – uncle of Swift's cousin Thomas, and son of the late Poet Laureate – were for example 'calculated for the meanest Capacity'.[47] Swift adopted a loftier stance. He surveyed the political history of ancient Athens and the Roman republic to support the now conventional post-revolutionary view that the state required a balance of elements: the monarch, the nobles and the commons. Where this equilibrium was lost, the consequences were never good. Swift's particular contribution was to argue that tyranny by no means resulted only from an individual dictator disturbing the balance. Far from it: he could cite examples of tyranny in Athens and Rome produced by people collectively exceeding the constitution's limits on their powers. This, he went on to suggest, was the nature of the emergency England and her sister kingdoms faced in 1701.

The politician Swift defended – and whose neck was eventually saved many weeks before Swift's *Discourse* was printed – was a jurist of imposing credentials. Lord John Somers had made his name long before he was made a peer, by defending the Seven Bishops: a churchman of Swift's strict and intellectual disposition would be inclined to admire him. After establishing a formidable reputation at the Bar during the 1680s, he proved equally capable in high office, serving as William's attorney general, lord keeper of the great seal and eventually as lord chancellor. Above and beyond any particular brief, meanwhile, Somers acted as one of the general master-builders of the post-revolutionary constitution, a role he consolidated by the part he played in drafting the eventual union with Scotland in 1706. All this he managed with an economy in speaking and writing that was rare in an age that valued rhetorical bulk: his closing address at the bishops' trial lasted a scant five minutes, but impressed all hearers. Middling tall, somewhat brown-skinned and 'of a grave deportment', Somers was, a contemporary noted, 'easy, and free in conversation': 'He gained such a Reputation of Honesty with the Majority of the People of *England*, that it may be said, very few Ministers in any Reign ever had so many Friends in the House of Commons; or could go to the City, and, on their bare Word, gain so much Credit.' The same writer alleged, however, that Somers was 'something of a Libertine'. Swift, who would dedicate *A Tale of a Tub* to Somers when the book was finally published, later decided that Somers possessed every eminent quality except virtue; and observed pungently in his notes on the description quoted above that Somers's father had been an utter rogue.[48] Yet, in the beautifully accomplished dedication to the *Tale*, we see the earlier impact Somers's intellect and personality had on a man who was always hard to impress and who so often delivered his sincerest compliments by means of a backhand. Swift assumed the voice of a bookseller, neutral and unassuming in everything but his approach to sales, who had sent out inquiries as to who might be the best subject for a dedication. All those he asked named themselves, but then gave Somers's name as their second. The bookseller, hoping for some pungent tale of courage or a scientific breakthrough to put at the front of the volume, is rather disappointed to hear from everyone the same story of Somers's 'Wit, and Eloquence, and Learning, and Wisdom, and Justice, and Politeness, and Candor, and Evenness of Temper in all Scenes of Life'.[49]

If Swift's political loyalties seem somewhat clouded in the first years of the new century, it is partly because such commanding personalities made a better showing on the scene than others who represented, or claimed to represent, the ideas and interests that Swift himself would later defend. Tories, notably Rochester, Seymour and Howe, seemed tawdry and opportunistic beside Somers's striking intellect and practical good sense, and Swift trusted him and his entourage to act rightly. In a savage passage in one of the digressions from the *Tale*, on madness, Swift's virtuoso calls for Howe, Seymour and other 'topping' Tories to demand that inspectors be sent to Bedlam, with a view to recruiting civil and military (not to mention ecclesiastical) officials from the ranks of the insane.[50] The consequences would be no different, Swift suggested, if those Tories were entrusted with real power. Over the coming decade, when personalities Swift felt he could respect emerged on the Tory side, his political allegiance would swing into what was probably its true place.

In the breathless summer of 1701 Somers seemed more like the latest in a long line of English ministers whose fates had been decided either by a monarch's displeasure or the mob's hatred. To the minds of most of Jack Howe's followers on the street, the technicalities of Somers's misdemeanours were as irrelevant as his learning. In the event, the Tories overplayed their move: the London riots triggered memories in the public at large of mob activity leading to national disaster. This was the history of 'popular Encroachments' to which Swift, capturing the conservative mood of the majority, alluded at the end of his *Discourse of the Contests and*

*Dissensions*. In Kent, always a sensitive county, the Grand Jury and Just-ices of the quarter sessions sent a petition to the Commons, urging them to bury party differences and grant supplies for the war that loomed ahead. The ensuing Tory uproar featured arrests and counter-petitions. In July, King William set out with the man whom, against all appearances, he had chosen as his apprentice, to conduct negotiations at The Hague. Wil-liam now was tiring; while his somewhat unlikely disciple, the Earl of Marlborough, was only touched with grey beneath his high and massive wig, and his greatest days lay ahead. Marlborough's fellow general and future comrade, Eugène of Savoy, had just completed a sterling contain-ment operation against the French, commanding Austrian forces at the Battle of Carpi. In the meantime, early in August, two ladies packed their modest belongings and travelled westwards through England towards Ire-land. Their self-appointed protector remained behind, at work on a political pamphlet that would in the end miss the heat of the moment.

The *Discourse* would be Swift's first major outing as a writer. The book that might otherwise have been his full-length debut, the *Tale of a Tub*, still lay in a manuscript seen by a few at most. Silenced for now, the *Tale* testified to the sense of writerly vocation Swift had held for many years, his desire for a readership and, perhaps, his impatience to display his true imaginative flair. Simultaneously the lateness of the book he actually sent this year to the printer, just falling shy of the bigger mark it might have made, suggests a lingering hesitancy, the delay brought about by perfectionism. 'Choose any subject you please, and write for your private diversion,' he advised a younger acquaintance in 1704, 'but be not hasty to write for the world.'[51] It seems to have taken a while for Swift to have conquered this Horatian attitude towards his own produc-tions; early on, he needed to be pushed, and, though he must have worked fast on the *Contests and Dissensions*, he may have thought more than twice before finally letting the pamphlet go. Throughout his career Swift left comments on the sometimes traumatic experience of having work published. In letters he frequently distanced himself from books and pamphlets his correspondent knew perfectly well were his. Like many writers of the time he expressed anger at booksellers who pirated his material, and printers who mutilated his text. The position of the writer, though, was one he explored more circumspectly in all but a few places – such as a passage in his late poem 'On Poetry: A Rapsody'. Here advice is offered for the debutant pamphleteer, having published a poem anonymously, who sits scanning for reactions, as discreetly as he can, as his pages are perused in a coffee-house.

> Be sure at *Will's* the following Day,
> Lie Snug, and hear what Criticks say.
> And if you find the general Vogue
> Pronounces you a stupid Rogue,
> Damns all your Thoughts as low and little,
> Sit still, and swallow down your Spittle.
> Be silent as a Politician,
> For talking may beget Suspicion,
> Or praise the Judgment of the Town,
> And help your self to run it down.[52]

The advantages of anonymity were obvious as unsparing comments were let fly above the pots of coffee and chocolate. Swift would subsequently display great pride when one of his papers became the talk of the town, and mortification when the words of a dunce were mistaken as his. And when he stood back it was irksome to contemplate the sheer volume of material leaving the presses, to be sold off (or not) by booksellers or hawkers in the streets. It might be recalled that he had recorded the fate of such productions all too vividly in *A Tale of a Tub*, as their pages found their way to be wrapped around food, were used as lining or hung up in the lavatory.[53]

# 7

Broadly speaking, Swift opposed any change to a political apparatus that had received its last necessary modifications at the time of the Glorious Revolution. Approaching such questions, he was largely Sir William Temple's pupil in placing infinitely more weight on personal than on social or structural forces. Yet he was acute when it came to observing how the minutiae of inter-personal actions must eventually build up into large-scale determinants. The first few chapters of the *Discourse* provide warnings from antiquity of how assemblies can behave as tyrants. Towards the end, however, he found his theme for the next decade and more: a profound dislike of political parties, which he discovered to be the root cause of the present troubles. Forcing individuals to give up their own views on separate questions for the sake of a 'party line' could only, Swift argued, have a stultifying effect on the problem-solving that was required of committees or assemblies. When people are free to think for themselves, he observed, the group quickly sifts the good ideas from the weaker. When party members are forced to use their vote for the sake of some overriding strategy, the worst sort of nonsense is often accepted. The insight in the following passage has never really received its due:

> For, let us suppose five Hundred Men, mixed, in Point of Sense and Honesty, as usually Assemblies are; and let us suppose these Men proposing, debating, resolving, voting, according to the meer natural Motions of their own little, or much Reason and Understanding; I do allow, that Abundance of indigested and abortive, many pernicious and foolish Overtures would arise and float a few Minutes; but then they would die, and disappear. Because, this must be said in Behalf of human Kind; that common Sense, and plain Reason, while Men are disengaged from acquired Opinions [i.e. 'party doctrines'], will ever have some general Influence upon their Minds.

For centuries, the political system had been supposed to work by consensus. Whether or not it ever really had is open to dispute; but this was the goal that most of Swift's politically active contemporaries, even strong Whigs or Tories, held as their ideal. Here, almost uniquely, Swift applied some remarkable intuition to resuscitate a dry mantra. Even as the party system slowly made itself indispensable to a state drifting towards modernity, by standing back a little from the fray Swift could see the ludicrous results the system might bear. The optimistic premise of the paragraph above is untypical for Swift, admittedly; and it is immediately qualified. When people in groups are free to think for themselves, the small stock of common sense they share will prevail, simply because it is mutual to all: 'Whereas, the Species of Folly and Vice are infinite, and so different in every Individual, that they could never procure a Majority.'[54] The point would be one Swift would rephrase many times. When people act reasonably, they act in similar fashion, to similar ends; separate persons, meanwhile, will be bad in their own unique way. But, overall, in the right conditions, the *Discourse* suggests that the shared stock of goodness is greater than the multitudes of individual ills, a cause for modest hope.

Somers was saved, however, not by 'common sense' but by the very principle Swift decried. The former Lord Chancellor belonged to the most organized political elite in the land: a self-selected group of Whig peers known to all as 'the Junto'. These included Somers himself, the intellectual chief; Charles Montagu, Baron Halifax, the financial mastermind (and designer of the Bank of England); Edward Russell, Earl of Orford, former lord of the admiralty, vanquisher of the French at La Hogue in '92; and

Baron Wharton, of 'Lilliburlero' fame, political showman and party organizer supreme. Together the Junto oversaw the policy and tactics of the Whigs as a parliamentary and social force. A minority, it would seem, in strict numerical terms, the Whigs were more coherent as a movement than their Tory counterparts. Whereas the Tories were essentially broken between their conformist and Jacobite sections, the Whigs were united on the principles of the Glorious Revolution, and had claimed the achievements of 1688–9 as their own. They could be more flexible in their attitude to their own champion, King William: while a Tory would always be hamstrung by ideas of how a king should be regarded and served, the Junto's view of monarchy allowed them to see William as one more piece on the board. Directed by the Junto, the Whigs sensed that party strength was the secret to success: even when they lacked a majority in the Commons, as they did during the Impeachment crisis, the discipline among their pawns enabled them repeatedly to turn an issue in their favour. Their dominance in the House of Lords, meanwhile, gave them a permanent advantage. And so in 1701, by the time Esther Johnson and Rebecca Dingley took up their lodgings near the old walls of Dublin City, patient campaigning below the level of Tory hysteria had all but steered Somers and his fellow accused Whigs out of danger. Party politics saved them as their supporters in the Lords completely outmanoeuvred the Tory-slanted Commons.

By the time Somers was all but safe Swift was still writing his account of the *Contests and Dissensions*, with its finely judged denunciation of party and beautifully phrased verdict on the species of vice. But if he wrote with an eye on possible patronage from the Junto, he mistakenly rejected outright their basic expectation of any supporter. 'I would be glad any Partizan would help me to a tolerable Reason, that because *Clodius* and *Curio* happen to agree with me in a few singular Notions, I must therefore blindly follow them in all.'[55] The 'Reason', any of Wharton's practised partisans might have answered, lay in what they might assume was Swift's motive for writing in the first place – a payoff, material, political or social. But Swift expected such reward as a perfectly merited but still secondary consequence of his defence of common sense: he had not yet accepted, and perhaps never would, the need to score points in the game he had entered.

For another reason, the *Contests and Dissensions* is an incongruous sight in the thicket of controversy of this moment. Or rather it was Swift who had strayed into an improper habitat. By supporting the impeached Whig lords and voicing caution about the possible tyranny of assemblies, he implicitly countered a movement within the Church of England he might have been expected to support. As Rochester's High Tories settled into office, King William was pressed by clergymen to restore Convocation, the two-tiered synod that had traditionally met, at Westminster, at the same time as Parliament. Indeed a vociferous and dexterous faction of the 'inferior clergy' claimed that Convocation was as important constitutionally as Parliament itself. This faction was led by the donnish Francis Atterbury, and stimulated by his wit and scholarship: indeed it was a natural extension of the 'Christ Church' circle mentioned earlier in connection to *A Tale of a Tub*. The King had long ruled without any Convocation being held; and Archbishop Tenison of Canterbury supported that arrangement, as did most of his pliant colleagues on the episcopal bench.

An unmissable disparity was emerging between the inferior and superior clergy, both in quality and politics. The lower ranks were consumed with grievances at the direction of policy over the past decade. They were also unhappy with their lot. Priests depended for their income on the tithes raised by agriculture in their parishes. They did the bulk of the work that maintained the Church, provided counsel, guidance and mediation for their communities, yet in many cases could barely live on their incomes. The landed class to which they were bound had been hard hit by poor harvests throughout the 1690s, but even more so by the increasing yearly Land Tax, the source of William's war-chest. The mounting sense of injury and desperation led to the clamour for the King to recall Convocation. He gave in when his trusty Whig ministry collapsed and Rochester took power. For a brief space in time, the Lower House of Convocation ran amok. Atterbury was an indefatigable activist and, as a satirical writer, was arguably equalled only by Swift himself. He was, it might be recalled, the ghost-writer behind the tract that had ridiculed Richard Bentley in the row over the *Epistles of Phalaris*. Swift, as mentioned earlier, had commemorated this struggle in his 'Battle of the Books'. Although Bentley would have the last word, Atterbury's involvement in the episode gave abundant proof of how style, at least in the short term, could triumph over science. Now this impressive polemicist took on the Bishops' Bench. The men in mitres were flustered, and saved from defeat only by Archbishop Tenison regaining his nerve just in time. The rebellion was contained when William ended his Tory experiment, dissolving Parliament and Convocation with it.

The alignment of Swift's politics in the *Contests and Dissensions* looks odd against this background. An accomplished but still minor work has therefore attracted a great deal of debate. In its own time the book could equally disgruntle rival bands of interpreters. It opposed the party 'system', while tacitly backing a Whig leader and thus interests opposed to those of Atterbury and his followers in the Lower Convocation. Those who had time to follow the subtext of Swift's little book could have made out a slight against the efforts of his clerical brethren. Perhaps if he had held an English benefice, and thus been involved more directly in the 'Convocation Crisis', his essay on ancient policy might have turned out differently. His subsequent campaigning on behalf of the Irish inferior clergy would demonstrate the strength of his affinities. Perhaps the central point to take is, again, the aversion he expressed to thinking determined purely by 'party'. By approving of Atterbury's goals he did not necessarily favour his means.

The ongoing Somers crisis, and Swift's discreet, delayed intervention with his *Contests and Dissensions*, meanwhile distracted from another literary project he was considering on a larger scale. During his time away in Ireland he had returned, perhaps out of estrangement, to the subject of English history. Inspired by a pre-Conquest chronicle written by Temple, he thought of picking up the story in the early Norman era. A sheaf of notes dating from perhaps as early as 1697 mark the origins of the mooted work; but then at some point, seemingly on Berkeley's choosing him as chaplain, he began writing what amounts to a series of character studies of William Rufus, Henry I and Stephen.[56] His purpose was explicitly didactic, in demonstrating the strengths and fallibilities of rulers, and their characteristic mistakes. His principal materials, and thus his focus as historian, consisted of the personal properties of his chosen figures. For Swift (as for Temple), history is made by rulers, and the individuals who challenge or guide them. He shows no hesitation in diagnosing moral or psychological weaknesses or strengths. So of William Rufus, England's William II, a king he clearly admires for his robustness and resolve, Swift observes: 'His vices appear to have been rather derived from the temper of his body, than any original depravity of mind.' Swift the historian, while condensing battle scenes, was also clearly moved by a good adventure. He captures with a singular mixture of economy and flair the moment when Rufus calls his followers to embark with him, in the height of a tempest, to wage instant war on an enemy across the Channel. In the space of a few words he gives Rufus something irresistibly Shakespearean, and makes a hero of the King:

'They that love me, will follow me.' He entered the ship in a violent storm; which the mariners beholding with astonishment, at length in great humility gave him warning of the danger; but the king commanded them instantly to put off to sea, and not be afraid; for he had never in his life heard of any king that was drowned.[57]

History and its giants would be a constant source of arguments and allegory for Swift, and the reader of *Gulliver* looking through these sketches for a *History of England* can hardly fail to notice the concealed art with which scenes are set and characters are presented. Just as the *Travels* would pose diligently as a work of hard fact, Swift's abandoned chronicle refuses to admit how much good history owes to phrasing and storytelling.

In the volumes he compiled of Temple's works, meanwhile, there was much to give Swift a hint from beyond the grave that his mission might indeed lie with history-writing. In Temple's preface to his very readable *Introduction to the History of England*, he repeated a complaint he said he often made, 'that so ancient and noble a nation as ours . . . should not yet have produced one good or approved general history of *England*'.[58] Holinshed and the other Tudor chronicle-makers seemed horrifically rustic; the efforts by antiquarians such as John Aubrey were not widely appreciated by non-devotees; the literary masterpiece of English seventeenth-century historiography, the first Earl of Clarendon's account of the reign of Charles I and the 'Great Rebellion', had not yet been published. The prize of Temple's posthumous, imagined approval was a keen incentive for Swift to strive to be the historian his dead master had looked for, and made it painful for him to let go of the book he hoped to write. He did forgo it, though, declaring that meaningful research was too difficult from his Irish base; and less consciously, perhaps, his journalism proved more satisfying as he emerged from Temple's fading shadow.

Together, nevertheless, Swift's historical fragment, along with the *Contests and Dissensions*, rehearsed his approach to political problems of both past and present. His premise – one he shared not only with Temple but with countless other, lesser writers – was that events were determined by faults or virtues in key personalities and the level of harmony circumstances allowed in the constitution of monarch, peers and commons. Social and intellectual change was simply abhorrent to Swift, as it was still a difficult concept for most. Change was to be measured as deviance from a desirable and proper norm, an admittedly unbeatable force that still must be resisted. In Swift's view of developed human life, powerful selves either preserved or corrupted a static ideal, an abstraction he, like many others, would never concede was an invention of their forefathers. The paradox Swift identified that complicated such a view is that a 'great' historical figure – a Louis XIV, a William of Orange or, as the future would show, a Marlborough – is invariably the slave or puppet of an emotional or other quality lying outside intentional control. Louis le Grand, the Sun King smiling with his wooden dentures from Versailles upon the advances of his troops through the Dutch 'barrier', was in the thrall of his fathomless ambition; the generals and diplomats he sent to further it were mastered simultaneously by fear of their king and a craven desire to please him. King William, leading Marlborough through The Hague, refining his statecraft and patiently assembling another alliance against France, was also caught in such strings. His passionate, lifelong opposition to Louis and attachment to his homeland blinded him to the separate needs of his island kingdoms, convinced though he was that defeating the French was in the long-term interest of all Europe. He was led on, too, by an urgent need to equal his distinguished predecessors in their opposition to tyranny from the south. As for his ambivalent pupil John Churchill, Earl of Marlborough, although fifty years old he was still in many ways an unknown quantity. William had been struck by Churchill's mixture of delicacy and doggedness in diplomacy, a singular ability to read a politician's insecurities and transmit his own heartiness in return, when they first met at the Binnenhof more than twenty years before. Since then, their relationship had weathered times of harshness and mistrust, and, despite Marlborough's proven ability in the field, his place as William's true successor was far from apparent. His unique gift for managing a battle had not fully shown itself, nor his love of gold and glory, which awaited Swift's scalpel in just under a decade.

There was a subtler aspect also, which is rarely pointed out, to the sense Swift shared with Temple that history lay in the hands of such titans, for better or worse. The elements of humanity, for Temple as for Swift, remained constant. Yet for both writers the people at the forefront of history were closely related to their cultures and circumstances. As Temple put it in one of his historical works, the 'virtues and dispositions of Princes and Magistrates [are] derived, by interest or imitation, into the customs and humors of the People'.[59] Here 'derive' is used in its now lesser known sense of diverting or transmitting a flow or force: which is to say, people not only follow but are influenced, arguably shaped, by those who hold power over them – which in obvious consequence makes the study of princes and magistrates overwhelmingly important. Despite its limitations, Swift and Temple's view of history had greater realism than William Molyneux's, for all the legalistic detail he brought to the case of Ireland. Molyneux exhibited the same confidence in statutes he brought to the laws of nature, but he could not account for the moments of impulse that so often dictated further events, scenarios in which a monarch such as Louis threw aside his treaty commitments, or the passionate outrage that greeted Molyneux's own book at Westminster: his more scientific mind could show only how these moments were wrong in law.

Swift's chosen companions, Johnson and Dingley, felt remote from such questions as they sought their bearings in Dublin in late August 1701. Swift himself was delayed from joining them, first by his literary work and second by the wait for the new Lord Lieutenant. Rochester procrastinated: partly through concern that his welcome in Ireland should pay him sufficient respect; partly in order to disable any movement in favour of war with France; and largely too in expectation that, given the disturbances at home, the King would award him still higher office as a peace offering for the Tories. In the last week of August he relented, and proceeded in full state with his entourage to Chester. The viceregal retinue was obliged to idle at inns near Holyhead, however, until the winds changed, which they refused to do until 17 September. By that time, Swift had polished up the *Contests* and left it with a printer, and his two female friends had grown 'much discouraged to live in Dublin, where they were wholly strangers'.[60] Rochester was greeted in Dublin with sumptuous and painstaking ceremony; Swift with relief by Misses Johnson and Dingley. Hard work with humans awaited the Vicar of Laracor, not so much in his very light pastoral duties, but rather more in the delicate task of consolidating his place in the new Governor's court. The job was not an easy one, given the Whiggish bent of his newly published essay. As he later admitted, he had to convince his clerical colleagues that Johnson and Dingley's arrival was not a 'frolic', but his sense of his own propriety was so strong he was willing to defy all gossips and critics. Any censure was soon silenced, he claimed, by Esther's 'excellent conduct' – and, he might have added, by the formal respects he assiduously paid to them both, in an effort to dispel the impression of a romantic attachment to one. At the same time, he needed to soothe their upset spirits. More problematically still, while disavowing any marital interest in twenty-year-old Esther, he would need to mark a territorial claim over her, for 'her person was soon distinguished.'[61]

# 6. Drifting with Whigs, 1702–1709

> Besides, who that hath a spirit would write in such a scene as
> *Ireland*?
>
> – *Swift, letter of 1704*[1]

## I

As King William mustered support against France in 1701, the monarch whose kingdoms he had seized did him an unlikely and indirect favour. From the spring on, the exiled King James was fatally weakened by a series of seizures. The last of these 'fainting fits' occurred on Monday, 22 August, while he worshipped in the chapel of the chateau at Saint-Germain. Emaciated and ailing for some years, he had devoted himself to a life of retirement and repentance since his sponsor, the Most Christian King of France, acknowledged the Prince of Orange as King of England in 1697. James's comforts were amply provided for at the chateau, which had been the unwanted home of exiled Cavaliers and his mother, Henrietta Maria. King Louis, her nephew, had generously renovated the incredible palace to accommodate the Jacobite Court. So the ousted King reflected on lost chances in the gorgeous parterres; but then, in time, declaimed gratitude to God for having taken his kingdoms and purged him of pride. While his courtiers enjoyed the Italianesque flourishes and many luxuries of Saint-Germain, James fasted and prayed there. He maintained a private correspondence with many officials and other dignitaries across the Channel, who kept in touch for their part as an understandable form of insurance. The austere personal regime took its toll, nevertheless, and the hale former Lord Admiral and notorious adulterer grew hollow in the cheek. The fits of 1701 brought tremors, immobility, lungfuls of blood. He disavowed all further ambitions, and, as he lay dying in September, pardoned his enemies so frequently that their guilt seemed even fouler to his frightened supporters and grieving wife. His final weeks brought a blend of drama and ritual, as he embraced his son through crimson-soaked sheets and priests chanted at his bedside, with altars set at both ends of his chamber. While renouncing power, however, he accepted a promise from King Louis that ensured nothing but trouble for the future.

There was a personal touch in Louis lending James Saint-Germain: the Most Christian King was born in the chateau in 1638. He was an elderly man himself now, and saw that even in bed a king could rarely die in peace. Visiting James the day after he collapsed in the chateau's Sainte-Chapelle, he alighted from his carriage at the gates, so the noise of hooves and wheels in the courtyard would not disturb his dying relative. James lingered longer than expected, although the formal medical tortures of blistering inflicted by cinchona bark, a Jesuit remedy imported from the New World, did little to help. Louis visited him several times more. On the third occasion, James's priests and nuns witnessed a premeditated outburst: Louis had given the matter great thought, and had decided in conscience that he must recognize James's son, James Francis Edward, as the rightful King of England, Scotland and Ireland. James sighed appreciatively from his pillow; his priests gave thanks.[2]

The scene was of course instantly publicized, and nothing contrived by any grandee – not even so skilled a manipulator as Wharton – could have united the English public so forcefully once more behind William. Here was a direct challenge from France to the settlement of the three kingdoms. War was now inevitable and, to the majority in both parties who had accepted the revolution, morally necessary. Louis's conduct incapacitated the war-sceptical Tories. Why he chose to do so remains mysterious, since they were so useful to his purposes, but he evidently made his calculations on a grander scale. The effect of doing so, nevertheless, was all but immediate: he brought the conflict with William back to a point of crisis. Perhaps the ageing Bourbon King sensed it might be his last campaign, albeit one he could only entrust to his generals and direct from Versailles.

It was not, though, to be William's campaign. After weathering the Howe–Seymour storm, bringing Parliament back under the control of his Court, and seeing a favourable result to the general election held in January 1702, on 21 February he had an accident while riding and broke his collarbone. It was said that his horse tripped on a molehill, and Jacobites for many years would toast the maker of the mound, the 'gentleman in the black velvet coat'. A generation later, Swift preferred to make

what seemed a tribute to the King's steed. As such, deliberately or unconsciously, he distinguished his distaste for the Williamite legacy from
outright Jacobitism. William was thrown by a horse called 'Sorrel' and
the trusty Houyhnhnm servant who bids farewell to Gulliver as a 'gentle
Yahoo' was also a 'strong Sorrel nag'.[3] Swift had his own memories of
William, his mentor's visitor at Moor Park, and when the accident
occurred, he had yet to acquire his confirmed hostility to monarchs
imported from Continental houses. Nevertheless, given the treatment of
the Church over the previous decade, he is unlikely to have shared the
extremer grief of King William's staunchest revolutionaries. For such
stalwarts, the equestrian statue of William on College Green in Dublin
– which would be much bespattered and insulted by those who felt
betrayed by his reign – now acquired a morose demeanour. It had been
unveiled with huge pomp only the summer before.[4] Typically, the injured
rider insisted on returning quickly to work, but, while his injuries healed
well at first, a fever proved mortal on 8 March 1702.

In France, James Francis Edward, henceforth 'the Pretender' to all
Loyalist Englishmen, was proclaimed the rightful heir. Europe was soon
at war again. Technically, French backing for the Pretender was not to
be a *casus belli*, since late in the day Versailles withdrew its official support for James Francis by means of a courtly refinement of terms. As
Swift pointed out nearly a decade later, 'they only gave him the *Title* of
King.'[5] This was barely noticed by English eyes, which only saw Louis
nurturing the Pretender; and indeed it didn't alter the practical help and
shelter France lent the Jacobite cause.

William's death arrested an otherwise all but irresistible surge in the
power of the Whig and moderate Tory interest. For William's successor,
his sister-in-law Anne, inclined towards the traditions embodied by her
ruffled Tory uncle, the Earl of Rochester. The Lord Lieutenant had
returned from Ireland in January, barely four months into his residency,
to oppose William's policy during the general election, and was soon
afterwards dismissed by the King. But Anne reinstated him, and he
remained her viceroy for almost a year, although without returning to
Ireland.

Swift remained in Dublin during the election campaign. He concentrated instead on acquiring an epithet to bolster his pretensions in the
Church. In February he was awarded his doctorate in divinity at Trinity
College. Newly made doctors were usually spared the raucous rituals of
initiation that junior members of the college endured when they took
their Bachelor's or Master's degrees. The clerics who proceeded to the

D.D., as Swift did now, were, as one might expect, a more solemn body of scholars. Nevertheless, there were still keen card-players and considerable gourmands among them, and custom required that a new Doctor of Divinity pay not only a fee for his degree but also 'treat' the college common rooms to food and liquor. These expenses totalled £44 for Swift, a substantial chunk from his annual income of no more than £250. It was money well spent, however, for one looking to advance himself in the Anglican establishment.[6] Yet among the greater troubles he caused, the velvet-coated gentleman threatened to make a hollow investment of Swift's doctorate.

The King's sudden death prompted a flurry of urgent action. For when the sovereign died, the Royal Court, the Privy Council, the ministry and its dependent organs of state died too, since all these consisted of servants to the King or Queen. William's demise set off a great push for 'place'. Clergymen were obviously not to stand aside at such a juncture. This was the time for them to stake their claims to the next appropriate opening. Some of those vying for state positions were sufficiently assured of their own importance to expect reappointment or even promotion; at the top, Marlborough, for instance, was unassailable. Conversely, some knew the game well enough to expect very little from Queen Anne. For most middling- and lower-placed aspirants, the succession meant an opportunity, indeed an obligation, to get their name heard. Swift joined these multitudes by sailing once more for England in April 1702.

Anne's coronation was a huge affair. Westminster Abbey, and key locations around the metropolis, were festooned at unprecedented expense and with almost suffocating density; poor Anne herself, long unwell and now overwhelmed by her new precedence, was hard to see and hear amid the finery that clothed and the hangings that glorified her. As sometimes happens in history, an overdone pageant was being used to cloak widespread misgivings. There was no heir; none, at least in the sense of a figure who could raise a cheer and offer continuity. It is difficult to accept how recently a portrait of Anne had shown the Court a woman who seemed confident, unaffected, mature in mind and sound of body. In a beautiful and intimate portrait of the mid-1690s, she shelters her blond and delicate-featured five- or six-year-old son. His name was Prince William, Duke of Gloucester. There is a fine counterpoint between the mother's broader and the child's longer face; both have the same rosy lips.[7] This was the family line that would save England if, as seemed likely then, the King's failed. Yet the young Prince died in 1700, and Anne – in fact chronically weakened by difficult pregnancies – even after the worst extremes of grief had passed, was never quite the same. Her Court returned to mourning each year on the anniversary of Prince William's death. Her beloved husband, Prince George of Denmark, trusty but undynamic, a natural consort, and her best friend, Sarah Churchill, the Countess of Marlborough, provided vital threads of love and life; yet, despite these confidants and although Anne would develop painful symbioses with her closest servants and first ministers, she would always seem one of the loneliest monarchs. She stands squarely in her later portraits, draped in cloth of gold, clasping her sceptre – a vision of solidity that belied frail nerves.

Although her anxieties grew in proportion to her corpulence and fragility, she would always prove firm-willed if her manipulators pushed her too far. Even her domineering uncle, Rochester, soon found her resisting his directions. She was decidedly High rather than Low Church, and her principles were staunchly backed by a close set of clerical mentors. Leading these was the Archbishop of York, who would prove no friend to Swift (and no admirer of satire). Still, Anne was no militant sectarian: she would always refrain until her final months from releasing the hounds on the Dissenters. Conflict made her wretched; she was in essence a conciliator. There was a fair amount, then, in her first speech to Parliament as queen to bring the English together. The great drawback to having Anne as monarch was the precipice that all could see lying ahead after her death. An emphatic Act of Settlement in 1701 had nominated a distant German, Sophia, Electress of Hanover, as next in line. The 72-year-old but very sprightly Electress was a granddaughter of James I, which was enough. The priority for England's legislators was keeping the Crown Protestant. Most uncomfortably, this goal obliged them to bypass the forty or more Catholic claimants, with James Francis Edward at their vanguard, who were closer in blood to Anne. To legitimists, these Catholics would always be truer candidates than anyone from Hanover. Since most assumed Sophia would die before Anne, the more likely successor was Sophia's son George: forty-two, with barely a word of English to his name, but with a canny understanding of the constitutional snares that might deprive his family of its prize. Further bills would need to be passed by Parliament before the Hanover claim was entirely fast in law; but the still greater task would be to cement public support for the likely foreign monarch. Genuine reverence was all but impossible to inspire, and the lack of it would lead to Britain becoming a more modern constitutional state – and thus more alien to Swift.

Developing one's links with Hanover was a priority for all the king-dom's greatest political players. Such tactics at present, nevertheless, were relevant to a much higher sphere of hope and influence than Swift's. His job for now was to get a foot on the ladder of the current establish-ment; there was much jostling, and not a minute to lose.

Some, though, abstained from joining the throng. Another young writer, Joseph Addison, was a promising candidate who didn't stir, partly because he was abroad, and partly because he rightly saw he had little chance of gaining much from this round of patronage. Swift was to hon-our Addison as one of his choicest acquaintances, both for his morals and for his wit. It was true that Addison was more or less a man without an enemy. An extremely shy, somewhat ascetic yet still cordial soul, he had been marked out for special treatment by teachers and benefactors alike. As a student at Queen's College, Oxford, he had published a Latin verse that so impressed William Lancaster, one of his tutors there, that he was immediately recommended for a demyship (a 'half' fellowship) further down the High Street, at Magdalen. He welcomed the move, and grew so attached to the grounds of the college that a leafy meadow-side path behind the great square tower there is still named after him. He took his Master's degree and proceeded to a fellowship, having been spared the usual condition of having to take holy orders. In 1702 he still was technically a fellow at Magdalen, but was on the last lap of a grand Continental tour that, again, he had been given unusual leave to pursue. When Queen Anne took the throne, he was living in Geneva.

Although he was so far away, the moment is apt to bring him into Swift's story. Born in 1672, Addison was five years younger than Swift, but much better placed. He was the son of a Royalist clergyman with some eccentric tendencies but a breadth of experience that far exceeded the parochial existence of Swift's revered grandfather. Lancelot Addison had spent the lean years of the mid-century wandering the earth as he waited for better times and a decent English benefice. He had lived as a chaplain in Dunkirk, and then spent eight years in Tangier. The spell in North Africa resulted in two fascinating books on 'West Barbary', and gave rare latitude of vision to the erudite theological works he produced after returning to England. Joseph Addison's birthplace was the rectory at Milston, a hamlet in Wiltshire where Lancelot was parson. His char-acter combined something of his travelling father's scope with a reticent, intensely studious instinct. He quickly displayed an aptitude for lan-guages and a love of literature, and manifested a painfully sensitive streak from an early age. His family told the story of how, as a very young child, he was so afraid of censure that he ran away to the woods, gathered what berries he could and took shelter in a hollow tree until a search party discovered and returned him to his frantic parents. The Alpine crossing through the 'eternal snows' of December 1701 unsurprisingly came as a shock to a gentle disposition (although the horror he expressed at the peaks was perfectly conventional for the time): 'My head is still giddy with mountains and precipices, and you can't imagine how much I am pleased with the sight of a plain.'[8]

His delicacy had not prevented him from getting on well, though, with men of very different characters and politics. He had been the friend of Richard Steele, his long-term future collaborator, during their schooldays together at Charterhouse. Addison's precision and rectitude was a stabilizing influence on Steele's more rumbustious and sensual impulses, and the very same qualities recommended him strongly to the senior Oxford scholars who accepted and protected him. He was cherished by Dryden for the compliments and commentaries he offered on the ageing, Roman Catholic and now unpatronized poet's translations of Ovid and Virgil. Dryden needed the sales these arduous works brought in his final years, having been frozen out of the Royal Court on account of his conversion to Rome, and was grateful for the young poet's genuine respect. Simultaneously during the 1690s, Addison's chaste, courteous style, deployed in praise of King William, brought approval from Whig leaders, notably Lord Somers and Charles Montagu (from 1700, Lord Halifax). The latter became Addison's chief sponsor.

Addison's literary gifts were narrower than Swift's, and arguably purer; his outlook, meanwhile, was broader and more tolerant, and his judgement of the world in many respects more rational. His academic career offers an unmissable contrast with Swift's sulky, self-sabotaged showing at Trinity College. His perceptions reflect the stability of his upbringing: there were no protective kidnappers lurking in his buried earliest memories, no presiding formative sense of unwantedness. The better scholar, arguably a better-adjusted person, Addison would always lack Swift's imaginative singularity.

During Swift's English stay in 1702, 'the vanity of a young man prevailed', and Swift acknowledged that the allegorical *Discourse* on ancient Greece and Rome was his. He received appreciative notes from all of the lords who had escaped impeachment; indeed, he 'grew domestic' with Lord Halifax, who was briefly threatened by another crisis. Setting a pattern for the future, Swift now attached himself to Addison's patrons just when their ability to help him was reduced, and with of course none of the guarantees they had given Addison.[9] After visiting Moor Park in July, he spent most of August at Berkeley Castle, where he was charmed and newly inspired by Lady Betty. He then returned to Ireland, having set a rough pattern he would follow for another decade. Trips of varying length to England would relieve prolonged spells in Dublin and his country parishes. With Esther Johnson and Rebecca Dingley in place, and following him at a chaste distance on his Irish circuits, and with his Church livings providing a modest but sufficient income, his Hibernian existence was more or less defined. Notwithstanding the great furies of Archbishop King – who now held sway in the Dublin diocese and had plunged into a labyrinthine lawsuit to affirm his jurisdiction over the capital's other cathedral, Christ Church – the mood of Irish Anglicans was for a time unusually upbeat. The charming and magnificent Duke of Ormond, grandson of the troubled Civil War hero, took over as lord lieutenant. In 1704 a keystone of Swift's uncompromising politics was set in place when the Test Act, forbidding non-Anglicans from holding public office, was passed by the Irish Parliament. A lingering doubt in Swift's mind, however, was that, while further legislation very efficiently trampled on the last clutching fingers of Roman Catholic autonomy, not enough was being done against the Dissenting sects.

Swift wintered in England from November 1703 to the following May, and was distraught by the leniency the 'fanatics' were demanding and getting. This was the political climate in which he finally launched his *Tale of a Tub*, dedicated to Lord Somers, in 1704. There was a discrepancy, though, between the tremendous elegance of the dedication to Somers, cloaking its *sprezzatura* in a tradesman's bustle, and the *Tale*'s fierce partisanship against the sects, and for Swift this was to become a breaking point. If the Whig hierarchy continued to patronize England's Protestant Nonconformists – which was, arguably, the foundation of the true Whig movement – then Swift would need to part company.

## 2

Yet, if Swift was never a true Whig himself, many of his close associates were, and this made his dilemma personal as well as ideological. As a Protestant, he owed the absence of a Papist monarch in Ireland to King William's campaign and the subsequent settlement. Whig propaganda painted all Tories as fifth-columnists and Jacobites, ready to welcome King James with the first favourable wind; and, despite the hyperbole,

Jacobites did nestle at the Tory fringes. But the label seems always to have brought doubts. By instinct Swift was closer to a personage such as the Lord Lieutenant of Ireland he attended from the autumn of 1707 to the early summer of 1709: Thomas Herbert, the Earl of Pembroke. A sponsor of learning, 'meek in his behaviour, plain in his dress' and with a cruel stoop to his posture, Pembroke was reckoned 'a lover of the Constitution of his Country, without being of a Party, and yet esteemed of all Parties'.[10] Around this time Swift described himself in similar words. Another leading figure of whom he grew still fonder was James Butler, the second Duke of Ormond, Pembroke's predecessor at Dublin Castle. Ormond, like his grandfather, the first Duke, seemed to transcend petty divisions of party. He seemed pure soldier and courtier, bearing the standard of an earlier age. With such exemplars in mind, Swift preferred to argue, and would for some years still, that the terms 'Whig' and 'Tory' were redundant when it came to worthy substance: a true loyal subject did not require the distinction. Yet, despite strenuous efforts, the ongoing game of political chess, played out on an edgeless board, defied the rules Swift tried to set for it. Some pieces were white, the others black. Ormond might well have transcended party, but his associates did not: they were principally Tory; and the Duke's future, to Swift's horror, lay with the Jacobites and the Pretender.

One of Swift's relatives and earliest biographers quoted the following passage, from a pamphlet written in 1709. Here Swift is writing in the persona of an Irish Member of Parliament addressing a counterpart in Westminster:

> Whoever bears a true Veneration for the Glorious Memory of King *William*, as our great deliverer from *Popery* and *Slavery*; whoever is firmly loyal to our present Queen, with an utter Abhorrence and Detestation of the *Pretender*; whoever approves the Succession to the Crown in the House of *Hanover*, and is for preserving the Doctrine and Discipline of the Church of *England*, with an *Indulgence* for scrupulous Consciences; such a Man, we think, acts upon right Principles, and may be justly allowed a *Whig* . . .[11]

But in the last point wishful thinking was straining reality. Whigs were of course observing Anglicans, because the law obliged them to be. The true defenders of the Church of England, its Irish branch, and the doctrine and discipline of both were to be found among the Tories. The Whigs by tradition were the party of Dissenters, Nonconformists, 'fanatics'. This divide was rendered more complex in practice by the reality of how masters and servants and neighbours got on with one another. As Swift observed later, Whig lords and gentry tended to treat their Anglican chaplains much more courteously than Tory patrons who professed allegiance to what was often called 'The Church Party'.[12] His ongoing support from the Earl of Berkeley, for all Swift's grumbles, was a case in point. Prizing wit and manners in his acquaintance, for now Swift found more congenial company among the Whig intelligentsia. However, the agreement on essentials could be stretched only so far. As the early 1700s progressed, the Whigs were inclined to repeal the Test Act to satisfy their grassroots supporters. Swift opposed this movement with increasing bitterness, even as he dedicated successive publications to luminaries of the Whig Junto. He was torn: the Whigs vouchsafed an Ireland free of popery, but were too inclined to the other extreme; while mainstream Tories, he convinced himself, were as sound when it came to basic, Williamite 'revolution principles' as any Dissenter. Swift expressed his earnest concern at the failure to defend the Established Church in a series of papers that were sometimes comic in approach – such as his superb *Argument against Abolishing Christianity* – but entirely serious in their aim and content.

Swift was redoubtable, as he had to be, in defending his interests. His prebendary's stall and his livings a half-day's ride from the capital made him financially secure at least, and better off by far than the majority of clergymen on the island. His country parishes required some early outlay – once again, there was no house for him – but produced a very reasonable income soon afterwards; and as prebendary at St Patrick's he was incorporated into the central machinery of the Church of Ireland. He was hardly overtaxed by his duties. There was no need for him to live permanently in County Meath, and his life in Dublin combined access to influential circles with ample time for study and writing, not to mention long trips to England. A glimpse of the pleasant group of friends he left in Dublin on these visits emerges in his letters to one Reverend William Tisdall in the winter of 1703/4.

In December he wrote in the midst of a crisis over a move to block the Dissenters from recognition within the state. In the nights after a crucial bill was debated and rejected, he told Tisdall, 'I noted the dogs in the street more contumelious and quarrelsome than usual . . . a committee of Whig and Tory cats had a very warm and loud debate upon the roof of our house.' He could afford the light touch of humour. He was inclined to favour the bill, and, although his prominent Whig acquaintances, the Earl of Peterborough, the Bishop of Salisbury and Lord Somers himself, said there could be no harm to the Church if it were rejected, he had been spared the need to question their assurances. On the back of his earlier *Discourse of the Contests and Dissensions*, he had been 'mightily urged by some great people to publish my opinion'. For now his mind turned warmly to his Dublin friends, especially 'Mistress Johnson'. With a love of a good hoax that would manifest itself regularly, he gave the Reverend Tisdall a good way of outwitting her: 'it is a new-fashioned way of being witty, and they call it a *bite*.' She was a vigorous moralist, and clearly took it to heart when something lax or outrageous was proposed. Swift instructed Tisdall:

> You must ask a bantering question, or tell some damned lie in a serious manner, and then she will answer or speak as if you were in earnest: and then cry you, 'Madam, there's a *bite*.' I would not have you undervalue this, for it is the constant amusement in Court, and every where else among the great people; and I let you know it, in order to have it obtain among you, and teach a new refinement.[13]

He would prove less than pleased, on occasion, when his turn came to be 'bitten'. He despised banter as much as he knew Johnson did. It was not altogether advice he could swear was the best he might offer.

A couple of months later, on receiving Tisdall's reply, Swift wrote back to him as one who was his first friend 'after the ladies'. Just a little tartly, he suggested Tisdall might think differently of both them and himself if he had read *their* letters to London. Tisdall had set up his 'establishment' near the ladies' home; Swift – teeth somewhat close together – said that he was pleased. He imagined the scene of Tisdall's visits, describing Esther Johnson's 'chamber' in William Street as a 'Little England'. Swift assumed the voice of their tutor and guardian, instructing his deputy: 'I am mightily afraid the ladies are very idle, and do not mind their book. Pray put them upon reading; and be always teaching something to Mrs Johnson, because she is good at comprehending, remembering, and retaining.' An atmosphere of companionable card games and pun contests is evoked. Esther is praised for her skill in the latter, and chided for taking it to excess; she had choked on a crumb, and her first word on regaining her breath had been a pun. Her housemate, Dingley, is pardoned for her blunders, her defects of wit. Both had been 'bitten' by Tisdall's provocations; well done on that, wrote Swift. But the ladies, he mentioned, had informed him of some blunders

made by Tisdall himself. He apologized for not having replied sooner
– 'I have been so long and so frequently pursued with a little paltry ailment of a noise in my ears that I could never get humour and time to
answer your letter.' He skirted, icily, around the point on which Tisdall
evidently wanted a clear declaration, advice and, in some form, permission; instead, he offered hints on how Tisdall might advance his career.
He should do what Swift manifestly hadn't: meditate long on some
theological issue, 'some worthy subject', and not think at all of 'writing
for the publick'.[14]

Tisdall had fallen in love with Esther, or at least had singled her out
as a bride; and he asked for Swift's help in securing a match. Perceiving
rightly how close Swift and Esther were, he also felt obliged to ensure
he would not face Swift as a rival. Swift's response was to wonder
coolly at Tisdall's audacity. A letter or two may be missing from the
time before the surviving correspondence resumes, in April 1704. Swift
was categorical in rebutting Tisdall's claim that he was behaving
unkindly, assuring him 'that there is more unaccountability in your letter's little finger, than in mine's whole body. And one strain I observe in
it, which is frequent enough; you talk in a mystical sort of way, as if
you would have me believe I had some great design, and that you had
found it out.'

Swift had already mastered a way of plucking the rhetorical plumage
from an opponent's argument as if it were a songbird for a pie. He
implied Tisdall's phrasing had something in common with the blustering
Fluellen in *Henry V*: not at all the least point of interest in this final letter
to Tisdall is Swift's familiarity with Shakespeare. The letter shows Swift
teasing, inquiring, echoing the presumptions and errors of his rival;
offering to 'talk starchly', like a false prude, inviting his correspondent
to reflect on his mistakes, but above all assuming an air of unassailable
probity. He would use such tactics on much stronger antagonists, but
was perfectly willing to deploy them on a stripling. The letter reveals his
unfair advantage; it displays Swift, too, as more than a bit of a bruiser
– a writer who fought, and aimed to conquer.

He took on the proportions of a grandee of Brobdingnag. 'I am
extremely concerned to find myself unable to persuade you into a true
opinion of your own littleness,' he told the suitor coolly. Tisdall, he surmised, had grown 'mighty proud', and with good reason, if Esther had
indeed accepted him. But she had not, nor was she likely to. He assured
him that Tisdall had nothing to fear from Swift making a proposal of
marriage – although 'if my fortunes and humour served me to think of

that state, I should certainly, among all persons on earth, make your choice; because I never saw that person whose conversation I entirely valued but hers.'

He objected not from personal interest – he was willing even to 'make overtures' on Tisdall's behalf to Esther's mother – but from his conviction that Tisdall was blatantly inadequate. How could such a person suppose he was worthy of Stella? He would not even condescend to banish Tisdall from the pleasant realm of William Street; the challenge was beneath him. As a point of pride he even declined to dissuade Johnson from considering Tisdall's suit. The show of magnificent indifference in these letters is so powerfully made that one can forget that Swift is, in fact, seeing off his rival and defending his territory. The episode illustrates his strength of will in many aspects: holding on to his blessings, disposing of a challenge and – not least, perhaps – ensuring Esther retained the status that suited him best.[15]

He passed a long unbroken period in Ireland from the end of 1704 till almost the winter of 1707. In Ireland, this time was characterized by turbulence in Dublin, as Convocation, the ecclesiastical assembly, invariably displeased the Irish Lords and Commons; and by comparative respite in and around Laracor. He developed amiable contacts with his agent, Isaiah Parvisol, who collected his tithes and oversaw his land in his absence; with Joe Beaumont, a merchant of Trim who ran errands for him, dabbled with the mystery of longitude and other mathematical tortures and suffered periodic bouts of madness; and with the then Rector of Trim, John Stearne. These and other local friends helped to make up a table for cards – although Swift would soon enough hold all guilty of sins against him.

He was still a near-tireless walker and rider, and his parishes gave him extensive opportunities for exercise. Long, long stretches of his overland journeys through England, always through Leicestershire to pay his now ailing mother a visit, would be on horseback. He developed an intermittent fear, in fact, of coaches overturning. He would use his physical exertions to ward off ill-health; for his vertigo would strike without warning. He had mentioned his ear troubles to Tisdall, but they were clearly more than 'paltry'. He made notes of the bouts in his account books: 'Often giddy God help me,' is one typical record of ten days of trouble, at the end of which he made an extra purchase of brandy to diminish the symptoms – or at least to soothe his spirits.[16] Still following the old dictum of the Temples' – in fairness, of many contemporary medical authorities – he would remain convinced that fresh fruit brought on or worsened the hideous dizziness. It was sometimes all he could do at times to resist a plate of apricots. Yet the effort was worth it, since he dreaded the disgrace of an attack occurring while he was in company, and strove to prevent the condition interfering with his business. As for other fixed aspects of his life, Swift developed for his illness its own gossamer web of fine, barely visible literary meanings, spanning both his own work and the wider canon, setting puzzles and traps for the scholar. In a letter of 1724, in the midst of writing *Gulliver*, Swift described tinnitus filling his head 'with the noise of seven water mills'.[17] Besides being simply descriptive, these mills instantly transported his correspondent to the booming darkness in which Don Quixote and Cervantes believe they have encountered a band of angry giants – only to discover at dawn the sound is made by plashing waterwheels, not snoring colossuses. Swift himself, by association, becomes a tacitly Quixotic figure; and thus, implicitly, he makes light of his condition. Awful though it may be, he sees the disease for what it is, as Sancho at dawn sees not a ravening giant but a physical and familiar landmark. The strand of allusion connected with his illness also runs into Swift's fiction. In the second book of the *Travels*, when Gulliver is first captured by a Brobdingnagian farmer, the titan holding him tries to communicate, but his huge voice sounds in Gulliver's ears like the roar (or distinctive 'clack', as Swift had it elsewhere) of a watermill.[18] The echo of Cervantes makes Gulliver in turn seem like Quixote. The rest of Gulliver's stay offers an inverted parallel, however, since the Brobdingnagians are shown to be anything but the cruel and tyrannous giants regularly encountered by knights of old. Paradoxically, their civilization is the one Gulliver is most complimentary about, if one excludes his final obsession with the Houyhnhnms. If the folk of Brobdingnag damage or threaten someone as tiny as Gulliver, it is only because of how they are built – on the scale of a European waterwheel. They are absolved from conscious malice in the harm they do him. Swift came to treat his illness with similar resignation when its symptoms descended; but never lost his anxiety about the onset of an attack.

During the unusually long period Swift spent in Ireland in 1704–7, a signal change occurred in the relationship between England and Scotland. The challenge from the Pretender had placed the succession in crisis; and technically the Scots were free to name James Francis Edward as the heir to their throne. For the English guardians of the revolution settlement, almost no cost at all was too high for preventing this turn of events. The alternatives, at some point in the near future, would be war or a treaty of union binding the Crowns. On the Scottish side, despite deep instinctive opposition in many quarters, union with England was desirable for financial reasons. But it was a dilemma: in exchange for economic partnership, the Scots would have to sacrifice their Parliament. Thus, in the spring of 1706, a delegation of largely suspicious Scottish peers travelled south to strike a bargain. The negotiators occupied separate chambers in a Treasury building in Whitehall, the converted Cockpit Theatre – an aptly named venue for the fight that lay ahead, crowded with ghosts from earlier dramatic clashes. The agreement took shape not through talks but through ongoing transfers of formal notes. Lord Somers was consulted to resolve outstanding points of dispute, and confirmed his reputation as the leading constitutional expert of the era. With the further aid of bribery, and the surreptitious activity of spies (including Daniel Defoe) recruited by Robert Harley, the parties made a deal. The Treaty of Union, signed in July 1706, was ratified at Westminster in November, and in Edinburgh in January 1707.

However grudgingly many in Scotland accepted the union, in Ireland it provoked dismay. The economic privileges enjoyed by England over Ireland were now extended to the northern kingdom: Dublin was left in the role of Cinderella to London and Edinburgh's ugly stepsisters, with no fairy godmother in sight. In protest, Swift constructed a slightly overwrought allegory in prose, 'The Story of the Injured Lady'. The English lover had abandoned his Irish beloved. Casting Ireland as England's jilted mistress, however, brought romantic and carnal connotations Swift evidently felt uncomfortable pursuing; yet, by avoiding them, his conceit seemed coy. Conceivably Swift was also aware that an idea of Ireland as a beautiful woman married to a 'rightful king' was a motif in much Gaelic political poetry. The idea became something of a stock concept as time went on; in earlier seventeenth-century Irish poems, however, the personification is psychologically much more involving than Swift's attempt, since the verse is continually coping with the thought that Erin's sufferings are sent as punishment for her sins. In *aislingi*, Irish dream-poems, the vision of this woman as Ireland was increasingly associated with the hope that foreign rule one day might end.[19] Whether Swift had any conscious intentions with respect to that tradition, it highlights his basic discomfort with the tone his 'Injured Lady' obliged him to adopt. The mode of plaintive sincerity was not for Swift. He realized there was a problem – and left the essay in manuscript. Much more effective was his short poem 'Verses Said to be Written on the Union'.

The Queen has lately lost a Part
Of her entirely-*English* Heart,
For want of which by way of Botch
She piec'd it up again with *Scotch*.
Blest Revolution, which creates
Divided Hearts, united States.[20]

The lines are at once daring and cunningly reserved, leaving it for the reader to decide whether Queen Anne gave away the lost piece of her heart or had it taken from her. Unlike the Williamite revolution, which rescued the kingdoms from Papism, this one forcing them together was only sardonically 'blest'. Whatever the advantages, the treaty was a botched job when it came to national feeling – as the events of 1715 and '45, and the eventual clearances of the Highlands, would demonstrate horrifically.

For the present, the union placed all Irish business with England, including Swift's, on a still more urgent footing: for the pickings to be gained would be slimmer than ever. When Swift returned to England in 1707, he had a new mission. In 1704 Queen Anne had agreed that the portions of English clerical incomes known as the 'First Fruits and Twentieth Parts', which were paid to the Crown, should be placed in a fund to augment the livings of the poorer Anglican clergy; almost immediately, the Church in Ireland had begun petitioning for the Queen to extend this famous and long-appreciated 'bounty' to her Irish priests. Although a promotion continued to elude Swift, Archbishop King appointed him as one of the chief petitioners for the First Fruits. He had high expectations, and an equally high set of well-disposed acquaintances: Ormond and Pembroke (and key members of their respective entourages), Berkeley, supporters among the Junto lords. While these authorities were still failing to lift him in the Church, he was compensated by the fact that some of them, along with fellow wits, were beginning to recognize his talent.

A somewhat vagrant life, taking ship every couple of years, boolying to the country for the summer, suited him well enough. In the Irish and English capitals, Swift changed his lodgings frequently during these years. A room for him was still available in a relative's house, such as his uncle William's, in the city, if he cared to take it; it is probable he did not. As chaplain to Berkeley, he moved with the Lord Justice from Chapelizod to a berth in the ramshackle Castle as occasion required. Otherwise, he had to make do with digs in town and a cottage in a country parish. One address at which he made a careful point of not residing, however frequently he visited, was the tall terraced house on William Street where he had installed Esther Johnson and Rebecca Dingley in 1701. In both Ireland and England, meanwhile, he was quite often given the comfort of a guest-room in the mansion or townhouse of an acquaintance. Again, failing that, in London he would seek out a set that fulfilled his requirements of cleanliness, centrality and chimneys that spread as little soot as possible. Outside, the lace and powder of the beaux drew his contempt, and the faces of town beauties, bleached and rouged, revolted him. Swift himself, though, was careful of his peri-wig and gown, and the rootless life pursuing fame was not unhappy for him. During his stays in London he exchanged news and views in the principal coffee-houses, in the Rose Tavern on Drury Lane or in a decent chop-house; and when he felt indisposed he would send out for cutlets to eat at his own table.

Since London's first coffee-house was established in or around 1652 – a plaque in an alley off Cornhill marks the site – its successors had rapidly made themselves integral to civic life. As an institution the coffee-house had somewhat ambiguous puritanical origins, as a temper-ate alternative to the tavern. Before the Great Fire, most were to be found above another shop or office. The arrangements and clientele evolved radically in a short time, but something of the ambience described below was preserved, as the years went by, since, like any meeting-place, the coffee-houses furnished thoughts for sceptical and humorous observers of life.

> Mounting a few steps, we made our way into a big room which was equipped in an old-fashioned way. There was a rabble going hither and thither, reminding me of a swarm of rats in a ruinous cheese-store. Some came, others went; some were scribbling, others were talking; some were drinking [coffee], some smoking, and some arguing; the whole place stank of tobacco like the cabin of a barge.[21]

Over the decades, as they sprang up in scores across London, punch and wine crept on to the menu of many coffee-houses; playing cards, origin-ally prohibited, found their way on to the tables. In a coffee-house, on paying a penny for admission, one found refreshment, often teas and chocolate as well as the house's principal brew, a chessboard and a bible – but much more besides. First, there was company, and a choice of coffee-house invariably depended on the professional set or political

tribe that gathered there; and, second, there was news, from the mouths
of fellow customers and from the latest papers strewn over the tables
and benches. While varying greatly in character, the coffee-houses were
unified by the part they played in fostering freedom of speech. For this
reason, they were feared and vilified by government throughout the Restoration: Charles II nursed ambitions to close down the lot of them. The
coffee-houses had always been frequented by reliable and conservative
citizens, who preferred the non-alcoholic atmosphere; but they achieved
full legitimacy only in the 1690s, when it became common for some of
the foremost courtiers to take their coffee and snuff in a few select establishments.

By Swift's time, many coffee-houses had built up substantial archives
of past publications – official, poetic and polemical. Notices would typically be posted up all over the walls, offering rewards, calling for
information, issuing threats; and, while political or literary debate dominated the main smoke-filled lounge, all kinds of business might be
taking place in the shop's connecting rooms. Auctions were frequently
held there, deals struck and stocks monitored. The coffee-house became
the proverbial haunt of the confidence trickster, on the lookout for gullible strangers and novices. To all but a few humane and forward-looking
punters, meanwhile, some quite legal transactions performed over coffee
were unconsciously immoral. For sometimes a slave would be sold on
the premises, after an advertisement had invited potential buyers to
come to inspect the captive in the days beforehand. A human being
might be sold 'by the candle' with as little fuss as a batch of rare books,
an antique curiosity or a piece of furniture.

The coffee-houses were milestones and landmarks, public yet club-
like: one's post might be delivered there, a parcel dispatched or a sum
of money safely deposited for collection. Privacy, admittedly, might be
hard to come by, much less secrecy: proprietors were notorious gossips
and messages were easily traced. Robert Harley once spotted one of
Esther Johnson's letters waiting for Swift in a glass-fronted case where
envelopes and packages were stacked. Harley, one of the land's foremost spy-masters, noticed the similarity between Swift's hand and
Esther's. She still rounded her letters as her sometime writing-master
did, and Swift reported that Harley had asked, 'How long I was in the
habit of writing to myself.'[22] As his influence rose after 1710, Swift
visited the principal coffee-houses more rarely, from concern for security and distaste for meeting former associates. During this, his first
decade of mature literary activity and political canvassing, he fre-

quented them freely. His journals and letters also indicate that the crowd and chatter could test his patience. He was a fastidious critic of conversation, and in a late work declared that the worst talk he ever heard was at Will's, 'where the wits (as they were called) used formerly to assemble'.[23]

He had further sources of more personal welcome, as a regular guest in family homes. In one of these, on his stays in London, he had formed another major attachment; and, as it happened, coffee was indispensable to the relationship from the outset.

# 3

As she first sensed only vaguely, Esther Johnson had now a 'rival' to contend with, a younger woman for whom Swift's feelings were ambiguous. In addition, she and the woman were namesakes. Esther Vanhomrigh, whom Swift referred to as 'Vanessa' in his poetry and 'Hessy' at home, was the elder daughter in a moderately prosperous family of four children. In Dublin, Hessy's surname was apparently pronounced 'Vannummery'.[24] She was born in 1688, the year of revolution, and was thus some seven years Esther's junior. She was therefore not yet twenty, and Swift more than forty, when they became intimate. After the death of Vanessa's father, a wealthy Dublin-based merchant of Dutch extraction, the Vanhomrighs moved to London in 1707, and became part of the same circle of writers and politicians in which Swift also moved. In December, Swift joined them on the road to the capital at an inn near Dunstable. Hessy dropped her cup of coffee by the hearth. Stopping at the same place some five years later, Swift regretted not having a diamond to commemorate the moment in a windowpane. If that seems uncharacteristically romantic of him, it ought to be mentioned that he expressed it in a letter to Hessy's mother, and that he was sorry he couldn't write 'any' of the family's names in the glass.[25] He would never be one for carving hearts with arrows through them. Still, the spillage and the broken china were an omen; 'coffee' became his and Hessy's code-word for the time they spent in private together, and the dropped cup presaged much more than shattered crockery. By Swift's account at least, their friendship developed from the time of the incident at Dunstable. During his trips to England from 1707 on, he could also withdraw to a back room in Mistress Vanhomrigh's house, for coffee and sweets with her daughter Hessy.

In appearance Vanhomrigh was said to be less striking than Johnson. She also didn't fit as well in the respectable parlour-visiting circuit, and Swift's more narrow-minded acquaintances tended to dislike her. 'She was fond of dress: impatient to be admired: very romantic in her turn of mind; superior, in her own opinion, to all her sex: full of gaiety and pride.'[26] Yet, if you suppress the vinegarish and chauvinistic tone here, the sketch captures the vivacity that attracted Swift. On his side, he always spoke of her as his pupil.

> I think there is not a better girl upon earth. I have a mighty friendship for her. She had good principles, and I have corrected all her faults; but I cannot persuade her to read, though she has an understanding, memory and taste that would bear great improvement. But she is incorrigibly idle and lazy – thinks the world made for nothing but perpetual pleasure.

His experience with Jane Waring in the 1690s appears to have turned him decisively against marriage. His unconventional bond with Johnson had provided a soul-mate, under strictly regulated conditions. In his other dealings with women of 'marriageable age' he looked only for the corrective freedom a tutor might exercise. He failed to realize before it was too late that Vanhomrigh either believed these limits were a front or that she would be able to break through them. When financial difficulties overshadowed her family, it pained Swift to observe how Hessy 'lost a good deal of her mirth'; he suppressed the part he played in her growing sadness, or remained unconscious of it.[27]

'Hessy' Vanhomrigh was expansive and open-hearted as Esther Johnson was reserved and, to many, inscrutable. Yet, although distressingly little remains on the record in Johnson's own words, she was emphatically no person to be trifled with. She never interrupted or corrected others' common social blunders in their presence; yet she would tolerate no impropriety on the topic of religion or 'any breach of truth or honour'. Fools would find themselves treated to a merciless retort when they paused for breath from their gabbling. She knew people talked of her relationship with Swift, and defying them took moral courage. Her reserves at moments of physical threat were remarkable too. One night in her mid-twenties she donned a black hood and lifted the sash of the dining-room window; leaning out, unseen and unheard, she aimed the pistol she had carried with her at one of a gang of burglars trying to break in below. Dingley and the female servants they employed stood helpless with fear. In the street, the 'parcel of rogues' carried off the man Esther had shot, who died of his wounds the next day.[28]

While admiring beauty, fastidious, in fact, about hygiene and the decency with which it was maintained, Swift had little interest in turning a head that was merely beautiful. He bonded with personalities that recognized and in their own ways equalled his unusualness as a person. By the age of forty he had won the love – for want of a better word – of two women; and, while most accounts of his life point out the tutorial nature he forced on the association, Swift himself frequently described both Johnson and Vanhomrigh – Stella and Vanessa – as people he was unable to teach: in Vanhomrigh's case, because of her refusal to accept the role of mere pupil; and, in Johnson's, because of an independence of character he could only stand and admire. Vanhomrigh's voice will in time reach us quite clearly through the letters she wrote to Swift in the last years of her short life; but the real scandal of Johnson's historical existence, as with so many women in the early-modern period, is that her perspective has not survived for us in writing. We can only guess at it from echoes and reflections in the vast journal Swift wrote to her in the years 1710–14, from his subsequent descriptions and from the words of a few male visitors to his eventual home in the deanery of St Patrick's in Dublin. She has too often been interpreted as his suspended appendage, deprived of marital status, yet retained as a chaste consort. The facts as we have them equally support an idea of Esther Johnson as a woman who was for the most content to be liberated from drudgery and motherhood – although there is anecdotal evidence that Swift's dealings with Vanhomrigh did make her jealous.

Swift would prove quite comfortable with fame; but he treasured only discriminating compliments. Though wider recognition came later, he was not long in gaining the respect and admiration of some of the country's best writers. Among these Joseph Addison made his name in 1704 with a long poem in praise of Marlborough and his series of victories against the French. *The Campaign*, perhaps the most gentle-minded description of war ever written, captured the mood of the moment. In its most memorable passage, a portrait of Marlborough in the field, Addison drew on recent impressions of the great storm that devastated much of England in November 1703 as well as the hubristic paintings he had seen at Versailles of Louis XIV. In those high-set canvases, Louis is depicted as Jupiter, hurling thunderbolts; setting Marlborough amid chaos, Addison gave him a humbler, much more attractive air of seraphic blitheness.

> So when an angel by divine command
> With rising tempests shakes a guilty land,
> Such as of late o'er pale Britannia past,
> Calm and serene he drives the furious blast;
> And pleas'd th' Almighty's orders to perform,
> Rides in the whirlwind and directs the storm.[29]

Instead of displacing the Almighty, Marlborough acts as his agent: and there was truth in Addison's strong claims for the general's calm. Knocked from his horse, threatened by pikes, saved by a whisker from a cannonball that cut a lieutenant's head clean off, upon surviving any number of near-misses Marlborough never lost his focus on the battle. Since the triumph of *The Campaign*, Addison had accompanied Halifax on a mission to Hanover and published an account of travels in Italy. He was now a prominent member of the Whiggish Kit-Cat Club (along with Congreve), close to the Junto and well-beloved of all those loyal to the war, from Marlborough down. Inscribed in one copy of his *Travels* that Addison presented as a gift was the following dedication:

> To Dr Jonathan Swift, the most agreeable companion, the truest friend and the greatest genius of his age, this book is presented by his most humble servant the author.[30]

How did Swift earn this accolade from the unofficial laureate of the day? His *Contests and Dissensions*, his pamphlets on the state of the Church, all would appeal to the pious and serious-minded Addison – who, despite his greater 'tolerance', disliked the religion of the sects. Meanwhile in terms of sheer technique, Swift had already shown unrivalled range in highly structured longer works and impromptu miniatures alike.

One of Swift's regular chores when he stayed with the Earl of Berkeley was to read from some 'moral or religious discourse' to the Countess. Among her favourite improving texts was the book *Meditations* (or 'Occasional Reflections') by Robert Boyle. Swift himself was not such a great admirer of the work. During the trip he made in 1703 (although the date is disputed), he slipped a composition of his own among the leaves of Boyle's treasured reflections. Picking up the book, he turned to a page entitled 'A Meditation upon a Broom-stick'. Lady Berkeley expressed some surprise at the title, but Swift, 'with an inflexible gravity of countenance', delivered the short reflection on the sad and nasty fate of the average broom-stick.

> This single Stick, which you now behold ingloriously lying in that neglected Corner, I once knew in a flourishing State in a Forest . . . It is now handled by every dirty Wench . . . At length, worn to the Stumps in the Service of the Maids, it is either thrown out of Doors, or condemned to its last use of kindling a Fire. When I beheld this, I sighed, and said within my self SURELY MORTAL MAN IS A BROOM-STICK.[31]

The humbled broom with its shabby periwig of strands becomes a truly versatile metaphor of a man's pride and vanity. The short piece is essential to any anthology of Swift; far from immoral, as early readers found it, the hilarity is all at the expense of Boyle's rather tedious and predictable *Meditations*. On its own terms, Swift's 'Meditation' displays very well his habit of looking closely at everyday things and imagining them in an unfamiliar light. The faculty furnished material both for fantasy and for realism: he would draw on it to the utmost in the Brobdingnagian and Lilliputian sections of the *Travels* – observing, for instance, that an apple would seem like a 'Bristol barrel' to a person six inches high.[32]

But Swift had already written a sustained exercise in something like the vein of his 'Meditation upon a Broom-stick'. In 1704 *A Tale of a Tub* was published; and with it another favourite shorter work of Swift's, again dating from the late 1690s, 'The Battle of the Books'. In the latter, after much squabbling, the books representing Modern and Ancient authors fight a pitched battle, divided by the issue Richard Bentley and William Wotton had contested with Sir William Temple's defenders back in the 1690s. Other writers might have developed the allegory and grounded it, as Swift did, with physical detail. But Swift's powers of observation were consummate. One touch of genius was to imagine and show how a book might really become human-like. Here he describes the galled goddess Criticism taking bibliographical shape in the library, in order to speak with her son, Wotton. She wishes to avoid dazzling 'his Mortal Sight', and so:

> She therefore gathered up her Person into an *Octavo* Compass [the small format in which Wotton's works had been published]: Her Body grew white and arid, and split in pieces with Driness; the thick turned

into Pastboard, and the thin into Paper, upon which her Parents and Children artfully strowed a Black Juice, or Decoction of Gall and Soot, in Form of Letters; her Head, and Voice, and Spleen, kept their primitive Form, and that which before, was a Cover of Skin, did still continue so. In which Guise, she march'd on toward the *Moderns*, undistinguishable in Shape and Dress from the *Divine Bentley*, *Wotton's* dearest Friend.[33]

The battle continues until a rupture – or wound – in the text conceals the outcome of the ensuing struggle between Ancients and Moderns. Swift could not pre-empt the verdict of history; although it is grimly clear where he felt the moral superiority lay.

'What a vile trick has that rogue played on me,' exclaimed Lady Berkeley, giving way to laughter as the company roared at the joke on Boyle. Her daughter Lady Betty (later Germain), Swift's lifelong friend, remembered the moment well, the Countess having told her visitors about the devout text on a broom-stick. Swift, having 'pretended business', had withdrawn from the parlour, leaving the stage set. Yet on publication his 'Meditation' was widely viewed as a slur on Boyle, a 'great and pious man' (whom Swift dismissed as 'a very silly writer').[34]

With his *Tale of a Tub* and vignettes such as that on the broom-stick, Swift was taking quite some risks – with superiors both in the Church and in polite society. Queen Anne's chief spiritual adviser, John Sharp, the Archbishop of York, allegedly declared him unworthy of advancement. Yet the power of Swift's gift made indulging it addictive. By concentrating his intellectual powers on the popular presses rather than on theological debate, he was soon firmly established as a leading wit; one, indeed, who by 1708 might well have lacked an equal. The social bond was crucial, moreover: to Addison, Swift was equally 'the greatest genius' and 'the most agreeable companion'. It is worth bearing in mind that the many volumes of Swift's work may represent only a fraction of his wit, ripostes and hoaxes occasioned by the moment and lost to time in coffee-houses and other long-vanished venues, as wine was poured or beans crackled in the roaster. Along with Addison, Swift had made similarly powerful impressions on Matthew Prior, an accomplished poet and minor politician who was currently suffering for his Tory associations; Ambrose Philips, a dreamy draper's son from Shrewsbury who wrote accomplished pastoral; and Addison's oldest friend, the playwright and retired soldier Captain Richard Steele.

Steele was a volatile sort whose high-flown moral outbursts were not always backed up by his actions. He made up an odd couple of the classic kind with Addison, the burly, round-faced doer to his schoolmate's pallid aesthete. Addison apparently disliked to sit in a group of more than three; when he did he spent most of the evening in silence. Steele had the defiant ease of a trooper wherever you put him. He was also a helpless spender in constant search of a profitable venture. Not long after meeting Swift over dinner at Addison's in March 1708, Steele saw the possibilities that lay in a mind that could discern the oddest features in 'obvious and common subjects', should it be turned to the right medium. Steele's interest was catalysed when one of Swift's creations became the talk of the town. In January, an almanac by one Isaac Bickerstaff had predicted the death of another, very famous and highly contentious astrologer, John Partridge. 'I have consulted the Star of his Nativity by my own Rules,' intoned Bickerstaff, 'and find that he will infallibly die upon the 29th of March next.'[35] When Steele met Swift at supper on the first of that month, London was still reeling from Partridge's furious – and faintly, perhaps, alarmed – retort to this horoscope. Who was Bickerstaff, the city wondered? In early April, Partridge sought to have the last word by crowing over his adversary's mistake: he had survived Bickerstaff's prediction. But this only invited a final, killing rebuttal. The poor man, replied Bickerstaff; Partridge didn't realize he was dead.

Although little known now, the name Bickerstaff belongs among a highly select group of characters' names. Along with Don Quixote, Robinson Crusoe, Sherlock Holmes and of course Gulliver himself, Swift's astrologer took on a life far beyond the edges of his first creator's pages. 'Unauthorized' papers by Bickerstaff were soon cropping up everywhere, along with countless answers and amendments to his predictions, as they would for many years to come. Appropriating these responses, Richard Steele adopted Isaac as the voice of his enormously popular and influential magazine the *Tatler*. Pleased by the attention, Swift supplied 'hints' for Steele's early issues with a generosity he later regretted. When the *Tatler*s were bound up in volumes a few years later, Steele paid a somewhat laboured tribute: Swift was an 'agreeable gentleman' whose 'certain uncommon way of thinking' proved vital to the task Steele had set himself.[36]

Swift, despite his preferred anonymity, was very touchy about such matters. In 1710 further editions were brought out of *A Tale of a Tub*. One was a pirated version of the text, which enraged Swift on two counts: first by naming him, and second by claiming he had collaborated on the book. His co-author was said to be his cousin and old schoolmate Thomas Swift. The mere idea made Swift fume. He blamed his publisher,

Benjamin Tooke, for not getting the authorized edition into print quickly enough, and deduced that Thomas had been bagging credit where none was due: 'I cannot but think that little Parson-cousin of mine is at the bottom of this.'[37] In his vehement 'Apology' – that is, not a retraction but a 'reasoned defence' of the work – Swift addressed all those who had shown their ignorance by attacking the *Tale* as diminutive creatures. He spoke from on high, yet with a Brobdingnagian carelessness about his manifest superiority. 'They are indeed like Annuals that grow about a young Tree, and seem to vye with it for a Summer, but fall and die with the Leaves in Autumn, and are never heard of any more.'[38] This was his verdict on those who 'answered' firm-rooted books such as his. His attitude was gargantuan in its assurance.

The friendship with Addison and Steele nevertheless showed that Swift could be open to criticism – from a sufficiently respected source – and eager to improve a piece of writing. He followed Addison's guidance to rework one of his choicest and pleasantest poems, *Baucis and Philemon* – possibly the highest measure of his regard for the younger craftsman. In a work of 200 lines, 'Mr *Addison* made him blot out fourscore, add fourscore, and alter fourscore.'[39] Swift's poem adapted Ovid's tale of Jupiter and Apollo travelling to earth in the guise of mortals; conceivably the two 'brother hermits, saints by trade' are burlesque alter egos for Addison and Swift themselves. Arriving at a village, the deities seek out locals who will treat them hospitably, and are disappointed by all except an old couple. Having delightfully translated passages from Ovid himself, Addison was well qualified to judge Swift's proficiency; but he ended up cancelling passages exhibiting what Steele correctly saw was one of Swift's singular strengths – an unusual but still very concrete perception of ordinary things.

It would be unjust to suggest Addison's edit cancelled the poem's colour and homeliness entirely. Although his amendments have routinely been criticized, the revised version gives the best passages a prominence they lack in Swift's more copious draft. The two saintly travellers, disconsolate, at last arrive at the home of Yeoman Philemon and his wife, Baucis.

> And then the Hospitable Sire
> Bid *Goody Baucis* mend the Fire;
> While He from out of Chimney took
> A Flitch of Bacon off the Hook;
> And freely from the fattest Side
> Cut out large Slices to be fry'd.

This is one of the most welcome and nourishing suppers in English poetry. As a reward for the hospitality, the angelic guests transform the elderly couple's home into a church. The metamorphosis is wonderfully observed. The kettle rises up a chimney that widens into a steeple, and at the top swells into a church-bell. The spit-turner on the hearth, which has almost lost the art of roasting from lack of meat to practise with, becomes a clock. A chair becomes a pulpit; the bed splits into rows of pews. Philemon and Baucis gain the right clothes for a parson and his wife. After many cheerful years, at the brink of death they are turned into yews, side by side in the churchyard, having left the parish in a thriving state for their successors. And there they stand:

> 'Till once, a Parson of our Town,
> To mend his Barn, cut *Baucis* down;
> At which, 'tis hard to be believ'd,
> How much the other Tree was griev'd,
> Grew Scrubby, dy'd a-top, was stunted:
> So, the next Parson stubb'd and burnt it.[40]

Casual sacrilege, grief and decay for the survivor until eventual extinction: Swift's abruptly pessimistic expectations are given the floor at the end, with no note of appeal or outrage, since none would help or even be heard. *Baucis and Philemon* encapsulates Swift's generous love for the institution he served and the humaneness he believed it promoted; and it also makes plain the limits of his hopes for his parishes in Meath and the overall Church establishment. His bleak sense of what lay in store makes all the more striking his work as a builder, a planter and a gardener at Laracor, and as a tireless campaigner in London.

In its easy classicism and pointed yet understated doctrinal allegiances, the poem reflects Swift's immovably traditional outlook, while the Bickerstaff papers seem to indicate an edgier inclination towards modernity. The science of astrology was still widely credited: a generation earlier John Aubrey, a fellow of the Royal Society, had included the horoscopes, whenever he could find them, on all the worthies whose 'Brief Lives' he recorded. Swift, though, displayed no interest in his birth chart, which cast him (rather accurately, it must be said) as a wilful and prepossessing Sagittarius. Yet the ultimately conservative agenda behind the Bickerstaff hoax squared its world-view firmly with that of *Baucis and Philemon*. The pamphlets posing as almanacs attacked the forces of Nonconformism through the compelling association their joke created

between charlatanism and Whiggery, hypocrisy and Dissent. Quacks
were equated with the adherents of party in general: 'To mention no
more of their impertinent Predictions: What have we to do with their
Advertisements about Pills, and Drinks for the Venereal Disease, or their
mutual Quarrels in Verse and Prose of Whig and Tory? wherewith the
Stars have little to do.'[41] Yet his principal target, Partridge, belonged to
the Dissenting camp and had his allies on the Whig side. Partridge, naturally, had no crucial role in the state: he was an extremist, a radical, a
republican – allegedly a member of the Calf's Head Club, which celebrated the decapitation of Charles I each year with a grisly feast of
veal.[42] Still, for all Steele and Addison's admiration, these works already
signalled the issue that would push Swift away from his respected
friends. Addison, despite his own background as a clergyman's son,
could reconcile the old Church with the movement for reform with a
confidence unimaginable in Swift.

Church business remained Swift's first concern on his visits to London. *Baucis and Philemon*, first printed as two-penny pamphlet in 1709,
illustrates how his ecclesiastical and literary purposes could intersect;
but it could do little to get official wheels turning. The remittance of the
Irish clergy's First Fruits, some years now after Queen Anne's Bounty
passed the seal in England, was still no closer. Moves to liberate and
empower Presbyterians and the sects, in contrast, seemed to be gaining
strength relentlessly. By the spring of 1708 the conflict was intensifying
in Swift's mind between his cordial relationships with Whigs and his
core beliefs. Somers was by now the Lord President of the Council,
enjoying new respect for his part in handling the legal conundrums
posed by the union of Scotland with England in 1706. Junto lords had
pushed their way, against the Queen's Tory preferences, into government; Halifax, although outside the Cabinet, was still influential. Yet
they did nothing to help Swift personally or to further his work on
behalf of impoverished Irish Anglican priests; nor, as he must have seen
by this time, were they ever likely to, since doing so would go against the
very basis of their popular support. The true tendency of the Whigs was
illustrated best of all by a man Swift soon detested, the Earl of Wharton.
Swift had canvassed the Earl as part of his campaign to secure the First
Fruits for the Irish clergy, and had been received 'drily'.[43] Swift was not
alone in watching with despair as Wharton assumed the office of lord
lieutenant in Dublin. The new viceroy set about milking the kingdom of
assets and hard cash to restore personal funds he had depleted in English
elections. Painfully for Swift, his esteemed friend Addison accepted the

post of personal secretary to Wharton, on a reported salary – astronomical – of £2,000 a year. A career in Parliament also awaited Addison; an awkward experiment in libretto-writing for Thomas Clayton's unsuccessful opera *Rosamond* was behind him. His public career moved on as Swift's remained in the doldrums.

Swift's Whig friends did, nevertheless, open doors to further influential figures. The result was always disappointing, but the introductions were made. As summer came in 1708, Swift was given a further opportunity, perhaps the last and greatest: a meeting with the Queen's most senior minister.

Sidney, Earl of Godolphin, had been the Lord High Treasurer, the Queen's premier minister, for six years; but his career of political service stretched back to the 1660s. King Charles had said that he was never in the way, but also never out of it – a golden virtue in a mandarin. Through the reigns of three kings he was 'employed in the Management of the Revenue, which he certainly understood better than any Man in England'. This, according to one writer, was the 63-year-old minister who ushered Swift into a private room at St James's Palace in 1708: 'He hath an admirable, clear Understanding, of slow Speech, with an awful, serious Deportment; does more than he promises; an Enemy to Flattery, Shew and Violence . . . of a low Stature; thin, with a very black and Stern Countenance.'[44] Yet Swift was not overawed. In his account of the meeting he acquitted himself well in a difficult situation. The Irish vicar standing before Godolphin was of middle height for the time, perhaps five foot five; he had a high, rather doming forehead from which the hair beneath his wig was receding. His face was on the plump side, double-chinned, with large somewhat protruding eyes, sky-blue. His voice could sound sharp; and he seems to have taken careful control of his tone in the course of the interview with Godolphin.

The Lord Treasurer began by doubting that any of the English priests to whom their First Fruits had been remitted 'was a Shilling the better'; but he admitted, when Swift softly demurred, that the sums for Ireland would be small indeed for the Queen to grant. He proceeded, nonetheless, to say that this would happen only on two conditions. The first was that the money 'should be well disposed of' – i.e. among loyal, obedient priests, with no shade of popery in their preaching – and the second that 'it should be well received with due Acknowledgements.' They had come to the pith of the meeting – which, however, continued in political code, even though Swift refused or failed to take a hint. 'I then begged his Lordship to give me his Advice,' he reported to

Archbishop King: 'what sort of Acknowledgments he thought fittest for the Clergy to make, which I was sure would be of mighty Weight with them. He answered, I can only say again, such Acknowledgments as they ought.'

As Swift realized, though without spelling it out for his archbishop, the condition was ciphered. The due acknowledgement of the Queen's bounty was, in fact, to come from Swift himself on the part of his fellow clergymen; and it was to take the form of journalistic service on behalf of Godolphin's ministry. Unacceptably for Swift, this would involve campaigning for the repeal of the Test Act. He asked Godolphin's permission to attend him on some other occasion, and the minister granted it; but a consultation with the Lord Lieutenant later the same day convinced him he was on 'a cold scent'.[45] Another meeting with Godolphin the following year proved equally dispiriting.

In suffering such frosty treatment, Swift was one of perhaps scores of churchmen paying the price for a rebellious surge by the inferior clergy in the last years of William's reign and the first of Anne's. Instinctively, Godolphin's loyalties were for the traditional Church; his religious politics were at heart close to Anne's or those of her confidant Archbishop Sharp. Nevertheless, his patience and self-esteem had been worn thin. On succeeding Rochester as the Lord Treasurer, Godolphin had inherited the task of dealing with a highly resistant majority in the Lower House of Convocation and, in the Commons, a core of High Tories with extreme Anglican convictions. He had entrusted the management of these factions to the Speaker of the House, Robert Harley, a precocious organizer but a politician of indeterminate hue. Harley had bought off Atterbury, the leader of the lower clergy, with promotion to the bleak and meagre deanery of Carlisle. Harley was also formally recruited: he became a secretary of state. For a time, Godolphin and Marlborough were able to govern and command on a non-party footing. Preserving the traditionally minded approach that Harley would also adopt when he formed a ministry of his own, Godolphin was extremely sensitive to Tory charges that he was betraying the Church. The Archbishop of York once found him close to tears at the latest battery of criticism.[46] Godolphin was a great accountant and administrator rather than a political fighter, but his tenderness to accusations of apostasy and cynicism would bring about his downfall. Unhappily, the more frustrated he grew at the High Tories' tactics, the more he did to alienate them. The final straw had arguably come some years before, when Tories in the Commons had tacked a bill to penalize 'occasional conformity' on to the Land Tax Bill.

The 'tacked' bill made it a criminal offence for public servants to worship at a Dissenting meeting-house after receiving Anglican Communion. This was the issue on which Swift claimed he had been 'mightily urged' to declare his hand.[47] To preserve the cross-party coalition of moderates, the bill had to be stopped; but this placed in jeopardy the revenues the Land Tax would bring to fund Marlborough's campaigns in 1705. To Godolphin, this was treachery, pure and simple. He shunned the Tories and turned for support to the Whig Junto. The Junto lords were ready to receive him, since the crisis had been largely produced by their parliamentary choreography. The Whigs won a big majority in the general election of 1705, settling the question for now. Since then, Godolphin and Marlborough's relationship with Harley had begun to decline. And, while Anne still distrusted the Whigs, and loathed the Junto members personally, Godolphin was all ears to their warnings and unheedful of their feints.

Since Swift had been spared the obligation to defend the Tories' proposals on occasional conformity, he can have meant little more to Godolphin than a potentially useful minor pamphleteer and canvasser. His archbishop in Dublin was generally thought sound; while the constituency Swift represented, the lower Irish clergy, had a limited place in the Lord Treasurer's calculations. At the time Godolphin could never have guessed what an enemy he was helping to make of his and Marlborough's legacy. Swift's shift, indeed, towards active antagonism had already begun. Publishing anonymously, Swift grew more determined in his opposition to Whig policies. Towards the end of 1708, his *Letter . . . Concerning the Sacramental Test* appeared, a pamphlet in which he wrote against a Whig move to repeal the Test Act. He completely ignored the reasonable complaint that sincere Dissenters were unwilling to profane their beliefs by receiving Holy Communion, as the Act required, once a year in an Anglican Church. In the *Letter* one can easily forget that Swift was defending the Established Church and the controlling interest. For on the emotional side, he always convinces: whether writing ironically or forthrightly, his words flowed from an earnest sense of being under threat. His work was charged with inherited Civil War memories of siege and raid, and his own generation's fright at the revolution of 1688–9. Moreover, his defence of the Irish side of politics lent him righteousness, if again one remembers to forget that it was the Episcopal, Anglican minority that was closest to his heart.

His precept was that the desire to repeal the Test in Ireland stemmed from colonial greed, since the Test Act barred Whig-Dissenter adventurers from the benefits of Irish office. Profit was all that concerned them, Swift claimed. Yet the irony Swift summoned up in the *Letter* to define English attitudes to Ireland has a power independent of his historical situation. Whichever way one looks at it, England was treating Ireland as a door-mat. Swift's attack on political oppression and economic exploitation resonates as strongly now, in times of advanced corporate hegemony, as it did 300 years ago. His assault begins with a quote from Cowley, the poet he admired and imitated as a young man; the urgency and pathos of the argument stem from Swift's experiences in his teens and twenties.

> I do not frequently quote poets, especially *English*, but I remember there is in some of Mr *Cowley's* love verses, a strain that I thought extraordinary at Fifteen, and have often since imagined it to be spoken by *Ireland*.

> > *Forbid it Heaven my Life should be*
> > *Weighed with her least Conveniency.*

> In short, whatever Advantage you propose to your selves by repealing the *Sacramental* Test, speak it out plainly, it is the best Argument you can use, for we value your Interest much more than our own. If your little Finger be sore, and you think a Poultice made of our *Vitals* will give it any Ease, speak the word, and it shall be done; the Interest of our whole Kingdom is, at any Time, ready to strike to that of your poorest *Fishing Town*.[48]

The mash-up made from Irish innards is a perfect example of the blend of jarring content and style that would persist and perfect itself in Swift's finest protest writing: an extreme, often visceral idea is delivered with great verbal nicety and set in language showing rhetorical restraint. The literary ingredients of the *Drapier's Letters*, and even the late incendiary essays on the state of Ireland, are present in the 'poultice' Swift offers here with a medical man's easy precision. But why, the loyal servant continues, if I demolish my burning house in case the fire should even touch a corner of your stable, should I kiss your hand the next morning for the privilege of having done so?

A passage that manages to do so much at once, adopting the stance of prostrate victim and active bondsman, while delivering hits of excruciating moral precision, was quite beyond the range of Cowley, who, unlike other 'Cavalier' writers, was no friend of irony. Swift was quoting the epitome of a style he had emulated in his early odes, but had now definitively left behind him. The paragraph also demonstrates the loosening grip of William Temple, for Cowley's were values Temple exalted and elaborated. Swift had not only moved far away from Temple stylistically; he had also discovered an unbridgeable difference in their thinking. Temple had written that an individual's spiritual belief

> is no more in a man's power, than his stature, or his feature; and he that tells me, I must change my opinion for his, because 'tis the truer, and the better, without other arguments, that have to me the force of conviction, may as well tell me, I must change my grey eyes, for others like his that are black . . .[49]

As for the basic statement here, Swift agreed: you could not force believers to change their faith. Yet he would add that some religious beliefs were wrong and illegitimate, and those who held them had no right to undermine the established order. You could not change an individual's convictions, but you had the right to ignore them if they were harmful to the state. Whereas Temple's inclinations would take him in a pluralistic direction (perhaps much further than this otherwise conservative Englishman might wish), Swift was an absolutist. The fundamental thing on which Swift disagreed with Temple's ghost, and thereby with even moderate Whigs, was tradition. By being the Church of England, by being the Established Church, the Church of England was right. The logical extension of his position, to adapt Temple's terms, is that those who have grey eyes should simply be glad that their existence and vision are tolerated by those with black eyes, whose supremacy is vouchsafed by constitutional history.

Yet it doesn't do to paint Swift as simplistic and inflexible where his old master might now seem forward-looking and liberal. Swift's sternness towards non-Anglican Protestants allowed him to be lenient, as very few Protestants of any shade were, towards Roman Catholics. Whigs argued that Protestants should stick together to defeat the threat of Papism, pointing in the direction of Saint-Germain and the Pretender. Swift dismissed this as a ruse, a piece of cynical scaremongering. Anyone, he maintained, could see how utterly oppressed the Papists were in Ireland, where the greatest danger supposedly lay. He exposed the fallacy in the *Letter* using the sort of direct, parabolic language Temple had preferred, but with a steely comic rhetoric that was foreign to the mild-mannered baronet.

It is agreed, among Naturalists, that a *Lyon* is a larger, a stronger, and more dangerous Enemy than a *Cat*; yet if a man were to have his choice, either a *Lyon* at his foot, bound fast with three or four chains, his Teeth drawn out, and his Claws pared to the Quick, or an angry *Cat* in full Liberty at his Throat; he would take no long Time to determine.[50]

So much for the cattish Dissenters; the curious weary sigh that accompanies the passage comes from having to cite the authority of 'naturalists' to explain something so obvious. The passage also captures Swift's sceptical view of 'full' liberty, as opposed to the qualified, restricted sense in which he would later claim to have defended or 'avenged' it. For the moment, the political struggle Swift had entered was tied. The keenest Whig reformers, including Wharton, held back from abolishing the Sacramental Test where they might easily have gone further. In mid-April 1708 Lord Somers called Swift in to hear his views on the matter, which Swift 'gave him truly, though with all the gentleness I could'.[51] In the papers he wrote over the next year, including the *Letter*, he was less than gentle. In one, *A Project for the Advancement of Religion and the Reformation of Manners*, he argued with painful and rather pompous simplicity that the Queen should make piety fashionable by rewarding only the righteous; while in *An Argument against Abolishing Christianity*, he made much the same point but from the opposite extreme of literary sophistication. The *Argument* is a 'Diabelli Variations' of ironic writing – a stream of continuous elaborations on a single joke: Swift impersonates a gentleman who ventures to suggest that abolishing the Church might not have the beneficial effect intended by those in favour of the measure (whose motives are, of course, pure). Together, the pamphlets of 1708 saw Swift refining two roles he would assume frequently to still greater effect. The first part was that of correspondent, whose 'letter' to a friend or confidant – published without his knowledge or consent – makes use of irony but is written in all sincerity. The second was that of a proposer or projector, a part that worked best when the persona itself was an entirely ironic creation.

A question such papers raise is why Swift should have devoted his creative and literary as well as professional and political energies to opposing the forces of dissent. If Dissenters were as ignorant and mistaken as Swift was constantly either implying or bluntly affirming, why bother wasting on them such masterpieces of irony as the *Argument against Abolishing Christianity*? One possible answer to this question rests on Swift's hidden recognition of the intellectual quality of his opponents and also the fundamental unity of his character as a priest and clergyman. To take the latter point first, there was no division whatsoever between Swift's literary and religious ethos. In his anonymously published satire, and the preaching and lobbying his ministry involved, he had but a single goal: to support the traditional structures and sacraments of the Established Church and the moral order they fostered. This was what made his critics in the High Church, notably Archbishop Sharp, so unjust in their view of him. They couldn't see that, while the means of his satire differed from those of his clerical activism, the end was the same. It was, however, true that such literary 'means' were radical and innovative in themselves, and, while this makes them compelling for us now, they evidently dismayed and puzzled many of their first readers.

As for the quality of the opposition, this calls for a closer look at the make-up of the often dissimilar communities and tendencies that a Swiftian persona lumped together as 'fanatics'. Dissenters might belong to highly structured alternative sects and Churches. Presbyterians, looking to the Scottish Kirk for their ecclesiastical blueprint, or the Quakers, were cases in point, yet many further strands of coexisting, sometimes competing Protestantisms were to be found across the realm. Dissenters were by definition 'free-thinkers', and when Swift used that term he did so scornfully. However, a Dissenter might also be a lone and truly independent thinker whose writings, in letter and spirit, offered persuasive arguments for undoing the entire basic idea of organized Christianity. The free-thinker *par excellence* in this most frightening respect was a fellow countryman of Swift, a scholar with whom the phrase 'free-thinking' has sometimes been thought to have originated. His name was John Toland, a writer who by 1709 was largely identified with the Whig cause and indeed enjoyed heavyweight protection from some of that party's leading politicians. Yet Toland, born in Londonderry in 1670, was really a person who defied classification. He was the illegitimate child of a Catholic priest's mistress – most accounts describe her as a courtesan – and was christened, he claimed, Janus Junius. At school, he adopted the name John, although even this was apparently lengthened to 'John-of-the-books', as he demonstrated very early on his quick invention and prodigious memory. One of his priestly schoolmasters is reported as saying that arguing with young Toland was like entering debate with the devil himself. He had no trouble countering quips about his parenthood: the concubine of a priest, he declared, was quite unlike a woman of the streets.[52]

He converted from Catholicism; an act that, in all his arguments with

258 JONATHAN SWIFT

the High end of the Church of England, always supported the central thesis of his writing. People were free, Toland would suggest, to apply their natural reason to their faith. If he hadn't, he pointed out, he would still be a Papist living in spiritual blindness. The argument was easy to dismiss but hard to outreason if one retained the core Protestant idea of the priesthood of the individual soul. Neither was he a ploughman turned Leveller, decrying book-learning. Study in Glasgow, Edinburgh and Oxford, where he immersed himself in the Bodleian's unique collection of manuscripts, and later abroad, in a period that brought him extensive European contacts, made an imposing scholar of Toland. In the early 1700s he made his name as one of the leading guardians of the Good Old Cause of English republicanism, with biographies of Milton and James Harrington, and a clarion call in *Anglia libera* supporting the Hanoverian succession as the best defence of parliamentary liberties. Yet Toland's greatest insult to the traditionalist world order had come in 1696 with his first and most famous work, *Christianity Not Mysterious*. It caused even an erstwhile supporter such as John Locke to distance himself from the 26-year-old iconoclast. Toland's future briefly looked perilous, until a powerful clique of Whig patrons realized the service he might do them, as a polemicist and provocative biographer. In time, he also developed a working relationship with Swift's future friend and flawed hero Robert Harley. To summarize a systematic but complex and surprising piece of writing, Toland asserted that there was nothing in the Bible that ordinary people couldn't figure out for themselves. This was not such an unfamiliar thesis; yet the verve and economy Toland displayed in pursuing it were novel and, for his opponents, seriously unnerving. He was saying that the organized Church had for centuries got away with mystifying and fogging over truths that could be transparent to all.

With this Toland joined a grand tradition of English heresiarchs stretching from Wycliffe to Blake. Like many prophets of holy simplicity, and a forebear particularly of Blake in this respect, Toland's appeal for lucidity would take him on a path towards ambiguous and often perplexing individualism. He would end his career in essence reversing the message of *Christianity Not Mysterious*, deep in research on (and possibly the living practice of) English Druidism, and writing works he published in editions of barely dozens of copies – works he admitted could not be read by all. Yet the first and strongest blow this champion of idiosyncrasy struck was to suggest that institutionalized religion was a sham. The suggestion was made in *Christianity Not Mysterious* with comprehensive logical variety and a great deal of rhetorical guile. One example from hundreds of passages demonstrating Toland's empathic intelligence is the following, from his introduction. He understands, he says, the reluctance to leave old ways behind.

> How fond are we all apt to be of what we learn'd in our Youth, as the Sight or Remembrance of the Places where we past that agreeable Time, does strangely affect us! A Mother is more charm'd with the lisping half-form'd Words of her prattling Infant, than with the best language, and most solid Discourses.[53]

A critic with Swift's attitude to infancy could resist the effort to sentimentalize the maternal bond; but it is harder to shrug off the idea that so much of adherence to old things derived from a love of familiar, long-cherished objects and customs – such as the relics Swift himself would preserve from the vicarage of his grandfather Thomas in Goodrich.

Swift appears to have worked his way back to *Christianity Not Mysterious* more than a decade after it first appeared. Before then, however, he was well aware of Toland by reputation and also by the polemical works that frequently appeared from the muddy waters of Grub Street. Toland is of course just one of many writers who incensed him on a yearly basis. Matthew Tindal's barbs against the English Church and clergy in his *Rights of the Christian Church* (1706) for many months made him itch to reply directly; yet, although he compiled extensive notes and drafted some fine belligerent paragraphs, he did not.[54] To do so, he figured, would mean joining an indecent wrestling match. Swift's preferred tactic was to filter pinpoint shots against such writers while writing in persona, and while in the midst of dealing with a topic somewhat removed from theirs – thus exploiting the blind spot to ensure a hit. Thus in *An Argument against Abolishing Christianity*, his neutral-minded, disinterested essayist points out that cancelling the Christian faith would mean depriving 'the Free-Thinkers, the strong Reasoners, and the Men of Profound Learning' of something to pontificate about. 'For who would ever have suspected *Asgill* [John, a lawyer and deist] for a Wit, or *Toland* for a Philosopher, if the inexhaustible Stock of Christianity had not been at hand to provide them with Materials.'[55]

At such moments, Swift was, in fact, being led to raise his game, to use literary technology more advanced than the old artillery of controversy, so prone to misfire. Adversaries such as Toland could and would not be silenced by declarations such as the following, even though it encapsulates Swift's moral position towards all forms of dissent:

Sects, in a State, seem only tolerated, with any Reason, because they are
already spread; and because it would not be agreeable with so mild a
Government, or so pure a Religion as ours, to use violent Methods
against great Numbers of *mistaken* People, while they do not manifestly endanger the Constitution of either.[56]

This would not suffice as an answer against *Christianity Not Mysterious*, a book that, published just a year or two before Swift put his own
startling debut into finished shape, is virtually an anti-*Tale of a Tub*. The
negative image in form and style of Swift's satire defending the authority
of the Church of England, Toland's book is an ardent treatise proposing
that individual minds can experience revelation for themselves. Wisely,
perhaps, Swift avoided engaging such works on their own terms; instead
he adopted their idiom and used it against them. His strongest response
to Toland and less gifted free-thinkers would always take the form of
satirical fiction – in the digressions of the *Tale* or Bickerstaff's disarming
exposure of politically driven charlatanism – rather than direct theological debate. Arguably, his avoidance of outright engagement hints at
latent uncertainty, and he could be accused of just snorting derisively at
tenets that were spiritually precious to their adherents. Yet, for reasons
that for Swift were equally profound, his satire aimed to remind readers
that, actually, Christianity *was* mysterious, and that claims by lone
voices to have solved its unfathomable questions were arrogant, simplistic and ultimately ridiculous.

The further he went into such arguments the more he realized how
they affected his political allegiances. On reading another Nonconformist tract in 1708, he wrote to an acquaintance (the poet Ambrose Philips)
who would prove a solid supporter of the Whig side. 'By the free Whiggish thinking,' Swift told Philips, 'I should rather take it to be yours. But
mine it is not; for though I am every day writing my Speculations in my
Chamber, they are quite of another sort.' A crisis would have to come;
although as yet the pull of loyalty exerted no urgent tension on such
friendships. Philips was touring the north, and Swift jovially hoped to
see him return soon 'very fat with Yorkshire ale'.[57]

# 4

Disappointments in his official missions were tempered by a cordial
reception in literary London. Even the works that by Swift's standard

seem relatively poor, such as the *Project for the Advancement of Religion*, more than satisfied the standards of the time. Commenting on this little treatise, an early *Tatler* declared that 'the man writes much like a gentleman, and goes to heaven with a very good mien.'[58]

It might not be surprising for a writer already so distinguished, not to mention such an accomplished social figure, to have his portrait painted. Accordingly, during his English sojourn of 1709, Swift sat for Charles Jervas, an artist some eight years his junior who was steadily making his name. Jervas had been embraced by Steele and Addison's circle, in which Swift encountered him. In the *Tatler* of 18 April, Steele praised Jervas for capturing the 'different perfections' of two ladies then idolized in town, and referred to him as 'the last great painter Italy has sent us'. A Dubliner by birth, Jervas benefited from the somewhat narrow criteria then required for perfection in his trade: 'nothing could be better imagined,' Steele murmured, 'than the dress he has given her of a straw-hat and a ribbon, to represent that sort of beauty which enters the heart with a certain familiarity.'[59] As for the Italian connection, Jervas had done diligent work abroad copying antiquities and collecting Renaissance drawings, and had a robust attitude to the artistic culture that had nurtured him. When one Raphael he fancied was detained by a direct papal order, he threatened to petition for the Royal Navy to bombard the port of Civitavecchia on which the Vatican depended.[60] Swift naturally was spared the need for rustic accoutrements in his portrait, since his aim was to present himself formally and impress, rather than to catch off guard the hearts of those viewing.

It is a pleasant scene to contemplate: Jervas, of a similar build and complexion to Swift, though deprived a little of air and exercise by his long studio hours, ushering in the Reverend Doctor, exchanging niceties and taking up his chalk; Swift, arranging his black garments and settling himself, resisting the little surge of pleasure the occasion brought. It was self-flattery, he knew – and he paid for it by holding his head at the odd angle that was natural for a moment, when something caught the ear or eye, but painful for much longer, and would mean a stiff neck the next morning.

The picture took Jervas some time and evidently some care. It was not completed until Swift returned to London for what proved to be a prolonged stay in the autumn of 1710. In one of the early letters of the great series that became the *Journal to Stella*, Swift described setting out for Jervas's studio on his 'shaving day'; and the jowl he presents in the portrait, as he gazes off to one side, is indeed smooth and almost glowingly white. He mentioned that in this second sitting Jervas gave the picture 'quite another turn', suggesting that at first he brought out a different facet of his subject. The Swift we see in this, the earlier, and better known rendering by Jervas, is very much the cleric: he is unpretentious to a fault, his dark gown and the sober background contrasting chastely with his starched preaching bands and rather radiant, almost cherubic plump face. Needless to say, in accordance with the aesthetic expectations of the time, there is no suggestion of the grogginess caused by Swift's recurring giddy fits. The expression is instead just faintly humorous, perhaps retaining a suggestion of the earlier 'turn' the painting took. For the side Swift himself certainly wished to emphasize was his dependable solidity as a churchman, not the mercurial and often disturbing wit of the author of *A Tale of a Tub*. He was a priest first and foremost, petitioning for the First Fruits, and willing to accept a preferment for his services. Recognition in these respects was presumably what counted when Swift said of the painting, 'we must get the approbation of the town.' Notably, when Jervas painted Swift again nearly a decade later, the prospects of further advancement having gone quite cold, the writer's secular achievements would figure much more prominently. The emphasis of the earlier painting might thus have come at his direction, rather than Jervas's. He would be pleased with the end result in its own right; unaware of how often his image would be reproduced even in his lifetime, he wished he was rich enough to order a copy to send home.[61]

Swift was forty-two the year the portrait was begun. The smooth brow and clear skin below almost sensuous eyes could easily belong to a man fifteen years younger. Pointedly, the canvas is clear of any status symbol: the bust in its feigned oval, isolated in darkness, is that of a parson, nothing more. This begs the question of whether Swift had – or felt he had – outgrown his place as Temple's dutiful secretary or as Berkeley's less placid chaplain. In these years, his contact with Moor Park grew faint, only to revive and come under terminal strain in the autumn of 1709. Completing the labour of almost two decades, Swift published the final volume of Sir William Temple's works, the third part of his *Memoirs*. The book met with a shriek of protest in print from Temple's sister. Lady Giffard declared that Swift's publication was unauthorized, and not based on Temple's own papers. With freezing dignity, Swift retorted that the copies he had spent years making of the originals had been checked by Temple and reflected his final intentions. He also clarified that he in no way pretended to have received any greater kindness or confidence from Temple than his late master's family or friends

– adding witheringly, 'I have but too good Reason to think otherwise.'[62] Tempers having cooled, Lady Giffard approached him more amicably some years later; but Swift spurned her advances. He maintained formal and polite relations with other members of the family, except when they crossed him: he would make short work of an insolent nephew of Temple, then Viscount Palmerston, in 1726.

Swift's ego was moderately pampered by people he admired; but his ill-will towards the lassitude of some was hardening. The thing about his portrait was that it represented the true Swift: the Church did matter to him more than his masterful miniatures. The people who really understood him – who really got what his *Tale of a Tub*, in all its surface brilliance and complexity, was saying – would see that there was no contradiction between his calling as a priest and his career as a wit. He enjoyed helping Steele, a fellow Dubliner by birth, though there were moments too when he regretted this prodigality. He sought the company and regard of people who saw him in a true light, and appreciated the scale of his talent. Conversation with these friends, and with 'Hetty' Vanhomrigh – who was already pressing for some sign of commitment – provided his chief comfort through the following winter. In the spring of 1709 one of his most famous poems was published in the *Tatler*. This was his 'Description of the Morning', capturing the city at the moment when drab things seem brilliant in untired sunlight. The dawn flashes on the windows of a few stray cabs:

> Now hardly here and there an Hackney-Coach
> Appearing, show'd the Ruddy Morns Approach.
> Now Betty from her Masters Bed had flown,
> And softly stole to discompose her own.
> The Slipshod Prentice from his Masters Door,
> Had par'd the Dirt, and Sprinkled round the Floor.

The vices of the town are all hidden; Westminster has yet to awake. The sins on display are all venial – and was Swift so very different from Betty, in thought if not deed, as he left another meeting with Hetty in the back room of Mrs Vanhomrigh's house? The speaker is invisible, not part of the scene; he does not mingle with the maid, the apprentice or the others who presently appear. With regard to Swift, it should be recalled that the figures crossing the stage of his morning city belong to a class he was determined never to join. His sister Jane had displeased him permanently by marrying her Dublin tanner. But such haughtiness is absent from the

'Description of the Morning': fellow feeling from the author would be stretching it too far, but the apprentice is not painted unsympathetically. By now Swift lunched with ministers and Members of Parliament; but there was a time, before Temple, before ordination, when he might not have escaped an indenture. And not that long had passed since he and Esther had technically been among the servants at Moor Park.

The absence of comment, explicit or implied, is notable. The poem is nothing more than a collection of actions, human events as regular in the city as sunrise. A 'youth' is sweeping the gutters at the road's edge frayed by carriage wheels; the bass voice of a man selling coal is drowned out by a singing chimney sweep, and a madwoman's scream pierces the air. A jailer stands at the gate of his prison to welcome back the inmates he has let out on a night's thieving. Bailiffs prepare; 'And Schoolboys lag with Satchels in their Hands.' We can fill in the rest: the early riders and strollers in St James's Park; the mess of mansions in the half-ruined precincts of Whitehall; the dome of the new St Paul's, just completed, huge enough to bake a raft of royal Brobdingnagian pies inside, curving pale against the sky.[63] The day is not yet up and running, and Swift offers no judgement on what he has caught sight of in its first movements. The verses are hardly an aubade, greeting the dawn. Yet the poem seems to be saying that this, at daybreak, is the best we may expect, so let us make the most of it.[64]

Life was transitory: amid the swathes of scornful remarks on relatives, and the stinging backhands he often administered to close friends, it is sometimes forgotten how deeply Swift grieved. In May 1710, at his Irish parish of Laracor, word reached him from Leicester that his mother had died more than two weeks earlier, 'after a long sickness, being ill all winter, and lame, and extremely ill a month or six weeks before her death'. As he always would, in bereavement Swift put away the satirical mask. 'I have now lost my barrier between me and death; God grant I may live to be as well prepared for it, as I confidently believe her to have been! If the way to Heaven be through piety, truth, justice, and charity, she is there.'[65] He had been a good son in return, visiting her in Leicestershire on every visit to England. Written in his account book – and appropriately drawing a quietus – these were generous words for a woman who, although no doubt because of harms she bore, had spent little time caring for Swift as a mother. The memorials of Abigail Swift have frequently been searched for possible causes of her son's personal difficulties; but he never reproached her for anything but marrying his father, and even then, long after she died. On a visit to Dublin during

Swift's early years in the priesthood, she told her landlady that she was expecting a male admirer. Soon afterwards, Swift was introduced as such when he called at the house. 'The doctor smiled at his mother's humour,' and visited her dutifully each day she remained in the city.[66]

# 7. Recruited by Tories,
## 1710–1714

I neither can nor will have patience any longer; and Swift you
are a confounded son of a —. May your half acre turn to a
Bog, and may your Willows perish; May the worms eat your
Plato, and may Parvisol break your snuff-box.

– *Sir Andrew Fontaine (Swift's good friend), writing in*
*June 1710*[1]

I

Early on a late-autumn morning in 1712, two parties of men met to settle a dispute the traditional way. The duel was somewhat unconventional
in that the challenge was issued by the person who had given the affront.
Charles Mohun, baron, known equally for his fighting and philandering,
had provoked James Douglas, the fourth Duke of Hamilton, over an
ongoing legal row. For a decade, Mohun had been fighting Hamilton in
the courts to keep his inheritance, the estates left by an heirless relative.
The Duke also laid claim to these properties, and there seemed little
prospect of an end to the suit. Mohun, who had been tried for murder
more than once, had the reputation of a cold-blooded scoundrel. In
1693 witnesses had seen him hold an unarmed actor down for a friend
to stab through the chest; but the Baron had friends in the House of
Lords, and they saw to his acquittal. There had been similar affairs since,
and when Mohun decided to put their long-running case to the sword,
Hamilton was obliged to answer the call. The place, The Ring at Hyde
Park, a broad paved circular promenade, provided both an arena for
the contest and a screen with its surrounding trees. The duellists met at

seven, with seconds and servants, chose their weapons and closed quickly and furiously. Hamilton had fifty-four years to Mohun's thirty-six, but, after several passes, ran his adversary through. The Duke was pulling himself and his sword free when he was wounded in his turn.

It was thought at first that this injury was done him by Mohun, lying on the ground beneath him and shortening his sword to pierce the Duke's shoulder through the back: so, at least, ran the version which Swift first heard and reported. But the geometry such a blow required was soon dismissed as unreal. A few days later John Hamilton, the Duke's second and kinsman, a colonel in the Scots Foot Guards, gave testimony that lent added passion to the hue and cry pursuing the killer. The colonel claimed that Hamilton had been stabbed in the back by Mohun's second, one George Macartney. The Duke's men carried him towards a nearby tea-shop, the Cake House, just beyond The Ring, but he died on the grass before they reached it. His body was taken by coach to Hamilton's town-house in St James's Square, where his widow was still sleeping.

The core of the quarrel was a cold matter of land and money: the disputed property of Charles Gerard, the second Earl of Macclesfield. But Mohun had stoked the argument by bringing in differences in polit-ics and personal conduct, and these proved explosive. The legal dispute turned into a question of honour, and it was this that dictated the short, cruel proceedings on the ground at Hyde Park. In the air, however, was a larger conflict. The duel took place in a period of exceptional political ferocity. Mohun was a Whig, a Kit-Cat regular, and Hamilton a Tory – in addition, a Tory with Jacobite sympathies. Macartney had recently been thrown out of the army for 'drinking confusion' – that is, solemnizing a curse over a toast – to the Tory-dominated ministry, and making an effigy of the Lord Treasurer out of a stick. Macartney was not a personal friend of Mohun, but he was more than reliable in a fight and a proven 'Tory-hater'.[2] Mohun and his attendant diehards were all the evidence the Tory press required of a broader Whig plot. On the Tory extreme, the conspiracy was seen as one directed against the ministry and, in the near-royal person of a duke, against the established order itself.

The duel stank of faction. The fallout combined all the defensiveness, indeed paranoia of the ruling party with the desperation and murderous resentment of the ousted side. The duel was also an eruption of the lethal animosity that underlay political debate: it showed where England had come from – a clash of swords – and where it would return, should the constitution fail. Lives and basic livelihoods were at stake, as well as

precious honour. By November 1712 the Tories had dominated government for two years. As they undid the policies of their Whig predecessor,
the Whigs and their allies lost their places at Court, military commis-
sions and lucrative administrative positions around the three kingdoms.
Influence subsided in one quarter, and rose elsewhere. The booty of the
state, in short, was seized and dealt out anew, and the result was hatred
expressed and violence held just about in check. Close to the very centre
of the struggle was Swift.

The day the Duke died, Swift visited Elizabeth, Duchess of Hamilton,
at the apartment near her home where friends had taken her for peace
and comfort. A sympathetic mob had gathered outside the Hamiltons'
house, ready for the word that might send them on a vengeful spree.
When Swift sent his servant for news, the man could hardly move
through the crowd, and found the Duke's footman in tears. Later, he sat
two hours with the Duchess. Swift had been on good terms with Hamilton, whom he called a 'frank honest good natured man' – and who
would joke with him by stepping on Swift's clerical gown as he followed
him downstairs – but still closer to his wife. The Duchess had visited him
when he was sick. She had personally sewn special pockets into the lining of a luxurious golden snuff-box the Governor of Dunkirk had sent
him as a present. He was deeply struck by her sorrow: 'I never saw so
Melancholy a Scene . . . She has moved my very soul.' He was anxious
she should not hear the 'Grubstreet screamers' bawling out the news in
order to sell broadsides.[3]

The papers had immediately cried up the private quarrel as a party
affair. The old battle-lines were pretty much as they had always been: the
Tories claimed to be the High Church party, on the whole, while the
Whigs leaned towards the Nonconformists, although in individual cases
such alliances were often purely strategic. But in two years the Tory-
packed ministry had done more than deprive their enemies of domestic
sinecures and block the sects. Robert Harley had also moved to close an
enormous source of employment and opportunity abroad. The government was ending Marlborough's war. The Whigs had always been closer
to the newer moneyed interest that had lent the Crown the massive sums
it needed to sustain the war. Yet a majority in the country appeared to
have decided that the gain of fighting King Louis had finally been out-
weighed by the human and financial losses. Despite some resounding
triumphs – Blenheim in 1704, Ramillies in 1706 – no definitive victory
had come. The profit of the war, in any case, was felt to have benefited
individuals and minority interests; and none stood higher than the com-

mander-in-chief of the Grand Alliance opposing France, John Churchill, Duke of Marlborough.

No mere edifice or title could do justice to Marlborough's stature in his homeland. Instead it was monumentalized by the staggering house built for him at the Crown's expense at Woodstock, Oxfordshire. Blenheim Palace was raised in tribute to the baroque tactics Marlborough displayed in August 1704, which resulted in some 30,000 Franco-Bavarian troops lying dead in the fields surrounding the village of Blindheim in what is today Germany. Early public enthusiasm for the palace project faded as campaigns in successive years made little headway within the borders of France and Spain. But Marlborough's position seemed unquestionable. In the field, he presided over scenes of unthinkable destruction of people and buildings, 'burnt according to the laws of war', all justified by strategy;[4] at home, he held sway over Parliament, Whitehall and St James's Palace. All he lacked, in many eyes, was a crown: and he might have been more widely suspected of coveting it, had he not been nearly sixty, sonless and, for all his love of glory and wealth, conservative in nature and a loyal friend of the Queen.

The Queen herself was in many respects a reluctant monarch, hurt by loneliness and loss. Unlike William, the outright politician she succeeded – and disliked – Anne had no formal training in statecraft or the humanities that informed it. History, geography, rhetoric – these were all foreign languages to her; she could, though, speak French like a native, having been sent to Paris as a poorly three-year-old for treatment on her eyes. She was shy and naive, and lent heavily on Sarah Churchill, the Duchess of Marlborough, for the support first given during the years when her children had died and her brother-in-law the King had tried to freeze her out of the state. Anne was never strong physically, and seventeen pregnancies – all resulting in miscarriages or young deaths – took a heavy toll: from her mid-thirties she could walk only a short way without help. For most of her life she was variously connected with and estranged from a cast of aspiring male protectors – William, Marlborough, and also the father and half-brother she kept in touch with but officially renounced. The one true stalwart in her life, her husband, Prince George of Denmark, had died in 1708. Despite her frailties and troubles, her quiet ways brought strong affections out in Court and country alike. 'She was in her own Nature extremly dilatory and timorous,' wrote Swift, yet 'upon some Occasions, positive to a great degree'.[5] The unassuming, but strong-willed invalid became a queen 'of blessed memory'.

Anne and Marlborough were bound by an old friendship that frayed as the war for Spain continued. The link was originally forged by Anne's sometime closest and rather domineering companion, Sarah Churchill. In time, a falling out between the two women spelled the end for Marlborough's pre-eminence. The original bond was supported, though, by personal sympathy and agreement on key questions, since both Anne and Marlborough belonged more to the High Church, Tory side of the political scene. Back when William III's foreign lieutenants dominated the English commands, Anne had supported Marlborough at considerable political risk: he was at one point a fugitive from a charge of treason. Times had changed, however, since the early 1690s. By 1709, when moderates on both sides in Parliament had begun questioning the point of fighting a war that by then seemed unendable, Marlborough was the champion of the Whig ascendancy. A marriage had sealed the pact between military and ministry. Marlborough's elder daughter had married the Earl of Godolphin's only son, Francis. As the foremost balancer of the nation's books, Godolphin was an unlikely zealot for a war of such cost, and, as a natural Tory, he was a strange bedfellow for the Whigs of the Junto in Anne's ministry. But he was far from singular: since, quite apart from Marlborough's successes in Flanders and beyond, spectacular though they often were, the war was an ongoing victory for the financiers on which the Crown relied. The Treasury could barely cover the interest on a rising annual debt that, many observed with increasing panic, would take generations to repay. As Swift pointed out, while monarchs had invariably overspent, the very concept of a standing 'National Debt' did not exist until William of Orange took the throne. 'The Expedient ... of raising Money upon the Security of Taxes' was supposedly thought up by Gilbert Burnet, Bishop of Salisbury, a powerful Whig clergyman, and the subject of several satirical roastings at Swift's hands.[6] The realization of the concept was the work, however, of leading Whigs, notably Sunderland. The Whig-slanted government, with Godolphin as their figurehead to ensure national unity, had gained a near monopoly on power. In tandem, a class of lending and investing 'stock-jobbers' enriched themselves.

The Whigs maintained that the war against Louis was necessary to stop France controlling the length and breadth of Europe and to protect British trade. Their opponents noticed that 'no peace without Spain', an ever more provocative mantra, might grant similar powers to the rival heir, the Holy Roman Emperor, Charles VI. The strain of the war told horrendously on the British populace and purse, but those who opposed it had to fight a stupefied sense of acceptance in the public, a state of collective narcosis; only another great win for Marlborough's army could rouse them. As Swift remarked to Stella, 'Few of this generation can remember any thing but war and taxes, and they think it is as it should be; whereas 'tis certain we are the most undone people in Europe.'[7] Public support for the war had been declining for some years, though, by the time he wrote those words in 1711. A sleeping readiness for change manifested itself in 1709, when the mood of the nation was disturbed by the treatment received by a troublesome priest.

The clergyman in question was a red-faced High Church Tory of the clearest stamp: the Reverend Henry Sacheverell, best known at Oxford as a bully and a drunk with dubious Latin. He was an unpopular fellow at Magdalen, and Addison's sometime friend. A jowly, heavy-browed man in his mid-thirties, to whom the two-humped crest of a periwig gave an especially pugnacious character, Sacheverell had been firing off sermons for years against Whigs, Dissenters and Catholics. Preaching in the November of this crucial year he rolled all his favourite topics together for the benefit of the Lord Mayor and Aldermen. He gave his audience blood, thunder and spittle on the subject of the 'false brethren' undermining the Church. These conspirators included most of the current government, but especially his lordship 'Volpone' ('the fox'), a popular nickname for Godolphin. They were fanatics, declared Sacheverell, reincarnations of the worst rebels of the 1640s. The sermon touched nerves that could always be easily inflamed in his supporters and targets alike. Against the advice of Lord Somers, Godolphin decided to press charges against Sacheverell. In doing so, the cunning of the fox deserted him: impeaching Sacheverell raised a storm of rioting across London, supposedly in defence of the cleric's sacred person. Swift, for his part, would always view Sacheverell with the distaste due to a rabble-rouser; he was later prepared to put in a word for him and even his brother, but declared that 'he shall be none of my acquaintance.'[8]

The Whig ministry had lost the confidence of both monarch and public. The Queen was guided now by a newly ascendant ex-minister who had lost office not long before. Harley, the former Secretary of State and Speaker of the House, advised Anne on a series of dismissals culminating in the ejection of Godolphin himself in August 1710. Swift, whom Harley was at that time persuading to take on the role of propagandist for a new administration, was exultant. He celebrated Godolphin's fall in a broadside, 'The Virtues of Sid Hamet the Magician's Rod'. The poem seized on a central prop in the humiliating process Godolphin had to endure. As the outgoing Lord Treasurer, he was commanded to break his staff of office. In his triumphant lines, Swift endows this rod with magic properties – it allows Godolphin to perform miracles in patriarchal fashion – fish for men, put people to sleep and divine seams of gold – but before being snapped ends its life as a rod for the statesman's own backside. 'My lampoon is cried up to the skies,' Swift reported, and Godolphin gave him a cold stare.[9] Meanwhile the Treasury was put into commission and Harley became the Chancellor of the Exchequer.

Six years older than Swift, Harley was the son of a Presbyterian who had fought on Parliament's side in the Civil War. Harley had also married into a Whig dynasty of the middle rank. Over a number of years, however, he had migrated from the Whigs and 'Commonwealthmen' to the moderate Tory wing. In particular he recognized the function the Established Church performed in giving cohesion to the moral framework of the state, and so presented himself as an orthodox Anglican. It was said that he would entertain clergymen in the morning but go back to his roots with his family by attending a Nonconformist meeting in the afternoon. Swift was the sternest of judges in such matters, but did not find his new patron wanting. In truth inconsistencies were there if one looked. At key moments over the years, the new first minister had been instrumental in determining measures and policies of the greatest importance: in fixing the Electress of Hanover as the successor to Queen Anne, for example, or in drafting the Articles of Union with Scotland in 1706. It was hard, too, not to suspect that any alliance for Harley was largely a matter of expedience. Those with any memory at all could remember how closely he had worked with Godolphin in the barely distant past.

An insider could nevertheless testify to the fatal turn a political career could easily take. Harley was a short and, in his early days, a slender man, and, although broader in stature by the time he was made chancellor, just short of fifty years old, he never lost his nimbleness in a tight political corner. He had a deep love of secrets, and he funded a network of informants in sensitive or volatile locations across the land. Among the agents on his books was a somewhat sceptical yet nevertheless co-operative Daniel Defoe. When Harley had served as the Speaker of the House a decade earlier, an observer commented that 'No Man understands more the Management of that *Chair* to the Advantage of his Party, nor knows better all the Tricks of the House.' Robin the Trickster, as he was known, 'is skilled in most Things, and very Eloquent', the same writer judged;[10] but since those words were written Harley had survived a political scandal that had cost a traitor his life in 1708. He had only escaped a charge of treason himself by the honesty of the man condemned for placing secret correspondence in enemy hands. Leading Whigs visited William Gregg in Newgate, offering him a pardon if he accused Harley of conspiracy. Gregg heroically refused, and went to the gallows; Harley escaped with his life if not his position as a secretary of state. Crucially, he retained the Queen's trust. Drawing up at Kensington a few days after Harley left office, Godolphin met his carriage leaving the palace. Godolphin subsequently reproached the Queen with near-open fury; but she straightened her smile, reminded him of his place, and saw to it that in future Harley was admitted via a back staircase.

## 2

Harley worked stealthily and steadily to ensure his revenge; undermining Godolphin in the Queen's eyes; supporting a new royal favourite, Abigail Masham, to unseat the Duchess of Marlborough and counteract another important enemy, the Duchess of Somerset; and gathering opposition to Godolphin. On becoming chancellor in autumn 1710, Harley's overall initiative took the form of moderation in matters of State and staunchness in support for the Church. It was the perfect combination to win over Swift, who was again in London to lobby for the Irish First Fruits. At the end of September, a friend and factotum of Harley, Erasmus Lewis, arranged for Swift and Harley to meet. In gratifying panic, Swift's Whig associates made a 'lamentable confession' of their failure to treat him decently; but too late. Soon Swift told Esther Johnson that 'The Tories dryly tell me, I may make my fortune, if I please.' He affected not to understand them.[11]

A few days later, Swift left his hardly salubrious lodgings and came to an arrangement with the new first minister. A blazing Indian summer had given sudden way to frosts and freezing winds that caught the town short. Swift was as surprised as any, and made a note of the change in his journal to Esther, but the new weather marked a shift in his newly blooming fortunes. Everyone wanted to meet him: 'I have more dinners than ever,' he reported. Yet the greatest piece of news was a private interview with Harley – either in his chambers at St James's or his townhouse off Piccadilly – who received him 'with the greatest respect and kindness imaginable'.[12] At the weekend Swift received assurances about the First Fruits; he was also moved to lend the aid of his pen to Harley's new ministry. He was forty-three years old. In private, he had begun an intimate counterpart to the extended writing project to which he now committed himself. Alongside poems, pamphlets and volumes in defence of Harley's political endeavour, Swift would build up the series of uniquely open letters that constitute the *Journal to Stella*.

The year 1710 was decisive for him. By the end of October he had taken on the task of writing a regular polemical newspaper for the government, the *Examiner*. He made the most of the paper's title by presenting himself as an impartial scrutinizer of affairs of state. His authorship was supposed to remain an absolute secret. Inwardly and publicly, albeit anonymously, he professed his independence of mere party allegiance, and did not scruple to send another offering to the *Tatler*. This was his 'Description of a City Shower', a sister poem to his earlier description of morning. The 'Description' was again preoccupied with an everyday situation, an urban squall. In an especially deft moment, as the first pats of rain hit the ground, Swift captures one domestic action by comparing it to another:

> Brisk *Susan* whips her Linen from the Rope,
> While the first drizzling Show'r is born aslope,
> Such is that Sprinkling which some careless Quean [a prostitute,
>      but here a maidservant]
> Flirts on you from her Mop, but not so clean.

The whipcrack of those shaken and gathered sheets is something anyone, in any age, has heard. The poem becomes involved in Swift's perennial war on muck; it encounters too the paradox of how cleanliness in practice can make dirt all the more evident by force of contrast. For soon a deluge is falling, but, instead of washing away the city's filth, it only brings it to the surface.

> Sweepings from Butchers Stalls, Dung, Guts and Blood,
> Drown'd Puppies, stinking Sprats, all drench'd in Mud,
> Dead Cats and Turnip-Tops come tumbling down the Flood.[13]

In such refuse, an unavoidable sight for all, could be seen the basic materials of life and its aftermath. As these lines were being touted and praised about London in mid-October, Swift's awareness of this stream of rubbish should be borne in mind. At the same time, he was being courted vigorously by Tory elders and other friends of Harley's ministry. He was becoming friends with Lewis, the official who had introduced him to Harley, and Matthew Prior, a former attaché who expected promotion from the new men in office, and who was credited in Swift's hearing with the cruel lines on Godolphin, 'Sid Hamet'. Prior was known on Grub Street as the antagonist of Dryden, having collaborated on a skit of the old poet's fable *The Hind and the Panther*. In all, an exclusive fold of wits and politicians now adopted Swift and lauded his accomplishments. He was drawn into the 'Saturday Club', made up of Cabinet ministers and other choice public men. In time, when the distinct character and discriminating basis both of its mission and its membership were lost, the Saturday Club was succeeded by another fellowship of 'Brothers' (with some blurring of the lines between them). For his 'brothers', praising his writing was made easier by the fact that almost all of it had been published anonymously: the compliments were paid ostensibly to an empty chair. 'The Virtues of Sid Hamet the Magician's Rod' especially delighted them – albeit for obvious reasons of party. Charles Mordaunt, Earl of Peterborough, a lean ageing general celebrated for taking Barcelona almost by accident, insisted on reading the poem aloud. Harley nudged Swift at the hits scored by each successive line.[14] Peterborough, rakish, previously quite Whiggish, unapologetically pragmatic in his politics, nevertheless became a firm friend and favourite of Swift.

Yet, below the surface, an undercurrent of rubbish preoccupied Swift's imagination at this time. Notwithstanding the bonhomie, the description of the shower, and the mildewed, battered city it pounds, is an unsettling counterpoint to this chummy scene amid heavy silver cutlery and fine-cut glass, drolleries exchanged as the bottle circumnavigated the table; the poem contrasts sharply too with the high-handed rhetoric Swift was about to unleash on the government's enemies. His head was turned, his vanity touched, but the 'Description' suggests he was someone who could never be transported completely by rising in the world. Things he found repulsive held him, paradoxically, to earth, since he could not avoid them or remove them from his mind: a consciousness, never sentimental, of the poor and mortal in the streets outside; unease at the flick of a maid's mop, and the marks it could not remove; the puddled earth; unspeakable riverbeds.

It should not be forgotten that this was a world Swift did more than observe and describe; it was one he had to hurry and often splash through on his daily rounds. There are a great many anxious references in the journal to the cost of a cab or a chair, occasional outbursts against rain and mud, and thanksgivings for the dry weather that allowed him a good walk. On almost any day, meanwhile, the thoroughfares were jammed. Among the many glimpses his *Tatler* offered of urban living in the early 1700s, Steele's paper gave a characteristic snort at how:

> [the] horses and slaves of the rich take up the whole street; while we Peripatetics are very glad to watch an opportunity to whisk across a passage, very thankful that we are not run over for interrupting the machine, that carries in it a person neither more handsome, wise, or valiant, than the meanest of us.[15]

Swift is to be pictured among such scurrying peripatetics, philosophers on foot; but sometimes also taking a seat in the splendid 'machine' of a duke or minister.

As winter set in during 1710, Swift set about defending the ministry's business. The government was, like any at that time, technically a coalition; and, while Swift addressed churchmen and traditionalists, another, arguably shrewder and worldlier writer kept moderate Whigs and Dissenters on board. Swift would not have welcomed the Nonconformist Daniel Defoe as a colleague any more than he would later openly admit the influence of *Robinson Crusoe* on the *Travels*. But the vastly experienced and definitively non-Tory professional was essential to Harley's plans to keep the moderate Whigs and Dissenters behind the new ministry. And what sold the project for Swift, so far as secular things were concerned, was also moderation. It *is* in a sense wrong to speak of him switching sides from Whig to Tory, since he despised the notion of belonging to a party. He began his first edition of the *Examiner* by declaring his approach: 'It is a Practice I have generally followed, to converse in equal Freedom with the deserving Men of both Parties.'[16] Even though his friendships with Whigs such as Addison were soon to cool, this sentence was perfectly true of Swift in the last months of 1710. Yet Swift's predecessor at the *Examiner*, Henry St John, was governed by a tendency that was in direct conflict with the old mode of consensus – one based on seeking means by which the men of one party might serve their own best advantage.

St John styled himself as Harley's political partner, though he was always the lesser of two equals. In February 1708 he had resigned his post as secretary at war, ostensibly in support of Harley – when Harley's exit left him no other real option. He had then awaited the moment to return to power; which, again, truth told, meant waiting for Harley to complete his delicate undermining of Godolphin. St John's contribution was to bring with him the support of the Tory base in the Commons: the ungovernable rump of men who, in modern parlance, would be called the 'backbenches'. St John had first attracted serious attention in the early 1700s by attaching himself to this faction. He stood out easily: none of the rustic Tories he sat among could match his urbanity or eloquent verve. He had a reputation as a rake and a man of leisure; and, despite the harm it did him at Court and the hurt it caused his wife Frances (née Winchcombe), who adored him ruefully till her death in 1718, he cultivated his image as both.

He was thirty-two when he took ministerial office as a secretary of state in 1710. A portrait dating from about 1712 displays a stout and rather podgy-faced grandee, with strong signs of his fondness for the bottle and the board showing through the obligatory drapery of periwig and shimmering silks. He was an adept in charming and impressing women, and his charisma worked well on fellow members of the House too. While Harley was widely reckoned the best tactician in Parliament before the rise of Walpole, Swift here and there implies that the younger, more flamboyant minister had a rhetorical edge on his chief. Fatally, though, St John lacked Harley's level head and skills as an organizer. He had the rhetorical flair to carry a debate, but not the shepherd's patience in gathering the flock for a vote, or the composure a drawn-out crisis required. Harley saw this, and, although he needed him, doubted St John's judgement and stamina from an early stage. St John became the minister responsible for northern Europe, and thus for the bulk of the diplomatic effort regarding the war against France; but Harley reserved the key decisions, and much of the daily business in this field, to himself. And, while St John effectively spelled out the consensus-seeking aims of the ministry in the inaugural *Examiner*, no senior figure did more to undermine it. He was soon pressuring Harley to exploit the large majority the Tories won, with the full backing of the Crown, in the autumn of 1710. The job ahead, though, was hardly under way; and Swift would be instrumental to it.

By supporting Harley, Swift was only announcing a concern for the old order he had harboured all his adult life. Whiggery was threatening the balance, and so finally he had to show his colours. He was putting on, rather than changing, his coat. Some friends and associates on the Whig side could be forgiven for regarding him as a traitor, but there were some bridges Swift could burn with impunity. The Temples' old friend the Duchess of Somerset, who would be instrumental in turning the Queen against Harley in a few years' time, had already branded Swift 'a man of no principle either of honour or religion'.[17] Swift would finally vent his dislike of her in one of his most vicious epigrams.

He always bore himself as if unafraid of upsetting anyone. But there were losses Swift regretted: his prized intimacy with Joseph Addison, sealed in many evenings over wine and olives, could never be regained. Addison was pulled into ever more regimented party duty by his election to the Commons in autumn 1710. In December, his eyes weary from paperwork, Addison noted that Swift was 'much caressed' by the new ministry, and dined almost exclusively with Tories.[18] Swift became a stranger to their old Whiggish hangouts, particularly the coffee-houses; the Kit-Cat Club was now a dangerous venue for him. He and Addison hardly ever called on one another now; and when it became apparent that Swift was writing the *Examiner*, an open breach was only just avoided. In poetry, prose and person, Addison was one of the Whigs' chief publicists for the war; Swift (although his character was incomparably more belligerent) became the most articulate champion of peace. By very early in 1711 Swift told Johnson sadly that 'all our friendship and dearness are off: we are civil acquaintance, talk words of course, of when we shall meet, and that's all.'[19] Over the following months Swift insisted that the separation was Addison's fault, not his.

His stay in London would stretch to years, rather than months, although he often told Esther she might expect him back in Dublin soon. Despite his workload he was an exhaustive correspondent, and never more fastidious than in writing as 'Presto' to the female friends he addressed as 'MD'. The journal he wrote for Esther and her companion, Mrs Dingley, reveals him as a critical but experienced metropolitan. After all, he had been making his home in temporary digs, off and on, for more than a decade. Like many room-hunters before and since, his chief concerns were cleanliness, quiet, convenience and decency. The addresses he mentions – on King Street, Suffolk Street, Pall Mall or Leicester Fields, to name a few – all put him a middling walk or short cab ride from Westminster. His accommodation was plain yet comfortable: in the *Travels*, Gulliver suggests that a room of about twelve by sixteen feet, with sash windows and perhaps two closets, would be standard for a 'London Bedchamber'.[20] A typical apartment in a house on St Alban Street, which gave Swift the use of the main parlour for receiving 'persons of quality', cost him eight shillings a week. The lodging which suited him best, though, was one he vacated fairly early on, five doors down on Bury Street from the London residence of Mrs Vanhomrigh. There he was an ever welcome guest, and a room for private chatter and laughter with Hessy was readily available. In short, he lived humbly but quite comfortably; alone, but rarely short of company when time permitted: an existence typical for the floating population brought to London for business in the courts or Parliament. Like other short-term residents, he was mindful of coins, cursing the clouds for the shillings they cost him in carriage and sedan fares. Like many too who lived out of a travelling trunk, he had his rituals and methods for minimizing luggage and clutter. Whenever he moved, he would box up all the books he had acquired since arriving – except for a half-shelf of essential works – and send them off to Ireland. Thus he arrived at each new address 'naked' of clutter – until his love of bookshops led to volumes heaping up again.[21]

Writing to Johnson one snowy morning in January 1711 – 'vengeance cold' – he complained to her that he needed a candle, and must write 'on the dark side of my bed-chamber ... for the bed stands between me and the window, and I keep the curtains shut this cold cold weather'.[22] He was no constant prisoner, meanwhile, of modest lodgings: a frequent guest in grand houses, he got used to accompanying Harley and St John on their trips to Windsor. What he saw there was of interest to Johnson, who shared his pleasure and interest in landscaping, and he reported his impressions in some detail. He had an eye for trees rather than flowers, admiring, for instance, a double row of elms at the verges of a two-mile avenue bisecting the vast main grounds of Windsor, and 'a delicious park just adjoining the castle'. His journal is peppered with assurances to Johnson that he is taking every opportunity for exercise, while usually directing her to do likewise. Her latent frailty concerned him: her breathing, her eyesight, her weight. His own health was still unstable. The old demons, vertigo and deafness, crept up on him periodically, and were a near-constant threat. Their perpetual imminence worried and tired him. His head would feel 'stufft', and too sudden a turn would cause his surroundings to keep spinning – 'but if it grows no worse,' he remarked, 'I can bear it very well.' He still followed the precaution of restraining his love of fresh fruit. His autumn entries record his torture at harvest-time: 'I envy people maunching and maunching peaches and grapes, and I not daring to eat a bit.' [23] Yet the volume and urgency of his work could simply not allow a prolonged attack.

He seems to have known when a bad fit was coming, and had tactics for stalling or minimizing it with rest and various panaceas. Brief attacks were clearly more frequent than full-out onslaughts of vertigo: 'this morning, sitting in my bed, I had a fit of giddiness: the room turned round for about a minute, and then it went off, leaving me sickish.'[24]

Such scares at various moments of the day were common, and he hated worrying his two friends in Dublin about them, 'but one fit shakes me a long time,' he admitted.[25] The winters left him weak and made him yearn for spring; but then the summers tormented him with heats his stout and dark-clad frame could hardly bear and, worse, the fresh fruit he strove to deny himself. 'I do venture to eat a few strawberries,' he confessed, but the connection seemed undeniable when his syndrome revealed its full force.[26] At such times, harsher purgative cures were deemed necessary: 'I have been much out of order of late with the old giddiness in my Head. I took a vomit for it 2 days ago, and will take another about a day or two hence. I have eat mighty little Fruit, yet I impute my disorder to that little, and shall henceforth wholly forbear it.'[27]

If he could not regulate the symptoms – however much he tried, with his assortment of dubious draughts, often sent to him by friends – he managed the stress by sticking to as fixed a routine as possible. He worked early, unless he had dined very late, socialized from about mid-day, visited his printers as and when necessary, and fraternized with political associates in the evenings. His last act of the day was usually an account of its happenings to Esther and Mrs Dingley. Those who have diagnosed Swift as a sufferer of Asperger's syndrome would probably seize on his disgruntlement at having his morning writing disturbed, or his precise requirements as to bed and hearth; but most who have had to work to tight deadlines in unhomely settings would admit to similar feelings. He was also not so singular in disliking a cold room, and making a moderate fuss about his attire. He was meticulous about his shaving day, distrustful of barbers, and forever put out by the cost of maintaining appearances: 'It has cost me three guineas today for a periwig. I am undone!'[28]

Much of the day went on solitary toil – his weekly essay for the *Examiner*, plus miscellaneous assignments as the political situation demanded. To produce the amount he did, though, he wrote and revised his papers quickly; words promptly answered his call as soon as his 'topicks' were clear in his head. One great modern scholar of Swift's manuscripts noticed that he would rest his pen on the page when he paused, leaving a trail of idiosyncratic dots – which suggests that instead of tracking back to finish and refine, he would wait a second till the exact phrase presented itself.[29] A large part of his time, with regard to his journalism, went on consulting with ministers or other informed parties. It is clear too that he lent a hand in drafting memoranda, parliamentary bills and keynote documents such as the Queen's Speech. These labours called for concentrated spells alone and intense spates of meetings, briefings, informal soundings. He was comfortable in all modes – so long, it seemed, as they did not overlap. When he was working, he resented a knock at the door. At liberty, he sought out friends and acquaintances, eagerly making new connections.

'What Puppyes are mankind,' he told Stella. 'I hope I shall be wiser when I have once done with Courts.' Yet it was as a courtier that Swift by now largely saw himself. He liked to say that he used the Court, at whichever royal residence it gathered, as he once did a coffee-house – as a place where he could meet people he would not otherwise see for months, and dispose of unwanted social obligations without discomfort, effort or expense.[30] The Court in truth was indispensable to Swift's networking and lobbying activities; yet perhaps it is only Pope, observing the scene at Hampton Court, who can illustrate the mixture of suspicion, fascination and cautious delight this great murmuring confluence held for Swift.

> Hither the Heroes and the Nymphs resort,
> To taste awhile the Pleasures of a Court;
> In various Talk th' instructive hours they passed,
> Who gave the *Ball*, or paid the *Visit* last:
> One speaks the glory of the *British Queen*,
> And one describes a charming *Indian Screen*;
> A third interprets Motions, Looks and Eyes;
> At ev'ry Word a Reputation dies.
> *Snuff*, or the *Fan*, supply each pause of *Chat*,
> With singing, laughing, ogling, and all that.[31]

'All that', one might have thought, was precisely what Swift loathed; and it was, whenever it was practised by a cheat, a scoundrel or a strumpet – but his letters to Johnson also show how much the social stir excited and intrigued him. Like poor Pope, though for different reasons, he was a demi-outsider. He could never quite be a part of it, age and profession and personality putting him outside the fold of beaux and beauties, but he could take a hand of cards and relish a good rumour. He loved to be among fashionable people, and could be comfortable with them; though to avoid impropriety or humiliation, he requested that ladies who were interested in meeting him made the first approach. Beyond, meanwhile, the supposedly civilized setting captured by Pope, he was more than aware of the evil niches of the town to which the same company in some cases resorted. In such quarters, his gown and bands were armour, if he walked there by accident. There were corners, moreover, he would be careful never to visit. The Earl of Rochester had once described a night-time ramble in St James's Park, where the distinctions of rank were lost amid the trees:

> And nightly now beneath their shade
> Are buggeries, rapes, and incests made.
> Unto this all-sin-sheltering grove
> Whores of the bulk [a seat outside a shop-front] and the alcove,
> Great ladies, chambermaids, and drudges,
> The ragpicker, and heiress trudges.
> Car-men, divines, great lords, and tailors,
> Prentices, poets, pimps, and jailers,
> Footmen, fine fops, do here arrive,
> And here promiscuously they swive [fornicate].[32]

Rochester's lines date from the early 1670s; but the array of humanity, and the locations London furnished it with, had changed little in the intervening decades. They would surface explicitly only later in Swift's writing career, as objects of fascinated disgust. And it was this swiving side of life, or rather the individuals who surrendered to it, that perhaps discomfited him most. He reserved what he regarded as the depravities of the sexual drive for perhaps his cruellest social criticism: he would attack the libido through an anti-sexual yet still bizarrely pornographic set of poems about ageing, disfigured prostitutes. Strikingly, neverthe-less, he had none of the inhuman and chauvinistic presumptions with which most men of his day (and many down to the present time) regarded sexually active women. In July 1711 he heard that a move was being made to obtain a pardon for a convicted rapist, on the basis of what he called 'an old notion', the idea that the woman will always have in some way encouraged her attacker. Swift showed progressive thinking on a point still raised in modern rape trials: ''Tis true, the fellow had lain with her a hundred times before; but what care I for that?' He inter-vened personally with St John to ensure that the sentence was carried out: 'and so he shall swing,' he informed Stella contentedly.[33]

In his urban movements he was rarely completely alone. A clumsy and often riotous shadow in the first half of the *Journal* belongs to Pat-rick, his Irish manservant. Patrick was strong and dogged, and not without guile; but almost every mention Swift makes of him comes with a curse. Patrick was a heavy drinker, often stiff and bruised from falls and fights in taverns. Swift was afraid to let his often trembling hands come near him with a razor. The poor man seems to have bodged everything he touched, from trimming a candle too short, so that its grease stained Swift's paper, to overfilling the inkpot or breaking the key to a trunk. He would disappear just when he was needed, wake his master too early after a long night of work, or forget to take the laundry and leave Swift without fresh linen. Yet the duties Swift needed him for were not those a more delicate valet could perform. Patrick, to put it plainly, was Swift's 'muscle': however angry he made Swift by getting into scraps and damaging things, he could take a thump from a footman and return it with added force. He could exert pressure if it was called for, and visit houses and taverns where Swift could not afford to be seen. He also had a survivor's knack for getting to know an entire neighbourhood. Swift never would admit to liking him, but he gives a strong sense that half of London's maids and porters did. And more than once he was glad to have the huge Irishman's company on a long walk home through darkness. As the political bitterness deepened, and as more and more potentially desperate characters found themselves compromised – ruffians such as Macartney, the slayer of Hamilton, and countless other ex-army grudge-bearers – Swift's person as well as his reputation became subject to threats. The friends he enjoyed in high places were all very well; but they made a bodyguard necessary in the town's parks and alleyways.

## 3

Writing in his digs, from the autumn of 1710 onwards Swift's business for the weekly *Examiner* was more to take the offensive than to justify or explain positive aspects of government policy. For many months to come, in spite of royal disfavour and their recent defeat at the polls, the fallen Whig hierarchy still felt the deeds to power were in their name. 'Those Junto pigmies if not destroyed will grow up into Giants,' the picturesque Earl of Peterborough warned Swift, wishing he might lead an old-fashioned charge against them.[34] For Swift, then, the first task was to discredit the previous regime; a delicate one, and not only because of the coalition's internal politics. Rubbishing Godolphin's administration by necessity involved attacking a man who, for all his faults, was both a national hero and serving commander. The assault on Marlborough required tactical thinking on a par with that of the general himself. The solution presented itself in the rhetorical tone that came to characterize the *Examiner*: a presiding attitude, that is, of objectivity and moral superiority. There were no cheap hits to be scored here: Swift's method instead was to offer a critique of lapsed greatness. This was frequently given within an absolutely brilliant satirical framework: as, for example, when he countered those who claimed the Duke had been poorly rewarded for his services. Here Swift's device was to compare the barely imaginable fortune bestowed on Marlborough with the humble tribute a victorious general of ancient Rome could have expected. It thereby reduced a complex political and moral question to the level of brass tacks and cold measurements, and suggested a technique that would serve Swift extremely well over the years – most extensively in his *Drapier's Letters* and most shockingly in the *Modest Proposal*.

'He is covetous as Hell, and ambitious as the Prince of it,' declared Swift of Marlborough in his journal. Winston Churchill, Marlborough's definitive but also fervently supportive biographer, found nothing to dispute in this judgement apart from the infernal dimension. The Duke himself, however, denied the charge: in a mortifying audience with the Queen in December, he had insisted he was neither ambitious nor covetous. Anne answered her old friend by saying it was a shame she could not politely turn her back on him; as it was, the sanguine matriarch hardly stopped herself from laughing in his face. Writing to his ladies in Dublin, Swift could afford to be lenient: 'Yet he has been a successful general, and I hope he will continue in his command.'[35] He was, like Harley (and unlike the Tories champing for Marlborough's head), being pragmatic. It was not at all clear that Marlborough's leadership might not be needed in Flanders for many years to come. It was imperative, nevertheless, that Marlborough be lamed politically, and Swift kept up the campaign in the early months of 1711, as a 'monstrous deal of snow' fell on London. The snow, Swift recorded, gathered dirt and acquired a layer of ice 'like a pot-lid'.[36] Still, he had as much stomach for a winter campaign as the suddenly beleaguered general. Swift's 'Letter to Crassus', for the *Examiner* in February, addressed the Duke as the living equivalent of the Roman general who had, along with Julius Caesar and Pompey, hijacked the Roman state through their 'First Triumvirate'. Crassus had also amassed an illegal fortune unrivalled in the ancient world. His military skills, like Marlborough's, were undisputed, and these Swift set aside in assaulting his target's avarice. Following convention, not once in the paper is Marlborough's name mentioned; the target was so obvious that Swift abstained from even the most tangential allusion to it. His preliminaries to the letter itself, a cool and surgical discourse on the vice of covetousness, furnish good examples of the Parnassian hauteur Swift brought to his task each week: he would treat the Duke more roughly (though by no means so damagingly) in cruder sorties such as his verse *Fable of Midas*.

Direct onslaughts were incompatible with the bearing of Swift's *Examiner*. The following paragraph illustrates the air of neutrality he cultivated.

> The Divine Authority of Holy Writ, the Precepts of Philosophers, the Lashes and Ridicule of Satyrical Poets, have been all employed in exploding this insatiable Thirst of Money; and all equally controlled by the daily Practice of Mankind. Nothing new remains to be said upon the Occasion [the topic of avarice]; and if there did, I must remember my Character, that I am an *Examiner* only, and not a *Reformer*.[37]

He preferred to discourse of things rather than persons; but, since offences carried more often than not a whiff of well-known perpetrators, he could hardly prevent inferences from being made. Only a slight nuance in the final sentence above, the faintest of gestures calculated for the initiate, betrays what Swift was actually doing: he *was* reforming, not just examining; but he was also assuming a persona, taking on a role. As 'the Examiner', he was not saying anything he did not believe, but there were infinite ways of doing that. As with his performance as Bickerstaff a few years before, Swift had to 'stay in character', and was doing so magnificently. Behind the scenes, despite his thickening skin, he was hurt by libels from new enemies. 'One Boyer, a French dog, has abused me in a pamphlet,' he fumed, at a swipe from a rival paper; but he was comforted that 'the minister promises me to swinge him.'[38]

In his *Examiner* essays Swift took an expansive view of the previous twenty years, and dropped the diplomatic stance he had taken in his political papers from 1701 onwards. When one looks closely, his dislike of the general trends in State and Church was present in his writing since his debut, *A Discourse of the Contests and Dissensions between the Nobles and the Commons in Athens and Rome*. Now it became explicit. Looking back over a period roughly equivalent with his own adult life, he found betrayal and corruption in all public affairs: and things had reached such a pass that the country itself had been mortgaged. 'It may be worth inquiring from what Beginnings, and by what Steps we have been brought into this desperate Condition,' he invited his readers. The Williamite revolution and subsequent settlement had undoubtedly rescued the nation, and the noblemen, gentlemen and clergymen who invited William of Orange to England and attended him on his expedition had acted in good faith. They had not, Swift was sure, intended to open an era of perpetual revolution. Then two terrible changes occurred. 'An under Sett of Men, who had nothing to lose, and had neither born the Burthen nor Heat of the Day' gained the confidence of the King.[39] These understrappers convinced William that he could not trust the Church of England, and thus the Court began 'caressing the Dissenters' and undermining the Established Church. How cruel, Swift observed, since none had stood up more bravely against James's papistical designs than the Anglican clergy. The handful of Nonjurors who could not accept William as the King deserved pity, he suggested, rather than contempt, for taking their allegiance to hereditary principles so far. The other grave change had gone hand in hand with the first. The turn away from the religious establishment, in Swift's view, was simultaneous with a displacement of the old basis of power, the landed interest. Instead of living on its harvests and manufactures, the country was now kept afloat on vast loans from the City.

The debate was about more than pulling Britain out of a long war or reducing the national debt. It was about the foundation of the state itself, and, ultimately, a clash over what the revolution and settlement of 1689–90 was really supposed to have achieved. To Swift, and (broadly speaking) the Tory interest, the civic and clerical establishment's move to support William was a one-off – in other words, the revolution was an exception, not a precedent. The clergy in particular had gone along with William's accession 'like Men who are content to go about, for avoiding a Gulph or a Precipice, but come into the old strait Road again as soon as they can'. Yet Swift now conceded there was no returning to that straight and narrow way (regardless of whether they had really ridden on it previously):

For, as in the Reign of King Charles the First, several well-meaning People were ready to join in reforming some Abuses; while others, who had deeper Designs, were still calling out for a *thorough Reformation*, which ended at last in the Ruin of the Kingdom; so, after the late King's [William's] coming to the Throne, there was a restless Cry from Men of *the same Principles*, for a *thorough Revolution*, which as *some* were carrying it on, must have ended in the Destruction of the Monarchy and Church.[40]

In Swift's eyes it was still a Roundhead plot: the regicides were alive in spirit in the Whig ascendancy of William's reign and in the early years of Anne's. For Swift personally, the trials of his grandfather, the Reverend Swift of Goodrich, still called for vengeance – and there were few concerned with the larger arguments whose perspective was untrammelled by similar inherited grievances. Indeed, in an unpublished essay, Swift had strongly argued that one should always look for the personal motive behind an author's public opinions. When Milton wrote his treatise in support of divorce, Swift claimed, everyone knew this was an 'occasional' work because the poet 'had a Shrew for his Wife'.

> Neither can there be any Reason imagined, why he might not, after he was blind, have writ another upon the Danger and Inconvenience of Eyes. But, it is a Piece of Logic which will hardly pass on the World; that because one Man hath a sore Nose, therefore all the Town should put plaisters upon theirs.[41]

That the same principle might also operate in his own case was a question Swift could handle: his motives might be personal but his reasoning was sound, and disinterested – unlike Milton's on divorce, or the Whigs' on continuing the war. Enemies, though, disputed his objectivity. Francis Hare, Marlborough's chaplain, back-handedly complimented Swift's most devastating attack on the war effort as 'a Masterpiece of Cunning, not the work of a Vulgar Hand, or of a *Swift* pen'.[42]

While the principles of the paper were undoubtedly his own, the voice of the *Examiner* was not, or not exactly. From the outset, Swift took on the character of an aristocratic observer. His speaker had all the attributes of a man of considerable property, with a coach and townhouse, tenants and an agent to manage his estate.[43] He was a four-square Church-of-England man, a respecter of the clerical estate and the Restoration prayer-book. The *Examiner* was concerned with polity, rather than mere politics. He was anxious for the books to be balanced; yet, with tradition and the right-minded nation on his side, he could roundly commend the government's plan to build fifty new churches in the metropolis. A paper devoted to this scheme offered grave, majestic applause late in May 1711, at the height of Harley's popularity.[44] The *Examiner*'s independence allowed him to brush aside the charge that he was supporting the ministry for gain or influence, and also to assume the grander bearing his often supercilious judgements demanded. His utterances were those of a patron, and certainly no hireling, of the government.

'The Examiner' was a person of honour, then, who typified the best and deepest qualities of the country. In response to jibes, this refined yet worldly landowner declared in an early paper his wish that he might 'tell [the world] my Name and Titles at Length';[45] but remained anonymous with good reason. He provided a necessary screen to the middling cleric, living in digs, who impersonated him in print.

The presence of mind required of Swift in sustaining this act is shown more strongly if the floor is given for a moment to the voices pitted against him. The rhetorical poise of the *Examiner* can make it seem, from this distance in time, that Swift's arguments were unassailable, and that his foes were reduced to silence by them. Instead, his success in the ongoing skirmishes over the change of ministry and the turn towards peace is to be measured by the volume of replies he provoked. Quite a few of these focused on Swift himself, and they too scored their points. The jab at his character in the following came from a long-term sparring partner:

> When that worthy Gentleman [Swift] was first put upon writing his Weekly Paper, it was presently given out by the Wags of his Party, that he was to maul the Whigs: Scandal was the only thing he pretended to ... His Acquaintance answer'd for him, that he had a Conscience exactly suted to such an Undertaking, and a Complexion to carry him thro with it: That he wou'd stick at nothing; but the highest Rank, the most conspicuous Merit wou'd be no Security against his Insolence.[46]

The author of these words was either Arthur Mainwaring, widely respected as a literary and political sage, or one of his assistants. For a time, when Swift's anonymity was still more or less intact, Mainwaring had employed Addison to write a *Whig Examiner* against the Tory paper. The cut and thrust required for such work did not suit Addison, who was clearly pained to find out that his adversary was someone he liked, trusted and admired. The extra sting in the passage thus comes from the writer's inside knowledge about Swift's 'Acquaintance'. Swift could only suspect that his much esteemed friend had rubbished both his character and conscience. As salt to the wound and proof of the insult, when the *Tatler* was published in book form, Steele dedicated the collection to Mainwaring.

Avarice was exhausted as a subject: 'nothing new remains to be said.' Marlborough was as unpopular at home as Crassus once was, with Plebeians and Patricians alike: yet there was still a pressing need to write against him. As 1711 progressed, the Duke gave one last proof that, however beset he might currently be at Westminster, he was unrivalled in the field – and thus far from finished for his supporters in England. After years of stalemate, in August he cut deep into enemy territory on a march that wore his men to the bone but – so records have it – spent not a single one of their lives. This was his celebrated incursion over Marshal Villars's 'Non Plus Ultra Lines', a label that had long seemed simply geographical, but now sounded almost risible. The Allied push culminated in the brief siege and capture in early September of Bouchain in northern France. At any other juncture, this would have been a victory to have made Marlborough's position as 'Captain-General' his for life, as he asked it might be – and for the reward to seem both fitting and sensible. But the public at home, however much it loved a triumph, really had lost stomach for the war it was funding in taxes and flesh: in Swift's analysis the 'landed' interest, which now sided broadly with the Tories – and idolized Queen Anne – was getting the better of the 'moneyed' interest. Swift's part in winning the publicity war over these questions was reflected by the respect, confidence and friendship that Harley, St John and most of the governing party now placed in him. 'They call me nothing but Jonathan,' he informed Johnson in February 1711; 'and I said, I believed they would leave me Jonathan as they found me.'[47] Nevertheless, as his success mounted – measured by audible panic and rage from the Whig contingent – he could not help his hopes rising. Militarily, Marlborough was still supreme: and that, Swift's journalism had argued, was quite as it should be. Yet politically the general was vanishing in smoke.

There were setbacks – battles lost, prisoners taken. At almost the same time as the Duke's last wonder, Harley's grasp of strategy seemed wanting. As a concession to the Tory conviction that England was better off waging war by sea than by land, he and St John authorized an ambitious marine operation to capture French Quebec. Brigadier-General John Hill was placed in command of 7,500 troops;[48] Admiral Sir Hovenden Walker took charge of the naval side of the enterprise, transporting Hill's expeditionary force in more than 60 vessels, escorted by 10 ships-of-the-line. Disaster followed. In August, fogs and gales addled the fleet on the Saint Lawrence River. Eight of General Hill's transports were wrecked, with an estimated 800 lives lost. Hill and Walker agreed to abandon the mission forthwith; and they returned home to ridicule. Hill, a friend of Harley and his ministry, and well liked by Swift, had displayed little of Marlborough's pluck and nous – but he shared with the

Duke a soldier's love of promotion and a trophy. He was rewarded the following year with a lord lieutenancy of the ordinance, and the governorship of Dunkirk, to general public disapproval. The Quebec Expedition was a bad blow for the government's popularity and in the longer run for Harley himself. It supplied material for prominent articles in his eventual impeachment.

Luckily for Harley, the government could still take the credit for Marlborough's success at Bouchain; and the Chancellor had done much, in the meantime, to restore confidence in the public finances. Harley's finest achievement to date was in damage limitation, stabilizing the budget while maintaining subsidies for the war. This was no small success, given the staunch refusal of Whig financiers to lend money to the government. The juggling act could not be long sustained; yet in company both Harley and St John maintained a carefree demeanour. 'I always find them as easy and disengaged as schoolboys on a holiday,' Swift reported.[49] Such conduct by St John was part of his mandatory breeziness as a self-declared free man. In Harley, calmness in the moment lay more with temperament and strategy: he could weather almost any emergency by thinking many moves ahead – often almost seeming to ignore the alarm of his allies in the present, at the risk of straining their nerves too far. The burdens of the war and the revenue pressed down on him; but peace would ease that weight. His goal lay with the overtures he was making to France.

Across the Channel, at Versailles, there was still of course 'the mighty king' who had, as Swift described him in the late 1690s, 'for the space of above thirty Years, amused himself to take and lose Towns; beat Armies, and be beaten; drive Princes out of their Dominions; fright Children from their Bread and Butter; burn, lay waste, plunder, dragoon, massacre, Subject and Stranger, Friend and Foe, Male and Female'.[50] Yet the truth was that Louis, now in his mid-seventies, was finally tiring. In the summer of 1711, as Marlborough saw and took his chance, and as Hill and Walker sailed towards catastrophe, a well-trusted official travelled privately to France. He was received for secret talks at the highest level, at which some basic agreements were reached. On his return, however, he was detained by Customs as a suspected spy, and his cover was blown. The unofficial emissary was Matthew Prior, and his mission had been to sound out peace terms. His identity, and the likely substance of his business in France, quickly spread through the press. The Whigs were appalled by a motion for peace they were certain was treasonous; and they declared the outrage should be felt universally. Without question, the news struck hard at the hopes of those who had tied their futures to the expectation of a long war; but they had had a year to prepare themselves.

Swift, who had by now retired as Examiner, saw there was no sense in denying the movement for peace, however shocked some might be at how close it now seemed. He decided to float a pamphlet confirming the rumour entirely. As ever, his method involved assuming a 'character' – this time neither of Examiner nor Reformer, but of Eavesdropper, more specifically in the guise of a French gentleman hired by Prior (in Swift's fiction) to assist him on his travels. This temporary companion writes to a friend, spilling all he knows about the mysterious Englishman. The suggestive name of the writer, the Sieur de Baudrier, should have alerted all readers to the dubious provenance of the text; but hundreds at least evidently failed to see any sign of a hoax. In any case the English travel-ler (who in the best traditions of espionage is also self-possessed, quietly spoken and coolly resourceful) gains access to some of King Louis's highest-ranking courtiers. Nothing material of the negotiations is of course disclosed, since Swift at this time had only a vague idea of what any possible treaty might contain. But the opportunity is taken to reveal how blighted and tired France was looking at this time, and also how blinkered the French were, in an implied comparison that did the Eng-lish great credit. On their journey, Prior remarks upon the general misery and poverty he observes beyond the carriage windows, at which his fel-low traveller:

> made bold to return for Answer, That in our Nation we only consulted the Magnificence and Power of our Prince; but that in *England*, as I was inform'd, the Wealth of the Kingdom was so divided among the People, that little or nothing was left to their Sovereign; and that it was confidently told (tho hardly believed in *France*) that some Subjects had Palaces more Magnificent than Queen *Anne* herself.[51]

Here with startling economy Swift scored points at the expense of the enemy at home and abroad, the French monarchy and the lustfully greedy Whig aristocracy, while piping a very loyal note for the modesty and integrity of the Queen. He was playing the same game he would take to extravagant lengths with the *Travels*: testing the credulity of his readership with fiction presented as fact, and relying on the gullible to betray themselves – for the hit in the passage above was too neat for the discerning to believe such elegant skull-cracking could be entirely

accidental. Swift was therefore amused when Prior, for all his sophistication, missed both the wit and the policy in the *New Journey to Paris*. The
two-penny pamphlet, 'a formal grave lie', as Swift described it, appeared
on 11 September 1711, and sold a thousand copies the same day (a huge
number). Swift followed St John to dinner at Prior's that evening, by
chance or design. Prior, who, to Swift, resembled a 'lean carcass',[52] brandished the paper at him as he entered the parlour, and spoke disgruntled
words about English freedoms of speech. The ritual of never acknowledging Swift's authorship genuinely confuses the issue of whether Prior
had guessed the *New Journey* was his. The gesture suggests he had, but
Prior was not amused. Swift took the pamphlet, calmly perused his own
handiwork and later told Esther: 'I read some of it, and said I liked it
mightily, and envied the rogue the thought.'[53]

St John might have been privy to this particular joke; but Harley kept
him away from much sensitive work. A year into government, the partnership was cracking. The main cause was the exposure of the two men's
inequality. St John was horribly upset when, in May 1711, Harley was
ennobled as the Earl of Oxford and Earl Mortimer, and then a day or so
later made the Lord Treasurer. 'I hope he will stick there,' commented
Swift; 'this is twice he has changed his name this week.'[54] With Swift and
his 'brother' wits, Harley refused to be addressed as 'My Lord'. Still, the
highest accolade, a knighthood of the Garter, was also predicted for him,
and was in time granted. St John gritted his teeth and paid his compliments; but envy raddled him. He too received a peerage, but only a
viscountcy, for which he took the title Bolingbroke. Matters were worsened by the wording of Harley's patent, which many found pompous in
the extreme. Gauchely so, it was said; but this was of no comfort to St
John, whose family prided itself on a line stretching back to the Conquest.
Though he missed a greater title and office, he possibly resented Harley
even more for a wound the Chancellor had received earlier in the spring.

The injury had made a hero and near-martyr of plain Mr Harley, as
he still was when he suffered it on 8 March 1711. The hurt was inflicted
with a pen-knife in the hands of a desperate Frenchman. Antoine, Marquis de Guiscard, a refugee in his fifties with an English pension of £400
a year, had long been an associate and informant of Godolphin and
Marlborough, and had for a time commanded a regiment of fellow ex-
patriots. Harley, though, had little use for him, and had trimmed his
pension; this prompted Guiscard to exchange treasonable letters with
the enemy in hope of reconciliation. On the day of the attack, Guiscard
faced questioning in St John's official chambers. Harley and a number of

other ministers and privy councillors were present. As the hearing went on, Guiscard muttered and cursed; and Harley, seated just behind him to one side, told him to mind his manners. Guiscard pulled out the pen-knife – which later passed to Swift, and which he kept as a relic – and plunged it into Harley's chest. In some accounts, Harley was saved by the thick embroidery of gold thread his sister Abigail had sewn on to his coat, which broke the blade; a second thrust, however, pierced flesh. As Harley collapsed, St John leaped forward with his sword drawn, and stabbed Guiscard. The would-be assassin received wounds from 'five or six more of the Council' before a senior peer bade them stop, so that Guiscard could face the consequences – and give up details of any wider conspiracy. St John, who apparently went wild, was restrained, and had his sword broken. As the situation calmed, and a surgeon examined Harley, it emerged that the attacker had fared much the worse of the two. Guiscard's little blade had jammed on a rib, and left Harley only a shallow cut, half an inch deep, which healed nicely over the next few weeks. Meanwhile every care was taken to preserve Guiscard for the hangman. 'I pray God he may recover to receive his Reward,' wrote Swift, 'and that we may learn the Bottom of his Villainy.'[55] A penniless marquis who appears begging in rags in the *New Journey to Paris* may well be a vengeful portrait of Guiscard. Yet, not long before the attack, Swift had actually put in a word of support with St John for this 'fellow of little consequence'; in fact, they had passed by one another in the Mall an hour before the questioning. Guiscard offered no greeting.

Swift was playing cards in a gentlewoman's parlour when he heard the news. It clearly shocked him to the core. He ran immediately to St John's house, where he met Frances, the wife of the Secretary of State, hurrying off in her chair for further news. Swift hired a chair himself, borne in his cabin on poles held by two sturdy runners, and travelled away from Westminster to Harley's house. There the minister was sleeping and, according to his son, apparently out of danger. Swift was left in profound shock. He wrote promptly to Archbishop King with a detailed report, valuable both for its account of the incident and the light it throws on Swift's inner state: 'I have read over what I writ, and find it confused and incorrect, which your Grace must impute to the violent Pain of Mind I am in, greater than ever I felt in my Life.'[56] The same strength of feeling comes through, although more ambiguously, in Swift's shorter account for Esther Johnson. 'I am in mortal pain for him . . . Pray pardon my distraction; I now think of all his kindness to me.' He sent Patrick loping off for news at first light the next day.[57]

Harley's death would have placed Swift's position in some doubt; but he had other protectors. Self-interest is obviously not what moved him, as he bolted across town for word of Harley's condition, and sat feverishly at his table to relate what he had learned. Anyone who reads Swift's *Examiner*s, his poetry and occasional journalism from the preceding months will see how utterly he had plunged himself into Harley's cause. Ending the Whiggish war and saving the Church from the Dissenters were plainly his first concern. While waiting in Harley's house to hear the first news of his condition, he wrote four rough lines on a scrap of paper. They were addressed to the first minister's surgeon.

> On Britain Europes safety lyes
> And Britain's lost if Harley dyes
> Harley depends upon your skill
> Think what you save or what you kill.[58]

A measure of Swift's distress was his use of 'Britain', a word he hated.

Swift's record of the Guiscard incident shows just how capable he was of deep idealism, along with steadfast and very woundable intimacy. It was really only now – as Harley convalesced, as the Whigs began muttering that the whole thing was staged, and as even St John spread a rumour that Harley had orchestrated the attack – that Swift realized how fond he had grown of the injured first minister. He pitied his friend's rheumatism, and was familiar with all his quirks – noticing, for example, how the minister was also hard of hearing on the left side, always turning his right ear to receive a servant's whisper.[59] A more or less complete easiness had developed between them. Swift's noontide visit to the Lord Treasurer at home one morning in October was evidently fairly routine: he found Harley eating broth in his bedchamber, 'undressed, with a thousand papers about him'. He noted that his friend had a 'little fever', and that his eyes were all bloodshot; 'yet he dressed himself, and went out to the Treasury.'[60] The scene was typical of countless similar meetings. This is not to say, of course, that Swift was Harley's confidant in the most secret official business; but, then, nobody was, and certainly not St John, the new Viscount Bolingbroke. The rift between the Earl and Viscount, as they became when Harley recovered, distressed Swift greatly, since the Secretary of State had also thoroughly charmed him, but above and beyond his love of persons was a passionate attachment to the enterprise. He wished the two leaders would see beyond their differences and take their task in greater earnest. The attempt on Harley's life by Guiscard, though, only added to the bitterness between Harley and St John, Lords Oxford and Bolingbroke as they became. From the opposition side, rumour was rife that Oxford had staged the whole incident; with the added gain of removing a French insider who might spill compromising facts about the ministry's collusion with the enemy. At around this time John Toland, a sometime cooperator with Harley – and a sincere adherent of civil liberties he saw the government betraying – believed such stories and repeated them. There was one slander, however, that Harley could not forgive, and it was floated by his fellow minister. St John let it be known that he in fact had been Guiscard's real target: the knife was meant for him, and thus he was the true martyr – an interpretation that, as Swift immediately saw, gave St John all the danger and glory of the episode and Harley only the pain.[61]

# 4

As the autumn of 1711 slipped into winter, the initiative for peace and the question of the next year's campaign built up a state of agonizing tension over Christmas – for everyone, it seemed, except the Lord Treasurer. The shape of the treaty with France, in which the ministry had all but disregarded the other members of the Grand Alliance, prompted a bitter rearguard action from the Whigs and Dutch representatives. Former members of the Whig Junto, collaborating with a former Tory, the Earl of Nottingham, insisted that no agreement could be reached with France unless Spain was kept entirely out of French hands. 'No Peace without Spain' became a crushingly effective motto; yet, for all that, Marlborough was stripped of office at the end of the year, and a relatively minor official, one Robert Walpole, a Whig whose abilities had already been noted by many, was another political casualty. A climax, however, came with a crucial vote carried for the government thanks to a cunning and controversial ploy by Harley. At a time when membership of the Lords was strictly capped, he persuaded the Queen to create twelve new peers. This gave him the majority he needed in the Upper House. The measure, arranged in time for New Year, involved allowing a number of eldest sons to come up early to Parliament; but, all the same, it was a startling gambit. Swift, on learning of it, was almost furious with Harley; over Christmas he had suffered ecstasies of anguish, and believed the government would fall. It was possibly Harley's masterstroke, encapsulating all his talents and flaws. Yet, despite the victory, it left his colleagues feeling shut out and resentful – since they had borne the worst of the stress, while the success was his alone.

The creation of the peers was felt as a puzzling, troubling tactic. Harley claimed that his goal was a return to an older politics, one in which party would no longer be the presiding force. The radical means he was prepared to use, however, clashed with his conservative aim. Relieved though he was, Swift confessed to being staggered by Harley's manoeuvre. 'In above twenty Years that I have known something of Courts and Ministers,' he wrote to Archbishop King, 'I never saw so strange and odd a complicated Disposition of affairs.'[62] He adopted, as he did so often, the air of an old hand on the manor of high politics, whistling at a wonder. The remark is one of those he made from time to time that indicate how he cherished his identity as a courtier. But he was genuinely rattled. While he placed the blame for the crisis squarely on the Whigs, and in time criticized the negligence of the Queen herself, Harley's audacity blindsided him. The affair left him more disposed to be angry with his chief, even as their friendship grew.

The force of such an episode on London's political community can only be sensed by retaining an awareness of how small a territory its active members shared, and how claustrophobic were the chambers and corridors in which they confronted one another. The Palace of Westminster as it stands today gives exactly the impression of renovated timelessness that its architects, Charles Barry and Augustus Pugin, designed it to convey; yet it contains no memories older than the mid-nineteenth century. The palace Swift knew, which burned down in 1834, was still properly speaking a palace, albeit one much altered and no longer home to royalty. Entering Westminster Hall, staring up at the frozen acrobatics performed by the timbers of its roof, is the only means of shadowing Swift's allies and opponents, and their countless predecessors in English statecraft. The palace itself was a much more modestly scaled affair than the Victorian structure that replaced it. The current building would take a good deal more gunpowder than was stashed in the cellar with Guy Fawkes. Pugin's Gothic Revival façade reproduces (and enhances) the lost medieval crust, but not the practical compactness of the original structure. The House of Lords was packed into a little hall, known as the Queen's Chamber, at the south end; the Commons held its debates nearby in St Stephen's Chapel, with the opposing sides of the House glaring and grumbling from the lines of its pews. These overstuffed, inhospitable rooms provided the stage for Harley's coup at the end of 1711.

It was a short-lived victory, as perhaps such triumphs always are, and would be thoroughly avenged. Yet the Whigs for now really had been routed. The chief scalp was undoubtedly that of the national hero, Marlborough. Swift was credited, not least by Marlborough himself, with inflicting the worst damage on the General's reputation. Marlborough's career was ripe for myth, and based, like the best legends, upon blood-sodden fact. His string of astounding successes had made him the most successful figure in English arms since Cromwell, and – given the scale of the operations he directed – quite possibly ever. He would loom much larger in English history now were it not for Wellington, who aspired to match him. Marlborough was well organized to a fault, frugal with resources and unsparing with effort, and always aware of the diplomatic dimension. He remained superbly courteous to his allies even as the Dutch in particular enraged his staff and troops by stalling and backbiting. On the march, he took great care of his men; in battle, he was generous with their lives for the sake of the greater objective, but often careless of his own with the same end in mind. He was invariably to be found on the front line. After Ramillies, the public seized on the image of their general being pulled from the mud and helped back into the saddle by a courageous aide, Colonel James Bringfield, whose head was struck off a second later by a cannonball aimed at Marlborough. The incident was commemorated in a grisly pack of illustrated playing cards as a moment that encapsulated both the devotion Marlborough attracted and his personal courage. Yet, at home, the *Examiner* had made him appear stingy, selfish, corrupt – and more than faintly treasonous in his ultimate ambitions.

In the run-up to the great crisis of December 1711, Swift had undermined the pro-war movement with a powerful and hugely controversial critique of the alliance against France. In *The Conduct of the Allies and of the Late Ministry in Beginning and Carrying on the Present War*, successive editions of which sold out within days, Swift took on more than the Whigs and the 'Monied Men' of the City. He alleged ineptitude and malevolence towards English interests on the part of the Dutch and even Marlborough's great comrade, Prince Eugène of Savoy. Swift's argument was bolstered with facts that till now had been sealed up in secret dispatches. The Dutch Swift found especially exasperating. He had long disliked them as a nation, for the Dissenting sects they fostered; while the recent concessions and privileges they forced from England infuriated him. Their demands for subsidies, their unwillingness to commit troops or funds, and above all their insistence on a protective borderland chain of 'barrier' cities, to be prised from France at a huge human cost, were utterly out of proportion to their status, as Swift saw it, as a minor power. When the vote on Spain was won, Swift allowed himself still greater vehemence against The Hague. He opened his waspish *Some Remarks on the Barrier Treaty*, published early in 1712, by asking how a rational alien might view the relationship between England and the 'States General' of the Netherlands.

> Imagine a reasonable Person in *China*, were reading the following Treaty, and one who was ignorant of our Affairs, or our Geography: He would conceive their High Mightinesses the States General, to be some vast powerful Commonwealth, like that of *Rome*, and Her Majesty [Queen Anne] to be a Petty Prince, like one of those to whom that Republick would sometimes send a Diadem for a Present, when they behaved themselves well.[63]

It was of course England, Swift silently clucked, which would be sending no more crowns to Amsterdam for the present. Funny though the passage is and trenchant as the *Remarks* are as a whole, the earlier book, *The Conduct*, has the greater power and drama. It was written when success on the question of ending the war was doubtful at best. The work was narrated in the manner of a privileged insider, but behind it was a private citizen who was staking his all on the matter. One should remember that if Harley had lost the vote in the Lords, the collapse of the ministry would have been inevitable. In that case, paragraphs such as the following by Swift could have landed him in prison. He was attacking England's finest soldier, the country's staunchest allies and the entire foreign policy of the national saviour, William III.

> In that whole chain of Encroachments made upon us by the *Dutch*, which I have above deduced, and under those several gross Impositions from other *Powers*, if any one should ask, why our G[enera]l continued so easy to the last? I know of no other Way so probable, or indeed so charitable, to account for it, as by that unmeasurable Love of Wealth, which his best Friends allow to be his predominant Passion. However, I shall waive any thing that is Personal upon this Subject.[64]

The restraint exercised upon a victim, *post mortem*, merits an admiring gasp from the reader: a grand political kill is granted 'personal' dignity – burial rites. The effect is amplified when one recalls that this is very much David standing over Goliath.

Marlborough was injured grievously by the charge of avarice and double-dealing. The story of his humbling and removal into exile is long and involved. In brief, as with the war he directed in Europe, operations were being orchestrated against him on more than one front. Years had passed since the Duchess of Marlborough, once the Queen's chief confidante, had been outmanoeuvred by a new favourite, a poor relation no less, her cousin Abigail Masham. Since then the Whigs had worked to unseat Masham in favour of another lady-in-waiting, Swift's foe Elizabeth, Duchess of Somerset, but she and her husband suffered indignities of their own in the great reversal at the close of 1711.

As for Marlborough, he was quite clear on Swift's part in his downfall. Swift reported how 'the Duke of Marlborough says, There is nothing he desires so much as to contrive some way how to soften Dr. Swift.'[65] Swift eventually passed word to the Duke that he had stopped 'many a bitter thing against him' from going to press.[66] At moments, in the aftermath of Marlborough's fall, he came close to regretting his part in it. This did not, however, prevent him from lowering Marlborough further in the public eye in subsequent works. He was at pains to make clear that he had never questioned Marlborough's abilities as a general; yet he was quite unimpressed by martial accomplishments when a soldier's character proved wanting – especially one who had opposed or offended him. Some years earlier, he had roasted Baron Cutts of Gowran, a patron of Steele and a military hero of the 1690s, who was nicknamed 'The Salamander' for his indifference to the heat of battle. Swift explored the comparison further, describing the spots on John Cutts's powder-burnt coat as if they were lesions, and pointing out the slimy amphibious trail left by his lustful pursuits: a twentieth-century editor of the poems was scandalized by the invective.[67] On a grander scale, Swift was as merciless with Marlborough's ambition and avarice as he had been with Cutts's supposed lechery. He was, of course, helplessly biased. The strikes on Cutts, Marlborough – or Godolphin, Nottingham or any of the Junto – were heartfelt but strategically motivated. They were political incendiaries, however much Swift intended them as absolute moral pronouncements. For he could overlook Viscount Bolingbroke's flagrant womanizing, but not the Earl of Wharton's; and forgive similar tendencies in the Earl of Peterborough, one of the most notorious political turncoats of the age.

The humbling of Marlborough brought a deeper Tory hue to the Harley–St John ministry. The pick of Marlborough's honours went to an Irish peer Swift virtually idealized. Marlborough's successor as the

Colonel of the First Troop of Foot Guards, Commander-in-Chief of the
Anglo-Dutch forces and, most prestigiously, Captain-General was the
Irish viceroy, the Duke of Ormond. Two years Swift's senior and a seasoned courtier and soldier, profusely and shamelessly in debt and a
popular lord lieutenant, Ormond belonged to a set of peers who had
been young at the time of the revolution and had acquired great influence
early. He was a Tory by family and instinct, intelligent and well-read
though not scholarly – sometime chancellor of Oxford – and suspicious
of the Williamite succession from the outset. Ormond was reconciled to
the revolution settlement, characteristically, only by a long-standing prior
friendship with William himself. His Tory bias was clear throughout the
early 1700s, though running Whigs to ground had no appeal for his
expansive, winning personality. Some considered him weak-willed, but
he had a proven presence of mind: it was Ormond who had prevented St
John and others with swords drawn from killing Guiscard where he
stood after his attempt on Harley's life.

With Ormond taking over as field commander in 1712, the contours
of Court and government shifted decisively. The era of Godolphin was
finally over; and he marked the end with his own, dying of kidney stones
in the early autumn. Exhausted, ailing, Godolphin had kept away from
the scene of power since being pushed offstage. For weeks after his death
he lay unburied for an undignified interlude till enough Whig Garter
knights could be mustered to carry the pall.[68] He was mourned sincerely,
though, by his onetime colleague Marlborough.

By then Ormond had endured a test of diplomatic rather than military nerve. At the start of the campaigning season he was instructed
informally by St John to avoid giving battle. Obeying meant angering
the Dutch and imperial allies, who hectored Ormond to attack with the
same insistence they had so often used in holding Marlborough back. As
negotiations with France moved on, by May Ormond was officially
bound by restraining orders. The alliance effectively broke in July 1712,
when Ormond led British troops away from the Dutch, and unsurprisingly found all doors in the region closed to him. The Whigs were aghast
for the same reason that the inhabitants of English shires were rather
relieved. Here was a general for peace, not for war. In a much debated
coup, Ormond occupied Dunkirk, which was to be demilitarized under
the terms of the peace the powers tried to thrash out at Utrecht. The
Dutch town hosting the negotiators was best known for the firearms
manufactured there, but in the remoter past it had lent its name to the
Union of Utrecht in 1579. With this initiative the breakaway provinces

of the Low Countries had formally rejected the authority of Spain. The summit gathering in 1712 may have hoped to conjure the ghost of the earlier stand taken against an expansionist monarchy. In the present instance, the allies presented a less than united front to the aggressor. Swift in fact sought to deepen the division.

With the removal of Marlborough, Swift's task might have seemed complete; but far from it. He had remained very active polemically. He was not as delicate with some of his targets – Whig lords, former Junto men and turncoat Tories – as he had been with Marlborough. A prominent example from earlier in the campaign was his handling of the Earl of Wharton, the former Lord Lieutenant of Ireland. Here was a man who freed Swift from all ambivalence: Wharton had treated his tenure in Ireland as a simple opportunity to recoup funds he had spent on the Whig cause at successive elections. After shunning Swift's overtures on behalf of the Irish clergy two years earlier, Wharton changed his tune towards him in 1710 when the Whigs lost power: 'he affected very much to caress me,' Swift recalled, silently gratified by the chance to shun Wharton in his turn.[69] He went on to give him a taste of the whip. Swift reminded the public that Wharton, who was still best known as a Restoration debauchee,

> hath some Years passed his Grand Climacteric [the 'crisis' age of sixty-three], without any visible Effects of Old Age, either on his Body or his Mind, and in Spight of a continual Prostitution to those Vices which usually wear out both . . . He seemeth to be but an ill Dissembler, and an ill Liar, although they are the two Talents he most practiseth, and most valueth himself upon.[70]

Swift's 'Character' of Wharton continues in this vein. It was less effective, arguably, than the haughty statue-toppling Swift performed for the *Examiner*; yet such attacks obviously had consequences beyond their specified targets, on Swift's relationship with those who still admired and followed the powerful figures he assaulted in print. His friendship with Addison, Wharton's former secretary, chilled into the merest civility in passing during these months. On his side Swift asserted that, however they differed now in politics, his sense of Addison's character was unchanged: 'there is no man half so agreeable to me as he is.'[71] Swift too, however much he had grown in influence, was essentially the same. Once there was a proven agreement of minds, if time and opportunity allowed, a friendship always followed. During the summer of 1711 he had moved out to Chelsea, for fresher air and more walking, where he lived near Francis Atterbury, his fellow clergyman and wit. Atterbury, round-faced, bewigged, sharp-nosed, was the Dean of Carlisle and then of Christ Church, Oxford, and later Bishop of Rochester. 'A little black [that is, dark-haired] man of fifty,' in Swift's miniature, he was a 'good pleasant man', but also 'cunning enough' and 'one that understands his own interests'.[72]

In person, the Bishop's manner was brisk, eloquent and compelling, his diction crisp and donnish; in the pulpit, he appealed to the heart, and was celebrated for his emotive preaching. Like Swift, Atterbury was no hermit, but was native to the clubby, old-school network through which the English Church functioned socially and professionally. In the early 1700s he had led the push to re-establish the old power of Convocation, deeply upsetting the Bishops' Bench until Whig manoeuvres snuffed out his efforts. Since then he had moved still closer to the Tory extreme. While frequently professing admiration, Swift was in two minds about him, though on becoming neighbours the two men quickly made the most of common ground, and passed agreeable evenings at Chelsea. Still, there were points of controversy to settle or evade. Swift might have asked Atterbury why he allowed Lord Godolphin to buy his support with the paltry deanery of Carlisle; but, then, he knew the answer. On his side Atterbury might have demanded to know why *A Tale of a Tub* was dedicated to Lord Somers.

Neither was a person to be much distressed by the odd jab. Both were weathered pugilists with selective ideas of mercy. Atterbury admitted treating an adversary 'barbarously' in satire as occasion demanded.[73] Wit had its own laws of collateral damage. Swift could always rely on a companion of such evident cultivation to appreciate his choicest productions; while one with Atterbury's bellicose tendencies would also enjoy his cruder tackles. During Swift's years of ministerial influence, these bone-crushing moves frequently came at moments of relief, when a political battle had been won and an advantage secured. He lay in wait, for example, for the Earl of Nottingham, who had gone over to the Whigs on the issue of Spain; when France made a key concession on Dunkirk in 1712, Swift reported that the famously dark-complexioned Earl, nicknamed 'Dismal', had gone into hiding there as a chimney sweep. After long days and weeks of writing tautly argued political tracts, he could not resist a spot of malevolent fun. Nottingham's efforts to bring peace to the Church in 1689 were disdained or forgotten by Swift, or eclipsed for him by collaboration with the Whigs. Swift's name, meanwhile, was well known to 'Dismal'.

By autumn 1711 he felt he had reached his zenith; although in fact he grew in stature for another two years. The emergency over Spain had yet to reach its crisis, the ministry seemed – for a spell – secure, and his part in strengthening the public confidence it enjoyed was widely recognized. His own official Church business might be caught in red tape, and delayed by the sheer volume of more pressing matters; but Harley assured him that it would be seen to in due course. Inundated though he was with other affairs, Swift's original mission never lost its importance for him; indeed, he considered it much more an achievement for the long term than some of the more spectacular successes in which he was involved. The remission of the First Fruits and Twentieth Parts would spare Irish priests from handing over to the Crown their first year's income on taking up their livings, and from a subsequent tax that claimed a 'twentieth' part of their revenue each year. It would save many of his colleagues in the lower Irish clergy from actual poverty. And Swift would be credited with this moral victory alongside, in time, those won for posterity by the *Examiner*. In short, the vagrant wit of former years was now one of the most influential men in the kingdom; and so he was offended but also amused by some homely and well-meant advice from Archbishop King. It was the clerical equivalent of father telling son it is time to settle down: 'God has given you parts and learning, and a happy turn of mind . . . you are answerable for those talents to God: and therefore I advise you, and believe it to be your duty, to set yourself to some serious and useful subject in your profession, and to manage it so, that it may be of use to the world.'[74] As Swift complained to Esther, the Archbishop missed a certain irony with these remarks. King himself, after all, despite knowing all his talents, had done nothing to help him. 'A rare spark this, with a pox!' he observed. He was writing late, and went to bed in a temper; punctuating his emotion, 'it rained most thunderously' from early the next day.[75]

King's letter has been taken as evidence of his failure to understand Swift; but he knew what he was talking about, and to whom he was speaking. Had he believed that Swift was already disposed to penning a theological treatise on some point of learned controversy, the 'useful subject' that excited Swift's scorn, King would not have felt the need to tell him to get on with it. For he was right. If Swift were to gain his eventual bishopric or more, he would need to do what the other bishops had done: then King could do his bit to help him. Satire and politics, in Church terms, were what natural philosophy was to other successfully promoted members of the clergy: a hobby, and a much more dangerous one, at that.

Replying to King from Windsor Castle, where he had accompanied his ministerial friends, Swift adopted a tone that was courteous, but unmistakably grand. We should remember that in the background was a relationship of more than a decade, one that neither man cared to throw away. Disagreements rumbled at intervals, but there was respect and restraint on both sides. King largely appreciated Swift's dedicated petitioning. Meanwhile Swift, although nursing complaints, thought highly of King. In an entirely anonymous setting he had praised him as one of 'the greatest and most learned prelates of the age'.[76] Here, however, we find prelate and priest at a moment of courteous conflict. Swift thanked His Grace for the compliments in his letter; but he described himself as 'a Man floating at Sea', a Ulysses of the Church who cannot yet know what he might do if he ever found the shore. He claimed that he anticipated little reward for his labours. On returning to Ireland, he expected to encounter contempt, especially from the Whig-dominated establishment in Dublin; but he assured the Archbishop that such disdain would mean little to him. He professed to miss his 'one scurvy acre' (presumably at Laracor). Swift found wealth enough, he puffed, in knowledge of his virtues. He put himself above the mere clamour for profit and place.

> I am as well received and known at Court, as perhaps any man ever was of my Level; I have formerly been the like [referring, it seems, to his former intimacy with Lord Somers and other leaders of the previous regime before his prolonged absence in 1704–7]. I left it then, and will perhaps leave it now (when they please to let me) without any Concern, but what a few Months will remove . . . I have been pretty well known to several great Men in my Life; and, it was their Duty, if they thought I might have been of Use, to put me into a Capacity of it; but, I never yet knew one great Man in my Life, who was not every Day swayed by other Motives in distributing his Favours.[77]

The letter to King reveals the defences Swift raised against disappointment; 'great Men' had consistently used but not rewarded him, and his one comfort was knowledge of the work he had done. But the letter conceals the proud way Swift had of putting himself at a disadvantage. In his dealings with Harley and St John he angrily turned down all offers of financial payment, which he found demeaning. At the same time he found it excruciating to apply formally for any Church promotion. He insisted instead on equality, cancelling dependence on his part – and expected preferment to materialize as a reflection of his worth.

A soured view of past and future was offset by excitement in the present. A taste of Swift's pleasure in high society can be got from his account of dinners, walks and meetings with the great and powerful at Windsor – where, he insisted to himself, there was no disparity. He was as much the Brobdingnagian as any of them or, like Gulliver, had lost sight of men of his own 'level'. He was fairly immune to the lure of material comforts. He prized his place at a great feast, but even then would sometimes eat in the kitchen at Windsor to avoid exposure. As for fine dining, despite a fondness for good wine, he had no need of elaborate dishes: as he reminded Johnson rather proudly, 'I have a sad vulgar appetite.'[78] He could enjoy a great occasion wholeheartedly. A journal entry written a few days after his reply to King captures both his exhilaration and a lingering insecurity at joining a group of nobles on an outing on horseback from Windsor. 'I borrowed coat, boots and horse,' he explained to Esther and Mrs Dingley – noting precisely, and admiringly, that the borrowed coat was of 'light camblet, faced with red velvet, and silver buttons'. He had been grumpy, having hurt his hand beating Patrick his servant, and somewhat apprehensive about his appearance. His hired horse, he declared, was not worth eighteen pence; but the sunshine played on the auburn-topped trees and the castle walls, the chequered scene of grove and meadow captured by Pope, and his heart soared. 'It was the finest day in the world, and we got out before eleven, a noble caravan of us.' This was where he belonged.[79]

# 5

Much of Gulliver's *Travels* is implicitly 'about' Swift's years as a ministry man: the book is a kind of secret history, in Padraic Colum's phrase,[80] alluding incessantly to the vice and short-sightedness that finally undid Harley's government. One broad correspondence between this period of Swift's life and the *Travels* lies in the pages where Gulliver answers the King of Brobdingnag's inquiries about European civilization. Gulliver is soon put on the defensive about English culture and politics. Swift had taken on a similar role with respect to the leviathan of the English public. In the course of 1711–12 his advocacy of official policy was at its most comprehensive and also closely argued. In *The Conduct of the Allies* and *Some Remarks upon the Barrier Treaty* he set about vindicating completely the ministry's negotiations for peace, negotiations that would culminate in the treaty signed at Utrecht in 1713. Swift's defence of Harley's policy culminated in a book-length *History of the Four Last Years of the Queen*, written largely at Windsor in the winter of 1712/13, but never published in his lifetime.[81] These and the many other, shorter works written before Swift returned to Ireland were the last in which he argued positively on behalf of an administration. His later polemical campaigns would all be critical, resistant interventions. And so Gulliver seems bereft of the support of his creator as he recounts the terrible sagas of European and British history to his host the King. Brobdingnag, memorably, is not impressed with what he hears. He declares: 'I cannot but conclude the Bulk of your Natives, to be the most pernicious Race of little odious Vermin that Nature ever suffered to crawl upon the Surface of the Earth.'[82]

This position, however, was not quite Swift's in his ministry years; unless we note that, technically, Brobdingnag delivers his awful verdict on 'the bulk' of Europeans, the majority rather than the whole. With that Swift might well already have agreed as he neared the end of his service for Harley: he was drawn to humanity's exceptions, the emergent trees above the canopy. The giant still looming at the back of his mind was arguably Sir William Temple, despite some dismissive references to him in the course of the *Journal*. Watching St John at work, Swift contrasted the minister's carefree competence with the 'splutter' his old master would make about almost being a secretary of state at the age of fifty.[83] The break he had made with the family at Moor Park by now seemed absolute, yet memories of Temple's conduct could still dictate the way Swift reacted to high and mighty behaviour in the present. On once being treated offhandedly by St John, he sought him out the next day and warned him: 'Never to appear cold to me, for I would not be treated like a school-boy; that I had felt too much of that in my life already (meaning from Sir William Temple).'[84] Temple still seemed the headmaster; and Swift was also, in a sense, pursuing Temple's vocation as courtier and essayist, arguing for diplomatic over military means.

Swift disliked having to concede that his endeavours were exhausting, but his journal records the strain they placed on body and morale. Regular colds and bugs were, as now, an unavoidable part of a busy urban existence; but at various periods Swift was staving off collapse. His giddiness troubled him frequently, and the lingering threat of a fit was taxing in itself. Yet the lowest point physically seems to have come in the early spring of 1712, when he developed crippling pains in his shoulder – a vulnerable spot, given the endless hours hunched over his writing table – which he suspected of being 'rheumatic'. He tried various medicines and compresses until the pain became sheer agony, writing proved impossible and he was left barely able to move. The bulk of his work on behalf of the ministry was by then completed, after an exceptionally hard stretch on his long defences of the arrangements for peace; but when a lull came, his health broke.

Pathogens were not the only threat to his person. Although his articles and tracts were all published anonymously, his identity as the government's chief apologist was soon widely known; and in the prevailing wildness that climaxed, arguably, in the bloody duel between Hamilton and Mohun in the autumn of 1712, Swift became a target. In the spring that year, as his shoulder first began to pain him, London was terrorized by a gang of vicious assailants calling themselves 'the Mohacks' (or Mohocks). For a spell in March, every night brought assault and mutilation to unarmed or hopelessly outnumbered victims. The 'race of Rakes', as Swift called them, would hand out beatings, stab, or slit mouths and noses. Such bands were not unheard of in earlier decades; maimings by groups of Cavaliers, usually in the pay of Charles II or a number of his chief courtiers, were one of the ugliest features of life in the Restoration capital. The personnel, the prey and the circumstances of such attacks were invariably political in nature, and this was the case again now. The Mohacks matched Swift's profile as 'rakes' – dissolute and volatile men, frequently ex-military, almost exclusively gentle or noble. There was an aristocratic quality to their group, and an unmistakably Whiggish prejudice evident in their choice of prey. They fell upon people whom they knew or suspected of having Tory sympathies or connections. A slash on Swift's face, or one of the Examiner's earlobes lopped off would have pleased them greatly. Swift compared the 'barbarities' of the Mohacks with those of rebel Irish houghers who were attacking livestock in Connaught at the same time.[85] He seemed unconscious of how the comparison, while cutting down the Mohacks' pretensions to glamour, aligned their victims with cattle slaughtered in protest against the shortage of land for tillage.

The background of violence in and out of official chambers, situations like that in which an armed minister of state could take justice in hand and gouge an assassin with his own sword, are a reminder that the London of Swift's day was not so far removed from the city where Christopher Marlowe was knifed in a dining-house. Duelling was as much a problem in Anne's time as it had been in Elizabeth's. Although his clerical gown exempted Swift from receiving or answering a challenge to 'the fields', he was still bound by a masculine honour code; and so continued to walk the streets in defiance of any Mohack trailing him. But, still, he confessed that here and there the thought of the gang had cost him cab fares he would normally have saved by walking. Hanging about a coffee-house, Patrick heard open talk that the gang was after his master; and Swift was glad to have the trusty heavyweight beside him on a night when, leaving a supper at Prior's house at midnight, he could not find a carriage. They reached home safely, but Swift admitted being 'afraid enough of the Mohocks'.[86]

The Mohacks disappeared suddenly, though, just a week or so later: the heirs and younger sons who deemed themselves above the law seem to have been scared when one of their comrades, a 25-year-old baronet, was arrested. Those connected with the ministry or known to be Tory in colour still feared conspiracy, however. On a Tuesday morning in November 1712, Swift was at one of his frequent amiable meetings with the Lord Treasurer when an odd-looking band-box was delivered up to the bedchamber where the two men sat. The post suspended their business for some minutes, and the talk of politics and literature they mingled with it. Experience made the men treat the package with caution. On opening the box, which contained another, Harley said he saw a pistol. Swift immediately took the package and carried it to a window.

Prising open the lid a little more, and cutting the pack-threads with his pocket knife, he discovered a delicately prepared and perfectly lethal booby-trap. Fortunately, the battering it had taken on the journey from the post office behind Ludgate, down to the Lord Treasurer's offices in Chancery Lane and then to his townhouse in Buckingham Street, had slightly dislodged the mechanism. The bomb consisted of a small fire-arm, primed and cocked, fixed in the middle of the box by two nails, with two inkhorns full of gunshot. Each inkhorn formed a barrel, at either end of which was attached a sack of gunpowder and a quill containing wildfire, a mixture of woodshavings, paper and other flammable material. To make doubly sure, one of these latter tubes was bent towards the pistol's firing pan, to act as a fuse.

The government's principal rhetorician now acted as a bomb-disposal man. His conduct was a measure of how long he had been living on his nerves. With an astonishingly cool head and steady hand, Swift set about inching the inkhorns and their explosives through the opening in the box, which he could not widen for fear of twitching the thread that ran from the lid to the trigger of the firelock. The device played devilishly on a natural instinct to remove the pistol first, in effect the detonator. Doing so, however, would disturb the nails supporting it in such a way that a secondary connection would have fired the gun, immediately igniting the inkhorns. These would have discharged their powder and shot through both sides of the box – blasting whoever was holding the package and anyone standing beside or nearby.

Some of the objects in Swift's account of the assassination attempt carry distinct biographical charges of their own. The nature of the parcel, though a logical choice for containing a bomb, is weirdly suggestive. It recalls the band-box in which, Swift claimed, he was carried to Ireland as a child.[87] Then there is the pen-knife he used to cut the string and wrapping: was it the same one used on Harley a year before, and that Swift had retained as a form of relic? Yet the oddest element in this half-hour of heroism is Swift himself. He took on a role in which few would imagine him. The nameless 'gentleman', as Swift referred to himself in his statement for the press on the incident, was someone who, at the deepest and most instinctive level, clearly felt that the minister in the room with him was worth dying for. Predictably, the Whig papers suspected a stunt, and a bid on Swift's part at self-advancement. 'God help me,' Swift wrote to Johnson, sounding quite worn out. 'What could I do; I fairly ventured my life.'[88]

Esther Johnson's long-distance support was vital to his spirits; he looked forward eagerly to a letter from 'MD', and chided at delays – which could stretch to many weeks. MD, though, was not code for Esther or 'Stella' alone. The unfailingly intimate letters of the *Journal to Stella*, as the collection has always been known, constantly addressed both Esther *and* Rebecca Dingley. Even in reading a letter, Esther was chaperoned, and all charges of misconduct forestalled. The involvement of a trio in the letters does, however, give them an airiness and a width that a one-to-one correspondence would surely have lacked. Swift's tone in addressing the women is never less than powerfully affectionate, and entirely at ease; but there is never a pronounced dip into yearning, or any stronger and less manageable current of feeling. The letters may well indicate the function Mrs Dingley served in person as well as on paper, in not only guaranteeing propriety but also acting as a safety valve on unruly emotions. She opened out the claustrophobia of a dialogue, but also provided containment. And, while Swift's greater concerns and tenderness were always for Esther, he constantly envisaged his readers as a pair. When he imagined himself with them, he took an arm of each:

> If I was with you, I'd make you walk; I would walk behind or before you, and you should have masks on, and be tucked up like any thing,

and Stella is naturally a stout walker, and carries herself firm, methinks
I see her strut, and step clever over a kennel [a wide ditch or gutter];
and Dingley would do well enough, if her petticoats were pinned up;
but she is so *embroiled*, and so fearful, and then Stella scolds, and Dingley stumbles, and is so daggled.

The three friends had few secrets from one another, one senses: 'Have
you got the whale-bone petticoats among you yet?' continues the passage above, alluding to the great hooped farthingales that were then
reappearing in London. 'I hate them; a woman here may hide a moderate gallant under them.'[89] Just occasionally, there are hints of a more
carnal inclination. One freezing February morning, Swift wrote: 'I wish
my cold hand was in the warmest place about you, young women, I'd
give ten guineas upon that account with all my heart, faith.' Here, it
seems, was Swift at one of his lesser known Byronic moments.

In Bury Street there was, however, a woman for whom Swift clearly
held high regard and who was willing to provide the lawful pleasures of
a wife. Esther Vanhomrigh had idolized Dr Swift for nigh on six years,
from not long after their first meeting in 1707; and Swift admired her in
return. Yet whatever passed or failed to pass between them, he stalled at
allowing the relationship to progress, let alone formalizing it with marriage. His writings suggest distaste for the physical act of sex, but one
could hardly say he was oblivious to the erotic side of life. On occasion,
as above, he could acknowledge corporeal urges with surprising heartiness. However, the obvious brake on further intimacy with Vanhomrigh
was the other Esther, Mrs Johnson in Dublin.

His letters to Vanhomrigh, as to Johnson, lurch disconcertingly from
an avuncular to a cavalier tone. 'I long to drink a dish of Coffee in the
sluttery,' he wrote to her from Windsor in August 1712. The 'sluttery'
should not be taken too hastily as a venue for illicit sexual activity; in
Swift's time 'sluttishness' denoted slovenliness.[90] He chided her for laziness and threatened to slip back to London incognito, and catch her
napping.[91] The letter was no billet-doux: its eroticism, if that is what it
is, is indistinct, a component of its humorously prudish and didactic
tone. Swift was in any case paying attention to the entire Vanhomrigh
establishment, not only the eldest daughter. He instructed Hessy to pay
his compliments to her mother, who welcomed his teasing attentions. A
fortnight later he sent the family a haunch of venison from the castle –
and was worried that his letter would smell of the meat when it arrived.
Impulsively Vanhomrigh thought she and the family might go to Wind-

sor and visit him there. Swift welcomed the idea, and even worked out the cost of it for her. Yet he squirmed at having her too close. A mutual acquaintance, the crucial ministerial aide Erasmus Lewis, let Hessy know that Swift had resolved to leave Windsor the moment she arrived. It was a joke, of course, and in her next letter Vanhomrigh treated it as one ("'tis a noble Res[olution]', she wrote; 'pray keep it . . . that I may be . . . accessory to your breaking it').[92]

In his heart of hearts Swift did *not* wish to see Vanessa amid Windsor's tufted trees and springing corn. For some time he had regarded the castle and its grounds as a privileged refuge; and physically, with its landmark round tower upon the central bailey, its stout outer walls and long approaches, it protected him with stone and distance from the sordidness of Grub Street. Emotionally, however, Windsor's strength as a bastion was ever more questionable, as mutual hatred and rivalry for the Queen's favour consumed his high-placed friends. Their enemies in any case travelled with them when the Court moved from the city, and Swift was always tense with vulnerability about his status. At dinner once in the kitchen – 'to avoid overmuch eating, and great tables' – he cringed when he was recognized by a gentleman porter who remembered his face from Moor Park. The servant said no more, and Swift was relieved, though he found him 'very pert'.[93] His younger, effervescent friend rolling up at the castle would subject him to much greater tortures, insinuations of the kind he feared the most. One can imagine St John's eyebrow arching on hearing of Hessy's arrival; and, still more clearly, Swift's tightening lips and blanching cheeks. So he was solicitous when the trip was cancelled – 'Is your Journey hither quite off?' – but an undertone of relief is quite audible.[94] He had given Vanhomrigh a hint that he preferred their friendship to remain discreet.

Since there was (in *his* mind) no impropriety, Swift could not be said to have betrayed either of the Esthers. 'Mrs' Johnson clearly did accept the boundaries he laid down. As such, he could sustain relations with Vanhomrigh on the same terms with a clear conscience; or, indeed, with a dozen women. But Vanhomrigh missed the point, or wouldn't accept it. She refused to let him go. As it became obvious during 1713 that Swift would soon leave London (although, in the event, he quickly returned), she fought for him. By June, when he had gone to Dublin to assume a new if rather unwelcome dignity, she was pleading for the slightest of news about him. She had heard he was unwell; and he was. She wrote passionately: "'Tis unexpressible the concern I am in . . . ever since I heard . . . your head is so much out of order.'[95] No answer came, probably because Swift was not only extremely busy, but also 'very sick'. She charged him with neglect, with cruelty. His bout of vertigo gave her an occasion to be in touch again, and she seized it. 'Why don't you tell me that [which] you know will please me,' she wrote. 'I have often heard you say that you would willingly suffer a little uneasiness provided it gave another a vast deal of pleasure.' This was the fourth letter Swift had failed to answer; and he did not reply for another month, chiding Vanhomrigh for her 'splenatick' words. He was in the country, 'riding here for life', and preferring a 'field-bed and an Earthen floor' to the great house in Dublin that had just been presented to him.[96]

## 6

From the late spring of 1713 permanent residence in Ireland seemed likely, if not now then soon, and Swift told Hessy that he planned to forget everyone in England and write as seldom as possible. She was to be the only victim of this clinical decision: the cut with her was to be decisive, as her behaviour had proved so alarming. In the late summer he was back in England, however, and spent two months at Windsor. With the castle walls protecting him, he seems to have used this interlude to draft a long poem explaining and justifying his attitude to Hester.[97] He gave it a classical and allegorical form: its fiction was a quarrel of nymphs and shepherds, which Venus is called to resolve. The nymphs accuse the shepherds of poor form in matters of love; the shepherds' counsel argues that female love is no longer what it once was and should be: that is, 'a Fire celestial, chaste, refin'd'.[98] Venus, scandalized by the idea that mortals might stop loving altogether, decides to try the question by conducting an experiment. She tricks Pallas Athena, the goddess of wisdom, and creates a female child endowed with every feminine grace but also every masculine virtue: and it is the latter, Swift's poem is in no doubt, that brings an individual any substance worth loving. In time the young woman, Vanessa, falls in love with her middle-aged tutor, Doctor Cadenus.

> *Vanessa*, not in Years a score,
> Dreams of a gown of forty-four;
> Imaginary charms can find
> In Eyes with reading almost blind.[99]

Swift, never exact with dates, represents the age difference in broad terms. In November, 1713, Swift was forty-six; Vanessa twenty-five. In real life Cadenus was thus twenty-one years Vanessa's senior, and is a 'gown': one innocent, moreover, of any carnal thought towards her. Swift is frank in revealing the smaller thoughts that pass through the mind of his counterpart. The older master is troubled by the gossip his besotted pupil will excite; how men in coffee-houses will jeer at the near-sighted old codger seducing a young woman – and a fairly wealthy one too – with his book-learning. At the same time, Cadenus's rather chilly heart is flattered; but the deterrents are too strong. He refuses to return Vanessa's love in kind. What he offers instead is the gift that Swift used the poem to present to Vanhomrigh: that of friendship. He would love her, he suggested, as he did Harley, or other admired companions. Love, says Cadenus, is an illusory compound of feelings, and often a screen for mere lust:

> But Friendship in its greatest Height,
> A constant, rational Delight,
> On Virtue's Basis fix'd to last,
> When Love's Allurements long are past;
> Which gently warms, but cannot burn;
> He gladly offers in return.[100]

Swift would use similar language in one of his most passionate and personal letters, mourning the death of Esther Johnson.

*Cadenus and Vanessa* then draws a curtain on the upsetting interview. Vanessa has used all her rhetorical skills (given her by Pallas Athena, but trained up, of course, by her teacher) to make Cadenus relent: whether he does, Swift leaves a mystery at the end. The outcome with Esther Vanhomrigh herself was much less ambiguous: Swift evidently refused to meet her demands. His offer of the constant rational delight of friendship also seems to have been conditional on her giving up her expectations. *Cadenus and Vanessa*, meanwhile, was acknowledged early on as one of Swift's finest achievements in verse: the familiar confidence with epigram extends magnificently to cope with the mythical apparatus framing the central couple's trauma. The dialogue between Cadenus and Vanessa shows a subtlety and economy unseen in Dryden, the vaunted master of the allegorical fable. The characters are beautifully painted, and Swift takes the utmost care, it seems, in drawing Vanessa/Hessy. She is hardly human, yet, unlike many other inventions by Swift, she acquires depth through the account of her childhood. She sparkles on the page.

The widespread fascination with the poem, which lived a long and varied life in manuscript copies before appearing in print in 1726, was also with the persons it concerned. By 1713, however shadowy, Swift was a public figure: he was known and feared as a writer. *Cadenus and Vanessa* became something of a collector's item for the light it cast on the inner life of the Doctor. Swift accepted the publicity, and affected indifference when it was finally printed without his permission: 'It was a task performed on a frolic among some ladies' – a mere parlour game, that is, to divert female company; and 'printing cannot make it more common than it is.' It was, he insisted, 'only a cavalier business'.[101] On her side, Vanhomrigh, who was dead by the time the poem saw print, also resigned herself to public speculation; indeed she may even have cultivated it for the slight comfort it brought during the lonely, angry years ahead. The biographical and literary aspects of the poem are peculiarly symbiotic. The circumstantial background to the conflict between Cadenus and Vanessa gives the poem pathos and also its occasion; at the same time, the supreme control of apothegm and argument both parties display seals off more violent and wrenching memories. There is no hint in Vanessa's speeches of the pleading desperation revealed in Vanhomrigh's letters to Swift of June 1713. Nor is there any suggestion of the deeper aversion Swift might have had to conventional partnership – except, possibly, early on, in lines explaining why the shepherds have lost their interest in women. Their difficulty, these Platonic herdsmen claim, lies with the way most women nowadays

> . . . only know the gross Desire;
> Their Passions move in lower Spheres,
> Where-e'er Caprice or Folly steers.
> A Dog, a Parrot, or an Ape,
> Or some worse Brute in human Shape.[102]

This was a commonplace male complaint about female sexuality. But the safety in numbers Swift seeks here is suggestive. Disgust at the biology of sex – the anatomical fact that women were technically compatible with all men, however 'Brute' – perhaps bears some relation to Swift's prudery towards other 'lower' passions; his desire, in other contexts, to be distinct and above purely material considerations; to be an island entire in himself. Leaving aside such implications, *Cadenus* also reveals him as an unrivalled propagandist. In Vanessa, he had fashioned a role for Vanhomrigh to assume, if she chose, as one who surpassed common physical transactions. The interpretations later given to the work nevertheless relished determining the very opposite.

That he felt uneasy about his relationship with Vanhomrigh comes across through the distinct shortage of references to her in his ongoing *Journal* to Esther Johnson, and occasional concealment of their meetings. His letters home to Dublin are uniquely transparent on all other matters. He also evidently had some buried rationale, some code that was based on a tacit arrangement with Johnson – or at least his understanding of such an arrangement – that satisfied his morality in this respect. Only the reticence of the *Journal* indicates a conscience less than completely at ease.

The effort to maintain a mental peace between other contradictions was part of regular life for Swift during these years. From our perspective, we would surely have to ask how Swift could tolerate Roman Catholics and some Nonconformists in person, and even make a close friend of a Papist such as Pope, and yet suspend his view of their humanity when they pressed for emancipation and a repeal of the Test Act. For his contemporaries, other questions were more pressing. How could the Reverend Dr Swift also be the satirical author of such apparent mockeries of religion? How could a Tory spokesman seek to retain his close friendships with Whigs? The answers seem to lie in the way early-modern society regulated social bonds: a relationship that was possible in one context, or in one set of conditions, was immediately frozen in another, or when circumstances changed.

Humour and invention, transmitted through the press, was one means of fostering a bond between entirely diverse parties. The publication of *Miscellanies* by Swift in February 1711, gathering papers, poems, jokes and oddments from the previous decade, could only unite the community of wit in admiration for its contents. The event was spoiled for him, as it happened, by piracy rather than politics. A nefarious bookseller, the 'unspeakable' Edmund Curll, brought out an unauthorized Swift *Miscellanies* in May. The book was a hotch-potch of things Curll had previously pilfered, such as the 'Meditation upon a Broom-stick' and a reissue of the annotated *Tale of a Tub*. Swift was angered for the sake of his text and still more for his reputation – he had little or no stake in any profits the legitimate volume might have made. Whereas the authentic *Miscellanies* printed by John Morphew was of course an anonymous work, 'that villain Curll' put Dr Swift's name on the title-page as a means of boosting sales.[103] As it happens, when the bona fide work appeared in February, he had already affected complete ignorance when the town attributed it to him. 'Some book seller has raked up every thing I writ . . . but I know nothing of it,' he complained self-indulgently to the ladies in Dublin – forgetting that he had already told them the previous October that the *Miscellanies* was almost ready for printing.[104] With the ensuing publicity, the secret gratification came at a high price, since his hopes of favour in the Church were endangered yet again. He minded less when Curll sold off old copies of the stolen *Miscellanies* as a second edition in August 1714 – by which time Swift was a dean, and his aspirations to anything greater were all but crushed.

Why, a simple-minded moralist might ask, should anonymity be allowed to protect Dr Swift's clerical career, if he was indeed the author of such profanities? Swift's logic lay as ever in an appeal to a higher principle, in this case artistic as much as doctrinal: his writings were in no way profane. Despite its avant-garde technique, *A Tale of a Tub* was in fact a heartfelt defence of the Church. This, he knew, was an argument lost on lesser minds, and so he had to publish anonymously; yet plagiarists such as the 'unspeakable' Curll disregarded both Swift's rights over his creative property and the pragmatic boundary he raised between his activities as priest and writer. His complex resentment against the bookseller would fester as years went by.

Most of the items in the early *Miscellanies* – authorized or not – harked back to a period when Swift urgently cultivated a cross-party community of discerning minds. One could laugh at Bickerstaff whether one's vote was Whig or Tory; and although few seemed to get the High Church message at the heart of the *Tale of a Tub*, its digressions and involutions offered delight to anyone who could grasp the ironies behind them. Swift's writing of more recent years could not sustain the truce this earlier work required. As the wedge between Tories and Whigs was driven ever deeper, it became all but impossible for him to maintain the stance he preferred as one indifferent to party politics. He and Addison tried commendably, however, to stay on polite terms. Only in the savage last months of the Queen and her ministry in 1714, when Swift fought a bitter duel in print with Steele, did the link dry up completely. Swift retained his high esteem for Addison, who gave striking proof of his own talent for comedy and observation in a new paper, the *Spectator*, again edited by Steele. The *Spectator* naturally favoured the Whigs, as did Addison's tragedy *Cato*, the premier of which became a huge party event in spring 1713. Addison had worked on the play occasionally for nearly a decade, and Swift remembered seeing an unfinished draft some years before. He slipped into Drury Lane one morning to watch a final rehearsal, and was mortified on his former friend's behalf. 'There were not above half a score of us, to see it; we stood on the Stage & it was foolish enough to see the Actors promptd every moment, & the Poet [Addison himself] directing them, & the drab that acts Cato's daughter [caught] out in the midst of a passionate Part, & then calling out, "What's next?"[105] His concerns proved needless, and not only because theatrical companies were well used to mastering their lines and pasting a production together in the last hours before performance. Addison's drama of the final days of Cato, statesman and stoic, was turgid with political symbolism. Party hacks and grandees on both sides were desperate to appropriate this meaning for their conflicting purposes. Although Addison's preferences were obvious, Bolingbroke pulled off a coup on the opening night by calling Barton Booth, the leading man, up to his box and handing him fifty guineas – for his portrayal of a champion of liberty. With this he outraged the Whigs in the audience by identifying the play's villain, Julius Caesar, the aspiring dictator, with Marlborough.

Swift's note on the faltering rehearsal captures his view of both political illusion and high-flown emotional writing. There is a Joycean touch when he observes the *prima donna* Anne Oldfield stalling in the middle of a purple passage, and yelling for a prompt. The effect intended by the poet is cathartic; the actuality is 'foolish'. The *Journal* as a whole makes it plain on every page that Swift's distaste for bombast stems from a deep well of genuine feeling, for people and issues. It wasn't authentic emotion, but amplification that he disliked.

The circle connected with Steele's old *Tatler* would always bring a sharp pang to his chest on behalf of a departed resident of Grub Street. When Steele dropped the paper, which had been a sensation, Swift tried to help a younger writer to continue it. William Harrison's abilities proved limited, though, and, despite generous support from Swift, he struggled. 'The jackanapes wants a right taste,' Swift admitted. 'I doubt he won't do.'[106] Later he used his influence to obtain serious diplomatic responsibility for Harrison as an assistant and courier, but his young friend was brought low by the perilous existence of one with no fixed income and no certain support from the powers he served. Swift's words to Archbishop King on the ingratitude of 'great Men' were trenchantly borne out by the case of this young writer and official.

Early in February 1713 Swift was shocked to find Harrison scuttling from door to door, in bad health and without a penny. Swift at such moments was always at his best, although this time too late. He hastened to extract £100 from Bolingbroke, which Harrison was owed for his services, and had the note in his pocket the next morning when Harrison's manservant answered the door in tears. Harrison, unable to pay for simple medical care, had died that night in his draughty garret. Swift's skills as a parson immediately came out: he organized a decent funeral, consoled the 'poor lad's' mother – and sermonized, more than a little, in high places where lavish feasts were held. At home, he was devastated, and admitted it in the company of paper, pen and candle. 'No loss ever grieved me so much,' he wrote to Johnson; he was unable to eat, and unable to end his letter with anything less melancholy. 'I send this away to night and am sorry it must go while I am in so much Grief.'[107] They buried Harrison shortly afterwards; and there but for the grace of God, felt Swift, lay any poor hack whose masters were forgetful. As the political conflict entered new and incredible degrees of fierceness, Swift showed in his *Journal* how some were tacitly aware that there were limits to the tensions the social fabric could sustain. So he and Addison would still take a turn together on the Mall when they met now and then.

# 7

By the spring of 1713, with peace all but secured, and the ministry apparently safe, it appeared that Harley could dispense with Swift's services. As summer came, Swift left for Ireland. On and off for three years, he had been promising Johnson that he would soon be home, often expressing vexation with the Court and the Parliament. Another factor in his departure was the turn internal politics had taken. The split between Harley and St John, widening since the row over honours in the wake of the Guiscard affair, was common knowledge. It was an 'evil which,' Swift said, 'I twice patchd up with the hazard of all the credit I had, [but] is now spread more than ever'.[108] His affection for both ministers made him a suspect figure, if not to them personally, then certainly to their rival camps. Ostensibly, however, what took him back to Dublin in 1713 was a reward for his labours. The prize was important and valuable, but it dismayed him. He had been appointed dean – the senior priest – of St Patrick's Cathedral in Dublin. When it transpired that no other post would be forthcoming, he was anxious to secure it. But he was crestfallen: the promotion meant banishment from England. 'I confess I thought the Ministry would not let me go,' he wrote to Johnson, the day his appointment was confirmed. 'But perhaps they can't help it.'[109]

As ever in Church affairs, Swift's appointment had been possible only when a number of others had fallen into place. The preferment had come, after a tortuous wait, when the incumbent Dean, John Stearne, was moved on from St Patrick's to a bishopric. Swift was treated cruelly by his political chiefs. At several times over the past few years his rise had been spoken of as certain when a number of prestigious and lucrative English deaneries became available. But these had all been needed to buy off clergymen of much more doubtful loyalty than Swift. In the six months before it was confirmed that he would take over in his home cathedral, at least three such posts were all but dangled before his eyes. In April 1713 Swift could take it no longer, and presented Oxford with his ultimatum: he would leave for Ireland forthwith unless 'something honourable' were given to him.[110] To his critics, he seemed grasping; yet, amid the undignified push and shove for benefices that most clerics took as part of their calling, Swift had been extremely restrained. After years doing vital service on behalf of the Church and the ministry that had sworn to protect it, he was beginning to feel ridiculous. Oxford's general answer to all Swift's pressure on the subject of clerical appointments was that the Queen could or would never make up her mind; and here he either lacked self-awareness or simply desired to avoid the blame. Of the two, monarch and minister, each slowed and troubled by poor health and heart-strain, Oxford was easily the champion prevaricator. He loved to hold the Court in suspense, to hoard information and withhold decisions until the last possible moment. He had also, perhaps, taken Swift at his word in his proud refusal of remuneration.

At one level Swift was greatly relieved to have at least 'got' St Patrick's, but the failure to obtain a real plum, a deanery in one of England's principal cathedrals, left him sore. The formalities in Dublin had to be observed, and so in June Swift made the long westward ride – with a trip en route to a distant cousin but with no stop-off, this time or ever again, at his mother's home in Leicester. He was angry and anxious, worried that his vertigo might strike on the way. He encountered one or two of the many predictable hitches the journey involved: there was the tricky business of shipping a horse, and arranging a new saddle, which needed mending when he reached the other shore.[111] In Dublin he felt little joy taking the oaths inside the cathedral's high cavern. Seeing Johnson after so long was the only true consolation; but even that pleasure was complicated by the distressing attentions of Vanhomrigh from England, which ate at his conscience and stretched his temper. He spent no longer than a fortnight in Dublin, where he was ill, and then rode out to Laracor with a stock of new remedies for his head. There he took advantage of the pastoral retreat he had mentioned often to Stella and others over the past few years.

In writing every page dispatched from London, he was surrounded by many thousands of his fellow creatures – in the rooms above and below his curtained bedchamber, the streets outside, the busy shops and taverns, the passages and halls of St James's or Westminster. Many in that teeming vicinity would have paid good money for a look at the private correspondence of the infamous Dr Swift. Removed to Laracor by a hard ride, a long sailing and bad Irish roads, his pen moved serenely over a sparse table, with indifferent labourers and tradesmen scattered throughout the far surrounding townlands. The peace was a relief; it was also somewhat galling.

A letter written early in July illustrates how restoring, nevertheless, Swift found the outdoor life: tellingly, it was written to Esther Vanhomrigh, a sign of his willingness to keep their friendship open, and share his heartfelt, spontaneous pleasures with her, even as he laid down severe limits to the contact they might have in future. He was gratified by the concern her notes poured out for his health. He had, he admitted, been very sick; but out here he was benefiting from constant riding and gardening. The hard earthen floor of his makeshift parsonage pleased him more than the 'great house' in Dublin that was newly his. 'My River walk is extremely pretty, and my Canal in great Beauty, and I see Trout playing in it.' With a touch of perversely triumphant self-denigration, he said that minding his willows and trimming his hedges was work more suitable for a 'country vicar' than acting as a cow-herd managing the factions at Court. The state of the islet on his garden's stretch of river concerned him; cattle kept wandering over it. In the meantime he was also overseeing workmen as they redug a ditch. His erstwhile masters, he implied, might do as they pleased. The letter combined a strong taste of 'now they'll see' with an air of sincere relief; and in it Swift resumed the avuncular role he found safest with Vanhomrigh.[112] In the meantime, despite the note of splendid and defiant isolation, he was by no means alone all day. He talked with his curate, rode over to greet the quality at Trim (the Justices were holding assizes); he visited the local prison, where he left a small donation. He also met Joe Beaumont, who kept an eye for him on his affairs at Laracor, and who, despite his long depressions, kept up his interests in higher mathematics. To Swift's increasing concern, Beaumont's fascination with the problem of longitude would make ever greater inroads on his sanity.[113]

Oxford and Bolingbroke allowed Swift to remain in Ireland only a little longer than it took the ink to dry on the paperwork necessary for the transfer of his deanery. Physically improved, and seeing how ominous the cracks in the ministry had grown, Swift made a show of resisting their appeals. Still, despite these grudging noises, he was eager to be gone. The autumn saw him back in London lodgings, as the land he had left behind him rumbled with dissent. In Dublin the antagonisms of Westminster were playing themselves out in conflicts that fleetingly erupted into physical violence. Luckily for Swift, he was back at Lord Oxford's side before the worst of it erupted.

For some years now the Lord Chancellor of Ireland, Sir Constantine Phipps, an ally of Bolingbroke, had been trying to force strong Tory measures on Dublin's predominantly Whig mayor and aldermen. Phipps's position was strengthened in tandem with Bolingbroke's, and their alliance grew firmer as time passed. In the autumn of 1713 Oxford appointed Charles Talbot, Duke of Shrewsbury, a moderate Whig, as the Lord Lieutenant of Ireland. Shrewsbury, described by Swift as 'the finest gentleman we have', was a natural mediator.[114] As the Lord Chamberlain, he was both a senior Cabinet minister and intimate servant of the Queen, and offered a bridge between moderate Whigs and Tories. For that very reason, he was distrusted almost equally by the powerful extremes of both parties, the leading Tory high-flyers and Junto Whigs. Yet, at the age of fifty-three, he was a proven minister and emissary. He had stepped in as the Ambassador to Paris after the death of Hamilton, and undergone the stress of seeing through the peace. At home, his English dukedom made him a statesman of the highest rank, while an Irish peerage as the Earl of Waterford gave him a strong territorial presence in the kingdom he was being sent out to run. He was admired almost universally as a living manifestation of the Renaissance aristocratic ideal, and his personal history gave him a strong aversion to extremist solutions. His father had been killed in a duel by the Duke of Buckingham, with whom young Talbot's mother was having an affair. An adamant but non-fanatical supporter of King William, whom he served faithfully, Shrewsbury had gone through spells of intense political activity and expensive retirement before returning to the Cabinet in 1710 and taking on the terribly delicate embassy. On paper, he was an outstanding, non-partisan choice as Irish viceroy; but his conciliatory talents were to be hard stretched. On the ground, a man like Shrewsbury could do little but look on helplessly.[115]

In Dublin, Phipps was now trying to force a Tory mayor on the city corporation, and the aldermen and the Irish Commons – soon roundly controlled by Whigs – were having none of it. Shrewsbury reached Dublin Castle amid election hysteria. Whig supporters flooded into the

Tholsel, the medieval merchants' hall and exchange in the heart of the old city, where a poll was to be held. The Tholsel was one of the points in Dublin where classes and separate ethnic groups converged: on Sunday mornings the Lord Lieutenant or his substitute and attending officers stood on a first-floor balcony to receive a salute from the Lord Mayor and aldermen on their way to service in the cathedral. Business in this district, even within the aisles of Christ Church, rarely ceased even on a Sunday. On certain weekdays country people might be selling 'friezes and linen cloth'; and there was generally such a throng that, as one traveller noted, 'you can hardly pass among them without danger of being lousy.'[116]

A fair deal of pushing and shoving was therefore normal in and about the Tholsel even during quiet spells: such conditions were typical for an early-modern hub. On this particular day in 1713 they escalated easily into riot. Whigs occupied the Tholsel and refused entry to Tories, and a pitched battle set in. The Tory supporters rushed the diminutive, venerable but stoutly built structure, and the mayhem soon spread. Troops opened fire on the mob, with at least one fatality. The electoral stage was torn apart and planks from it were brandished and flung. In the aftermath, the helplessness of Shrewsbury's position became apparent. The eventual poll displayed the latent Whig strength in the country. Afterwards, against Shrewsbury's advice, an uncompromising Cork-man, Alan Brodrick (soon Viscount Midleton), was elected as the Speaker. Within a few weeks, the Whigs of Dublin identified Shrewsbury as no friend of theirs on account of his refusal to muzzle the Tories. On the other side, Phipps and his followers were apoplectic at the preference the viceroy seemed to show the Whigs. The Tories thus began to deal directly with London. Shrewsbury found the Whig majority in Parliament refusing to vote supplies, while the Tory majority on the Privy Council ignored his directions. Respectable stalwarts of Anglo-Irish society such as Mistresses Johnson and Dingley reviewed the news by staring into their teacups, and refusing to hear any criticism of the Crown or the Church. At this interval Swift's two closest friends, though long settled in Ireland, perhaps also regretted his failure to gain an English berth, as Tories and Whigs took one another by the throat. Every occasion, every public appointment, was defined by the feud. When the Primate of All Ireland, Narcissus Marsh, died, the obligatory sentiments of respect and regret were hard to hear above the thunderous manoeuvring that immediately ensued to decide his successor. The Dublin Tories moved faster, and it was one of their men, Thomas Lindsay, who became the new Primate.

Ireland, it seemed to Shrewsbury, was close to ungovernable; and the viceroy's position to most in Dublin was becoming untenable. Yet he suspended the crisis with a standard tactic, proroguing Parliament, and in fact remained as Lord Lieutenant until another political turn displaced him. The barely receding tensions of 1713, meanwhile, marked out the battleground Swift would be forced to live on when he returned to Dublin. If the ministry failed, the large house waiting for him by St Patrick's would be no calm refuge.

As the Harley–St John alliance crumbled around him, moreover, Swift saw that he might be left to the wolves. On rejoining the scene at Westminster he soon realized the ministry was more than embattled; it was all but imploding. At Christmas in 1713, the Queen fell frighteningly ill, and reports of her death were greeted with joy in Whig parlours and coffee-houses. When Anne heard about these celebrations, she was hurt and furious; and now ordered Harley to push harder on High Church policies to frustrate the Whigs. This was the antagonistic direction Harley had avoided, with a few concessions, since 1710, and he was unwilling to change now. The Queen's revengeful course was exactly the one St John, however, with wider Tory backing, was eager to pursue.

St John still drew his strength from the ranks of the October Club, that vaguely masonic Tory association with Jacobite roots, known also as the 'High-Flyers', which seemingly accounted for almost a third of the Commons. The October men served effectively as his personal parliamentary militia. This was a faction Swift had, following Harley, always tried both to dissuade and reassure.[117] But the 'Octobrists', rural squires almost to a man, united by their hatred of Dissent, the crippling rises in the Land Tax during Marlborough's wars, and the London financiers who had profited from those campaigns, had long followed the urbane Bolingbroke as their unlikely chief. With a steady gang in Parliament bolstered by recent success at the polls, Bolingbroke was also making inroads at Court. Swallowing his earlier resentment at not being made an earl, and with the fast-fading Queen suppressing her qualms over his irregular personal life, Viscount Bolingbroke was edging out the Earl of Oxford as the chief royal favourite.

The rift in the government was blown wide open in April 1714, when a leading moderate Tory (and the Speaker of the House), Sir Thomas Hanmer, shifted his support to the opposition in the very middle of a crucial debate. Swift had worked much with Hanmer in the course of compiling *The Conduct of the Allies*. Oxford was left exposed; he made vague, barely intelligible overtures to the moderate Whigs. But Whigs of every hue were merely counting down the weeks or even days until the Queen lay on her pall and a new German king, who despised the Tories, arrived to put them back in power. In a desperate gambit, Oxford joined Bolingbroke in urging the Pretender to convert to Anglicanism and so make his claim for the British throne.

Swift, oblivious to these back-room dealings but traumatically conscious of the ministry's collapsing façade, was still battling. In March, responding to his pamphlet *The Publick Spirit of the Whigs*, a royal proclamation offered £300 as a reward for anyone disclosing the author's identity. The sum was a long way from the highest granted in such cases, but amounted to a very decent year's income for most: more than enough to tempt a witness from Grub Street. Behind the scenes, the assault was widely known to be Swift's – in particular by Richard Steele, the pamphlet's foremost personal target. Steele, now an MP, had written stridently but sloppily against the government and the peace. His earlier friendship with Swift was dead, but relations had improved in previous months, and there is some evidence that Swift sought a truce. Provoked by swipes from Steele's essays for his new paper, the *Guardian*, however, Swift made a sadistically long job of exposing his opponent's poor style, patchy reading and overriding egotism. Privately, he was deeply wounded by personal references Steele made in the course of the row. In passing, meanwhile, Swift also insulted the Scots as 'a poor, fierce Northern people', and said there could be no possible benefit for England in a union with them. His old prejudice against the Covenanters of the English Civil War rose up and landed him in trouble. Years before, with a sharp quibble on the Greek *skotia* ('gloom'), he had defined Scotland as a 'Land of Darkness' in *A Tale of a Tub*.[118] The Scottish lords residing in London – nothing more, to Swift, than a pack of scroungers – bayed for amends. Swift sneered at their touchiness: could they deny that they had forced England into the Union by threatening to make their own choice for the Scottish Crown upon Anne's death? With the Hanoverian succession under threat, Swift argued, thanks to blunders by Godolphin in managing the business, the English had no choice: there was no other advantage for them to gain, he insisted, from such a union.

Swift was genuinely frightened by the danger in which the affair placed him. He was distressed too, though not altogether surprised, by the coldness of former friends. Lord Delaware, the Treasurer of the Royal Household, till then 'always caressing', would barely return Swift's greeting until the crisis had passed and the risks of associating with him had faded.[119] That was politics. Yet, as the lairds called for the culprit to be branded, only his two friends and sponsors at the highest level could save him, conceivably from the pillory.[120]

He could not rely on such protection much longer. The last days of Harley's ministry were made explosive by rebellion from the Tory back-benches, and by St John scheming to steal the last of the goodwill the Queen bore her Lord Treasurer. Swift was far from alone in urging Oxford and St John and their camps of supporters – a dwindling camp, in Oxford's case – to recall the case for unity. The Duchess of Ormond, addressing Swift as 'brother' as the ministry's club convention dictated, reminded him of the story of the arrows: easily broken when single, unbendable when bound together.[121] Late in the game, Swift made a final attempt to bring the two leaders together by forcing them to share a car-riage, just the two of them, on their way to Windsor. This gave them four good hours to settle their differences; yet, two days later, both told Swift that 'nothing was done.' Convinced in the end that the partnership was beyond repair, and the government doomed, Swift announced that he was leaving. It was roughly a year since his last departure, to be installed as dean in Dublin. One evening in June, it chanced that all three sat together one last time. On taking his leave, Swift later said he asked them two questions: first, whether the 'mischiefs' that had soured their work might not be reversed by two minutes' frank talk; and, second, would the ministry not disintegrate in two months if the present state persisted? Bolingbroke, the more open of the two, answered 'yes' to both. Oxford, who 'had stronger Passions than the Secretary, but kept them under stricter Government', demurred; and merely asked Swift if he was free for lunch the next day.[122]

Harley was no longer himself. He had lost Tory backing for delays in measures and promotions for which the Queen, newly contrarian in her final months, was in fact responsible; while his habitual air of secrecy, and a tendency to 'refinement' and over-complication that Swift for one deplored, brought justifiable blame. Oxford declared, though, that he finally lost all credit with the Queen in May 1714, when he granted a request from the Hanoverian Resident in London that the future George II, the Hereditary Prince of Brunswick-Lüneburg, might take his seat in the Lords as the Duke of Cambridge, a title he received in 1706. Oxford had no choice but to accept that the Prince had every legal right to do so. Although Prince George himself cancelled the request and recalled Baron Schütz, the trouble-making envoy, all enemies of the Lord Treas-urer could be satisfied with the damaging affair. The Queen sensed vultures circling, and was furious with Oxford for issuing the necessary writs. Oxford was almost past caring. His customary reserve had sunk almost to stupor since the previous November, when his eldest and favourite daughter, Elizabeth, Lady Carmarthen, died. At that time only a lingering sense of duty prevented him from resigning; as months passed, and as further stratagems occurred to him, he became obdurate, and tightened his grip on the white staff of office that Bolingbroke coveted so much. Oxford's health declined too, and after years of raucous argument in Cabinet, he gave in without fighting when Bolingbroke finally persuaded the Queen, who was close to death, to dismiss her chief minister at the end of July 1714. The way, it seemed, stood clear for Bolingbroke – and a Tory 'revolution'.

Yet the Viscount's triumph was very brief. A clique of moderate Whig lords moved quickly to ensure that Oxford was succeeded as the Lord Treasurer by the Duke of Shrewsbury, the Lord Lieutenant of Ireland. Bolingbroke had been outmanoeuvred in an instant; and he knew the game was up as soon as the unfortunate, apoplectic Queen acquiesced with shallow breaths to Shrewsbury's appointment. Her head by then had been shaved, and she was bled at intervals. Those gathered around the bed hourly expected the next convulsion to be her last. Beyond the palace, many in London assumed that she was already dead. In the version of events that reached Swift, it was Bolingbroke himself, suppressing his gall, who nominated Shrewsbury for Anne's approval.[123] In Swift's patently unfair assessment, Shrewsbury had merely been waiting for the moment to plunge his knife home in Oxford's chubby back. 'The Duke of Shrewsbury hated the Treasurer, but sacrificed all Resentments to Ease, Profit and Power; and was then in Ireland acting a Part directly opposite to the Court.'[124] In 1713 Shrewsbury had more or less typified all that Swift looked for in an ideal courtier; and certainly one who had been in leading councils since his early twenties would be no naive player. An abstract glance at his portfolio of employments might have suggested that the handsome, slightly frail Duke was touched with megalomania, for he now held the posts of lord chamberlain, Irish viceroy and the 'prime' ministerial duties of lord treasurer. But Swift was forgetting that Shrewsbury took all of these jobs, from 1710, in order to defuse huge arguments. This last and highest appointment, which brought him hurrying back from Dublin, was again given and accepted, wearily, for the sake of consensus. Since his secrecy, unpopularity and alcoholism meant that Oxford could hardly expect to retain office, Shrewsbury being made the Lord Treasurer marked the greatest victory over Bolingbroke that circumstances would allow the stricken leader. He had beaten his junior tormentor at quite literally the last gasp.

A few days later, all Bolingbroke's plotting was made irrelevant by Anne's death. In one of his last official acts, Oxford proclaimed the new King, and was subsequently hissed through the streets by the mob. The Elector of Hanover succeeded Anne as George I; and the way was opened, not for a Tory remodelling of the state, but for the Whigs to retake power. By the time the evenings grew short, both of Swift's friends had been turned out into the wilderness – deserts in which they could at least avoid one another. For some months yet, Oxford and Bolingbroke were spared reprisals as dormant splits appeared within the triumphant Whig party. As for Swift, his duties in Dublin beckoned; and, as far as the wider political scene was concerned, it would be a long time before he could stop reflecting on what had passed, and hoping it might still be put right.

# 8. The Phantom Academy

Who can deny that all Men are violent Lovers of Truth, when
we see them so positive in their Errors?

– '*Thoughts on Various Subjects*'[1]

## I

The importance of these ministerial years to Swift's outlook can hardly
be overestimated. Ultimately, however, the period became most significant because of the massive shock he suffered when it ended. A decisive
trauma ensued, for, although initially depressing if not devastating, the
failure of the Harley–St John alliance set him free, personally and creatively: personally to nurture the most important relationship of his
adult life – a relationship without which all the teeming detail of Swift's
*Journal* would be lost to us; and creatively to write without the strictures
of a party line. Free of the whip, Swift would be able to indict as he
pleased, but also to educate and entertain at liberty, and tackle injustice
on his own terms. Dejected as he was in August 1714 by the prospect of
his future in Ireland, awaiting him was a decade and a half of regener-
ation, action and unequalled literary inspiration.

The story of Swift's years as a party writer would fill a large volume
of its own. They were hugely important years for him: they constituted
the one time he felt close to fulfilling his deepest ambitions. As such they
provided considerable fuel for his future vengeful and defiant exertions.
So, before going with Swift to apparent exile in Dublin, this chapter will
look again at his final months as a ministry man, and review his Tory
years in London with a survey of relationships, plans and resources that
would remain part of his future. Contact with some friends would fade,
but their influence endure; while some surviving relationships, regardless of absence, would provide active support and inspiration. Although

his friends in government were swept from their perches in the Whig purge that followed the accession of George I, Swift had built up another layer of connections while resident in London, a safety net of contacts and associations; and these brought personal, artistic, and, in some cases, technical and logistic support, if not the political influence and preferment he coveted.

By the early summer of 1714 Swift was extracting himself from certain Court circles, albeit only with the idea of teaching them a lesson. A sense may be gained of a more enduring level of contact and influence from a visit he received in July, scarcely a month before Oxford's ministry (and Bolingbroke's hopes) boiled away for ever. His guests were not seeking him out in London. He had quit the city at the start of June, having given up hope of Oxford taking action or Bolingbroke calling off his conspiracy. Instead, Alexander Pope and Thomas Parnell found Swift in the remote hamlet of Letcombe Bassett in Berkshire, three miles away from the market town of Wantage, birthplace of King Alfred.

Swift had taken up the invitation of a prolonged visit from the Reverend John Geree, the Rector of the parish. The link with Geree went a long way back, for he too had lived in some capacity with the Temples. He ran a little school from his house, and was proud that the small number of his pupils afforded him time and energy to pay each one a great deal of individual attention. However, he admitted he would be grateful if Swift could put in a word here and there that might boost his roster to ten or twelve boys. He hoped that his current five boarders would not discourage Swift from visiting his 'poor Habitation'. He promised him a horse, a garden and a 'pretty good library'. Swift was happy to accept the invitation and also to help, having offered long before to do whatever he could for Geree.[2] He arrived at 'Upper Letcombe' in early June 1714. Determined to cause his friend the least trouble possible, and perhaps embracing the radical change of pace, he would not hear of Geree changing his domestic routine. Thus he sank immediately into an unfamiliar rustic and near-solitary personal regime; and after just under a week with Geree, he confided to Esther Vanhomrigh that he was in danger of catching the spleen – that is, sinking into irritable depression.[3] Despite their unhappy spell the year before, when Swift began resisting closer contact with Vanhomrigh, friendly exchanges continued. He took care to help with the troubles she found managing her finances after the death of her mother in January. But, as bereavement and debts enveloped her, so her need of more attention and involvement from Swift only increased.

Geree undoubtedly belonged with another kind of creature to the busy, Court-wise folk Swift had grown used to in London. Swift loved him well, he told Hessy, but his host was 'such a melancholy thoughtfull man' that it was getting on his nerves. There was no conversation or cards to absorb his anxieties. They got up at six each morning, and had their main meal at noon; and this would keep Geree going until about eight, when he served some bread and butter with a glass of ale. Swift had sent him wine back in April, and they would share a pint of it every other evening before Geree turned in at ten. For the intervening hours, while Geree taught, Swift was left to himself. He read, he claimed, much of the day; but most of his books he had already shipped to Dublin in six large boxes. Writing, as ever, took its share of the day, as did a long walk. For this he gave his host, not heeding his protests, a guinea per week. Two or three of these guineas had parted from Swift before the space for reflection and exercise, and the restorative power the country-side always had for him, started to do him some good. Too much of the time passed in the hope that the courtiers and officials he had left behind him were sorely missing his help and considering their sins. A letter from the publisher John Barber told Swift that 'Every body is in the greatest Consternation at your Retirement, and wonder at the Cause.' But if they were guessing why he had left, then he could only doubt that they had taken his point – that they must stop their petty squabbling and pull together to avoid disaster. Less gratifying still was Barber's report of Bolingbroke's merry reaction to Swift's departure. He surely had got the message of Swift's turning his back on them all, but, sensing victory at last over Oxford, made fun of it.[4]

Swift was left with the rectory's low ceilings and uneven floors, the simple guest room and plain tableware; the voices of Geree's five pupils in the house; and the miles and miles of fields and soft hills surrounding Letcombe's little Norman church. At that point in his stay there was no woman to chat with for diversion. Geree's wife was visiting her father twenty miles away. It is just possible that Mrs Geree may not have welcomed their visitor as wholeheartedly as her husband. During their engagement, a couple of years earlier, the Parson had sought Swift's advice on what to do about marriage 'when it was too late to break off': the record is ambiguous as to whether Swift transmitted his anti-conjugal philosophy on the matter of poor young couples marrying.[5] But these were background issues. The place was a blank canvas for his memories and feelings, relieving him from the pressure of events while lending him the freedom to review the struggles of the past few years.

When he gathered his thoughts to write of what was passing in London, the crisis seemed unreal. The feuds that were scuttling the ministry seemed all the pettier, all the simpler to drop, in the face of what was at stake. A much younger contemporary of Swift, a fellow at Trinity, had recently argued that the universe had no actual being except in perception. That is, according to George Berkeley, when we stop looking at or hearing a thing, so far as we are concerned it ceases to be. Its existence is only maintained because God is constantly looking at it. Swift, who later admitted that he found Berkeley's theories a little 'too speculative', had gone to great lengths in presenting this philosopher at Court.[6] An abstracted, rather shy but charming man, Berkeley had some difficulty making his presence felt, possibly because he doubted the ultimate veracity of his or anyone else's being. In April 1713 Swift had recommended Berkeley strongly to the ministers, and had sent them copies of his extraordinary books. He had also taken his young friend out and treated him to dinner in an ale-house.[7] A good chop put one back in touch with matter. But might Berkeley's staggering idea be correct? It was, in a sense, another way of arguing Spinoza's case that God is the only true 'substance' in the cosmos – an idea slightly easier to grasp. Away from London, in any case, when he studied the government's problems from the void of Letcombe, Swift found them rootless, phantasmagorical. He reinforced his long-held view that Oxford and Bolingbroke could put matters right if they only resolved to do so.

He was soothed somewhat by friends writing to complain of his neglecting them. A number of these belonged to a group that had grown up within Swift's frankly vast political network during Oxford's years in government. His relationship with them up to this point forms a sort of subplot to his main political adventure. They were closely connected to the Court, and in one case intimately with the Queen herself, but met increasingly for refuge from the trials of public life. They called themselves, informally, members of the Scriblerus Club. The two younger friends who turned up at the parsonage at Letcombe in early July made up a scout party from this select little unit, and Pope reported back on what they discovered. The Dean received them at the back door of the Gerees' home and greeted them in surly fashion. Both guests were younger than Swift. Pope, just four and a half foot tall, was a stooping, pale, emaciated figure, yet jocular and animated; the other, Thomas Parnell, was handsome, amiable, yet at moments sombre and abstracted. Introductions were made; Mrs Geree had by this time returned and greeted her guest's friends more courteously than he did. When the company had settled, toasts to Bolingbroke, Oxford and absent confederates were drunk over wine and cider. Then Swift made coffee – having roasted the beans himself, though monitored by Mrs Geree as he did so – and politics dominated the chat.

Pope and Parnell complimented his rustic set-up; but Swift denied he was happy, except for the relief of being away from Court. He had just said the same thing in writing to another member of Scriblerus, one unable to make the trip.[8] It was a source of stubborn delight, however, to insist on how out of touch with world events he was. He had only learned that the elderly Electress Sophia of Hanover had died from a fellow he met at a neighbouring farm.[9] Although eighty-three, Sophia had still been widely expected to outlive Queen Anne. As it was, Anne survived her by a matter of weeks. The Electress was caught out in a squall in the garden she had commissioned at Herren-hausen, and collapsed. Some murmured that an insolent letter from Bolingbroke had upset her so much she fell sick. Sophia's son George, the new Elector, would now succeed Anne directly – unless by some twist Bolingbroke (and, less willingly, Oxford) could persuade the Pretender to turn Protestant. Such matters were far from being Swift's concern any more, especially since 'country Politicks are doubly insupportable.' He was too busy sighing with his neighbours over the lack of rain and the price of hay.[10] 'As for the methods of passing his time,' Pope recounted, 'I must tell you one which constantly employs an hour about noone.'

> He has in his window an Orbicular Glass, which by Contraction of the Solar Beams into a proper Focus, doth burn, singe, or speckle white or printed Paper, in curious little Holes, or various Figures . . . I doubt not but these marks of his are mysticall, and that the Figures he makes this way are a significant Cypher to those who have the skill to explain 'em.[11]

Pope wrote in the accepted manner of Scriblerus, a society dedicated on his instigation to cultivating redundant and wayward learning. Swift's experiment was less scientific than vengeful. The specks on the sheets he burned with his customized glass had once been the names of acquaintances: Pope watched him scorching away that of Thomas Hanmer, Speaker of the House and tempter of Bolingbroke, and also the printer John Barber. Swift also idled with his ray by defacing a number of proclamations against the Pretender, and also the text of Bolingbroke's incendiary and ultra-Tory piece of proposed legislation, the 'Schism' Bill.

The absent fellow Scriblerian addressed in Pope's subsequent letter was John Arbuthnot, physician to the Queen. For a month now Arbuthnot had been chiding Swift, through the post, for his 'proud stomach' on flouncing out of town and failing to write to his friends. They became acquainted, it seems, late in 1710 or early 1711: stays at Windsor and frequent encounters at St James's and Kensington gave their friendship plenty of time to develop. Arbuthnot, an extremely tall man prone to overeating, was a Scot and a Tory on the moderate side, notwithstanding that his brother Robert, a banker, was a Jacobite exile prospering in Rouen and Paris. Political agreement made passing time with Swift and Harley all the easier for Arbuthnot, since he shared their love of history and recondite knowledge. Closer to the softly spoken and sanguine Lord Treasurer in temperament than to the more forthright new Dean of St Patrick's, he shared the love both had of a good joke. As for Swift, the Doctor found pun-contests an all but inexhaustible source of amusement. Arbuthnot meanwhile was a polymath; a trusted committee man in the Royal Society, an antiquarian and a publishing mathematician and numismatist. His *Tables of Grecian, Roman, and Jewish Measures, Weights and Coins*, last updated in 1709, was accepted as a standard work. In addition, besides being pretty much the most important physician in the land, he was also the acclaimed author of a serial comic bestseller. Arbuthnot had created John Bull as an allegory of England in the person of an honest if occasionally slow-witted squire. Bull's *History*, which recounts his dealings with his domineering neighbour Lewis Baboon (Louis XIV), did much to persuade the public that the national interest and honour might not be best defended by persisting with the fruitless war. Arbuthnot's conceit covered domestic politics as well, since another thorny presence in Bull's local sphere, indeed his home, is his sister Peg, who represents the Scots. The John Bull pamphlets became viral reading across the kingdoms, while stirring resentments in each; but, although more phlegmatic than his friend Dr Swift, Arbuthnot cannily employed a similar comic tactic in entering political debate. Like Isaac Bickerstaff in 1709, John Bull made it difficult for all but the most resolute antagonist to keep a straight face. Like everyone, Swift followed the series avidly and exchanged comments with Johnson on its occasional dips in quality.

Alongside Swift and Arbuthnot, Thomas Parnell – 'the Parnellian', as they called him – was a more modest participant when the Scriblerus Club met in St James's Palace, a location that allowed the Earl of Oxford to join the meeting, or at a coffee-house in the City; but so in truth was Oxford, who enjoyed the jokes to the full but could not contribute on an intellectual or literary par with others present; and so too, for the moment, was another junior member, John Gay. When Parnell and Pope visited Swift at Letcombe, Gay had just left for Germany, clicking his heels, as secretary to the new envoy to Hanover, the Earl of Clarendon. Delighted with his salary and the opportunity, Gay credited the appointment to Swift's influence: 'You begin to be an able Courtier,' Swift replied tartly, concealing his delight as robustly as he did his string-pulling on Gay's behalf.[12] Gay was moderately well known as a writer of pastoral and the author of *The Mohocks*, a one-act satire on the aristocratic gang that had terrorized London in 1712. Regardless of his output and growing reputation, and his three years' seniority, his close friend and sponsor Pope still regarded Gay as his pupil and indeed his 'elf'.[13] The three senior Scriblerians' esteem for Gay and Parnell was a considerable tribute to the latter pair's wit, but also to their companionable natures. All members of the club felt it was as much their duty to rally around Parnell as it was to canvass for a post at Court for Gay. Parnell, a priest with an Irish living, was still clouded by the loss of his wife three years earlier. Swift, who had secured a preferment for Parnell in St Patrick's and, like the others, respected his work in verse, noted to Johnson that 'the poor lad is much afflicted.'[14]

In 1714 Thomas Parnell was thirty-five, and John Gay, twenty-nine; Alexander Pope, delicately shrewish where Parnell was robustly morose and Gay light-headed and amiable, was twenty-six that year. Yet it was fairly clear to all members of Scriblerus that he belonged to another order of talent than that of the other younger men. The select society itself was his idea. His initial project of founding a periodical composed entirely of quackery proved impossible, due to the club's collective lack of time, and gradually turned into a comic novel about the life of a child of arcaneness, Martinus Scriblerus. Each member made his own contribution, although by Swift's account the work was chiefly Arbuthnot's. Gay was 'too young' and Parnell 'too idle', and, despite giving the initial 'hint' for Scriblerus, he claimed that Pope 'has no Genius at all to it in my mind'.[15] Certainly Arbuthnot's massive command of contemporary scientific literature, of every promising, proven and ridiculous variety, gave him an advantage. In excusing Gay on grounds of youth Swift was really demurring at his lack of any further education beyond his West Country grammar-schooling at home in Barnstaple. Pope, the youngest of the group, was an autodidact: but his unsuitedness to the Scriblerus story, as Swift saw it, stemmed from the 'Genius' that drew his talents in another direction.

Swift made just one reference to his younger friend in the pages of his huge journal of letters to Johnson. It was a peremptory notice and instruction. 'Mr Pope has publishd a fine Poem calld Windsor Forrest; read it. Nite [good night].'[16] By 1714 Swift, like a good many others, could see that Pope's work was already a touchstone for any future attempt in English verse. Pope was highly offended when a respectable critic by the name of Thomas Tickell passed over his *Pastorals* and instead singled out the offering of another poet, Ambrose 'Pastoral' Philips, printed in the same volume. This fine piece of discrimination – or the lack of it – became a standing joke on Grub Street, one that Pope himself supported in a nail-gratingly ironic contribution to Steele's *Guardian*. In the meantime the foul personal attention Pope was starting to receive, which spared neither his physical frailty nor his Roman Catholicism, was a skewed testimony to the power of what he could do and had done already with the language, all – or at least mostly – within the miraculous limits of a heroic couplet. By 1714, when he relaxed at Letcombe with his friends, the bulk of his early accomplishment was already complete. He had made a conspicuous debut, like a good Virgilian, with his youthful *Pastorals*; the Horatian *Essay on Criticism* had soon followed, as had the first version of perhaps his best-known poem, *The Rape of the Lock*. Pope had steered as well clear as he could of the Whig–Tory feud. He had lodged with the painter Charles Jervas, a fervent Whig; he had written the prologue to Addison's *Cato*, and was still amiably connected to Steele and Addison. Yet such associations could not stop him writing in praise of the Tory peace negotiations in another classic of Augustan anthologies, *Windsor-Forest*. Again in pastoral mode, here Pope joined public and personal preoccupations with near-invisible stitching. The poem is the finest tribute to the Oxford administration's central achievement, the Peace of Utrecht. Pope's dedicatee was the Tory Secretary at War, George Granville, or Lord Lansdowne as he had become in 1712, in Oxford's New Year detachment of controversially created peers.

The treaty signed in April 1713 had in many respects set the calendar back to 1700, albeit at the cost of hundreds of thousands of lives. Philip, Duke of Anjou, Louis of France's grandson, was confirmed as the King of Spain, though on the condition of renouncing any claim to the French Crown. Other young relatives of Louis were similarly disqualified from pretensions to Spain on Philip's death. Such a basic agreement angered the

Whigs, and also renegade Tories such as Nottingham, who cherished a plan to dislodge Philip altogether from Madrid. In *Windsor-Forest*, Pope had carefully praised the devastating victories England's 'eager sons' had won in the country around so many European villages ('thoughtless towns', he called them). Yet the fate of so many 'vigorous swains' is typified unmistakably by Pope in the easy-going late-summer slaughter taking place as the hunting season opens in the environs of Windsor.

> See! from the Brake the whirring Pheasant springs,
> And mounts exulting on triumphant Wings:
> Short is his Joy! he feels the fiery Wound,
> Flutters in Blood, and panting beats the Ground.[17]

The image of the tumbling bird sets off another of an infantryman, crumpling under gunfire: there is a simple perfection even in the phrase 'fiery Wound', typical of the unobtrusive aptness shown throughout the poem. Although Pope avoided the party-political front, and ran no gauntlet as Swift had with *The Conduct of the Allies*, his writing in *Windsor-Forest* is arguably much braver and stauncher, since, unlike Swift, he cut through to essential injustices: the massacre of labourers to procure glories for dukes and princes. Pope also struck firmly at what most in England accepted was one of the genuine prizes of Utrecht. As the European territories and overseas interests of Spain were shared out among the allies, Britain seized the *asiento*, the monopoly granted by Madrid for the sale of African slaves to its American colonies. Pope was ahead of his time in declaring his abhorrence of such arrangements. He called beyond the limits of any particular treaty to an egalitarian spirit of peace.

> Oh stretch thy Reign, fair *Peace*! from Shore to Shore,
> 'Till Conquest cease, and Slav'ry be no more;
> 'Till the freed *Indians* in their native Groves
> Reap their own Fruits, and woo their Sable Loves,
> *Peru* once more a race of Kings behold,
> And other *Mexicos* be roof'd with Gold.[18]

Swift's great tirade against slavery at the end of the *Travels* was many years away, when his spirit was freed of ministerial concerns. Yet Pope launched his, in the passage quoted above, at a moment when he had none of the official protection Swift could rely on, and when the commercial return on his writing was still not certain. He had a great deal to lose in going beyond the standard lines of praise for or criticism of Utrecht. He was, it must be said, still covering his tracks, in making no concrete comment on any particular article of the treaty, or indeed in saying anything with which anyone could really disagree. Even magnates trawling in fortunes from plantations in the West Indies could pray piously each Sunday for an end to slavery. Pope's poem is thus politic as well as 'political'; for this and for its consummate artistry *Windsor-Forest* belongs high above the other workaday verses written to condemn or, like John Gay's *Rural Sports*, to commend the Peace.

How well Swift's ministerial campaigning emerges in comparison with Pope's dexterous clarion call is something for each of their readers to decide. Pope's early experiences of anti-Papist prejudice and suppression (he had just about the most unfortunate surname a Catholic could possibly have) made him side with the victims of slavery in a way that Swift, the child of an embattled controlling minority, could not. Swift's priority as a government writer was to save the institutions he saw as guarantors of basic social cohesion. It was also to stop a horrific war and disable a profiteering oligarchy. The *asiento* did not figure largely in his thinking about the peace – the goal of which for him was to forestall the utter ruination of the British and Irish economies. He scoffed, though, at the Dutch for their willingness to overlook articles they found dubious in the treaty in a bid for a share of the African trade: for the monopoly was not, as the Whigs claimed, merely a 'Trifle'.[19] There is a disquieting touch of pride in that remark, as if Swift classed this new gain as a straightforward economic achievement. His eyes set on the fray, Swift did not condemn that trade at the time the *asiento* was acquired. It is striking that he eventually allotted Gulliver several years of profitable involvement in slaving, seemingly to show that there could be blood on the hands even of such an everyman (he may, admittedly, have given Gulliver a Dissenting past for much the same reason): yet by the end of his fourth voyage Gulliver fiercely condemns slavery. This and Swift's allegiance to what is, in a crucial respect, a criminal regime should probably make us look at the tags inside our clothes, and reflect on the conditions in which they were probably made. His involvement with Harley's ministry raises questions that haunt many who try to do some good in public life while accepting the compromises brought by collective responsibility and external economic or other 'corporate' influences, and at times losing sight of their consequences.

When Pope and Parnell visited him, Swift was not viewing events *sub specie aeternitatis*, from the perspective of eternity, as the younger poet could; or, rather, he believed that he was, and that the boiling prism of political society in the Queen's last days actually showed things in their ultimate aspect. As Oxford and Bolingbroke tore up their life's work over a trifle, a personal disagreement, Swift tried to see to the core of what had gone wrong, and also nursed hopes of being able to transmit their achievements to posterity. For a long time he hoped he might be appointed Historiographer Royal. This was a post that made the holder official historian to the Crown, and thus technically brought control of how the Crown's substantial archives would be interpreted. Besides his ambitions as a chronicler, ambitions that would largely go unfulfilled, Swift's hankering for this modest honour was surely touched by a sense of how important the role might be in the Earl of Oxford's eyes. In day-to-day politics, Harley's lust for information was sated with his network of spies; in his domestic capacity as the maintainer of a great house, the Earl directed this charisma for knowledge, at huge expense, to a collection of books and manuscripts that was fast becoming one of the largest and most precious in the land. Just as Harley's agents reported from problematic boroughs across Britain and Ireland, so the scholars and booksellers in his hire would notify him of leads on unique transcriptions in obscure attics and auctions. It says a great deal that Oxford lavished as much energy and money on this library, which formed the basis of the Harleian Collection in the British Library, as he did on his cellar. Swift therefore assumed the Lord Treasurer would take care to place the position in special hands. He was ready to receive it as a sacred trust.

But the office of Historiographer Royal had always been little more than a sinecure, as Arbuthnot reminded Swift, mildly ticking him off for caring so much about it. The job had been created largely for the sake of James Howell, the amicable yet factually unreliable Cavalier chronicler and epistolarian. Since 1710 Swift had had great plans for developing the post, and in time saw in it a means of sanctioning his sweeping and for now unpublishable history of Anne's last four years. By mid-July 1714 these ambitions had been added to his other defeated hopes. Arbuthnot had put in a word for him to Lady Masham, still the Queen's confidante – but she, although sending her compliments, would do nothing in his interest.[20] The position and its £200 a year were given instead to a man called Madox, whom no one seemed to know (but who in fact proved conscientious).[21] Swift growled, but was prepared for the blow.

Slowly and painfully he was reverting to thinking of himself and his acquaintance in purely individual terms, no longer as the representatives of officialdom or confederates in a more nebulous historical mission. His friends were now bound to him by common traits, doubts and virtues alone. The process was strongly indicated by a noble and moving letter written to the weakening Lord Treasurer early in July. Swift began with a startling egalitarian assertion. He had, he wrote, never allowed a difference in power or title to create any real difference between men. Yet, 'being now absent and forgotten, I have changed my mind.' The Earl of Oxford had a thousand people who could claim to admire him as much as Dr Swift did; as such, Swift could only expect 'a thousandth part' in return for the true affection he gave Oxford. Despite Swift's commitment to brevity, the conceit showed his skill with baroque expression when he cared to use it. He continued:

> And the misfortune is still the greater, because I always loved you just so much the worse for your Station. For in your publick Capacity you have often angred me to the Heart, but, as a private Man, never once. So that if I lookt towards my self I could wish you a private Man tomorrow.

Swift wrote in the likely expectation that these anomalies of regard were soon to be equalized. Both he and the Lord Treasurer, now nicknamed 'Dragon' by friends on account of his mildness, were on the verge of becoming private men again. Naturally no real privacy, a term Swift would always use pejoratively (insisting on its classical root, denoting a state of 'privation' from public affairs), could ever be the Earl and statesman's lot. Yet Oxford's impending dismissal gave Swift a final chance, albeit purely rhetorical, to put both on the same footing. With this neat piece of levelling done, he could assure Harley as a comrade that his friendship had nothing to do with place-seeking or ambition before making his bow and withdrawing from the levee. The collapse of the government restored the equality Swift had foolishly imagined to exist between them at the height of the minister's power. He praised Harley for never allowing rank to come between them: he was never afraid to disagree with the Lord Treasurer, 'nor am now in Pain for the manner I write in.'[22] Not long afterwards, with the letter dispatched, Swift was in fact a little discomfited to think of its very open sincerity. As at other moments of crisis in his long life, he had expressed himself in a way that most – mistakenly – might consider deeply un-Swiftian; with a forthright if artistically nuanced declaration of feeling. His letter to Oxford was 'very odd and serious', he confessed to Arbuthnot in another the same day.[23] But the thing was sent, and he had meant every word; and Arbuthnot soon informed him that Harley, the Dragon, 'seemd mightily pleasd with it'.[24]

Swift meanwhile knew that he too could not be reduced to utter 'privacy'; it was more than a year since he had assumed the powers and dignities of his new office as dean, following and directing cathedral affairs through the post. Yet, as he returned to laying plans without the comfort of thinking the government might back them, it would be as well to consider what schemes Swift had nursed before events conspired to ruin them.

## 2

As he became ever more active as a Tory partisan, Swift nurtured a pipe-dream that, to his mind, offered a means of reconciling party differences, at least for the leading intellectuals of the kingdom. One of the several paradoxes in his politics was that, even as he became synonymous with the Tories, he sought an escape from the new party-riven establishment, yearning for a time that had never really existed, when government was carried out by a dependable consensus between the monarch's councillors in Parliament. As he insisted in numerous papers, including his *Examiners*, there was no essential difference in principles between Whigs and Tories. At a simpler level, he missed his bright Whig friends, and the convivial times of the previous decade: Addison in particular was a painful loss. He also regretted being unable to do more for others, notably his old acquaintance Congreve. Early in his collaboration with Harley's ministry, Swift had had high hopes of the informal Society of 'Brothers' organized around the Lord Treasurer and Secretary St John. A stated aim of this fraternity was the patronage of 'men of genius'.[25] Yet its meetings quickly decayed into occasions for canvassing, recruiting and mere opposition-bashing. In late June 1711, when St John was still only contemplating a club for members with 'wit and learning' or 'power and influence', Swift sounded out Oxford on a scheme of his own. 'I am proposing to my lord to erect a society or academy for correcting and settling our language,' he told the ladies in Dublin, 'that we may not perpetually be changing as we do.' Francis Atterbury, of whom he saw much that summer, applauded the idea. Oxford himself, Swift reported, took to it 'mightily'.[26]

The Lord Treasurer, as in almost any enterprise, stalled before taking matters further – excusably, surely, in this case, given the pressure of balancing the nation's accounts while securing a viable peace. Still, Swift presented his suggestion to the public the following spring, in a pamphlet dedicated to the Earl of Oxford and entitled *A Proposal for Correcting the English Tongue*. He only hinted at his subsidiary goal of bringing together minds; the main objective, as he told Johnson a year earlier, was to halt linguistic change. Swift lamented flux in English, which took the form of neologisms and grammatical disintegration. 'I have never known this great Town without one or more *Dunces* of Figure, who had Credit enough to give Rise to some new Word, and propagate it in most Conversations; although it had neither Humor, nor Significancy.'[27] If the influence of a dunce could corrupt language, then, conversely, the financial and social 'credit' of learned lords could reverse or at least delay the process. A society with a royal charter, similar to the Académie française, should legislate for the English language, fixing grammatical rules, while approving or removing words and expressions as its high council saw fit.

Although Swift's target was the reform of language, the *Proposal* says much about his assumptions regarding the nature of the world. If his political orientation puzzles some readers, it should be recalled how sincerely Swift believed that complex autonomous phenomena could be altered and amended by a little conscious and concerted effort on the part of the Court, the commonwealth in its entirety or the rational mind of an individual. The conviction had already been aired in his *Project for the Advancement of Religion*, which won Steele's praise in the *Tatler* in 1710; there he had argued that the Crown could outlaw immoral conduct by denying patronage to anyone who misbehaved. Vice would, in consequence, become unfashionable and die away accordingly. The belief in the ease with which human life might be repaired in fact lends a sense of high tragedy, and of religious mission, to Swift's satire. All the evils and absurdities exposed in *A Tale of a Tub*, Swift was suggesting, existed only for a lack of due care and effort. Although such a view might seem to sit oddly with Swift's reputation as a pessimist, it actually reinforced the deepest of his suspicions about human nature. If people might improve the world, from outright harmful acts to sloppy grammar, by such simple steps, their failure to do so indicated that they were just lazy, ignorant or actually malign, and preferred things as they were. *Ergo*, men and women were essentially corrupt.

The severe restraints and expectations Swift placed on himself and his own urges fed his certainty that developed minds such as Harley's and St

John's could stop disliking each other, and thus save the government and the kingdom, if they only chose to do so. Equally, the stylistic demands he placed on any squib or note he wrote, and his own taste for good speech and writing, could be adopted and implemented by all if they were only well directed.[28] Ultimately, the fall of England might be prevented if everyone (including the Irish and the Dutch) could be induced to see sense. The unguardedly plaintive note of the phrase in his letter to Johnson back in 1711, 'that we may not perpetually be changing', indicates the wish and need behind his attitude on these questions. He felt a deep desire for stasis, a moratorium on the pain that life's flow constituted.

Swift's plan to unite Whig and Tory wits in the common fight against bad phrasing went amiss. He took the extremely rare step of putting his name to the *Proposal*. As such, the proposed academy was publicly associated with a prominent Tory. This was made all the more reprehensible by the French model the scheme inescapably imitated. One or two writers fleetingly gave Swift's ideas serious critical thought, gesturing in the direction of the still unformed modern insight that linguistic life stems from social, environmental and unconscious factors beyond the absolute control Swift thought was possible.[29] On the whole, the Whig press cudgelled what they saw as a Tory plot to bring in French notions with the mooted peace; the Pretender, of course, would not be long behind. The mere idea of *improving* the English tongue sounded distinctly unpatriotic. Swift insisted quite genuinely that his essay was 'no politics, but a harmless Proposall'. The plan was delicious to him. Late in May 1712 he got a taste of the fraternity his academy might have offered when he dined outside with fifteen members of St John's disappointing brotherhood 'under a Canopy in an Arbour' in the Earl of Peterborough's garden.[30]

Swift's readers, though, can be grateful that essays such as the *Proposal* and the earlier *Project for the Advancement of Religion* did reach the light of day. They bring out the ache behind his eventual satirical narrative of a man adrift; more immediately, they help to explain the panic and dolour that overtook him in the last months of Harley's ministry. Furthermore, although the theories in the *Proposal* might look sketchy even in the light of contemporary thinking on linguistics and society, they gave Swift a base from which to strike at palpable instances of poor thought and expression. As so often, though his larger logic might be flawed, his identification of an opponent's fault is unerring.

Overbearing, rhetorically sloppy and coarsely emotive, Richard Steele was a major offender – at least so far as his writings concerned Swift's ministry of language. In the course of 1713, their long-festering relationship switched into open hostility. Steele opposed the peace and was outraged at the treatment of Marlborough and others he regarded as heroes in the national cause: Swift was of course a leading maligner. During April and May, suspecting rightly that Swift was still contributing to the *Examiner*, Steele sniped at his former friend as a 'miscreant' in one issue of the *Guardian*, and as an 'unbeliever' in another. Swift had been replaced at the helm of the *Examiner* by Delarivier Manley, with whom Steele had once had an affair. Lowering the tone of the debate for good, Steele dismissed both opponents with a jeering broadside: 'It is nothing to me whether the *Examiner* writes against me in the character of an estranged friend or an exasperated mistress.'[31] With this, their friendship finally lay in shreds.

The last trace of amity was extinguished in a furious exchange of letters in which both men felt they had right on their side. Swift was extremely hurt, as always, at the charge against his Christianity. At the time when the row played itself out, he had just been appointed dean, and a creeping doubt as to his worthiness for the place – despite his high and self-righteous expectations – may have made him especially sensitive. He felt doubly wronged by Steele, since he not only believed he had persuaded Harley to let Steele keep his sinecure as a commissioner of the Stamp Office, but was now assured and taunted that his good offices in that respect were entirely irrelevant. Harley needed Steele for his own purposes, and Swift was ignorant of the tentative, pragmatic link his master fostered. Swift's insecurities emerged violently when he learned that, according to Steele, Harley and St John had laughed at him for his pomposity. Steele cast him, suddenly, as the lone boy in the playground. Swift ground his teeth: 'I was laughed at only for your sake,' he riposted.[32] He charged Steele roundly with 'vileness', a slur that excited the anger of a trooper against one he could not call out for a duel. Steele denied that he was the servant of any party – rather ridiculously, since he had identified the Whig view entirely with his own, but sincerely nevertheless. And he too invoked the shadow of lost friendship and mutual regard: 'I do not speak this calmly ... out of terror of your wit or my Lord Treasurer's power, but pure kindness to the agreeable qualities I once so passionately delighted in in you.' The argument had lost all touch with Acts of Parliament or treaty articles: it turned on betrayal, the undoing of comradeship and mutual esteem. In his final reply, which closed the correspondence, Swift insisted he had always avoided mentioning or alluding personally to Steele in print: it was his colleague-turned-adversary who had broken the unwritten pact. In a postscript, he also claimed that he had gone so far as to compliment Steele publicly in his *Proposal for Correcting the English Tongue*.[33]

The remark is curious and possibly untrue. In the *Proposal*, Swift compliments:

> An ingenious Gentleman, who for a long Time did thrice a Week divert or instruct the Kingdom by his Papers; and is supposed to pursue the same Design at present, under the Title of *Spectator* . . . This Author, who hath tried the Force and Compass of our Language with so much Success, agrees entirely with me in most of my Sentiments relating to it.[34]

In May 1713, almost a year after the *Proposal* was published, Swift intimated that Steele was the 'Gentleman' he meant here.[35] Yet the compliment in its home context applies much more aptly to Addison. Steele had very decently acknowledged his debt to his more accomplished friends in the collected edition of the *Tatler*; and the best issues of the *Spectator* have always been accredited to his chief collaborator. Complimenting Steele in such terms would have appeared a gross hyperbole. Originally, Swift was wooing Addison to support his projected academy; a year later, he used the remark as moral capital in his spat with Steele, effectively claiming gratitude from two sources for his tribute to a single 'Author'.

Steele threw himself into front-line politics. He gave up his governmental sources of income, including a pension he received for having been gentleman waiter to the Queen's consort, Prince George, and began a series of crudely written yet effective pamphlets against the government and the Peace of Utrecht. Soon after his election as MP for Stockbridge in the general election of September 1713, he alleged the government was deliberately failing to destroy the fortifications at Dunkirk, gained for Britain in the Utrecht Treaty, as part of a murky conciliation of the French. *The Importance of Dunkirk Consider'd* alarmed the country, and sold well. Steele continued to beat the same drum in issues of his newest creation, a paper called the *Englishman*. Addison had briefly taken over his duties with the *Guardian* while Steele went campaigning, but the journal was dropped, abruptly, in the autumn. Steele's next big-hitting publication was an incendiary pamphlet called *The Crisis*, which drew attention to the Queen's poor health and cried up the danger of a Jacobite challenge to the succession. Steele reprinted pages of statutes, labouring his constitutional point in an enormous appendix. Soon after *The Crisis* was published, the Tories began working to expel Steele from Parliament, and he was forced to give up his seat, on a charge of sedition, in March 1714. In an open challenge to the evasions made possible by anonymous and pseudonymous publishing, the tactics of Dr Swift and his cohorts, Steele had defiantly signed *The Crisis* with his own name. It proved to be a phenomenal bestseller.

Swift answered each of Steele's major pamphlets. If the gentleman complimented in the *Proposal for Correcting the English Tongue* really was Steele, Swift now removed entirely all suggestion that his imagined academy might have held a place for that 'ingenious Gentleman' or others who shared his opinions. The first, *The Importance of the Guardian Considered*, was an artful piece of character assassination: a professional hit masquerading as the work of an amateur. Steele had written *The Importance of Dunkirk Consider'd* as a letter to the Bailiff of his constituency of Stockbridge. Swift now addressed the same gentleman, in the mode of a concerned informant, and pointed out the duplicity and egotism of Stockbridge's new representative at every possible turn. While insisting that 'I owe him no Malice', Swift proceeded to mention all of Steele's crimes. Intellectual mediocrity, though, was the most prominent failing he found in his enemy.

> To take the height of his Learning, you are to suppose a Lad just fit for the University, and sent early from thence into the wide World, where he followed every way of Life that might least improve or preserve the Rudiments he had got. He hath no Invention, nor is Master of a tolerable Style: his chief Talent is Humour, which he sometimes discovers both in Writing and Discourse; for after the first Bottle he is no disagreeable Companion.

Barely a page in, the illusion of external observer is dropped, and a voice speaking from personal acquaintance takes over. Swift assiduously avoids tainting Addison through association with Steele, by mentioning the benefits Steele has gained from their 'continual Conversation and Friendship'.[36] Steele, however, is portrayed as one eternally ineligible for membership of Swift's academy for correcting the English language. It is as if Swift tried to strike out all suggestion that the passage celebrating the *Spectator* in his *Proposal* could possibly refer to Steele; as, in a moment of weakness, he had told him it did.

In *The Publick Spirit of the Whigs*, his answer to *The Crisis*, which got him into trouble with the Scots, Swift continued in the same vein, writing with exactly the balance and expansiveness he knew Steele could never muster. Denouncing the leading Whigs yet again, he declared:

> I am sensible it is of little Consequence to their Cause, whether this Defender of it [Steele] understands Grammar or no; and if what he would fain say, discovered him to be a Well-willer to Reason or Truth, I would be ready to make large Allowance. But when with great Difficulty I descry a Composition of Rancour and Falshood, intermixed with plausible Nonsense, I feel a Struggle between Contempt and Indignation, at seeing the Character of a *Censor*, a *Guardian*, an *Englishman*, a *Commentator* on the *Laws*, an *Instructor* of the *Clergy*, assumed by a Child of Obscurity, without one single Qualification to support them.[37]

It possibly didn't occur to Swift that yes, perhaps the Whig grandees actually *did* think that Steele's grammatical deficiencies were 'of little Consequence to their Cause'. Furthermore, if that is their view, Swift exposes himself to a troubling implication of his own argument. He may well possess all the qualities and 'qualifications' Steele lacks, and thus is entitled to assume the roles his opponent has usurped. Yet if those talents prove to be irrelevant, as he concedes they might, what is there to prevent the world from regarding Swift himself as another 'Child of Obscurity' – as much an upstart as Steele, his fellow countryman? With the stately demonstration of his stylistic superiority, Swift was engaged in a battle his greatest enemies weren't remotely interested in fighting. The halting prose of *The Crisis*, read avidly across the shires, had already won the war over the succession.

Swift's supposed victory over Steele, in the crucial pamphlets of late 1713 and early 1714, set something of a pattern in his last year of writing for the ministry. He was writing the best prose and raising the loudest laughs; yet ultimately he was fulfilling objectives his adversaries, and even the Machiavellian Bolingbroke, cared little about. Unlike Swift, it perhaps mattered less to such enemies if people laughed at them behind their backs. He could hardly imagine that what for him was excruciating torture, humiliating mockery from one he considered his friend, was for others – for thick-skinned, impetuous Steele – something to be shaken off and forgotten.

The republic of letters, despite Swift's efforts, thus remained riven. A wit retaining the goodwill of the majority on both sides was rare indeed.

Such an exception was William Congreve, Swift's younger schoolmate. The gentle-hearted dramatist had withdrawn somewhat since his decade of near-constant fame in the 1690s. The spite that loaded the debates his plays provoked, over the rules of dramaturgy and the morality of theatre itself, seems to have made writing for the stage distasteful to him. So in the early 1700s he turned to a more introverted form of writing that, while bringing less acclaim, perhaps better suited his temperament. He worked on words for music, from individual lyrics to entire librettos. In the meantime he maintained his connection with the theatre and aided the ill-starred movement to establish an English opera: his *Semele*, with music by John Eccles, was to have been performed on the opening night of the new Queen's Theatre in the Haymarket in 1705. But the project petered out, another show was put on at the lack-lustre opening, and Congreve's *Semele* was never performed in his lifetime.

Stating his preference for ease and quiet, Congreve adopted the lifestyle of a beloved yet semi-retired celebrity. His patrons and associates were overwhelmingly Whig: he was a stalwart of the Kit-Cat, the darling of the Marlboroughs and Somersets. Although he might have been expected to suffer under the new ministry, Harley made a point of reassuring him, in the early spirit of coalition, that he was in no danger of losing the modest sinecures that now formed the basis of his official income. In the same spirit, Swift prided himself on having helped: 'I had often mentioned him with kindness to lord treasurer.' After meeting Harley on one occasion, Congreve confided to Swift that he was treated with much greater kindness than he had received for many years. Harley gave Swift the pleasure of bearing the news to Congreve that his modest revenues were safe.[38] The playwright remained in more or less the same state for the duration of the ministry. Cutting-edge work proved beyond him as his health failed: he suffered badly with gout, and developed cataracts. His friends among the Whig magnates were unlikely to let him sink into real hardship, and so it seemed, since he enjoyed a lifestyle that, although quiet, manifestly required several more hundreds a year than he earned from the state. On the Treasury books his place as a commissioner for the licensing of wines brought only £200.[39] Later, Swift decided that Congreve was an example of an artist selling out politically to procure security: until he accepted Whig sponsorship as a young man, claimed Swift, Congreve often lacked a shilling to pay for a 'chair' – the covered seat lifted on horizontal poles by two bearers that was a standard form of transport in the city, and cheaper than a cab.[40] For that he could hardly blame Congreve, though; and he feared for him in inconstant times. He was especially touched when the playwright helped his unfortunate protégé Harrison by writing an edition of the new *Tatler* series for him despite the strain on his weakened eyes.

By the end of the summer of 1714, the times seemed to show that a bragger such as Steele had judged the situation perfectly. Even Congreve, much more admirable in Swift's eyes, had only to wait for his patrons to regain office. He was soon made the Secretary of Jamaica (with special dispensation from living in the colony), on a comfortable £700 a year. Though Swift with his deanship could be said to have done just as well – even better, bearing in mind the circumstances – that was not how he viewed the matter. He identified himself instead with other survivors of the fallen regime.

## 3

It was remarkable to Swift how enemies of the Church – even those who held high office within it – were so often also foreigners to syntax. His struggles in the second half of 1713 were not with Steele alone. He also took up his pen against one of the Whigs' episcopal patriarchs. Gilbert Burnet, Bishop of Sarum, had irritated him for years. A Scot by birth, Burnet had been much favoured by King William. During the 1690s he became perhaps the foremost trimmer on the Bishops' Bench. In his writings, historical and theological, he crushed ecclesiastical principles into a crude dovetail with the revolutionary settlement. He later brazened out a great deal of sardonic commentary from other sections of the clergy, since during the reign of James II (who hated him) he had vocally supported the Test Acts. He had then survived exile and implication in the Rye House Plot against Charles II. He had a habit of inciting a strong dislike. Swift's early hero, Archbishop Sancroft, had refused to consecrate Burnet when William appointed him the Bishop of Salisbury in 1689. Yet he could be seductive: he was an impulsive, sensual character, and his wife was an heiress of noted beauty. He was troubled at the moment of decision but afterwards invariably content with it. His writing nevertheless made a great show of introspection and self-questioning. The work for which he is best known, the *History of His Own Time*, turned the era into a narrative of his personal spiritual formation. In 1713 he was seventy, still going strong despite the Queen's fervent disapproval, though, as it happened, with only a couple of years to live.

In Burnet, Swift found a natural enemy. Like so many of his foes, the Bishop was initially well disposed towards the author of *A Tale of a Tub*, and for a time Swift respected him. When Swift's defence of Somers and the other impeached lords, the *Discourse* on ancient Athens and Rome, appeared in 1701, many suspected Burnet as the author. In one of several apparently cordial meetings, Burnet admitted that he was forced to disown the work very publicly to avoid being impeached himself. The root of Swift's growing odium was Burnet's leadership of the Whigs dominating the Bishops' Bench in the Lords, who favoured a deal with the Nonconformists. Swift's adherence to the opposing tendency, the High Church politics of the lower clergy, would only strengthen with time. Back, however, at that delicate time in 1701, when Somers and the other Whig leaders seemed to dangle 'great preferments' in front of Swift, his view of their intentions was clouded and his own path unclear. When he recounted the period in which he published the tract that led Somers and the others to court him, he described himself in terms that might have fitted the younger Burnet. 'Although I had been for many years before no stranger to the court, and had made the nature of government a great part of my study, yet I had dealt very little with politics, either in writing or acting.'[41] Like Swift as a youthful clerical courtier travelling to Kensington Palace in 1693, in 1663 Burnet had been entrusted with a delicate, if more dangerous mission: his mother had sent him to plead for the life of his uncle, Archibald Johnston, Lord Wariston, the architect of the Scottish Covenant and subsequent revolt of the late 1630s. The resemblance may only be pushed so far, as the two men's politics held little common ground: annotating his copy of Burnet's *History* later in life, Swift branded Wariston an 'abominable dog' and 'a fit uncle for such a bishop'.[42] Luck and personal inflexibility denied Swift the rapid rise that Burnet's fortunes brought him. Burnet was a proven survivor: and, on making himself indispensable to the Williamites, he set about mangling Church doctrines. His pen forced the Trinity and the Thirty-nine Articles of the Anglican Church into disagreeable conformity with the new regime. He beckoned, in short, in a direction Swift could never take. He remained a peculiar image in negative of the younger man who became his critic: pliable where Swift was adamant, versatile and opportunistic where Swift's nerve and conscience froze. Interestingly, while Swift was in some respects a man in search of his paternity, Burnet was the victim of aggressively over-principled and maniacally involved fathering: he was the son of a noted Edinburgh attorney who combined the unflinching tendencies both of a Puritan and a resolute Episcopalian. His son the Bishop simultaneously followed and resisted the direction of his father.

During Anne's last years, Burnet had begun reissuing his earlier works with new introductions – books and pamphlets that, his enemies noted, mainly provided occasions for berating the current trends in government. The strategy culminated in November 1713 with the separate publication of Burnet's introduction to the third volume of his *History of the Reformation of the Church of England* in advance of the work itself. Although the ploy was mocked, it served its purpose well, and it needed countering – for the introduction was, like Steele's *Crisis*, a major intervention in the party struggle, albeit for a more limited readership. Venting the annoyance of many years, Swift now responded with a baroque extension of Burnet's method: *A Preface to the Right Reverend Dr Burnet Bishop of Sarum's Introduction . . .* Earlier in 1713 Swift had made short work of another theological writer, William Collins, in a brusque dismissal entitled *Mr Collins's Discourse of Free-thinking*. In dispatching Mr Collins, Swift was in rather poor derisive form. In his sally against Burnet, catalysed by the sense of emergency, he did better. His 'preface' to Burnet's introduction was arguably crude at moments, but effective nonetheless.

> I was debating with my self, whether this Hint of producing a small Pamphlet to give notice of a large Folio, were not borrowed from the Ceremonial in *Spanish* Romances, where a *Dwarf* is sent out upon the Battlements, to signify to all Passengers, what a mighty *Giant* there is in the Castle . . . I have seen the same Sort of Management at a Puppet Show. Some Puppets, of little or no Consequence, appeared several times at the Window, to allure the Boys and the Rabble: The Trumpeter sounded often, and the Door-keeper cried an hundred Times, until he was Hoarse, that they were just going to begin; yet, after all, we were forced some Times to wait an Hour before *Punch* himself in Person made his Entry.[43]

Puppet-shows, to be found in humble market squares and village commons, on street corners or amid the bustle of Covent Garden, always fascinated Swift. More than once in his writing marionettes appear as models of real people, accompanied by grim conjecture about the nature of the puppet-master. Swift's own puppeteering in the passage above turns Burnet into both the Dwarf on the battlements and Punch at the fair, and reveals there is no real giant behind the castle walls. Yet the energy expended on Burnet in this pamphlet suggests an adversary of imposing stature, even if he was (to Swift) a cheat. For Swift, Burnet was guilty of exactly the same scare-mongering to which Steele had stooped. He was crying out at dangers that, as Swift assured himself, could not be real: the Pretender swooping in, and a Popish uprising. Swift's faith in Oxford and Bolingbroke was such that any secret deal with the Pretender was also out of the question. The true threat, Swift declared hoarsely yet again, came from the elements Burnet and Steele were sponsoring: the Dissenters, the Presbyterians, the fanatics. He rejected the idea that Burnet, Steele and the Whigs held their fears of a Papist take-over as genuinely as he did his of the Low Church faction. He was blithely unaware that Oxford and Bolingbroke were corresponding with James Francis Edward and his Court at Bar-le-Duc, and offering him the Crown if he converted.

Here, then, in Burnet, was another confirmed traitor: and here too was another mind unqualified to enter Swift's phantom English Academy. For, as Swift suggested in his *Preface*, 'I would advise him, if it be not too late in his Life, to endeavour a little at mending his Style, which is mighty defective in the *Circumstances* of Grammar, Propriety, Politeness and Smoothness.'[44] Although his private notes on Burnet's works are gruffer ('Dunce', 'Strange inconsistent stuff', 'This wants grammar'),[45] the thesis in the text is consistent: defects in style, Swift proposes, are inextricable from deficiencies in knowledge and morality. It was, though, a principle Swift could suspend at other moments if he wished. Notably Oxford, his beloved lord treasurer, was known to lose track of a sentence, but 'In drawing up any State Paper no man had more proper thoughts ... Although his [Harley's] Style were not always correct, which however he knew how to mend, yet often to save time he would leave the smaller Alterations to others.'[46] By others, Swift principally meant himself. He had dusted off and redrafted several crucial documents, including the Queen's Speeches to Parliament, during Harley's tenure. The signal difference between a Harley and a Burnet in this respect, notwithstanding the gulf between them in principle, was that Harley had the humility to seek help. It didn't occur to Swift, or if it did he resisted the thought, that Harley and Burnet were as political animals very similar, both being consensus-builders, seeking broad agreement of the largest possible majority, akin particularly in their various efforts to reconcile High and Low elements in the Church. They were both mediators of a kind Swift could support only if there was near-absolute agreement between them and his own personality and strictest principles. He did not expect perfection: he could forgive St John's misdemeanours, as his oratory was superlative, and he could pardon Harley's sloppy grammar, since his aims were so commendable. But he rarely gave the benefit of the doubt.

Indeed, by trashing the style of his opponents, something he could do with undisputed comic brilliance, Swift sometimes avoided the need to take an argument to deeper levels. In a superbly funny pamphlet of 1712, he pretended to be the Earl of Wharton writing a letter of thanks to another Whig cleric, William Fleetwood, Bishop of St Asaph, on behalf of his friends at the Kit-Cat Club. Fleetwood had reissued four old sermons in a slim volume, and in the preface took every opportunity to praise the former ministry and lambast the current one. Swift let the devil out. His impersonation of Wharton, thanking Fleetwood for services rendered, has diabolical, hilarious zest. He takes Fleetwood, who is better than any old prophet, as relieving subjects of their duty to obey their monarch:

> This you say is the Opinion of CHRIST, St *Peter*, and St *Paul*: And 'faith I am glad to hear it; for I never thought the Prigs had been Whigs before: But since your Lordship has taught them to declare for Rebellion, you may easily persuade them to do as much for Prophaneness and Immorality; and then they, together with your Lordship, shall be enrolled Members of our Club.

Again, Swift tweaks at the pride of the writer by pointing up the shortcomings of his style. No greater insult could there be, in Swift's mind, than the admiration of a lout such as Wharton. A passage where Fleetwood heavily repeats the word 'such' sends Swift's Wharton into an ecstasy.

> Who can read, unmov'd, these following Strokes of Oratory? Such was the Fame, Such was the Reputation, Such was the Faithfulness and Zeal, to Such a Height of Military Glory [Swift/Wharton is quoting Fleetwood here] . . . I am resolved to employ the *Spectator*, or some of his Fraternity (Dealers in Words), to write an Encomium upon SUCH. But whatever Changes our Language may undergo (and every thing that is *English* is given to change) this happy Word is sure to live in your immortal Preface.[47]

The criticism behind this bravura is not altogether fair. Such repetitions as the Bishop uses here were standard rhetorical devices (the figure in question here is called anaphora), and manifestly practical for a speaker or writer used to addressing large congregations. Yet Swift's real feeling reveals itself in the remark that all English things are 'given to change'. Mistakes in grammar and diction were symptoms of a much more general malaise: in his mind, those who cared so little about using language properly were equally uninterested in preserving the qualities and traditions it expressed. They were mindless vehicles of the widespread change that Swift felt all about him, and that he devoted so much energy to opposing.

Swift's ardour in the cause of his academy might well seem incongruous in the mind of a reader who recalls the great satire on scientific institutions in the third part of the *Travels*. There, in the Laputan-controlled capital of Lagado, professors of 'speculative learning' exhibit their schemes to the sceptical voyager. Gulliver's attitude in this section swings sharply into line with Swift's: he is appalled by what he sees. One professor of language aims to remove all the polysyllables from speech, and another wishes to abolish language altogether, to prevent the corrosive effect that speaking surely has on human lungs. In a famous piece of intellectual slapstick, Swift's professor urges that people should carry the things they intend to express around with them. Naturally, the academic observes, men of weightier affairs will have to employ sturdy bearers of the bundles of objects needed to communicate their thoughts. The particular butt of Swift's joke here is a doctrine espoused late in the previous century – one that had surfaced with variations in other epochs – that all language boils down to a correspondence of things and words. Yet Swift is not mocking the idea of an academy of language per se, and thereby reversing his view of earlier years. The academy of Lagado instead enshrines more or less all of the intellectual vices that Swift's English Academy, had it been founded, would have set about removing.

These evils are encapsulated in a device that reflects a subtle and prophetic intuition on Swift's part of how thought, language and historical context are bound together. Gulliver reports that one of the academic projectors has built a machine consisting of a frame containing a network of metal wires. Each wire bears a row of a great many wooden tablets, each of which is inscribed with a word. In total, a massive grid, some twenty foot square, is composed, which its inventor claims possesses all the possible forms and combinations of his language's entire vocabulary. When the wires are turned, an infinite series of sentences, most of which will be pure nonsense, may be generated. Gulliver points out that the signs on the near-numberless pieces of wood are set together without any notion of order. The inventor nevertheless asserts that when all the randomly created sentences are eventually taken down, they will comprise a universal theory of knowledge.[48] From a modern perspective, the episode puts Swift in the literary company of Huxley, Borges and Eco; but that should be set against the extremely prescriptive view of language and knowledge that the passage nevertheless puts across. For it never ceased to be Swift's belief that English might and should be regulated by a panel of qualified authorities. His academy would consist of the very element the Lagadon machine-builder demotes and excludes: the learned, articulate mind endowed with a balanced sense of linguistic history, usage and above all syntax – that is, 'order', the factor lost entirely from the lumber of the language-frame. The language-machine is, of course, like a Postmodern artifice, unbuildable; yet the mesh of intellectual, verbal and social forces it reduces to mere babble is something Swift takes almost for granted. Wanting, however, are the prudent literary and linguistic judges who can guide those forces towards coherence and durability. Instead of the semi-literate boys who turn the machine's countless handles – the equivalents, perhaps, of hacks such as Steele and the bishops of Salisbury and St Asaph – Swift would appoint guardians of a calibre who might actually make the goal of the Lagadon machine a reality. For he supported putting a 'frame' around language, but his would be a flexible, discriminating one.

Thus the academy of Lagado, by the time Swift came to create it, might seem to epitomize all that academia should not be but generally was. Yet Swift, as so often throughout his book, does not remain long in agreement with his narrator. After visiting the schools of languages and speculative learning, Gulliver is next dismayed by political theorists who propose that those who make up courts and ministries should be chosen on the basis of abilities and virtues rather than of nepotism and time-serving. The professors of politics seemed 'in my Judgment wholly out of their Senses; which is a scene that never fails to make me melancholy'.[49] As such, Gulliver is made to speak precisely against the idealistic politics Swift tried to propose in the early 1700s; one of those moments ensues in which Gulliver's integrity and consistency as a dramatic character crackle and break up, causing us to question the illusion of Swift's fiction and the opinions we might presume it encodes. We are subjected, conceivably, to a twitch in the mind of Swift: is Gulliver's scorn for 'extravagant and irrational' optimism actually right? Is it, in fact, Swift's soured mature view of politics?

By the time Harley's ministry floundered, and the first germs of the *Travels* perhaps took root, Swift had formed a very real sense not only of how the higher nebulous organs of state were administered but also more basic civil institutions. In February 1714 he was elected a governor of the Bethlehem Royal Hospital in Moorfields, better known as Bedlam, along with his friend Atterbury. His impending relocation back to Ireland made it impossible for him to attend governors' meetings regularly, but his election marked a silently significant step for him. The treatment of lunatics had already preoccupied him metaphorically and, as he aged, it became a point of great personal interest. Swift implicitly feared the forces that might be turning the handles of his mind's undoubtedly nimble, but manifestly fragile, cognitive and sensory machinery. The spectacle of the deranged was as casually engrained in London's urban imagination as that of extreme violence is today on evening television, for the mad-house had always been open to the fee-paying public. In a *Tatler* of June 1709, Bickerstaff describes a standard excursion: 'I took three lads, who are under my guardianship, a-rambling in a hackney-coach, to show them the Town; as the Lions, the Tombs, Bedlam, and the other places which are entertainments to raw minds, because they strike forcibly on the fancy.'[50] Swift mentions taking a similarly heedless tour of 'all the sights' back in December 1710.[51] The phrase 'raw minds', however unintentionally, is an apt one not just for the young sightseers but also for the inmates *seen* on such occasions – manacled to the walls, railed and whispered at from the other side of iron bars. The sight of a resident of the hospital 'tearing his Straw in piece-meal, Swearing and Blaspheming, biting his Grate, foaming at the Mouth, and emptying his Pispot in Spectator's Faces' was clearly familiar to him from earlier occasions. Swift himself could mention a visit paid to Bedlam in the same insouciant breath as a puppet-show seen a little later the same day. Puppets and the chronically insane were already fixed items in his figurative lexicon. In *A Tale of a Tub*, his spokesman had jauntily suggested that the asylum might be a source of officials and officers for the state and armed forces.[52] The implication that the jest might be crudely reversed, and that all too many bearers of public responsibility might easily change places with the unfortunates in the asylum, only deepens in his work. Accordingly, his need for a fellowship, offering refuge from unreason and asylum in its basic sense, increased as the political emergency worsened.

# 4

Occasionally Swift's desire to raise a Camelot in defence of the English language was appeased by the ministry's club – all members of which, regardless of rank, Swift addressed as 'Brother' (and their auxiliaries as nephew, niece and sister). Yet the English Academy project, soon buried, pained him with its failure. Swift had to console himself with a narrower, like-minded few. He was no different to the bookish person of any era in finding relief and companionship in a shared love of letters and an enjoyment of word-games. He would happily spend an evening 'punning scurvily' with a friend or two, and share the best (or worst) of what passed with Johnson and Dingley – for the two women were keen punners in their own right.[53] He was also delighted when the activity could be combined with his love of a practical joke. In March 1713 his old college tutor St George Ashe (now the Bishop of Clogher), visiting London, graced the parlour with an effort he considered a masterpiece. 'If there was a Hackney Coach at Mr Pooley's door, what Town in Egypt would it be; why it would be *Hecatompolis, Hack at Tom Poley's*.' Yet, as Bishop Ashe turned red and breathless at his own hilarity, Swift plotted a 'bite'. He instructed his younger friend Sir Andrew Fountaine, a regular in the Vanhomrighs' family circle, to write to poor St George's brother Thomas at home in Dublin, telling him of the prize pun; Thomas was then to send the Hecatompolis gag to his brother, presenting it as his own. Sure enough, St George was both disappointed and wonder-struck that both he and his brother could have thought up the same pun independently. Ashe was 'sadly bit', Swift told Johnson, but the stunt failed to become the talk of the town as he had hoped.[54]

Swift had got to know Fountaine, a long-standing follower of the Earl of Pembroke, years before in Ireland. It may have been through Fountaine, an easy-going socialite, that he first became such good friends with Mrs Vanhomrigh and her family, since their early visits to the widow's household clearly coincided. Fountaine's presiding interest, meanwhile, was one Swift could respect but didn't share. He was an avid and authoritative antiquary and art-collector, and, with a light-hearted pragmatism Swift lacked altogether, responded to the crisis and impending Hanoverian succession, in 1714, by departing on his second grand tour. During these travels, he was said to have 'out-Italianed the Italians themselves' in the deals he struck to augment his collections.[55] Another, still younger friend, whom Swift liked equally for his pleasant manners and his cap-

A Woman mangled in so horred a maner, that it was not possible shee should be knowne, & after the Villaine washed his handes in her bloode, was taken by the Troopers adiuged to be hanged leaped of the lader & hanged him selfe like a Bloodey Tyger.

Companyes of the Rebells meeting with the English flyinge for their lives, falling double before them, cryinge for mercy, thrust theire Pichforkes into their Childrens bellyes & threw them into the water.

1. (*left*) Atrocity propaganda from James Cranford, *The Teares of Ireland* (1642). An example of the acts Protestants across the British Isles believed were being committed by Irish Catholics on a mass scale in Ireland during the rebellion of 1641.

2. (*below*) A slightly stereotypical depiction of an Irish cabin, published after Swift's death (in Arthur Young's *A Tour in Ireland*, 1780) but corresponding to descriptions of peasants' houses before and during his lifetime.

3. A 'wild' Irish man and woman from John Speed's 'Map of the Kingdom of Ireland' (1616); another enduring English image of 'mere' or 'native' Irish people.

4. 'The Battle of the Boyne', by Jan Wyck (1693), depicting a hugely important event in Swift's youth, William of Orange's victory over James II, and also a landscape Swift knew well.

5. (*top*) South-east view of St Patrick's Cathedral, by W. Smith (nineteenth century). The cathedral as Swift knew it, apart from the pointed spire, which was added after his death.

6. (*bottom*) The High Street and Market Cross, Kilkenny, showing the town where Swift spent his schooldays.

7. Swift, by or after Charles Jervas (1709–10); perhaps the most famous image of the writer.

8. Sir William Temple, by Gaspar Netscher (1675), the writer and diplomat who employed Swift as his secretary in the 1690s. Swift's early admiration for Temple soured somewhat in later years.

9. Portrait of a young woman, possibly Esther Johnson (early eighteenth century), Swift's closest companion until her death in 1728.

10. Portrait of a young woman, possibly Esther (or Hester) Vanhomrigh, attributed to Charles Jervas (early eighteenth century). Vanhomrigh and Swift's long relationship began with the breaking of a coffee cup in 1707.

11. Alexander Pope, by or from the studio of Michael Dahl (c.1727). Swift's esteemed friend, widely regarded in his lifetime and afterwards as the finest poet of the day.

12. A less familiar view of Swift, in relaxed attire, by Isaac Whood (1730).

13. North prospect of St Patrick's Cathedral, by Jonas Blaymires.

14. Swift's *Travels*, frontispiece from the first edition, 1726. The image of Gulliver encouraged the resemblance early readers established between the character and his author.

acious yet unassuming intellect, was an Anglo-Irish absentee landowner. Charles Ford, who was thirty-two in 1714, owned property in the country near Swift's parish of Laracor, but lived for the most part in London on the rents from his estate. A large body of Swift's correspondence was written to Ford, and its volume reflected the trust Swift placed in him. His importance to Swift's literary career would subsequently be vital, when he took responsibility for the manuscript of the *Travels*. Swift had known the chatty, apparently small-framed bachelor since about 1708, and only a few years passed before he was treating him like a favoured son.[56] In 1712 he procured for him the post of Gazetteer, which brought the management of the government's official (and often quite dull) newspaper. The job had previously been Steele's, but Swift had negotiated for Ford a rise in the salary to £200 a year. It was a plum; 'yet the Puppy does not seem satisfyed with it,' Swift complained to Johnson.[57]

Swift belonged to various circles and circuits of friendship, some overlapping, some coinciding with professional or literary associations, and others not. A full account of them, reducing Swift to one more figure in their midst, would fill an ample (and diverting) book of its own. He was less enthusiastic, however, about the best-known group to which he belonged than its instigator, Pope. This was largely because the Scriblerus Club took from the outset the form of a contrarian, ironic society, whereas Swift's plans for an academy were in deadly earnest. Pope's initial idea for an academy of useless learning may have seemed to Swift too much like a skit on his grand idea. Swift the great teaser and master of irony intensely disliked others making light of his serious designs. Still, the camaraderie and the conversation were irresistible, and he became a regular member of what slowly became a distinctly fugitive cluster.

Swift needed friends and associates who were willing to enter into his hoaxes or play the part he assigned them in his domestic dramas with Harley and St John, his friends and enemies at Court and sometimes the public at large. Back in 1711, dissatisfied when Harley sent a personal note of apology for affronting him with an offer of £50, Swift dispatched Erasmus Lewis, senior official in the secretarial office, to demand 'further satisfaction'. Lewis, the apparatchik who had first introduced Swift to Harley, obliged; and a few weeks later Harley expressed his regrets in the manner Swift required, prompting him to say that 'I should think he loves me as well as a great minister can love a man in so short a time.'[58] The tiff and the ritual of resolving it helped set the seal on their friendship. Swift was rarely short of a willing co-actor in such performances.

At times he required a large assembly at Court or a ministerial levee to go along with them. A Whig cleric described with disgust one occasion, in an antechamber at Windsor in 1713, when Swift assumed the airs of a 'master of requests'. He granted favours and declined them as he pleased. He pestered one aristocratic and well-funded group to offer large subscriptions for Pope, 'the best poet in England', who had begun a translation of the *Iliad*. They must all cough up, he told them; 'for, says he, "the author shall not begin to print till *I have* a thousand guineas for him."' Shortly afterwards Swift strutted into prayers with the Lord Treasurer.[59]

Swift may have given in to the temptation to swagger at such moments, and we have his own word on the liberties he sometimes took with powerful, vastly wealthy, titled persons. Yet we should also bear in mind the resentment and envy that colours the above account, written by a fellow clergyman who 'could not help but despise him'. Swift was quite aware that he attracted dislike, and in all probability augmented his high-handed manner to increase the displeasure of all those who saw him as an upstart. A vehement poem written during his stay at Letcombe in 1714 suggests that what most goaded such observers was the way he didn't behave like all the other 'country vicars' flocking to Court. He had forgotten his station as a minor priest: 'He mov'd, and bow'd, and talk't with too much Grace; / Nor shew'd the Parson in his Gait or Face.'[60] Yet Swift defied the very idea that he should merely act the rustic cleric: he was more than that. He insisted instead on the traditional dignity that a member of the clergy could claim as an able courtier in the highest setting. Swift may not have been guiltless of the pomposity and pretension he is charged with by a supporter of the opposition; but the tone the writer gives him should be offset, in our minds, by the heartfelt and vulnerable commitment revealed in Swift's journal for Esther Johnson. There, oddly enough, Swift really does 'show the parson' in himself, as well as the would-be political fixer, in his eagerness to use his influence to sort out people's problems.

The opportunity to perform, to show off his gracefulness as speaker and conversationalist, clearly delighted him, and he had no fear of making begrudgers in the audience suffer at the sight of his splendour. On occasion, though, in his political dramas, he was willing to let another player direct the scene. He tolerated Matthew Prior's anger at the *New Journey to Paris*, in which he gave the game away on Prior's secret peace mission, since he firmly believed his comic impromptu had helped to save the day. Almost every major event in Swift's career as self-appointed minder of the ministry had a similar touch of staging to it. His sufferings over every mishap made him fail to see how similar he was to the guileful Lord Treasurer, whose love of drama and secrecy was legend.

Personal vignettes Swift could handle over tea at St James's, in Harley's dining room or a tavern in Westminster; but the management of the larger theatricals by means of which his books and pamphlets reached the world naturally called for a disturbingly large number of back-stage technicians. Unfortunately Swift could not transmit his writing solely through the intellectuals and policy-makers with whom he most identified. He was naturally obliged to work with printers, involved himself closely with them in the process of publication, and cursed their blunders when they disturbed the *mise-en-scène*. Dismissing the dyer's hand, he refused to subdue his nature to the element he worked in. Pope noticed that one of the names Swift burned away with his 'Orbicular' lens at Letcombe belonged to a man who had risked imprisonment for publishing one of Swift's works. The rays Swift focused on his moniker were John Barber's punishment for fumbling the affair with Steele and *The Publick Spirit of the Whigs*. Of all the people with whom he developed close contacts, printers and the hacks of Grub Street were those he expected to dance exactly to his tune.

Such expectations were unwise. London's booksellers and printers were shrewd by necessity, often as learned as their authors, frequently unscrupulous, dexterous and, if successful, ruthlessly pragmatic. Almost all had their blind spots, being human; sometimes for a hated rival, occasionally for a particular brand of books, and in many cases for the cause of Tory or Whig. It would be wrong to suggest that Edmund Curll, long singled out as the chief villain of the trade, was typical of his profession; but he did possess qualities that proved vital to success. First, he was indiscriminate and self-promoting, publishing anything from guides on apothecary, which advertised cures he sold from his own premises, to pornography (*The Way of a Man with a Maid* was one of his early titles) and religious meditations. By the time the Tories foundered, Curll was in his mid-thirties, and had mastered his trade. Established since 1710 at the Sign of the Dial and Bible on Fleet Street, he sold as many of the latest bestsellers as he could – all pirated and offered for sale, along with his mercury-based syphilis pills, at a competitive price. Curll had an avid eye for literary potential and a profound disregard for an author's copyright. He had already brought out his own unauthorized *Tale of a Tub* and other works by Swift, adding a key that explained points of difficulty and revealing Swift's authorship to the masses. Many authors had suffered the same treatment, and it awaited Gay and Pope. A shadowy figure in the record, Curll seems to have faced his vendettas blithely. Curll's piracy had also angered the more respectable end of the business, embodied by Jacob Tonson; yet even Tonson, the grand old man of London publishing, would not let a grudge get in the way of a sound investment. The book trade worked by booksellers and their printers sometimes sharing authors, as they did other 'resources', when demand for a work exceeded the capacity of a single workshop. Two years after Curll made off with a manuscript by Matthew Prior, Tonson collaborated with him on a collection of Latin poetry by Thomas Hill.[61]

Printing and bookselling in the early 1700s, then, were trades in which grievances were loudly aired but could be swallowed and forgotten for the sake of a scoop or another opportunity. Swift could hardly fit easily into such a professional milieu. It brought out his tendency to polarize things. For him, resentment at betrayal, barring some massive and self-abasing act of atonement, was in all but exceptional circumstances to be carried to the grave. Making and mending their differences, printers were thus caricatures, so to speak, of a tendency Swift observed in humanity at large. In return, he could treat them cordially, conspire with them intimately, respect their craftsmanship and ingenuity when immersed in the detail of copy and proofs; but then curse them heartily when they acted according to their kind. He mirrored their pragmatic inconsistencies with heartfelt dualisms that gave rise to conflicting remarks in his letters and writings. Barber, whose name was tortured with fire at Letcombe, was actually on reasonably friendly and respectful terms with Swift, as was the author and journalist who became Barber's mistress, and lived with him intermittently above his shop on the corner adjoining Old Fish Street and the top end of Lambeth Hill.[62] 'Mrs' Delarivier (or De la Rivière) Manley had been brought up in a family of Royalist gentry. Her father's Civil War record was rewarded with a high-ranking commission on Jersey in 1667, and Delarivier was christened after the Governor's wife. In a childhood spent moving from one posting to another, she was befriended by books. Later, with little else to live on but her wit – on being abandoned by her husband, a bigamist, in 1694 – she took to professional writing. She was tireless and prolific, turning her hand to essays, history, dramas and novellas. Her fortunes were repeatedly hit by scandals. She was led astray from good prospects by flirting with the son of her protector, the Duchess of Cleveland (Barbara Villiers, a mistress of Charles II); her intimate letters were published without her permission. Such mishaps nevertheless provided

inspired ideas for her works. Her relationship with Richard Steele provided much material for the first volume of her best-known fiction, *The
New Atlantis*. By the time Swift got to know her, as his assistant and
then as his substitute on the *Examiner*, 'Dela' Manley thus had a packed
lifetime of intrigue, bad luck and cruel treatment behind her. In 1712 she
was, said Swift, 'about forty, very homely and very fat', and at that
moment he was impressed with her: 'she has very generous principles for
one of her sort; and a great deal of good sense and invention.'[63]

One of her sort: a fallen woman, publicly known over the years as the
lover of Steele and now of Barber, and thus disrespectable; and also a
hack, a writer of a lower order. Swift was anxious that a line should be
clearly perceived between his work for the cause, *pro bono*, and the
output of such denizens of Grub Street. Physically, Grub Street rambled
north-west towards Moorfields in the liberties beyond London's old city
walls. As an address it was synonymous with the poverty, dirt, over-
crowding and discomfort of St Giles-without-Cripplegate, the parish
containing all but the uppermost third of Grub Street. The street took its
name from the *grube*, or ditch, for rubbish running parallel to the northern city wall. Bedlam Hospital was found a few roads south-east along
Fore Street. Long depressed, long a haven for fugitives and pariahs, and
also a venue for idle and disreputable pursuits, the area became associated with hack writers – Pope's myriad 'dunces' – for the cheap rents it
offered them and their publishers. Culturally and almost spiritually,
meanwhile, Grub Street was more than just a thoroughfare: it was a
state of being and a moral topography all in itself.[64] Yet by 1712 the
whole eco-system of Grub Street appeared to be facing extinction. In
June that year the government imposed a half-penny tax on newspapers
printed on a half-sheet. Those printed on a whole sheet were taxed a
penny. The plan, St John's, was to crush the prospering libel culture;
'They are always mauling lord treasurer, lord Bolingbroke and me,'
Swift complained, with a hint of pride at making up the third in this
government trinity. His feelings were mixed, since the tax seemed to
spell the end of a vibrant, shameless and creative tranche of writing that,
in part, appealed strongly to him. 'No more Ghosts or Murders now for
Love of Money'; he would lose, like countless others in the kingdom, a
great amount of idle reading. He made haste to send a few last half-sheet
compositions to the press before the tax was levied. Some titles folded,
as designed; but Grub Street proved resilient. 'These devils of Grubstreet
rogues . . . will not be quiet,' Swift fumed to Johnson a few months after
the tax came into force. His outrage poured out in fierce denial that his

creative self, as distinct from his social outer crust, was in truth largely 'one' of Manley's 'sort' – indeed, a specimen of still greater genius, application and cunning. Swift was no serf of Grub Street, but its non-resident overlord.[65]

Poor Manley suffered constantly from poor health and poverty from which Barber, while enjoying her favours, did little to protect her. In 1712, when Swift wrote his qualified praise for her, he expected news of her death any day: she lay ill with a dropsy and bad legs. In July 1714 she was sick again, though apparently 'in no danger', and saving money by living in Finchley. When Charles Ford heard from Bolingbroke of a friend ailing in the country, he assumed the minister referred to Swift; Swift did not record how he took the irony of his and Dela's living in similar circumstances. After Dela succeeded him at the *Examiner*, he was generally anxious that the descent in style should be generally recognized; and at some point she did or said something that made him dislike her very much indeed. A shameful and surely unnecessary poem about her, 'Corinna', has always been attributed to him. It runs through the common knowledge of her life in jaunty stanzas.

> At twelve, a Wit and a Coquette;
> Marries for Love, half Whore, half Wife;
> Cuckolds, elopes, and runs in Debt;
> Turns Auth'ress, and is *Curll*'s for Life.[66]

The closing line acknowledges the ubiquitous 'unspeakable' printer, who both pirated her work and defamed her reputation. The verses were published in Swift's *Miscellanies* of 1727, a collection he oversaw, and so their authorship cannot really be disputed. By then Manley had died (in 1724) and his active association with her lay in the distant past, though the poem is hardly more excusable for that. It is evidence of an undoubted callous streak, probably the memorial of a remark about him attributed to Manley, and shows how he could stoop to a rotten-egg fight if the need arose. Manley's damning offence, in Swift's eyes, was her betraying his friend Barber by working for the 'unspeakable' Curll. It was in 1714 that she 'turned Auth'ress' (Swift's contempt is unmistakable) and wrote her semi-autobiographical *Adventures of Rivella*, published under Curll's imprint. Her relationship with Barber presumably ended at this. Manley's reward, one typical for Curll's 'authors', was impoverished reclusion at Finchley; and the enmity of Swift, among others.[67]

Still, little quarter was given or asked on Grub Street. For although

Curll stands out in the period as the great rogue among London's stationers, Barber didn't get his nickname 'Tyrant' (from the Duke of Ormond, no less) for nothing.[68] Curll was obviously biased and malicious in his *Impartial History* of Barber's life, describing a penny-pinching and socially pretentious bully, and published for the sake of gloating posthumously over a long-standing enemy, but much of what he includes is corroborated. Swift himself may have experienced something of Barber's dictatorial conduct. Yet the two worked regularly together from the time Swift took over the *Examiner*, which Barber published at a very decent profit. Curll mentions how Barber, who was also a printer of the *London Gazette*, would force one of his writers to double as a corrector – a horror that would never have occurred in Curll's own printing house – and keep him working on the sheets until three or four in the morning.[69] Swift's letters to Johnson frequently record long and late meetings with Barber, and often with Dela, and throughout his correspondence exhibited great concern for exactly such details in the text. When it came to fine print, he was Barber's match as tyrant; as he could be, as 'Corinna' bears out, in haranguing fellow writers and former colleagues.

The bond between Swift and Barber was their common attachment to the ministry; the prize for Barber, less disinterestedly, was the profit guaranteed by the *Examiner* and the government *Gazette*. Occasionally the business proved risky to both: Barber may well have spent time in prison for bringing out *The Publick Spirit of the Whigs*, the consequences of which for Swift might equally have been greater. Barber and Manley, meanwhile, were just two of Swift's accomplices weighing up such hazards against gains and principles in the battle for good copy. Another of his regular collaborators, Benjamin Tooke, was Barber's partner in printing the *Gazette*. John Morphew, the printer of *The Conduct of the Allies*, truly hit the jackpot by courtesy of Swift, in its astonishing run of sold-out editions. Morphew also took over reprinting Swift's issues of the *Examiner* in collected form. Such a marketable writer excited goodwill and envy in equal measure among the publishing fraternity, in which political and commercial dedication were often equally sincere. A figure with Swift's authority in Westminster, meanwhile, could also call on lesser scribblers to do his bidding.

One of those whom Swift claimed, contestably, as his minion was Abel Roper, a Tory journalist and bookseller. Roper, two years older than Swift, had weathered the eras. He is credited with being the first to print Wharton's lyrics to 'Lilliburlero', and, like all survivors in his line of work, had a keen sense of how to excite the public. Roper spent most of his career in a scrap of one kind or another: in 1700 he had seen off one rival, Richard Kingston, in a brawl that he commemorated in *A Full Account of a Terrible and Bloody Fight*. Assaults and death-threats became par for the course, as in 1712, when he had his wig pulled off and was beaten in the street by a peer who disliked him; and an MP declared that he would cut Roper's throat. Roper had been running a news-sheet called the *Post Boy* since 1695. Although Tory by politics, he was fiercely anti-Jacobite, an attitude that put him very roughly in the same camp as Swift. It also placed him in a running battle in the streets where the newspapers were delivered and distributed, with his chief Whig competitor, George Ridpath's *Flying Post*. Both appeared several times a week, and were restless clashing chariots in the mad race to define each turn of events and policy. Swift often complained about the shoddiness of these papers. Occasionally he contributed a paragraph or short article to the *Post Boy* in order to be sure that an incident was set forth in the truest or most expedient light. Sometimes too he manipulated Roper's paper for tactical purposes of his own.

One notable example is a neat piece of rescue work Swift performed back in April 1711. Writing to Swift of Guiscard's attack on Harley, Archbishop King admitted that those accusing the minister of colluding with the French had surely been proven wrong. However, he observed that 'some whisper', dropping a quotation from Tacitus, that Harley was using Guiscard as a screen to cover his overtures to France.[70] The line King cited implicitly compared Harley with Gaius Calpurnius Piso, who used Faenius Rufus as a tool in his plot to murder and seize power from the Emperor, Nero. King claimed he had been misunderstood; but the gaffe was costly. The Archbishop not only risked discrediting himself with the ministry, but also jeopardizing the cause of the Irish clergy.[71] Moving quickly, and displaying the command of the medium he had already achieved, Swift managed to 'scratch out' the passage repeating the story in the *Post Boy*. King sent grateful thanks; and almost a month later, perhaps having let the Archbishop stew a little for his own good, Swift informed him that he had spoken with Harley to repair the damage done to His Grace by 'infamous rascals' in Dublin. Nevertheless, the ministry had it on good authority that King had indeed made the classically slanted jibe against Harley.[72] Swift emerges from such incidents as something of a proto-spin doctor. Without question he appreciated the power of news; and he took no little satisfaction from having such superior sources. Sadly, these sources too often qualified him to dispel reports of promotions he had won. In March 1712 Esther heard a story that he had gained the lucrative deanship of Wells, one that was soon disproved. She attributed the leak to Roper. But this was impossible, said Swift; for 'Roper is my humble slave.'[73]

Or was he actually yet another of Swift's masters? Contributing to Roper's rag left a sour taste. 'I have been drawing up a Paragraph for the Post boy,' he told Esther on 17 November 1712, 'to be out to morrow, and as malicious as possible, and very proper for Abel Roper the Printer of it.'[74] The touch of malice, such as it was, came at the end of his account of the duel in which the Duke of Hamilton was, arguably, murdered. He closed his paragraph with a gravely offhand 'N. B.' on the subject of the provocateur and assassin: 'This is the 4th person that my Lord Mohun has had the Misfortune to kill.'[75] Uneasy though they made him, Swift's contributions to the lower echelons of the popular press were invariably made with a concern to lift the taste and accuracy with which a topic he held dear was related. His most obvious intervention in this respect was the report he filed of the letter-bomb attempt on Harley's life – which the Whig press instantly saw as a fabrication on Swift's part with a mind to becoming the Dean of Wells – or gaining a similar place. Another, briefer, quite disinterested and very touching example of his work as newsman is his obituary notice in the *Post Boy* for his friend Anne Long. Swift had known Long for some years before his ministerial period, and she had charmed him with her beauty, good judgement and intelligence. She was admired by many, and subject to gossip for her closeness to the alleged mistress of Lord Halifax; but nothing for Swift, strikingly, could touch the personal sainthood he bestowed on her. He was upset, however, when she made 'two nasty jests' in a letter from King's Lynn, where she had fled and assumed a false name to avoid her debts. The letter turned his stomach, but he attributed her coarseness to the bad manners prevalent in her distant place of exile.[76] He pitied her from the heart as her fortunes worsened, and when she died late in 1711, of an asthmatic complication, he was broken. 'I never was more afflicted at any death,' he wrote – this was before young Harrison died in his garret – on a melancholy Christmas morning.[77]

His notice of her death in the *Post Boy* succinctly and imperatively set the tone in which she was to be described, cancelling all mention of illicit liaisons, her long struggle to maintain appearances without being forced into giving or receiving compromising favours, and two years of loneliness: 'She was a Lady very much celebrated here for her Beauty, Virtue and good Sense; and is extremely lamented by all who knew her.'[78] The succinct and reserved sentence deserves comment not only for what it suppresses, but the self-restraint Swift showed in confining himself to it. He mourned for Long with great but contained affection. He paid personally for a tablet commemorating her in St Nicholas's Chapel in King's Lynn. None of her former ostentatious admirers at the Kit-Cat Club could equal his devotion to her. In a private grieving memorandum he described her as 'the most beautifull Person of the Age . . . of great Honour and Virtue, infinite Sweetness and generosity of Temper'.[79]

Such sentiments were not, preferably, for printing in the 'gutter' press; but such journals as the *Post Boy* had their uses. They did work that someone had to, and to which Swift himself often, rolling up his sleeves, had lent a hand with his own superior papers. There must have been times when he returned to his digs, with the smell of the fish market near John Barber's house lingering in his nostrils, and wondered whether his efforts were worthwhile. Yet while he complained when they crossed his purposes, there was much amid London's booksellers, printers and even the city's hacks he undoubtedly admired. Whether, looking ahead, one thinks of Gulliver's handiness and pragmatism, or the craftsmanship of Irish manufacturers he defended, Swift looked for industry and efficiency in all walks of life. Writing on the causes of the ministry's decay, he observed that nothing was more harmful to a professional reputation than a neglect for 'Time, Place and Method', regardless of one's good intentions: 'Which hath made me sometimes say, to a great Person of this latter Character, that a small Infusion of the *Alderman* was necessary to those who are employed in publick Affairs.' He recalled seeing the same person (Bolingbroke) once try to cut a sheet of paper with too sharp a pen-knife. The blade moved so jaggedly that the clumsy minister spoiled the sheet. Swift suggested that he watch how the clerks in his office performed the same task with 'a blunt piece of Ivory'. A little strength and a steady hand made the job easy.[80]

Whatever he lacked in social finesse, John Barber made up for with this requisite 'infusion' of business-like practicality: indeed, the 'Tyrant' had spells as an alderman and lord mayor ahead of him. The men in his printers' workshops exhibited this quality too, operating the timber-framed, six-foot-tall presses, picking out font from the letter-cases with stunning speed and dexterity; applying the pads to the form in which a page was set on the 'coffin', or bed of the apparatus; rolling the rounce of the machine over dampened paper, keeping the pressure even as the font bit and the ink took hold without a smudge or tear; and then repeating the whole process, for page after page, volume upon volume. Those pages, in their sepia-tinted columns on paper now crinkling, are works of beauty in their own right. As for the writers, even the hacks of Grub Street had to put in leg-work, tailor their prose to a basic standard and meet a deadline. Though Swift might have denied such workers a place in the committee room of his hypothetical academy, he was aware of how effective they were when well directed.

# 5

At Letcombe Bassett in the summer of 1714 Swift was far, physically at least, from the world of courtiers and printers. Mentally he was nowhere else but the passages of St James's, Kensington Palace and Westminster, and the chock-a-block trading streets of the City. By mid-July he was already refining his skills at connecting and pulling strings in this world from a distant location – a talent he would need to develop further when he returned to Ireland. The plans he laid for publishing one last piece of work reached such a degree of elaborate stealth that in the end his pains were wasted.

His *Some Free Thoughts upon the Present State of Affairs* illustrated how impossible he found it to pull his mind away from the grim endgame. He could be reassured that his own goal had been achieved: the remission of the First Fruits to the clergy of Ireland had been granted, and a board established in 1711 to oversee the use of the funds in improving churches and clerical homes. Yet his ambitions had long gone beyond that; it seemed to him that a mighty chance was being squandered. However inevitable the outcome seemed from spring 1714 – with the political death of Lord Oxford, the 'Dragon', a daily expectation – there were endless possible sequences of moves that might bring it about, and each carried a tantalizing potential for reversal and redemption.

The title of Swift's *Free Thoughts*, given his contempt for free-thinking, is haggardly ironic, a reflection of the limits to which he had been stretched. He was writing the pamphlet as a privileged insider; but his opening sentence expressed a wish commonly felt by outsiders to government and administration. Elegantly, Swift captured a desire for simplicity and transparency in affairs of state. 'Whatever may be thought or practised by profound Politicians, they will never be able to convince the reasonable part of Mankind, that the most plain, short, easy, safe and lawfull way to any good End, is not more eligible, than one directly contrary in some or all of these Qualities.'[81] Swift was writing against 'profundity', against far-fetched schemes and against the secretive way of doing business that was his friend Harley's hallmark. In making the remark, Swift felt no guilt at his own enjoyment of a good spider-like scheme: he was not suggesting that politicians give up their cunning. His opening pages are largely given over to justifying the maxim above, and the thrust of his subsequent argument is that the ministry could still survive if its leading members would only decide that it should.

The call for rationalization was never heard, mainly because Swift failed to heed his own argument. He trammelled his essay in a byzantine plot to ensure his authorship remained a secret. He believed his *Free Thoughts* would be most effective if readers had no clue they were his. So first of all he sent the manuscript to Ford, urging him to change any word or phrase he repeated too often, and then to forward the pages 'by an unknown hand' to Barber: 'have nothing to do with it, though there is no danger.'[82] This was on 1 July 1714. Ford replied on the 6th, stating that he had done nothing to the text apart from cancelling a few archaic *e*'s in Swift's spelling. Though Ford questioned the wisdom of including a passage that was less than wholly respectful of the Queen, the manuscript had been sent according to Swift's instructions. Unless Barber was 'a very great Blockhead' and missed the need to publish quickly, the printed text would soon be back in Swift's hands. The latest clamour in Parliament, Ford reported, was over damage the peace would inflict on Britain's trade with Spain. Tory and Whig merchants alike were up in arms, the knives were readier than ever for Oxford, and Bolingbroke was already mustering his Cabinet.[83] Every vote on such a question made a loss of confidence and dissolution of Parliament ever more likely, bearing out the following claim in Swift's *Free Thoughts* on the need for Oxford to drop his 'Mysticall manner of proceeding' and for Bolingbroke to swallow his aspirations: 'A Ship's Crew quarrelling in a Storm, or while their Enemies are within Gun-Shott, is but a faint idea of this fatal infatuation.'[84] The comparison was faint because the danger Swift saw in the Whigs was so immense and deadly to the national interest. Further letters confirmed the rise of Bolingbroke, now widely seen as 'the man of mercury' (the phrase, coined by Erasmus Lewis, made a play on the cures for the pox on which promiscuous St John possibly relied).[85] Indeed, a jaunty note reached Swift from Bolingbroke himself, in which the Viscount reassured Dean Swift of his constant friendly wishes while at the same time making it clear that he was managing perfectly well without him. Gaily he promised to send another hamper of wine to further the 'dear dean's' secluded contentment.[86]

In mid-July Swift was confounded by a 'splutter' in the progress of his pamphlet.[87] Barber had departed from Swift's script and added a Machiavellian subplot of his own, by handing the manuscript over to Bolingbroke. And there the matter stuck. At first Bolingbroke seemed content to let publication go ahead after merely altering a few passages that were critical of him. Then either he had second thoughts or he was too preoccupied with spearing the dragon. The *Free Thoughts* remained his captive. Ford urged Swift to send him another copy of the text, if he had one, so that a wholly uncensored version might reach the public before Oxford was finally ousted. The parliamentary session had ended, and his dismissal was looked for at any moment.[88]

The text Bolingbroke might have authorized turned Swift's even-handed and at moments magisterial analysis of self-destructive politics into a propaganda document supporting his purely expedient pro-gramme. Praise of Oxford was cut. The emphasis instead lay with the spirit of Swift's closing assertion that 'the only way of securing the Con-stitution in Church and State . . . will be by lessening the power of our Domestick Adversaries.'[89] This statement, shorn of all qualification, tal-lied perfectly with the agenda Bolingbroke had adopted to win over the Tory core of Oxford's government. It manifested itself in hateful legisla-tion that Oxford himself loathed (and that he permitted his brother to oppose in the House of Commons). Bolingbroke had put forward a Schism Bill, which, if made law, would prohibit Dissenters from estab-lishing their own schools. Swift's censored essay, if published, would now imply that such measures reflected the will of the majority. In a fierce debate, the Earl of Nottingham, that staunch Anglican who had entered a league with the Whigs, opposed the bill in terms that expressed High Church principles much more ably than Swift had done. In his speech Nottingham also took aim at the Dean himself. The Earl, wrote Swift, was 'fam'd for tedious elocution', but Nottingham spoke trench-antly in defending the rights of parents to educate their children as they saw fit. He laid a share of the bill's crimes upon Swift: 'I tremble when I think that a certain divine, who is hardly suspected of being a Christian is in a fair way of being a bishop, and may one day give licences to those, who shall be entrusted with the instruction of youth.'[90]

For Swift this accusation typified the hypocrisy of those who objected to a lowly clergyman being politically active and influential.

> Now *Finch* [Earl of Nottingham] alarms the Lords; he hears for certain,
> This dang'rous Priest is got behind the Curtain: . . .
> That *Swift* oils many a spring which *Harley* moves.[91]

Nottingham was owed a little vengeance for the way Swift had mocked and discredited him in the crisis leading to the great vote on ending the war for Spain; and, in return for the injustices he had suffered from Swift's pen, he committed a number against Swift; first, by charging his enemy with atheism, and, second, by assuming that he supported a bill that really he detested. In a letter to Charles Ford on 25 July Swift confessed in gentle terms his distaste for the Tories who stood ready to take over government, and that he was 'displeasd' with their 'Creed Scheme'.[92] The Schism Bill was also apparently one of the phrases on which he concentrated the beams from his magnifying glass. Such private criticism hardly stands as a denunciation – but shows typically how Swift's humanity and sense overcame collective doctrine when a wrong was being done. The desires of the simple-minded utmost Tories, drinking home-brewed ale at meetings of their October Club, had never been his: they were as selfish and stupid in defending their parochial interests as the Whig hardliners were in shouting up the war with Spain and high finance. When it came to it, Swift had no wish for the *Free Thoughts* to appear in a version sanctioned by Bolingbroke.

At the end of July, Swift enjoyed a brief excursion to friendly territory. He was invited by Lord Oxford's recently married son, Lord Harley, to meet him and his wife, appropriately enough, at Oxford. The journey took him to what most in the Whig camp viewed as a High Church plantation. He was cheered by the young couple, and comforted by the melancholy solidarity he found among the dons he met. He was fond of young Harley, who was witty and scholarly, and an apt student of Scriblerus. Together they talked of politics but also of Pope, and toasted Arbuthnot '6 glasses before the usual time'.[93] Swift knew the city as a fond but infrequent visitor; he had taken his Master's degree there, during a pleasant spell of leave from Moor Park. In spending the scanty amount of time required to keep term, he had evidently wandered widely through the cool green and stony places. The visit of July 1714 was a social trip of just three days. It was probably long ago that he had brushed past some gravestones bearing the name 'Gulliver' in the churchyard of St Mary's in Banbury, a parish he always associated with Puritans.[94]

Down in London, the Lord Treasurer's ministry was expiring painfully. Within a day or so of Swift's departure from Oxford, it was over. After much acrimony, the Queen told the Earl to surrender his staff of office. Arbuthnot and Lewis had watched him cling with surprising obstinacy to this symbol of power in his last month as first minister. The Dragon 'dies hard', Arbuthnot had confided to Swift, 'kicking and cuffing about him like the devil'.[95] Oxford had made the run-in as hard as possible for Bolingbroke. On the very day he gave up his seals, he wrote to Swift as one who tomorrow would be 'a private man' once more, thus answering the appeal to their friendship Swift had made a few weeks earlier in terms of equal force: 'I believe in the mass of souls ours were plac'd neer each other.'[96] The Queen meanwhile spared no humiliating detail of their final interview when she announced her decision to the Court. Oxford now suffered much the same strangely triumphant, strangely gleeful malice she had shown Godolphin, his predecessor.

As for Bolingbroke, he had reached the summit – only to learn how short a time one is often granted there. He had assembled the makings of a secretariat – Bishop Atterbury was tipped to take over as the Privy Seal – but in truth had little definite notion of how to proceed. He was essentially an opportunist, driven by ambition and his loathing of Oxford. The detail of his manifesto, and his elaborate theories of a 'country party', would occur to him only during years of exile spent abroad and at the sidelines. The Secretary had the prospect of becoming the 'Prime Minister' only fleetingly before Shrewsbury overtook him and the Queen left the country's future open by dying, painfully and rather angrily. It is interesting that Bolingbroke still confided his shock quite naturally to his friend 'Jonathan', writing impulsively:

Dear Dean.
The Earl of Oxford was remov'd on Tuesday, the Queen dyed on Sunday . . . what a world is this, & how does fortune banter us?
    John Barber tells me you have set your face towards Ireland. Pray don't go. I am against it, but that is nothing.[97]

Queen Anne's grasp on life had been precarious for so long that her death when it came was paradoxically a shock. In her last year she drastically reversed the policy of balancing the factions at Court and in Parliament that had largely characterized her reign. She was wounded badly by the Whig jubilation, even among her personal guard, which greeted the mistaken report of her death at Windsor the previous Christmas. In response – in revenge – she became ever more inclined to give the Tory extreme a free hand; although she held back, until the session ended, when it came to giving the Lord Treasurer his notice. More critically, Swift would point out that she had failed to fill four major Irish bishoprics with suitable men. In the privacy – the continuing privation

– of Letcombe Bassett, soon after her death he set down a harsher opinion of the Queen than he had previously ventured. 'She was in her own Nature extreamly dilatory and timorous; yet upon some Occasions, positive to a great degree.'[98] In truth Swift was simply putting into words a characteristic that courtiers had long observed in the Queen: the defensive stubbornness she called on as a last resort, when her more wilful and assertive generals, prime ministers and ladies in waiting put her under pressure. The effort of coping with such aggressive personalities, while forever looking among them for signs of real affection, was as exhausting psychologically as her illnesses were physically. 'I believe sleep was never more welcome to a weary traveller than death was to her,' was the verdict of her physician Arbuthnot. She died on 1 August. Arbuthnot felt that her last days were cut short by the 'contention amongst her Servants'. But she had perhaps wished to hold on and observe, for one more time and almost *in extremis*, the anniversary of her son William's death on 30 July. She had maintained the yearly custom of a day of mourning at Court. In any case, her final collapse came so suddenly that she left her will unsigned. Arbuthnot, like many of her servants, was left without the modest legacy he expected, a loss he bore philosophically.[99]

On his side, Swift had got his reward, his deanship, however it disappointed him, in good time. Like most at Court, though, he had lost chances he felt entitled to regret. His greatest single critic among the upper clergy had died earlier in the year. John Sharp, Archbishop of York, was 'the crazy prelate' who had denounced Swift to the Queen as the author of the *Tale of a Tub*, and thus unsuitable for positions of high sacred trust. (Interestingly one of his successors to the See of York would treat the creator of *Tristram Shandy*, Laurence Sterne, much more leniently.) Swift floated the story that Sharp had begged his pardon, before the end, for doing him this injustice, though such moral satisfaction came rather late in the day: 'Poor York! The harmless Tool of others' hate . . .'[100] Still, with Sharp, Queen Anne's most trusted clerical adviser, dead, he might expect another preferment from Bolingbroke's new ministry if not from Oxford's. But all such speculations ended, at least for the present, when Anne breathed her last. There would be no honours from the Whigs who were poised to take back their controlling share of government.

Lady Masham, Anne's servant, confidante and Arbuthnot's friend, agreed with him that the stress of the last few months had proved fatal to the Queen. She was more forthright, though, in laying the blame.

Forsaking all laws of polite hospitality, she had spoken bitterly to Oxford in her own parlour when he paid her a visit in early July. 'You never did the Queen any service,' she had hissed, 'nor are you capable of doing her any.' The beleaguered yet impassive Earl bore the tirade with his customary phlegmatic calm, and even returned for a supper at the Mashams' to which Bolingbroke was also invited. The Earl had a delayed sense of drama. He made no reply to the lady-in-waiting herself, but reported her speech to all others who would listen. Soon afterwards, Ford recorded sadly, all of Oxford's supporters were cursing Lady Masham as a 'bitch' and 'kitchen-wench'.[101] Such scenes Swift was glad to have missed during his country sojourn. Lady Masham was rumoured to hate Swift almost as much as the Duchess of Somerset, the Temples' old friend and for a long time his enemy – a red-haired and murdering 'hag', as he now (allegedly) described her.[102] Yet he received a very fond and mournful letter from Lady Masham just two days before Anne's weary journey ended. In it she praised his 'charity and compassion for this poor lady who has been barbarously us'd'.[103] Anne was present to the end through the hopeless sessions in which her council had wrangled over the government's future in Oxford's absence: certainly this was cruelty to the afflicted. In her letter Masham also pleaded with Swift that he should not abandon his friends and go to Ireland. This was, of course, while the Queen was still alive, just: after Anne died, he had little choice. The dog-days of 1714 brought more puzzlement and introspection for Swift, and a long series of good-byes, mostly by post.

He lingered at Letcombe; he hardly knew why – for news, for a miracle. He had packed up his suits and linen and sent them to Ireland, and was left, he said, in 'rags'.[104] Yet he retained his self-possession. Among the most notable of his letters was a dignified reply to Bolingbroke, which quite ignored the flippant and rather frantic tone of the disappointed Viscount's note. Triumph had been so close to the younger man Swift had admired so much. Presently Bolingbroke was excluded from the list of nineteen commissioners the Elector of Hanover authorized to manage the realm until his coronation. Bolingbroke's political life was frozen; and with talk of impeachment already rising for irregularities and malpractice during his time with Oxford in office – in fact a simple, brutal matter of political liquidation – his options were narrowing by the day. His battles in both Houses and on the back stairs at Windsor, Kensington and St James's; his refusal to give up his casual sexual liaisons, surmounting even the prudish Queen's reservations – all his feats had come to nothing. His reply to Swift's solemn missive still fizzes with the tensing nervous energy of a cornered champion. He cursed Swift for writing to him 'in so grave a style' and with 'a heart void of all tenderness'. He bade him go to Ireland, 'since it must be so', but also stammered his demand for Swift to return in order 'to bless – to bless me and those few friends who will enjoy you'.[105] Both he and Oxford remained in London, though both mentioned plans of withdrawing to their estates, and canvassed weakly to renew their powers after the impending succession.

Swift accepted he must go to Ireland. In just over a month he was once more writing rather archly to Viscount Bolingbroke, who by then had been formally dismissed from all his offices. With a brilliant turn of wit that must have smarted greatly before it made his reader laugh out bitterly, Swift congratulated the 'man of mercury' on the 'greatness' he had achieved on ceasing to be a royal servant. Before then, however, a much more awkward leave-taking, again carried out in writing, had stood in his way. He had chided Hessy Vanhomrigh on coming unannounced to him at one of the houses where he had passed the remainder of the summer in a string of visits. They had had an awkward encounter: perhaps even barely friendly on his part. Afterwards he warned her seriously that now he was going to Dublin such mischief must not be repeated. 'If you are in Ireland while I am there I shall see you very seldom. It is not a Place for any Freedom, but where every thing is known in a Week, and magnifyed a hundred Degrees.' The remark and its anxiety are strange when one thinks how Swift refused to let Irish gossip bar him from seeing Esther Johnson as often as he liked. The scrutiny he feared most, then, of his relations with Vanhomrigh was probably that of Mistress Johnson.

There was no choice but to go, since, as the Dean of St Patrick's, he must take the Oath of Allegiance to the new sovereign. 'These Publick Misfortunes have altered all my Measures, and broke my Spirits,' he told Vanhomrigh. Still, he promised her his lasting 'Esteem and Friendship', and even expressed the hope that he would be back in London by early winter.[106] He was not, then, breaking with her; but his departure proved the decisive step in the end of their old protected intimacy. The agreeable life might have continued, if Swift's affairs really had allowed him back to England that year. Instead another dozen would pass before he entered London again, and by then 'Vanessa' would be dead.

Swift can be envisaged with a sad and puzzled tension on his slightly pudgy features, sweating freely in his dark clothes and regulation horsehair wig, as he avoided the political cannibalism that overtook his friends, while managing relations with his two Esthers. He had time for a little self-portraiture too, during these last months in England. He pictured his plight in two striking poems. 'The Author upon Himself' was a controlled yet still vehement harangue. The other was a surprisingly cordial imitation of Horace. In it, Swift voiced only longing for the retirement he had found and was experiencing, in fact, somewhat uneasily.

> I often wish'd, that I had clear,
> For Life, six hundred Pounds a Year;
> A handsome House to lodge a Friend,
> A River at my Garden's End;
> A Terrace Walk, and half a Rood
> Of Land, set out to plant a Wood.[107]

These very English lines look for comforts that might, if Swift chose, have been immediately forthcoming in Ireland. He had his dean's more than moderate income to make use of, and land at Laracor to tend. Yet the real business of Swift's poem (as of Horace's) is not leaving 'court and town' but establishing to savvy city folk what a mild-mannered and unambitious fellow he is. As Westminster's minions imagine Swift hatching plots and deciding the fate of the nation in his carriage rides with Lord Oxford, we hear him talking with his friend about the weather, their literary interests or struggling equally to make out the lettering on signs they rattle past. The poem gains a genuine wide-eyedness from its biographical background; from Swift's complete ignorance, most notably, despite his love of a state secret, of how Oxford and Bolingbroke had urged James Stuart to turn Protestant and accept the British Crowns.

After all these country months he was in good shape for the drawn-out ride westwards, towards the Welsh coast, as early autumn beckoned. He was a few months short of forty-seven years. Had he never reached Dublin, or had he vanished from English letters on arriving there, he might be remembered now as a great technical refiner of the language's prose. His reputation would be that of a chiefly conservative writer, fighting for old-worldly causes that all too often had reactionary sources and tangents. A Tale of a Tub would sit as an avant-garde anomaly among his popular comic miscellaneous pieces, from the Bickerstaff papers to the great urban 'descriptions' in verse. Personally, meanwhile, he would survive in more detail than any contemporary figure, due to the ongoing commentary provided in his reams of letters home to Johnson and her trusty friend Dingley. If his career had ended here, as in

1714 Swift himself believed miserably it would, we would know enough to avoid misrepresenting him. The skewering satire, the alternating stylistic magnificence and plainness that perhaps epitomize what we mean by 'Swiftian', had all been displayed and tested; his harshness, his capacity for resentment and self-pity, his loathing of modernity were also proven. But so too was his generosity as a friend, colleague and supporter, his warmth of regard and fellow-feeling, his enjoyment of the present and his commitment to preserving the better things of this world. His 'conservatism', as we call it, at the risk of terrible anachronism, stemmed from living memory of the Civil War. For Swift, conservatism meant saving the institutions – the constitution of Church and State – that to his mind and a great many more stood between the nation and societal collapse. As such, he was absolutely dissimilar to those defining themselves as conservatives in our own time, on the basis of their commitment to 'market principles'. Yet it is best to place him in his own day, where his motives are amply explained on their own terms in his political writings and the extraordinary *Journal to Stella* – a document that we should never forget is really no diary at all, but one half of a dialogue, and a unique record of a love and friendship.

# 9. Small Dominions

> After venting all my Spite,
> Tell me, what have I to write?
>         – 'Epistle to a Lady'[1]

## I

The reprisals that followed the ministry's implosion, the death of Anne and the accession of George I were shattering for all those associated with the Tory side. King George excluded all associates of Oxford and Bolingbroke from high office. Aided by royal patronage and coercion, the Whigs gained near-total control of the House of Commons early in 1715. They proceeded on a course of vigorous repossession and repressive legislation. Charges of treason were drawn up against the leading former ministers. To control the public, a soon-notorious Riot Act was quickly passed, endowing the militia with brutal powers in response to anything resembling mass protest. Amid the shock of it all, Swift disdained to comment on the predictable rewards that greeted the Whig loyalists: from a knighthood for Richard Steele to a soon fulfilled promise of a complete return of honours to the Duke of Marlborough.

The Tory reaction was largely, if understandably, irrational: Swift's friends were afraid of the pillory, the gallows and the axe. Bolingbroke and Ormond astounded their friends and followers by bolting for France, to join the Pretender's Court. Bolingbroke, who soon bitterly regretted the move, became James's secretary; Ormond took up a command in an invasion attempt that stirred wild fears across the islands but ended in disaster. Swift was furious when his diocesan superior, Archbishop King, lightly suggested that Swift might be a Jacobite himself. Meanwhile, in contrast to those fleeing and hiding, Oxford in Swift's eyes displayed impressive courage. He stood his ground; and was committed to the

Tower to await his trial for whatever crimes the new government could substantiate against him. Oxford was content enough there, with reasonable comforts, books and regular visitors, and commented that his neighbours the lions and ravens made a nice change from the House of Lords. He knew the political and procedural obstacles that would bar his worst enemies from taking his head, and was prepared to take his chances. Swift seems now to have regretted profoundly his earlier criticism of Harley; he addressed him as 'ablest and faithfullest First Minister' and the truest patriot the age had produced.[2] Arguably the relief Swift felt when Harley was eventually released, in 1717, freed his energies for a larger fight against the ills of the world. But, for the present, there was little to do but concentrate on his new responsibilities in Dublin.

When Swift's appointment as the Dean of St Patrick's was announced in 1713, a fellow clergyman stole up to the cathedral and tacked a sheet of verses to one of the great wooden doors. The lines were cynical about the causes of Swift's promotion.

> This Place he got by Wit and Rhime
> And many Ways most Odd;
> And might a Bishop be, in Time,
> Did he believe in God.[3]

The poetaster making this Lutheran gesture was one Jonathan Smedley, an army chaplain and a priest with a small parish in County Cork. He was about four years younger than Swift, and this act of protest signalled the beginning to a long-running antipathy. Swift received a 'scoundrel sermon' from Smedley late in 1716, and complained about having to pay the cost of postage (as the addressee always did, in the pre-stamp era); but ignored him publicly for the time being.[4] After many years of disappointed sycophancy, Smedley later embarked for riches in Madras. Only then did Swift hail him as 'the very Reverend *Dean Smedley* / Of *Dullness*, *Pride*, *Conceit* a medley'.[5] In 1714, Swift had acknowledged how his varied and sophisticated literary work exposed him to stupid accusations:

> *Swift* had the Sin of Wit, no venial Crime;
> Nay, 'twas affirm'd, he sometimes dealt in Rhyme.[6]

He *was* a poet, and the creator of ironic pseudo-universes that converged in scathing commentary on the unfortunate world he inhabited; but the supposed 'Sin of Wit', as Swift maintained in his every daily action, did nothing to compromise him as a priest. In his conduct of business at St Patrick's, he immediately gave Smedley the lie. By the end of 1714 few who saw him at work nursed any notion that he would be an ungodly or inefficient dean.

The move to Dublin in the late summer 1714 brought Swift a mixed-up experience that was both humbling and aggrandizing. He was back in the provincial capital, the scene of all his earliest resentments, and would be stuck there for as far ahead as he could bear to look. The contrast between the Irish and English settings only pained him. He asked Esther Vanhomrigh, who had trailed him achingly across the Irish Sea, how their home town seemed to her. She took lodgings in Turnstile Alley, a lane off College Green near Trinity. She also had a mid-sized country property, inherited from her father, about a dozen miles west of the city, where she and her sister Mary set up a more permanent household. 'Does not Dublin look very dirty to you?' Swift wrote. 'Is Kildrohod [Kildrought; called Celbridge by the English] as beautifull as Windsor?' He recalled miserably an exquisite set of rooms he had enjoyed there in August 1712, with windows looking out upon Eton and the Thames.[7] At the same time his present accommodation was hardly all that squalid. For after years of living in digs and shifting his boxes across town, he was now the master of one of the finer houses in all Dublin, and manager of a large ecclesiastical estate.

Tradition has it that a substantial church devoted to St Patrick has stood on or near the site of the present cathedral since at least the ninth century. The building programme that fortified the Norman Church, physically and symbolically, led to this Gaelic chapel being reconceived on grander lines. Towards the end of the twelfth century the Archbishop of Dublin, John Comyn, earmarked the church for expansion: it was to become a sacred college, and was formally consecrated as such with a great show of medieval pomp on St Patrick's Day, 1191. Over the next generation, the church evolved in scale and law into a cathedral.[8] As its priests, novices and servants increased in number, the expansion and enrichment of the structure was a parallel work in progress. By the first days of the Reformation, when Thomas Cromwell ordered the cathedral chapter to remove their much loved images of saints from internal niches, St Patrick's had become the grey-blue giant that was familiar to Swift: 300 feet in length, the nave almost 70 and the cross all but 160 feet in width. The tapering spire visible today was added a few years after Swift's death; but at 120 feet the north-west steeple, built of blue Irish limestone and carrying a freight of eight bells, had more than enough presence to dominate a much lower, smaller city than the one we know today – even though the cathedral sat in a basin below Dublin's old walls. The cathedral interior, however, differed considerably from the long, open space worshippers and visitors enter now. From the Middle Ages until the mid-nineteenth century, physical subdivisions emphasized the liturgical and administrative purposes of separate areas of the cathedral. A screen wall divided the nave from the choir. The arms of the transept, the transverse section that gives any cathedral its cruciform shape, were split from the central crossing by an arrangement of galleries. In the southern transept, this construction gave clerical meetings greater privacy, since that part of the structure served as the cathedral Chapter House. The Lady Chapel, at the east of St Patrick's, functioned as a separate church for a congregation of Huguenot exiles, and was screened off from the main body. Swift's cathedral still offered height and vastness in its nave to instil wonder at the magnitude of the creation. Elsewhere, it was a more compartmentalized, labyrinthine structure, more suited to the needs of a large working community, offering spaces for quiet conferences as well as solitary prayer.[9] 'It is a very lofty building,' wrote one visitor, 'with three aisles; the middlemost one is a noble one.' The nave was invaluable to Dublin's establishment because it allowed more or less all members of the civic authorities and government to pack inside its walls. It could host large assemblies such as those gathering on Lenten Sundays, when the whole university processed to the cathedral in their gaps and gowns, behind a servant bearing the Provost of Trinity's mace of office.[10]

In its tradition and situation the cathedral was peculiarly suitable for a dean such as Swift. The early constitution of St Patrick's set its character in something stronger than stone. Centuries before, Archbishop Comyn had permanently bestowed a large tract of land, defined in his day as 'eight void spaces' around the churchyard, measuring almost six acres in total, upon the cathedral chapter, to develop as they saw fit. The needs of the community were paramount; the working and monastic, rather than ceremonial and episcopal, nature of the complex was emphasized by the addition of a mill. Within this 'close' of many acres, split by charter and tradition into parcels of land for the church's various officers, the Dean and not the Archbishop presided. It was the Dean, in Church parlance, who had powers of 'visitation, enquiry and correction'. The Archbishop was only lord of the adjacent 'liberty' of St Sepulchre's – created in the Norman carve-up of Dublin and the surrounding territory.[11] In the old days, the Dean had been elected by and from among his fellow canons of the cathedral chapter. The character of this body of men was firmly Anglo-Irish. For many hundreds of years, membership of the chapter had always been denied to any Gaelic Irish priest.[12] Since the Reformation placed Church patronage firmly within the power of the Crown or its approved subordinates, that tradition of autonomous promotion from within had been weakened; but it persisted in spirit with the frequent choice of a dean, as in Swift's case, who had come up through the ranks. Having belonged to the cathedral chapter as a prebendary since 1700, Swift had strong ideas on how to assert the authority his new post invested in him. The cathedral's founding ethos as a collegiate and evangelical organ put it historically in tune with his temperament. Even its status and location encouraged a natural sympathy, grudging though it might have been initially, between St Patrick's and its new dean. For St Patrick's was the 'second' cathedral of Dublin, after Christ Church, where the Archbishop had (and still has) his throne. This technical pre-eminence did not mean that Christ Church was dearer to Archbishop King's heart. He had fought a long and bitter legal battle with the chapter of the older cathedral, and the bad blood had yet to wash away. Yet St Patrick's, a place of learning by nature and a cathedral almost by historical accident, was something of an architectural outsider. It hovered in its suburban expanses with the air, depending how one looked at it, of an outcast, a sentinel or even a besieger.

Like so many pillars of the ecclesiastical establishment, St Patrick's suffered rough treatment during and after the Civil Wars of the seventeenth century. Inside, attempts since then at renovation would uncover signs of past splendour: the great stone ceiling, painted azure and studded with stars of gold, had long needed taking down when it was finally dismantled in the early 1700s. The character of the close, surrounded by a thick wall, had also changed over time. A century before Swift became dean, merchants had embedded themselves and their shops within the close as they had within the structures of Christ Church itself. War and subsequent reforming waves had then banished these traders. By Swift's day the close held a fine library endowed by Primate Marsh, an almshouse, as well as the manses of the Chancellor, Archdeacon, Prebends and the College of the Vicars Choral. These officials were gradually vacating the site; by the early nineteenth century the Dean lived in near-aristocratic isolation. In Swift's time, the close still held a bustling and often contentious community of churchmen and their servants, pulling things down and putting others up, gently remoulding the rituals by repeating them so often, managing their portion of space and influence, and testing their elbows on one another's ribs. From the moment Swift re-entered this clerical kingdom as its senior priest, he was determined to bestow it to his successors in the best possible state.[13]

He lost little time in making his presence felt, even before he returned permanently to Dublin. At the close of 1713 he had felt obliged to discipline the Vicars Choral, the priests who were permanent adult members of the choir St Patrick's shared with Christ Church. They had attempted to renew a lease on some very valuable land near St Stephen's Green. The parcel had already been granted, however, to the Earl of Abercorn, whose city residence sat on the western side of the Green.[14] A delicate matter of friendship and party politics was involved in the affair, and Swift was incensed that the Vicars should try to dispose of cathedral property without his (or, technically, the whole cathedral chapter's) permission. The choristers were meddling in affairs that did not concern them – for their own benefit, Swift claimed. He wrote in harsh terms to the head of the Vicars Choral, John Worrall, and threatened to turf out any one of them who granted any lease on their own authority, for their own gain; 'and [I] shall think the Church well rid,' he declared, 'of such men who to gratify their unreasonable Avarice would starve their successors.'[15]

In all other key respects, Swift was a robust supporter of the choir. His periodic deafness and poor hearing gave him little personal taste in music, or so he claimed; but he had no intention of letting musical standards slip at St Patrick's. He would make every effort, in coming years, to secure the best available choristers. But the affair over Abercorn's tenancy showed the cathedral how the new Dean meant to proceed. The Vicars Choral had their base in a college just to the west of Swift's deanery, in the cathedral's southern cloister, and he had no qualms about upsetting such close neighbours. Moreover he had been a member of the chapter for long enough to know that the Vicars Choral, temperamental artists as many of them were, could often be trouble. The cathedral statutes compelled them to remove their hats whenever they passed the Dean, but this was a rule some were evidently prone to forget. They were also specifically forbidden by charter to strike one another with either hands or feet – another requirement they sometimes overlooked. The long-standing and distinguished organist Daniel Roseingrave had been disciplined for beating up a fellow chorister in his previous posting, at Gloucester Cathedral; and then tussled violently with Robert Hodge, the man he replaced at St Patrick's.[16] Swift became firmly attached to John Worrall and his wife Mary, but saw from the outset that a firm hand would be needed with certain elements in the cathedral family.

His confidence in dealing with occasional miscreants belied a latent personal insecurity. He could make short work of correcting the Vicars Choral because he felt right was so inalienably on his side. In disposing of all Church property, Swift would always place stable longevity over short-term gains: thus Abercorn, not only a valuable ally for the Church but also the long-standing lessee of the disputed patch off Stephen's Green, was to have his claim upheld. But when there was a question of pure personal status rather than principle, Swift could be more uncertain. Again, an episode in late 1713 is illustrative. Swift was asked to preside over the Lower House in the Convocation of the Church of Ireland that was to meet, in tandem with a new Irish Parliament, in the autumn. The Dean of St Patrick's often assumed this function, as 'Prolocutor', and it was held to be an honour. As such, a little campaigning was needed in order to be sure of election. But Swift baulked at this: he couldn't face the possible humiliation of failing to get enough votes. 'I will have nothing to do with it . . . I should make the foolishest figure in nature,' he told one loyal deputy, 'to come over hawking for an employment I no wise seek or desire, and then fail of it.'[17]

In material terms, there was much to support his new place in the world. Although he spent much of 1714, amid his other troubles, in considerable stress and anger at his 'proctor' Parvisol's poor management of his finances, the Dean's revenue was considerable – more than sufficient to make him comfortable for life. The deanship also made him one of the city's more substantial householders. The dean's house lay within the liberty walls when one turned in off Bride Street, a thoroughfare running south-east, and passed the more obviously palatial episcopal residence. Facing the house on its northern side, the eastern end of the cathedral lay in view. The deanery had been substantially improved as recently as 1713 by Swift's predecessor, John Stearne, and had long been an impressive property. A survey of 1546 described it as 'a capital messuage with gardens and other necessary edifices'.[18] The building Swift lived in was destroyed by fire in 1781, but records show that it was fronted by a large lawn (or even a small park), with further, smaller grounds to the back, and with ample stables and a courtyard on its southern side.[19] An 'English horse' he brought over with him when he was first installed took a while to adjust to these new quarters: poor 'Bolingbroke', as Swift called him, sickened in the unfamiliar climate, and was sent to grass (although evidently returned for some years' further service). Swift, upset, complained in September 1714 about the shortage of decent hay and horses.[20] The house itself was spacious; and, although Swift took to living quite privately, with a select group of friends as his regular guests, there was plenty of room for hosting dinners and gatherings. The unaccustomed roominess, indeed, seems to have made him slightly uncomfortable in the first months of his deanship. A young acquaintance indicated the size of the house by mentioning one of the features the Dean found most amenable. The deanery was large enough to need two back staircases, as well as the 'great stairs' that Swift would run up and down when the weather prevented him from walking or riding.[21]

To run his new establishment, he needed more servants than he was used to organizing. He found it within himself to evict his predecessor's cat, which he claimed had 'almost poisoned the house', but not an elderly handmaid who had long been employed at the deanery. The selection and training of servants proved exasperating. He could be an exacting master but from the outset paid wages higher than average. In addition he gave each servant four shillings a week for their board (a real benefit, by the standards of the day), even though meals were provided for them most days in his kitchen. A crucial recruit early on was his housekeeper, Mrs Brent, a Presbyterian lady whose religion was evidently no impediment in Swift's eyes. He had known her for years: his mother had lodged with her when she visited Dublin.[22] In time, Mrs Brent would dine with him at the big table on the evenings when he had no imposing guests – and such evenings were evidently frequent. Memories, perhaps, of Moor Park, and the surly treatment he had later received from the Temples, reminded him that some helpers deserved more respect than they generally received. He was far from being a snob with his staff, then, and, though his tendencies were authoritarian, he saw that to err was human. It was typical, for example, that his stable lad should break 'the very letter of a proverb' and stacked the hay on a rainy day, leaving it to smoke like a chimney. Yet 'the little subaltern cares of life', as he elegantly styled his 'many important nothings' to be done at home, brought their pleasures too. The joiner hired to fit shelves for Swift's library could not finish in a fortnight what he promised to do in six days, but the bookcases themselves were a prospect he enjoyed, as was a new fireplace he commissioned.[23] After nearly a year in residence, we find him describing the house as too large for him and the people inside it too many, but also instilling something of the order he desired. The minimum of fuss and distraction was the founding principle of his husbandry, at least in the account he gave to Pope.

You are to understand that I live in the corner of a vast unfurnished house; my family consists of a steward, a groom, a helper in the stable, a foot-man, and an old maid, who are all at board-wages, and when I do not dine abroad, or make an entertainment (which last is very rare) I eat a mutton-pye, and drink half a pint of wine: My amusements are defending my small dominions against the Arch-Bishop, and endeavouring to reduce my rebellious Choir.[24]

First, though, he had to endure an autumn, winter and spring of disorder and unrest in these 'small dominions'. The worst of his enemies, after his troublesome health, was his own lingering sense of failure. When he seated himself on the decanal throne in the southern aisle of the cathedral – fittingly close, for a dean of such piercing expectations, to the site of the long-abolished prison of the diocesan Inquisition – he could excusably congratulate himself on holding one of the great clerical titles in the kingdom. The prebendaries sat in stalls about the 47-year-old dean. The astronomical effect of Gothic architecture, here with forty huge pillars sustaining the cathedral from choir to nave, was of course always designed to dwarf the most prominent of worshippers. To look at such a wonder of stone from Swift's perspective, however, was to see its vulnerability to time and neglect, and to feel the burden it brought; he denied that he felt in any way enlarged by his promotion. Even as his congregation grew accustomed to this stocky, blue-eyed and ever more bristly browed minister as the dominant man in the cathedral, he felt his new honour compared poorly with the influence and thinly veiled prestige he had held at the Court of Queen Anne. Soon after he arrived in Dublin, it startled him one day in September when a messenger presented himself with such elaborate courtesy that he assumed the man would be plying him to put a word in with someone in power or a similar, familiar favour. Then, on seeing that there was no other business than a letter to be read, Swift recalled abruptly that the Queen was dead, the ministry had fallen, and he was 'only the poor Dean of St Patrick's'.[25] He expected no further promotions.

His deanery became both an elite salon and a fortress of sanctity. He read prayers strictly every evening, and all servants were obliged to attend. When illness, especially an attack of deafness, stopped him reading from the liturgy, he would withdraw at about ten to perform his devotions in private. A younger friend noted how worn and 'fouled with the snuff from his fingers' were the edges of his prayer-book's pages. Obscenity was not to be tolerated; Swift lamented profanity in works he could otherwise commend. Curses he censured immediately; 'for he detested all immoral or impious men, and could not endure the hearing of any thing that tended to levity in religion, lewdness, or any immorality whatsoever.' His severity seems to have carried over into his near-obsession with cleanliness – or else both stemmed from the same ruling and inflexible principle. 'He was cleanly even to superstition. His nails were always close pared, and every second day he shaved himself, though troublesome, as he complained his hair was hard as hogs bristles, and he washed his feet as often.' He exercised rigorously. He changed his under-linen daily, a singular habit at this time, and even when weather, health or work kept him indoors would don his gown each morning.[26] A spot on his person, let alone his character, was unbearable to him.

## 2

The greatest comfort was of course the reunion with Johnson, who still lived in the city with her faithful friend, Rebecca Dingley. They now lodged on the far side of the river from Swift, however, on Mary Street, a respectable thoroughfare running parallel to the Liffey. St Mary's Church, on the corner of Jervis Street, was a landmark in the neighbourhood, its plain external walls concealing a galleried interior of rich wooden carvings. Johnson and Dingley's route to Swift probably took them across Essex Bridge, splendid in design but slightly dilapidated. According to one historian this was 'the focal point' of Dublin for the next hundred years, opening the city's fine and still quite recent stone quays to the viewer who paused on the span:[27] the rows of well-off, fashionable houses on lower Capel Street stretched northwards from the bridge. The ladies' address on Mary Street lay safely within the same busy, largely genteel grid.

Although not far removed by carriage or by foot, the distance between Johnson's apartment and Swift's deanery was enough to impose a public sense of their very separate addresses. Swift and Johnson met only at respectable visiting times, and were hardly ever alone together in a room. Yet, with the due proprieties observed, their emotional proximity was unbroken. 'Stella' was a regular if not daily visitor at the deanery. Over the coming months and years she and Dingley would generally follow Swift on his movements between city and the country, though very rarely staying under the same roof and, except when travelling, hardly ever see-

ing him in disreputable morning hours. Little can be said of a definite
nature about his happy return to this fixed orbit with Johnson, precisely
because his letters to her dry up at this time. As is the way of correspondence, Swift's in the autumn of 1714 speaks of the absences he found
painfully significant: but he also in fact avoided writing too much to
friends whose company he missed most. Though Arbuthnot in particular
would chide him for the lack of contact, the Whigs controlled the post
and were monitoring all Tory correspondence; the times invited caution.

One demi-presence, based partly in Dublin, thrilled and tortured him
above all. Esther Vanhomrigh, having followed him and set up home at
Celbridge, insisted on seeing him often. Swift had told her repeatedly
that this would be impossible; yet hurried, half-distant, half-impassioned
notes from him indicate that for a while they did meet intermittently in
the later months of 1714. His feelings for her were still largely paternal,
or avuncular, and the disorder of her finances stressed his fastidious soul.
In July, he inferred correctly that she had been shaken deeply by a touch
on her shoulder – that of a bailiff – and had arranged for her to borrow
short-term funds from one of his publishers, Benjamin Tooke.[28] As winter set in, after he carefully avoided a detour to Celbridge on a country
visit that took him to Trim, they evidently met on a number of occasions
in her lodgings in Turnstile Alley. In contrast with the cautionary letters
he had written her over the past two years or more, the tone of Swift's
notes to Vanhomrigh during these months is quite ardent. Five days after
his previous visit, he promises to see her tomorrow – and declares that
he would visit ten times more often if it were only 'convenient'. In
another he insists that he will see her in a day or two, and that 'it goes to
my soul not to see you oftener.'[29] Vanhomrigh's letters, meanwhile, carried the note of outrage and offence they would strike until the end of
her friendship with Swift and indeed her life. She knew better, she admitted scornfully, than to demand that he find the courage to acknowledge
feelings that she still believed mirrored hers for him. Amid all her
material troubles, she asked merely for a stable and open friendship –
and asked what shame there could be in his seeing her to give her advice
from time to time. She clearly found it insupportable that his new station in life should cause him to shrink from the magnificent individuality
that had won her early admiration. 'Now when my misfortunes are
increased by being in a disagreeable place amongst strange, prying,
deceitful people whose company is so far from an amusement that it is a
very great punishment, you fly me and give me no reason but that we are
amongst fools and must submit.' She reminded him of his maxim that if

one did what was right the world's opinion meant nothing. Swift had difficulty observing it in his present situation. Her letter arrived when he was hosting some company 'on a Saturday night' and threw him into a state of confusion. Replying on Monday – that is, having left her to fret all weekend – he weakly repeated a rumour he had heard that very morning from the mouth of a woman who performed some 'business' for him. He put dashes in his letter, censoring the crucial words: 'she heard I was in — with one —, naming you.' In love – or in town? With one – what? He hardly needed to say. 'I ever feared the Tattle of this nasty Town.'[30]

The gossip was all the more sickening because of the thought that Esther Johnson surely was no stranger to it. Dublin itself, with its odious 'Tattle,' seemed to sap and diminish him, while galvanizing his shame. After a further haughty reply from Vanhomrigh, the correspondence is largely interrupted for some years, with the exception of a single note here and there; but when it resumes with the next set of surviving papers, from 1719, it leaves little doubt that the relationship had continued on much the same basis in the interlude. The lacuna in the records of Swift and 'Vanessa' stands for lost exchanges made up of rebukes and remissions. In the last note of 1714, Vanhomrigh scolded Swift for visiting only when he could get the better of his inclination to hide from her behind his curtain of propriety. Yet she had also fallen into a further, more damaging pattern. She would almost always apologize for her reproaches in the same note, indeed at moments beg him to forgive her for existing. She was caught in the sad turmoil of a person who could not shake her obsession or admit that it was an illusion. Neither, on his side, could Swift. He did not show her the mercy of cutting her off completely: he would always insist that he would see her when he could.

The affair reveals him in some respects as very mortal. He liked two women very much for very different qualities – and was equally adamant that he could live with neither. But at the same time he displayed with Vanhomrigh a peculiarity that does at one level support the theory of some that he suffered from Asperger's or another syndrome on the autistic 'scale'. Despite the intimacy and freedom that both he and Vanhomrigh had once celebrated in their conversations over coffee in chambers such as the original 'sluttery', there are hints in their letters that they weren't perfectly in tune with one another. In her notes late in 1714, Vanhomrigh wrote movingly of how she dreaded his 'frowns' and his 'killing, killing words'. Swift's response to such accusations was generally bemusement, or, as he put it himself in December 1714, 'confusion'.

Yet the diagnosis of Asperger's – the definition and understanding of which are so rooted in our own time – isn't actually necessary to get an idea of the personalities interacting here. Swift, despite his gift for enjoyment of conversation, had always been reserved. By the 1720s, when he was well known to a new set of younger friends, one of them noticed that he would habitually express emotions in a very understated way. Even when highly amused, he would only smile, slightly, and never laugh aloud. His intonation too was almost constantly 'sharp, strong and high-toned' – which, to a delicate ear, might impart fixed anger or dislike.[31] The trait seems to have grown stronger in him with age. Earlier descriptions of Swift – typically that of Addison (who, admittedly, was similar to him in this respect) – testify to the charms of his company; and Vanhomrigh herself was evidently won over by them. The unlaughing and monotonous image of Swift should be placed against a warm tribute the Duke of Ormond had paid his sense of humour and his social skills as recently as 1715. He missed Swift because it was such fun being with him: 'You have left so sweet a relish by your Conversation upon all our pleasures that we can't bear the thoughts of intimacy with any person.' Yet he also sketched the depressed state which other friends were soon describing Swift as being in: 'Common report bespeaks you tired and melancholy, conversing with few persons, hating Ireland and yet making no attempt to come to England.'[32]

Whether autistic in nature or not, an immense concern for propriety, even in private company, gained more and more power over his personal expressiveness as he aged; and the shock of his transfer back to Dublin was possibly a decisive event. To Vanhomrigh, this increasing blankness must have been extremely distressing and hurtful, especially when her need for warmth exceeded her ability to revere dry wit. Yet what to her seemed a frown or a killing word was most likely intended by Swift as a neutral or even compassionate sign. For on her side, Vanhomrigh was extremely sensitive and strongly empathic: small changes of expression, the slightest tension in the facial musculature or an indeterminate tone carried great weight with her, and she 'mirrored' such flickers and shifts with powerfully sympathetic or hostile reactions. All the steadiness Swift enjoyed with Johnson, whose reserve he shared and exalted, was absent in his engagement with Vanhomrigh. As a couple, they were ripe for catastrophe.

'This nasty town', Dublin, while steadily expanding, was in many ways what it had always been in Swift's lifetime. The Irish capital had more celebrants now than when he was young; they pointed out the splendid public edifices finished or in progress. There were 'handsome structures' modelled on the masterpieces of Chelsea and Greenwich, a 'large and noble building' for the barracks; fine bridges, pleasing open spaces such as Stephen's Green; a smart Customs House and the quiet, slightly rundown grandeur of Trinity College. All the amenities of a capital were to be found, a theatre and recreation grounds and every manner of shop, with 'markets for live and dead cattle, fish, fowl, fruits, herbs, roots, &c.'.[33]

To Swift the town offered an endless stock of maddening absurdities. Over the coming decades, he would highlight other features of 'this beggarly city', such as the 1,500 houses standing vacant, while builders put up new ones on sites that could serve better purposes.[34] He was appalled by the noise and muck of the metropolis, but saw there was nothing for it but to take it in good part.

> Every Person who walks the Streets, must needs observe the immense Number of human Excrements at the Doors and Steps of waste Houses, and at the Sides of every dead Wall; for which the disaffected Party [a stock phrase for the Tories] hath assigned a very false and malicious Cause. They would have it that these Heaps were laid there privately by *British Fundaments*, to make the World believe, that our Irish Vulgar [people] do daily eat and drink.[35]

For as long as its identity would depend on the support and esteem of England, Dublin would remain an outpost, a neglected repository of lost ambitions; the lead duct in a brutally primitive assembly rigged up to drain the wealth and spirit out of Ireland. That it was also the scene of his formative griefs and disappointments would hardly clear Swift's view of the place. It would be some years yet before the old attachment brought him to fight for the country as his own, and acknowledge it as such by doing so.

He coped by exercising obsessively; and, above all, this meant riding. The Irish roads he lamented as 'deplorable' and 'barbarous' were no deterrent except when the rain made rivers of them.[36] His regimen was linked to the single greatest cause of his personal insecurity, his seemingly incurable problem with dizziness and deafness. Periodically bouts would still plunge him into a private vortex or strand him in profound silence. They only became stronger with the years and, when he was well, the constant semi-conscious anxiety of an attack doubtless contributed to the growing restraint others observed in him. He must have been

almost perpetually on his guard against a relapse. The cause of his condition, a loose bone amid the tiny structures of the inner ear, would
never be known to him; and, along with his self-imposed stringency
towards fresh fruit and occasional experimentation with various tonics,
maintaining physical fitness was still the chief measure he took against
his condition. Menière's Disease lay beyond the medicine of the day, and
ultimately could not be suppressed or escaped by hard riding. Yet, while
doubtless doing much for Swift's soundness of body in all other respects
– he would live into his late seventies – the rhythm, regulation and physical relief he found in exercise did much for the balance of his mind.
Despite his latent frailty, he was in no way a writer to wilt consump-
tively in a garret.

'In his person he was robust and masculine,' observed a friend who
got to know him in middle age; 'his deportment was commanding, and
his walk erect.'[37] The sureness with which he bossed canons of the cathedral and corrected lapses of good manners in his reception rooms was
supported by a certain stout muscularity, worked up by long hours in
the saddle. From his first autumn back in Dublin his habitual route, usually in the company of two servants, would take him out beyond the
new town on the far side of the Liffey, along the great strand that
stretched towards the hill of Howth. Out there he was no lost Joycean
artist with the wind whipping through cast-off trousers. Quite what his
meditations on horseback might have been is obviously a secret even the
Dublin seashore has long forgotten, but the exercise for Swift was clearly
essential to keeping his spirits in order. He escaped the city and its teeming signatures of all things that were there to breed, the ineluctable
faecality of the corporal. The understanding that grew up between horse
and rider possibly brought him his greatest experience of physical harmony. There was real urgency, as the year turned cold in 1714, in his
search for a reliable replacement for the Viscount of Bolingbroke's ailing
namesake.

There were two serious incidents on his rides in the course of his first
two winters back in Ireland. The first, late in 1714, illustrated the difficulties he was having at home, and the other, about a year later, the
rather graver problems besetting him from further afield. The first
showed up his servant troubles. On the last Sunday in December he
travelled to Belcamp, some five miles north of Dublin. His destination
was the ancestral home of Henry Grattan, the future patriot leader, on a
visit to Bridget (née Flemyng), the great-grandmother of the famous
Irish parliamentarian. Of Bridget's seven sons, Robert, the fourth, was

the Prebendary of Howth, like his father before him, with a stall in St Patrick's; the fifth, John, was the Rector of a nearby parish. When travelling in this direction, as he frequently did, Swift would cross the Liffey by ferry while his servants took his horse across one of the city's two serviceable bridges. On this day he found he had forgotten something at the deanery, and so retraced his steps there alone to retrieve it. The walk was a matter of perhaps twenty minutes to one of Swift's constitution, but the hour was near three and the sun was descending by the time he made it back across the river. On the far side he found his men standing woozily near a shop that sold brandy. They had quite clearly warmed themselves on a few seasonal tots. He took his horse at the door, and possibly also took a nip inside himself, since later he mentioned how Will and Tom, his groom and footman, helped him back into his cloak ('I love malt liquor,' he wrote in a later decade, 'but dare not touch a drop'[38]). He realized something was badly amiss when 'the two Loobies' put the mantle on him inside out. He rode on, and Tom refused or was unable to follow. Swift halted, waiting; and in time the lad galloped up wildly. Swift told him off and Tom sighed that he was indeed as drunk as a dog. They had now got out on to the sands, and Tom could barely control his horse. The servant was riding Bolingbroke, usually a delicate steed. Tom lurched at times into the sea and then back again close to Swift, now assuring his master that he was sober. The Dean gave him a taste of the whip and further harsh words; and they went on a while farther until Tom's nerve broke again and he sobbed that he was indeed very drunk. In time it all proved too much for Bolingbroke – Swift's constant lashing and cursing, perhaps, as much as Tom's wayward riding – and the horse began to protest. Tom was thrown, and Swift needed to call for help from a passing boy. In one last fury Tom fought off all of them – Swift, Will and their stand-in helpmate – until with a redoubled effort they got the bridle out of his hands. The stranger mounted Bolingbroke and the newly formed trio rode off, leaving poor Tom staggering in the dusk with the tide at his ankles.

They reached Belcamp before dark. Swift half expected Tom to reel after them to the Grattans' house, but he also feared that he might return to the deanery and rob him. Swift sent the boy he had recruited to St Patrick's with a note that, should Tom show his face there, the footman should have his valuable great-coat, boots and whip taken away and then be dismissed with a crown to tide him over. Typically Swift sent assurances that he would settle up Tom's outstanding pay himself when he returned. Furthermore he missed two items essential to his two great compulsions, hygiene and writing: he feared that his toothbrush and quill were in one of Tom's pockets, since he could find them nowhere in his bags.[39]

This to-do did not disturb Swift for long. Indirectly it led to his finding a footman who pleased him greatly. The replacement's name was Alexander McGee, who was soon known (for obscure reasons) as Saunders, and was for Swift not only the 'best servant in the world' but in time also a friend.[40] Along with Mrs Brent, the household controller, and a middle-aged cook-maid, Mary, a woman 'of a large size, and very robust constitution', her complexion roughened by smallpox, Saunders soon eased the pain behind Swift's regular grumbles about his staff. There were still, almost needless to say, incidents that became minor legends, but Swift's domestic kingdom began to settle. One day early in their association Mary brought him an overdone joint for his dinner. He asked her to take it downstairs and roast it less. She naturally protested that that was impossible; and Swift, having reflected that it is better to commit faults that can be righted, from that day called her 'sweet-heart'. Besides looking after the kitchen, Mary mended his socks and made his bed, and generally helped to ensure that, aside from the odd toothsome supper, he was very well cared for.

His other confrontation on the road, the following winter, was more dangerous and also more sinister because of the bad blood it revealed in the land at large. Swift was harassed on his favourite route by a young aristocratic bully with a strong Whig bias. While returning one day from Howth, a chaise drawn by two 'high mettled' horses rattled up aggressively behind him. The servant riding to Swift's rear had to jump off the road to avoid being run over; and Swift himself took his horse both left and right, attempting to give way. His groom, riding ahead, was powerless to help. The two gentlemen in the carriage, meanwhile, had no interest in merely overtaking. They followed Swift as he swerved from one side of the road to the other, and were evidently set upon turning him off his horse. By sheer luck, he managed to stay in the saddle and jump across a ditch. The chaise halted too, and Swift 'mildly expostulated' against the occupants. The scene recalls a near-fracas almost twenty years earlier, when Swift had stood his ground against a crowd sympathetic to a boatman he refused to pay on account of his foul language. Back then, however, Swift had been a minor clergyman, and his opponents equally nameless. Now he was politically notorious, and a public target. His riding habits were evidently well known. His assailants this time were also of another order. They were powerful and protected from the consequences of their actions, even if Swift were to be physically injured or worse. He was shocked to recognize the well-set young man who now began bawling at him. 'Damn you, is not the road as free for us as for you?' came the shameless retort to his protest. This was 21-year-old Cadwallader Blayney, the seventh Baron Blayney, who had once been represented to Swift as a 'man of some hopes and a broken fortune'. Among other favours, Swift had introduced him to Addison during Wharton's time as viceroy. Now Lord Blayney was calling to a servant for his pistol, and demanding to know if it was loaded. The man replied that it was and handed it to his master, at which Swift had no choice but to plead. 'Pray Sir, do not shoot, for my horse is apt to start, by which I shall endanger my life.' This supplication seemed to satisfy Blayney and his companion, and they ordered their carriage on. Swift was left shaken, keeping his horse as calm as he might on the safe side of his ditch.

With no hope of redress, while observing that neither law nor the 'colour of his peerage' could justify or excuse Lord Blayney's assault, Swift merely petitioned the Irish House of Lords for permission to ride safely on the Strand, and indeed on any road, 'for the recovery of his health'.[41]

## 3

Several more years of exclusion from the wider political struggle lay ahead for Swift. He was distressed by the Whig witch-hunt in Westminster, and conscious of his own status as a potential victim. The encounter with Lord Blayney on the Strand brought that home. This was no random aggravation of a clergyman: the young aristocrat had recognized Swift, and had sought to give him, at the least, a severe fright. The incident highlights the fact that, however much Swift vaunted his retirement in the cathedral liberties, he was a famous public figure. He remained the author of the *Conduct of the Allies* – notwithstanding his vestigial attempts to remain anonymous: that is, of one of the bestsellers of the century, a work that had completed the political defeat of Marlborough and his associates. The Dublin public had read and absorbed Swift's *Examiners*, and party allegiances had been stirred there as much as in London. Swift had not yet, it was true, occupied the pedestal the Irish population would offer him in a few years' time: for it was not yet apparent that he would stand up to defend the impoverished workers living in the streets near the cathedral, or the suffering tenants out in the country. But 'the Dean' was a personage known by sight and name.

At this point, during this interlude, it makes sense to reconsider what it was that Swift himself believed he would be fighting for in Ireland. Put simply, his goal was an idyll. He wanted Ireland to have what he believed England had. England, he imagined, despite the ravages of the Whigs and the depredations of time, still had a social structure on which decent life could grow. The basis of this structure was rural; England, Swift would always feel, rested on the prosperity of the land, and thus so should her twin Irish kingdom. The cellular building block common to the shires and the boroughs of England was the parish – and the nucleus of each parish was of course the priest. Taking this framework for granted, Swift argued that if life was good for English country parsons, it could only be better still for their neighbours.

A Vicar there of forty pounds a year can live with more comfort than one of three times the nominal value with us [Anglican priests in Ireland]. For his forty pounds are duly payd him, because there is not one Farmer in a hundred, who is not worth five times the rent he pays to his Landlord, and fifty times the sum demanded for the Tythes; which, by the small compass of his parish, he [the vicar] can easily collect or compound for; And if his behaviour and understanding be supportable, he will probably receive presents now and then from his parishioners, and perhaps from the Squire; who, although he may sometimes be apt to treat his Parson a little superciliously, will probably be softened by a little humble demeanour.

The life that was still possible for an ordinary English vicar was a subject of reverie for Swift.

The Vicar is likewise generally sure to find upon his admittance to his living, a convenient House and Barn in repair, with a garden, and field or two to graze a few cows, and one horse for himself and his wife. He hath probably a market very near him, perhaps in his own village. No entertainment is expected from his visitors beyond a pot of ale, and a piece of Cheese. He hath every Sunday the comfort of a full congregation, of plain, cleanly people of both sexes, well to pass, and who speak his own language [as many if not the majority of rural Irish labourers still did not]. He dreads no thieves for anything but his apples, for the trade of universal stealing is not so epidemic there as with us. His wife is little better than Goody [a 'simple' woman of the village], in her birth, education, or dress; and as to himself, we must let his parentage alone. If he be the son of a farmer it is very sufficient, and his sister may very decently be chambermaid to the Squire's wife. He goes about on working days in a grazier's coat, and will not scruple to assist his workmen in harvest time.[42]

This figure was not just the foundation of the English Church, plain, honest, diligent and conformist; the parson encapsulated Swift's vision of England. That vision was of course under threat from the Whigs and the moneyed men, and had been for years, but so long as the Church remained, this English existence would also. The passage above was written in the 1730s; but the humble paradise it described was the one Swift had always cherished and championed. It stemmed from the aura of the Reverend Swift and his ordeals at Goodrich; it drove Swift in his long campaign to secure the First Fruits for the Irish lower clergy. It manifested itself in Gulliver's wish to see 'some English yeomen of the old stamp' among the spirits brought forth for him at Glubbdubdrib: and at this moment in the Travels Swift both confessed a sense that his idyll was in truth defunct, and challenged his readership to keep it alive. When Swift finally described himself as 'liberty's avenger' in his epitaph, he was alluding in part to the 'Spirit of Liberty' Gulliver identifies in these yeomen, 'their Valour and Love of their Country': the virtue of a vanishing species.[43]

The overriding point behind Swift's evocation of England was that it was utterly inapplicable to Ireland. Swift's homeland had no settled parishes with well-fed, rooted farmers, and thus no stable income for priests. It remained a country of scattered townlands and isolated smallholdings, ruled over by disproportionately large manor houses. These big houses, in which Swift sought company and often stayed on rural visits, had the air if no longer the function and appearance of fortified outposts. Beyond, one had cottagers living in something often close to utter abjection; tenants who, being ethnically diverse, had little in common besides their hardship. Of these the majority were still native, 'mere' Irish Catholics, men in canvas tunics and leggings and women in shawls, both wearing brogues and the older among them still treasuring the versatile mantle that doubled as coat and blanket. Their hollow-eyed children were invariably sent begging for bread. Swift viewed these people with pity more than scorn. He suggested, in the late paper quoted above, that the native Irish had in fact conferred some 'politeness and civility' on the Scots arriving from the late 1500s on.[44] By the time of his exile to Ireland, the country was wretchedly ripe for a humanitarian crisis. Trade was crippled by English restrictions; agrarian land was increasingly given over to pasture. Despite his professed aversion to it, Swift would be drawn into defending the country in which he found himself confined. Rather than emancipation, however, he acted from an alternative, despairing, colonizing urge. He wanted Ireland to have parishes like those of England, and at the same time knew that such modest bliss was impossible.

There were, however, those in Ireland who certainly had plenty, and Swift spent a good deal of time as a guest in wealthy homes. Over the course of the eighteenth century, the Anglo-Irish gentry acquired a reputation for lavish and reckless hospitality. Swift is reported to have visited the house of Thomas Mathew in Tipperary, who made it his rule that visitors should treat the place as their own and help themselves to as much of his food and drink as they could stomach. The 'midnight orgies of Bacchus' nevertheless went on 'without in the least disturbing the repose of the more sober part of the family.' Thomas's mansion was a pleasure palace at the disposal of all and sundry:

> There were two Billiard-tables, and a large bowling-green, ample provision was made for all such as delighted in country sports; fishing tackle of all sorts; variety of guns with proper ammunition; a pack of buck-hounds, another of fox-hounds, and another of harriers. He constantly kept twenty choice hunters in his stables for the use of those who were not properly mounted for the chace.[45]

Hospitality was one of the local squire's traditional duties, but over the coming decades visitors from England concurred that the Protestant gentry of Ireland took it to excess. Descriptions abound, especially from later in the century, of carousers lying amid the wreckage of the previous night's feast, before taking to the hunting grounds to work up an appetite for another. Such accounts patently reinforce the impression that these freeholders were becoming 'Hibernicized' – for previously the native Irish gentry had been credited with the same indiscriminate generosity in their housekeeping: it was one of the traits, the same accounts imply, that had ruined them. Swift lamented this process. He felt its logical conclusion would be the English ending up in clay cabins with the worst-off Irish peasants.

The likes of Thomas Mathew – whose estates were massively encumbered by the time he died – would always be exceptions, ideal for supplying a colourful anecdote and supporting a stereotype. A general impression nevertheless existed that estates were managed poorly; and Swift would be ever more pungent in his disapproval of waste. As the century progressed, the fortunes of a tiny minority funded fantastic building projects. The gentry of Swift's later years, though, were more frequently caught in uncomfortable conversions of older structures. If the Anglo-Irish didn't directly move in to the square-walled medieval fortresses from which native Irish families were dispossessed, they either incorporated them into extensions or reused their materials. The results were frequently uncomfortable and ugly. A later observer, Jonah Barrington, described his ancestral home, the 'great house' at Cullenaghmore, as 'an uncouth mass, warring with every rule of symmetry in architecture'. Yet the inhabitants did their best to give Cullenaghmore the same crusty attributes that a similarly lived-in and neglected English residence might easily have possessed. The Barringtons' home, dating from the reign of James I, was built from the wreckage of a demolished castle, and the writer suggested its interior was all too typical. He grew up amid the remnants of generations known to Swift:

> Some of the rooms inside were wainscoted with brown oak, others with red deal, and some not at all. The walls of the large hall were decked (as was customary) with fishing-rods, fire-arms, stags' horns, foxes' brushes, powder-flasks, shot-pouches, nets and dogs' collars; here and there relieved by the extended skin of a kite or a king-fisher, nailed up in the vanity of their destroyers. A large parlour on each side of the hall, the only embellishments of which were some old portraits, and a multiplicity of hunting, shooting, and racing prints ... The Library was a gloomy closet, and rather scantily furnished with everything but dust and cobwebs.[46]

Adjusting for the slightly earlier period and differences in the scale of individual properties and standards of housekeeping, a great many of Swift's Irish acquaintance can be located in similar conditions. When you forgot the small castle from which the house was raised, you might have been in England – where periodically there were also tenants living on the edge of starvation. Yet all the cultural unity Swift still attributed to England was missing. As one historian put it, the Anglo-Irish gentry would always be an 'uncomfortable excrescence' in the land they dominated.[47]

Swift could only see Ireland from the view of a Protestant household; but the view of England he applied as a model for Ireland was also distorted. Needless to say he overlooked the moderate dreariness and exhaustion from labour to be found in an average cluster of rural English parishes, such as those comprising Plympton in Devon, 'a poor and thinly inhabited town, though blessed with the privilege of sending members to Parliament'.[48] Swift was more than capable of acknowledging bleak prospects – though he gave short shrift to those who complained about hard work. Part of his argument was that England gave adequate, not excessive, comforts to an ordinary clergyman and the ordinary souls he was there to guide. The distortion lay rather in the stasis Swift sought for in England. The parochial order Swift imagined in 1730 was, in his mind, all but the same as it had been in 1630; that timelessness, indeed, was crucial to the point he was making. Yet his idyll denied the very rift he had spent the years from 1710 fighting over; a canyon in English society that had opened in the course of the Civil War and decades of subsequent conflict. The English shires in 1714–16 were not the settled parcels of peace he sometimes claimed they were. The Tory–Whig, Anglican–Nonconformist split was everywhere, and thoughts of civil war seemed entirely apt as the Hanover Court established itself. In the riots breaking out across the country – although concentrated in the south-west – rival effigies were burned, churches and meeting-houses attacked. The sometimes tenuous relationship between parson and squire could be much less stable than Swift pictured it, and the vicar himself, the farmer's son, was by no means Swift's dependably unifying figure. The High Church priest could be a Presbyterian target, and a rabble-rouser. Both sides had their heroes, from King Billy to Henry Sacheverell. The latter courted controversy, though he did his utmost to distance himself from the burning and looting that greeted King George's coronation. England in 1715 was in the grip of an emergency, though not the one described by the proponents of the Riot Act. Government was not about to fall: indeed, its local powers were enhanced by the notorious statute which stipulated death for any in a group of more than twelve, 'unlawfully, riotously and tumultuously assembled', who remained after the Riot Act was read to them. The emergency was social in nature, the outcome of an insuperable breach between clashing Churches. Swift had played his part in widening that division; and he remained best known for his services to the High and Tory side of it.

For the time being, he concentrated on Church affairs, and they remained vexing. Archbishop King had spoken quite candidly to colleagues and officials of the antagonism he expected from Swift. He was determined to stock the cathedral and diocese with as many of his own recruits as possible.[49] The Archbishop frustrated Swift in these matters because he deeply suspected the Dean of being a Jacobite. The extent of King's suspicions, with the rebellion of 1715 in the background, became apparent to Swift only in the course of 1716. For a long time Swift had proceeded naively, sharing his views on appointments with a superior who was scheming all the while against him. Two men Swift particularly wanted to help were Thomas Walls, the Archdeacon of Achonry, and his friend and fellow Scriblerian Thomas Parnell. His support for the latter was snubbed almost immediately: Swift had wanted Parnell to get the prebend he vacated on his appointment to the deanery. On the strength of Swift's recommendation, King was even prepared to reverse his own earlier support for Parnell, a man he clearly valued. The battle over Walls was more drawn out. Annexed to the cathedral, meeting in one of its chapels, was the parish of St Nicholas Without. Before he was made dean, Swift had desired this benefice for himself, and bore a lasting grudge against his predecessor, Stearne, for not seeing that he got it. Later Swift earmarked this pleasant urban living for Walls, a man whom even the Archbishop acknowledged was 'grave and good'.[50] This character reference was given, however, before King was aware how much an ally Walls was of Dean Swift. Amicable relations and established trust certainly existed between Walls, a pious yet warm-hearted, reliable and inoffensive person, and his more waspish superior. In February their households happened to exchange horses for a period: Walls complained quietly of Bolingbroke's 'shyness', and Swift retorted that the Archdeacon's mare had almost thrown his servant, Will, a half dozen times. In short, Walls was a much valued subordinate and friend, whom Esther Johnson also liked and respected.[51] For over a year of guarded wrangling, King used his influence among the prebendaries to thwart Swift's aims. And this was only one skirmish in which Swift came to suspect foul play.[52] As the spring came, he sought help, writing to Bishop Atterbury for some advice on his powers as dean. Swift knew the constitution of St Patrick's intimately, but the majority of his prebendaries would still contradict him on points of order at meetings of the chapter. He asked Atterbury to tell him more about the standing of deans in English cathedrals on which the foundation of St Patrick's was based.[53]

In the course of 1716 Swift was most attentive to his parishes in Meath. Riding out to the country brought accustomed relief, though in February he found his gardens and grove at Laracor 'sadly desolate'.[54] He visited his churches throughout the year, reading prayers and preaching, as was his habit while in Ireland whenever cathedral business and his health permitted. A cherished scheme was his plan to buy an additional plot of land, some twenty acres, for his glebe at Laracor. He was using money granted him for the purpose by the overseers of the Irish clergy's First Fruits. It pleased Swift to think of having supplemented the living for his successors. By the autumn, the purchase having been approved, he was impatient to have the deeds confirmed so that he would not miss the year's planting.[55]

Absorbed though he was by such distractions, by far the greater part of his time required him in Dublin. Conversation with Johnson and a few others there eased his spirits somewhat; yet he was vexed and depressed by his troublesome priests. Atterbury's reply to his inquiries, delayed by the Bishop's gout and a savage political battle in London, had come in April. Atterbury had confirmed Swift's view of his legal position: the strong powers peculiar to his position as Dean of St Patrick's were more generally reinforced by Tudor statutes. Yet much, Atterbury warned, would always be determined by points of 'decency and convenience'. He counselled Swift not to push too hard. In his reply, expressing gratitude for Atterbury's response to an 'insignificant letter', Swift did not pick up on this note of caution. The chapter were opposing him, he claimed, purely out of different party principles – Whiggish inclinations – at the bidding of the Archbishop, who mistook his authority. As the Dean, Swift legalistically proclaimed, he had the deciding voice in both proposing and vetoing candidates for offices. Even in matters of canon law, it was the Dean who was entrusted with punishing all offences except heresy and one or two others. He closed his letter to Atterbury in a partisan voice favouring belligerence, scattering sardonic comments on new abuses in the Church and urging him to continue carrying the fight to the Whigs in the House of Lords. 'God never gave such talents,' he assured Atterbury, 'without expecting they should be used to preserve a nation.' This was a fine compliment from the greater writer of the two; yet he failed to take the advice that made Atterbury the higher-reaching politician.[56]

His retreats to County Meath brought mishaps and lapses of health that physically reflected his low morale. In May, riding to his parishes inflamed a painful sore. At Trim he stayed in the home of the Rector, Anthony Raymond, an old acquaintance. Raymond was a friend Swift had been sometimes too proud – and too busy – to see much of in London. Years before, Swift had complained of the 'plaguy trouble and hindrance' he feared when the country Rector called at his city digs. On that occasion, Raymond had stayed late, even though Swift was struggling with a cruel cold.[57] But although Swift felt his Irish neighbour preened himself a little for superior manners and dress, back in Meath, Raymond was an amiable, hospitable and trusted companion. Swift, as he generally did, gave a good man his due. Raymond had resigned a fellowship at Trinity on accepting his rectory, though he still hoped to publish a history of early-medieval Ireland. Dr and Mrs Raymond's home seems always to have been open to Swift in winter, when the manse at Laracor was too cold and clammy. Now Swift's injury brought him to their door at the time of year he had often fantasized about from London. 'Oh, that we were at Laracor this fine day!' he had written to Johnson in the spring of 1711. 'The willows begin to peep, and the quicks to bud.'[58] On returning permanently to Ireland, Swift showed such day-dreams had been in earnest. He spent as much time in his parishes as he could. Confined indoors in May, having managed to find only a half-sheet of paper to write on, he worried about a window left open near his hogsheads in the deanery cellar. At such moments the loyal Archdeacon Walls continued to act as his reliable factotum.[59]

In mid-June his patience broke. Subterfuge and threat alike had failed against the clergymen resisting him in the cathedral's chapter house; so he turned again to the Archbishop, their suspected puppeteer, with an outburst of noble candour. He had heard that King was leaving for England in a few days' time, for a customary and necessary period of lobbying on behalf of the Irish Church, and if possible to visit a spa for the sake of his gout. Accordingly Swift wrote to him from the country. After wishing him the best on his mission and for his health, Swift stated his grievances. He pointed out how every minister he deemed worthy of preferment, King had discounted. He gave two examples at length, one of them Walls. All his friends, Swift said, had known long before he did that he was out of favour with the Archbishop. Swift admitted he could hardly fail to see a further pattern: it was an open secret in the diocese 'that several clergymen have lost your Grace's favour by their civilities to me'. Swift protested that he wasn't complaining – that would be beneath any man of spirit; but his letter still reads as the dignified plea of one being treated as if they have the equivalent of playground lurgies. It will strike a chord with anyone who has felt first vaguely outcast, then somewhat at odds and finally downright persecuted during their first months or years in a job. Instead of pleading for justice in particular instances, Swift's next move was to appeal to King's better self, asking 'merely to know whether it be possible for me to be upon any better terms with your Grace, without which I shall be able to do very little good in the station I am placed'.[60] He finished the letter by candlelight in the early hours of the morning.

The Archbishop, sixty-six years old and thirteen into his episcopate at Dublin, was a proven manager, where Swift was a sensitive artist. King was also, at heart, deeply amiable and humane, fond of company and recreations, and genuinely concerned for the welfare of his juniors and their congregations. The good-humoured expression in his final portrait, rare in an age of pallid, chubby solemnity on canvas, reflects the quick-witted and strong-willed character preserved in King's correspondence and writings. His narrow, pointed nose and pronounced cheekbones gave his wide yet rather small-chinned face an impish look – much more suggestive of ludic and acerbic tendencies, in fact, than the more rotund, impassive countenance of Swift. Yet Swift was much the more delicate of the pair, and, although King could not indulge such a temperament, he had no wish to torment it unreasonably. Using a device common in disputes between masters and servants, monarchs and parliaments, he wrote briefly telling Swift that he was 'heartily sorry' that some of their colleagues and acquaintances had clearly done so much 'to sow dissension' between him and his dean. As for the clergymen Swift had instanced, he stated quietly yet firmly that he had acted in all good faith; and he closed by expressing his hope that he could convince Swift soon in person of his wish to live and work constructively alongside him. Behind the letter, hurriedly written yet consumately professional, a keen political campaigner's intelligence may be detected – one that has realized his competitor is oblivious to the larger game being played, and is thus not consciously an opponent. King had been blocking Swift as part of his general strategy to pull the Irish Church back from disaster. He took Swift to be a Tory of the highest kind, close to being if not indeed a Jacobite fifth-columnist, and he assumed that the men Swift supported were of the same cadre. Thomas Lindsay, the ageing Primate of All Ireland, was also a Tory – though not an outright 'discontenter'. King saw that the goals of such clergymen would clash violently with the vision the Whigs of Westminster had for the Irish Church (and Ireland generally), in a fight they could never win. He refused to let them bring the Church itself down with them. King would never entirely drop his suspicions about Swift's politics – but he may have been truly surprised to see how personally Swift, with all his experience at Court, had interpreted his tactics.

Swift remained touchy. Knaves ruled. Alexander Pope, vilified by envious dunces for the huge success of his translation of the *Iliad*, reported that profane versions of the Psalms of David, printed by Curll, had been attributed to him.[61] Swift sympathized; the criminal profiteering of Curll infuriated him too. While he still held influence, he had long meditated an attack that would claim the bookseller's ears, 'but the rogue would never allow me a fair stroke at them, though my penknife was ready and sharp.' That year Pope's choice of weapon was (non-lethal) poison rather than a blade. With Elizabethan directness he invited Curll for a drink, in order to settle their differences, and then slipped an emetic of near-instant effect into the bookseller's cup. He described the resulting tortures with glee and at length. Pope had written to Swift in expansive form, for, despite the scratches left by foes and critics, he was still partly elated by fame and financial security. Swift's responses to his friend's witticisms were more caustic: he gave another of many scathing verdicts on Ireland, and his letter had a general undertow of gloom. 'I love you never the worse,' he told his friend, 'for seldom writing to you.' He had much less to say that was worthy of report: 'I can assure you the scene and the times have depressed me wonderfully.'[62]

The ongoing business of land purchase took Swift frequently to Meath in late November and December. He was unable to join Johnson and Dingley travelling north, to County Down, to spend Christmas at the home of John Stearne in Dromore, south-west of Belfast. Swift blamed his lack of a horse strong enough to take him such a distance, yet work also detained him, and a certain aversion may have played its part.[63] He had been involved in the tortuous negotiations that led to Stearne's promotion as the Bishop of Dromore. Stearne was thus another name on Swift's list of friends who owed him their gratitude and good-will, and against which he had carefully recorded slights and betrayals. Yet Johnson rated Stearne highly; she and Dingley had valued his company during Swift's long absence in London. Swift, though, went no further than Trim during the festive season of 1716.

A trace remains of a meeting, or failed meeting, with Vanhomrigh that December: whether it represents a frequent custom or a rare event is uncertain. He was anxious as ever after seeing her – or almost seeing her, since his note does not make it clear whether they actually met, nor does it cast any light on the exact circumstances that worried him so much. He was concerned, though, that their mutual acquaintance, the Provost of Trinity College, would believe she had visited him (presumably at Trinity) only in order to see Swift. The circumstances behind Swift's terse note are most unclear, but his worry seems excessive, given that he appears not to have been at the Provost's rooms when Vanhomrigh called, but visited him the following day. He exhorted her to think of some excuse, for 'I hate any thing that looks like a Secret.' He sent sympathy, though, for the troubled health of her sister, Moll.[64]

Managing tension between Vanhomrigh and Johnson, while keeping both within bounds he could handle, took up much of his considerable willpower and emotional strength. It was manifestly Vanhomrigh who caused him more trouble. Swift tried to fix and delimit their relationship in public perception, to attribute her presence in the room to any other reason but attachment to him. Yet Vanhomrigh remained a figure in the background, calling on almost all of Swift's Dublin acquaintance, in the city and at their country homes. She was known as well to acquaintance passing through, such as Ford or the painter Charles Jervas, whom Swift avoided earlier in his stay, but greeted cordially as 'Friend Jervas' when his departure drew near. Jervas was apparently a good match in conversation for Vanhomrigh's sometimes sparkling, sometimes vituperative repartee: Swift mentioned how the painter's 'eloquence and vanity' sometimes needed holding in check.[65] Jervas, moreover, may well have taken both into his studio, though obviously at different times. A supposed portrait of Vanhomrigh has long been attributed to Jervas, and the young woman in the painting (now in the National Gallery of Ireland) undoubtedly has an air of Vanessa. Her wide, challenging eyes stare out directly, with an expression of sardonic primness on her flushed, rather wide face. The woman has dark hair – though Swift suggested she was fair – drawn back from her forehead; she wears a fine gown of blue satin, with a frill and bow of white lace. Her bearing is formal yet relaxed; she has nothing to hide. If her smile were just a fraction broader she might openly convey the sense that she finds the whole business of posing a joke. When the painting was made is uncertain, but on this visit of 1716 Jervas may well have tried to persuade Swift, a reluctant sitter, to be sketched again.[66]

He spent Christmas at Trim that year quietly but not unhappily. 'This would be a very good Place for you,' he wrote to Walls, 'for there are no cards nor diversions, only you cannot smoke or drink ale.'[67] Swift himself was always eager to dispel or prevent an attack of spleen with a punning contest or some other parlour game. The loss of Johnson's company, in this as in so many other respects, was always heavy. She would invariably come out with the best thing heard in any evening, no matter how clever their companions were. One recent *bon mot* during Jervas the painter's time in Dublin highlighted both her wit and intransigent Tory politics. A visitor had asked Jervas where he lived in London: 'Next door to the King,' Jervas replied, no doubt chuckling at himself. His house was near St James's Palace. But Mr Jervas was mistaken, observed Mrs Johnson. He lived next door only to the *sign* of a king: shop and tavern signs, in the absence of regular house numbers, were generally used for postal directions, and George I was reduced to one such marker. Johnson won the louder laugh by far, and probably a refined huzzah, for her follow-up.[68]

In his room at Trim, Swift exhaled sarcastically when word came of Johnson and Dingley's safe return from Dromore: they spoke of nothing, he guessed, but Bishop Stearne's big house.[69] The New Year brought a scattering of fresh problems along with ongoing concerns. His excellent curate at Laracor, Thomas Warburton, had secured a good parish of his own in Armagh, which put Swift in need of another deputy. He instructed Walls to find him a large choice of good candidates, though he conceded that 'we are much out of parsons here.' Notably, he wanted a curate who could do more than read from the prayer-book. It was vital to Swift that a priest could preach well. At Trim, the growing strangeness of his friend and associate Joseph Beaumont, 'poor Jo', still wrestling with the problem of longitude, continued to disturb. One unspecified incident forced Swift to send Beaumont's brother-in-law to town to take him in hand.[70] 'I am endeavouring to persuade Jo that he is mad,' he reported a few days later.[71] In mid-January, Archbishop King's reply arrived to the tense, hurt letter he had written before Christmas. A bad cough and cold had delayed King from writing, though he seems also to have been guided by an intuitive sense of the need for some cooling-off time. The relationship of dean and archbishop would begin to climb from its nadir – with just occasional explosions along the way.

# 4

A bothersome consequence of being 'a person distinguished for poetical and other writings', as Swift described himself, was the way this reputation disguised the warmth and sincerity of his affections, and his sensitivity to criticism or teasing. A quarrel in the autumn of 1718 illustrated how wit was sinful indeed when he was the wrongful victim of its sting.

In mid-1717, near the height of his joy and relief at the escape of his friends from Whig custody, Swift had befriended a brilliant young raconteur. A classicist and schoolmaster, Thomas Sheridan endeared himself to the 'Presto' side of Swift's personality. He was almost giddily witty, personable to a fault, extremely clever and more than a touch reckless. That year Swift turned fifty, and Sheridan reached the age of thirty. His family origins were native Irish, although the Sheridans had long ago conformed to the Anglicanism that made the politics behind Thomas's witticisms firmly Tory. After a fairly humble Dublin schooling, he had arrived at Trinity College much later than the average freshman, aged twenty. He had impressed his tutors, though, and won a distinguished scholarship. In or around 1711, the year he graduated, he took the step Swift regretted most in all his colleagues and protégés: he married a sweetheart from his native County Cavan. Sheridan's marriage to Elizabeth McFadden proved even more miserable than most Swift criticized as improvident. Thomas had no money to speak of – had no benefice, was not even yet ordained – and the dowry McFadden brought from her parents' small estate of Quilca would prove unequal to the couple's tastes and expectations. They had a greater problem still: not many years of married life had passed before the Sheridans realized they couldn't stand each other. Elizabeth harried Thomas for his poor business sense and he scolded her for lack of kindness. Dislike mounting to hatred still brought children, however, and Sheridan, having taken the cloth two years before, opened a school in 1714, though its income barely covered their expenses. It brought other rewards, nevertheless. His little academy on Capel Street, close to the hub on the northern side of the Liffey, made his name famous in Dublin.

As a teacher, by the standards of the time, Sheridan was superb. Swift, admittedly with an itch on his conscience, later pronounced him 'the best instructor of youth in these kingdoms, or perhaps in Europe; and as great a master of the Greek and Roman languages'. More concretely, he recalled that Sheridan could tell at first sight what sort of pupil a boy would be: an adept, a drudge or a pest. He apparently disliked using the cane, preferring, said Swift, 'to shame the stupid' and leave the punishment of idlers to the violence of their classmates. Sheridan himself, with habitual droll candour, explained his methods as varieties of tyranny. 'Heaps' of grammatical rules would baffle and subdue; bursts of terrifying temper would sap resistance. Yet Sheridan's other qualities also reached the classroom. He was an astounding storyteller with 'a fruitful invention'. The gems and *nugae* he mined from a vast range of sources, ancient and modern, came to fill many volumes in his study. He was also, Swift affirmed, a talented writer. His verse and prose were full of humour, though neither were 'sufficiently correct'.[72]

This failing had as much to do with decorum as grammar and style.

Swift was immediately enchanted with Sheridan, and made him welcome at the deanery. Johnson grew very fond of him – and 'entertained him also as she would a brother'.[73] He and the Dean soon fell into the habit of exchanging comic, riddling verses. These *jeux de lettres* could involve some rough hits, and Swift clearly expected Sheridan to take what was coming to him as the junior man. Sheridan, however, was too used to maintaining his dignity in the classroom, with mockery and violence as he saw fit. A year or a little more after they became friends, he began to go too far. A couple of surviving poems show Swift demanding that Sheridan mind his manners. The root of their falling out early in the autumn of 1718 was a dispute over whether a woman might aptly be compared with a sieve; the Dean thought so, the schoolmaster not. Then Sheridan extended the dispute to a contest over the quality of Swift's verse in general.

> Oft have I been by poets told,
> That, poor Jonathan, thou grow'st old . . .
> Thy rhymes, which whilom made thy pride swell,
> Now jingle like a rusty bridle.

He continued by declaring that Swift's verse now limped along on gouty feet.[74] Swift was entitled to cry foul because this was a parley of 'left-handed' poems – written with deliberate wobbliness (note the deliberate metrical lumpiness in the lines above) – fighting at a disadvantage. Swift was stung too by the idea that his powers were fading with age. This must have struck home. It was four years since he had been active in the press, known by all as the nemesis of Marlborough's pride and avarice. It was also natural for a writer so long dormant to wonder if his best work was behind him. Swift's replies swatted Sheridan in turn, but much more gently; for the most part they were concerned with calming the battle. Affectionate references to Sheridan as Phoebus carry just a slight sardonic tinge, with a genuine warning in the use of the myth. The poems are good ones too, even while maintaining the left-handed rule. The rhymes creak, as does the metre at times, but look how nicely this one plays out the moment of Swift's receiving Sheridan's latest letter.

> I can't pray in quiet for you and your verses –
> But now let us hear what the Muse from your car says.
> Hum – excellent good – your anger was stirr'd:
> Well, punners and rhymers must have the last word.

The positioning of that 'Hum', for all his verve, was arguably beyond
Sheridan. Swift continued with admonition rather than attack:

> But let me advise you, when next I hear from you,
> To leave off this passion which does not become you:
> For we who debate on a subject important,
> Must argue with calmness, or else will come short on't.

The poem warns Swift's Phoebus that if he rhymes too much in his carriage he may end up swinging from a cart – the proverbial wagon pushed
away from beneath a condemned man's feet.[75]

Sheridan, a man of pure mirth, was too caught up in the joke, and
perhaps too secure in the friendship, to realize how offended Swift was.
Swift answered with suspended rebukes: he was too proud to share hurt
feelings with the younger man. Yet his repeated appeals that Sheridan
tone down his insults show how far he was ready to go to avoid snub-
bing him. They had got to know one another during a delicate period for
Swift. The summer of 1717 saw his leader, Oxford, released from captiv-
ity. February 1718 brought the death of Swift's onetime tutor and old
friend, St George Ashe, Bishop of Derry.[76] Addison, who liked and knew
Ashe well, wrote condoling with Swift on the loss of one 'who has scarce
left behind him his equal in Humanity, agreeable conversation and all
kinds of learning'.[77] Swift left his feelings unrecorded. Ashe had taught
Swift at Trinity, and remained an understated yet constant and amiable
presence in his correspondence and close Irish social group. Swift had
sometimes played the odd prank on Ashe, but only of the kind that if
anything highlighted the Bishop's fondness for a joke. Respect was
maintained, and benignity guaranteed. This was the master–pupil relationship as Swift conceived it when he met and grew fond of Sheridan.
The passing of Bishop Ashe would naturally stir the thought that Swift
was now the senior, semi-paternal figure with regard to men of Sheridan's age: and there was something inextinguishably boyish in Sheridan's
character. Sheridan's conduct, as Swift saw it, violated the terms of this
subtle contract. He denied Swift the older man's role, and jibed him like
an equal, a schoolmate.

Here and there in Swift's papers, meanwhile, one finds occasional hints
of how he felt his mortality, and the burdens of his intermittent illness. A
note in his account book in May 1718 records a 'terrible Fall'. The sombre
comment that only God could see the end of such suffering was offset by
the typically tough reflection that he was feeling a little better.[78]

Fairly early in their relationship Swift had written a tender Latin epigram to Sheridan, praising him as a creative spirit and as a tutor. He sketched the schoolmaster as both sage-like and mercurial. A wave of Sheridan's golden staff – the life-giving, dream-inducing caduceus of Hermes – could open heaven and earth to the mind of an apt student.[79] A foreign language could sometimes release Swift from the obligation English imposed on him either to irony or to emotional restraint; he allowed himself to write a passionately complimentary letter in French to Vanhomrigh a little later. A Latin poem written after she died would be unrecognizably despondent. Sheridan clearly brightened days and evenings; it may have been that Swift saw something in his new friend that indisputably resembled himself, and felt an urge to nurture and support it in his friend. Above all Sheridan appealed to Swift's sense of vocation and civic-mindedness. Swift commended him first and foremost as a teacher. Memories of Kilkenny, of Trinity, would rise and wound him in the coming years, and he would set them down in acrimonious memoranda. He always felt that the elders of Trinity had taken a dim view of him; and as the years passed he returned that view with his unmatchably baleful stare, as the career of its new provost progressed. Richard Baldwin, a militant Whig, was put in charge of the college in 1717 and became notorious for keeping a mistress. She suffered for her lover's sin: on one occasion the undergraduates ran her out of the gatehouse. Whatever his other faults, by contrast with 'dear Baldwin chaste' (as Swift styled him)[80] and his growing band at Trinity, Sheridan encapsulated what an educator ought to be. Affection for the student in Sheridan mingled with serious regard for the tutor.

Thus Swift laid himself painfully open to insult and rejection. He had also, as he knew, been dazzled before by a mercurial character, the carelessly injurious Viscount Bolingbroke. On his side, Sheridan was far from being a politico; he was redeemed, in fact, only by his innocence of malign intent, his blithe unawareness of harm done and his unnerving dedication as a jester. He steamed on with a long poem that enraged Swift further. In it Sheridan imagined the funeral of Swift's muse, which he had already pronounced dead. Swift himself would, with ironies and self-deprecations of his own choosing, envisage reactions to his death; but the idea of his inspiration dying was little short of inconceivable. At the interment Sheridan set forth, however, the chief mourners were a train of asses and owls, '&c.'. He distributed copies to everyone he knew.

Swift had never known a situation quite like this. He had been hurt before by people he cared about, but never struck so, as he saw it, by a cherished subordinate. When slighted by Jane Waring, he had responded with icy scorn. He had dealt with the loss of Addison by allowing contact to freeze up. Steele he had lambasted in the press. His enemies at Moor Park he had simply spurned. When it came to Archbishop King, whom he couldn't escape, he had appealed to his sense of justice. Sheridan, he decided, could only be chastised indirectly.

He applied to another friend. This was the Reverend Patrick Delany, a junior fellow at Trinity, and from this period on another of Swift's stalwarts. Sheridan, it seems, had made the introductions. Delany, four years older, was an accomplished scholar and wit, with a growing reputation as a preacher, but in character he was quite unlike the volatile schoolmaster. Equable, diplomatic and judicious, he had a much stronger strategic sense of the moves that would benefit his career; a less colourful and appealing person, but also one who scattered less shrapnel when he spoke. Swift respected Delany as a sensible man to about the same degree as he simply liked Sheridan. In early October 1718 he hoped that Delany might take Sheridan aside and tell him to ease off. Delany would, however, bear a message from Swift in the form of a dignified and in places quite wonderful poem. It began with a serious compliment, addressing Delany as 'the Man I long have sought'. It continues with a very interesting discussion of the ingredients of appropriate comedy.

> Three Gifts for Conversation fit
> Are Humor, Raillery and Witt:
> The last, as boundless as the Wind,
> Is well conceiv'd though not defin'd;
> For, sure, by Wit is onely meant
> Applying what we first invent.

Wit, that is, thought Swift, belonged to a faculty of judging and deploying the discoveries of intellect. It arguably belongs with the part of rhetoric that was once called *dispositio*, 'arrangement', as much as with the faculty the specialists called *inventio* – the discovery of good materials for speech. These were the skills that were failing Sheridan at present. Humour could flourish only when wit picked out and articulated the insights and jokes that were apt to a given conversation. Raillery, meanwhile, was a manifestly inferior quality either in a person or in a writer. It was the mode of communication for boors at the tavern:

> that clan of boist'rous Bears
> Always together by the Ears;
> Shrewd Fellows, and arch Wags, a Tribe
> That meet for nothing but to gibe;
> Who first Run one another down,
> And then fall foul on all the Town;
> Skill'd in the Horse-laugh and dry Rub,
> And call'd by Excellence, *the Club*.

Such were the lordly louts who had almost driven Swift off the road a couple of winters before; such too had been many of the bluff 'October' squires catapulted into Parliament in 1710. Swift and Delany belonged to a morally higher layer of society and discourse. Not only elegant and enjoyable, 'To Mr Delany' demonstrates how Swift felt that there was no contradiction in a churchman being a wit, if he was one in the true high sense of the word.

After lauding Delany, the poem then starts gently to chide. If his friend agreed with these thoughts on the nature of wit, as Swift knew he must, why did he excuse Sheridan's raillery at the present time? The final couplet shifted to the imperative: 'If he be Guilty, you must mend him, / If he be innocent, defend him.'[81] Positive though he was, Swift hesitated before sending the verses to Delany. He worried, as he admitted in the note he eventually attached to the poem, that 'I may be thought a man who will not take a jest.'[82] While he pondered, though, Sheridan's indecencies (as Swift saw them) only worsened. Swift was provoked into calling Sheridan a goose, with 'base quills'. Sheridan retorted with goose-like viciousness rather than goosy stupidity:

> Tho' you call me a goose, you pitiful slave,
> I'll feed on the grass that grows on your grave.[83]

Swift had borne too much already, and after more brooding a fortnight later the poem to Delany was dispatched. Delany took the hint immediately, and handed the poem on to Sheridan (although Swift had directed him not to, in the poem itself). Delany recorded in his posthumous defence of Swift that Sheridan was so mortified that he burned the sheet of verses. Thus he proved to be unlike the other, grander 'man of mercury' in Swift's life.

A sad postscript to the saga was given by Thomas Parnell, Swift's younger fellow Scriblerian, in the second half of October 1718, as the quarrel with Sheridan reached its crisis. Parnell never really got over the loss of his wife, who had died seven years previously. It was no accident that of all Parnell's poems, the one picked most often by pirate anthologizers was a 'Night-piece on Death'. In this, his strongest feelings were voiced if not appeased. Contemporaries spoke of him as an alcoholic, although in an age when men such as Swift thought very little of a pint of wine, they may have been suggesting his weak and melancholic frame coped badly with drink. He had settled in Ireland, where, after disappointing him in the acquisition of a prebendary's stall in St Patrick's, Archbishop King provided the modest vicarage of Finglas, just outside Dublin. Earlier in 1718, Parnell had visited England; he fell ill and died at Chester on his way back. He was the first member of Scriblerus to die, and his death on the road confirmed Swift's gathering thoughts on the rare and temporary nature of friends. Parnell and Ashe, two lost companions, punctuated Swift's effort to rescue right relations with Sheridan while still preserving his dignity. The point was underlined the following year by Joseph Addison, with whom Swift had renewed a bond of understanding and lasting respect. He died in June, worn out by politics and by now estranged from Steele, after weakening for some time.

'The truth is,' reflected Delany, 'Swift kept every friend, and I believe every man living that he conversed with, in some degree of awe: and no man that I ever knew of, if he were so disposed, would yet dare to flatter him.'[84] Therein was the source of Sheridan's error. Morally and emotionally Swift projected utter robustness, a steel-proof disdain for the opinions of lesser minds. Sheridan was not alone in misreading him. The Dean's air belied the strength of his attachments and the surprising delicacy of his temperament.

# 10. Bursting Bubbles

I cannot but warn you once more of the manifest Destruction
before your Eyes, if you do not behave your selves as you
ought.

*– The Drapier's first letter*[1]

I

There was no question of lowering his guard, however, especially beyond
the 'dozen persons' in Dublin with whom he claimed to speak regularly.[2]
Though he still shunned the sphere of broader politics that remained a
province of knaves and traitors, the Church, as ever, presented a rather
fearsome battleground. The pendulum had by now swung right away
from the High Church faction; indeed, it seemed to have risen beyond its
acme on the opposite side, and frozen in mid-air. The Latitudinarians,
the wing of the Church favouring moderation towards reasonable Dissenters, were setting the agenda. Their champion was nevertheless a
bishop who managed to upset everyone, reformers and traditionalists
alike. Benjamin Hoadly, Bishop of Bangor, was more a political philosopher than a theologian. His true gospels were arguably John Locke's
books on government. Yet in 1717 he reached new levels of controversy
with a published sermon expounding the view that the Church could
expect to have very little authority or jurisdiction over legal, political or
social matters in the mortal world. Properly, Hoadly argued, the ecclesiastical realm was confined to questions of the next life, questions that,
as Hoadly observed, it could also influence only to a limited extent.
Hoadly's writings anticipated, far into the future, a wholly secular state,
but even in the mid-1710s left little doubt as to which had the greater
control over everyday moral and practical life, Church or government.
The 'Bangorian Crisis', taking its name from Hoadly's diocese, was the

greatest theological row of the century. As an emergency measure, Convocation was prorogued and, barring a brief session in 1741, did not meet again until the mid-1800s.

A Krakatoan uproar such as this had long been brewing. The Sacheverell Affair and the Convocation Crisis of 1702–3 had given warning tremors. It wasn't as if Hoadly's ideas were terribly original; but this was the first time they had been broached so trenchantly by a churchman, and a senior one at that. Hoadly, destined ultimately for the golden See of Salisbury, had been a loyal Whig writer since early in Anne's reign, and was close to the senior ministers Sunderland and Stanhope. Painfully for clerics such as Swift, the Bangorian furore defined the path on which their Church was ultimately set. The door for the Dissenters was open. No revival of old pre-Civil War powers, let alone the medieval sway their offices once held, could be imagined by Atterbury and his High Church cohort. The war had been lost; tactically, barring divine intervention, all that could follow were skirmishes to make the Low Church victory as sour as possible. Even conservative Whigs had little taste, really, for Hoadly's vision. Crucial to the rancour he provoked was the ill-feeling evident in his writing. He had much to be angry about, since his life was physically painful to him. As a student at Cambridge, Hoadly had caught smallpox and then had been maimed by the unspeakable treatments of a rough-handed surgeon. His cure had left him severely broken in body. He could preach only while kneeling, and moved on crutches. His disabilities invited additional hatefulness from his opponents; as Alexander Pope knew, a physical handicap was all too readily interpreted as a sign of moral defect. Hoadly, though, was ready for all comers, and stood his ground in any polemic.

Hideous though the future seemed, the more immediate problem for Swift was the Whig ministry's practice with regard to the Irish Church. From time immemorial, Westminster and often Lambeth Palace had viewed the Church of Ireland as a convenient receptacle for an overflow of English ministers. On top of that, some of the Irish bishoprics brought much bigger incomes than many of the English ones, in grotesque disparity with the impoverished majority of Irish vicarages. English clerics who could take the loss of status and the distance from home travelled contentedly enough to occupy sees in Irish counties. Most of these incomers were philosophical about the exchange of home comforts for greater wealth. Much of the year could always be spent in London, in any case. This practice went completely against the original Elizabethan vision of an Irish priesthood for the Established Church in Ireland, the

vision that had, incidentally, led to the institution of Trinity College and
other Irish centres of learning. Such developments led to Swift and Archbishop King realizing how much they had in common, and brought
them to work more closely together. More particularly still, the tide of
immigrant bishops pitted Swift against the imported Welshman charged
with the diocese of Meath, where his parishes lay.

Sixty-five or so years old, his constitution toughened by the climate of
India and ocean travel, Bishop John Evans lived in a near-permanent
state of outrage. Ireland was choking with Tories, he felt, and everywhere they baited him. Evans wrote regularly to the Archbishop of
Canterbury, William Wake, and his letters are soaked in vitriol. As it
happened, on crossing to Ireland in 1716 he had vacated the See of Bangor soon occupied by Benjamin Hoadly. He had been a firm supporter
of Marlborough and the Whig Junto against the Peace of Utrecht.
Evans's fury with the state of the Irish Church is at first hard to square
with his reputation as an adventurer. For nearly fifteen years he had
served as a chaplain in Madras for the East India Company, during
which time he had made investments of his own and traded shrewdly.
His success attracted envy from mercantile colleagues, who dubbed him
the 'politic padre' and, with a sudden onset of piety, wondered if such
flagrant money-making was appropriate to 'a man of his coat'.[3] Evans
had returned home, acquired degrees in divinity and used his fortune to
boost his prospects in the Church. Further business ventures might be
expected in his biography, and Evans assuredly was dauntless in his pursuit of extra revenues wherever he was based. Yet he took his ministry as
seriously as he did his finances; it appears that he saw no need to distinguish between the two. He was convinced to the core not only by the
standard Whig doctrine on the revolution, but also by the more inclusive
Whig thinking on the shape of the Church. He saw enemies everywhere,
in the shape of Jacobites and crypto-Papists. It is striking that, even as
such priests reached the ascendant, they, like their High Church colleagues and enemies, were convinced that all might be lost in a moment.

'Dublin and his Dean', that is, King and Swift, were marked men in
the eyes of Evans and his allies. The Dublin duo hated all things English,
the Welshman informed Canterbury.[4] Evans's self-righteous anger was
not at all soothed by the regularity with which he beat King and Swift in
contests over preferments – in ensuring, for example, that St George
Ashe's See of Derry went to a confirmed English Whig, William Nicholson. King and Swift reciprocated Evans's dislike. The enmity was a sadly
ironic one, since there was potentially less that divided them from Evans

than there was between him and radicals such as Hoadly. Yet their differences were more than enough to stoke a steady rancour: for Evans, Ireland was a colony to be stacked with Englishmen. For 'Dublin and his Dean', Ireland was a kingdom to be tended by home-grown Irish ministers. This meant that Swift's little church at Laracor, where he or his curate generally had a congregation of only fifteen people – 'most of them gentle, and all simple', in Swift's phrase – was a site for a much wider conflict.[5]

Evans and Swift had their first public contretemps in June 1718. Evans had summoned the clergy of his diocese for inspection, or a 'visitation', at Trim. In a speech to the assembled clerics, Evans 'reflected with some roughness' on certain ministers present who shared the principles of Dr Swift. His real target, shrewdly, held his tongue until an assembly the following day, when protocol permitted clergymen to respond to the Bishop. Swift stood up and spoke 'with great coolness of temper; but at the same time, with much severity, and fine satire'.[6] More than a few jaws evidently dropped among the audience, while the Bishop himself pursed his lips and turned a stately shade of puce. Later in the summer Swift's friends ganged up on the Bishop. Bishop Stearne was to deputize for the Primate of All Ireland, Thomas Lindsay, at a visitation in August. Evans, Nicholson and other Whigs braced themselves for a clash of croziers; but the numbers were too even – and their respect for the Primate's authority prevented any outbursts or butting of mitres. The ill-feeling between Evans and Swift naturally lingered. A year later, the Bishop's blood pressure soared at Swift's intentionally provocative request that he ordain a man who was an obvious Tory. Swift could easily apply to another bishop, and did; he was merely playing with Evans's volatile temper. This was in May 1719, and, on receiving word that Evans had rejected his ordinand, Swift wrote to inform his bishop that he would never again be attending his visitations. He was quite plain in refusing any further 'injurious treatment', even though the moral victory had clearly been his in the previous year's formal altercation. He advised His Grace to remember that on such occasions he was addressing a fellow clergyman, not a footman. 'I cannot help it, if I am called of a different party from your Lordship: but that circumstance is of no consequence with me, who respect good men of all parties alike.'[7] He spoke the truth; he and Addison, for example, had put themselves back on good terms before Addison died. Indeed, Swift's close friend the late Bishop Ashe had been a moderate Whig.

The points that could be scored in such encounters carried some satisfaction; yet, in the larger fight, though acknowledging it was unthinkable, Swift, King, Stearne and other High Churchmen were obviously on the losing side. Each major ecclesiastical vacancy in Ireland was invariably filled by an English Whig; who then set about bolstering his party's network in the parishes or diocese he controlled. Primate Lindsay's days were numbered. Swift and King, meanwhile, although learning to collaborate, still sometimes handicapped one another by tacitly competing over appointments. Swift seems to have seen, if not accepted, that the most he could do was to be assiduous in the cathedral business which took up most of the days – particularly, as he somewhat evasively told Vanhomrigh, the sociable hours of the afternoon. Otherwise he would engage in man-to-man clashes such as those he fought out, inconclusively, with Bishop Evans, when necessity arose. Though he barely realized it yet, this still left him a huge store of unused energy, and gradually, his frustration with what he could do for the Church left him available to stand up in defence of the Irish kingdom – that is, his vision of the Protestant kingdom of Ireland. The important thing to appreciate is that, for Swift, fighting for Ireland meant defending something smaller, less significant by far than the Church that encapsulated his whole sense of moral and social order. Though defending Ireland would make him a resounding voice for what now seems basic human justice, in his eyes it initially meant settling for less.

Contrasting images of Swift arise at this time. Writing to Charles Ford – now lodging at the sign of the 'Blue Periwig' off Pall Mall, having spent some time abroad – he offered a valetudinarian self-portrait. It was the end of 1719, and Ford had nagged him for not replying to a letter. Swift responded in the vein of an essayist: 'I do not think that Men who want their Health are answerable for Lazyness and Indolence. If they keep the same Affection for their Friends, no more in justice ought to be required. Indeed I fear, when Life grows indifferent every Thing grows so too.' He had just got over a long attack of his dizziness when he suffered 'a pitifull broken shin'; the bruising broke into a sore and he was confined to the deanery and the house's gardens for another month. 'Thus in Excuse for my Silence,' he wrote to Ford, 'I am forced to entertain you like an old Woman with my Aylments.'[8] He found himself in the mood to muse, however, and later in the essay admitted that no cloister could seal out politics entirely. Almost subliminally, he betrays the sense of a wish to reach a wider public. His complaints to Ford suggest that his heaps of ecclesiastical business were not just burdens but obstacles, impeding him from some other endeavour.

The variations in Swift's mien resulted partly from his medical condition. The prolonged bouts of vertigo and deafness that came at least half-yearly might lay him out for weeks or even months on end; he would be lost in spinning caverns, full of silence or blurry sound. But when the attack abated, or at least when the giddiness receded, he could then return to being a sound-bodied, very fit man still only in his early fifties. He was also not above using his sickness tactically, in order to excuse himself to Vanhomrigh or cloying visitors; one acquaintance who made him increasingly ambivalent was a clingy, whinge-prone, self-serving and generally quite unreasonable local squire, Knightley Chetwode. Swift could disguise or exaggerate his physical weakness as the social moment required.[9]

He is captured quite differently by another formal portrait completed at about this time.[10] It was by Jervas yet again; but, whereas the earlier study of 1710 showed Swift primarily as clergyman, this later, richer and more generous interpretation depicts him as a literary personality – indeed a dignitary of letters. Swift is sitting at an angle to his desk, on which rest volumes of Lucan and Horace. The setting seems to be his 'closet', an intimate, in fact almost poky chamber. There is no hint of luxury; Swift, abhorring ostentation, would have said he had none to show. Yet there is still something quietly luminous about the seated figure, even though no trace of idealization is present in his features or the furnishings. He is manifestly older than the priest Jervas painted eight or nine years earlier; bewigged and plump-faced, the hemisphere of his chin rests in a collar of fat. His eyebrows have grown bristlier. There is even a hint of the stubborn beard that he was heard to liken complainingly to hog's hair. It is the face of a man you have seen in the pub, looking up from a newspaper as you brush past his table; and, where you might expect a huffy look of annoyance or even hostility, instead you catch a glimpse of unnerving intelligence, humanity and suspended humour. How Jervas has worked this into his canvas is hard to define. Swift's eyes are paler than sky-blue; his nose is straight, his gaze even, and there is just the slightest curl at each end of his mouth. The light catches the top of his high, domed brow, drawing attention to a hairline receding beneath the peaks of his long wig but also giving an almost angelic touch to his head, like a furled-up halo. The same light brings a sheen to his clerical coat.

This is neither Swift the doughty horseman nor the unfortunate chronic patient. There is no sign of beckoning, but none either of the prickliness those who knew him learned quickly to respect. This is a man of fascination and chaste charm – one who might be admired and loved. Jervas painted Swift this time as Johnson and Vanhomrigh appear to have seen him.

'Nor is the love I bear you only seated in my soul,' Vanhomrigh told him, at a time of great strain for her; 'for there is not a single atom of my frame that is not blended with it.'[11] A man so irascible and often so openly cynical about such statements made him an unlikely partner or idol for a woman who was so prepared to make them to him. Yet, while Swift always seems to have declined any settled physical relationship with Vanhomrigh, he could sometimes mirror her statements of passionate esteem in his own, more cautious manner. With the people to whom he was most attached, Johnson, Oxford and Sheridan being other key examples, Swift was willing to brave a profession of affection; but that did not change his basic fear of doing so. In general he followed the pattern he had set long ago with what now, if he ever thought of it, must have seemed a very slight and transitory connection: his liking for Jane Waring during his time as a young minister in the north of the country. The pattern was one of building directly loving words into ironic frameworks, dovetailing affectionate comments with jokes, or delivering them by means of an indirect compliment that needed reading backwards. Here and there, however, he did give way to profusion. In a long letter earlier in 1719 he set Vanhomrigh above all the female sex. Swift wrote impulsively in French, which he seems not to have checked, declaring how she embodied all that he could look for in a mortal: virtue, good sense, spirit, tenderness, '*l'agrément*', and strength of soul.[12] When he approached the verge of writing something similar in English, he almost always sounded edgy. The grief and perplexity Vanhomrigh expressed at his changes in tone, in writing and in person, not to mention his frequent silences of more than a month, are very understandable.

Swift still protested that his visits to her, his contact with her, had to be clandestine; and with this the visage of the urbane, gently superior being on Jervas's canvas falls away to reveal the priest tormented by the idea that he is behaving immorally, and scared of the humiliation that must follow disclosure. 'If you knew how many difficulties there are in sending letters to you, it would remove five parts in six of your quarrel,' was his snappish opening to a letter of August 1720. He continued rather unctuously by saying he would make no promises in future, so as to be better and not worse than his word.[13] On her side, Vanhomrigh was no more a simple victim than Swift was *un homme fatal*. In her surviving letters, Vanhomrigh adopts the tone of a wronged lover, but also seems to relish the pursuit involved in loving Swift, and the resistance it encountered. A fondness for pestering emerges on her side, as a defensive use of teasing does on his. The more he insisted on a necessary distance between them, the more she swore to be tenacious: 'I was born with violent passions, which terminate all in one – that inexpressible passion I have for you.'[14] She refused to take him as the fussy, anti-social, painstakingly moralistic middle-aged man he never disguised from her: to 'Vanessa', he would always be the elegantly maturing spirit depicted for posterity by Jervas. The violent feelings to which she attested possibly barred her from loving someone who would do her bidding quietly. Both, in their different ways, imply a certain painful pleasure in their ongoing struggle: Swift fleeing, Vanhomrigh advancing. In short, either party in the friendship is liable to be stereotyped – Swift as an abuser of affection, and Vanhomrigh as a bit of a stalker. The truth of the matter, if there can be a single truth to such things, will never be known.

Visiting her in town cost him agonies; while the price of not calling on her was a heavy conscience. In the spring of 1720 Vanhomrigh decided upon a tactical withdrawal. She and her ailing sister Mary ('Moll', 'Molkin' or 'Malkin' to Swift) began to spend most of their time at the country house in Celbridge. This lay within easy riding distance for Swift and his menservants when the miry roads and his health allowed, and also offered him a discreet approach to her door. A local rector, one Dr Arthur Price, had allegedly paid addresses to her, and Swift would surely have heard of an engagement with relief as well as a pang of regret; but Vanhomrigh spurned such attentions. Only Swift's would do, if her notes may be trusted. Soon after the move, Swift wrote to entertain her with a sheaf of verses by her 'friend' who was surely his own alter ego, Cadenus. The advice in the poem certainly sounds like his:

> Nymph, would you learn the onely Art
> To keep a worthy Lover's heart,
> First, to adorn your Person well,
> In utmost Cleanliness excel . . .

Disquietingly, Swift flirts with the role of lover he eschewed in reality, in a way that suggests an unhappy swirl of answering feelings on the part of his lonely reader. With the point about hygiene, Swift intended to puncture any pastoral illusions Vanhomrigh's country setting might have engendered: 'I reckon by now the Groves and Fields and purling Streams have made Vanessa Romantick, provided poor Molkin be well.'[15] Yet the

lines also recall the cruel and impossible demands he had warned Jane
Waring, long ago, that he would make of any spouse. Keeping his heart
was implicitly impossible; no woman – no earthly creature – would ever
fulfil his standards of 'utmost Cleanliness'. Except, perhaps, Stella –
Esther Johnson – and of course keeping her clean meant never touching
her. Far to the north, Jane Waring lived as a single woman, still in poor
health. She died later that year, as it happened, in November.[16]

<h1 style="text-align:center">2</h1>

Before the summer ended, a mutual acquaintance arrived in Dublin. In
August, Swift reported that 'Glass Heel' was in town. This was almost
certainly Swift's long-term filial correspondent Charles Ford, the former
Tory Gazetteer.[17] The glass heel referred to the fashionable footwear of any
self-respecting beau – heels of amber were also acceptable – and made a dig
at the priorities of the dapper, propertied bachelor. Since the collapse of
Oxford's ministry, Ford had toured the Continent and, when in London,
remained in close touch with Swift's old association of like-minded, bookish men. His visit brought questions for Vanhomrigh from a key operator
in Swift's former team, John Barber, the bookseller and alderman. Barber
had lent Vanhomrigh a considerable sum some years before, and Swift was
determined she should not worry about it. Barber was still a prominent,
indeed rising figure in municipal life, and his businesses were thriving. 'If
Heaven had lookt upon riches to be a valuable Thing,' Swift said of his
wealthy friend, 'it would not have given them to such a Scoundrel.' Vanhomrigh replied, speaking fondly of Swift's goodness and generosity, and
with touching joy at the prospect of a visit. She also mentioned how glad
Mary would be. Ford's estate at Woodpark in Meath, on the road to Trim,
would place him and Swift a short ride from the Vanhomrigh sisters' house.
The expectation in the summer heat was suffocating. Swift had elicited
raptures from Vanessa by imagining for her the long history that their
acquaintance could fill. The 'exact Chronicle of twelve years' would run
'from the time of spilling the Coffee to drinking of Coffee' through to the
present age with a chapter of 'hide, and whisper'.[18] Vulnerable, delighted
and demanding in the same breath, Vanhomrigh dashed off an ecstatic
note asking whether the idea of this history had 'crowded' on him spontaneously, or if he was just trying to please her.[19]

    The visit evidently took place, and passed happily. Swift, though, saw
mortal illness in the younger sister, Molkin Vanhomrigh. 'I am much con-

cerned,' he admitted. He recommended his own method for tackling ill-health and spleen – plenty of vigorous exercise, possibly not the best remedy for a case of consumption. He wrote from the deanery in a sombrely tender vein after a delay that was sheer anguish for his friend, the 'white witch'. Events were darkening the clouds of autumn: in London, stocks had gone into freefall, and he was relieved that Vanhomrigh had been prudent with her savings. Barber had taken Swift's hint as to his money and replied from London with assurances that since Mistress Vanhomrigh was a 'person of honour' she should give herself no trouble about the debt. On a point much more important to her, Swift promised gravely that his 'kindness and esteem' for her would never change. He pleaded yet again that she ought not to 'quarrel and be governor' – to become 'Huff', a character he sometimes imagined – when a few weeks passed without a letter. More words in the letter took on the eternal tone of the adulterer uttering genuine desire and regret for a lover he will never abandon everything to join. He expressed the wish to be with her, and appealed gruffly for sympathy. 'I am getting an ill head in this cursed town for want of exercise. I wish I were to walk with you fifty times about your garden, and then – drink your coffee. I was sitting last night with a score of both sexes for an hour and grew as weary as a dog.'[20] Vanhomrigh's sense of such expressions was achy and bewildered: she would never understand. Swift, she felt, could make his life – both their lives – better at any moment. Instead he chose to be a dog while the winter rains approached and her sister began to die.

References to coffee as code for something much more are everywhere in these letters. On reading them more than forty years later, Horace Walpole had no qualm in asserting that coffee meant sexual intercourse. The theory found many adherents over the years. Dedicated Swiftians, indeed, may also be divided into two camps, on the question of a carnal or a virgin dean. The arguments on both sides are compelling, though the equation of caffeine and sex reflects a somewhat unscholarly if altogether human wish for a trace of fulfilment in a somewhat bleak pattern of events. The same motivation on the part of his readers drove the search for evidence of a secret marriage between Swift and Esther Johnson. A Swift who married Stella and who 'lay with' Vanessa, in Walpole's phrase, also becomes a little easier to locate in the routine spectrum of drives and vices: he was a man who loved two women. Leo Damrosch, a recent biographer who favours the idea that Swift's love for Vanhomrigh was romantic and erotic, observes that coffee and sex were commonly associated, since some coffee-houses were regarded as 'temples of Venus'.[21] Swift could still, nevertheless, have exploited a bawdy undertone while writing of an experience that remained crushingly dissatisfying for Vanhomrigh. Drinking coffee was quite evidently something he expected her to do by herself.[22] Those who see Swift as asexual (such as Irvin Ehrenpreis) find that his only self-evident meaning in his talk of coffee is a perk, a peccadillo, a harmless buzz – the thrill provided by another kindred nature. There is much innuendo in the Swift–Vanessa letters, but innuendo rarely refers to a consummated urge. Accordingly, Swift has been understood as someone who adopted the tone and poise of a lover but resisted the deed – or even felt repelled by it. His sexuality apart, the notion of physical liaison with Vanhomrigh presented serious practical problems. It required a whole host of accomplices: Ford might be trusted to be silent, but her servants and even her sister perhaps could not. The role of Mary, or 'Molkin', is a further enigma: Swift speaks of having written to her as well as to Vanhomrigh, which recalls the often puzzling trio made up by Dingley in Swift's addresses to Johnson. As with Dingley, the constant third party may have acted as a sort of ventilator on the intimacy – and thus turned his more suggestive comments into mere gallantries; unless, that is, Molkin facilitated or even participated in whatever sexual play or contact might have passed between Swift and Vanhomrigh. At one point Swift upset Vanhomrigh by writing what she called a 'Love-Letter' to Molkin; but it is impossible to know whether taking it as such was mere archness on the part of all concerned, or something more.[23]

Whatever the deniers say, there is an unmistakable afflicted sexuality running through their correspondence. It is there in the sustained and direct pleas on Vanhomrigh's side – 'I am sorry my jealousy should hinder you from writing more love-letters'[24] – and, on Swift's, since his notes to her *were* evidently received as love-letters, with their provocative, burbling whispers of coded references, sometimes carrying messages from 'Cad', his alter ego Cadenus, sometimes speaking of Vanhomrigh as another person, 'Huff' or the 'Governor', with whom greater freedoms were possible. At moments he made his very obscurity carry a note of erotic intent: 'Cad bids me tell you, that if you complain of this puzzling you with difficult writing he will give you enough of it.'[25] The libidinous energy of the letters – teasing, pleading, threatening, punishing, sharing and consoling – is undeniable, so the possibility of a physical affair between them cannot be ruled out; and it is surely incredible that such manifest longing, obsessive attachment and guilt could have lasted so long if desire hadn't overpowered Swift's reluctance at least at moments in their drawn-out relationship.

It is the mystery, perhaps, that makes his connection with the two Esthers so fascinating. The pattern of contact with Vanhomrigh stayed as it had been since 1714 – irregular – unhappily for her. In October 1720 Swift invoked the usual obstacles as excuses for not repeating the visit to Celbridge. One of his reasons, though, was novel. 'Glass Heel' was taking up a great deal of his time. Ford, as Swift hoped Vanhomrigh must realize, was a walking expression of how complicated his position was. If Vanhomrigh was well acquainted with this funny urban single-ton, so too was Mistress Johnson; and Ford's fondness for word-games and the classics, his mixture of cheek and asceticism and (above all) his loyalty to the old Church establishment, put his character more in tune with hers than with the more wayward woman at Celbridge. Some years later, Ford entertained her and Dingley as his guests for half a year at his estate. A function of Swift's intimacy with Ford was presumably the extent to which he could be relied on to compartmentalize relations with the two women. For so far as Swift was concerned, there could be no interaction between them; and in this, presumably, he was protecting Johnson, or at least felt he was. Conceivably, he was obeying her. How-ever his relationship with Vanhomrigh fluctuated, theirs remained constant, based on almost daily meetings. This steadfastness was marked by a relatively new custom: every year since about 1719, Swift would write a birthday poem for Stella. An early exception had come in 1720, when an onset of giddiness prevented him from observing the ritual. He compensated for the lapse with a poem of thanks later in the year: 'To Stella, Visiting Me in My Sickness'. In this, he extolled her as perfection, stolen from heaven and transcending gender. He also gave a moving, good-humoured picture of her care:

> How would Ingratitude delight,
> And how would Censure glut her spite,
> If I should *Stella*'s Kindness hide
> In silence, or forget with Pride.
> When on my sickly Couch I lay,
> Impatient both of Night and Day,
> Lamenting in unmanly strains,
> Call'd every Pow'r to ease my Pains,
> Then Stella ran to my Relief
> With cheerful Face, and inward Grief;

> And, though by Heaven's severe decree,
> She suffers hourly more than me,
> No cruel Master could require
> From Slaves employ'd for daily Hire
> What *Stella*, by her Friendship warm'd,
> With Vigour and Delight perform'd.[26]

The lines to Johnson are self-deprecating and intimate in a way the letters to Vanhomrigh, though sometimes expostulatory, never are. The man lying on the couch can be frank about the suffering he causes with his groaning, because the offence is already forgiven. He tacitly accepts comparison with a 'cruel master', it seems, in exchange for the amnesty granted by Stella. Yet there are limits; one might not push the cause of her 'inward grief' (or Heaven's 'severe decree') beyond the immediate humorous circumstances.

Swift's verses for Johnson's birthday on 13 March 1721, though sprightly, arguably bear a touch of recent sorrow from Celbridge. Towards the end of February, Mary Vanhomrigh died, plunging her sister into a distress that Swift found difficult to counsel. Despite seeing Molkin so sick the summer before, he was shocked. He had seen both women in Dublin the previous weekend. 'I observed she looked a little ghastly,' he admitted, but her death seemed very sudden.[27] Another hiatus in contact with Vanhomrigh may have followed. His surviving letters to her from later in the year are solicitous about her health and state of mind, but also plead for her compassion. He asked her not to be cross. She must fight the spleen, he urged, as he did. 'The wisest men of all ages have thought it the best Course to seize the Minutes as they fly, and to make every innocent action' – he hesitated before settling on 'action', having entirely crossed out two earlier choices of word – 'an Amusement.' Were the pleasures of such harmless acts the 'coffee' of life? Regardless, 'without health you will lose all desire of drinking your coffee, and be so low as to have no Spirits.'[28]

Despite the segregation he enforced between Vanhomrigh and Johnson, the shadow of Molkin tinged his poem for Stella that March. Johnson was forty; and, he noticed now, mortal. Two years before, he had made a joke about the weight she had put on since her teens; how wonderful it would still be if the gods could split her into two people who each possessed half her wit, wisdom and beauty.[29] The poem for 1721 offered an elaboration on the theme of Stella's excellence outlasting physical decline. The poem is less finished than the earlier offerings;

but paints a miniature of his friend in just one line. For a second the jocundity of a mild conceit freezes, at the chastening glimpse of Stella with 'An angel's face, a little crackt'.[30]

Late in December 1719 Swift had told Ford that he had been writing only 'Verses . . . all Panegyricks'. He was being wryly inapt. Aside from the birthday poems, neither of his most considerable efforts were works of praise or celebration. Instead they were something like admonitions to the carnal community from which Swift purportedly excluded himself. The year 1719 was one of two grim satires published later but copied out by Johnson at about this time. The first, 'The Progress of Love', tells the story of a young woman who seems the very image of chastity until she elopes with the butler. The other, 'The Progress of Beauty', explores female trickery as the ruling principle of a woman's face and body. It opens with the moon, Diana, rising in a 'frouzy' mess, and then detects an exact parallel between her 'cloudy wrinckled Face' and the ruin of a 'nymph' called Celia:

> To see her from her Pillow rise
> All reeking in a cloudy Steam,
> Crackt Lips, foul Teeth, and gummy Eyes,
> Poor Strephon, how would he blaspheme![31]

Strephon is the generic swain who courts the nymph. The recurrence of 'crackt' in the later birthday poem would be upsetting if Swift didn't make it clear that Stella, unlike Celia, doesn't disguise the signs of age in her 'angel's face'. Stella might be unique among women at one extreme; yet Celia is surely singular at the other. Swift lavishes descriptive detail on her nightly process of self-reconstruction with the help of pencil, paint and brush, and a cementing coat of white lead. She is a prostitute, and she waits until midnight to leave her garret. The illusion of her beauty relies on her not being seen in daylight. 'She's wondrous fair!' cries one fop who sees her, behind glass, in the cabin of her chair. When the moonlight does eventually light up her 'rotting' figure, Swift reveals her as a wasting victim of syphilis – for whom total disintegration is the only final prospect. The threading of rhymes in Swift's quatrains makes Celia's fate seem all the more inevitable.

> No Painting can restore a Nose,
> Nor will her Teeth return again.
> Two Balls of Glass may serve for Eyes,

> White Lead can plaister up a Cleft,
> But these, alas, are poor Supplyes
> If neither Cheeks, nor Lips be left.[32]

For many critics over the past three centuries, the 'Progress of Beauty', along with the kindred poems Swift composed later on, is proof of a misogynistic and even depraved nature.[33] The 'Progress' may perhaps always be read as a condemnation of women using cosmetics, wrongfully leading men to find them beautiful. It mocks the right of those who are older and those who are branded by social convention as ugly to lead sexual lives. But if that was all there was to the 'Progress', it would be a much less strange and far more boring piece of work than the one we have. Instead, the 'Progress' and its later companion poems are fascinating exercises in diverse cruelty. Celia herself does not appear as an object of hate. She is presented as a being who needs her cosmetic camouflage in order to survive. Her physical disintegration is treated without any sentimentality, but not without a certain sympathy. She is who she is, even if she is a caricature; and Swift's target with that caricature seems not so much women as sexuality itself – or, more precisely, the limits to which people are prepared to deceive themselves for the sake of their libido. Swift's mature work repeatedly smashes down the walls people set up between their drives and emotions. In the *Travels*, he attacks cultural egotism about the superiority of human beings, spiritual and biological, by confronting his contemporaries with the image of the Yahoo: in effect, he said, 'Look, this animal is also human.' The 'Progress' is a work of similar provocation. In order for the human person to be sexually desirable, it must not be disgusting: but with 'rotting' Celia he forces upon readers an image that is both appalling and sexual – and leaves individuals to sort out the resulting psychological mess for themselves. Celia's disguise is ultimately maintained, he suggests, by a mass social hypocrisy: a willingness to tolerate deceptive appearances for the sake of securing sex on demand. For Swift's final stanza points out that the only way of putting Celia out of business is for there to be an impossibly constant supply of fresh 'Nymphs' (that is, young prostitutes).

> Ye Pow'rs who over Love preside,
> Since Mortal Beautyes drop so soon,
> If you would have us well supplied,
> Send us new Nymphs with each new Moon.[34]

With this ironic invocation Swift recognized the lengths to which pro-curers of women were willing to go to replenish their market. Far from condemning women as innately deceitful or concupiscent, these lines are surely more a denunciation of the voracious sex trade – with power and relevance in our age of 'human trafficking' as much as in Swift's. Even if new nymphs were to reach London's brothels 'with each new Moon' – those 'supplies', Swift is saying, would be insufficient to make Celia redundant, or to stop an aroused male from convincing himself she is 'wondrous fair'.

The stance on prurience in the 'Progress' has an added force because Swift was criticizing the degenerate extremes of a drive he had rejected, it seems, more or less entirely. He was not writing as the potential cus-tomer of an afflicted woman such as Celia, or any prostitute, but as the celibate – or more or less celibate – Dean of St Patrick's. Guilt about any sporadic lapses, on his rare visits to Vanhomrigh, would surely only have reinforced this position with an element of muted self-chastisement. By the time he became a Dublin legend, Swift was well known for support-ing disabled and disfigured women beggars who peddled trinkets or sweet-breads or plied some other innocent trade. The 'Progress' is a demonstration of what he felt such women should have been spared.

3

The bid for England had failed. When it sank in that his future would keep him in Ireland, Swift had sworn that he would have nothing to do with domestic politics. A little later he had reiterated this vow against 'meddling' in Irish business in a letter to Ford.[35] His seclusion from broader campaigning had been highly expedient in the frightening atmosphere of 1714–16, though it always had a touch of what to Van-homrigh he called Mistress Huff. He was giving the cold shoulder to public life in Ireland and, if anyone was paying attention, England too. Politics, however, was to draw Swift slowly back into the open. The Whigs pressed on with aggressive reforms to Church and State. The Jaco-bites continued to make noises off. Swift's friend Atterbury, Bishop of Rochester, was now up to his neck in English operations on behalf of the Pretender. Bolingbroke had repented of his impulsive flight to the men-dicant Jacobite Court; he was negotiating for a return to England, asserting his loyalty to Hanover and in the meantime trying to make some money from investments in French stocks. In England a Jacobite

plot went ahead. A large sum of money was raised to buy, as the Jacobites thought, Swedish assistance in another expedition to England. The
plans faltered, but then, thanks to a covert visit to Madrid by the Duke
of Ormond, proceeded with Spanish backing. Protestant weather saved
England yet again; the Jacobite fleet was wrecked off Finisterre. However, the government soon faced a tempest of its own in the form of a
gigantic financial implosion. The 'South Sea Bubble' would claim the
careers and even lives of several leading ministers.

For Swift, the unprecedented collapse in stocks in the autumn of 1720
and its terrible public impact vindicated all his old prejudices. The 'Bubble' has significance for his work beyond his immediate responses to the
public impact of the immediate crisis. In the *Examiner* he had many
times decried the idea of basing an economy on credit rather than on
property – or, in contemporary parlance, on 'money' rather than on 'land'.
The Tories, as we know, in his mind stood for land; the Whigs for money.
Yet the realities of public finance since the late seventeenth century, in
particular the runaway expense of warfare, meant that no state (as now)
could function without considerable private credit; and it was a Tory
lord treasurer, Swift's leader, Oxford, who had authorized the founding
of the South Sea Company in 1710. The company's charter was based
on a simple enough deal: in return for a monopoly on South Sea trade
– soon opened up by the gains of Utrecht – the South Sea Company
would take over a proportion of the national debt. This relieved the
burden on the Bank of England, and also siphoned some of the bank's
profits away from its Whiggish board members. For seven years, the
company traded on fairly conservative lines, aided by the steady growth
in liquid capital that followed the Peace. Then, in 1718, its directors
made a bid to take over the entirety of the national debt, and to pay a
handsome fee, in addition, for the privilege.

Though sorely tempted, the King's ministers dared not place national
finances in effect under the roof of a single trading house; though they
did still grant the South Sea Company a vastly increased share of the
debt. No British corporation, not even the old East Indian firm, had ever
betted so substantially on its own fortunes. The South Sea directors were
inspired, though, by the success of the Scots banker John Law in France,
where the sale of debt had resulted in an instant boom. Viscount Bolingbroke was one of a great many enriched by the French Mississippi
Company on the back of Law's luck; and he had the sense to cash in his
winnings. In London, the South Sea board relied on countless investors,
big and small, putting in the funds needed to cover the debt in return for

stock that only soared in value. They removed any ceiling on the company's potential profits by conveniently setting no limit on the amount of stock they would be entitled to sell in exchange for the annuities. The price of company shares thus rose towards the heavens; thousands of dependent speculative ventures also sprang up, so quickly that in June 1720 the government passed an emergency 'Bubble Act' prohibiting unauthorized companies exploiting South Sea capital. It was too late. In August the stocks began to decline, and in the autumn they plummeted. The trades dependent on the stocks, in the now familiar web, soon also faced ruin.

Swift's sympathies for the victims of the bubble were strictly rationed. His first concern was for the Irish investors deprived of their entire incomes, and for the craft-workers and labourers who faced dispossession and starvation in consequence. Like many in Ireland, his anger was sharpened by further legislative tyranny at Dublin and Westminster. The year 1719 saw a further penal law passed that sanctioned a felon's branding for unauthorized Catholic priests; a strong body of opinion was in favour of castrating them. Efforts to repeal or at least relax the old laws blocking exports of Irish livestock, cloth and other produce were strictly rebuffed. A Tillage Bill, requiring owners to cultivate a (very modest) proportion of harvestable land, was quashed, in order to protect the vast imports of English grain. Worst of all, though, was the Declaratory (or Dependency) Act of April 1720, which now at last explicitly set out Ireland's status as a colony – subject not only to the monarch but also to the 'Lords and Commons of Great Britain'. The Act brutally determined the key point that William Molyneux had contested many years earlier: that while a monarch living in England might hold sovereignty over Ireland, the Parliament at Westminster did not. Now, ruled Westminster, it did.[36] And not only the Irish legislature but also the judiciary was effectively rendered lame, since, as with its English equivalent, the Irish House of Lords sat as the highest court in the land. The Irish Lords' judgements now counted for very little, since their counterparts in England could technically overrule them.

Swift, along with Archbishop King, was indignant, and their mutual anger made their alliance firm at last. Typically, though, Swift did not blame his younger friend Ford for the lack of empathy and understanding he displayed on the matter. When Swift wrote to Ford in early April, he was just recovering from a fit of giddiness that had forced him to lie down for five hours on the night of a dinner he had given in the deanery. He had called on one of the Grattan brothers to deputize as host while he lay miserable upstairs. Thus, on taking up Ford's latest letter and reading his 'friendly expostulations', he lacked the spleen to be cross with one he always treated as a favoured nephew. 'I believe my self not too guilty of veneration for the Irish House of Lords,' he admitted, 'but I differ from you in politics. The question is whether People ought to be slaves or no.'[37] This quiet, confidential sentence is all the more striking for bypassing issues of custom, law or propriety, principles to which Swift usually appealed. Here he had gently but directly referred the matter to a basic ethical question. Or, to adapt the academic jargon Gulliver uses in urging the King of Lilliput not to make a province of the neighbouring kingdom of Blefuscu, he adduced the 'topicks' of 'justice' rather than 'policy'.[38] It marked the beginning of a new period.

The bursting of the bubble in 1720 made the incapacitation of Ireland all the more terribly obvious. Previous embargos on Irish products had to some extent stimulated invention. Yet, unlike England, the country had virtually no means of reviving or at least patching up its economy, and no power of redress against the corrupt financiers. Given its newly declared dependent status, any measures the Irish government took to boost or protect the kingdom's trade would be interpreted as competitive acts against England. In response, late in May 1720 Swift burst back on to the scene of public writing with an incendiary pamphlet offering *A Proposal for the Universal Use of Irish Manufacture*.

The essay picked up an idea advanced more innocently many years earlier: that Irish people should only wear garments manufactured in Ireland. This was made an act of defiance, with the added benefit of discouraging immodest foreign dress, which Swift would regularly encourage in future years.[39] The title of 'A Proposal' suggests a return to one of his favoured early modes, the mock-expert thesis; but the text itself, short and explosive, takes on the voice of someone more like a tavern wit. His persona rattles sharply and at times a bit haphazardly between topics and angles on topics. The aim is less to spell out a point than to deliver a punchline, which he does unerringly. The central tenet is delivered early on: 'Upon the whole, and to crown all the rest, let a firm Resolution be taken, by *Male* and *Female*, never to appear with one single *Shred* that comes from *England*; *and let all the People say, Amen.*' But the real business of the piece is in branching off from this idea to recount pithy anecdotes and set up shrewd witticisms. The essay rasps in its unbowing pursuit of causes the author knew to be lost and measures he knew were impracticable. There was little good in calling on the newly disabled Irish Houses of Parliament to pass resolutions against the wearing of imported clothes, declarations that would be immediately quashed by Westminster; and the Irish cloth-making industry was actually in no state to cope with the demands of quantity and quality the 'universal use' of native goods would place upon it. Such realities were beside the point, which was to rouse the town with a splendid entertainment and an appeal to basic justice. Absentee landlords, English legislators, English tradesmen whining disgracefully about the 'impositions' Ireland placed on their trade, imported bishops and Whiggish ex-military 'adventurers' all got a lash of Swift's whip; but so did dim-witted Irish shopkeepers and their customers for fetishizing the 'fopperies' brought in from a nation Swift came close to declaring an enemy. The attitude gelling the patchwork of remarks is the barfly's demand that all his hearers should be able to take a joke. So some gentle fun is even had at the expense of Swift's now staunch ally, Archbishop King, who had led the way by going out 'clad head to foot in our own manufacture'. Since the Proposer had already admitted that the Irish wares would need a good deal of improvement before his plan could take full effect, this was tantamount to saying that the Archbishop was willing to risk ridicule in badly made and ill-fitting clothes for the sake of his country-people's welfare. But this was a decoy before the real sting was launched: 'under the Rose be it spoken, *his Grace deserves as good a Gown, as if he had not been born among us.*' Here, spoken in binding sincerity (*sub rosa*), were words aimed at Ireland's blown-in English clergy – the likes indeed of Bishops Evans and Nicholson.[40]

As Swift knew full well, the worthies of the town who were loyal to England would be quite incapable of taking such a joke. A show of good humour, indeed, might be viewed as treasonous. Containing the strength of protest on the back of the Declaratory Act was a massive task for the Act's supporters on the Irish Privy Council, in Dublin's Parliament and courts. They might have brushed off the *Proposal* as mere banter – self-evidently the work of Dean Swift, as Bishop Nicholson observed – but instead they took the bait. Viscount Midleton, the Irish Lord Chancellor, 'took alarm' and set legal proceedings in motion. Swift's printer Edward Waters found himself in court for sedition. His trial was held in the 'large and fine building' housing the 'old' Four Courts, in the grounds of Christ Church – about which, the leading praiser of the city later conceded sheepishly, 'nothing more can be said, but that there has been and is now good Lawyers and fine Orators', even though the law courts were now 'in a manner only form'.[41] Vestigial though they might be in any case weighing English against Irish authority, the sessions could still be dramatic. Waters's trial was sensational for the corruption of proceedings. Swift recorded how the near-apoplectic Chief Justice, William Whitshed, displayed remarkable stamina in forcing the jury. '[He] sent them back nine times, and kept them eleven hours, until being perfectly tired out, they were forced to leave the matter to the mercy of the Judge, by what they call a special Verdict.' Whitshed's conduct was saddening, Swift reflected, since in cases involving no conflict of party or nation he had always been a good judge. At one point in Waters's trial the Chief Justice had gone so far as suddenly to declare, hand on heart, that the 'author's [that is, Swift's] design was to bring in the Pretender'. There was no mention made of the Chevalier James anywhere in Swift's text. But for printing the 'factious and virulent pamphlet' Waters was sent to prison.[42]

Swift, who remained untouched despite his authorship being an open secret, felt obliged to get Waters out; and the stress of canvassing for his release forms the background to his correspondence with Vanhomrigh in the same period. Visiting her at Celbridge evidently provided some much needed joy and relief. He lobbied Lord Molesworth, a firm Whig who was nevertheless in agreement with him over the outrage of the Declaratory Act; and also applied to an old Tory colleague, Sir Thomas Hanmer, the Speaker of the House of Commons in the time of Harley and St John, and, conveniently, father-in-law of the incoming Lord Lieutenant, Charles Fitzroy, Duke of Grafton. His appeals involved swallowing some reservations and past resentments. Swift had burned Hanmer's name with a magnifying glass at Letcombe Bassett in 1714; and he marked down the Duke of Grafton as 'almost a slobberer without one good quality', but he at least proved malleable;[43] and some months later Waters was set free on Grafton's personal orders.

Quite unlike the leaders he admired – Harley, St John, Atterbury – Swift refused to accept collateral human damage as a consequence of his own actions. In rescuing Waters he proceeded with his characteristic grouchy humaneness. In some respects, as Swift indirectly admitted in his account of the ordeal, the campaign for Waters was an easier fight than others he had taken on. Swift reckoned that his *Proposal* had proved 'agreeable to the sentiments of the whole nation', and the support he received from a grandee such as Molesworth suggests he was right. The row over the court case obviously gave the pamphlet still more publicity than it might otherwise have won; and the strange, magical by-product of its comedy was to put Irish citizens of different party loyalties in agreement on its basic stance. There is a risk of overstatement, but the pamphlet opened a channel of understanding between Swift and Whigs with whom he had previously had no common ground on Church politics, his first concern. As he explained in the same 'letter' in which he gave his view of the Whitshed–Waters debacle, an English Whig 'is a creature altogether different from those of the same denomination here'. He recalled how Joseph Addison, an English Whig and a man of the finest calibre, had been appalled by the brutish and anti-clerical profaners who greeted him as a kindred spirit during his time as Wharton's Irish secretary. He was being inconsistent, of course, since Addison was an individual he considered altogether an exception. But, supporting the distinction, another friend pointed out to him that the Anglo-Irish breed of Whigs got their irreligious, 'fanatical genius' because they were descendants of 'Cromwell's soldiers, adventurers establish'd here, who were all of the sourest Leven'. These were tough, uncompromising, single-minded soldiers' children who saw no paradox in taking land from its inhabitants and then defending it as their own. They were not all ungodly, in fact, but they were mostly Dissenters. Yet the spirit of the Good Old Cause, the disdain for overlords who trampled on the rights of commoners, was exactly the energy Swift evoked in his essay on Irish manufactured goods. Such Whigs would have no doings with Swift's Anglican Church, but they might follow his lead on the rights of their adopted country. Swift also noted that since there were so few prizes left to contend for on the basis of party, 'the great motive of quarrelling was at an end'.[44] In April 1721 he noted to Ford that 'many of the violent Whigs profess themselves perfect Jacobites' in reaction to England's treatment of Ireland.[45]

A legitimate question exists as to what Swift even meant when he spoke up for Ireland. Swift is often understood to have defended the Anglo-Irish establishment rather than the common people of Ireland. True though this point is, it still calls for qualification. In his earlier works defending the English 'landed' interest he might equally be charged, from a modern democratic perspective, with having little thought for the millions of labourers who made up the great majority in England. Far from flinching at this accusation, Swift might even have failed to see the criticism that, for modern democrats, the remark essentially entails. His *early*-modern conception of 'country' was really one of a social order regulated by a balance of Crown, Church, commons and nobles. The 'lower sort' – that is, the majority of people alive at the time – were assumed to benefit from a prosperous balance between the three old estates of the realm. This was, in fact, a guarantee of national liberty.

But what this actually involved, for Swift himself, was more or less the most generous settlement he could conceive of bestowing. He didn't view Ireland as a mere extension of England or a reservoir of property and raw produce. He defended Ireland as a kingdom that was entitled to the same rights and benefits as those enjoyed by the inhabitants of its 'sister' English kingdom.

This defence in any case largely took the form of a sustained barrage against the Irish Ascendancy itself for the inane laws and customs it allowed. Swift's *Proposal* of 1720 consists predominantly of an attack on the stupidity of those running the island. 'It is the peculiar Felicity and Prudence of the People in this Kingdom,' it began verbosely, 'that whatever Commodities, or Productions, lie under the greatest Discouragements from England, those are what they are sure to be most industrious in cultivating and spreading.' Instead of promoting agriculture, penal laws forbade the cultivation of land for tillage; vast tracts were converted to pasture for wool that couldn't be sold. The criticism of the Irish might easily be countered as unjust: these measures were imposed, after all, by the will of English interests. Yet the standard of fairness and wisdom Swift invokes in this opening paragraph is the statute law of England, which strictly provided for the encouragement of agriculture, as the basis of a self-sufficient state; and this is the level of protection, he implies, that ought to be extended to Ireland and all who lived there.[46] Putting everyone in Irish woollens to use up the surplus was a desperate remedy, an absurdity even, which only signified how far out of order the country had grown.

Thousands in Ireland lived permanently in danger of starvation, and Swift was in no doubt where the immediate blame lay. Here is the voice of the Dean of St Patrick's in the cathedral pulpit:

A great Cause of this Nation's Misery, is that Egyptian Bondage of cruel, oppressing, covetous Landlords, expecting that all who live under them should *make Bricks without Straw*, who grieve and envy when they see a Tenant of their own in a whole Coat, or able to afford one comfortable Meal in a Month, by which the Spirits of the People are broken, and made for Slavery; the Farmers and Cottagers, almost through the whole Kingdom, being to all intents and Purposes as real Beggars, as any of those to whom we give our Charity in the Streets.[47]

Yet a regular theme, developed in the same sermon, was the imbecile addiction to luxuries, especially the fancy goods brought in from abroad, which Swift's *Proposal* labelled 'fopperies'. Widespread beggary and fashion-led pretension were perversely allied in Swift's mind, as they were for like-minded conservatives. Swift had the hatred of an Eliza-bethan Puritan towards such items and the vices of pride, vanity and lust they fostered. Compelling the Irish to wear second-rate goods manufac-tured at home thus had the extra spiritual benefit of an act of penance.

As for the response to Swift simultaneously indicting English tyranny and Irish passiveness, there was little doubt. A great cross-section of the Irish public, 'native' and 'colonial', took him as their own. He became their defender, soon known to many purely as 'The Dean': 'the pamphl-et, proposing the universal use of Irish manufactures within the kingdom, had captivated all hearts . . . He was looked upon with pleas-ure and respect as he passed through the streets.'[48] Apotheosis as the 'Hibernian Patriot' was just a few years away; but, more importantly, with respect to Swift's view of life about him, his loyalty to Ireland had been tested so far that it finally broke loose from his standard rhetorical posture of contempt towards his homeland. He maintained both for the rest of his days, regardless of the contradiction: a disdainful air and a militant affection.

The knock-on effects of the South Sea crisis, which wiped out savings and mortgages across Ireland, threatened this dejected kingdom not only with a major depression but widespread famine. At the end of 1720 Swift decided to make his literary presence felt once more, at the source of the problem. Ten days before Christmas Swift sent a long poem to Ford in London. As with the *Proposal*, his goal was provocation. On unsealing Swift's letter in his lodgings at the Blue Periwig, Ford unfolded the verses written close together in two columns on the sheets within; 'as correct,' said Swift, 'as I can make it.' He directed Ford to forward the text, copied in an unknown hand, to a printer who might then, he said airily, 'do what he pleases'. Despite the aristocratic gesture, he made it plain to Ford that he had worked hard on the poem and wanted it care-fully printed.[49]

He was writing now about the South Sea debacle. Swift had no reser-vations about criticizing the greed and gullibility of the investors, but he also captured the public mood in singling out the company directors as the villains of the story. In Swift's lively poem 'The Bubble' (or 'Upon the South Sea Project', as it was titled in many printings), the little fish in this polluted sea of speculation are guilty of devouring other little fish; but the directors are the whales that 'eat up all'. 'The Bubble' is also a poetic critique of the very concept of a stock market. The voice that presides at the beginning of the piece is that of a mountebank, stirring up the punt-ers: Swift's charlatan invites us to drop a coin in a pot and watch it increase in size the more water is poured over it.

> Thus in a Basin drop a Shilling,
> Then fill the Vessel to the Brim,
> You shall observe as you are filling
> The pond'rous Metal seems to swim;
>
> It rises both in Bulk and Height,
> Behold it mounting to the Top,
> The liquid Medium cheats your Sight,
> Behold it swelling like a Sop.

The confidence people placed in South Sea money was nothing less than the avaricious faith required to believe in the notion of this ballooning silver soufflé. Swift comes back to the optical illusion of objects magni-fied by water later in the poem. The chinking of sweaty coins in eager pockets rings loud throughout the performance, as Swift brings earth-quake and tidal wave to London's stock-jobbing hideouts. The chief coffee-houses are all hit, and so is the den of traders in the alley opposite the fine, arcaded and utterly panic-stricken Royal Exchange:

> There is a Gulph where thousands fell,
> Here all the bold Advent'rers came;
> A narrow Sound, though deep as Hell:
> CHANGE ALLY is the dreadful Name.[50]

'The Bubble' offered readers in London the delight of an imagined, apocalyptic revenge: Ford saw to it that the poem was brought out by Benjamin Tooke in January 1721. It was quickly reprinted in Dublin, where an avid readership waited. With this Swift made his own work the butt of a dig he had made against publications imported from London in his *Proposal* of the previous year. 'It is wonderful to observe the Biass among our People in favour of *Things*, *Persons*, and *Wares* of all Kinds that come from *England*. The *Printer* tells his *Hawkers*, that he has got an *excellent new Song just brought from London*.'[51] In 'The Bubble' Swift made no distinction between the plight of the English and Irish gamblers who had been brought up short by the crisis: an equal measure of blame was applied to all, and the main condemnation reserved for the company board. Implicitly, the Court and ministry were also accused: for key members of both the government and the royal family were guilty of insider-dealing, and neither the public nor the Commons were in much doubt as to who they were. It was all too much, in any case, for one leading minister, Secretary Stanhope. A former general in the wars with France, Stanhope had weathered almost every sort of fight the age might throw at a person. He had survived Marlborough's battlefields unscathed, and had been passionately involved as a denouncer of High Church hypocrisy in the trial of Sacheverell. The only assault he proved unable to throw off was the charge of being a cheat. He collapsed and died of a stroke in early February; predeceasing Marlborough, his old commander, who was also slowly dying. Stanhope had been expected to succeed him as the King's captain-general.

While the ministry found itself encircled and bewildered, in Dublin Swift decided that his own name also needed clearing. Early in January 1721, as 'The Bubble' became required rebel reading, Swift allowed his pen to vent some of the grievances he had nursed during six years of silence. He wrote an essay defending himself against the contradictory accusations mentioned earlier, insisting he was neither Whig nor Jacobite. In it he declared his support for the Glorious Revolution, his support for an annual Parliament, his reverence for the memory of Queen Anne, his opposition to the 'moneyed interest', his adherence to *habeas corpus*; and reflected dourly that he would never lose a thought on the major politicians of the day 'while there is a cat or spaniel in the house'.[52] Though set forth with magnificent offhand panache, these words were not exactly true; nor was his wish to live peacefully in obscurity. He gave the essay the form of a letter to Pope, whom he saw as a fellow sufferer charged wrongly with sinning for wit; but he suppressed it, and twenty years later Pope confirmed that he had never received it. The letter exuded a sense of victimhood understandable in a man often struck with deafness and vertigo, but which didn't tally with the vigorous political offensive he had led over the previous eight months.

## 4

In the way of old cities, the people who shared a trade in Dublin tended to cluster together in the same streets and neighbourhoods. Close to St Patrick's, in streets built to the west of the cathedral over the later decades of the seventeenth century, communities of weavers had settled. Historically the area had long pulled in crafts-people and trade because, for a time, by living in the liberties they were not obliged to join a guild; nor were they accountable to the Dublin Corporation.[53] At this time, though, the substantial cluster of cloth-workers near the cathedral close put Dean Swift in the vicinity of some of those hit hardest by the financial crash. Early in April 1721 Archbishop King estimated that 1,700 families, or about 6,000 people, were in danger of starving for want of trade and employment. Swift noted that this estimate excluded the droves that had left Ireland to find work abroad. The total number of those affected by the crash in Dublin would therefore be much greater. The number had, admittedly, been reduced by the outbreak of a lethal fever in the city's poorer neighbourhoods in the spring of 1720. King's figure was officially accepted, and Dublin Castle allotted £100 towards their relief; a token sum, but enough to stimulate others. Special collections were held in churches around Dublin, and a benefit performance of *Hamlet* put on at Dublin's Theatre Royal on 1 April. The play's pervading mood of 'something rotten' in the state reflected public feeling perfectly. The playhouse, a regular site of tumult, was located in Smock Alley, down by the river on Blind Quay.[54] Swift seems not to have attended in person, but did compose an epilogue for the occasion; it was twinned with a prologue by Sheridan.

> Who dares affirm this is no pious age,
> When Charity begins to tread the Stage:
> When Actors, who at best are hardly Savers,
> Will give a Night of Benefit to Weavers?

Both poems read out in the theatre picked up on the idea that Irish people should wear only Irish cloth. An anonymous 'Answer' was printed shortly afterwards, mocking the notion that women could ever be persuaded to give up their foreign-made finery.[55] But on this point Swift was becoming dogmatic: when a kingdom was reduced to rags, he told Ford, its people had no choice but to wear them.[56]

Those among his acquaintance who had escaped ruin – and who lived beyond earshot of starving families – were beginning to complain of ennui about the crisis. Bubble fatigue was setting in. Comfortable now in his Duke Street home, yet seriously weakened by asthma, the poet and diplomat Matthew Prior wrote to Swift that 'I am tired with politics and lost in the South Sea.' Old poets were correct, he added, in comparing the howling of the waves to the cries of the mob.[57] However they pained him, the begging appeals Swift heard in the streets were in many ways preferable to the noises of water-wheels and cataracts that filled his head when deafness overtook him. He stood out from friends in the Scriblerus crew or the wider Tory 'Society of Brothers' for his engagement. Writing from France in high summer that year, Bolingbroke chid him for getting involved. Bolingbroke hoped the weavers and judges would go after Swift in person the next time he tried 'to talk sense or do good to the Rabble'. He may have stung Swift's sense of valour by alluding to his 'proxy', Waters the printer, recently released, who needed 'iron ribs' to endure the trouble Swift had brought him; but his point was that Swift should never even have dirtied his hands in the business. Such words came easily enough now to Bolingbroke, who had purchased a chateau at La Source, near Orléans, with his gains from the Mississippi Company. (His indirect benefactor, John Law, was now on the run and reported to be hiding in Copenhagen.) Bolingbroke was fond too of the palatial family home of his new wife, the Marquise de Villette, delightfully situated near Nogent-sur-Seine in the Aube region.

Bolingbroke wrote learnedly yet breezily to his 'Dear Jon', discoursing on Plato, Tacitus, Horace and his beloved Cicero; and he urged the Dean not to become too preoccupied with money. Throughout a correspondence that would stretch nearly twenty years into the future, Bolingbroke urged on Swift the virtues of fortitude, satisfaction with retirement, and the joys of friendship. He did so now even while working hard to regain his English estates and the right to return to public life at home. 'I mourn for Ireland,' he told Swift, 'but I pity you more.' Ireland, he pronounced, with vivid contempt, was like the bruised Indian servant of a colonial master who had cut his own throat.[58] For Swift, whose early half-unwilling hero-worship for Bolingbroke never disappeared, such airs were a necessary part of the former minister's aristocratic, cavalier persona. He welcomed the opportunity to write back with his finest courtly bearing, to quibble over points of Latin metre and post-Socratic thought, and he relished doing so all the more to one who offered such a strong link to the time when Dr Swift had 'credit' in the highest places. And Bolingbroke's views in fact gave Swift the chance to ply contrary arguments on teaching and protecting 'the rabble', and thereby to understand his own position better.

Swift's round of usual business with the cathedral and his growing commitments to public causes still left time spare. On visits to the country especially, there were long hours alone, when he was well, that could be filled by reading in an armchair. A good memory for phrases – rather than dates and figures – and decades of brow-beating at school and university kept the classics alive in his mind. As he told Vanhomrigh, he was also more than willing to dip into works he happily denounced afterwards as 'trash'. His reading at this time suggested a strong interest in travel-writing. In 1720 he had read Thomas Herbert's *Relation* of his voyages to Africa and the Middle East. The book was published almost a century earlier: Herbert was modestly famous in history as the nervous guardian appointed by Parliament as Charles I's 'secretary' during the martyred King's last months. Herbert periodically embellished the account he had written of his travels as a younger man. With savage relish, Swift made a note in his copy of the *Relation* that 'if the book were stript of its Imper-tinence, Conceitedness and tedious Digressions, it would be almost worth reading.'[59] Yet the *Relation* clearly influenced and informed Swift's imagin-ation in the sea-allegories of 'The Bubble'. Another source amid the many travel-books he read is entirely possible, but he seems indebted, for exam-ple, to Herbert's sighting of shoals of flying fish, leaping in such multitudes that at times they 'darkened the body of the sun'. Herbert describes the fish – 'beautiful in its eye, the body, though no larger than a small herring yet big enough for those complemental fins, which so long as moist serve as wings' – in contexts of dead calm and piracy, both of which have echoes in Swift's poem.[60] Exploiting the descriptive precision Herbert's text afforded him, Swift likened these flyers to subscribers leaping for South Sea benefits, even as predators lurk above and below:

> So fishes rising from the Main
> Can soar with moistned Wings on high;
> The moisture dry'd, they sink again,
> And dip their Fins again to fly.[61]

The natural detail preoccupied Swift more here, it seems, than tidying the verse. One can see how Pope or Addison, for example, might have questioned the entirely colloquial yet still slightly loose repetition of 'again' in the quatrain.

Such details were signs of open-eyed, pragmatic interest in his sur-roundings, his aversion to the abstract and the arcane. For quite some years now Swift had been mentioning travel plans. Invitations to Eng-land stood constantly open, and he had also thought a trip to some Continental spa, perhaps the one at Aix-la-Chapelle, might be good for his condition. Yet, because of business, ill-health and some trepidation about venturing on to Whig-controlled English soil, he had never acted on these vague intentions. His interest in Irish landscape and geography suggests the pleasure he might have taken in visiting foreign lands; and, as he neared his mid-fifties, he may have wondered if he would get the chance to see more of the world. The spare-time reading of travel books such as Herbert's was also, though, a course of research for a literary project that was slowly taking shape in his mind and, more gradually still, on paper. These informal researches took in works of greater pedigree. In the midst of the struggle over the *Proposal for the Universal Use of Irish Manufacture*, Swift concluded a retrospective of Herodotus, undertaken many years since he had first read through *The Histories*. As with Herbert's *Relation*, he felt compelled to put his verdict, dated 6 July 1720, on the title-page of the century-old Genevan edition in his library. He praised Herodotus, the 'pater Historicum', for his neutrality and fairness, and the power of his judgements to communicate both moral and political wisdom to a discerning reader. He did admit, though, that the volume of detail and digressions could get slightly tedious at times.[62]

The rereading of Herodotus was highly relevant to the incipient work on which Swift meditated; for the father of history, in drawing on his own exploration of the eastern Mediterranean, is also the father of travel-writing. Touches from Herodotus would find their way into Swift's text in myriad and often paradoxical forms – such as the distinctly Scythian practice of the Houyhnhnms in the collection of Yahoo-skins, which seems to draw on customs observed in Herodotus's fourth book. The two main lessons, positive and negative, Swift seems to have taken on returning to the *Histories* were the importance of a credible, unbiased narrator or chronicler, and of keeping the material on track. The first surviving sign that Swift was actually applying these lessons to a book of his own, one that would be both a memoir and a travelogue, dates from mid-April 1721. At the end of the letter fulminating to Ford on the fate of the Irish weavers, Swift announced: 'I am now writing a History of my Travells, which will be a large Volume, and gives Account of Countryes hitherto unknown; but they go on slowly for want of Health and Humour.'[63] Seven years of confinement in Ireland had sent Swift's imagination wandering over horizons that were invisible, as yet, to any other inhabitant of the earth. Later on he would be addressed, by admirers, enviers and loathers alike, as 'Dean Gulliver'. His letter to Ford suggests that, at least at the outset, he had identified himself with his still nameless voyager. The first samples from this work in progress would reach chosen friends over the next twelve months.

The year 1721 also put Swift at loggerheads again with his diocesan in Meath, the irascible Evans. Neither man learned anything new about the other from the confrontation. Swift memorably characterized the Welsh bishop as uniting the 'hasty passion' of his countrymen with 'the long, sedate resentment of a Spaniard'.[64] Quite oppositely, his relationship with Archbishop King, tested and perhaps proven by earlier disagreements, had strengthened into further mutual respect, confidence and indeed friendship. Swift was prepared to admit that King must now almost pass for a Tory. Their cooperation was born of necessity: so few allies of any real authority or strength existed that each man realized the other's trust could not be squandered. Their separate, yet concurring statements and initiatives during the plight of the weavers confirmed a common purpose in civic affairs. They found themselves broadly in agreement too on opposing an initiative to found a National Bank of Ireland: it was an idea Swift in particular would have found entirely comic were it not for the risk he saw in it, namely of presenting brokers and swindlers with another great opportunity to ruin honest people. In a chatty and humorous letter to King in September, Swift sympathized with the Archbishop's near-solitary opposition to the bank in the Irish House of Lords. They clearly now conversed as two hoary, jaded warriors for their faith. 'I am a plain man,' Swift told his superior – one who would gladly see fifty bishops hanged if he might have prolonged the life of one lost colleague of the old stamp. He returned witticisms from His Grace about the qualities of female company – quite possibly King was teasing him about his liaisons with Johnson and Vanhomrigh: 'I am afraid the clatter of young ladies' tongues,' he answered coolly, 'is no very good cure for a giddiness in the head.' Then he ended the letter grimly, breaking off an anecdote with a piece of news that had just reached him in Gaulstown, near Kinnegad, close to the border between counties Meath and Westmeath: Matthew Prior, who a few months before had informed him that 'the cough does not diminish', was said to have died in Cambridgeshire, where he had visited the Harleys' grand home at Wimpole. 'I pray God deliver me,' wrote Swift, thinking of the grief that would hit him if the report were confirmed, as it shortly was. A doubt was growing as to how many friends in England he might never see again.[65]

Swift was writing to King from the country near Trim. He had spent a long summer staying at Gaulstown House in Westmeath, the spacious home of one of the uppermost families in the local oligarchy. George Rochfort had received the house as a wedding gift from his father, Robert, a former attorney general of Ireland and the Chief Baron of the Exchequer. It was a firm Tory manor; the Whigs had muscled the elder Rochfort from office after the accession of King George. Safe in the knowledge he was among a clan of allies, Swift had settled in for a long vacation. He thanked his hosts – and insulted a fellow clergyman – in a verse 'Journal' of more than a hundred lines. The poem leaves no doubt that Swift became an integral member of the household. It joked that he would be up at seven, padding the landings in his nightgown, to waken the family. After some early study followed by a lazy breakfast, he would join George Rochfort and his brother John, nicknamed Nimrod because of his passion for hunting, in a boating expedition on the house's lake. 'To the oar' becomes a refrain of the poem. A younger priest, the long-nosed Reverend Daniel Jackson, would absent himself, preferring to stare at spawn in the ponds or stitch up holes in his breeches. Lady Betty, Rochfort's wife, is heard at various moments nagging the men – for staying too long with their books or too long in their boat. The family gathers and settles, and disperses, in the course of the day's fixed rituals:

> Now Water's brought, and Dinner done,
> With Church and King, the Lady's gone;
> Not reckoning half an hour we pass,
> In talking o'er a moderate Glass.

The forms must be observed – the toast to an ailing Church and a suspect king; the evening prayers – and the rituals are as unobtrusive and comfortable as elderly armchairs. The late afternoon yields time for another boat ride, sating Dean Swift's need for exercise. The company observes the sunset. Talk, and supper, still lie ahead, and then:

> 'Tis late, the old and younger Pairs,
> By *Adam* lighted walk up stairs.
> The weary *Dean* goes to his Chamber,
> And *Nim* and *Dan* to garret clamber.

There were, though, lively exceptions to the daily round. On one of their rows round the lake, Swift seems to have taken a tumble out of the boat – a moment he passes over for the sake of brevity. In this charming, rough-cut poem Swift was nonetheless willing to digress at length on the 'pedantry unmerciful' of Dean William Percival, Arch-deacon of Cashel:

> How haughtily he lifts his Nose,
> To tell what ev'ry School-Boy knows.

Percival had crossed Swift in 1713 by becoming the Prolocutor of the Lower House of Convocation – a position Swift had expected to assume without a contest. Here he took a gratuitous bit of revenge against this unwitting rival, and indeed against Percival's wife, who, he assures us, was just as much a bore. Percival was provoked to 'answer' the poem, ineffectually, when it was distributed, for Swift had sketched him perfectly as the guest who will not pause from speaking for a breath or a stroll, or quietly drink his tea to let others watch the sunset in peace.[66]

Swift was becoming accustomed to portraying himself in poems, and also to remaining in character on such visits. Privately, he implied that both being and being with 'the Dean' was sometimes a strain. Although Reverend Jackson is very much the 'outsider' in 'The Journal', a lugubrious letter from Swift in October addresses him as one of the very few at Gaulstown whose company he found easy. He was sure too that, despite Rochfort importuning him to stay on, the family were 'weary of a man, who entered into none of their tastes, nor pleasures, nor fancies, nor opinions, nor talk'. This the poem flatly contradicts: and such sourness only impinges faintly on 'The Journal' at the end, when Swift implies that he must vacate his room and give up his quilt for a favoured pair of guests.[67] Asking which version of the summer is true, the jolly or the estranged, the answer of anyone who enjoys a public role, however modest, but is grateful to slip out of it, would surely be 'both'. Swift could revel in his persona while at the same time resenting those who mistakenly believed that there was nothing more to him. On his ride home through miry roads, with one servant ahead and another following, he was glad to let his field of vision widen. He stopped to gaze at the salmon falls and a twelfth-century castle at Leixlip, where he spent the night, eight miles from Dublin. Averse to losing a minute, he was on horseback at first light, and walked into St Patrick's in time for morning prayer. 'There's a Traveller,' he told Jackson.[68]

The confidence between them would last some time. They shared local acquaintances: Jackson knew Swift's friend and occasional agent, Joe Beaumont of Trim, the frustrated mathematician whose mental state remained volatile. The following spring Swift informed Jackson that Beaumont was in London, and had gone completely mad – 'riding thro' the Street on his Irish horse with all the Rabble after him and throwing his money among them'. Swift requested the Secretary of the board of Bedlam Hospital, of which he was still a governor, to have Beaumont sent there. As with other colleagues, his friendly relations with Jackson cast light on a closely knit provincial community – and how a 'traveller' could find distinctive human specimens a short ride from his own parish.[69]

## 5

Swift was still recovering from repeated and prolonged attacks of his aural complaint, 'disordered with noise in my ears and deafness', when the huge news reached Ireland that the King's ministry was headless. Swift had discovered a new treatment for his standing ailments: a clove of garlic steeped in honey, placed in the ear on the advice of his tailor, seemed to restore his hearing.[70] On 19 April 1722 the Earl of Sunderland, the King's senior secretary of state, died of pleurisy at his house on Piccadilly. The returns were just coming in from a tiring general election campaign. Sunderland had exhausted himself fighting the influence of a rival who, it pained him to admit, was also his saviour. Portly, unassailable, unequalled in debate and practical management, Robert Walpole had rescued Sunderland in the Commons from a charge of corruption the previous year. Walpole had for some time been in the wilderness: with Stanhope and now Sunderland dead, his moment seemed to have come, as key officials and allies of the late secretary were left to their fates. A timely bout of smallpox and a suicide disposed of two other figures tainted by the South Sea crash. A more formidable opponent for Swift's wit now seemed to have his chance, and Walpole seized it. Certainly, another hapless Jacobite rising in April that year was a wonderful opportunity for him to prove that he was the man to save Britain from this resurgent threat.

Swift's friend Atterbury distanced himself from this latest conspiracy, while hoping that it might succeed. His wife died that month after a long illness, and the Bishop secluded himself in his Westminster deanery. He was disconcerted by the gift of a miniature dog, a pup named Harlequin, sent by the Pretender's minions in Paris to bring some cheer to Mrs Atterbury's final days. Harlequin, who was lamed in transit, was equally a device placed by double agents, notably the Earl of Mar, to incriminate Atterbury. A focal point of subsequent government inquiries was establishing the identity of Harlequin's intended recipient. The Jacobites' projected invasion, which Atterbury had hoped would capitalize on the uncertainties surrounding the election, was another unqualified disaster, disintegrating before it could pose any actual danger. Equipment for 10,000 Jacobite troopers, costly but ultimately useless, lay untouched in a Brittany harbour warehouse.[71] Ormond had put himself many times beyond bankruptcy in the personal loans he had taken out on behalf of the mission, all to no end: for the Spanish authorities were ready to detain his transports, and all English officers in French regiments were firmly confined to barracks. As soon as the tip-off came through, Walpole was able to seize power. All of Sunderland's lieutenants, notably Secretary of State Carteret, were obliged to pledge themselves to Walpole or risk denunciation. The country was briskly roused to a state of emergency; and, as the year warmed, fortune brought further gifts in human form to Walpole's office. One minor link in the Jacobite chain, an Irish priest who acted as copyist, tried to sell the little information he possessed. Walpole, who had no scruples about ordering torture, encouraged the belief that the priest knew more than he had so far divulged. While the Reverend George Kelly, an agent with real knowledge, withstood questioning bravely – having proved handy with a pike while resisting arrest – the paper evidence Walpole needed was supplied by an unfortunate, partly deranged adherent of the cause. Christopher Layer, who had met the Chevalier in Rome, had concocted a plot all by himself, and put it in writing. Walpole had no hesitation in using the pure fantasy in Layer's papers as evidence against Francis Atterbury, the man the new chief minister firmly believed was the foremost Jacobite agent in England. Atterbury's last public act as the Dean of Westminster was to serve at the state funeral of the Duke of Marlborough in early August 1722.

Atterbury had been little more the Duke's admirer than Swift, who was spared the hypocrisy of mourning clothes. Indeed, Swift launched one last, post-mortem offensive against Marlborough, free of all the restraints his task for the *Examiner* had brought a decade earlier. After gloating over the smell of the corpse's loosening bowels and the absence of true love at the graveside, Swift delivered one of his most cutting perorations in verse:

> Come hither, all ye empty things,
> Ye bubbles rais'd by breath of Kings,
> Who float upon the tide of state,
> Come hither, and behold your fate.
> Let pride be taught by this rebuke,

> How very mean a thing's a Duke;
> From all his ill-got honours flung,
> Turn'd to that dirt from whence he sprung.[72]

Swift played no direct part in the Jacobites' plots, or the investigation that hunted down Atterbury; and he suffered little personally himself apart from the habitual suspicion that all prominent Tories must be Jacobites. This is not therefore the place to narrate at any length Atterbury's solitary months in the Tower, agonized by gout, in unusually comfortless conditions for such a prisoner; nor his spirited response to his captors, and his eventual consummate defence, in Parliament, against Walpole in person. He did not give his prosecutor an easy victory. Atterbury, forced by his gout to move on crutches, was perfectly willing to use his fists and shake men by their collars or their ears if occasion demanded; and he was admired by Londoners for giving his bulky overwhelming sadist of a jailer, Colonel Adam Williamson, a shove that laid the bully out on his backside. At the climax of Atterbury's trial, the duel between the minister and the accused sealed Walpole's reputation; for in besting – just – such a sharp-witted and uncontrollably eloquent opponent, with an unquestioned mastery of fact, the King's newly established premier demonstrated that there was no one in the realm who could equal him in debate. Swift followed the affair at a safe distance from the deanery parlour, from the houses of friends and – for long stretches – from his sick-bed. Had he been closer to the scene, he might, like Pope, have been called to Westminster to testify to Atterbury's character. Pope, pale and unwell, gave a nervous but conscientious performance at the stand on his friend's behalf. Outside the packed confines of the chamber, it was easier to revile the unconstitutional proceedings as a farce. The outstanding piece of evidence against Atterbury was Harlequin, the little dog that had arrived for his wife from France. Swift echoed the judgement of many in denouncing the ministry's case as resting on a broken-legged, spotted luxury pet:

> I ask'd a Whig the other Night,
> How came this wicked Plot to Light:
> He answer'd, that a Dog of late
> Inform'd a Minister of State.
> Said I, from thence I nothing know;
> For, are not all Informers so? . . .
> WHIG: But you must know, this Dog was lame.
> TORY: A weighty Argument indeed;
> Your Evidence was *lame*. Proceed . . .[73]

As it happened, and as it is easy to forget, the Bishop *was* guilty as charged. Correspondence proving that he was by far the most lucid and capable of the leading Jacobite operatives (at least in England) came to light more than a century later. Swift appears to have suspected as much; nowhere, at least, did he directly rebuff the accusations levelled against Atterbury. Yet the evidence on which Atterbury was found guilty, by a special Act of Parliament, indisputably was as lame as poor little Harlequin. The trial was later bookmarked in the annals as a prime example of corrupt procedure. Such enlightenment came too late for Walpole's vital witness, Christopher Layer. Although manifestly out of his wits, Layer was convicted of high treason and sentenced to the worst punishment the law could still inflict. A discreet word from on high seems to have ensured that he was already dead when taken from the gallows to be drawn and quartered.

The months passed for Swift with familiar tensions: with party strife, conspiracy and panic rumbling overheard, cathedral business filling the days; and, in the innermost chambers of heart and mind, a seemingly permanent antiphony between Vanhomrigh and Johnson. There were quarrels with both. Stella, he suggested, in one of his yearly tributes to her, was prone to persisting stubbornly with a point on which all her friends could see she was wrong. She also tended, he said, to take out the angry passions she concealed from the world on those who were closest to her. Versifying these observations, Swift described faults of which he was resolutely unconscious in himself:

> Your Spirits kindle to a Flame,
>  Mov'd with the lightest Touch of Blame,
> And when a Friend in Kindness tries
> To shew you where your Error lies,
> Conviction does but more incense;
> Perverseness is your whole defence.[74]

Yet such spats with Johnson were never of a kind that might unsettle the essentials of a relationship. A testimony to their abiding closeness, and his relative distance from Vanhomrigh, is to be found in the record of Swift's investments at this time. He purchased Talbot's Castle, a large fifteenth-century house at Trim, on the site of a long-desecrated abbey by the River Boyne. Designating the building a castle was to flatter it slightly, but it was a large enough manor; a long, narrow building of grey-brown stone with lancet windows and tall chimneys, it is still inhabited, and stands on slightly higher ground behind the striking ruin of Trim Castle. Beside it rises an afflicted bell-tower, the forty-foot tapering Yellow Steeple, a remnant of St Mary's Abbey. In its prime the abbey sheltered a miraculous healing statue of the Blessed Virgin. Although local tradition holds Cromwell's troops responsible for leaving nothing of St Mary's but its tower, probably little remained of the structure, and nothing of the sacred effigy, after the first destructive zeal of the dissolution. The slanting Yellow Steeple, in any case, named for the colour of its stone at sunset, had already acquired its current form by the time Esther Johnson paid £65 for Talbot's Castle. The guides at Trim still tell the story of how she then sold it to Swift for £200, saluting the sharp business instinct the transaction seems to reveal in them both: for documents in the Registry of Deeds in Dublin show that Swift redeemed the sum at a profit when he sold on the property for £223.[75] Swift provided Vanhomrigh with advice and helped ease loans, but nothing in the record shows him working with her as he did with Johnson in this instance – as a unit, partners, to mutual benefit.

His friendship with Vanhomrigh was unhappy at the root, and all the more passionate for it. Johnson seems to have accepted the form of association Swift desired; Vanhomrigh challenged his limitations outright. She wanted more of him, and he wouldn't change to suit her. Yet he claimed, in some letters, that he would have been happier if they could have been closer. Through the summer of 1722 their letters displayed the established pattern of loving-torturing sentiments. Both complained of deep melancholy; each attributed unhappiness to the displeasure or unhappiness of the other. If Vanessa was sad, wrote Swift, then he must be as well; if Swift was angry with her, wrote Vanhomrigh, then she could only be miserable. She also found it cruel in Swift, writing from Clogher, to wish he was in Dublin with her, where they might meet at some discreet place and 'pass 3 or 4 hours in drinking coffee in the morning, or dining tête à tête, and drinking again till 7'. By such an appeal he could only disarm any gathering will on her part to break off with him; saying such things was holding out hope only to dash it. How often, anyway, had such prolonged contact been possible in Dublin? Vanhomrigh's letters cry out at precisely the lack of such long days together. Swift named 'Kendall' as their rendezvous, possibly the house of a bookbinder of that name in the vicinity of Vanhomrigh's city lodgings. He complained that for some days he had felt as splenetic as she did on most, but urged her to be happy, recommending 'Reading and Exercise for the Improvement of your Mind and Health of your body;

and grow less Romantick, and talk and act like a Man of the World'. He claimed to be glad she was seeing people, but implied that he envied them. A few lines later he reminded her again of scenes and bric-à-brac from their story together; the porcelain in her mother's old house, 'the indisposition at Windsor', an incident beside a bookstall somewhere in London. He ended, in French, on an ardent note: 'believe that I will always be all that you desire – adieu.'[76]

His billet-doux provoked an excited response. 'Cad! I thought you had quite forgot both me and your promise of writing to me.' She was in the city, dealing with a lawsuit arising from her still labyrinthine family affairs. Every sentence in her note contained a barb to hook on Swift's conscience and temper. Having reminded him he was negligent, she scoffed at the idea that mere socializing could ever bring much satisfaction. She had visited the house of a 'great lady' she didn't care to name, where the ladies and beaux were prinked to what she assumed they thought was perfection; she wished Swift had been there to see them (thus reprimanding him for his absence). 'Their forms and gestures,' she declared, 'were very like those of baboons and monkeys: they all grinned and chattered at the same time.' She only desired that she could be in the country with – and a long row of dashes suggested no one else's name but his. She was shocked when one of these 'animals', some gallant, snatched her fan. This threw her into such a panic that she expected he might pick her up and carry her to the top of the house, as another ape had made off with a certain friend of Swift's. She was alluding to the moment in the *Travels* when Gulliver is snatched away by the Queen of Brobdingnag's pet monkey. Swift had either sent or read to her some pages from what would become the second part of his ongoing fiction. (Word of the project was getting around his wider circle, in hints from Swift himself and from his closest friends. 'I long to see your travels,' Bolingbroke had written in January.)[77]

Vanhomrigh revelled in the confidence and the superior stance she could then share with Swift. Beyond the transient intimacy, though, reality seemed bleak. She charged Swift with the burden of improving it. 'I do declare that I have so little joy in life that I don't care how soon mine ends. For God's sake write to me soon, and kindly, for in your absence your letters are all the joy I have on earth . . . Cad, think of me and pity me.'[78] Swift may have put off replying for as much as a month, and his response was both imploring and testy. He had moved on to County Armagh, where he took up the invitation of a long visit to Robert Cope, the Parson of Loughgall. They had met in London years earlier, and this was not the first time Swift had spent some weeks with Cope, his wife and family. The Copes had nine children, and Swift described the priest to Ford as 'the most domestick man you ever saw'. He saw a lot of them; it poured with rain, day after day, confining him to the parsonage. He reviewed Vanhomrigh's letter with young shouts and thudding footsteps outside his bedchamber door.[79]

He enjoyed her account of her trip to the grand house, and said he saw similar behaviour from such mandrills daily; but it was best to endure it and treat it as an amusement. 'The worst thing in you and me is that we are too hard to please, and whether we have not made our selves so, is the question.' He withheld the tone of an estranged partner that had leaked out in his previous message, in June, and replaced the screen that defined him as Cadenus, tutor, not lover. They differed in one thing, he said – though he then proceeded to name two distinct points. He, unlike her, did not quarrel with his best friends; and there were ten remarks in her letter that were obvious provocations, each more than enough to spoil someone's day. 'We differ prodigiously in one point,' he asserted again: she courted misery and the spleen, while he ran away from them. He expected she was back in Celbridge now – and he was positive that during the recent bad weather, unable to walk or ride, she had only sat in her chamber and mulled over her sorrows. He, on the contrary, had made use of it 'to read I know not how many diverting Books of History and Travells'.[80] This was the 'abundance of trash' he admitted having got through in another letter to Ford a few days later; but it was diverting trash. Despite their common critical trait, the differences between Swift and Vanhomrigh were never plainer than in this last, as it proved, surviving exchange. She was a person existing in and exploring her emotions to the full; he, on the other hand, generally tried to avoid them. Grief, 'spleen' and longing were powers that scared him. Yet he was able to find satisfactions that proved beyond Vanhomrigh, in external things. Shortly before moving on to Armagh he had travelled all the way along Lough Erne, the longest lake in Ireland, and, with an invalid's gratitude, had enjoyed both the landscape and his renewed strength moving across it.[81]

No answer survives to this letter or to his final one to her, written on 7 August 1722. It is full of similar things, but also veiled exhilaration at the ordeals and inconveniences of his 'northern journey'. He had ridden 400 miles since their last meeting – presumably in late May; and another 200 must follow before he saw her again. He was mucky and smelly and expected 'no Christian family' in Ireland would let him over the threshold. He suspected lice had infiltrated his linen; multitudes of ticks – the creatures were unfamiliar to him – were swelling on his skin. Some he had pulled off; others he would scratch out soon. The air he adopts is one of bearing evils with good grace, but there is an unmissable buoyancy, and boyishness too, in his letter. He had grown immune to regular drenchings, getting lost and sometimes going hungry. On setting out from his hosts at Loughall, he would go whither 'I do not know, nor what cabins or bogs or in my way'. The priest in his mid-fifties was free of cathedral affairs, politics and his deanery sick-bed. He tut-tutted now on Vanhomrigh's social niceties, her deliberate difficulty to please: the one thing she had in common with 'Glass Heel' (Ford, who avoided Ireland as much as he could) was their belief that Swift was the only person worth speaking to on the whole island. Yet this was the shabby, windswept and sunburnt rider who thought of her idly on horseback and was 'in mortal fear of the Itch'.[82]

To Vanhomrigh, weary with law business and pining for her roving correspondent, such preachy and yet latently carefree stuff must have been infuriating. Her reply is lost, if she wrote one; they may never have met again. This time it might have been Swift, alarmed by her silence, who sought out Vanhomrigh, assuming their usual occasional coffees would resume in the autumn. In any case, nine months later she would make her will, with no reference to him. There have been speculations of some ultimatum from her, some climactic breach; yet all the record shows is an end to communications. And it was Vanessa, so far as can be told, who let them end. Rather than showing her frantically appealing for some form of acknowledgement or commitment, the archives reveal two letters from Swift that lack an answer. Vanhomrigh had most likely contracted the tuberculosis that killed her sister Mary; and it may just be that discovering her illness prompted her to take the step at last of shrugging off Cadenus, and her illusions about him. The loss of their semi-traditional summer meeting gave her time to gather the will to make a break at last. The weeks that Swift conjectured she spent in silent, melancholy thought at home in her chamber – while he walked, rode and read 'diverting books' of the sort he recommended – gave her the space and silence in which to decide.

6

Coming in from a walk during Christmas that year, Swift found a welcome and surprising letter had been delivered and left on his table. He had not been in touch with John Gay since as far back as 1714; yet this was not, the page of friendly writing assured him, due to any change of affection on the writer's side. Gay inquired after him constantly, and had felt guilty every 'post-day' for almost nine years. 'I have not profest to you that I love you as much as I ever did, but you are the only person of my acquaintance, almost, that does not know it.' Mild-mannered, warm-hearted and companionable as ever, Gay had been severely rattled by the South Sea crisis. A handsome edition of his *Works*, published by sub-scription under Pope's auspices, had given him a very decent nest-egg. The list of subscribers attests to how universally liked Gay was – gran-dees of every hue signed up for copies; even Walpole put his name down for two. The money raised grew for a time into a substantial fortune as the stocks rose. When they fell, Gay was all but ruined, until some deter-mined burrowing by Pope recovered just under half of the thousand he had invested.[83] These hundreds would tide him over but could not vouchsafe his long-term comfort. At present, he was lodging with his friend Lord Burlington, and scouting as ever for employment and patronage. Great men sent their civilities, but not much solid help. 'They wonder at each other for not providing for me,' he quipped, 'and I won-der at 'em all.' Gay suffered from 'cholical' symptoms that the waters at Bath had so far failed to cure. Socially he was the opposite of sedentary, but physically lacked Swift's stamina for exercise: he was a little fat, and Swift suspected that he drank bad wine.

'You find I talk to you of myself: I wish you would reply in the same manner.'[84] Gay was the most guileless of Swift's old writer friends. Swift wrote back delightedly in January 1723; one can almost hear him chort-ling. He rebuked Gay, however, for the torture of old awoken memories. It would be three months or more, he wrote, before he could take any pleasure again from wine, company, riding or his gardens. Gay revived England in his mind's eye: 'there I made my friendships and there I left my desires.' Gay might hardly recognize him: he had aged; his studies and his writing had gone into decline. He apologized for not visiting London – but what a figure he would be there, having taken shelter from his disappointments in stupor and a 'scurvy sleep'. This pleasantly reproachful exordium complete, and the old days lamented, Swift went on to advise Gay that the best thing he could do would be to follow him to Ireland. He made the same case to Ford, who was in Ireland, in a birthday poem written later the same month.[85] Decent wine could be got, the cost of living was lower, and a sinecure might be found with some official or other. The horrors of Hanoverian–Whig rule also surely made the move enticing. He concluded in his most affectionate tone, made all the warmer by the habitual accompanying irony: 'I wish I could do more than say I love you . . . Take care of your Health and Money; be less modest and more active, or else turn Parson and get a Bishoprick here; would to God they would send us so good ones from your side.'[86] The letter is one of many documents making it readily imaginable why friends liked this somewhat detached, eccentric and frequently ill-humoured clergyman so much; so painfully, in Vanhomrigh's case. He liked them in return with an embattled tenderness. The trick to knowing him was not demanding more; something most of his similarly minded, bookish friends, sharing his limited sense of private companionship, found easy to do. They knew better than to push beyond the border of his public self.

His thoughts on how such a self should be managed were by now well developed. The task was particularly urgent in the case of women, he felt, because they were in general very badly instructed. In February 1723 he drew up 'A Letter to a Young Lady, on Her Marriage'. The woman Swift addressed had very recently married John 'Nim' Rochfort, the younger brother of Swift's host at Gaulstown in the summer and autumn of 1721. The unmarried Dean had no doubts at all of what Deborah Staunton's new life would require of her. He knew her family well, and his regard for both the Rochforts and Stauntons prompted him to write. Her parents had done well, he said, in keeping her out of the world's view till now. She had avoided picking up countless bad habits. But they had failed, like many otherwise entirely respectable families, to cultivate her mind. To that end Swift now offered counsel.

The letter that follows is an essay by Swift on his own feminine ideal. Largely, the trick the 'very young' Mrs Rochfort must learn is to avoid resembling the majority of women. She must not lose her virginal shyness too quickly; he hated the way new wives became forward and domineering in company as soon as they were married. She must not behave too fondly towards her husband in public, or even in front of servants: it made decent people extremely uncomfortable. They attributed it either to hypocrisy or concupiscence. She should lose the 'violent passion for fine clothes' that was impoverishing the Irish wool trade. She would be surprised by how gentlemen had less respect for women dressing expensively than paying a little more attention to the 'cleanliness and sweetness of their persons'. 'I shall only add, upon so tender a Subject, what a pleasant Gentleman said concerning a silly Woman of Quality; that nothing could make her supportable but cutting off her Head; for his Ears were offended by her Tongue, and his Nose by her Hair and Teeth.'[87] By this stage, after a few paragraphs, it emerges that Swift is playing an edgy game with decorum. He is capitalizing on the licence his role and status as 'the Dean' allows him in connection with the family, while pushing close, at moments, to effrontery. His safety cushion is a culture of steadfast bigotry towards women: decapitating a silly woman was an idea to be laughed off in any parlour. Yet Swift is making such remarks in order to provoke one woman to be different, rather than to say that all women are the same. His criticism of women's normal talk and behaviour only intensifies as his 'Letter' continues.

> And when you are among yourselves, how naturally, after the first Compliments, do you apply your Hands to each others Lappets, and Ruffles, and Mantuas; as if the whole Business of your Lives, and the publick Concern of the World, depended upon the Cut or Colour of your Petticoats? As Divines say, that some People take more Pains to be damned, than it would cost them to be saved; so your Sex employs more Thought, Memory and Application to be Fools, than would serve to make them wise and useful. When I reflect on this, I cannot conceive you to be human Creatures, but a Sort of Species hardly a Degree above a Monkey; who hath more diverting Tricks than any of you; is an Animal less mischievous and expensive; might, in Time, be a tolerable Critick in Velvet and Brocade; and, for ought I know, would equally become them.[88]

There are chastening thoughts on how short-lived the young woman's beauty will be, and how she will need to work hard to keep her husband's friendship and respect. She should therefore listen carefully to men of learning and experience when they speak of science, history or 'Travels into remote Nations'. Overall, she should be wary of falling too much under the influence of other women, be they great ladies or favoured chambermaids. Women, Swift declares, corrupt other women.

The puzzling thing about the 'Letter to a Young Lady' is that it avoids becoming no more than a mosaic of moralistic, chauvinistic sententiae, albeit one wrought with Swift's superlative craft. His point isn't that women are intrinsically weightless: society, he said, not biology, made monkeys of them. However hard they study, Swift says, they can never hope to equal the 'perfection of a schoolboy': but that is because they lack the education of schoolboys, not their intellectual potential. By the age of seven or eight, Swift and boys like him had a fluency in Latin to be envied by any twenty-first-century postgraduate classicist. Swift's point is that girls were drilled in being silly and superficial, as boys were trained in parsing. Morally, he saw no difference between the sexes. 'I am ignorant of any one Quality that is amiable in a Man, which is not equally so in a Woman. I do not except even Modesty, and Gentleness of Nature. Nor do I know one Vice or Folly, which is not equally detestable in both.'[89]

It even bothered him how women he knew made a virtue of showing fear at the sight of a cow, a spider or a frog. He admired Johnson, after all, for taking pistol in hand and dealing resolutely with a burglar who had tried to force a window in her house. Thus the harsh statements against women in the 'Letter' exhibit an idiosyncratic strain of misogyny. Swift was taking the liberty of criticizing female traits as he would do failings in men: with the aim of correcting, not defining.

The 'Letter' is not, though, the work of a reformer. Instead, it is curdled and clouded by Swift's problems with women, sexuality and the body. Displays of intimacy or relaxedness, pleasure in dress and adornment – these are traumatically abhorrent subjects. So if his advice for the young woman he addresses formed the basis of a social programme, it would involve limitation, not enablement. The 'Letter' hisses at moments with explicit violence – as, for instance, when Swift meditates on 'bold, swaggering, rattling Ladies, whose Talents pass among Coxcombs for Wit and Humour'. 'I have often thought that no Man is obliged to suppose such Creatures to be Women; but to treat them like insolent Rascals, disguised in Female Habits, who ought to be stripped, and kicked down Stairs.'[90] Women behaving like rascals should be beaten like cross-dressing rascals; yet such brutality exceeded the measures Swift might have prescribed for coxcombs and beaux, whose existence he accepted as a sad fact of human life. Here we are in the region of the Houyhnhnms and the methods they consider using on the Yahoos. The justifying principle is that humans behaving like beasts may be herded and slaughtered like beasts. This was a rationale Swift satirized in others but also recognized rarely in himself. Like some of his other writings about women, the 'Letter' reveals this exterminating instinct in an unreflected state. Recalling a remark from the previous summer, it might be said that Swift lacked either sincerity or self-awareness when he urged Vanhomrigh to behave more like a 'Man of the World'. It would have disgusted him, had she done so.

There is little question which of the two women closest to him corresponded more to the standards set out in the 'Letter to a Young Lady'.

Johnson was the incarnation of those standards; Vanhomrigh was a stray comet, skirting Swift's planetary system in an orbit that might prove destructive every time she reappeared. Though by no means a 'bold, swaggering, rattling' lady, Vanhomrigh does not come across as the reticent maid Swift sketched as the model for his young reader. One observer described her as being 'full of pertness, gaiety and pride'.[91] She was opinionated, forthright and potentially uncontainable. The awkward story was told of one occasion when Johnson and Vanhomrigh visited the same house: Stella sat silently while Vanessa 'displayed her talents'.[92] Johnson took vengeance, allegedly, with a neat poem about a jay striving to match the song of a linnet. However anguishing such encounters may have been for all three, Swift's mixture of fascination and angst at Vanhomrigh's rogue tendencies casts light on the ferocity of his imagining, in the 'Letter', a woman stripped and kicked down the stairs. In an unacknowledged fantasy, he was raising his boot over such a woman to crush the attraction or insecurity she might arouse in him.

Managing the cathedral often worsened his mood. The Chancellor of St Patrick's, Theophilus Bolton – another opponent – was made the Bishop of Clonfert. The usual follow-on resulted, with skirmishes among the senior clergy and hostility from London. Despite their alliance, Swift and King still differed at times over candidates. So an 'ugly chapter-business' preoccupied the Dean at winter's end. Time was also taken up by his leechy and provocative friend Chetwode, who was embroiled in a legal clash with the government, and whose invitations and visits always required some invention to avoid. Late in March, however, Swift put the cries and smells and Dublin behind him and took to the road. Ford was still in Ireland, and had invited Johnson and Dingley to spend the spring and summer in his house at Woodpark. Swift stayed some days or even weeks as well, and noted how Johnson quickly grew accustomed to Ford's lavish hospitality. Ford kept a better table than his friends were used to sampling. A collector, connoisseur and amateur scholar, 'Glass Heel', or 'Don Carlos' as Swift also styled him, stocked his cellar and library alike with only the best of things. Swift complimented him as a host by describing Johnson's daily increasing pickiness.

> A Haunch of Ven'son made her sweat,
>   Unless it had the right *Fumette* [a rich meaty stock].
> Don *Carlos* earnestly would beg,
> Dear Madam, try this Pigeon's Leg;

> Was happy when he could prevail
> To make her only touch a Quail.
> Through Candle-Light she view'd the Wine,
> To see that ev'ry Glass was fine.[93]

Swift himself did not remain with Johnson and Dingley amid such opulence for the whole summer. The cathedral called him back to Dublin, though he hoped not for long. He was moreover planning another long riding holiday, this time in the south of the country, which for many years he had wished to explore.[94] The trip fell in with the effort he had told Gay he planned to make each summer in order to build up his strength, through riding and walking, for an expedition to England. 'The onely Inconvenience is, that I grow old in the Experiment.'[95]

He may have left Woodpark, where Johnson was safely occupied, for another reason besides work and recreation. As spring passed, Vanhomrigh had accepted she was dying; she drew up her will on 1 May. There is no evidence that Swift visited her, but with Johnson in the country he might travel to Celbridge unmonitored by the observer that most worried him. In the will, his name was omitted from seventeen beneficiaries of token sums. This has often been interpreted as an act of spite by Vanessa. The named recipients included little-known relations and servants, but also men of influence such as Archbishop King and Erasmus Lewis. The silence between Swift and Vanhomrigh from August 1722 may be understood in endless ways. Resentment on her side, and anxiety about scandal on his, does seem likely. Yet Vanhomrigh's denying Swift a legacy might equally have been, in fact, one last small work of consideration and obedience to his fears of Dublin's gossip and Stella's jealousy. The best way of mortifying him would actually have been to bequeath him everything.[96] There is also the possibility that the will mattered very little to Vanhomrigh, and that she left out Swift's name as a sign of the document's inconsequence. As it was, she shocked the chattering city by carelessly bequeathing most of her estate to her executors. One, Robert Marshall, was her lawyer; the other, George Berkeley, the Dean of Derry, she hardly knew. When the will was proved and her property auctioned, her fortune amounted to nearly £5,000.

Vanhomrigh was thirty-five when she died, on 2 June 1723. The day before, Swift wrote to Cope about his preparations for his southern journey. By midnight on the 2nd, there had been time for the news from Celbridge to reach him. In a brief note to Chetwode, sympathizing about legal troubles, Swift reported that he would be departing immediately: 'I am forced to leave the town sooner than I expected.' As such he would be neither in Dublin nor in Trim for the funeral or the reading of the will; nor to hear Berkeley's report, on having read through the letters kept by Vanhomrigh, 'that they contained nothing, which would either dishonour her character or bring the least reflection upon Cadenus'.[97] A sentence from Swift's parting lines to Chetwode resonates beyond its context of difficulties in business: 'It is worse to need friends, than not to have them.'[98]

Berkeley's remark is representative. The philosopher was almost invariably gentle and humane. Yet the majority of Vanhomrigh's male mourners and subsequent memorialists were all in basic agreement as to her instability and generally 'defective' character. The Earl of Orrery declared she was 'happy in the thoughts of being reputed Swift's concubine: but still aiming and intending to be his wife. By nature haughty, and disdainful, looking with the pity of contempt upon her inferiors, and with the smiles of self-approbation upon her equals; but upon Dr Swift with the eyes of love.'[99] Swift's friend Delany felt Orrery's words were 'such as might do honour to the best pen, and most upright Christian heart'.[100]

Swift took his grief far south, and gave no hint of it in the letters that survive from that summer and autumn. It is better not to have friends than to need them, he had written – a maxim that allowed the still more painful truth that when one loses a friend, the need will usually remain. At the coastal village of Schull in south-west Cork he was moved to write lines describing the stark and destructive grandeur of the black cliffs and the sea beating against them. His description of the cliffs' descent imagined them toppling forward into the abyss.

> Lo! from the top of yonder Cliff, that shrouds
> Its airy Head amid the azure Clouds,
> Hangs a huge Fragment; destitute of props
> Prone on the Waves the rocky Ruin drops.
> With hoarse Rebuff the swelling Seas rebound,
> From Shore to Shore the Rocks return the Sound.[101]

The lines above do not contain Swift's exact words, but those of a translator commissioned for an early printing. Swift in his original text turned away from English, and evoked the scene in Latin. It is a unique effort amid Swift's poetry, and one of which he was particularly fond and proud. The mood is elegiac, but the circumstances that have brought the observer to gaze at the cliffs remain unspoken. Swift was denying and detaching himself from his need of a friend who was dead. Yet the manner he brought to his subject was exactly Vanhomrigh's. Usually for Swift, nature is an obstacle or a resource, a consolation, an annoyance or a facilitator of exercise and industry. In 'Carbery Rocks' he responds to it as a near-cosmic force that dwarfs him. He responds to it as the 'Romantick', the quester he had discouraged in Vanhomrigh the previous summer. His view moves downwards, from the cloud-covered summit of the cliff, with a huge and terrifying overhang, to a 'dismal orifice' in the cavern at the base, both open to and sucking in the day as it does the waves; then his eye moves suddenly up again, and catches a woodcrest nesting perilously near the top. And this is just summer – the waves of winter will set loose a power greater even than Jove's thunderbolts. All creatures straying near will be exterminated; fishermen weary Neptune with their prayers. 'Carbery Rocks' avoids even faint reference to a Vanessa-like figure; any such allusion would have kept Swift from ever printing it. As it is, the poem is more than a work of mourning: it is a strange piece of literary fellowship with his dead friend.

But, although its high emotionalism might be reminiscent of Vanhomrigh, Swift had explored the cliffs near Schull for the sake of diversion and exercise, his two main weapons against spleen. The investigation almost cost him his life, claimed Delany:

> His curiosity carried him to the brink of this dreadful precipice, and not content with what information his eyes could give him, as he stood over it, he stretched himself forward at his full length upon the rock, to survey it with more advantage. And attempting to rise up again, when his curiosity was as well gratified as it could [be], he found, as he told me, (for I had it from his own mouth), that he lost ground, which obliged him to call, in great terror, to his servants who attended him . . . to drag him back by the heels: which they did, with sufficient difficulty, and some hazard.[102]

Such a moment has terrible comic potential for an unsympathetic listener, especially when the subject is a person such as Swift – who was sure to have seen the funny side of this undignified scramble of men, had he not been the one being tugged from the abyss by his heels.

As for Swift's poem about the scene, all sense of this incident is absent from the tone and treatment of the subject matter. 'Carbery Rocks' obsesses powerfully instead with an element that will at any time engulf anything that comes near. And more or less anything, the poem suggests, will at some point get drawn in. The fishermen watching the precipice from a safe distance today may be smashed on to the rocks at its base tomorrow; and will, in any case, inevitably be claimed and consumed by the energy represented by the rocky mass and surging cataracts. That energy is not simply 'death', but a sump of all possible dreads and despairs. It is not what you feel when you slip at the clifftop, but what you see when you see the cliff. It might be bereavement; it might be the life-shrivelling religious and social conventions of the time that brought shame to Swift and Vanhomrigh's relationship.

The poem comes close to doing what Swift normally prohibited: speculating on the nature of last things, ultimate mysteries, deeper levels of thinking and feeling. It is like a page of Miltonic juvenilia, taking an imaginative direction Swift never otherwise felt able or inclined to pursue, but that his university Latin showed he might.

It was nevertheless a page to turn over, and forget as best he could with a fresh leaf. The end of the summer sent him letters from Bolingbroke and Pope; Sheridan pressed him to visit his crowded family residence at Quilca. As he had the previous year, urging Vanessa to be patient, Swift delayed the autumn journey as long as he could. 'No, I cannot possibly be with you so soon,' he told Sheridan, writing from Clonfert in the west. 'There are too many Rivers, Bogs and Mountains between.'[103] The grumble was affected. Such landscapes absorbed him more than they hindered him: 'this is no ill country,' he conceded, praising the local Bishop's recent effort to have ditches dug. The brief dispatches on his summer wanderings hint that, like the character he was now in the midst of creating, he was at home in *terra incognita*. Presumably he took the developing *Travels* with him on the road, since the vacant time was perfect for adding to the manuscript.

In Dublin, St Patrick's and the unavoidable disturbances of a parliamentary session awaited him. Along with the excitements of battle he could regain the solace of his closest friendship. Johnson must return from Ford's pampering at Woodpark. In his poem teasing her (and thanking Ford) for the luxuries she had enjoyed, Swift wrote amusingly of her contempt and disappointment on returning to her sparser lodgings.

> The Coachman stopt, she lookt, and swore
> The Rascal had mistook the Door:
> At coming in you saw her stoop;
> The Entry brusht against her Hoop:

Each moment rising in her Airs,
She curst the narrow winding Stairs:
Began a Thousand Faults to spy;
The Ceiling hardly six Foot high;
The smutty Wainscot full of Cracks,
And half the Chairs with broken Backs . . .[104]

Rarefied tastes on a limited budget will always offer good stock for comedy; and the lines catch very well that universal moment of turning the door-key, after a long trip away, and returning to the burdens of home. The lines mean more too, because of the personalities and their foibles. Swift had never liked those large whalebone hoops women wore beneath their skirts; there is a quality of 'I told you so' as Stella's farthingale brushes on the narrow entry. Swift was quite possibly making another of his probably unwelcome comments about her weight and need for exercise. There is a further undercurrent all the more powerful, and genuinely oppressive, for its lack of direct articulation. The run-down details are domestic, yet for a moment on the narrowing winding stairs Stella seems to be cursing more than just the furnishings. A note of anger against her settlement, her limited situation, against Swift's grief for a woman other than herself, can be heard for a second before the joke continues; anger barely expressed and hardly acknowledged, but present and sensed.

Despite her six-month isolation at Woodpark, Johnson could not have missed the gossip and rumour that surrounded Vanhomrigh's death, nor the sadness, however he suppressed it, of her host. Ford had known Vanhomrigh since the early days, and was fond of her. Johnson also knew Swift far too well not to guess the thoughts that dominated him during his long absence in the south. There was more for her to suffer. A few years later, when Swift's poem *Cadenus and Vanessa* was illicitly published – traditionally, yet apocryphally, on Vanhomrigh's posthumous order – Johnson had to endure the praise and speculation it excited. The allegory of Swift and Vanhomrigh's relationship became the talk of the town yet again. One day in company a stranger said to Johnson 'that Vanessa must be an extraordinary fine woman that could inspire the Dean to write so finely upon her'. 'Mrs Johnson smiled, and answered that she thought that point not quite so clear; for it was well known, the Dean could write finely upon a broom-stick.'[105] She was alluding to the parodic homily Swift had written twenty years before in the Berkeley household. Her response is a masterpiece both of loyalty to Swift and vengeance on her rival. Of all the comments and expostula-

tions attributed to Johnson in connection with Vanhomrigh, this one
bears the stamp of authenticity. It belongs with the other *bons mots* of
Stella collected by Swift and others. Yet it also prompts a contrast with
the contents of Vanessa's letters. No remark by Vanhomrigh has such a
killing mixture of timing, breadth and precision. Johnson's one-liner
confirms her as the genuine counterpart of Swift. It embodies the truth
that we can only suppose placated her while it enraged Vanhomrigh and
possibly troubled Swift. Johnson was his first choice. A story that they
were secretly married, supported by no evidence whatsoever, nevertheless expresses what everyone who knew them perceived: Stella was his
closest companion, the nearest to a wife that he could bear. And this
leaves the uncomfortable likelihood that his insecurities kept Vanhomrigh, as a secondary and occasional confidante, as a kind of reserve.
While he clearly felt deeply for her and grieved, the loss of Stella would
be of another order. It is even questionable whether Swift could have
completed the *Travels*, or had the strength to fight Walpole's government, if the other woman had been taken first. Instead, Johnson lived
just long enough to see him into immortality.

## 7

In 1723 Swift published a pungent tract on a question of ecclesiastical
management. His *Arguments against Enlarging the Power of Bishops in
Letting of Leases* opposed the traditional yet newly exploited practice
many bishops had of giving long leases on diocesan lands. The practice
involved a humble fixed rent being paid in exchange for a more considerable initial payment. If farms were leased on perpetual fixed rents
('fee-farm') for long periods, this naturally meant that the revenues of
the Bishop's successors would be severely compromised when the lands
increased in value. The swindle was especially harmful in Ireland, for
reasons Swift explored at some length.

The *Arguments* reads partly like a paper Swift might have written in
1713 or even 1706. The blend of subtlety and ebullience, the staunch
High Anglicanism underlying the ironies, the plenitude and economy of
the language, at once eloquent and yet plainspoken – these and other
qualities of the essay were all present in Swift's work early on. Yet in the
*Arguments* a more recent tendency emerges again: we find a writer reasoning (and cajoling) from the viewpoint of basic principles of justice,
rather than a man of his time artfully defending a point of Restoration

creed or an act of penal legislation. This is the voice of an examiner, but one who has the eye of a farmer, the memory of a scribe and the arithmetic of a book-keeper. As he debates the commonplace idea that Irish land has risen in value, his authority comes from years of walking and riding the length and breadth of the country, and of tending for his glebe in Meath. He sounds like a man now rooted in Ireland.

> I cannot see how this Kingdom is at any Height of Improvement, while four Parts in five of the Plantations for 30 Years past, have been real Dis-improvements; Nine in Ten of the Quickset-Hedges being ruined for want of Care or Skill. And as to Forest Trees, they being often taken out of Woods, and planted in single Rows on the Tops of Ditches, it is impossible they should grow to be of Use, Beauty or Shelter.

He was explicitly addressing his allies, members of '*our Party*'; i.e., Tories, and Tories with a genuine care for the 'Church established, and under the Apostolical Government of Bishops'.[106] The *Arguments against Enlarging the Power of Bishops* illustrated how Swift had stood his ground doggedly. He would claim there had been no substantive change in his essential views since he first entered into orders: and also that those views reflected the best interests of all in England and Ireland. Yet the paper also showed how far he had come. Despite the strong show of churchmanship, he was calling out to old Whiggish resentments against a heavy hand in Dublin Castle. He was now explicitly contesting a point that affected the basic interests of all those inhabiting the island: the *Arguments* was launched against a move made in Parliament that year to repeal an old Act, passed during the reign of Charles I, limiting the period for which ecclesiastical lands might be leased. A handful of (English) bishops stood to gain from large payments up front, and their immediate tenants might get on comfortably, while their sub-tenants, the people actually working the land, paid rack-rents and lived one failed harvest away from starvation. Against this state of affairs Swift's churchman proposes a strong culture of fair-minded ecclesiastical landlords, accepting payment in produce rather than cash, to offset the falling value of money. The economics of the case are cloudy; Swift's appeal is to equity as much as to tradition.

In the paper on leases, Swift warmed up for what proved an epic struggle the following year, when the government attempted to enforce 'debased' brass coins on Ireland in place of good silver. In purely economic terms, the scheme should not have been at all detrimental; yet

Swift and his allies were right in reading motives of colonial disdain and profiteering. The great campaign belongs with history rather than with biography; for the essential change in Swift, which led him to take on Robert Walpole in the guise of a humble tradesman, had already occurred and been demonstrated. He had shifted.

In his letter of August 1723, Pope reassured Swift that 'Whatever you seem to think of your withdrawn & separate State, at this distance, & in this absence, Dr Swift still lives in England, in ev'ry place & company where he would choose to live; & I find him in all the conversations I keep, & in all the Hearts in which I would have any desire.'[107] These words were a balm for Swift's badly upset ears. They soothed exactly the pain he had expressed to Gay, in January, on being reminded of his old life in England. That is where – and when – he felt he would always belong. At the same time, it bothered Swift that this could never really be so. As he declared to Ford, in urging him to settle permanently in Dublin, London was no place for the right-minded, amid 'swarms of Bugs and Hanoverians';[108] where the Whigs seemed likely to rule for ever. He was pledged to Ireland for as long as he could foresee, and in attacking and criticizing it, he spoke with the freedom allowed to a helpless child or parent he could not abandon. In addition, in his 'withdrawn and separate state', life with Johnson mixed affection with a strong dose of critical repartee. He was more comfortable and fulfilled with Stella, giving him a flick of his own wit from time to time, than he could be with Vanessa and her sometimes extortive language of compliment. For roughly the same reasons, and against every outward protestation he made to the contrary, Ireland suited him better. This is not to say he stopped being angry, or even stopped believing he hated the place. But it was there that he really achieved something of the ubiquity Pope gave him in his letter; for it was in Ireland that he was able to write a book that could speak to everyone.

The difference between Swift and the personage he might have become in England is shown up by the contrast offered by another famous Anglican cleric. Towards the end of June 1723 Francis Atterbury was sent into exile for his crimes against the state. Unwell and embittered, he arrived at Calais aboard the HMS *Aldborough*. On the Thames a flotilla of small boats manned by well-wishers had seen him off; now he was left abruptly in the harbour with his family and luggage. He had been stripped of all his English titles, and a few years of frustrating service on behalf of the Pretender were ahead of him before an ugly breach, and his death soon afterwards in 1732. At Calais, he learned that another

distinguished Englishman was in town. Viscount Bolingbroke had
arrived, and would shortly embark for home to receive his full pardon.
He had profusely assured the government that he had broken off all
contact with James and his agents. His letters to Swift in recent years
had all proclaimed his devotion to retirement and the small consolation
of knowing kindred spirits existed in the world. At the same time, and
with little inner conflict, he plotted his return to the thick of the fray. He
would soon be the doyen of the Tory opposition. From his hotel room in
Calais he sent an apology that ill-health would prevent him seeing Atterbury and his party. Atterbury was amused by the switch that was taking
place without a meeting of the two parties concerned. 'Then, I am
exchanged!' he is supposed to have said. Unhappy lodgings awaited him
in Brussels and then Paris, where he could understand most of what was
said but could express himself only awkwardly in his unpractised French,
a torture for one of England's foremost wits and public speakers.[109]

Swift never had Atterbury's flair as a preacher, which a *Tatler* of 1709
attributed to his 'soft and graceful behaviour', his 'person' and a 'peculiar force' that swayed both reason and feeling: 'when he thinks he has
your head, he very soon wins your heart.'[110] Swift had once hoped he
might cut such a figure in the pulpit, and that people might now and
then ask on Sunday mornings, 'Pray, does the doctor preach today?'[111]
He had long ago given up such aspirations, and whenever he mentioned
copies of his sermons he usually told friends to treat them as rubbish.[112]
He might have been no super-preacher to draw the crowds, but he took
his pulpit duties seriously, and was a hard judge, as dean, of other ministers in his cathedral: 'As soon as any one got up into the pulpit, he
pulled out his pencil, and a piece of paper, and carefully noted every
wrong pronunciation, or expression, that fell from him.' Hard or scholastic words faced almost as severe a reprimand as any trace of
indecency.[113] Yet his own sermons were quite frequently political in
nature, and at moments their thoughts express his entire philosophy of
life: as, in the following, from a sermon on the Trinity:

> It would be well, if People would not lay so much Weight on their own
> Reason in Matter of Religion, as to think every thing impossible and
> absurd which they cannot conceive. How often do we contradict the
> right Rules of Reason in the whole Course of our Lives? *Reason* itself
> is true and just, but the *Reason* of every particular Man is weak and
> wavering, perpetually swayed and turned by his Interests, his Passions,
> and his Vices.[114]

There in brief is the basis of his lifelong objection to the free-thinking of Dissenters; and also the justification of his satirical activities. He was free in his non-professional writing to sport with the illusions and lapses of individuals' reason, because Reason itself was absolute and the province of God.

These words on the Trinity also stand as a rebuke to the conduct of one such as Atterbury. Swift shared the exiled Bishop's doctrinal convictions, and his adherence to the Tory cause as a means of resecuring the old status of the Church. He admired the other man's gifts. Yet he lacked Atterbury's fanaticism and arrogant self-assurance. On the basis of his own judgement, Atterbury was willing to aid and abet a military rebellion, a course from which Swift's memories of the revolution – and inherited traumas from the Civil Wars – would always make him recoil. He would never abandon his true Church; he just saw the contradiction involved in actually taking lives for it.

Instead of trying to make his words and actions fit a single theory, we can understand him better by seeing that his sympathies were drawn in sometimes conflicting directions. There was even a difference between what he *thought* he believed in and what he was prepared to put into practice. In his early *Examiners*, he had declared himself in terms that largely echoed Bolingbroke's rhetoric; nevertheless, he always felt uncomfortable with the extremes of 'squirearchy' in which Bolingbroke saw his opportunity. From 1714, he would always sign himself a Tory: but what he meant by that varied. Obviously it signified a fierce allegiance to High Church principles, but also a more personal devotion to the Lord Treasurer he had served. This never diminished. He venerated the Earl of Oxford – who, on his release from the Tower, rarely or never replied to his letters. When the elderly and battered statesman died in 1724, Swift reverently relayed the version he had received of his old master's passing. 'Lord Oxford died like a great man, received visits to the last, and then two minutes before his death, turned from his friends, closed his own eyes, and expired.'[115] Such a vision of dignity, stately and saintly, belonged to a higher moral realm for Swift than the sectarian Toryism Atterbury supported on behalf of the Church. Swift loved Oxford because, despite his cunning and foibles, the Earl's politics were closer to his. Swift's Tory creed was one he felt all reasonable Whigs could ascribe to. After the fall of the Tories in 1714, Atterbury's zealotry hardened, while Swift's vision gradually broadened – though he actually denied, in letters, the widening of his sympathies that his published writings suggested.

In Ireland, his stance towards Whigs of an older, plainer stamp, rougher yet fairer than the new breed of profiteers, relaxed. In times of greater evil such compromises prove necessary; and Swift proved capable of making them. He could never go further than tolerance; that is, he could never contemplate supporting a repeal of the Test Act or the other discriminatory and penal atrocities of law. Notably, however, in his book of travels, he gave his alter-ego a Dissenting background. Gulliver, moreover, is educated at Emmanuel College, a traditional Puritan command-post. Making the hero a Tory High Anglican would have taken the book in the direction of bathos and (further) charges of Jacobitism. As it was, while Gulliver became in Swift's eyes a figure of fun, he could often speak the truth and see lucidly.

Atterbury was exiled, and so was Swift – to remoter nations than Ireland. On his way, he moved towards a position of more radical but also more constructive rebellion than Atterbury could contemplate. Most people, to Swift's mind, were stupid and harmful; they sought conflict and complication where none – as in the questions of religion – were needed. It was necessary to upset them, often, to point out their mistakes. He was also obliged to defend them from the rapacious instincts of their rulers.

# 11. Dean Gulliver

Unhappy Ship, thou art return'd in Vain:
New waves shall drive thee to the Deep again . . .
'Twill not avail, when thy strong Sides are broke,
That thy Descent is from the British Oak.
— *Swift, 'Horace, Book I, Ode XIV'*[1]

I

When Swift's ship neared the harbour on 22 August 1726, Dublin welcomed him as a hero. He was 'The Patriot', the first citizen of the city. The bells of St Patrick's rang out in his honour, and other neighbouring churches echoed the peal. Bonfires were lit in the vicinity of the cathedral; hardly a street in the town lacked his portrait, hung up as a sign over some shop or tavern. The son of Swift's friend Sheridan had it on good authority that the 'principal citizens' and heads of the city's guilds and corporations went out to greet him in 'a great number of wherries' adorned with streamers and colourful and intricately decorated banners. On shore, a 'multitude' met and accompanied him in a free-form procession all the way back to the deanery. The 'rejoicings' lasted into the night. 'Hibernicus', the regular commentator for the *Dublin Weekly Journal*, understood that copies of his recent essay on the topic of ingratitude were rolled and filled as firecrackers by the good people of St Patrick Street, 'by which means they became an instance of that virtue they were written to inculcate', he observed complacently.[2] Swift took it all as his due; and a little gold watch in his bags, with a special chime to mark the hours of night for an invalid, meant more than all the fuss and finery that lined his path.

He was exalted as 'the Drapier', the modest man of the world who, in a series of incendiary 'letters', had exposed a pernicious attempt by the government to impoverish Ireland. Walpole's plan had been to introduce halfpennies made of an inferior alloy into Irish currency, thereby debasing the coinage, while private English interests made vast fortunes from the patent to mint the change. That, at least, was how Ireland viewed the matter. The coins themselves seem, in fact, to have been at least equally as good as the English ones, so far as their metal composition was concerned, and better than those found hitherto in Ireland.[3] A currency, however, depends on the confidence placed in it by those who use it, and the Irish public quickly made their feelings known: the plan was greeted with the scorn and protest merited by other abuses. A vast affair, the debacle over 'Wood's ha'pence' is well summarized by an early (and generally shrewish) commentator on Swift's life:

The popular affection, which the Dean had hitherto acquired, may be said not to have been universal, till the publication of the Drapier's *letters*, which made all ranks, and all professions unanimous in his applause. The occasion of those letters was a scarcity of copper coin in *Ireland*, to so great a degree, that for some time past the chief manufacturers throughout the kingdom, were obliged to pay their workmen in pieces of tin, or in other tokens of suppositious value. Such a method was very disadvantageous to the lower parts of [economic] traffic, and was in general an impediment to the commerce of the state. To remedy this evil, the late King [George I] granted a patent to William Wood, to coin, during the term of fourteen years, farthings and halfpence in *England* for the use of *Ireland*, to the value of a certain sum specified. These halfpence and farthings were to be received by those persons, who would voluntarily accept them. But the patent was thought to be of such a dangerous consequence to the public, and of such exorbitant advantage to the patentee, that the Dean, under the character of M. B. Drapier, wrote a letter to the people, warning them not to accept Wood's halfpence and farthings as current coin. The first letter was succeeded by several others to the same purpose, all which are inserted in his works.

At the sound of the Drapier's trumpet, a spirit arose among the people, that, in the eastern phrase, was *like unto a tempest in the day of the whirlwind*. Every person of every rank, party and denomination, was convinced, that the admission of Wood's copper must prove fatal to the commonwealth. The Papist, the Fanatic, the Tory, the Whig, all listed themselves volunteers under the banner of M. B. Drapier, and were all equally zealous to serve the common cause.[4]

And so all these factions greeted him with acclaim when he returned from the long-delayed, long-avoided trip to England he eventually made in the spring and summer of 1726. To the government and its supporters in Dublin, he was no figure to be adulated, but indubitably one to be reckoned with. During his stay, Walpole himself had tried to taint Swift's public image by inviting him to dinner, and encouraging a rumour that Swift had sued for favour with his ministry. Swift denounced the lie: he had in fact made surreptitious advances to Walpole, though not on his own account but on John Gay's, which the Prime Minister had cheerfully decided to misunderstand. Swift had been in politics long enough to know when he had been stung, but the damage was limited.

The nation-wide push against Wood's patent was diamond-tipped by Swift's letters from M. B. Drapier, a plain-dealing yet clever and entirely imaginary businessman with a shop in Dublin's busy St Francis Street. The matter of the halfpence stoked passions of colossal force, and Swift's feat was to keep these under control in the practical observations of his letter-writer. The chief difficulty Swift faced in the letters was putting across often quite technical points about the shoddy manufacture of the coin, and the fraud he felt it constituted, in language that a tradesman might credibly use and weavers would understand. Swift solved this problem by changing the addressee with each successive letter in response to the crisis. The first letter had a simple incendiary attraction – at its core was the suggestion, similar to the one in Swift's earlier *Proposal* on Irish cloths, that the country resort to passive resistance by simply boycotting the tainted coin. Subsequent letters, though, obliged Swift to respond in some detail to official reports on the quality of the metal and the legality of the patent itself. The third letter was therefore addressed 'To the Nobility and Gentry of the Kingdom of Ireland'. With the range and precision of his arguments, historical and economic, Swift arguably stretched the consistency of the Drapier persona; but the Drapier's language, even at his most oratorical, might always conceivably have been used by a merchant with a grammar-school education. Intellectually, M. B. Drapier was on a par with many of Swift's fellow alumni from Trinity who had entered trade, and also with Gulliver – though his reasoning is invariably far more acute. The consistency of Swift's persona mattered less, regardless, than saving the kingdom; and by the time the later letters appeared the Drapier had become a figurehead for Swift in any case.

The campaign gathered its momentum over several months. The arrival of a new and reasonable lord lieutenant, John Carteret, in the autumn of 1724, in time gave the 'Anti-Wood' lobby the initiative. By the following summer Carteret was advising London to revoke the patent – though not, as the Corporation of Dublin and the Drapier had urged, to give Ireland its own mint. By then, however, Swift had drastically expanded the symbolic field of the conflict. In his fourth letter the Drapier made explicit what all had sensed throughout: the fight was for more than farthings: it was about the status of Ireland as a kingdom. 'A People long used to Hardships, lose by Degrees the very Notion of *Liberty*; they look upon themselves as Creatures at Mercy; and that all Impositions laid upon them by a stronger hand are . . . *legal* and *obligatory*.' A pinpoint strike was thus delivered on the moral integrity of the Declaratory, or 'Dependency', Act against which Swift had railed years before. 'I *depend* only on the King my Sovereign, and on the Laws of my own Country,' the Drapier declared. 'I am so far from depending upon the People of *England*, that, if they should ever *rebel* against my Sovereign, (which God forbid) I would be ready at the first Command from his Majesty to take Arms against them.'[5] Such words were a measure of how far the constitution had changed in Swift's lifetime, for they swore fealty to principles that Whig rule and political theory had rendered redundant. Ireland was no longer a king's to dispose of; it was England's. Yet, by saying this was wrong – indeed, illegal – Swift courted further trouble with the executive. An absurd proclamation was issued offering £300 – the same price, incidentally, put by Parliament on his head just over ten years earlier – for anyone disclosing the identity of the Drapier. In the official reports of the Irish Privy Council it is obvious that Swift's authorship of the letters was known in every tavern in the city. His printer, John Harding, was imprisoned; yet he could not be brought to make Swift's secret a matter of record. Doing so, he must have sensed, would have paralysed the presses – for if the Drapier were unmasked, nobody would risk putting such 'free thoughts' in print again. On the governmental side, the prospect of a very public trial for sedition with a defendant as rhetorically capable as Swift was nothing to be savoured. Thus a near-repeat performance of the judicial farce with the printer Waters three years earlier ensued, complete with paroxysms from Chief Justice Whitshed. This time, instead of rejecting the Grand Jury's verdict, Whitshed simply discharged and replaced the jurymen. Swift noted that the family motto emblazoned on the judge's coach was *Libertas & natale Solum* – 'Freedom and my native country'; ironic, he observed, since Whitshed was betraying both.

> *Libertas & natale Solum*;
> Fine Words; I wonder where you stole 'em.[6]

As for Swift's printer, John Harding had borne questioning bravely but was less fortunate than Edward Waters. He died in prison in 1725. A popular storm rose up over the trial; and by December 1724 the movement to resist Wood's halfpence had essentially won the day. The new Primate of All Ireland, Archbishop Boulter, a strong government insider, conceded the matter was hopeless. For his part, Lord Carteret had succeeded in avoiding mass violence, and also strengthened the regard in which the government's chief opponent held him. Swift was prevented by illness, circumstance and (probably) strategy from meeting the Lord Lieutenant until January 1725. It behoved him as the Dean of St Patrick's to pay his compliments, but legend had it that, on one abortive visit, he left a note at Dublin Castle questioning the point of the formality.

> My very good Lord, it's a very hard task
> To wait so long and have nothing to ask.

Swift is said to have written these lines on a card he tucked in a window of the Castle. They provoked a genial couplet, placed in the same casement, from a former lord mayor of Dublin:

> My very good Dean, there's few come here
> But have something to ask or something to fear.[7]

Swift might firmly insist that fear and supplication were equally irrelevant to his visit, which was an act of pure courtesy. But a gentlemanly understanding prevailed. He and Carteret had first been acquainted in what Swift sometimes felt now was a prior incarnation, when he was resident in London, and he admired the viceroy – all the more for Carteret's lack of amity towards Walpole. Here was a governor of the old school, with something of Ormond's statesmanship and fairness. The two had met when Carteret had entered public life more than a decade earlier, and now the Whig lord reciprocated the rebel band-leader's esteem in an accomplished return of complimentary reproaches. If Swift thought the viceroy had forgotten or now disregarded him, His Excellency chided the Dean in return for insulting his intelligence. 'I shall not be testy,' Carteret promised, 'but endeavour to show that I am not altogether insensible of the Genius which has outshone most of this age.'[8] Such cool, elegant praise by one of the most accomplished diplomats of the eighteenth century gives an idea of the height Swift's reputation had reached by the mid-1720s, just as the adoration of his weaver neighbours in Dublin indicated its strength and breadth. Lord and Lady Carteret became Swift's devoted friends even as they maintained a show of public difference over every issue, from the ongoing currency crisis to Church patronage. Swift would defend Carteret in a spirited *Vindication* of his time in office.

The Dean's eventual call on Carteret in January 1725 was a matter of great public excitement. Swift reported how 'the town has a thousand foolish stories of what passed between us; which indeed was nothing but old friendship without a word of politics.'[9] Bureaucracy and ceremony imposed necessary delays before victory could be acknowledged. During the summer Swift busied himself with a final Drapier's letter, which would urge the country to seize the moment and press the English to relieve Ireland's outstanding grievances. Yet, when the revocation of Wood's patent was finally proclaimed in August 1725 – Swift heard the news on the last day of the month – he thought again, and cancelled publication. Had he proceeded, Carteret might well have had a few words 'of politics' to say at their next meeting, since the unpublished letter went to new lengths of insubordination. Dublin, meanwhile, rejoiced, and, teasingly, the Irish House of Lords spent a full two days debating (and so delaying) an Address of Thanks to the King for commanding Wood to surrender his grant.

Swift approved of the Lord Lieutenant's statesmanship, his wit and his learning. Accordingly he became a moderately frequent guest, despite the initial comedy, at the tumbledown fortress that constituted the symbolic target of his campaign as the Drapier. Dublin Castle must always have loomed large in his imagination. There was no possibility of its withstanding a full-scale military assault, and viceroys had long been in the habit of lodging their families in a mansion in lush parklands beyond the city proper; yet its bulk, its permanence, its nearness to every current of life in the old Dublin gave the Castle all the presence of an established possessor. The medieval, much patched-up residence itself, reached via a drawbridge and gatehouse complete with the obligatory clanking portcullis, was 'without much magnificence on the outside', according to one observer. The courtyard behind the walls did, however, boast a 'handsome guardhouse', accommodating the Governor's permanent troops in relative comfort; these received the viceroy and his government 'with colours flying and drums beating' whenever he entered the complex. Then, behind one of the windows where Swift left his sardonic note, the hall of the house presented a noble flight of stairs with several stately rooms beyond; one of these, the Presence Chamber, contained a canopied chair, in effect a throne, embodying the Lord Lieutenant's near-princely status as the monarch's delegate. Behind the house was a 'broad terrace walk, the length of the building', with a multi-levelled garden that was explored by means of marble staircases and a little bridge over a diverted stream: the flower-pots, lawns, gravelled paths and lime trees had been arranged and planted a generation earlier by the Earl of Romney, the infamous aristocrat Swift had known through Sir William Temple.[10] To the Williamite establishment the Castle now embodied, Romney remained a hero, famed for his part in inviting the Prince of Orange to rescue the Stuart kingdoms from popery. To Swift, he had seemed a hypocritical lecher, and still did so, if he thought about him as he toured the Castle's walks and greens. There is no reason why Romney and a hundred other spectres should not figure in our thoughts, however, if we contemplate these visits. The layout of the world he valued is recovered when Dean Swift is placed within these walls, and pictured bowing to the viceroy, taking the seat a servant pulls out for him at table, or standing among other dignitaries – in fur-collared gowns, in clerical garb, in regimentals – and quite distinct from the many Castle minions in their uniform frock-coats and wigs. Seeing Swift here, curt and unsmiling, amid the trophies, the suits of armour and the tapestries, is for a moment also to fix his ambivalent political coordinates from 1725 on. Arriving as a dignitary, and expecting to be treated as one, he was touring the centre of the regime he supported and belonged to; but he was also infiltrating the stronghold of a power he had beaten in the field.

The climb-down over the Irish coinage scheme was the first defeat for Walpole's ministry, and one of only two policies on which the wily, merciless Prime Minister was bested in the course of his long administration. It was arguably the first time in British history that a purely popular campaign of protest reversed a political decision of central government. Mighty reputations were brought to the block to pay for Wood's banished brass. Yet Walpole himself felt it as little more than a tremor in his demagogy; a greater bother for him was a breach in the ranks of his Whigs in the course of 1725.

Throughout 1724–5, while raising a whirlwind, Swift still had energy and time to work on another half-secret fiction. Gulliver's *Travels* abounded with jokey coded references to Swift's fight on behalf of the Irish economy. The floating island of Laputa in particular is an unmissable allegory of the Hanoverian Court in its drift from one part to another of the King's dominions, descending occasionally to flatten resilient regions.[11] The island's core technology is a loadstone exploiting the magnetic pull and push of the earth below, huge in size yet in shape 'resembling a weaver's shuttle'.[12] This flying allegory of the Hanover regime is metaphorically powered by an industry it has trammelled and exploited, in a kingdom it has reduced to a province. Certain passages from the Laputa voyage were among those Swift's publisher felt obliged to cancel in 1726 for safety's sake.

It was Gulliver, not thought of preferment from Walpole, that finally brought Swift to England in 1726. He travelled to arrange the printing of his book, and departed before it appeared in his publisher's shop. He was received with genuine delight by old friends who for many years had known him only through their memories and his distinctive broad handwriting. Pope, pugnacious yet delicate with tubercular bones, made his home at Twickenham Swift's unofficial headquarters for the duration of his trip, open to all trusted allies who cared to visit him there. The beloved cronies of long ago, Arbuthnot and Gay, with whom he concluded his stay in London, embraced him at last. He was charmed by Pope's love and companion, Martha Blount. Bolingbroke received his bow with glinting eyes and offered his white, gout-afflicted hand; they spoke as comrades now. Bolingbroke sent his compliments to 'the three Yahoos of Twickenham', in an arch note giving proof that he was privy to Gulliver's progress.[13] As a keen 'improver' of lands, Swift was absorbed by Pope's landscaping and the strange embellished tunnel, below a road traversing his property, which he styled his 'grot'.

Henrietta Howard, friend of the Princess and mistress of the Prince of Wales, lived nearby, and Swift got on well enough with her, although their friendship brought none of the political gains he had contemplated on beginning it. A tactical initiative on his part instead resulted in, at one level, a genuine and pleasing confidence with an intelligent courtier whose company he enjoyed; at another, it brewed a great resentment in him when she demurred from doing some actual good. Knowing a talent for trouble when she saw it, Princess Caroline also sought him out, and he was proud of the condescension required on both sides: he was making as much a concession as she was, he felt, by going to see her. The Princess admired a gift of Irish plaid Swift had sent Mrs Howard, claimed it for herself, and then ordered the poplin to be made into

gowns. She failed, however, to send Swift a pair of medals she had promised for his costly gift. Although charmed at first, he came to dismiss
both Caroline and Howard as having 'neither memory nor manners'.[14]

The joys of long-missed company, and the pride of public recognition
notwithstanding, England failed to enchant. He had misgivings on
departing, and they only grew as reports warned him that Esther Johnson was probably dying. Never strong, she had returned in the past few
years to the near-permanent sickliness Swift remembered in her as a
child. As the summer came in 1726, she sank further, with a feverish
complication of some chronic pulmonary ailment. In July, Sheridan sent
word to Swift that she was moderately better. For perhaps a day, Swift
was deceived. Another trusty helper, John Worrall, the head of the cathedral choir, told him the truth – and Swift replied with a letter of anguish.

> What you tell me of Mrs Johnson I have long expected with great
> Oppression and Heaviness of Heart. We have been perfect Friends
> these 35 years. Upon my advice they both [she and Dingley] came to
> Ireland and have been ever since my constant Companions, and the
> Remainder of my Life will be a very melancholy Scene when one of
> them is gone whom I most esteemed upon the Score of every good
> Quality that can possibly recommend a human Creature ... indeed
> ever since I left you my Heart hath been so sunk, that I have not been
> the same Man, nor ever shall be again, but drag on a wretched Life till
> it shall please God to call me away.

The only power England now had to keep him, faced with such a future,
was in affording him a miserable refuge from the sight of his friend
dying. If there was no chance Johnson would recover, he instructed Worrall to renew his licence of leave to remain in England. 'I would not for
the Universe be present at such a Tryal of seeing her depart.' She would
not lack friends to care and comfort her, he said, but 'I should be a
Trouble to her and the greatest Torment to my self.'[15] His prevailing
instinct, that is, was to be safely away from the sound of Johnson's
coughing and calling, and the sight of her pallor and sweat. The preoccupation with his own pain, rather than with the lonely trauma of his
afflicted friend – a woman who had left a normal life behind for his sake
– puts Swift in a bad light here; and the innermost, inexpressed reaction
of steady, dependable Worrall, whose wife was nursing Johnson, after
breaking the seal on the letter, would be a valuable guide. But if he was
abandoning her, he was committing the sin of one abandoned repeatedly

through childhood: by his family when his nurse 'abducted him', by his nurse when she returned him to his family; and by his guardians again when they dispatched him to Kilkenny. The voice in this and one other letter in July that year is not of a near-sixty-year-old, but of a child screwing his eyes to shut out the darkness. Fear of grief led him to avoid Stella's sick-bed as he had Vanessa's three years before. In comparison the death of Vanhomrigh, though it had moved him deeply, seems very much a rehearsal for a worse bereavement still.

It turned out that the crisis of Johnson's health in 1726 was also merely a rehearsal for the ultimate loss he was now forced to contemplate. Some five days after writing to Worrall, he elaborated on the mantra that had come out when he learned that Vanhomrigh had died: it was better not to have a friend than to need one. Almost better, indeed, not to be born at all, or to be left with the 'poor casual remains' of a life.

> I think there is not a greater folly than that of entering into too strict and particular a friendship, with the loss of which a man must be absolutely miserable; but especially at an age when it is too late to engage in a new friendship ... pardon me, I know not what I am saying; but believe me that violent friendship is much more lasting, and as much engaging, as violent love.[16]

At a moment of abject openness, Swift suggested he had known both these forms of emotional violence.

When Johnson pulled through, reality told Swift that it was only a matter of time until the fatal lapse came. Another twenty years of life for her, in fact, made little difference to the fear in which he lived of losing her. For now, the last corrections to the *Travels* – on the advice of the surviving Scriblerians – could be put into the manuscript; a manuscript he had had copied by an unknown hand, most probably in Ireland.[17] A letter to the printer in the name of Richard Sympson, Gulliver's cousin, was copied out by Gay – with whom Swift was staying by the first week of August. A representative sample of the text was then sent, with elaborate secrecy, to Benjamin Motte, a respectable publisher who had taken over the business of Swift's onetime collaborator Benjamin Tooke. In the letter, Swift as Sympson demanded £200 for the whole work; Motte, baulking slightly at the size of the figure, agreed to pay it within six months of publication. 'Sympson' agreed, and asked that the book appear before Christmas.[18]

Then Swift was gone, back to his life in the deanery. In July he had admitted to Sheridan: 'This is the first time I was ever weary of England, and longed to be in Ireland, but it is because go I must; for I do not love Ireland better, nor England, as England, worse; in short, you all live in a wretched, dirty Doghole and Prison, but it is a Place good enough to die in.'[19] Quite often, actually, in his *Journal to Stella*, he had complained of his weariness with England; but, while claiming to love Ireland no more than before, he admitted the novelty of having come to accept it, 'Doghole' though it was. And the truth was more than that: he had given the country the benefit of his violent friendship.

Pope wrote with morose fondness of a 'sensation like that of a limb lopp'd off' without Swift in his eccentric household. Miss Blount and his venerable mother, a staunch Papist, missed the Dean.[20] Swift knew that, while Pope could at times be somewhat artificial, he was no stranger to disability – 'You pay dearly for the great talents God hath given you.' By the end of August, he was back in his Irish Antipodes, looking at folk about him as if they were utterly unknown to him, and wondering again how he had ever come to such a place. How far one could come 'in a few hours, with a swift horse or a strong gale'.[21] Lurking in his written meditations as the autumn drew on was the sense of being a stranger to himself: the oddity of Dublin may in many respects have been a reflection of the unfamiliar way the city now perceived him, as a saviour. The image was incongruous. His large eyes had acquired something of the staring prominence they would have in his final years and, despite every resistance he made at accepting it, they had grown dimmer. Swift's friends nagged him regularly to wear his spectacles, and he recognized their concern in his story: Gulliver's save him from the rain of arrows striking him as he tows away the Blefuscan navy. But his lenses offer no protection from the charges of treason that await him in Lilliput. What glasses, Swift implied, could shield *him* from the shots of his enemies in Dublin and London? Delany noted gravely that it was difficult finding a pair, in any case, large enough to cover 'the natural make of his eyes'.[22]

## 2

Dublin was packed with places to talk, do business, gather news and pass it on: for many, the most obvious place was the main aisle of Christ Church Cathedral, where, as in the old St Paul's of London, trading and gossiping continued even during service. Another form of venue was offered by the coffee-houses, and these were generally oriented and defined by some larger structure. The greatest concentration, at least of those with the latest reports and speculations, and frequented by the leading wits and traders, was to be found in the vicinity of the old Custom House on the quayside or behind on Essex Street. The Custom House, the predecessor of what is often called Dublin's finest building, offers a sharp point of contrast between the architecture Swift knew from childhood, and the more grandiose imperial vision that was just emerging as he entered old age. The Custom House of Swift's time, where his letters were routinely stopped by government agents, was a more reticent, more practical affair. Four storeys high, including its attics, it had three stout chimneys sprouting from a steep roof; an unassumingly proportioned portico, with a set of narrow archways at the base of the front's central section, gave the necessary touch of civic grandeur. It was neatly edged with coigns, and fretted at the eaves with entirely functional corbels. It was a building that belonged in a Dutch mercantile town, and expressed the sort of city Dublin was, historically, before it was obliged to enforce ideas of empire through its façades and boulevards. The coffee-houses and meeting places where Swift's exploits as 'The Dean' were discussed and recorded belonged to the older yet slowly altering culture of this largely vanished city, in which distinct patriotic ideas of an independent Ireland had yet to gain momentum.

Up Essex Street, the Lord Lieutenant's Council Chamber had stood, in a large house reached via 'a handsome pair of wooden steps', until a fire destroyed it in 1711;[23] a more popular and enduring presence at ground level was the 'Wooden Man' (also known as 'The Upright Man'), a totemic effigy to be found near Eustace Street until years after Swift's death. In 1753 a jocular petition was sent to Dublin Castle on the Wooden Man's behalf, rejecting the imputation that he had long been 'harbouring idle and disorderly persons'. Nevertheless, in this locus, where fists flew quite regularly after dark, Dublin's flâneurs mingled with the city's men of business. Dempster's, Bacon's and the Merchant's were only a few of the most prominent establishments. One was named after an elephant that had been put on display in the neighbourhood, then accidentally incinerated and subsequently dissected by avid natural philosophers.[24] As in London, a good coffee-house allowed its clientele to combine their refreshment with other business or interests: thus the Grecian by Essex Bridge sometimes served as an auction-house, and the Cocoa Tree was conveniently located above one of the city's best bookshops. Any of these offered a large variety of newspapers – most only a few sheets, or a single broadside in length – the better class of which provided news not only from Dublin but also London, interspersed with briefer dispatches from the Continent. A paper of quality would have a long discursive essay: in mid-December 1726 readers idled over a meditation on 'things unusual' in the *Dublin Weekly Journal*.

In this edition 'Hibernicus', an Ulster Presbyterian called James Arbuckle, who moved about the city on crutches, reflected on Europe's attitude to the 'barbarians' of the other three continents. 'The many volumes of Voyages and Adventures, of Itineraries and Pilgrimages ... afford us very little Ground of triumphing over them, either as to the Natural Superiority of our Understanding, or the Purity of our Virtue.' To the learned, the thought was rather commonplace – if, for the most part, strictly hypothetical; but it might have been stirred in Arbuckle's mind by a sensational volume that had been advertised in the paper's 'Just Publish'd' section for some weeks now. Along with *The History of the Conquest of Mexico* and *The Lives and Amours of Queens and Royal Mistresses*, readers were informed of:

> Travels into Sev'ral Remote Nations of the World. In IV Parts. *viz*. A Voyage to Lilliput. II A Voyage to Brobdingnag. III A Voyage to Laputa, Balnibarbi, Luggnagg, Glubdubdrib, and Japan. IV A Voyage to the Country of the Hoyhnhums. By *Lemuel Gulliver*, First Surgeon, and then Captain of Several Ships. Sold by G. Risk, G. Ewing and W. Smith in Dame Street.

The spelling of the distant places was unorthodox – although the more easily pronounced variant on Houyhnhnms surely had something to recommend it – because the Irish edition was almost certainly unauthorized. As in most notices the book received, Lemuel Gulliver is named as author and appears as real a person as the dentist Samuel Steel, whose advert for his practice always filled the bottom corner of the *Weekly Journal*'s last column. Almost every week Mr Steel reminded the public that he eased the toothache with unrivalled skill and gentleness, cleaned teeth, 'be they never so foul', offered tips on preserving them, and furnished hopeless cases with dentures 'so neat' they seemed real and might be worn 'several Years, without being taken out of the Mouth'.[25]

Arbuckle went somewhat hot and cold on Swift. Like the rest of Dublin, he had lauded the Drapier; his paper, backed by the powerful Whig Lord Molesworth, informed the nation of the debt it owed the Dean himself. Yet, as a Presbyterian, there was only so far and for so long that he could get along with the champion. A crude and fatally unpopular broadside against Swift in 1735 would make mud of his name amid the patriots for the rest of his days; yet Swift publicly (and generously) expressed admiration for some of Arbuckle's later work, a just tribute to a man of reading, principle and perception. Arbuckle was one of myriad minor writers to whom Swift would offer battle and in some rare cases reconciliation. At present he was still one of Swift's wholehearted supporters in the Whig camp; over previous years he had solicitously recorded ups and downs in Swift's health. Back in the last weeks of 1726 he had, however, ignored a piece of Swift-related news that was widely reported elsewhere, notably in a paper run by a young publisher, George Faulkner, with whom Swift was later closely connected. On 30 November, to mark both his birthday and the Drapier's victory, a large number of gentlemen had marched up to the cathedral to join prayers and to sing hymns. Outside afterwards, a small fiesta was held: 'a splendid entertainment' was performed, featuring song and instrumental music. The bells again rang in Swift's honour, and bonfires were lit at various points throughout the city. Faulkner printed a stately report of the celebration in his *Dublin Journal* (not to be confused with Arbuckle's *Weekly*) on 3 December.

Twenty-four years old, Faulkner had only finished his apprenticeship two years previously and had not yet been made 'free' of the city or his guild. Yet he was already well settled in business, operating at present from the hub by the other cathedral, in Christ Church Yard. His name would be for ever associated with Swift's, although by this time they may have had no personal contact. In 1725 Faulkner's shop had run together a collection of the Drapier letters, issued as *Fraud Detected; or, The Hibernian Patriot*. Faulkner was a true devotee of his trade: an obsessive worker who badgered and bargained until he got his way, his eyes fixed on obtaining good copy for the best possible deal. A few years later, silly neglect of an injured shin in the midst of work led to his losing a leg. The disability did nothing to slow him down, and he was soon distinguished for his quick, piratical gait. Faulkner made good use of his tenacity to cadge Swift into letting him print the first compilation of his works, printed in four volumes – with predictably hypocritical huffs of protest and disavowal from Swift himself – in 1735.

Faulkner's *Hibernian Patriot* and Arbuckle's more circumspect *Journal* give a fair idea of the range within the consensus of support Swift could motivate. He only wished the same unity could be mustered in other struggles against London. Hopes that it would, he knew, were unrealistic: a few weeks later Arbuckle's editorial was fulsome in praise of the English, urging his Dublin readers to imitate their self-declared overlords. But in general 'Hibernicus' bears out the comment quoted earlier that Swift really had brought Tory and Whig, Papist, High Church and Fanatic, together – notwithstanding his omission of the city's birthday tribute to Swift. There were, after all, other stories to pursue. On the same day Faulkner reported the procession and street celebrations, the most eye-catching item in his Presbyterian rival's issue was 'news from Guildford': a woman there had apparently given birth to a rabbit. She was brought into town for examination by learned physicians.

The journals showed, however, that Gulliver's *Travels* were ubiquitous, and a lucrative publishing property. In London, Swift had quite overpowered the reading public's imagination. John Gay, writing in mid-November after recovering from a fever, gives the most coherent of the many accounts Swift received of Gulliver's reception.

> About ten days ago a Book was publish'd here of the Travels of one Gulliver, which hath been the conversation of the whole town ever since: The whole impression sold in a week, and nothing is more diverting than to hear the different opinions people give of it, though all agree in liking it extremely. 'Tis generally said that you are the Author, but I am told, the Bookseller declares he knows not from what hand it came. From the highest to the lowest it is universally read, from the Cabinet-council to the Nursery.[26]

From the outset the *Travels* attracted the wide spectrum of readers (and listeners) it has held for centuries now. There were notable and discrepant individuals among Gulliver's early admirers, however: the Duchess (now dowager) of Marlborough, sixty-six years old, having hated Swift religiously since at least 1710, was now reportedly in 'raptures' over the work and swearing how she had misjudged the author. The sell-out was remarkable for a work of 700 pages priced rather highly at 8s.6d.

The objectivity in Gay's letter was naturally feigned. Having assisted Swift (along with Charles Ford) in preparing the manuscript for publication, he was writing pointedly here for the benefit of the post office letter-openers retained on the Secret Service fund, and also playing along with Swift's show of ignorance about Gulliver. John Arbuthnot in his more business-like way reported the same provocation and excitement, and gave precious evidence of how the *Travels*' reality-device had taken in many. A trustworthy earl, 'no inventor of stories', had talked with the master of a ship who informed him 'that he was very well acquainted with Gulliver', but lived at Wapping '& not in Rotherhith', as the printer claimed.[27] Pope urged Swift to make the most of his new pre-eminence. 'Surely, without flattery, you are now above all parties of men ... Don't fancy none but Tories are your friends.'[28] Pope's arguments had convinced Swift to charge Motte £200 for the copyright;[29] a timely demand, now the first impression had run out, for small fortunes were soon being made on bootlegged editions.[30] A similar point was made more roguishly by another old comrade: the Earl of Peterborough, the Whig-turned-Tory-turned-would-be-Whig, and sometime captor of Barcelona. The Earl accosted Swift as a wizard, a Protean magician shifting his shape from Drapier to ship's Surgeon and 'sometimes a Reverend divine', but settled on addressing him as 'Captain Gulliver'. All Swift need do now, Peterborough joshed, was to master one of the kingdoms' most popular street-entertainments. 'The Capt indeed has nothing more to doe but to chalk his pumps, learn to dance upon the Rope, and I may yet live to see him a bishop; verily, verily, I believe he never was in such imminent danger of preferment.'[31] Peterborough was alluding to one of the funniest passages in the early chapters of the *Travels*, where Gulliver soberly describes the displays of acrobatic lackeying necessary for any successful courtier in Lilliput. What was true of Lilliput was in this case, as in so many others, true at home. Peterborough's letter captures for us the delight clearly felt at the sheer cheek of Swift's fiction. Never had Europe's culture of grovelling and corruption been lampooned so brilliantly.[32]

In all, the *Travels* caught the mood of a world ripe with wonders. Both Peterborough and Swift's new friend Mrs Howard mentioned the story of the unfortunate woman of Guildford whose poor child was thought a rabbit. Like Peterborough, Prince George's mistress wrote to Swift as Gulliver, and received two jovially conceived letters in reply: one from Swift as Swift, voicing perplexity at her note – confusion he cleared only on investigating a copy of the *Travels* for himself; and another, delightfully, from Swift as Lemuel Gulliver, thanking her for her faith in his good intentions. He offered her the crown of Lilliput, which he had saved from the flames he controversially extinguished.

According to Gay, the majority of readers felt that the *Travels* contained no 'reflections' on individuals – and would thus escape charges of libel or sedition. Anticipating a long critical tradition, he reported how many felt 'the Satire on general societies of men is too severe'. One particular corpulent East Anglian, though, could hardly avoid detecting a decidedly personal edge to Gulliver's severe criticisms of 'Chief Ministers'. Swift's text was even watered down for the first edition.

A *First* or *Chief Minister of State*, whom I intended to describe, was a
Creature wholly exempt from Joy and Grief, Love and Hatred, Pity and
Anger; at least makes use of no other Passions but a violent Desire of
Wealth, Power and Titles: That he applies his Words to all Uses, except
to the Indication of his Mind; That he never tells a *Truth*, but with an
intent that you should take it for a *Lye*; nor a *Lye,* but with a Design
that you should take it for a Truth.[33]

Though obviously intended for George I's first minister, Swift's attack is
also undoubtedly directed beyond Walpole; much of his distant anger
against 'Volpone' Godolphin, the old Fox, can be felt in the passage.[34]
Here Swift also risked being understood as criticizing his onetime leader,
Oxford. He had loved the Earl, now dead two years, until the end; and
was on excellent terms with his scholarly minded son. Some confusion is
unavoidable since Walpole resembled Oxford in guarding his cards,
keeping a tight hold on all strands of power and operating in a general
atmosphere of mystery. Both chief ministers, the Whig and his Tory predecessor, had developed their own spy networks. Indeed, perhaps some
of Swift's suppressed exasperation with Oxford really is an ingredient of
Gulliver's outburst against political leaders. It should be recalled how
Swift told Oxford he liked him all the more when he was deposed as the
Lord Treasurer; since whatever faults he saw in him as a minister he
found few in him as the man who was his friend.

From early December, critical commentaries began appearing. There
was a marked dislike of the 'filthy', scatological passages. One early
critic and decipherer took the simple opportunity of an all-out denigra-
tion of Arbuthnot, Pope and Gay; another was genuinely distraught by
the vision of humanity in the fourth voyage, 'so monstrously absurd and
unjust'. Some balance was struck in a 'key' to the *Travels* by Abel Boyer,
offering acuity in exchange for some grateful plagiarism – since long and
lucrative passages from the text accompanied his explanations.[35] Then,
as now, however, sales had an eloquence of their own. The *Travels* were
a phenomenon. Motte was exhausting his printers to meet demand, and
the brigands of the trade had full pockets too. Translations in Dutch,
French and German would appear in 1727.

Bonfires and fanfares in his neighbourhood; acclaim and wonder-
ment brought in by newspapers and the post; yet the acclaim rang rather
flatly behind the deanery windows, dimmed by Swift's echoey ears and
a worried heart. He had made the house much more his own since he
first moved in twelve years ago, when he complained it was too big and

empty. Portraits of old friends, presents he demanded they send, now hung on the walls, along with prints and other trifles he had gathered over time. One was a mezzotint of a thinker Bolingbroke also claimed to admire, Aristippus, celebrated by Horace as one who could adapt himself perfectly to every circumstance and every station of life, high and low, accepting greatness and misfortune alike.[36] But it was hard to be like Aristippus when the person you loved most was dying, and knew it, and when you lacked the courage to watch till the end. Johnson had survived 1726, but was terribly weakened. Swift had plans for another journey to England; another flight from grief.

At the height of her recovery, just before winter, Johnson was still 'very lean and low'.[37] By January she was sinking again, and would never really regain her strength. In March, Swift wrote what proved, as they both perhaps already suspected, to be the last of his birthday poems to her. The opening lines cast a charm and call for a freeze on reality:

> This Day, whate'er the Fates decree,
> Shall still be kept with Joy by me:
> This Day then, let us not be told,
> That you are sick, and I grown old,
> Nor think on our approaching Ills,
> And talk of Spectacles and Pills;
> Tomorrow will be Time enough
> To hear such mortifying Stuff.

Yet the poem is thickly shadowed with the anxieties it tries to allay. The lines react to Johnson's unheard voice, the voice now of a terminally ill person, in Swift's attempts at comfort. She was wondering what life meant and what her own life amounted to; she was holding on only for the sake of her friends – some of whom she accused, directly or implicitly, of unkindness. They were unkind in making her keep going; and perhaps, the poem senses, for other reasons. Swift tackled the first, existential streak of angst with a genial request:

> From not the gravest of Divines,
> Accept for once some serious Lines.
> Although we now can form no more
> Long schemes of Life, as heretofore;
> Yet you, while Time is running fast,
> Can look with Joy on what is past.

She had lived well, virtuously and charitably, courageously and authentically, Swift told her; the world was a better place for her presence. Did she think her good acts were mere 'empty shadows . . . That fly and leave no marks behind?' Unfortunately the terms of the question imply the answer. He could pat her hand all she wished; on 13 March 1727 the dying woman reached the age of just forty-six. Although disparaging himself as a divine, he could only speak as one. The poem is all about good deeds lodged in heaven's memory; no mention is made of dreams or wishes nurtured on earth, or the disappointments Johnson appears to have expressed. As for the charge of unkindness, Swift urged her to 'take pity on your pitying Friends'.

> Me, surely me, you ought to spare,
> Who gladly would your Suff'rings share;
> Or give my Scrap of Life to you,
> And think it far beneath your Due;
> You, to whose Care so oft I owe,
> That I'm alive to tell you so.[38]

This last poem for Stella bears out Swift's claim about the toll of 'violent friendship'. Desperation was being smothered on both sides; at the same time the poem tries to set a seal of peace on what must have been quite frequent reproaches. Johnson does seem to have 'spared' him, for a month after writing the poem he embarked – evidently with her permission – for England.

One reason for Swift's huge popularity in Ireland was the grinding hardship he had declared unacceptable. Had the country been less miserable, he would have inspired fewer supporters. And the hope he offered was frail and sceptical; he made no attempt to deny that all his efforts might prove futile, that Ireland might be beyond salvation, and that it might even deserve the desolation it faced. The state of things he left behind in April 1727 was only worsening. The Primate of All Ireland wrote of how, on his visitation that year, 'we met all the roads full of whole families that had left their homes to beg abroad, since their neighbours had nothing to relieve them with.'[39] Despite strong differences of party, the Primate's analysis of the situation tallied closely with Swift's. A period of wretched harvests was setting in, worsened (in contemporary eyes) by the long-standing trends of converting arable land to pasture for livestock, and the discouragement to agriculture from English legislation. The country now needed to import grain, and could barely afford it. The internal economy suffered from a chronic lack of silver and gold exacerbated by a punishing exchange rate. The English gold guinea was worth threepence more in Ireland than in England; in consequence, the Irish tended to make payments to England in silver, lowering further the country's supply of ready money.[40] Swift would observe dourly that the Irish situation reversed the maxim that the chief riches of a country are its inhabitants, an argument taken to its ultimate conclusion in the most notorious of his modest *Proposals*. There was simply too little at home to support the population; and thus people began leaving the kingdom in hordes.

Simultaneously, in a cruel irony, the position of those seeking to raise genuine concern was badly compromised. The clergy, who were the chief activists for Irish trade and self-respect, were widely seen as a large part of the problem because of the tithes that gave them their livelihood. In some ways this position has been continued by scholars who view Swift as caring only for the fate of 'loyal Protestant subjects' in Ireland. In part, undoubtedly, this was manifestly true: the Irish Catholic peasantry (and gentry) were barbarians to him, as they were the great 'other' to the colonizing landowners and their foot soldiers.[41] Yet the case, despite abundance of proof on its side, may still be overstated. Nobody knew better than Swift what a small fraction of the population such *loyal* Protestant persons constituted. Gritting his teeth, he was speaking up for a vast number who failed to match this profile. Doing so directly was naturally unthinkable: arguments voiced on behalf of the impoverished Catholic majority would have been treated as treasonous, the final proof, indeed, of the Dean's suspected Jacobitism. The question needs bearing in mind of what it was politically possible for Swift to say, notwithstanding his own strong anti-Catholic prejudices.

The Protestant institutions of the kingdom, with the Anglican Church established at its core, certainly comprised the constitutional framework Swift sought to preserve; and undoubtedly, as a firm supporter of the initial phase of the Glorious Revolution, he was willing to countenance great violence in the defence of that framework. But his pamphlets of the late 1720s show indignation on behalf of all those facing starvation, 'loyal Protestant' or 'wild Irish'. For as long as Swift could remember (and long before) the poorest of Ireland's vast Catholic majority had been living in unspeakable conditions. There was consequently a gruesome predisposition to disregard the Irish peasantry as direct victims of an emergency such as the dearth of 1727–30. Rather, they provided the measure of deprivation to which the enfranchised and entitled 'nation' of Ireland was now sinking. The great shock to Swift's generation in the late 1720s was that Protestant parishioners were approaching the subsistence level of Catholic peasants.[42] The picture was muddying; it was not always possible to say who the barbarians were any more.

The same basic concern for life, in all fairness, also emerges in some publications and dispatches by Swift's worst enemies in the Church. Yet the best and ablest clerics were limited in number, and the best of all were physically failing. Swift's health was always uncertain, and it was frankly a miracle that Archbishop King had survived a winter of pleurisy and rheumatic pain.[43] The Archbishop had spent much of his last sojourn in England at Bath, taking the waters. Similarly, on leaving the island again in 1727 Swift planned to combine political campaigning with private recuperation. He had resolved at last on travelling to the Continent in the summer and trying the cures on offer at Aachen.

Otherwise, Swift travelled for many of the reasons that had always taken him to England. It was only there that one could meet and influence people who ultimately directed those who held the strings in Ireland. Like the regions below Laputa, Ireland was remotely controlled. Meanwhile, as ever, he had affairs of his own to settle and friends he dearly missed. His old words about belonging in the land of his fathers, the land that 'made' him, still had much of their incanted force. He repeated them, since they were necessary in order to keep up appearances – in his own eyes as much as in anyone else's. His first action on arriving had a touch of exorcism about it. He travelled to Herefordshire and visited the parsonage designed by his grandfather, Thomas Swift, at Goodrich. Despite angry statements about them, he stayed in regular touch with relatives on both sides of the water, and was generous with his money when they needed it. The gift he brought to Goodrich was both costly and symbolic – a chalice used by the Reverend Swift and cherished by his family as a relic. Swift had had the heirloom newly inscribed before returning it to its home church: it now commemorated the old Royalist as one 'known in history' for deeds supporting the King. Swift's Latin here has been described as 'inelegant'; possibly the weight of the occasion was a little too much.[44] In part, there was relief to be had in passing on the heavy cup. It seems significant that the fragment of family history written by Swift dates from after this final visit.[45] The stories of the generations took their final shape, with salutary and pejorative ends in mind. His paternal grandfather becomes the beatified patriarch; his sons become the guardians who fail in their trust – Swift's father by marrying, his uncles by neglecting him. His maternal relatives are hardly mentioned. It is significant too, surely, that Swift set this account aside. The 'Family of Swift' ends with a complaint, an unsustainable one, about his failure as a younger man to gain the deanery of Derry. He abandoned the document there; the implied decision is that he had said enough, and that the vein of resentment was not worth pursuing further. The egoistical example of Bishop Burnet possibly discouraged him as a memoirist. Writing about the present may understandably have taken up too much of his energy for him to return to the autobiography.

Next in the spring of 1727 there followed a brief trip to Oxford before reunions with Pope, Gay, Bolingbroke and the second Earl of Oxford. At Twickenham he and Pope, when their illnesses allowed, worked on an 'authorized' collection of *Miscellanies* that would finally – they thought – put Curll in his place. As it had the previous summer, Pope's house provided Swift with a base for most of his stay, a point of safe return from his various excursions to the city, Cambridge and Richmond, among other ports of call. While maintaining private friendships, he also pursued a committed and cunning political agenda. Through his amicable contact with Mrs Howard, he hoped for more access to the foremost royal couple. In mid-May, Princess Caroline summoned him for an audience twice in one week, and he wrote proudly to Sheridan of their talk. 'She retains her old civility, and I my old freedom.' His skills as courtier exercising the privileges of counsel were undiminished. The Princess moreover indulged him in a game of spot the bashful author. She accused him, 'without ceremony', of having written a 'bad book', one which she and Prince George liked in 'every particular'. Purring, Swift 'gave her leave, since she liked the book, to suppose what author she pleased'. He left the palace satisfied, and the experience even gave some breeziness to remarks he later wrote to Sheridan on Johnson. She and Dingley were living at the deanery in his absence; but let them spend as much time in the country, out in fresh air, he directed. Johnson had caught cold, he was informed; and he replied that surely this didn't put her in danger. He was oblivious to the skill with which Caroline had massaged his self-esteem, naturally without any word of support on concrete political matters.

George and Caroline's public dislike of Walpole was enough for Swift. The opposition was finally gaining strength; Bolingbroke had even been granted an audience with the King. To Sheridan, dictating for fear of his well-known hand being recognized, Swift reported a new and strange situation: he found among his allies at last 'a firm, settled Resolution to assault the present Administration, and break it if possible'. He was lending the weight of his name and also the skill of his pen to Bolingbroke and his lieutenant, William Pulteney, the leading authors of a vibrant, well-written new paper, the *Craftsman*.[46] There was gratitude as well as personal pleasure, then, among such friends, at Swift's arrival – for his presence was totemic for the Tory cause. And Walpole, it seemed, was unnerved by the new confidence of his enemies. Swift gave credence to reports that the minister was 'peevish and disconcerted', and that he had marked the Dean of St Patrick's as an orchestrator of dissent. Swift was already inclined to trust Bolingbroke and others when they warned him against travelling to Europe, for fear that he might be assassinated. In May, he was almost buoyant, thrilled with the prospect of a fight, a bit vain, understandably wary, and more than a little naive. Almost touchingly, he still believed that a change of ministry might radically help the people of Ireland.[47]

The prospect of real change grew larger, very suddenly, and then faded in the course of a season. On 3 June, George I departed for his annual trip to Hanover; on the 11th he died of an apoplectic fit. For a moment, it looked as if the ministry might be dissolved and that Bolingbroke might have his chance, at long last, of taking over the Treasury. Yet an initial display of scorn from the younger George to Walpole – who arrived panting at Richmond, disturbed the heir's sleep, and was given to understand that he no longer held office – turned out to be misleading. Contrary to expectations, not least his own, Walpole remained the new monarch's English vizier. The main effect on Swift of the death in Germany was an end to his travel plans. He was all set for France, when the news arrived, but after weeks of hesitation called off his adventure. The friends who had before merely cautioned him against going now urged him to stay with 'great vehemence'. This was no time to be leaving the country, but rather a moment to be seized, crucially, by every show of attachment to the successor. Drifting to France might lead some to suspect Jacobite intent (despite the ruinous state of the Pretender's affairs); at best it looked flighty. Swift, bred in an age when such matters of form meant even more than they did in Georgian England, listened and was swayed.[48] His confidence had been shaken, too, by another tiff with Archbishop King. Politics, friends, St Patrick's, his age – he was sixty in November – all pulled him back from breaking the geographical limits of his lifetime. Only news of Johnson's death might have driven him away to France – into hiding, past caring.

His loss of resolve is clarified in the light of two of the many struggles that claimed him that summer. One was official, the other physical; both involved two familiar adversaries, and both exposed the very fragile sense Swift still had of his personal dignity. The first battle was short and explosive, and to a large extent unprovoked. Archbishop King had conducted his visitation of St Patrick's while Swift was away, and reprimanded the Dean for supplying no proxy in his absence. It was a matter of bureaucracy, and arguably King was somewhat pedantic in making a fuss. He postponed the revisit until Swift completed the necessary paperwork. Swift was incensed. He reacted as he always did when someone tried to correct or criticize him while assuming the role of higher authority. He dispatched a long, melodramatic rebuke, denying King's right to make such demands and heckling him in the now well-practised tones of an accomplished freedom-fighter. 'My proceeding shall be only upon one maxim: never to yield to an oppression, to justify which no precedent can be produced.' And then he exhaled all the ill-feeling which had rankled within him against King for decades:

> I see very well how personal all this proceeding is; and how, from the very moment of the Queen's [Anne's] death, your Grace hath thought fit to take every opportunity of giving me all sorts of uneasiness, without ever giving me, in my whole life, one single mark of your favour, beyond common civilities. And, if it were not below a man of spirit to make complaints, I could date them from six and twenty years past.[49]

There was little justice in launching such a tirade over an administrative lapse. But Swift was roaring inwardly at everyone who had been charged with nurturing and acknowledging him and who had failed him in both respects. The phrase 'my whole life' stands out in the sentences above, and in the full letter. King had neglected to give Swift his due for a career of (it was true) unstinting service to the Church; but he had missed what Swift really needed and deserved. He had failed to act the part of the father Swift never had. None of the rewards brought by the Drapier or Gulliver could compensate for the humiliations he had suffered as a result of this dereliction. As so often before, King seems to have intuited that Swift's rebuke was directed at someone or something other than him. He continued to treat the subject of dispute as what it was – an administrative point.

The other fight exposing Swift's insecurities was with a real and unrelenting enemy. In early August his sickness struck him down. As usual, there was little benefit in taking emetics or abstaining from the painfully delicious harvest of 'peaches, figs, nectarines and mulberries', though he did both. Deafened and whirling with vertigo, he sealed himself in his room at Twickenham, unable or refusing to see visitors. Along with intense physical discomfort he was mortified by the sight he presented to his noble friends. As the weeks of late summer passed, there was little improvement. Elsewhere in the house, Pope was working on the *Dunciad* and Gay on his *Beggar's Opera* – according to legend, in response to a 'hint' from Swift. When his vision cleared and stomach steadied, Swift also took up paper and pen, but could stay with neither for long. A wearied yet good-humoured letter informed Sheridan that 'I am now Deafer than ever you knew me, yet a little less, I think than yesterday.' He was alarmed at news that the new King and Queen would shortly arrive in the neighbourhood, that is at Richmond Palace, and he would be expected at Court. The prospect was unthinkable; tottering, in mid-August he left Twickenham for London, where he arranged for a cousin to have him nursed at her house in New Bond Street.[50] Mrs Howard sent merry sympathies to Swift on his disorders. He had promised to pay his respects in person when he could walk without staggering and was able to hear a musket let off.[51] She chided him on his flight – she had suffered many years herself with terrible headaches, 'and yet never was peevish with my self or the world'.[52] Swift replied genially, telling a story of how he first met Deafness and Giddiness, 'now two old friends', many years before in Surrey.[53] The cordial message is also important for what it omits to say. It was an accomplished display of tactical courtesy, since many months had passed since Swift had stopped thinking of Mrs Howard as a potential ally. At a personal level, he saw that she could be sincere and benevolent. But when Prince George became king, Swift feared that her increased scope as a courtier would gradually suffocate her 'private virtues'.[54]

An ageing man, deaf and walking drunkenly – when he could stand – and shuddering with the after-convulsions of the potions he drank to empty his stomach: this was the spectacle he could make of himself to Sheridan but it was not something he was prepared to show to Paris. His decrepitude would be reported and eagerly amplified in the many Whig journals. Furthermore, his literary judgement was also at stake. In July, he had corresponded with his French translator, the Abbé Pierre Desfontaines, who assured him that the city's literati eagerly expected his arrival – and that, indeed, 'all of Paris wishes to see you.' The optical language makes it hard again not to identify Swift with the exhibit Gulliver becomes in various remote capitals. Vexingly, however, there had been a problem with the translation, of which Desfontaines now sent Swift the second edition. Revising it, the translator felt impelled to censor coarser and misanthropic passages, which he had already trimmed extensively at the first attempt. Such rectitude, he felt, better suited French tastes.[55] He provoked a courteous yet spirited defence from Swift. They could agree, Swift conceded, that the taste of nations was not always identical; yet, where there were people of intelligence, taste as to judgement and knowledge would always be the same. Gulliver would hardly be road-worthy if he could appeal only to the minds of Atlantic islanders. Notably, he appealed to the verdict of 'les partisans de ce Gulliver', who had already declared the work immortal just as it was – it would outlive the conventions and customs Desfontaines found so important. This reference to critical opinion carried with it a faint note of uncertainty. Desfontaines was spokesperson for a literary culture that had set the rules for Neoclassical decorum; Swift stood for the view that human filth and depravity – the subjects Desfontaines was anxious to diminish – were inextricable from real life. In the state he was in, Swift had no wish, or rather lacked the strength, to take this argument to Paris, however much the city wished to gaze at him. He often regretted the decision.

Nevertheless, he kept the possibility open, because if one piece of 'fatal news' reached him from Dublin, he would still consider going to France – for what he then hoped would be his final winter. The sense of his own physical affliction was the milder of two grim spirits hovering constantly overhead; the other, more baleful, was Johnson's condition, and the constant thought that she might suffer a relapse. Two letters from Sheridan in the second half of August told him to prepare for the worst. While still at Twickenham, he said that no message could injure him more – except perhaps some declaration that he 'should be put to Death for some ignominious Crime'. The letter opened a shaft of nightmare, guilt and persecution. Thinking of Johnson's decline, Swift seems to have felt he was on trial for his own life: implicitly, the word of her death, when it came, would strike him like a heinous accusation. He was too sick to travel, but the knowledge of her pain made returning impossible; he couldn't face it. As with his conduct the year before, Swift once again invited charges of selfishness and moral cowardice: that no such accusations arrived, it seems, in correspondence from Dublin indicates how well he was loved – and possibly how much he was feared – by the deanery circle. His letter to King, berating the Archbishop for failing to act as a father, surely has some bearing on his state of mind with regard to Johnson. All the bravery he had shown in opening parcel-bombs, staring down pistol-barrels on the road and charging down the British government in the guise of the Drapier simply deserted him now. With no memories of real nurture, in this crisis of impending separation he could only nurse himself, and so forsook the woman on what was most likely her death-bed. At the same time, as the author of a book that so many had proclaimed immortal, after long years of what he felt was neglect, he had also possibly succumbed to the conviction artists sometimes have that their talents and sufferings entitle them to special exemptions and indulgences.

When Sheridan's next letter came, he kept it in his pocket for an hour, afraid to break the seal. Even his illness was now almost a comfort, 'for it would have been a Reproach to me to be in perfect Health, when such a Friend is desperate.' He asked what point there would be in recovering – 'to see the Loss of that Person for whose sake Life was only worth preserving'. Once again, writing at more length was beyond him. 'I am able to hold up my sorry Head no longer.'[56]

Despite thoughts of staying longer, in mid-September he made a sudden move to return. On the 12th he had directed Worrall to extend his licence to remain abroad for another half-year. The proprieties of the situation in his house also filled him with panic: few outside their network of helpers and friends in the liberty seem to have known that Johnson and Dingley were living in the deanery. They must be moved, he decided, for it would seem indecent if Johnson died in his home – base persons would draw slanderous conclusions. Self-consciously, almost absurdly, he gave these instructions in Latin – which would pose little difficulty for an enemy in the Church or Secret Service (and clerics sometimes worked for both organizations). His real intention was possibly to hide these words from Johnson, if she should get a glimpse of the letter.[57] Certainly such effort on his part to get her out of his house before she died there looks harsh from this point in time, regardless of appearances his friend was surely past caring about. Perhaps it was guilt about such thoughts that prompted him to leave London in a sudden rush just a week later. In any case, he seems to have sensed that his bout of giddy deafness was nearing the end of a cycle, and he resolved to make the most of it. The road itself may also have revived him, for his hearing slowly improved over the course of a journey that in other respects proved shattering. This considerable mercy aside, his one comfort on the trip would be a fine empty commonplace book he had stolen from one of Walpole's minions.[58]

## 3

He and his servant Watt started westwards by coach on 18 September. Their journey from London began in an inn amid the dark lanes of Aldersgate Street, within the old City walls.[59] They stopped at Coventry, and at Chester met one Lawson, the Captain of the royal yacht, 'a man of veracity'.[60] Lawson would be sailing for Ireland from the port of Parkgate, but could not say exactly when; fatally, Swift declined the offer of a berth. Instead he and Watt rode on towards Holyhead. They hired a most unsatisfactory guide, who grumbled at Swift's requests to see the sights along their road. It was a journey of three days, which master and servant broke overnight firstly at a place he called 'Ridland' (probably Ruthin), twenty-two miles by Swift's reckoning from Chester.[61] At Conway, he was recognized by the elderly landlady of an inn; he viewed the tomb of Nicholas Hook, born a forty-first child and the father of twenty-seven. Leaving Bangor, their next resting point, at four in the morning, he and Watt were undone by the rocky ways. Five miles from Holyhead, both horses lost shoes. Although it was Sunday, Watt found a smith, with whom they left the horses and walked on to an inn. There was no ale in the house; and with a fierce thirst and a growing temper Swift found a boatman to take him the last few miles along the coast to the harbour. When they arrived, they learned that the ship for Dublin, with unfortunate promptness, had departed just the day before. The next would be held up, it turned out, for more than a week.

If Holyhead felt disconnected, geography reinforced the sensation. The harbour town is tucked into a north-western extremity on a north-western extremity, on a dot of land separate from the island of Anglesey. It takes its name from the 'monstrous mountain' looming over it, the 'Holy Head' or 'Sacrum Promontorium'. Defoe on his Great Tour mentioned a common practice of climbing the promontory for a view of Ireland, a walk often disappointed by bad weather, as Swift's was, before returning or continuing south. The clouded sky and empty sea compared unfavourably with the piled stones found in Merioneth, which made Stonehenge seem ordinary.[62] Physically, Holyhead favours an experience of discontinuity; it is the stub of an atoll, a last stone in the sea, the remnant of a lost bridge between Albion and Hibernia.

That night the bumps and strains of his days on horseback communicated themselves in his sleep: Swift dreamed he fell twenty times from his saddle. The next morning brought his misery home to him. Holyhead was desolate, emptied by the recent sailing. The inn-keeper was a good woman but her establishment was squalid. He was almost out of clean linen, and a sweaty shirt had already done two days of duty. Worst of all, the previous batch of passengers had emptied Holyhead of wine. With no books to read, and no acceptable company, he whiled away both morning and afternoon walking on the rocks. The next day, when he went further still, he was diverted by water shooting several feet into the air from a blow-hole. By this time he had turned to his purloined notebook, and had begun to fill it with every thought and perception he could put into writing – the bare events of each day, ideas for essays, pieces of poems. Half consciously, he returned to the epistolary mode of report he had last used during his ministry years. His record of a week's baiting at Holyhead reads like one final *Journal to Stella* entry. 'Is this not strange stuff?' he seems to ask her at one point, with his old confidentiality. 'Why, what would you have me do?' Yet this journal was not addressed to her, or at least not constantly. He mentions his 'dearest friend' firmly in the third person.[63]

He would not admit it, but the situation did improve somewhat on the evening of his first stranded day, when the packet-ship brought his hostess eighteen bottles of claret. He ordered one with the 'raw chicken' he was served for dinner, and found it bad. Yet he ordered another with supper the following night.[64] Wine was one pleasure that left his conscience in peace. When an ignorant do-gooder proposed taxing luxury imports, Swift claimed he could part with tea or coffee or spices – and of course declared that 'foreign cloaths' should be burned – yet pleaded: 'I beg you will leave us our Wine, to make us *forget* a while our Misery.'[65] Swift was, however, far from taking his love of the grape to excess, at least by the standard of the times: a bottle sufficed, and as he told Pope: 'I can bear a pint better than you can a spoonful.'[66] Gulliver, calmly quaffing two half-pint Lilliputian hogsheads, each in one draught, gives a fair idea of Swift's tolerance to alcohol.[67] The Bacchic spirit, though, remained distant from his writing – the most crazed of his voices tend to speak with a grim sobriety. Voltaire, whom he had possibly met on this or his previous trip, was acute in rejecting the already popular idea of Swift as an 'English Rabelais'. A connection was there between the two satiric fantasists, he admitted, but without qualification it distorted the nature of both writers. Voltaire found Rabelais tedious, and blamed a surfeit of liquor for a lack of discipline. By contrast, he thought Swift's steady rationality compelling, even when the logic served absurdity.

When Voltaire maintained that 'Dean Swift is Rabelais in his senses' he meant that Swift was a sobered-up Rabelais. A measure of the historical difference between these two grand eighteenth-century names is that Swift had no reason to meet or acknowledge the still rather obscure French writer in his early thirties, living in exile for insulting a noble-man; but Voltaire's *English Letters* nevertheless might have offered him an independent defence against the doubts of Gulliver's French transla-tor. Desfontaines would surely have been nonplussed to read Voltaire's assertion that Swift 'possesses all the Delicacy, the Justness, the good Taste' that in Rabelais were wanting. Swift was grateful when a bottle took the edge off, but he was no 'intoxicated Philosopher'.[68]

The compliments of the avant-garde and the establishment alike seemed distant, indeed, at Holyhead in September 1727. Basic hygiene was high on Swift's priorities – higher even, possibly, than a glass of decent burgundy – and he demanded the same cleanliness and courtesy as he would have before his ascent to fame. Rewearing shirts and linen had always been a misery, and he had always despaired of his servants' ineptitude. The blunders of poor Watt – packing just a single cravat, mixing clean with 'foul' clothes in his bag, rubbing Swift's wet gown with a floury cloth, and thus caking it in plaster – would fill, said Swift, a history of their own. The inn's food was awful yet expensive; his room was dark and filled with smoke when the fires were lit. Such faults were basic wrongs against anyone of his station, he felt. Only a suspicion of a star-complex creeps into his notebook jottings. He expected better treat-ment from the Captain, one Jones, by virtue of the personage he had become: the skipper had treated him without 'the least civility', even though Watt had given him the Dean's name. He refused to sail until more passengers arrived. 'In short,' wrote Swift, 'I come from being used like an emperor to be used worse than a Dog at Holyhead.' Behind the supercilious air, though, was a terror of relapsing. He could still hear fairly well, but he felt his dizziness might return; and the thought of being incapacitated in his present location could not be borne. He would receive less care and mercy, he said, than a 'Welsh house cur'.[69]

Despite the rudeness of Captain Jones – and of an unfavourable wind – Swift *was* recognized, even at Holyhead. He claimed that his hat was worn out from being lifted and tipped to the 'poor inhabitants' of the town. His attention was sought even at long distance. A young hopeful by the name of Wheldon believed he had solved the stubborn problem of longitude. Wheldon had sent his proof to the leading authorities, including Edmund Halley, and had received 'not a Tittle of Answer'. He had heard that the famous Dean Swift, whom he mistakenly believed was proficient in the higher mathematics, was marooned at Holyhead, and wondered if he might care to relieve the boredom by perusing his calculations. Swift responded grimly. His old friend and agent at Trim, Joe Beaumont, either had driven himself mad by the agony of longitude, or focused his insanity upon it, and ultimately solved the great problem by taking his life. Moreover, Swift was acquainted with most of the men to whom Wheldon had applied. Halley, the great astronomer, John Keill, a distinguished Scots mathematician, and Isaac Newton – whom Swift despised for colluding, as the Master of the Mint, in the plot to defraud Ireland with base coin – had all told him at one time or other that longitude was incalculable. Swift's answer, printed afterwards in Faulkner's *Dublin Journal*, was brutally concise.

> I understand not Mathematicks, but have been formerly troubled too much with Projectors of the Longitude to my great Mortification ... One of my Projectors cut his Throat, and the other was found an Imposter. This is all I can say; but am confident you would deceive others, or are deceived yourself.[70]

John Wheldon has resisted history, never being identified. He chose, admittedly, a bad moment to approach Swift. Obsessing with a phantom such as the longitude puzzle seemed very much a waste of life. The shortness of time was all too apparent; although 'whoever would wish to live long should live here,' Swift wrote at Holyhead, 'for a day is longer than a week, and if the weather be foul, as long as a fortnight.'[71]

Five hours each evening of his stay lay heavy on his hands. As for Holyhead's vicar, 'a dog is better company', he declared spitefully.[72] During the day bad weather often kept him fretting indoors, and a break in the cloud launched him immediately for a long walk. On Wednesday, 27 September, the day Wheldon's letter reached him, he climbed the mountain behind the town, hoping to glimpse the Wicklow Hills. He paused for breath, unwontedly, fifty-nine times on the way up. At the top, to his sorrow, the haze of the day obscured the view, and presently it thickened to a 'furious shower' that overtook him on his way down. He took shelter in the cabin of an old woman sifting flour, who understood no English: it reminded him despondently of Ireland.[73]

Default sentences cursing Ireland and the Irish pepper the journal; yet so does invective against Wales and in particular Holyhead. The switch from one target to another shows that Swift's rage was largely separable from any of them. There were moments when he was almost reconciled, like Gulliver or Crusoe, to his lonely beach. The faults of the inn were undeniable:

> Yet here I could live with two or three friends in a warm house, and good wine – much better than being a Slave in Ireland. But my misery is, that I am in the worst part of Wales under the worst of circumstances: afraid of a relapse, in utmost solitude, impatient for the condition of our friend.[74]

'Our' friend: was it Sheridan he was writing to? Formal, cautious Delany? Or Johnson's chief attendants, plain, dutiful John Worrall and his wife? Perhaps a composite of all of them; the action of writing suspended his isolation, which was the main thing, and distracted him from his governing anxiety.

> I shall say nothing of the suspense I am in about my dearest friend . . .
> I will speak as if it were not in my thoughts; and only as a passenger who is in a scurvy unprovided comfortless place without one companion, and who therefore wants to be at home, where he hath all conveniences there proper for a Gentleman of quality.[75]

The location was almost irrelevant: the scurvy place that demeaned him might have been 'here' or equally 'there'. All he needed was something to be angry with: sometimes it was Wales, sometimes Ireland, sometimes the long-suffering 'dunce' and 'puppy', Watt. The trigger might as easily have been the mild officiousness of Archbishop King. The seedy Welsh hostelry offended Swift, but then offered him refuge. The deanery seemed one part of the great slave plantation that was Ireland, but then was 'home', a seat that gave him status and comfort, and friends. The values of place alternated, while the constants in Swift's view of his predicament were emotional. A sense of having been cheated, insulted and betrayed; a reader whose imagined trust and sympathy he counts on; and a 'dearest friend' whose imminent loss terrifies and plagues him (albeit one whose death-pangs he wishes desperately not to witness). These were old travelling companions.

His anger with Ireland differed entirely in nature from his hatred of, say, Walpole or Marlborough. The latter were specimens of vice – tyranny and corruption. He got angry with Ireland as he did when he got angry with a servant, and often felt badly about it afterwards ('Pray pity poor Watt, for he is called dunce, puppy and liar 500 times an hour, and yet he means not ill, for he means nothing').[76] Swift's hostility to Ireland, in fact, was the same as it had been that time when, in one account, he decided as a young child that he must have been a changeling. 'Sometimes he would declare, that he was not born in Ireland at all; and seem to lament his condition, that he should be looked upon as a Native of that Country.'[77] Ireland was his personal, emotional shorthand for all that was amiss with the circumstances of his life; a panoply of wrongs that included, incidentally, the sins of England. After a few days at Holyhead he realized there was a great deal of force in his anger that might be put to some use. Whenever he fell into a rage, he would turn his face towards Ireland, in order to stimulate the wind he wished would carry him over. This detail might be a metaphor for the use Swift made, throughout his life, of his pain and frustration. One fortunate thing was that people proved easier to influence than the weather.[78]

At Holyhead he paid unusual attention to his dreams – since other diversions were so scarce. They were largely 'nonsense', he decided, but one he recorded at some length. In it he imagined that Lord Bolingbroke and Pope were in 'my cathedral' at a full service, and the Viscount was going to preach. Swift could not find his surplice, and, though he offered his stall so that Bolingbroke could proceed more easily to the adjacent pulpit, he found that rogue members of the chapter had broken the seat. Then, amid the rabble, he saw Bolingbroke delivering his sermon. 'I thought his prayer was good, but I forget it.' He disliked it, nevertheless, when Bolingbroke quoted from the dramatist and wit Wycherley, Pope's old friend. A classic anxiety dream, it also illuminated Swift's attitude to the two spheres of his public existence, as clergyman and wit. Each had its proper language, and they should not be mixed.[79]

The yacht bearing Lord Carteret to Ireland was due to sail on 14 October. Despairingly Swift began to think they would go over together. Yet on Thursday, after a wait of four days, he was at last informed that wind and tide served. The focus of his anger lifted from the obstinate Captain, Jones, whom he invited to lunch – perhaps in atonement. 'So adieu till I see you in the deanery,' he told the nameless reader intended for his notebook, just before being rowed to the ship. He put off deciding which of his friends should receive his journal. But the ordeal wasn't over. Half an hour out, a sudden strong wind stopped the ship going on, and, despite the crew's best efforts, the storm forced it back into harbour at eight in the evening. To avoid 'accidents and broken shins' Swift stayed in his churning berth all night, and returned to the familiar inn the next morning. And in the end he opted to address the scribbles in his notebook to 'you all'.[80] Pope and Gay, gleaning the details of the night-mare from Sheridan, took this as including them as well as the benighted company at Swift's deanery. They were intrigued to hear of the book bearing 'a most lamentable account' of his travels; and sent sympathies for the further trauma that lay ahead when his ship, after a wait of several more days, was forced to drop anchor at Carlingford, many miles to the north of Dublin. A tough road brought Swift to the capital on horse-back. He was met, it seems, by Sheridan, concerned yet no doubt also a tad amused (as Gay and Pope would be, for all their fond anxieties), on the outskirts of the city.[81]

Awaiting Swift then was the sadness he would have given anything to avoid. Not even the trials of Holyhead lasted long enough to spare him watching over Johnson in her last months. He sat at her bedside, in a house very close to the deanery; and sometimes read a prayer composed specially for her. Three such prayers were later printed. They call on God to be merciful to the suffering woman: 'Give her Grace to continue sin-cerely thankful to Thee for the many Favours thou hast bestowed upon her.' But he implored the 'All-powerful Being, the least Motion of whose Will can create or destroy a World' to think of her 'mournful Friends'; especially, perhaps, one whose world would be all but engulfed when she died. There are possible traces of his last conversations with John-son, for he also asked that God 'forgive every rash and inconsiderate Expression, which her Anguish may at any Time force from her Tongue'. Her heart, he promised, was still with God; as he knew or hoped it was still with him, despite what she might say in the worst moments.[82] It took her six months to die, he acknowledged.[83]

Over the same autumn, his letters show him dealing with habitual affairs, clerical matters, a correspondence with friends and allies in England. He tried to persuade Pope and Gay to move to Ireland, and laughed at their comments on his terrible journey. How had they learned all they knew? He guessed that it must have been the devil or some force of poetic inspiration.[84] Benjamin Motte was proposing to print an illustrated edition of the *Travels*; Swift sent him some thoughts on images it might include. He also discussed the forthcoming volumes of *Miscellanies* he had prepared with Pope, of which four fifths was all his work and containing 'all the poetry I ever writ worth printing'.[85] In December, a letter arrived from Voltaire. It reads as from a person Swift either had not met or might not remember; yet someone 'who ows to yr writings the love he bears to yr language'.[86] He followed another custom by falling sick with his usual complaint, perhaps when the strain of watching, comforting and waiting became too much. At about eight in the evening on Sunday, 28 January, a servant brought a note to the deanery that told him Johnson had died two hours before. He had a few guests for supper, as he often did on Sundays; Sheridan may be counted among the party, with only a couple or few more who were strangers to his close Dublin set. Swift was still unwell. He did not go to Johnson's house; he never saw her dead. Instead, after the household had said prayers, he sat alone and wrote, for as he had said in his 'Holyhead Journal' and repeated now, in a deeply felt memorial of Johnson's life and character, 'What can I do but write every thing that comes into my head?'[87]

He continued writing solidly for three nights in the long hours before bedtime, jotting down all he could recover of her 'gracefulness, somewhat more than human', her 'civility, freedom, easiness and sincerity'; her 'most agreeable voice', speaking gently and only occasionally but never hesitantly except when confronted with strangers.[88] Monday, then Tuesday passed, and in the evening Johnson's requiem was held in the cathedral. Swift noted: 'This is the night of the funeral, which my sickness will not suffer me to attend. It is now nine at night, and I am reserved into another apartment, that I may not see the light in the church, which is just over against [i.e. opposite] the window of my bedchamber.' His inability to see even the glow from the chapel where her coffin was resting prompted contrasting thoughts; memories of Stella's bravery. He continued: 'With all the softness of temper that became a lady, she had the personal courage of a hero . . .'[89] He kept his vigil with pen and paper, and in a dozen pages preserved the core of what we know about Esther Johnson. He gave examples of her wit, her learnedness, her generosity and a marked tendency to show no mercy in the presence of a fool. He knew the document would at some point be made public, along with a few other memorials in manuscript; and as such he offered Johnson a tribute he had been unable or unwilling to give Vanhomrigh. Hunched over his page in the dark side of his house, he grieved for her as he had never been able to grieve over the death of his father or the seeming detachment of his mother. For a precious interval, the anger of a changeling against his place of exile dissolved into the fear and sorrow of a small child in the large unwelcoming homes of relatives; or of a very young boarder, dispatched to the hinterland of Kilkenny.

# 4

A large part of Swift's life died with Stella; but he responded to bereavement, over the next few years, with what proved his last great blaze of public creativity. He would spend much of 1728 and '29 in effective retreat, enjoying the comforts and company offered by a stately home in Ulster; yet politically his mind was fixed on a populace facing a stark choice between starving or emigrating. He was far from alone in grief and anger and the urge to fight: Archbishop King, confined indoors for most of the winter, wrote that 'the cry of the poor for bread is a stab to my heart.'[90] Hugh Boulter, the Primate, warned that 'some thousands will perish before the next harvest.'[91] Boulter, no friend to Swift or King, had nonetheless campaigned hard for emergency legislation to limit the conversion of arable land to pasture, and for compulsory transfers of corn to the north from the south of Ireland. The kingdom was stuck fast in a long stretch of dearth, a cruel shortage of fuel took many lives in the cold months, and no change in the country's basic economic paralysis could be conceived. Despair of improvement in the wider, public realm exactly mirrored the desolation of Swift's personal loss. Over the two years following Johnson's death, he set out his position on the essential injustice governing affairs.

The abrupt decline in the late 1720s should be seen within an enduring frame of rural poverty across the island. A sneery description of the crude cabin accommodating, with some variations, the hardest-struck peasantry in all Irish counties was essentially as true in 1728 as it was in 1689, the year it was published. There it was, recurring across the hillsides, 'built without either Brick or Stone':

> With Seats of Sods and Roof of Straw.
>  The Floor beneath with Rushes laid, [in]stead
> Of Tapestry; no Bed nor Bedstead;
> No Posts, nor Bolts, nor Hinges in door,
> No Chimney, Kitchin, Hall or Windor ...
> On either side there was a door
> Extent from Roof unto the floor,
> Which they, like Hedg-hogs, stop with straw,
> Or open, as the Wind does blow.[92]

Such 'hovels' had been all but innate as features of the landscape since long before Swift's childhood. The dire problem now was the chronic lack of food in them. A measure of the urgency created by the poor harvests of the late 1720s was that the conditions of the very neediest seemed to be falling further; while labouring people who may once have lived more or less comfortably before were being sucked into the old nadir.

It especially infuriated Swift to read English papers asserting blithely that Ireland was prospering, and that the Irish were ignorant of England's woes. *A Short View of the State of Ireland*, published in the spring of 1728 (written, apparently, the year before), laid out the perspectives that a country with Ireland's natural and navigational resources *should* have presented to curious visitors. Here is what 'the worthy Commissioners who come from England' might have expected to see on their ride around the kingdom:

> The thriving numerous Plantations; the noble Woods; the Abundance and Vicinity of Country-Seats; the commodious Farmers Houses and Barns; the Towns and Villages, where every Body is busy, and thriving with all Kinds of Manufactures; the Shops full of Goods, wrought to Perfection, and filled with Customers; the comfortable Diet and Dress, and Dwellings of the People; the vast Numbers of Ships in our Harbours and Docks, and Ship-wrights in our Seaport-Manufactures; the perpetual Concourse to and fro of pompous Equipages.

'Plantations' have barbed connotations in Irish history, as 'improvement' does in the history of rural areas across the kingdoms in the eighteenth century; yet the idyll Swift means to subvert of a state of general plenty is self-evident. Next comes the actual pomp he invites his English inspectors to take in on their survey:

> But my Heart is too heavy to continue this Irony longer; for it is manifest, that whatever Stranger took such a Journey, would be apt to think himself travelling in Lapland, or Iceland, rather than in a Country so favoured by Nature as ours, both in Fruitfulness of Soil, and Temperature of Climate. The miserable Dress, and Diet, and Dwelling of the People; The general Desolation in most Parts of the Kingdom; The old Seats of the Nobility and Gentry all in Ruins, and no new ones in their Stead; The Families of Farmers, who pay great Rents, living in Filth and Nastiness upon Butter-milk and Potatoes, without a Shoe or Stocking to their Feet; or a House so convenient as an *English* Hog-sty, to receive them. These, indeed, may be comfortable Sights to an English Spectator;

who comes for a short Time, only to *learn the Language*, and returns back to his own Country, whither he finds all our Wealth transmitted.[93]

By envisaging scholarly English visitors making notes on the Irish language, Swift brings native, or 'wild', Irish inhabitants into the picture, and thus implicitly extends to them his pity for the degrading spectacles lamented here. He called forth another touring rider, in a later pamphlet, discovering 'little to be found among the Tenants but Beggary and Desolation; the Cabbins of the Scotch themselves being as dirty and miserable as those of the wildest Irish'. The famed Presbyterian work ethic had folded under adversity.[94]

'The landlords, the unmerciful landlords, are the chief cause of this,' exclaimed Archbishop King.[95] Generally, Swift agreed – though he blamed legislators for failing to make appropriate demands by statute. He conceded that the dearth, the lack of improvement on farmsteads, might all be traced to the 'Ignorance or Greediness' of grasping individual freeholders.[96] Certainly the thesis had much to recommend it when, in the midst of famine, landowners prepared to export some of Ireland's slim grain reserves in the summer of 1728. Yet, in another paper that year, Swift took on the voice of an Irish country gentleman. His speaker/writer was a patriotic non-absentee landlord and thus close to Swift's ideal of how the gentry of Ireland ought to have conducted themselves. The choice of persona succeeded for similar reasons to Swift's early *Examiners*, for the character was both at the heart of a system, embodying the qualities necessary in those of similar station throughout the kingdom, but also above all of his society's petty divisions and corruptions. The gentleman is addressing the Drapier – and so, for those in on the joke, Swift is effectively talking to himself – and his main topic is the lack of lower-value coinage. He qualifies this grievance with a bitterly wonderful piece of rhetorical pre-emption.

It is true indeed, that under our Circumstances in general this Complaint for the Want of Silver may appear as ridiculous, as for a Man to be impatient about a Cut-Finger, when he is struck with the Plague: And yet a poor Fellow going to the Gallows may be allowed to feel the Smart of Wasps while he is upon Tyburn Road.

The problem of small change enables the fictitious letter-writer, and thereby his creator, to link together the suffering of all levels of society as Swift perceived it. Tradesmen and farmers could neither buy nor sell, and labourers could frequently not be paid 'until their Wages amount to a Double Pistole, or a Moidore'.[97] These were heavy gold coins of Spanish and Portuguese origin: to English eyes, their appearance in far-flung Irish parishes might have signalled the existence of some Jacobite treasure-trove. The reality was much less quaint. One such coin was to be divided among many labourers, as best they could, invariably at a local tavern, where they would pay a shilling just for changing the gold for silver and copper – which was rapidly squandered on ale. These were men who came running with knives and axes to quarter the meat when a cow or a horse was found dead on the road.

Such men and their families were not excluded from sympathy or protection in Swift's vision of things. But they could have no claim to power or status. Swift was attacking the old order for failing in its duties, not leading a charge to overhaul it. Answering a number of letters he claimed to have received from citizens pressing for action, he isolated three changes that would need to occur before any improvement might be seen. First (and foremost), Ireland would need to gain 'Liberty of Trade'; second, the Irish would need 'a share of Preferments in all kinds equal to the British Natives'. Third, absentee landowners taking as much as half the kingdom's revenue (modern figures give a lower, but still substantial estimate) to England would need to return. Swift saw no hope whatsoever either of the first or the third alteration taking place; the second he abandoned altogether, reinforcing his comment that 'there is nothing left us but despair.' The phrasing of this second in his list of necessary changes has further significance. By 'the British Natives', Swift was referring to those inhabiting the kingdom created by the union of England and Scotland, in opposition to the people of what was still technically another kingdom in its own right, albeit a dependent one. Legally, only those obeying the Test Act and communicating in the Anglican Church of Ireland could be entitled to any 'Preferments' – in the Church, the state or the army – that might be redistributed. And there lay the crucial distinction that informed his thinking about the Irish population. All were entitled to live and eat (and, conceivably, trade and make money); but only those who were true to the Established Church could aspire to a foothold in the official order. On this point he was as unaltered as the British themselves in their attitude to Irish trade.[98] He wasn't campaigning for old rules to be relaxed, but for them to be applied properly. As it was, all that remained to him were territories and governing authorities demanding different shades of his anger.

Together the 'Irish Tracts' of 1728–9 make Swift's visit to Goodrich in

1727 seem all the more like a valediction to his parents' homeland. The country Swift loved was a realm of the past. Now, his scorn for England was unabated: there 'our Neighbours and Brethren ... rejoice at our Sufferings, although sometimes to their own Disadvantage.'[99] Such hostility, however, is taken by Swift as a fixed, almost ontological factor. Underneath this cloud of English tyranny, he has plenty of anger to spare for the Irish themselves, from the 'peevish or knavish' farmers cheating the clergy of their tithes, the landlords charging rack-rents, tenants failing to rise above circumstance and improve their holdings, to the absentee landlords and the women who insisted on buying foreign clothes and trinkets. Of these, the last caught arguably the worst of his misogynistic vehemence:

> Is it not the highest Indignity to human nature, that men should be such poltroons as to suffer the Kingdom and themselves to be undone, by the Vanity, the Folly, the Pride and Wantonness of their Wives, who under their present Corruptions seem to be a kind of animal suffered for our sins to be sent into the world for the Destruction of Familyes, Societyes, and Kingdoms; and whose whole study seems directed to be as expensive as they possibly can in every useless article of living?

Such women fed on luxury, he claimed, as 'starlings grow fat on henbane'. He exempted 'a few' from his accusation, perhaps recalling Johnson's abstemiousness; 'let the rest take it upon them.'[100] Swift's only solution to Ireland's plight was that people tailor their expenses to their incomes, and middle-class women dressing themselves in Flemish lace flouted such parsimony. Yet the language in such a paragraph is ignited by something other than offended frugality; Swift explodes at the suggestiveness of such violations, the allure that might lead men or kingdoms to their undoing.

About two months before Johnson died, Swift told a mother mourning her dead child that she should not grieve, for life was a thing to be despised.[101] His ordeal during Johnson's long illness and his conduct after her death rejected this cold philosophy – a little late for the poor bereaved woman who received his condolences. Swift's work of the next two years was an extended defence of a slave's right to live. His papers were surely fuelled by the loss of Johnson, for the state of Ireland as he depicted it presented the lack of all the qualities she had taken to the grave – reason, wit, chaste beauty and decency. He grieved by raging, and raged by converting fury into the sardonic fatalism that pervades these pamphlets. Swift's reaction to the loss of Johnson also testifies to the rate he set on the things that remained in his life. He had always advised Esther Vanhomrigh to resist melancholy and the spleen, and this was a doctrine he applied with the help of long-standing supports. Practised manners, trusted friends and acquaintances, and long-established routines caught his fall. His illness was a shield against unwanted callers. He maintained his correspondence, and he allowed nothing lachrymose to enter his (surviving) letters. The region of his personality that Johnson had occupied simply shut down; the rest kept running. It cost him no effort resuming his avuncular gallantries to Martha Blount, for example, as early as February: 'I am afraid I continue in love with you, which is hard after near six Months' absence. I hope you have done with your rash and other little disorders, and that I shall see you a fine young healthy plump lady; and if Mr Pope chides you, threaten him you will turn Heretick.'[102] Despite nagging ill-health (and occasional complete collapse), he was remarkably active in the first half of 1728. He and Sheridan together began a weekly paper, the *Intelligencer*, possibly as a scheme of Sheridan's to divert Swift's feelings. It was founded on the concept of publishing news of 'important events and singularities' illustrative of folly and vice from around Dublin. The paper's 'office of intelligence', established at great expense, was to receive its information from agents at key sites of human fallibility:

> Some at the Play-house, others in Churches, some at Balls, Assemblies, Coffee-houses and meetings for Quadrille; some at the several Courts of Justice, both Spiritual and Temporal, some at the College, some upon my Lord Mayor and Aldermen in their publick Affairs; lastly, some to converse with favourite Chambermaids and to frequent those Ale-houses and Brandy-Shops, where the Footmen of great Families meet in a morning.

Only the city barracks and Parliament House were left unobserved, since the editors could find 'no *enfant perdu* bold enough to venture their Persons at either'.[103] These were the storehouses from which the *Intelligencer*, a short-lived but choice publication, would draw its material. They also offer a metropolitan cross-section of the places where Swift's name was spoken and his latest works discussed.

With Johnson dead, Sheridan was close to being Swift's favourite companion. He was impulsive, forgetful and spendthrift, but also endlessly witty and generous to a fault. He infuriated and enthralled his older friend in equal measure, and actually combined many of the flaws Swift claimed he would expunge from Ireland at large. In July 1725 the surest sign of Swift's high standing in the eyes of Lord Carteret had been the appointment of Sheridan to a comfortable living in Rincurran, County Cork. 'His greatest Fault,' Swift had told Carteret, 'is a Wife and seven Children.'[104] Dublin Castle saw the matter differently: Sheridan's mortal sin was being a notorious Tory. Yet the Lord Lieutenant disregarded the English followers who pointed out furiously that Sheridan was the Drapier's right-hand man.[105] Swift was overjoyed, having stretched his expectations from the viceroy beyond all reasonable limits. He proceeded to give Sheridan detailed advice on how he should establish himself in his new parish – only to see all his work destroyed by his protégé with a single sermon. On 1 August, the anniversary of George I's accession, Sheridan preached in Cork; for his text, he chose 'Sufficient unto the day is the evil thereof.' A Whig in the congregation – someone of 'no large dimensions of body or mind'[106] – made sure the event was reported at Dublin, and all further progress in the Church was sealed off to Sheridan. His name was instantly removed from the list of the viceroy's chaplains.[107]

Swift had astounded Sheridan by reacting good-humouredly to this howler. He offered advice as one 'discarded courtier' to another – writing, in fact, as a guest from the Sheridans' ramshackle property, Quilca, in County Cavan, while Sheridan himself was away. He made another of his pre-publication references to the *Travels*, urging Sheridan to look again at the description of the Yahoos, 'and expect no more from Man than such an Animal is capable of'.[108] The comment illuminates how generally Swift intended the Yahoos to be understood as a potential image of all humanity; and the letter as a whole shows him reasoning tactically, as a politician rather than as a Houyhnhnm. Yet he entered the incident in a prose sketch of Sheridan as a 'Second Solomon', who failed signally to display much wisdom whatsoever. The Cork fiasco joined a catalogue of slips and insults from Sheridan, in a paper compiled by Swift at separate moments and in widely varying moods. On one occasion in winter – probably late in 1728 – Sheridan promised to send his chaise to collect Swift in the country; but dispatched it late, and to a place thirty miles away from where Swift was staying.[109] When Swift described him as 'proud and captious', some such slur or oversight still clearly rankled. He in his turn upset Sheridan by pointing out how ready he seemed to disappoint firm friends if he might impress or gratify a good-looking woman. He was more just when he noted how a lack of judgement and discretion made Sheridan appear 'as if he were neither generous, honest, nor good-natured.'[110]

The disaster in Cork was mitigated only by the legal impossibility of Sheridan's being deprived of his newly gained living. For someone behaving sensibly, the income from Rincurran offered security. For Sheridan, whom Swift accused of raising and dressing his daughters as if they were countesses, it could not suffice. Having stayed with Sheridan on his rundown small estate in Cavan, Swift had begun a list of complaints about his friend's housekeeping that were indicative (he felt) of the man.

> But one Lock and a half in the whole House.
> The Key of the Garden Door lost.
> The empty Bottles all uncleanable.
> The vessels for drink few and leaky.
> The new house all going to Ruin before it is finished.
> One hinge of the Street door broke off . . .
> The Door of the Dean's Bed-chamber full of large Chinks.
> The Beauset [a large windowed cabinet or half-dresser typically holding
>     silver plate, in which lights could be usefully placed and reflected][111]
>     letting in so much Wind that it almost blows out the Candles.
> The Dean's Bed threatening every Night to fall under him.
> The little Table loose and broken in the Joints.
> The Passages open overhead, by which the Cats pass continually into the
>     Cellar, and eat the Victuals, for which one was tried, condemned, and
>     executed by the Sword.[112]

Swift had a way with the wayward schoolteacher of not kicking him when he was down – or at least not doing so directly. When Sheridan had offended him so badly in 1718, Swift had recruited the voice of his 'sweet-heart', Mary the kitchen-maid in his deanery, to deliver one of his (many) rebukes. The bond between them was too firm to break, as Swift showed by speaking a friend rather than as a censor at the very low moment Sheridan experienced in 1725. He knew that Sheridan could expect a hard time from his wife. Swift placed much of the blame on her, of whom he wrote with the same occasional misogyny that inflamed him when he thought of Irish ladies wearing foreign lace: 'a most filthy slut; lazy, and slothful, and luxurious, ill-natured, envious, suspicious; a scold, expensive on herself, covetous to others'. She was the prime example of a woman undoing a husband. Swift still remembered with outrage Sheridan's telling Johnson that all women were alike.

How could he compare Stella with 'the most disagreeable beast in Europe?'[113] The strength of Swift's reaction in itself suggested another, arising from a deeper source, a spasm triggered by the troubling thought that perhaps all women – even Johnson; even his mother – played this trick of love on men, and ruined them. His anger in writing of 'Solomon' suggested that even Sheridan had played it on him too. For he clearly loved the errant schoolmaster: Sheridan could never equal Johnson, but Swift's friendship with him was also a passionate one.

Sheridan lacked 'discretion': but this was exactly the virtue Swift declared was overrated in an essay for the *Intelligencer*. The piece was manifestly a defence of tendencies he shared with Sheridan. Swift's typification of a discreet parson, after a non-descript career at university – making it a rule never to laugh at a joke or make one himself – quietly creeps up the ladder of preferment towards the Bishops' Bench.[114] A very different ecclesiastical specimen was 'Eugenio', a gentleman's son: 'He had the Reputation of an arch Lad at School, and was unfortunately possessed with a *Talent* for *Poetry*, on which Account he received many chiding Letters from his Father, and grave Advice from his Tutor.' Here was a thumbnail portrait either of Swift or of Sheridan in boyhood. Their alliance was based on the 'towardly' spark they shared with the fictitious Eugenio. Admittedly, Swift's story had long ago departed from that of Eugenio or Sheridan, as it carried him to his eccentric prominence in Georgian society. In the *Intelligencer* piece, Eugenio is consigned to a wretched vicarage in Lincolnshire, where he is 'utterly undistinguished and forgotten'.[115] Sheridan, with his seven children, had not fallen – arguably, could not fall – to this extreme. But he was a purer example than either Swift or even Eugenio of the 'arch Lad' lacking a spot of forethought. He had rented a house outside Dublin at Rathfarnham, invested heavily in it and then, taking a sudden dislike to the place, let it fall to pieces. He had then signed a lease on the property for 999 years to avoid paying heavy damages for his neglect.[116]

Swift and Sheridan contributed initially to the *Intelligencer* on roughly alternating weeks. Neither had the spare time or energy to make it their central occupation. Swift used his essays, nevertheless, to deliver further thoughts on subjects he considered essential. Many picked up on themes of the *Drapier's Letters* and of course Gulliver. Preferment, the state of Ireland, the decline of the aristocracy as a result of shoddy and over-indulgent schooling, all took their turn. Dominating the third issue was an essay by Swift in defence of Gay's bounding theatrical success, *The Beggar's Opera*. Gay had set his 'ballad opera' in the haunts of London thieves: its main plot is taken up with the love-life of a highwayman, Macheath, who is engaged to Polly, the daughter of a procurer, fence and informant, Peacham. Yet Macheath is also engaged to the daughter of a Newgate jailer, Lockit, who conspires with Peacham to murder the thief and split his money. The scene shifts from Peacham's den to a tavern where Macheath is ensnared, and on to Newgate, where his life is spared by an appeal from the audience.

When Gay had first informed Swift of the play's success in mid-February 1728, it had already been performed fifteen times. A confirmed hit in those times might expect a run of five or six nights. Yet the public joy in Gay's comedy showed no sign of fading; he was told to expect at least another fortnight of shows.[117] All those who cared about the soft-mannered poet were delighted for his good fortune. He had recently been subjected to a little bit of humiliating vengeance from Walpole. It was said that Gay had written a satirical 'character' of the Prime Minister, though Gay denied having anything to do with it, and Walpole said he believed him; yet late in 1727, as the postings and pensions of the new Court were allotted, the chief minister rewarded Gay's reasonable hopes of a sinecure by making fun of him. Gay was offered the place of gentleman usher to Queen Caroline's daughter, two-year-old Princess Louisa. This would require him to do little for his £200 a year but walk in front of the little girl on state occasions, but the well-aimed big-boned Norfolk elbow in the ribs of his dignity was unmistakable – at least to Swift, who described it to Carteret as 'one of the cruellest actions I ever knew, even in a minister of state, these thirty years past'.[118] He was sure that the new Queen, Caroline, with whom he was bitterly disappointed, had also been privy to the jest. To be overlooked was one thing, and Walpole's goodwill could never be depended on; but Gay had been led, like Swift, to believe that Caroline held him in high regard. In 1727 he had dedicated his verse fables to her son, Prince William, and the book had been received with raptures at Court and promises of favour. Gay's *Fables* proved a classic of the eighteenth and nineteenth centuries, running through 350 editions before 1900;[119] yet then, as now, very few authors could live on their sales. In effect a state subsidy in the form of a place at Court or some other small public position was necessary for an artist to live with any comfort: arguably none had Pope's talent for combining commercial success with high literary merit. The proffered ushership was nonetheless a test of Gay's political submissiveness, and he found it beneath even his well-known modesty to accept the post. Instead he pushed on with his opera and presented it for performance at the Lincoln's Inn Fields Theatre. It opened on 28 January.

By the time of Gay's next letter to Swift, on 20 March, the play was still in the theatre – thirty-six performances, and counting; the run would extend to an almost unprecedented sixty-two. Gay reported how the previous week, when one of the actors fell sick, the theatre was forced to offer another play or else send the audience away: 'but the people call'd out for the Beggar's Opera, & they were forc'd to play it.' In his letters to Pope or Swift, Gay habitually urged them not to write him essays, but to speak of themselves and tell him how they did. He was constantly apologetic, however, about following this practice himself: 'I would not have talk'd so much upon this subject, or upon any thing that regards myself but to you; but as I know you interest yourself so sincerely in everything that concerns me, I believe you would have blam'd me if I had said less.' Like Pope, Arbuthnot, Bolingbroke (and, indeed, almost all of Swift's close English friends), Gay ended his letter by urging Swift to visit. In preparation, he had made a touching gesture: he had bought a second set of bed-sheets for his London digs, so that they would no longer need to send to Jervas the painter for his spares.[120] The warmth and thoughtfulness on such a point from the younger man (now in his early forties, and not in perfect health) shine another little ray on Swift's gathering reluctance to travel. Devoted though he was to the Scriblerian set – and his letters to Gay are almost paternal – it was difficult for a sixty-year-old, periodically unwell and fastidious perennially about hygienic and domestic arrangements, to countenance a lack of clean bed-linen. He was much more determined for now that Gay invest his earnings wisely; which, to his friends' relief, he did, and turned his hundreds into thousands.

Quite apart from the play's manifest allusions to Walpole's oligarchy – one of his nicknames occurs in Peacham's list of thieves, and Peacham himself is arguably an allegory of the minister – The Beggar's Opera troubled many who concerned themselves with the morals of society. Didn't it seem, murmured the general critical conscience, as if Gay were glamorizing a bloodthirsty underworld? For Swift such critics betrayed their idiocy. The play was a parody and a satire. Swift has often been credited with floating the overall concept of the opera in a letter to Pope more than a decade earlier: 'What think you of a Newgate pastoral, among the whores and thieves there?'[121] The remark was clearly intended as a suggestion for Pope's satire in verse: the form of a musical drama, which gives the Opera its magic, seems to have been Gay's idea entirely. Nevertheless, so far as Swift was concerned, the satirical approach was inseparable from the subject-matter, and he therefore dismissed the notion that Gay had thoughts of romanticizing the situation. Peacham, Lockit and Macheath often speak as if they are titanic figures of the ancient world. Even Swift missed some of the allusions, but thought that Macheath, just before his fantastical reprieve, might imitate Alexander the Great.[122] Characters in most operas were idealized, but Swift maintained that Gay was doing just the opposite, by showing the fates of 'abandoned wretches'. At the same time, in Swift's reading, Gay was suggesting how similar these cut-purses were to the much more powerful 'common Robbers of the Public' who were currently running the country. Gay shared the vision of a sickened state that Gulliver communicates to his master the Houyhnhnm:

> Hence it follows of Necessity, that vast Numbers of our People are com-
> pelled to seek their Livelihood by Begging, Robbing, Stealing, Cheating,
> Pimping, Foreswearing, Flattering, Suborning, Forging, Gaming, Lying,
> Fawning, Hectoring, Voting, Scribbling, Stargazing, Poisoning, Whor-
> ing, Canting, Libelling, Free-thinking, and the like Occupations.[123]

For Gay, as for Swift, the legal and illegal livelihoods listed above are all on a continuum. The larger analytical scope of the *Travels* (in, for example, the passage just quoted, which details the consequences of economic mismanagement) did not form part of Gay's conceit; yet another quality it shared with the *Travels* was its pure comedy. Accordingly Swift's *Intelligencer* piece on the *Opera* was also true to the boundless humour of the play, and identified its appeal to something universal in human nature. Gay's work also led Swift to make one of his principal statements on the goal and character of satire:

> There are two Ends that Men propose in writing Satyr: one of them less
> noble than the other, as regarding nothing further than the private Sat-
> isfaction, and Pleasure of the Writer; but without any View towards
> personal Malice: the other is a publick Spirit, prompting Men of Genius
> and Virtue, to mend the World as far as they are able. And as both these
> Ends are innocent, so the latter is highly commendable.[124]

Here in brief were Swift's two main strands of writing: the bagatelles he produced for friends or a limited circle, and the grand satirical projects with the aim of vexing, if not improving, society. *The Beggar's Opera* belonged firmly to the second, greater class. Swift reported that the Irish production had captivated Dublin: there was no end in sight to its run, with the 'house cramm'd, and the Lord Lieutnant severall times there, laughing his heart out'.[125]

Did Swift attend a performance? He was no connoisseur of music. It seems that he was confined to a detailed examination of the script in the deanery, his eyes coping badly with the small print, and perhaps asking Sheridan or some other regular to read passages aloud. In his *Intelligencer* essay on Gay he had defended the idea that a young priest was entitled to watch a moral drama at the playhouse, if he left his clerical habit and bands at home. Here he was partly vindicating his own practice in younger days, when he was evidently no stranger to the theatre. He could not, however, defend a clergyman sauntering in in his gown to stand openly with the 'vicious crew' one always found in the pit. For so senior a churchman, and such a famous one, a trip to the theatre incognito was now probably out of the question.

The positive side of Swift's literary reputation was now broadly established. He was a household name in Dublin and London as an unparalleled polemical campaigner; and the *Travels* was widely accepted as a book for the ages. In the highest panegyric, Swift was synonymous with his most famous personae. Pope was dedicating his *Dunciad* to Swift, and in January 1728 had sent a draft of the lines addressing his great ally for approval from St Patrick's.

> And Thou! Whose Sence, whose Humour, and whose Rage
> At once can teach, delight, and lash the Age! . . .
> Attend, whatever Title please thine ear,
> Dean, Drapier, Bickerstaff, or Gulliver.[126]

Publication of *The Dunciad* followed in May, and Pope tinkered with the passage on Swift for subsequent editions. In these revisions Swift remained the equal of Cervantes and Rabelais, and the unbinder of his country's 'copper chains', yet the insightful lines praising him at once as the scourge, teacher and delighter of his time were cancelled. The following lines presented another small, significant adjustment:

> Whether thou chuse Cervantes' serious air,
> Or laugh and shake in Rab'lais' easy chair,
> Or praise the Court, or magnify mankind.

Initially Pope had written here of Swift *extolling* mankind.[127] This later version still defended Swift against what became the standard charge of denigrating humanity, but with greater critical precision. The idea of Swift's writing *magnifying* his subjects, demystifying and scrutinizing them as it did so, tallied well with Swift's own frequent imagery of lenses and mirrors as metaphors for the media of satire.

As for the magnifying glass Pope turned on the scurrying termites of Grub Street, Swift had had his doubts about the wisdom of the project. It was a grave error, he reasoned, to preserve names that history would consign in due course to oblivion. One should never commemorate one's lesser enemies, for fear of their tainting future ages.[128] This rule was rendered both redundant and ironic by the future Pope's poem envisaged – learning and the civilized arts were doomed in the face of an eternity of 'dulness', ignorance and stupidity. The anxiety behind *The Dunciad* is that Pope was castigating the victors. As for the quality of the verse, however, Swift left Pope in no doubt as to his view of its excellence. 'After twenty times reading,' he informed him in July that year, 'I never in my opinion saw so much good satire, or more good sense, in so many lines.' And he adapted his policy towards the dunces by urging Pope to reverse his earlier rule of leaving out their names. They should all be identified, and Pope should make exhaustive notes for the lengthier *Variorum* edition he was busy preparing. Twenty miles outside London, he observed, nobody would know the 'town-facts' or many of the literary personalities involved; the same was likely to mar the poem's reception in Dublin.[129]

Swift's foes and Pope's themselves were rarely unaware they had been branded. A standard retaliation was to say the point scored was in fact no hit at all, and that the larger argument was poorly constructed. In some cases the replies and answers display a genuine sense of mystification: 'I have been long studying, and am still at a loss, in what *Classis* of Men to place Captain Gulliver as a writer.'[130] A prominent voice in a veritable horde hostile to Swift belonged to a clergyman who has been met in passing already. Jonathan Smedley, the Dean of Clogher, had tacked up verses berating the new Dean of St Patrick's in 1713, and thought no better of him fifteen years later. He and Swift, though known to each other only by sight, had launched spiked verses against each other in the course of the 1720s. In 1728, prompted by *The Dunciad* and the Swift–Pope *Miscellanies*, Smedley put out a book-length assault on both 'Dean Gulliver' and his 'Fellow-author'. He imagined them as a pair of ruthless hawks in a bird-kingdom of writers: 'Who, having prey'd so long, and struck their Talons so deep, into all their Feather'd kind, must expect that whole Aviaries of Quills will be let fly at them; that their very Eyes will be pick'd out; and that it is well, if they escape with

their Lives.'[131] *Gulliveriana*, as Smedley called his addition to the volumes of Swift's and Pope's *Miscellanies*, was a last charge. Smedley had
sacrificed all moral authority in Ireland by supporting Wood's Patent
against the Drapier in blatant hopes of favour; and, despite this concerted toadying, and his valuable benefices, he was heavily in debt.
*Gulliveriana* was a lavish work of malice performed to further fading
hopes. The loathing and envy betray genuine engagement, however, and
at some level a desire to deal with critical bemusement. Here and there
it also illustrates Swift as he must have been perceived by many as his
fame became unquestionable. The literary and clerical communities of
both capitals were too small for Smedley not to hear of Swift's ailments
and his brusque ways even with friends. Smedley gleefully distorted the
details he gathered, mixing character and author together: 'How Gulliver grew intolerably insolent and vain on account of his Writings;
insomuch that he turned light-headed, and in his mad Fits, abused every
body that came in his Way, sometimes spat, and sometimes piss'd in their
Faces, and kicked all the Dogs that he met, by which he was frequently
bit.'[132] Such passages do much to explain Swift's fear of public exposure,
especially during periods of illness, and his preference for the sanctuary
of his home in Dublin. The madness, arrogance and misanthropy caricatured by Smedley would persist in sketches of Swift through to the
twentieth century. Added to this was an allegation of godlessness; critics
searched the *Travels* assiduously for evidence of Swift 'ridiculing our
common creator'.[133] The final ingredient in the hostile view of Swift was
the idea of him as a roué. *Cadenus and Vanessa*, Swift's allegorical
account of his relationship with Vanhomrigh, had been printed and
eagerly pirated, and there was still a fairly widespread perception of him
as a rake. A mock-romance of 1728 cast Swift as a lustful Polydore, who
'was from his Youth amorously inclined; never without less than two
Intrigues upon his hands'.[134] Smedley grudgingly acknowledged that
*Cadenus and Vanessa* was Swift's 'best performance', yet he followed the
instincts of many with an accusing jab at the delicate passage where the
poem declines to say how the characters ended their story.

> But what Success Vanessa met,
> Is to the World a Secret yet:
> Whether the Nymph, to please her Swain,
> Talks in a high Romantick Strain;
> Or whether he at last descends
> To like with less Seraphick ends.[135]

If ambiguity existed as to Swift's liaisons with Vanessa, set forth here in allegory, Smedley still found plentiful matter for 'shame and sorrow'. With sordid relish, he decided that 'whatever happen'd between them two', Captain Gulliver was even less seraphic with regard to his other lady, Stella.[136] Shame was evidently foreign to Smedley's mind, and loving sorrow was an equal mystery.

There were scores of Smedleys for Swift to bear or ignore, yet *Gulliveriana* proved a parting shot. Smedley's finances prompted him to resign all his livings the following year and try his luck as an East India Company chaplain. Clergymen were known to have made great fortunes: notably John Evans, the late Bishop of Meath, who had shocked even Swift by endowing a large fund for the lower clergy of Ireland in his will. Swift sent Smedley packing with a poem for the *Intelligencer*, published in the spring of 1729: 'To all mankind a constant friend, provided they had *Cash* to lend.'[137] Given the former Dean's persistence, an answer might well have reached Swift from Fort Madras, had Smedley not died and been buried at sea on his way to India.

# 5

The streets around the cathedral, with their communities of textile workers, presented Swift with daily evidence of the hardship caused by the dearth and depression. The poorest of the urban population was as short of food as they were of employment; and, like Archbishop King, Swift heard the cry of beggars, seemingly in droves, calling out for bread. Outside Dublin, his main view of the rural disaster brought on by poor harvests was provided by a long sojourn in County Armagh. He was on good terms with an Ulster baronet of Scottish descent, Sir Arthur Acheson, forty years old and quietly spoken, who owned a large estate between Newry and Armagh as well as a Dublin townhouse on Capel Street. In the spring of 1728, Acheson invited Swift to stay with his family at their country home. The moving force behind the invitation, though, is likely to have been Acheson's lively and sociable wife, Anne, with whom Swift quickly established a friendship in his familiar role of tutor and teasing godfather. Acheson was a scholarly, introverted, faintly sedentary man, proud of his home and his ancestry – he was the fifth Baronet – but lacking wit or dynamism. The taciturn Ulsterman was by default one of the leaders of the region's small Anglican community. At some point, probably not long after midsummer, Swift journeyed up to the Achesons' grand house at Market Hill (now Gosford Castle).

The situation Swift witnessed in the wider country of Ulster informed much of the pathos and descriptive horror of his political writings during this period. The scenes he saw necessarily displayed the effects of the harvest crisis on a very specific section of the Irish population, since here one found, uniquely for Ireland, a Protestant (and largely Presbyterian, or Dissenting) majority. In Sir Arthur Acheson's words on his home territory, 'we have few or none of the Old Irish among us.'[138] Defining such a phrase now is somewhat contentious, yet by this he clearly meant the Anglo-Norman descendants as well as the Catholic 'natives' driven off the land by the original planters and in subsequent oppressions. The extremes being suffered there thus constituted a Protestant emergency, no doubt triggering inherited memories from the previous century; hence the consternation of the Irish Church and gentry more generally. For Protestant Ireland, the great dearth of the late 1720s mattered so much because it was an Ulster dearth, ravaging Protestants. In March, Swift had received a letter from a relative of Sir William Temple, prompting memories of another age. This was William Flower, whom as a young boy Swift had accompanied to London by river from Sheen. Flower, now living at his family home in Kilkenny, had never forgotten how Swift refused to pay the 'drunk and insolent' boatman, and had risked a drenching at the hands of the mob for his principles. Now he wrote offering to send gold as an anonymous donation to Sarah Harding, the widow of the printer who had died in prison, having refused to divulge the Drapier's identity on oath.[139] Swift himself had supported Mrs Harding in the business she had taken over on her husband's death, directing specifically that she be compensated for the cost of setting up the last, unpublished letter by the Drapier, and later using her press to issue the *Intelligencer*. Flower also reflected how 'the miseries of the North, as represented, demand the utmost compassion, and must soften the malice of the most bitter enemy.'[140] Flower's sentiments were typical of the Protestant Ascendancy mourning the trials of labouring Protestants in Ulster. These were the 'Irish' workers who might expect sympathy from the ruling classes, if any was to be forthcoming.

Swift was obviously in step with this governing mentality. The plight of labouring tenants would most likely mean all the more to him, given his long association with the region: this was the area in which he had first served as a priest, at Kilroot near Belfast Lough, and that he had

visited and re-explored frequently over the last decade and more. But
one crucial factor that distinguished his attitude should be held in
mind. As an Irish clergyman Swift was distinctive – distinctively Tory,
one might say – for his great contempt of Irish Presbyterians. He had
voiced this feeling scorchingly in the *Tale of a Tub* and his papers on
Church politics in the early 1700s. An essential difference in his and
Archbishop King's politics, and the basis of the Archbishop's distrust
when it came to Swift's judgement of appointments, was that Swift had
always considered the Dissenting population a much greater danger
than the severely contained Catholic Irish. Thus in 1728, Swift's pity
for the struggling Protestants of Ulster is actually as remarkable as his
compassion for the Catholic peasants he saw enduring similar hardships. In his strident papers from this time, humaneness conquers his
innate prejudice against both non-Anglican communities. And it is
notable how the poetry he wrote at Market Hill, adopting the voice of
Lady Acheson, puts him in cahoots with some of the 'Teagues' – a
planters' derogatory term for native Irish people – who were to be
found on Acheson's land.

> He's all the day saunt'ring,
> With labourers bant'ring,
> Among his colleagues,
> A parcel of Teagues,
> (Whom he brings in among us
> And bribes with mundungus.)[141]

Swift was in direct contact with people of every status and denomination in the environs of Market Hill. The northern crisis was thus, for him
at least, a disaster of all the Irish to be found in this area. So when he
cries out against the fate of the starving poor, except where he specifies
that they are Protestant churchgoers, they may be taken as heretics of
every hue as well as loyal Anglicans.

Whether Catholic or Protestant, native Irish or Scots, however, the
nature of the work confronting any agricultural labourer was a great
leveller. The planters commonly regarded the tools and practices of Irish
farming as lagging far behind those seen in England; but the terrain presented different challenges. The ploughs in use were evidently quite
rudimentary, but the common Irish spade was often better for digging
much of Ireland's boggy, stony ground, and a long-handled, narrow-
bladed 'loy' – with space on the blade only for the right foot to push (or

'kick') – was the standard tool. No four-wheeled cart, it has been claimed, was used in Ireland until 1755; but then again, a wheel-less 'slide car', made of two long shafts with a base of cross-beams and wicker-work, was often better suited to slick marshy surfaces. A frequent lack of equipment and organization was nevertheless a common complaint, and compounded Irish farming's other disadvantages.[142] As such, Swift was evidently willing to set aside his doctrinal prejudices and give diligence its due when he met with it. The Market Hill poem quoted above, typically again, shows him less suspicious of 'Teagues' than of 'Fanatics'.

Soon after his arrival, Swift had established himself on very familiar terms with his hosts. He got on well with Lady Acheson, worrying about her thin physique, lecturing to her on long walks they took together and prescribing daily doses of Milton, Bacon and improving literature for her free time. He also began freely making adjustments to their property, and the 'parcel of Teagues' mentioned in the lines above, supplied with cheap tobacco, are likely to have comprised his personally appointed team of workers. He planted trees, oversaw various 'improvements' (a key word for Swift in his later years) and in some cases uprooted established features of the Achesons' property. This he seemingly did with Lady Anne's blessing and with Sir Arthur's more muted acquiescence. There is a faint sense from the beginning of this close association that the Baronet was to some extent humouring his wife in his treatment of their guest. His reticent character made it hard to tell. The unspoken arrangement between Swift and the family was hospitality in return for the cachet of hosting probably the most famous and certainly the most controversial man in the country. For Lady Acheson, Swift wrote poems about his long stay that together would fill quite a sizeable volume of verse. One of the finest and most resonant in the set is a poem about the removal of an old thorn-tree at the gate of the mansion. In this Swift abandoned his customary couplets and showed that, like Pope, he could write in quatrains that recalled the balance and economy of the seventeenth-century lyric. With a measured archaism, he employs the older mode to describe an act of cultural vandalism carried out in the cause of practical necessity.

> At *Market Hill*, as well appears
> By Chronicle of antient Date,
> There stood for many a hundred Years
> A spacious Thorn before the Gate.

Hither came every Village Maid
And on the Boughs her Garland hung,
And here, beneath the spreading Shade,
Secure from Satyrs sat and hung . . .

But Time with Iron Teeth I ween
Has canker'd all its Branches round;
No Fruit or Blossom to be seen,
Its Head reclining tow'rds the Ground.

This aged, sickly, sapless Thorn
Which must alas no longer stand;
Behold! The cruel Dean in Scorn
Cuts down with sacrilegious hand.[143]

The Dean has taken up the axe – or directed his workmen to do so – on the orders of Lady Anne. Still an active horseman and walker, he was more than fit enough to do the job himself when his head and ears were free of their old symptoms. The text's silence on another point of view suggests that Sir Arthur, whom Swift portrayed as preferring the quiet of his library, might have been less keen to have the ailing landmark hacked down, even if it no longer blossomed. The chopping is symbolic: Swift is cutting back delicacies of sentiment, insisting on a pragmatism that matched the harshness of the age. In the background of the poem, beyond the terraces of Market Hill, is the rough logic engendered by famine. If the plant no longer yields anything or serves a useful purpose, chop it down. The same robust spirit guided Swift's other activities at Market Hill. Similar logic, pushed beyond the limits of sanity, would inform *A Modest Proposal* the following year.

The drawn-out joke in the Market Hill poems is of a guest whose presence had never been very earnestly desired: he arrived three days before he was expected, and in subsequent weeks and months outstayed his welcome. At one and the same time Swift thus preserved the self-protective image of his doggedness and inflexibility while exhibiting considerable social sensitivity. A guest who truly conformed to the character of the thick-skinned bullying self-appointed home-improver the poems depict would manifestly never have been capable of writing such self-deprecating poems. The unflagging figure of the 'relentless Dean' allows the infinitely subtler and mercurial literary creator to capture the attitude and manner-isms of his hostess, as she regulates both before his critical gaze: there is

ample testimony of the walks he urged her to take ('daggled and tattered, /
My spirit's quite shattered') and the course of reading he prescribed for her
('instead of new plays / Dull Bacon's Essays').[144] In a long and sprightly
'lamentation' in which Swift impersonates Lady Acheson, he allows her to
scoff at his trials of strength with Sir Arthur's tenants ('Who makes the best
figure / The Dean or the Digger?') and at the features he added to their
estate. His pretentiousness is set upon: his 'bower' is 'A hole where a rabbit
/ Would scorn to inhabit', and his precious arbour is all too easily destroyed
by a wild calf, to the glee of village girls who then plunder the briars in the
wreckage.[145] Another beautifully executed monologue written from her
perspective, 'Lady Acheson Weary of the Dean', mentions how his puppies
and horses are eating the family out of house and stable. Yet, while there is
a vivid graffito of the 'insulting Tyrant Dean' with 'Tallow Face', 'Beetle
Brows' and 'Eye of Wall', a more biographically truthful portrait is that of
the writer we don't get to see, the ethereally intelligent social observer
*behind* the poem – the Swift who held the entire respect of Gay, Arbuthnot
and Pope, and who could evidently animate considerable affection in the
Acheson household.[146] The poems set forth a figure of the Dean as a lazing
titan. He is the national hero – the Hibernian Patriot, no less – turned stubborn lodger, who rages, chides and frets, and ultimately wears his hosts
down. However, the subtext of the poems suggests this was precisely the
guise Swift was evidently able to slip off, for periods, at Market Hill, as he
did at his own retreat at Laracor. The Achesons provided a sheltered space
for the monolithically irascible Dean to relax his combative public stance,
and become an entertaining, amicable companion; a guest who was more
than capable of commenting on, making fun of and indirectly apologizing
for his faults. Therein lies the delicate act of gratitude the poems perform
so successfully.

On these first visits, he loved Market Hill. The Achesons treated him
with generosity and kindness, and also tolerated for many months his
growing eccentricities. A fortress built by the family in the time of James
I had been destroyed in the 1640s, and its replacement had no military
pretensions. The huge boxy castle that stands near the site of the great
manor house Swift knew is a creation of the nineteenth century; yet the
paths he plotted still lead through the woods of the townland the family
controlled. Here was the refuge he needed above all from the publicity
of Dublin. Market Hill gave him insight into the agricultural catastrophe but also comfort, seclusion and company in the balance he required.
His manners, perhaps without Johnson to check them, were becoming
stranger; the mixture of remoteness and rudeness often attributed to him

was now more firmly established. His health, meanwhile, was assaulted almost monthly by his aural disorder, and his hosts nursed and humoured him with great consideration. It was a relief to him when people were willing to shout, so that he could follow conversation, and the Achesons obliged him in this. 'I hate Dublin, and love the Retirement here, and the Civility of my Hosts,' he told Sheridan in August, whom he urged to join him there (and then take him home in his coach).[147]

Sheridan was in the south, pursuing slim hopes of another benefice in County Cork. When these were disappointed, instead of meeting professional or social obligations, he idled. In Dublin, he had missed the date on which schoolmasters were required to present themselves to the ecclesiastical registrar. Archbishop King was displeased. He had had words on Sheridan's behalf, and the Registrar had told him that Swift's friend was always late; and that 'the highest [that is, the most Tory] churchmen are commonly the most negligent.'[148] Meanwhile, in Armagh, Swift expected a visit. But Sheridan opted to take the waters at a spa called Ballyspellin near Kilkenny, and published a poem commending both the cure and a woman he either met or accompanied there. The ballad is a fun exercise in rhyme-finding, and after eighteen stanzas he claimed to have exhausted every serviceable echo of 'Ballyspellin'.

> My Rhymes are gone, I think I've none,
>     Unless I should bring Hell in;
> But since I am here to Heav'n so near,
>     I can't at Ballyspellin.

Piqued by his friend's non-appearance, Swift decided to prove him wrong. He wrote a ballad bludgeoning Sheridan's, rubbishing Ballyspellin, and labelling the female companion a grisette. He arranged for his poem to be privately published in Dublin, and distributed among their acquaintance.[149]

> How'er you flounce,
> I here pronounce
> Your Med'cine is repelling,
> Your Water's mud,
> And sours the blood
> When drank at Ballyspellin.[150]

The consequence of this public drubbing – exposing more than faintly flat_tatious tendencies in Sheridan – was another quarrel. Sheridan was mortified, and Swift was enraged by his subsequent petulance. He was constantly performing favours for the erratic schoolmaster. He had recently written to the Bishop of Cork on Sheridan's behalf; at Swift's request, Pope had read Sheridan's translation of Persius.[151] Such services, Swift felt, not even mentioning his benevolent seniority in respect to Sheridan, allowed him a little 'innocent merriment' at the younger man's expense. Sheridan thought differently. He called the ballad an affront, 'against all the rules of reason, taste, good-nature, judgement, gratitude or morals'. Swift assumed that he had been corrupted by his spa-side female friend, and noted the incident as another example of Sheridan being lured by a woman's smile 'as a child is by a new play-thing'.[152]

He was eager to be pressed to stay with the Achesons till Christmas. In fact he remained at Market Hill until the first half of December; and then, on concluding necessary affairs in Dublin, quickly returned to the north.[153] His desire for sanctuary made him brave enough to travel in one of the bitterest winters for years. At Christmas 1728 Dublin was covered in snow, and was punished with a terrible frost. The misery of the season highlighted the long-standing lack of fuel; coal was simply too rare and expensive for the poorest homes. The countryside, meanwhile, was no place to go if gentlemen wished to avoid the sight and sound of starving families. Armagh offered little more by way of pampering than his deanery, where he had a dedicated group of helpers to call on – from Mrs Brent, his Presbyterian housekeeper, to Mrs Worrall, who had diligently nursed Johnson. At Market Hill, though, he had the consolation of nature and his projects to improve the grounds; and, perhaps above all, he was free of the expectation that he do something to remedy the times.

In mid-January he at last felt he could demand no more kindness from the family, some of whom were possibly hoarse from speaking up to accommodate his bad hearing. He had been ill for about a month, but now admitted that 'my raggedness will soon force me away.' He was to return, however, in the summer, and a letter to Pope from Dublin in February 1729 explains why:

> I lived very easily in the country: Sir Acheson is a man of Sense, and a Scholar, has a good voice, and my Lady a better; she is perfectly well bred, and desirous to improve her understanding, which is very good, but cultivated too much like a fine Lady. She was my pupil there, and severely chid when she read wrong. With that, and walking and making

twenty little amusing improvements, and writing family verses by way of libels on my Lady, my time past very well and in very great order; infinitely better than here, where I see no creature but my servants and my old Presbyterian house-keeper.

His ears had closed again, and he was refusing to admit any visitors until his hearing fully returned; and even then he denied callers for a week or two after he was properly fit. The one advantage of periodic deafness was being able to feign an attack of it if occasion demanded.[154] That summer he was to advise Acheson on the conversion of an old stone cattle-shed into a malt-house; and he offered, it seems, to purchase a plot of land from his host. The parcel was to be called Drapier's Hill. The personalities Swift encountered and the schemes he began in the north were recorded in a further series of good-humoured poems, by turns refined and brusquely vernacular.

He stayed at Market Hill until October 1729. On the road into Dublin from the north he was met by crowds led by many of the city's notables. The bells rang, and one saw displays of 'illuminations' and bonfires with musical entertainments, a re-enactment of the greeting Swift received in 1726.[155] Although utterly untruthful with respect to Swift's participation, Dean Smedley caught the spirit of popular tribute:

> What great Fame Gulliver grew into among some simple People on account of his last pretended Atchievement: How the Ballad-Singers, and other Mob of the Parish he lived in, used to gather about him, huzza, sing Catches, and get drunk in his Honour; which Solemnities he took care to encourage, by presiding in them himself.[156]

To a blighted capital, any excuse for festivity might seem perfectly reasonable. But Swift was also a talisman. A decent harvest had come in at last, after three years, and there was almost the superstitious sense that he was responsible for this apparent mercy. His compatriots also had fewer defenders to thank: in May, Archbishop King had died, at which Dublin had mourned as if stricken with a 'general calamity'.[157]

Perhaps now there would be an end of eating the oats required for next year's sowing, or dining on scavenged meat and blood. 'Three terrible years of dearth,' he mused to Pope, in a letter in August; 'and every place strowed with beggars.' For Swift corn was chicken-feed, however, in the true scale of Ireland's problems; 'our evils here lie much deeper.' There would be no clemency from merchants when it came to the price of grain; the perennial neglect of the land would continue; the English trade embargos would persist. Absentees would still ship money out of the kingdom, and the Irish Parliament would remain vestigial. Swift's campaign as the Drapier had newly mobilized the Protestants entitled to sit in Parliament, but they had already diverted funds and willpower into irrelevancies. Work had begun on a grand new home for their sessions on College Green; the decaying mansion in which they had gathered since the 1680s had been pulled down, and earlier that year the Lords Justices turned out to lay the first stone with great ceremony.[158] For Swift this splendid Georgian construction would nonetheless stand as a work of architectural irony, suggesting power and autonomy where in his mind none could exist, where the Declaratory Act had indeed all but removed it. And perpetuating his more idiosyncratic grievance, women could still be seen wearing embroidered foreign cloths that were beyond the means of their families; 'their pride will not suffer them to wear their [country's] manufactures even where they excel what come from abroad.'[159]

His response, while the rest of the country drew breath as the harvest came in, was to castigate rather than cheer. He invented a maniacal parody of a long-term solution, a plan that would be especially painful for the island's vain womenfolk. For the purpose he created the best known and arguably most memorable of all his coolly spoken technicians and experts: the Modest Proposer who suggests that the children of the poor should be farmed as livestock. The result would create a profitable new market and deal with the problem of overpopulation at a single stroke. The comic mastery of the *Modest Proposal* lies partly with its timing. It delays the gruesome joke, beginning with a passage which is part description, part moralistic social analysis, and might be found in any of Swift's earnest writings during the period of dearth:

It is a melancholy Object to those, who walk through this great Town, or travel in the Country; when they see the Streets, the Roads, and Cabbin-doors crowded with Beggars of the Female Sex, followed by three, four, or six Children, all in Rags, and importuning every Passenger for an Alms. These Mothers, instead of being able to work for their honest Livelyhood, are forced to employ all their Time in strolling to beg Sustenance for their helpless Infants; who, as they grow up, either turn Thieves for want of Work; or leave their dear Native Country, to fight for the Pretender in Spain, or sell themselves to the Barbadoes.

The irony is as yet only detectable in the sanctimonious reference to the beggars' 'dear Native Country', and the satirical intention is cloaked as the opening paragraphs continue and the writer broaches his topic of how poor children might be made 'sound and useful Members of the Commonwealth'. Swift is relying on a cry of alarm from the reader when his persona finally lifts the lid on his big idea.

> I have been assured by a very knowing American of my Acquaintance in London that a young healthy Child, well nursed, is, at a Year old, a most delicious, nourishing, and wholesome Food; whether Stewed, Roasted, Baked or Boiled; and, I make no doubt, that it will equally serve in a *Fricasie*, or *Ragout*.[160]

The rest is a feat of elaboration on points taken to absurd yet wholly logical conclusions. The piece can bring you to laugh aloud at the grave enthusiasm and statistical precision of the proposer who believes, with the sincerity of a child himself, that he has had a truly great notion. 'How could someone imagine this?' students will sometimes ask a teacher on being given the text to read. To contemporary readers the *Proposal*'s illusion of authenticity was still more tenacious and, in consequence, the moralistic subterfuge all the more outrageous. Although stories of cannibalism during the nadirs of seventeenth-century warfare have largely been exposed as terrified hearsay, in Swift's time it was held as fact that people during the Thirty Years War had been reduced to eating human corpses.[161] And here, in Swift's brisk prose, was a scheme to industrialize this ultimate depravity, and redirect it towards children raised for the very purpose of providing meat. His persona was seeking to capitalize on an eventuality that, to an eighteenth-century European reader, was extreme but still, just, harrowingly possible. The less safe the period in which *A Modest Proposal* is encountered, the more dangerous and distressing Swift's feat of irony will seem.

Part of the shock lies in his creation of an exuberant utilitarian so unconscious of his amorality. Elsewhere, Swift himself had little space for tenderness: stern measures were necessary. If one's income sinks from £100 to £50 a year, what is there to be done but halve one's expenses?[162] If the thorn your ancestor planted at the gate no longer blossoms but simply gets in the way – pick up your axe and cut it down. And here is Swift being entirely sincere – apparently – in another essay of 1729, on how the 'poor native Irish' should be dealt with:

It would be a noble achievement to abolish the Irish language in this
kingdom, so far at least as to oblige all the natives to speak only English on every occasion of business, in shops, markets, fairs, and other
places of dealing . . . This would, in a great measure, civilize the most
barbarous among them, reconcile them to our customs and manner of
living, and reduce great numbers to the national religion, whatever
kind may then happen to be established. The method is plain and simple;
and, although I am too desponding to produce it, yet I could heartily
wish some public thoughts were employed to reduce this uncultivated
people from that idle, savage, beastly, thievish manner of life, in which
they continue sunk to a degree, that it is almost impossible for a country gentleman to find a servant of human capacity, or the least tincture
of natural honesty; or who does not live among his own tenants in
continual fear of having his plantations destroyed, his cattle stolen, and
his goods pilfered.[163]

Here Swift again tested the responses of his godly readers. Such a voice
is not so far removed from that of the Modest Proposer. It has all the
failures of reason characteristic of the wildest Swiftian persona. How
can one expect 'natural honesty' from people who are forced to live like
beasts? The phrase itself degenerates into oxymoron. This, seemingly, is
Swift's voice – that is, the voice of the historical, biographical Swift. The
text of this paper of 1729 takes on moral and literary complexity from
the fact that Swift affects to be writing out of compassion – or something close to it – *for* the native Irish. He – or the persona he adopts for
the occasion – would suppress their language entirely; but he would
include them in the benefits of a materially more comfortable existence
by forcing them to adapt to 'our customs'. In essence, he would bring
them into the nation; in his view, as respectable servants to Protestant
families they would be better off than they are now. Though it might
seem very much like a toned-down passage from *A Modest Proposal*,
Swift's intention here was to advance measures that would save the children of the 'barbarous' Irish from the roasting pot.

A little earlier in the same tract, by inviting his reader to suppose that
Papist peasants have an understanding 'just equal to that of a dog or
horse', and thus might be trained by benefits and punishments, he
comes across as someone who must be another of his invented lunatic
projectors. But we cannot be sure. He implicitly credits the poorest of
tenants with much more potential intelligence; he challenges standard
Protestant perceptions about the 'laziness, perverseness, or thievish dis-

position' of the wild Irish. He sees, in effect, that such traits are products of circumstance. His method for suppressing the language is to outlaw it in places of business, not to punish it with violence everywhere. He seems blind, or dismissive, of course, to what seems obvious to us, the prior claim such oppressed people had to the land that was taken from them, or their right to speak their own language. The idea is still taken to such lengths that it eventually exhausts one's ability to believe that Swift adhered to it completely. A persona, or at least the shade of one, must be at least partially active in this essay. For behind the extremist Protestant voice of the essay, as with the *Modest Proposal*, was a man who had suffered deep loss just two years before; who had seen the depressed rural populace with his own eyes; who had 'bantered' with Catholic labourers; and who tacitly, perhaps, was leading his readers to reflect on their prejudices. The views of Anthony Raymond, the scholar of Gaelic who had been his neighbour at Trim, would be obvious to Swift.

On the other hand, suppose the ideas of this essay are taken at face value, as Swift's own and sincerely held thoughts. He was no systematic thinker, and rejected outright the idea that he should be. Scripture and the Book of Common Prayer was for him precisely what saved one from having to think up metaphysical systems. But the 'defence' of the native Irish, a defence that to a modern way of thinking differs little from a programme of cultural extermination, clearly does bear the marks of long forethought. In order to save the children of Irish paupers from being farmed out to 'Persons of Quality and Fortune' – or meeting some equivalent destiny – harsh remedies are needed. The women of the island will need to give up their fine imported fabrics. The native Irish will need to sacrifice their language and, essentially, their culture; the smaller loss, since to Swift both Irish language and culture were 'barbarous' and were holding back the peasantry from leading better lives. The logic underlying this attitude is indicative of a cruel age, a time that regarded conquest as proof of moral superiority, but there is much to the argument that is peculiar to Swift. His attitude to the most impoverished sections of society is essentially this: in order to ensure basic survival, a person or a community should be prepared to give up or suppress the distinguishing marks of their identity. For someone of his experience and versatility this was not such a great demand, because it was one he had answered for himself in a way that shaped his entire personality.

The programme of suppression he had in mind for the native Irish strongly resembled the cumulative traumas of his early childhood. Swift had been torn from home and then sent back; his mother had seemingly forsaken him, and as an adult he had no (recorded) arguments with her for doing so. His earliest memories were of a labouring family's cottage in Whitehaven, and then of being the smallest, lowest presence in a much grander home in Dublin. This transfer back to Ireland had a very muddled meaning for him. It took him from poverty to relative privilege, yet also from nurture to neglect, and from England, his preferred homeland, to Ireland. What he was proposing for the native Irish was much more clear-cut and beneficial, to his way of thinking: they would be led, over the course of a generation, to exchange their 'savage' speech and customs for an Anglicized identity. Swift had done exactly this in embracing so strongly the utmost letter of the Anglican creed and heritage. He had done something more besides: he had doubled his personality in a way that alongside the strict and sombre churchman was an elusive wit and fabulist. The principle under-writing his psyche and thus his way of reasoning was that a person might endure the worst emotional deprivations and yet remain a person through it all, even if that meant splitting oneself deeply.

Speaking crudely, there was Swift the conformist and Swift the anarchic humorist, and together they produced the satirical writer. The psychology of our own age indicates there must have been a third and silent element to Swift: one that grieved at lack of love and a sense of belonging nowhere, craving status, stability and recognition to offset the gnawing effects of shame and insecurity. But there is no need to mention that third aspect here, for the crucial point is that Swift at an early age had solved, very creatively, the brutal challenge he recommended for the native Catholic population of Ireland – that is, adapt and survive. Unconsciously he expected the native Irish to use the same tactic of doubling-up that had got him through childhood: his main concern was that they could speak and deal in English 'at least' in public venues. With their outer selves perfected, in private, they might speak as they wished; as the Presbyterians might. And the private lives of Catholic natives could at moments seize Swift's interest, imagination and unofficial respect much more than those of Presbyterians.

As long ago as 1720 he had translated eighty-odd lines of a long poem in Irish, *The Description of an Irish Feast*. Written earlier in the 1700s, the poem celebrated a great gathering held by O'Rourke, the famous rebel of Elizabethan times. The text has always been attributed to Hugh MacGauran (Aodh Mac Gabhráin), and was set to music by the outstanding traditional musician of the century, Turlough Carolan, a blind harpist whom Swift had heard perform.[164] The humour of the original had self-evident attractions for Swift, as did the word-game of translation. The verse opened a circle of dancers Swift would never dream of joining in person but who captivated his attention nonetheless. His addiction to fitness comes through in his relish for their exertions:

> They dance in a Round,
> Cutting Capers and Ramping;
> A Mercy the Ground
> Did not burst with their stamping.
> The floor is all wet
> With Leaps and with Jumps,
> While the Water and Sweat,
> Splish, splash in their Pumps.[165]

Gauging the overall tone of Swift's *Description* is a testing task, for the act of translation itself is ambiguous. It seems both patronizing and fascinated in equal measure. Readers will find themselves asking, did his rendering of the Irish text indicate a 'walk on the wild side' in the safe form of a fiction – an excursion into a culture he regarded as 'primitive'? Or did it mark a more inclusive and open-minded attitude, however cautious, to the 'mere Irish' and their side of history? Swift's version supports no verdict on those points. It does, however, show that he knew enough Irish, though no doubt with the help of a literal crib, to work up his translation; and it also shows him involving himself in the art of the Irish original. Like his dealings with Catholic labourers at Market Hill, it offers a glimpse of him in contact with the people whose language he nevertheless suggested should be suppressed for their own good.[166]

Again, if we continue to interpret it literally, this proposal was still made with a view to putting the mere Irish above a condition of abject poverty – not, as in earlier colonial schemes, in order to disable the population. The idea can be helpfully placed in the context of Swift's rhetoric of reproach to the victims of oppression. He insistently berated the entire Irish population of Ireland for allowing British insults to pass. In 1729, 'St Patrick's Well', a spring near Trinity College famed for its sacred healing powers, mysteriously dried up. Assuming the voice of St Patrick – who had magically elicited the waters from the rock – Swift informed the Irish that the apparent death of the spring was a judgement on their degenerate state. The native Irish population were a disgrace, said the patron saint, to their distinguished and heroic ancestors. Swift's plan to stop Irish being heard in public conceivably belongs to the same vein of patriarchal rebuke.[167]

The attitude behind Swift's plan for Irish speech and customs was that of a sufferer turned enforcer, proposing the course of lesser cruelty. Put bluntly, Swift's hidden rationale was that since he had lost his Englishness – and much more – why shouldn't the Catholic peasantry give up their Irishness? Even so, his thinking on the largely impoverished Irish-speaking population stands out from that of other Protestants in the period. It is located somewhere between an idealistic tendency among some clerics to proselytize in Irish, or to 'Anglicize' Irish Papists through 'English Schools', and the brute culling instinct of many planters.[168] His measure of pure sympathy was strictly rationed for the Irish infants he spared from being 'offered in sale to the Persons of Quality and Fortune'. Rearing children for a refined table was no way, he accepted, of 'lessening the Number of Papists among us'.[169] It seems, however, even if an ironic persona is at work in his statements on the Irish language, Swift would not spare the children of Catholic beggars from giving up their parents' speech and habits of life. Nobody could be spared such aggressive moulding. His own existence had been a strenuous effort to preserve an adapted exterior; and he had also shown how, having assumed the necessary disguise, one might use words to raid the cattle of the great and powerful.

The conforming façade, however, was cracking. Friends who adored him, notably Sheridan, also smarted from harsh stings. It took an exceptionally steady, firm-footed friend, such as John Worrall or his wife, or his patient housekeeper, Mrs Brent, not to foster resentment at his frequent slights and verbal cuffs. Equals and superiors ran the regular risk of being cut down to size. Although there was no open breach, in his last visit to the Achesons he seems to have wearied even the devoted slender-figured and asthmatic lady of the house, for whom Swift's favourite nicknames were 'Skinny' or 'Snipe' – recalling similar terms he had once bestowed on Esther Vanhomrigh.[170] He forestalled objections by expressing them himself in the poems he presented to Lady Acheson or Sir Arthur, yet for all that he could clearly be rude and disregardful at moments of physical and personal boundaries. He was unconquerably opinionated and, although fastidiously clean – another source of tiring expectations – was sometimes physically off-putting. Gay pointed out to him that it bothered some people when he put his food in his mouth with his knife.[171] So during his last visit to his friends in the north he began to cast them off before they rejected him. He had decided not to build on Drapier's Hill. He had reached the conclusion, as well, that Sir Arthur was unworthy of his company. He was as silent and immobile as Swift was when his 'unsociable comfortless deafness' descended, though without that excuse.[172]

> What intercourse of minds can be
> Betwixt the Knight sublime and me,
> If when I talk, as talk I must,
> It is but prating to a bust? . . .
> His guests are few, his visits rare,
> Nor uses time, nor time will spare;
> Nor rides, nor walks, nor hunts, nor fowls,
> Nor plays at cards, or dice, or bowls;
> But, seated in an easy chair,
> Despises exercise and air.[173]

The happiness of a family, Swift suspected, was all too often an illusion. In 1732, Sir Arthur and Lady Anne separated. Swift appears to have understood why, and his sympathies were more with the lady. 'Mrs Acheson', as he styled her then, settled on an urban life that suited her better: 'she is an absolute Dublin rake, sits up late, loses her money, and goes to bed sick,' he reported.[174]

# 12. Indecency and Indignation

I have sometimes made it a doubt with myself, which was the
greater debasement – to be a swine in reality, or in poetry!
What can be so shocking, as to see the heavenly muse wallow
in the mire! sunk into the character of the basest of all the
brutes.

– *Patrick Delany*[1]

## I

All sorts would call on Swift at his deanery. For the sake of peace, after
being ill he would keep news of his recovery from everyone but a select
group of friends until a fortnight or more after regaining the freedom of
his house. Bedridden for long stretches, deaf and short-sighted, he would
be confined to a painfully limited set of perceptions – bed-posts and
curtains, the sheen on the floorboards, the blur of blue-grey stony colour
from the window looking out on the cathedral. The plain-minded clarity
with which Gulliver relays what he has seen in his remote regions reflects
a fieldsman's practical observations, but also an invalid's watching and
wondering. Sometimes the *Travels* even hints at the creative use Swift
made of his myopia, accustomed as it made him to bringing objects up
close, into giant proportions, or straining his eyes to see things further
away – to watch a servant, for example, 'threading an invisible Needle
with invisible Silk'.[2] With the book finished, published years ago, and
the sensation it caused dying down, vertigo and deafness remained his
companions; the immobility and the gazing continued. Swift, unlike
Gulliver, remained tied down, disturbed by sea-like sounds.

In this state he felt quite unlike the image of sardonic titan, regal wit
and mighty patriot that his supporters held of him. When hearing and
balance returned, he was able to act these parts again, and the house

would be open – if sometimes on sufferance – to the many who sought his counsel, company and approval.

The older he grew, the more he tended to welcome humbler visitors above the grander ones. The former were, for one thing, frequently less trouble. Tradesmen and manufacturers, it seemed, would occasionally come to pay their respects, and petition for his help in some matter. A visit from a delegation of weavers in 1729 allowed him to berate the nation again for not taking the limited action it might on behalf of Irish trade. He wondered 'whether those animals which come in my way with two legs and human faces, clad, and erect, be of the same species with what I have seen very like them in England'.[3] Over the next decade, as old age and poor health began to get the better of him, the species only grew stranger to him. He remained, however, the esteemed (and feared) focus of much fashionable admiration; and he was pleased enough to welcome it sometimes, at his traditional supper parties on Sunday evenings.

Some friends, mostly younger, he trusted would need no welcome. Sheridan and Delany were still his regulars. Slightly rarer might be a call from one or more of the Grattan brothers and their wives; more of an event, a visit from one of his country friends and hosts in Gaulstown or Market Hill. Among others in Swift's immediate town circle was a cleric in his early thirties. James Stopford was quiet, learned, moderately well-off and very fond of foreign travel; a fellow of Trinity, he had been a confidant and protégé at the deanery for a good many years by the time Swift commended him publicly in a wry pamphlet of 1730. Having the comfort of his fellowship and 'a little foolish land' to ease the lack of a preferment, Stopford had no drive to overcome his social awkwardness. In 1725, as Stopford embarked on a second Continental tour, Swift had given him a fond letter of recommendation to Pope: 'he is such a Youth as you could wish ... an humble admirer of Poetry and you, without any pretensions to the muses at least as he asserts.'[4] In it he urged Pope to introduce him to all the original Scriblerians and newer auxiliaries. Yet, when faced with meeting the first poet of the day and Brobdingnagian Gay and Arbuthnot, Stopford quavered. He put off delivering his letter to Pope until just before he departed for France. The poet was slightly offended, and Swift was obliged to make apologies on Stopford's behalf. He explained that Stopford, bashful to a fault, had also resisted his attempt to introduce him to Lord Carteret.[5] In one of his most emotional letters during Esther Johnson's serious illness of 1726, he had shared his deepest feelings with Stopford, addressing him repeatedly as his 'dear Jim'.[6] First names meant a lot to Swift, who generally avoided them in his letters, and who had been flustered with almost equal pleasure and suspicion, long ago, when Harley and St John took to calling him 'Jonathan'. Young Stopford taking such a liberty was obviously unthinkable. Yet, at his zenith in his mid-sixties, Swift reminded his putative superiors on the Bishops' Bench that they were all once 'young Beginners . . . known by their plain Christian Names, among their old Companions'.[7] Jim Stopford triggered an instinct both comradely and paternal in his terrifying maverick patron.

Like Sheridan, like Ford, Stopford was a candidate for being the son Swift never had. His gentle, unassuming character ruled out the spats and anecdotes Sheridan brought to Swift's biography, and he had none of the schoolmaster's glitter or quickness; he was a quieter, steadier presence in the deanery parlour. In the end, he proved to have an essential gift for success in a clergyman: he could avoid causing offence, and rose, despite his shyness, to become the Bishop of Cloyne.

Among the men, there were also relatively new female acquaintances. No women were admitted to the deanery, for propriety's sake, unless they had received 'very particular invitations'.[8] Swift became a confirmed supporter of Mary Barber, a poet, and Constantia Grierson, an autodidact of outstanding scholarly accomplishments. Barber had published rhymes in praise and imitation of Gay. Grierson had edited a pocket classics volume of Terence; in 1730, aged twenty-five, she was at work on an edition of Tacitus. Along with Mrs E. Sican, who had 'a very good taste of Poetry', these three women made up a 'Triumfeminate' that Swift commended to Pope. All were the wives of prominent mercantile citizens. Mrs Sican had given Swift a fine sturgeon as a present, sent anonymously with a few lines of verse, about six years earlier. Swift's attitude to the trio was gallant but not condescending. He was critical of the 'surly rich husband', a printer, who exploited Grierson's command of languages for his business but stifled her desire to write.[9] Another woman friend, a more flamboyant figure in Swift's story, said Grierson's gift was 'like the intuitive knowledge of angels'. Grierson put to shame countless dull males struggling over their books in Trinity College, although not for long; she would die, probably of consumption, in 1732.[10]

For a time, two epigrams pasted up in a front window of the deanery had promised Swift's guests good wine yet meat of poor quality.[11] Once inside, however, Swift actually saw that they were treated well, although he concealed his generosity as a host as he did his benevolence to servants and relatives.[12] 'His way was,' said Delany, 'instead of pressing or courting, rather to affect a kind of reluctance and fear of his being devoured by their eating and drinking with him.'[13] There was a grain of real angst, though, in this concern for expense, and it germinated rapidly towards the end of the coming decade. For now, Swift made theatre at dinner out of his parsimonious urges. A notable performance was recorded, long afterwards, by another young woman he befriended in the late 1720s.

When Swift first set eyes on Mrs Laetitia Pilkington, probably towards the end of 1729, she claimed he said, 'What, this poor little child married. God help her, she is early engaged in trouble.' Pilkington and her husband Matthew, a young priest and a gifted scholar, were both diminutive, and seemed like children to many who knew them. Mrs Pilkington was barely twenty, and when Mary Barber introduced them Swift assumed she was the older woman's daughter. Mrs Pilkington was also connected to Constantia Grierson. Dr John Van Lewin, Laetitia's father, a distinguished obstetrician, had taught Constantia the elements of midwifery, and, like her, was a southerner. The two women's early lives were otherwise dissimilar. Mrs Pilkington grew up in the relative comfort of a physician's house; Mrs Grierson had survived a childhood of great poverty in Kilkenny.

Mrs Pilkington was a keen poet, and Mr Pilkington, eight years her senior, a good musician and amateur painter. They were just the sort of people to brighten up an evening, and they were skilled at getting their feet under a table. As Swift's birthday neared in November 1729, Laetitia wrote a eulogy in his honour, which was borne to him by Delany via Barber. Swift asked for the Pilkingtons to be invited to a gathering Delany planned at his home at Glasnevin, just outside the city. Delany originally shared what became a spacious and elegant house with another fellow of Trinity, a physician and expert in demography called Richard Helsham; and at first they called it 'Heldelville', as a somewhat provocative amalgam of their names. They reduced the diabolic scent of this invention by renaming the place 'Delville', which Delany stuck with when he became sole owner in or around 1732. In 1729 work on what proved a lifelong (and very costly) architectural project was just beginning. Rather like Pope, whose work he adored and whose garden at Twickenham he was fully aware of, Delany was to aim for an effect of measured wildness in the grounds at Delville. In time his work would incorporate a portico known as 'Swift's temple', where the Dean took a grateful seat on summer visits. Delany had the motto *Fastigia despicit urbis* ('The heights despise the city') inscribed on the frieze – a little hubristically, since the demolished folly was engulfed by Dublin long ago. In any case, such adornments to the property lay in the future: in 1729, on an afternoon in early December, the garden was the scene where Mrs Barber, as Swift's 'chief poetess', introduced him to the Pilkingtons. Laetitia remembered, exultantly, meeting 'on a noble Terass, whose Summit was crowned with a magnificent Portico, where Painting and Sculpture displayed their utmost Charms', though in all likelihood she projected the later development of Delville on to that first encounter.[14]

It pleased Swift when a young woman's armpits didn't stain her gown. It interested him when they did, as he became ever less reserved about showing in his published verse.[15] A week later, he invited the couple to spend Sunday at the deanery. He was charmed by the pair of them. Mr Pilkington had something of Sheridan's bubbliness and learning; Mrs Pilkington was clever, spontaneous and funny. Swift had Matthew preach, and honoured him by reading the Communion service – without once looking at the prayer-book, Laetitia noticed. Like a true stalwart of the Carolean Church, he bowed to the holy table; a clear statement, in mime, of his Cavalier loyalties.

The gesture was significant, and Mrs Pilkington knew it was worth recording. The vaulted space of the choir was a site of long-standing disputes, in which Swift himself was a fervent participant. For the sake of opposing doctrinal and sectarian agendas, St Patrick's had been variously exploited and closed down, desecrated, decorated and ideologically altered in the two centuries since the Reformation. As in churches throughout the kingdoms, the cathedral had seen a running struggle over the placing of the table where Holy Communion was celebrated. It had been shifted from the east end of the choir, where the high altar – a word abhorred by Protestants – was placed in any Catholic arrangement, and set 'table-wise' by the pulpit, in the centre of the congregation. An enormous monument had then been installed by Richard Boyle, Earl of Cork, for himself and his wife in the very place where the altar had stood, a quarter-acre work of effrontery that was dislodged during William Laud's controversial return to older ceremonial customs. Swift, bowing to the Communion table in 1729, was acknowledging Laud; Charles I; the example of his ancestor, the Vicar of Goodrich; a former realm.

When the service ended, he was surrounded by beggars outside the church door. He distributed alms – clearly another personal ritual – to all except one elderly woman whose hands were dirty: water was hardly so scarce, he told her, that she might not wash.[16] There was a touch of familiarity here, suggesting Swift often gave to her, and that she would have better luck next time. The beggars in the purlieus of St Patrick's were all known to him. If they made some effort to follow a trade, however humble or even vestigial, they could expect his support. He was especially attentive to elderly and ailing unprotected women, and joked that he had a 'seraglio' dispersed across town. 'One of these mistresses sold plumbs, another, hob-nails; a third, tapes [ribbons]; a fourth, ginger-bread; a fifth, knitted, a sixth, darned stockings, and a seventh, cobbled shoes.' Some of these he encountered in public view; others he would find in 'by-alleys, and under arches', thus maintaining the sense of an illicit tryst. There was hardly a back-street in Dublin which lacked a member of the old Dean's harem. The joke was a premeditated piece of cruelty disguising philanthropy. He had an Elizabethan's scorn for 'sturdy beggars' and a medic's blunt concern for those in real trouble or pain. All the women in Swift's seraglio were sick or disabled. Again, like the roll-call in an abusive nursery rhyme, 'One of these mistresses wanted an eye: another, a nose, a third an arm, a fourth, a foot.'[17] To dispel all appearance of sanctimony he named each after her affliction. 'No Soul has broke his Neck, or is hang'd or Married,' Swift told Sheridan in 1733, with a sexton's cheerfulness; 'Only Cancerina is dead, and I let her go to her Grave without a Coffin, and without Fees.'[18]

Deformity, signs of rough usage, wear and tear – they fascinated Swift on the faces and bodies which passed him, especially women's. Creases, craters and dents, an increasing subsection of his writing would suggest, in his mind comprised something close to the reality of flesh, in the young as much as in the old. One of his jottings in 1730 sketched out the face of a prostitute, and lingered on the muddy textures of her freckled skin.

> Like a fly-blown Cake of Tallow,
> Or, on Parchment, Ink turn'd yellow:
> Or, a tawny speckled Pippin,
> Shrivel'd with a Winter's keeping.[19]

When the Pilkingtons filed into the deanery with the other guests for their first Sunday visit, Swift insisted that Laetitia step with him into his study. 'Well,' he said, 'I have brought you here to shew you all the money I got when I was in the ministry – but do not steal any of it.' He then opened a series of empty drawers. 'Bless me,' he exclaimed – in Laetitia's report – 'the money is flown.' The day continued in a show of regal eccentricities and exuberant confidences. He showed Laetitia his private museum, a stash of portraits and trinkets presented over the decades by acquaintances whose memories he treasured: people who were names from history for his young guest. A drawer in one cabinet was full of golden medals, and Swift allowed her like a child to choose two for herself.[20] He could not refrain from smiling when she chose a pair for their weight rather than their antiquity. At dinner, he played an inefficient tyrant, scolding the butler for snaffling a glass of his ale, and protested that his household was overrunning him. Seated at the head of the table, he watched the servants behind him in a large mirror on the marble-topped sideboard against the opposite walls. As years passed, this surveillance would become less and less a comic ritual, and his scrutiny ever more in earnest. Otherwise, all was done in the height of old-fashioned taste – the food was served, noted Laetitia, on nothing but silver plate. This was of course the first of many Sundays when the Pilkingtons would be joined by two or three clergymen who usually passed the evening with Swift: most probably Delany, Stopford and Sheridan. On one of these occasions, another guest made a striking entrance.

> There now came in, to sup with the Dean, one of the oddest little Mortals I ever met with ... Upon the strength of being an Author and of having travelled, [he] took upon him not only to dictate to the Company but to contradict whatever any other person advanced, Right or Wrong, till he had the whole talk to himself (for, to my great surprise, the Dean neither interrupted nor showed any Dislike of him).[21]

This ageing garrulous bachelor was Charles Ford, on one of his periods of Irish residence, to whom Swift could deny little by way of attention or tolerance. Swift saved his reprimands for the post rather than the hearth. Contact between the two men did decline, however, over the next few years, when Ford based himself solely in England.[22] Still, in joining companions such as Ford, introduced as they were under Delany's auspices, the Pilkingtons could not be classed by Swift's regulars as interlopers. They were children, and prompted sunny responses. Swift made a point of putting the same amount they had left on the collection plate into Laetitia's hand as he ushered them to their cab at the end of the evening.

There were enough of such occasions. There were also the evenings spent alone, coping with the reality of desolate feelings. In late February 1730 he complained to Pope of the very symptoms he had so often urged Vanhomrigh to resist.

> I am daily harder to please, and less care taken whether I am pleas'd or not. I dine alone, or only with my House keeper. I go to my Closet immediately after dinner, there sit till eleven and then to bed. The best company here grows hardly tolerable, and those who were formerly tolerable are now insupportable.

The last sentence is more a confession of the strain company placed on him – for domestic performances such as those he laid on for Laetitia – than a reproach he might have sustained against specific companions. He took the freedom to berate as one of his basic liberties. In the same letter he told Pope of how he found writing both rhyme and prose harder than ever; but also how he wrote whatever came into his head, and usually burned the results. He preferred to write in the evening than to take up a book, since reading by candlelight made his eyes sore. Here Swift's tone might be plaintive, but the emotion it communicates is a grudging acceptance of such evenings – when there seems nothing one can do but sit alone, ponder the ills of one's life and the world's, and reflect on what a burden it is to have visitors. The eager correspondence he maintained with Pope, or his evident delight in putting on a show at home for the Pilkingtons, manifestly belies the disaffection he expressed on this evening at the end of winter. His lurking melancholy simply needed its say. Despite his professed difficulties writing, verse and prose still ran irresistibly from his quill, over page after page. His unhappiness, as he admitted to Pope in telling him his news, stemmed from immediate as well as chronic causes. He was worried about investments he had made, money he had lent. Some claret he had bought with high expectations through Arbuthnot's brother Robin, a Jacobite financier and merchant based permanently in France, proved undrinkable. The disappointment was wrenching, since Swift claimed the cheapness of good wine comprised 90 per cent of the reasons that made Ireland habitable. He had written in protest at a bill to raise the duty on wine, but had thought twice before publishing his essay. Enacted just before Christmas, this measure cast a further cloud for Swift on the festive season. Then in January he had fought with the new Archbishop of Dublin, John Hoadly – the younger brother of the fierce Whig, Benjamin – over the ceremony of his enthronement in St Patrick's: when Hoadly refused to take his oaths before Swift as dean, Swift would not even sit at dinner with his new superior.[23] Still more profoundly, he was embattled with a new public slur.[24]

## 2

About a fortnight earlier, a gentleman had arrived at the deanery and demanded an interview that at first left Swift perplexed. His caller had come at the request of a mutual acquaintance, Joshua, Viscount Allen. The same day, at a meeting of the Irish Privy Council, Viscount Allen had angrily denounced a move to present Swift with the Freedom of the City, enclosed in the gift of a gold box. On hearing of the plan, Swift had let it be known – via Delany, it seems – that the box should bear an inscription recounting all he had done on behalf of the nation. The idea had first been mooted years before, but in mid-January, the Lord Mayor and the Corporation had ordered that a box worth a maximum of £25 should be fashioned accordingly. Since then Dublin had witnessed riots in protest against the continuing shortage of bread and work, and now Allen spoke scornfully at the council of this latest waste of public funds on a trinket for a trouble-maker. His father, though, had supported Swift's stand as the Drapier; and the present Viscount himself, as Swift recorded tartly, had once been eager for friendship at the deanery. In haste, as his words in council spread through the town, Allen dispatched his genteel messenger to St Patrick's to reassure Swift that his regard was actually unchanged. Swift, however, on gaining the facts, did not reciprocate. He replied (it was said) by saying that while he was sorry for Allen as a madman, he must renounce him since he was clearly possessed by the devil.[25] Biding his time, he transformed Allen into an absurd satirical figure. As 'Traulus', Allen featured in Swift's poetry and prose over the coming half-year. Swift wrote with venomous ease of a turncoat inept in even the basic arts of treachery, yet one who was able to 'sputter out the basest and falsest Accusations; then to wipe his Mouth, come smiling to his Friend, shake him by the Hand, and tell him in a Whisper, it was all for his Service'.[26]

Unsurprisingly, Swift had given fresh material for controversy in the debate that ensued over his gold box. Why he should feel the need to campaign so ardently for the gift was no mystery to those who knew him, even a relatively recent acquaintance such as Laetitia Pilkington: the answer lay among the treasury of splendid mementos she had inspected, under Swift's approving eye, on her Sundays in the deanery. He placed immense value in such relics; they had near-sacred significance for him without being idols. The city's present was to be a major exhibit in this private museum, and he wrote of the affair to Pope with a very sincere sense of injury. Exercising politic caution to obtain a public favour, though, was obviously alien to him, and over the previous few months, even as the debris settled around the political crater made by *A Modest Proposal* and his other resounding pamphlets of 1729, he had continued his bombardment of the Georgian regime. A poem that might in fact have led to prosecution, 'Directions for a Birthday Song' – in mock-honour of the King, telling the story of the Hanover takeover as sordid saga – was too dangerous to publish; but early February saw the appearance of 'A Libel on Dr Delany and a Certain Great Lord'.[27] In this Swift addressed the culture of corruption and cronyism that engrossed the British government. His starting point, rather uncomfortably for his mannerly disciple, was an attempt Delany had made to gain further patronage from the Lord Lieutenant. Delany pressed his suit in the form of a verse dialogue, 'An Epistle to Lord Carteret', which at once flattered and yet set up the poet as the viceroy's equal and companion.[28] Delany's unctuousness chafed Swift. He chided his younger friend in a vehement 'Epistle upon an Epistle'. He tutted:

> You can't, grave Sir, believe it hard,
> That you, a low Hibernian bard,
> Should cool your Heels a while, and wait
> Unanswered at your Patron's gate.[29]

The personal lecture in Swift's poem provided an opportunity for public comment. Swift's first essential point both in the 'Epistle', which he brought out at Christmas 1729, and in the 'Libel' two months later, was that Delany should be satisfied with the funds he possessed. He held a college living, the Chancellorship of Christ Church Cathedral, and would shortly acquire the equivalent post at St Patrick's. These, Swift suggested, must surely be enough: implicit, in fact, in the poems is some nettling at Delany's apparent ingratitude in greedily seeking more than Swift had helped him to procure. The second point Swift made was a general one. Delany, said Swift, ought to realize that nobody of real virtue or talent had a chance of serious promotion under such a debauched regime. Swift's friend the viceroy was pointedly exempted from these overall charges; Pope, meanwhile, was praised as the typification of true and unsupported genius. Otherwise, more or less every other recent recipient of honour or employment was chastised as a fawning, raw-tongued wretch. When the topic of Swift's award came up in the council chamber on 13 February – eleven days after the 'Libel' on Delany was published – it seemed to his critics that he felt licensed to spray muck at them while expecting gold in return.

Such effrontery was evidently too much for Viscount Allen. He paid for his criticism by becoming Traulus in two lampoons that showed no mercy. The very name 'Traulus' vindictively hit on Allen's habitual stutter by drawing on a Greek term for 'speaking shakily'.[30] The first poem is a dialogue between two well-known Dublin figures, a lunatic and a sound citizen. The lunatic, Tom, asks constantly to know why Traulus could have spoken so hatefully about Swift; the freeman replies that Traulus is mad. In the course of their speeches Allen is dragged through Bedlam, and declared by far the moral inferior of the most deranged inmates there, who spatter him indiscriminately with their excrement, and of whom even the worst can tell friends apart from foes. He is successively compared, at length and with relish, to a man possessed and a mad dog. With 'Traulus, Part One', Swift had left himself the option of a sequel; apparently feeling that Allen had still got off lightly, he followed it up with a second poem in which he dropped the feigned sympathetic attitude of Robin and Tom and let loose instead with sheer invective. Swift may have been stirred to over-kill when the Presbyterian writer James Arbuckle dared to point out his vainglory in the affair of the gold box and the desired inscription. Arbuckle's lampoon seems to have appeared in early spring.[31] By then Allen had also made a second speech against Swift, in the House of Lords. Dropping every show of friendship, he declared Swift a Jacobite and an enemy of King George and called for the printer of the 'Libel' to be prosecuted.[32] While the new Parliament House was still being built, the Lords and Commons sat in the Blue-Coat School on Oxmantown Green, a fine yet modest, wide-fronted building dignified by a clock-tower and an elaborate gateway bearing royal arms on its pediment. Swift could be satisfied that Dubliners older than Allen could recall how the structure at the core of the school had originally been a shelter – a 'hospital' in the original sense – for orphans, idiots and beggars. Such citizens could make their own comparisons to the present set of inmates.[33]

Despite his resentments against the unspeakable Curll and other piratical publishers, Swift had long been a master of print for publicity purposes. By the early 1730s he was a Richelieu of the press, dispatching his libels like militiamen and assassins, and his enormous popularity made him all but untouchable. For such a notorious critic of the establishment to receive any public commendation whatsoever was thus a blow for the prevailing order; yet at the end of May he did get his gold box. A compromise, admittedly, had been made. Hoadly, his archbishop, was also presented with a box, worth slightly more than Swift's, containing the Freedom of the City, and this happened the day before the Lord Mayor and aldermen filed obediently up to the deanery to bestow their gift. The government's man had therefore received the same, indeed a slightly higher honour. Nevertheless, given the imbalance of power, Hoadly, with the backing of the British state and Swift with that of the weavers of Dublin, there was little doubt where the moral victory lay. And Swift was better equipped to win any clash of propaganda. It was spring, and the weather may have allowed the ceremony to take place in the deanery garden. After the Mayor said a few appreciative words, and handed over the box, Swift gently handed it back to him, and asked that he first be allowed to speak. He went on to vindicate his entire public career in Dublin, working back from Viscount Allen's outrageous slander in the winter. He assured those gathered that he had done more for King George and more to hinder the Pretender than forty thousand of any 'noisy, railing, malicious, empty zealots' who made aspersions to the contrary. He ranged as far back in time as his journeys to England to secure the First Fruits for Ireland's lower clergy; his acts of private charity since becoming dean – lending money at no interest to save, he reckoned, more than 200 families in Dublin from ruin. He kept his most daring stroke till last, by publicly acknowledging his authorship of 'those books called the *Drapier's Letters*'. He spoke openly of the reward for £300 that had been offered to anyone who informed on the Drapier; and again, demonstrating how tender his pride was on such questions, alluded to the charges of sedition Allen had made against him in the Lords. There were ten thousand to one, he estimated grimly, whose opinions differed from the Viscount's. Early in the speech, he mentioned how the honour 'was mingled with a little mortification' due to the delay Allen and other miscreants had caused; and he concluded that it might have been decent for the city to have had a dedicatory inscription engraved on the box. To wry smiles, no doubt, and questioning looks, among the aldermen, members of the chapter and surely his listening servants, he then accepted the Freedom of the City – and to be sure that posterity received his exact words, preserved the speech in writing.[34]

It was in the summer of this year that he made his final visit to

Market Hill and dropped his plan to buy land on the estate. His friendship with Sir Arthur Acheson palpably cooled. Vertigo and dizziness continued periodically, and he fought them off as ever with his old precaution of long rides and walks. By the autumn he had returned to his 'old Cathedral formalities' – prayers at nine, and reprimanding his subordinates.[35] In October he replied expansively to a teasing, warm-hearted letter from Lord Bathurst – a friend and admirer he shared with Pope, Gay and, until recently, Congreve. Bathurst, who was then forty-six, was one of the twelve Tories raised to the peerage by Oxford's emergency measure of late 1711. He joked that Swift had stolen the best bits of his works from, among others, Dryden, Cervantes and Rabelais, and that he shouldn't be so proud for risking his neck and his ears. But Bathurst also offered an evocative measure of Swift's public impact by saying he had 'set kingdoms in a flame', and provided a valuable glimpse of how Swift's work affected such a reader. Bathurst confessed to feeling tired at the end of his tracts, though not with boredom but over-stimulation. His brain and imagination were heated by Swift's words as if by wine.[36]

Another year was ebbing, and Swift could still offset physical maladies with rigorous exercise, and political attacks with intoxicating creativity. This pattern would hold for several more years. He relied on his friends, who visited his home and invited him to theirs, and counted on being allowed to insult them – for their own good – with impunity. Delany, though, seems to have been stung, over time, by the various epistles, libels and panegyrics in which Swift bandied with his name. He saw 'sourness of temper' in his great friend. His satire, Delany felt, had always reflected an inflammation of debilitating passions. Reminiscing later, Delany suggested that these corrosive energies were by now slipping out of control, and he put the cause down to a single absence among the deanery set.

> And all these infelicities of temper, were remarkably augmented after the death of Mrs Johnston, whose cordial friendship, sweet temper, and lenient advice, poured balm and healing into his blood, and kept his spirits in some temperament [evenness]; but as soon as he was deprived of that medicine of life, his blood boiled, fretted, and fermented, beyond all bounds.[37]

Delany preferred to emphasize Johnson's sanguine, calming and empathic qualities; Swift's papers suggest that Stella's personality gave her companions something more. Restraint and decorum, benignity offset with an icy judgement of phrase when required – these were certainly key features he admired in her. Yet Swift also praised her audacity of wit, her single-mindedness and forthright courage. That is to say, she was something greater than a soothing presence in the parlour, the gentle patter of Swift's hand that Delany sought to commemorate. In that civilized arena she epitomized containment and gentleness, but she could also silence a fool with a single killer remark. Undoubtedly providing moral support, she brought it in the form of catalysis as well as equilibrium. She indisputably left Swift to a chasm of sadness that younger women friends such as Mrs Pilkington or Lady Acheson could brighten only intermittently. But Delany's view of an angry old man boiling over without her 'feminine' restraint, a view that contributed to a myth of lunatic frenzy in Swift's final years, was founded on a misunderstanding of the condition he died of, and also on some understandable resentment. Swift would dwindle, rather than explode; the question was not how long he would last before his 'spirits' consumed him, but how long he could keep going without the friend who had relieved his worst moments, pitted her wits against his and urged him on to his greatest accomplishments.

It was more than fortuitous, then, that at Christmas in 1730 he began to draw close to a younger relative who soon enough became his primary assistant and amanuensis. A guarded part of Swift's life was a pattern of stealthy benevolence towards his extended family. Rhetorically and publicly, his attitude to his relations was that of the young child complaining that he had been stolen from a better home in England: the Swifts and Erickes and their offshoots basically disappointed him. This, at least, was his default view of his family: conversely, the gift of a book he sent in December to Martha Whiteway, the daughter of his uncle Adam, was typical of his thoughtfulness in practice.[38] Her husband, Edward, who died probably soon afterwards, in 1731, appears to have been unwell, and Mrs Whiteway was touched by the present. Swift in turn was stirred when she preferred to treat the book as a loan, and returned it with a letter that impressed him. The exchange allowed him to get to know her better through his standard mode of making contact with someone he grew to favour: affection or interest disguised as bad humour. 'You might give a better reason for restoring my book,' he told her, 'that it was not worth keeping.' The handwriting on her parcel was strange to him. He thought it was a man's – which, for Swift, was a promising sign in a woman. It made him safe, or so he imagined, to proceed towards intimacy without his intentions being misunderstood. That sense of safety,

with Vanhomrigh and Johnson, had not been as secure as he wished; and
though his age and general attitude put him past such complications now,
there might have been rumours. Whiteway was a mature married woman,
forty years old, well-educated and extremely capable. He was sixty-three.
She lived in Dublin, but in a distant parish, and the cousins had seen very
little of each other while she raised her family. 'I am so ill a visitor,' admitted Swift, 'that it is no wonder we meet so seldom.' He assured her though
that he always thought and spoke well of her, as he had known her when
younger; 'for as to what you are now, I know little.' Visits began, and
increased after her husband died the following year. She became, over
time, Swift's main organizer, and significantly he adopted her with none
of the fuss or comedy that welcomed the Pilkingtons.[39]

Whiteway and a few other assistants should be held in mind when
Swift gives the appearance, in his letters and publications, of a blazing,
sinking, solitary figure. The cathedral's defender – or 'avenger' – of liberty had a quiet, versatile domestic team of supporters, who provided
practical and emotional ballast during his prominent struggles. These
contests naturally continued in 1731, when Swift gave proof that he was
quite prepared to brazen out even royal displeasure, and to a degree
even relished the controversy that followed.

That spring a tablet was to be placed in St Patrick's to commemorate
the Duke of Schomberg, a hero of the Williamite revolution. One of William's closest friends and lieutenants, the Duke was killed at the Battle of
the Boyne, and was thus a prominent martyr in the Orange pantheon.
For a long time Swift and his chapter had urged Schomberg's family to
sponsor the monument. With baffling parsimony, they continually
refused. So the canons of St Patrick's went ahead with a memorial paid
for from cathedral funds, and composed in what a newspaper proudly
called 'elegant Latin' by Dean Swift.[40] In the inscription, Swift was
entirely unafraid to declare that Schomberg's relatives were too mean to
stump up some money for the hero's stone.[41] 'The Dean and the Chapter
applied ardently, repeatedly, for the Duke's heirs to make arrangements
for this monument,' ran the epitaph, chiselled in gold letters on black
granite. 'The fame of his virtue had more meaning for strangers than ties
of blood did to his descendants.'[42] Overall, the tablet thus said a great
deal more about the stinginess and small-mindedness of a set of living
grandees than it did about the heroism of Schomberg. It was consequently
less a celebration of the Glorious Revolution than a very public insult to
the Hanover Court. It followed Swift's old agenda of wresting the glory
of that revolution away from the Whig faction that had exploited it to

attempt undoing the constitution. The result, Swift's memorial implied, was an aristocracy consisting of degenerate, historically ignorant ingrates. His point was aided by the personal qualities of Schomberg's heir herself. Frederica, Lady FitzWalter, and her husband Benjamin Mildmay were said to have a marriage 'as curious as that between two oysters'.[43]

The King and Queen felt the broader force of the slur, and were furious. Swift, who was sure he had nothing to look for in their favour, exulted in placing himself above mere resentment. 'I hear the relations are angry,' he wrote airily to Pope. 'Let them take it for their pains.'[44] But Swift had by no means heard the last of the matter: not least, he faced reservations from within the cathedral chapter about the quality of his Latin.[45] These grammatical and stylistic corrections were arguably much more upsetting for Swift than King George himself, meanwhile, who publicly declared that the epitaph was a plot on Swift's part to stir trouble between England and Prussia. At this Swift adopted the requisite tones of indignation and outraged loyalty, while being manifestly gratified by such spluttering from on high.[46] Friends such as Pope, however, more closely connected with the English Court, advised caution. Rather awkwardly, Swift required the goodwill and help of some he had already half declared his enemies a little later the same year. A person wishing to embarrass him had forged a crude letter in his name to Queen Caroline, pressing her in highly familiar terms to show some favour to his protégée, Mrs Barber. Such a tactical error (and such a badly written note) on Swift's part was unthinkable; and it slightly tarnished the fine stroke achieved with the Schomberg monument. But overall he was well able to bear this collateral damage.[47]

And meanwhile in his base of operations, the liberties of St Patrick's, the late autumn of 1731 displayed the cathedral and its chapter in full pomp and splendour. A lavish show was prepared for the feast-day of St Cecilia on 22 November. The occasion was overseen by the cathedral's volatile but long-serving organist and composer, Ralph Roseingrave, and Matthew Dubourg, 'Master of the Music attending His Majesty's State in Ireland'. The organ was accompanied by a chamber orchestra; the sound of strings recalled a short-lived attempt, when Swift was just a boy, to give cathedral services something of the grandeur Charles II had witnessed in the chapel of Louis XIV. Although a full orchestra was beyond the chapter's means to maintain on a permanent basis, the performance with the choir contained favourites including Henry Purcell's *Te Deum* and *Jubilate*, along with secular works such as concerti by Corelli. Dublin's music-lovers were thrilled with the ambitious programme, which stretched over a full day – from ten in the morning until four in the afternoon. Mary Granville, the diarist and writer (who later married Patrick Delany), testified to the general delight, reporting that the crowd in St Patrick's was the greatest she had ever seen.[48] Here was an event asserting the old civic status of St Patrick's, and also reviving distinctly Stuart customs of ecclesiastical music. The festival mingled pride with a note of defiance in a minor key; and it also brought some much-needed joy to the population.

So long as the arrangements did justice to his cathedral – and all due proprieties were observed – Swift was satisfied. His defective hearing disqualified him from hazarding much comment on the quality of the music itself. He jotted a few lines, self-deprecating, warm and funny, in a poem he left 'imperfect':

> Grave Dean of St Patrick's, how comes it to pass
> That you who know musick no more than an ass
> That you who was found writing of Drapiers
> Should lend your Cathedral to players and scrapers?

The rapt crowds packing the nave, the hubbub, the force in the air but tonal indistinctness of the singers and the 'scraping' violinists – these were more for Swift to endure than enjoy. He was left, rather like St Cecilia on her wedding day, 'singing' to himself in the privacy of his mind and his rough-cut poem. His greatest personal pleasure in the entertainment came from the whining protest he expected from old-school puritans who saw traces of the devil, the Pope and the Pretender in the elaborate festivities.[49] In his resilience, he certainly resembled the saint being commemorated. It had taken the swordsman three strokes on her neck, and a further three days, before Cecilia died. Swift's enemies in London must have felt the same might prove true of him.

3

His stock of anger was undiminished. Assaults on the remnants of what he counted civilization continued to enrage him, and in the early 1730s he maintained a steady flow of powerful papers in resistance. These works vary in tone from exuberant mockery to cold fury. They are somewhat less universal in appeal than the pleas he offered during the years of famine in the late 1720s, but their prose is as acute as ever. Countless passages continue to strike beyond their immediate contexts. So far, however, as Swift's predicament went, the larger war over Ireland's economic independence and status as a kingdom was in his eyes lost; but he would pitch his energies, for as long as they would last, into political and ecclesiastical skirmishes. He fiercely condemned a bill to force each lower Irish clergyman to reside in one parish, and give up his other livings. The move was ruinous to the clergy, he reasoned, and thus the whole social order, because the average Irish parish simply could not sustain a priest and his family as its equivalent in England might. The land was too poor, parishioners too few, hostile Dissenters too many. The bill prompted one of Swift's many warnings on the basis of the past century of history. Early 1732 saw Swift vigorously combating two bills introduced by the Irish bishops. One would force 'country clergy' to build houses on their glebes or face sequestration – 'an office,' mused Swift, 'which ever falls into the most knavish hands.' The other bill would allow a bishop to divide the parishes in his see into as many parcels as he liked. This would increase the Irish lower clergy from about 600 to many thousands of priests, who would expect 'to live with Decency and Comfort, provide for their Children, be charitable to the Poor, and maintain Hospitality'. Here Swift spelled out exactly what would be impossible if the bills became law.[50]

Swift was in no less doubt than ever as to the Church's foremost enemies. Within, they sat upon the Bishops' Bench. Without, they were to be found in the Dissenters' meeting-houses – and, of course, in the Whig-packed offices of state. In their lordships, he found the epitome of what a later age summed up in the phrase 'I'm all right, Jack.'

> There are no Qualities more incident to the Frailty and Corruptions of human Kind, than an Indifference, or Insensibility for other Mens Sufferings, and a sudden Forgetfulness of their own former humble State, when they rise in the World. These two Dispositions, have not, I think, any where so strongly exerted themselves, as in the Order of Bishops, with regard to the inferior Clergy.

Many people today, entirely oblivious to Swift's ecclesiastical struggles, might apply this statement to their mysteriously privileged managerial superiors. How much easier life is, he reflected, when one becomes a bishop! He had long known that he never would, barring some political miracle; and he spoke with solidarity for his less fortunate colleagues, in the knowledge that – despite his frequent grumbles – he possessed one of the country's richest deaneries.

> The Maintenance of the Clergy throughout the Kingdom, is precarious
> and uncertain, collected from a most miserable Race of beggarly Farm-
> ers; at whose Mercy every Minister lies to be defrauded. His Office, as
> Rector, or Vicar, if it be duly executed, is very laborious: As soon as he
> is promoted to a Bishoprick, the Scene is entirely and happily changed;
> his Revenues are large, and as surely paid as those of the King.

The 'fatigue' of ordaining new priests, he added, was as arduous as the
individual bishop cared to make it.[51]

So many years had passed since Hugh Boulter, His Excellency the
Primate of All Ireland, had entered this happy state that he was conceivably guilty of the complacency Swift attributed to his order. He had been
translated to the primacy (from Bristol) as far back as 1724, when he
succeeded the staunch Tory Lindsay, and thwarted Archbishop King.
Boulter was a quiet-mannered man, five years younger than Swift. A
portrait from the mid-1730s shows a fleshy, droopy face, long-nosed
and almost chinless, framed by the wig and vestments of his office. He
tended to drone on, in the Lords and in meetings. Personalities far more
dynamic than Boulter's will always seem bland next to one as phantas-
mally powerful as Swift's. He was in many respects the classic apparatchik
and backstage mover. His letters show that bolstering the controlling
Whig interest was his major objective in public office. Accompanying
the new Primate back in 1724 there came a writer who might be recalled
from Swift's 'government' period in London: fifty-something Ambrose
Philips, the poet and sometime dramatist, laboured unctuously as
Boulter's secretary. Despite friendly beginnings, Swift had had little if
any contact with Philips since they took an awkward stroll together in
the Mall late in 1712: Whiggish Philips, then known as 'Pastoral' for his
pictures in verse, but by now as 'Namby-Pamby' for his execrable lines
to aristocratic children, had looked 'terrible dry and cold' at Swift that
day, and Swift had cursed the Whig–Tory division.[52] He had never missed
him as he had Addison, however; and while wishing him no harm he
hardly welcomed his arrival in Dublin.

Both middling figures, primate and secretary, had considerable power
in the country Swift grudgingly cherished. Most of Boulter's time, it
seems, was taken up with political manoeuvring, and his activities
impinged on the deanery circle. In the mid-1720s he spared no trouble
in containing Delany, informing Newcastle, the Secretary of State, that
Swift's friend was 'a great tory, and has a great influence in these parts'.
He had tried to tempt Delany away from his influential position at Trin-

ity with 'a good country living'.[53] He also kept careful tabs on Swift himself. In 1726 he had warned Newcastle what to expect if Swift came to London. There could only be trouble, even though Boulter trusted that the Dean's notoriety would prevent him misleading all those whose principles were sound.

> The general report is, that Dean Swift designs for England in a little time; and we do not question his endeavours to misrepresent his Majesty's friends here, wherever he finds an opportunity: but he is so well known, as well as the disturbances he has been the fomenter of in this kingdom, that we are under no fear of his being able to disserve any of his Majesty's faithful servants, by any thing that is known to come from him: but we would wish some eye were had to what he shall be attempting on your side of the water.[54]

The above is representative of Boulter's long-winded personal style, and also his twitchiness as a bureaucrat: signalling a threat, dismissing its danger, suggesting anyway that 'some eye' keep it under surveillance. Generally, Boulter's career and correspondence confirm Swift's view that there were two strains of English in Ireland, those who 'happen to be born in this Kingdom' and 'the Gentlemen sent from the other Side to possess most of the chief Employments here'.[55] Boulter was one such gentleman and he sought to bring in many more. Breaking the 'Dublin faction' had been among his earliest priorities.[56] He had rejoiced at the first arrival of John Hoadly, as the Bishop of Ferns, much more than had Hoadly himself, who landed in feeble spirits with his family after a four-day voyage.[57] Boulter by no means confined his informing and lobbying energies to ecclesiastical matters. When Swift's old adversary Lord Justice Whitshed died, late in August 1727, Boulter expressed formal regret but immediately pressed the government to choose an appropriate candidate. The Primate justified his concern in terms that illustrate his basic perspective. He told Newcastle: 'There are so many Irish in the Council, and many of them more opposite to England than anyone there ought to be, that it is of the last importance to us to have two of the judges, who shall always be in the interest of England.'[58] Regardless of who or what exactly was English any more, Swift felt that the Irish judiciary and administration should serve the interest of Ireland. Boulter commented sadly how Whitshed had 'brought on himself a great storm of malice',[59] but Swift denied the dead judge's memory a grain of pity. He was in no doubt that Whitshed was responsible for the death of the Drapier's printer, John Harding. When accused of dishonouring the dead Swift retorted splendidly, lavishing classical grandeur on a Lilliputian no-good:

> Laying it therefore down for a Postulatum, which, I suppose, will be universally granted, that no little Creature, of so mean a Birth and Genius, had ever the Honour to be a greater Enemy to his Country, and to all Kinds of Virtue, than HE, I answer thus: whether there be two different Goddesses called Fame, as some Authors contend, or only one Goddess, sounding two different Trumpets, it is certain that People distinguished for their Villainy, have as good a Title for a Blast from the proper Trumpet, as those who are most renowned for their Virtues, have from the other; and have equal Reason to complain if it be refused them.[60]

Thus Swift satisfied Whitshed's posthumous claim for a last salute from the appropriate horn with one of his great oratorial denunciations.

Previously Swift had admitted that, in non-political cases, Whitshed had been a perfectly decent judge. Similarly, Boulter's papers show that the public good was not absent from his thoughts. He had acted sanely and humanely during the recent years of dearth, and supported a Corn and Tillage bill that Swift could not oppose in principle although he might despair of its having much effect in practice. Boulter was largely the architect of the ecclesiastical bills Swift fervently opposed in the early 1730s. At face value, the plan to redistribute parishes was not dismissive of the interests of the lower clergy, nor the status of the Church.[61] It was a measure to ensure an active minister was resident in each Irish parish. Boulter, though, anticipated a change Swift could not contemplate with pleasure, namely a reconciliation of the High and Low Protestants of Ireland. If Irish Dissenters could be brought into Anglican Churches by vicars they respected and were willing to support financially, then Swift's objections would be groundless.

Such redemptive points do not change Boulter's central case that Ireland was a territory to be administered for the benefit of England. And it was here that Swift sensed and engaged with an enemy. It is less important that his own position was more than a little inconsistent. He championed the claim of the English born in Ireland above that of the English born in England. This amounted to saying that the ills of Ireland began with the Whig ascendancy, while forgetting that he himself was the son of men who had arrived in all eagerness for the riches Ireland seemed to offer. Acknowledging his ancestors' share of the wrong was too much; better to draw a line in 1714 and condemn all that followed. Massaging the logic suggested by history nevertheless allowed him to blast his scornful trumpet at colonial executives such as Edward Thompson, the newly appointed Commissioner of the Revenue, who urged the Irish to accept a vast new tax scheme Walpole had proposed. Typically, Swift blamed the Irish themselves for putting up with such scoundrels, let alone honouring them.

> I will bridle my Indignation. However, methinks I long to see that Mortal, who would with Pleasure blow us all up at a Blast: But, he duly receives his Thousand Pounds a Year; makes his Progresses like a King, is received in Pomp at every Town and Village where he travels, and shines in the *English* News-papers.[62]

The best remedy he could offer was one that could serve as the last line of defence in our own time. Electors, he urged, should vote only for representatives who could impartially serve the wider interest. A government placeman such as Thompson, with a tidy salary, would never risk losing his sinecure as punishment for opposing an unjust measure by the authorities. For that reason, Swift pleaded with his 'brethren', such cronies should never be elected in the few constituencies where a genuine contest was possible. At the same time he admitted that an individual who could resist selling out would be something of a prodigy. 'I could sooner hope to find ten thousand Pounds by digging in my Garden than such a *Phoenix* by searching among the present race of Mankind.'[63]

The seeds of egalitarian argument in Swift are of course scorched by his scepticism towards human nature and the continuous revivals of Reformation and Civil War disputes that took place in his mind. These ongoing struggles distorted his perception, even as they flavoured his prose. One can hardly repeat too often that, for Swift, 1640s and '50s simply were not over. The early 1730s saw yet another push to repeal the Test Act in Ireland and open the way for the High and Low Churches to become equivalent and reconciled. In a number of papers answering this threat Swift laid out his historical arguments against the Dissenters at some length, and with one overriding point: they were not to be trusted. For the past century, be it under the name of 'Puritans' or 'Presbyterians' (not to mention the splinter group of 'Independents'), they had proven themselves a class of traitors. When Dissenting pamphleteers asked why their co-religionists should rise against any invasion by the Pretender, since their rights were so limited under the current regime, Swift took this as proof that yet again they expected to cast in their lot with the rebel party. The claim that Catholics were still the great threat to the realm he dismissed as a smokescreen, in what amounted to a plea for lenity towards them. 'The Papists are wholly disarmed. They have neither Courage, Leaders, Money, or Inclinations to rebel. They want every Advantage which they formerly possessed, to follow that Trade; and wherein, even with those Advantages, they always miscarried.' By historical reckoning, Swift put the danger posed by the Dissenters at three times that of the Papists. He totted up the damage done by the respective Churches. The Catholics of Ireland had tried to destroy Protestantism during the reign of James II; whereas the Dissenting sects had murdered Charles I, abolished the monarchy and also the Church.[64] These arguments had a deadly reality for Swift. His implacable dismay at the impending defilement of his Church was tempered now with anger on behalf of his country. At the outset of his central paper on the Test in this period, *The Presbyterians' Plea of Merit, in Order to Take Off the Test*, he commended the idea of experimenting with repeal in Ireland before bringing it across the sea. 'This I take to be a prudent Method; like that of a discreet Physician, who first gives a new Medicine to a Dog, before he prescribes it to a human Creature.'[65] Thus he gave the scheme an aggressively slow and bitter clap of the hand. By the end of 1733, he was again at the vanguard of an Irish movement in opposition to the government; and, despite the force and dexterity of the Dissenters' campaign, the motion to repeal collapsed in the Irish Parliament. Boulter, who supported the Dissenters and had been confident the repeal would succeed, was shocked by how suddenly the move for it imploded. But he admitted that once again Dublin had been brought to the verge of violent disorder. Agents from the Presbyterian fastnesses of the north came to town to lobby Members of Parliament; clergy supporting the Test were drafted in from the country to the same end. As these forces converged, it was agreed at an emergency meeting at Dublin Castle in early December that the Test could not be broken. The repeal might be defeated with such a majority that, as Boulter conceded, 'it was not so certain when such an union might be dissolved.'[66]

In the aftermath of the government defeat (as it was widely seen), a furious caller arrived at Swift's door. Richard Bettesworth was an MP and serjeant-at-law who had supported repeal. Swift had swiped at him in a triumphant poem that seems to have appeared just after Christmas

1733. The poem presented a fable on a piece of pretension: we are told that a barn and stable have been struck by a flood.

> Whole Ricks of Hay and Stacks of Corn,
> Were down the sudden Current born;
> While things of heterogeneous Kind
> Together float with Tide and Wind . . .
> A Ball of new-dropt Horse's Dung,
> Mingling with Apples in the Throng,
> Said to the Pippin, plump and prim,
> *See, Brother, how we Apples swim.*

Swift compared the brotherhood of dung-ball and pippin to the fraternity the Dissenters so often insisted on, hypocritically in his view, with members of the Established Church.

> And thus Fanatic Saints, tho' neither in
> Doctrine, or Discipline our Brethren,
> Are *Brother Protestants and Christians*
> As much as *Hebrews* and *Philistines.*

There was no mistaking who was fruit and who was manure in this family relationship; and Bettesworth, as a champion of repeal, was classed firmly with the latter.[67]

Stung by the laughter of the town, Bettesworth turned up at the deanery to demand satisfaction. The servants told him the Dean was visiting some friends, and there the Serjeant confronted him. It took Swift a moment to recall who Bettesworth was; from 'the singularity of the man in his countenance, manner, action, style and tone of voice' he remembered meeting him perhaps once or twice before, although he airily protested ignorance of Bettesworth's name. Bettesworth was having none of it. He knew that the verses were Swift's: the poem had summed up Bettesworth's skill as an advocate by saying 'half a crown o'er pays his sweat's worth', and nobody else, he complained, could have pulled off that rhyme on his surname (the second *e* in 'Bettesworth' is silent). 'I had heard of some such verses,' Swift admitted. Bettesworth was soon ranting. 'Over-warm and eloquent', his behaviour forced Swift to call for assistance (from John Worrall, it seems). Bettesworth, 'going on with less turbulence', then left.

Swift took advice and learned that Bettesworth was 'a peaceable man in all things except his words, his rhetorical action, his looks, and his hatred to the clergy'. [68] He reported the incident to Lionel Cranfield Sackville, the first Duke of Dorset and since 1731 the Lord Lieutenant of Ireland. Sackville had little stomach for the job, and had disappointed Walpole by failing to see through the repeal of the Test. The matter with Bettesworth, however, did not rest there. In early January, the *Dublin Journal* reported, a group of 'persons of honour and quality' called at the deanery to show their loyalty and offer their protection.[69] A larger and noisier number arrived some days later to make a similar pledge, which they had put down in writing: for they had heard that their 66-year-old champion had been threatened or even challenged to a duel.[70] Swift was upstairs, sick and dizzy; he sent down a grateful blessing. He still maintained that he didn't know Bettesworth's name, and so couldn't have thought of the offending rhyme with 'sweat's worth'. The inner sanctum at St Patrick's, and indeed the wider town, knew better. Swift then judged that an example should be made, as a deterrent to anyone who might imitate Bettesworth, and so hounded him with a further pair of vigorous lampoons. The first was called 'The Yahoo's Overthrow'. The broadside is one small instance of how the *Travels* was more than a book: it was an ongoing event, an unclosed epic that many besides Swift felt free to continue. Here Swift assumed the voice of a cheerful mob:

> On this Worrier of Deans whene'er we can hit,
> We'll show him the way how to crop and to slit;
> We'll teach him some better address to afford
> To the Dean of all Deans, tho' he wears not a sword.[71]

# 4

'He hath insulted us all by insulting the Dean,' sings the crowd in 'The Yahoo's Overthrow'.[72] Many years had passed since Swift had come to be a living symbol for Dublin's collective spirit, on the streets and in eyes peering out from the Castle. His stature and popularity were unaffected when he came out strongly against a bill that all propertied interests in Ireland except the clergy were determined would pass. At the same time, as the debate on repealing the Test raged on, a bill was proposed lowering the tithe on growers of hemp and flax. The trade in linen was the Irish economy's single success story; yet it was concentrated in the north, in the Presbyterian heartlands. Swift therefore opposed the bill not only for depriving poverty-stricken priests of their lawful (and divinely ordained) property, but also, less vocally, for supporting the faction of Irish society he hated and feared most. After all further opposition was made effectively impossible, for the sake of the record Swift published *Some Reasons against the Bill for Settling the Tyth of Hemp* in January 1734. Such a position was to be expected of him, as an old Tory, oddly though it sat with the great defender of Irish manufactures.

Still, one such essay could not alienate him from the thousands who looked to him for leadership on national, rather than ecclesiastical, lines. The previous spring, Walpole's plan to extend duties on wine and tobacco was defeated by a block of resistance in all the kingdoms. By abandoning his Excise Bill Walpole suffered the greatest reversal of his long demagogic rule. Though without taking a leading part, Swift had naturally stood among the prominent opposers, and his name was at the fore among those being toasted in the jubilation that followed in Dublin. As was by now almost a tradition at any setback for the English hierarchy, festivities broke out in the liberties of St Patrick's, with bonfires and music. On this occasion a dozen younger men had risked their skins – not to mention the fabric of the cathedral – and got a blaze going on top of the steeple. Another celebratory pyre burned in front of Swift's house; he was presented with a barrel of ale; and a mass toast was raised to 'that worthy patriot the DRAPIER, who saved our nation from ruin.'[73] Such celebrations continued as more or less yearly events on Swift's birthday.

Swift offered his admirers and subordinates often harsh love in return. One day, as they walked through a field he had purchased, admiring the fruit trees growing against a wall he had had built, dictatorially, to the highest feasible standard, he told Laetitia Pilkington that he was 'king of the mob'. When the workmen made their first attempt at the wall, as soon as they laid a stone of doubtful quality he would let them build three or four perches beyond it before ordering them to tear it back down to where the flaw had crept in. The same shoddiness met with identical treatment five or six times before the gang, chastened, took care that every stone they used was entirely sound. Swift was utterly unapologetic about making such requirements. He had warned his cook not to make mistakes that might not be corrected; here was the price of errors that could.

Pilkington was by now a favoured companion. As he did Sheridan, Swift treasured her for her ready wit. Quick as ever, she observed that if the workers hadn't learned their lesson, the wall would have become a project like Penelope's weaving on Ithaca – 'if all that was done in the Day was to be undone at Night.' Swift's custom at such moments was to mock her, as befitted a king of the mob, for finding a clever literary remark for every occasion. When they managed to get home by foot before a shower, he sent the sixpence that would otherwise have paid for a cab to 'the lame old Man that sells Ginger-bread at the Corner, because he tries to do something, and does not beg'.[74]

For the residents of the nearby liberties, Swift's posterity lay with this municipal presence, the Drapier: at once the scorner of government and the exacting patron saint of weavers, bricklayers, lame gingerbread-sellers and his handicapped seraglio. For Swift himself, being 'the Angel of Ireland' (Pilkington's phrase) was obviously insufficient.[75] The ultimate merit he sought could be awarded only by literary judges of the highest order. Though Addison and Atterbury had been minds of this level, personal doubts and differences tinged Swift's respect for them. For almost two decades his highest literary esteem for living wits had been reserved for Pope, Arbuthnot, Gay and Bolingbroke. Although he could relax with Sheridan, Delany and the 'Triumfeminate', for ultimate approval he looked to the survivors of Scriblerus. Privately, Swift might indulge his reservations about Pope by sharing with the Pilkingtons a blasphemous Latin expression in one of the poet's letters.[76] Publicly, he could only rue his friend's greater gift for verse.

> In Pope, I cannot read a Line,
> But with a Sigh, I wish it mine:
> When he can in one Couplet fix
> More Sense than I can do in Six:
> It gives me such a jealous Fit,
> I cry, Pox take him, and his Wit.[77]

Swift could not hope to rival Pope in euphony or allusive lightness; or the simultaneous mastery of the long verse paragraph and the apothegm contained in a perfect couplet. The 'sense' the two poets 'fixed' in their lines, however, differed in kind and in intent rather than in overall quality. Pope was a poet who ultimately despaired of civic action bringing any good; Swift was a poet who felt nevertheless the attempt to improve the *polis* needed to be made even if defeat were certain. As such, even in his great assault on the culture of his time, the evolving *Dunciad*, Pope treats the sonic and semantic materials of poetry as a buffering layer. Part of the point of *The Dunciad* is that Pope creates his own verse-model of Grub Street and its environs, in which he can mould the simulacrum of each dunce like a little victim of clay. Something similar might be said of all Pope's famous works, going back as far as the *Rape of the Lock* and the early pastorals. In his great verse epistles, perhaps even the *Essay on Man*, there is a sense that a gate to the outside has been closed: Pope and his addressees and interlocutors observe a holographic projection in the quiet of the garden or the library. Ugliness and horror are present in Pope's fictions, but are cleansed by his use of the medium. In Swift, despite his obvious powers as a fabulist, there is never this contained bubble, a glass case holding an artificial world. His poems are interventions, performances, not descriptive replicas. They go out into the streets, invade and rummage through real houses – much as Swift himself sometimes would when making a call. After checking the cleanliness of the kitchen and garret in their 'Lilliputian' residence, he told the Pilkingtons that he always made a thorough (and invasive) tour of every home he visited.[78]

In the early 1730s Swift wrote a number of longer poems that took his idiom in verse to its final extreme. They completed a group that, along with the *Tale of a Tub*, the *Travels* and perhaps the *Modest Proposal*, make up the works that readers and students are most likely to approach today. They provoked uproar on their first appearance, and have continued to inspire shock, revulsion, mirth and above all disagreement. Swift used the Pilkingtons as conduits for releasing these poems; and the couple's plummeting social reputation became tied up with the poems' notoriety.

The first and probably most famous of the group was a grand piece of self-fashioning, in which Swift becomes less and less ironic about his character and legacy as the poem continues. 'I have been severall months writing near five hundred lines on a pleasant Subject,' he wrote to Gay in December 1731; 'onely to tell what my friends and enemyes will say on me after I am dead.' He reported that he added two lines to it a week, cancelled four and altered eight.[79] The poem at hand, which he wrestled with much as he had his vexed ode on Archbishop Sancroft, decades earlier, was the 'Verses on the Death of Dr Swift'. The rhetorical prompt is a maxim from La Rochefoucauld on the essential selfishness of human beings: 'In all Distresses of our Friends / We first consult our private Ends.'[80] The opening passages, forming a 'proem', confirm this thought by revealing Swift's jealousy of his friends' talents, in a wonderful flow of inverted camaraderie.

> To all my Foes, dear Fortune, send
> Thy Gifts, but never to my Friend:
> I tamely can endure the first,
> But this with Envy makes me burst.[81]

Moving on into the main poem, Swift gauges the self-serving responses that will come when his final decline sets in. Urban commentators will agree how 'that old Vertigo' has plagued him for years, and now he 'droops apace': his memory has gone, he bores young people with the same constant cycle of stories from twenty years before. His gift of poetry is drying up, and he can hardly stomach a pint of wine.[82] After discoursing of the ageing, sinking Dean, these younger people 'Then hug themselves, and reason thus; / It is not yet so bad with us.'[83] One gossiper is sure Swift must die soon; and would rather he does so than disprove his prediction by lingering. The case alters when Swift imagines older, ailing citizens hearing of his afflictions:

> Yet should some Neighbour feel a Pain,
> Just in the Parts, where I complain;
> How many a Message would he send?
> What hearty Prayers that I should mend?
> Enquire what regimen I kept;
> What gave me Ease, and how I slept?
> And more lament, when I was dead,
> Than all the Sniv'llers round my bed.[84]

Swift proceeds with a vision of how oblivion will come: like lichen over a tombstone, as one friend after another forgets him, including the precious quartet of Pope, Gay, Arbuthnot and Bolingbroke.

> The rest will give a Shrug and cry,
> I'm sorry; but we all must die.
> Indifference clad in Wisdom's Guise,
> All Fortitude of Mind supplies.[85]

'I have heard the name,' says Barnaby Lintot, the famous bookseller, when a browsing reader inquires by chance for Swift's works. But they are lost in a mausoleum of volumes mostly by dunces.[86] By now Swift has moved some distance away from La Rochefoucauld's maxim; and quietly, in the closing panegyric section of the poem, he sets about searching for an antidote for it. For among a group gathered at the Rose Tavern in London Swift envisages at least one member of the company, impartial and 'indifferent in the cause', giving him his due. The maxim ultimately still holds true because this speakĕr is not Swift's friend or neighbour; he has nothing to lose or gain from Swift's demise. It can neither frighten nor comfort him. The extempore eulogist speaks selflessly. The Dean, this drinker affirms, was always well received at Court, but never craved the fellowship or compliments of dukes or princes. He 'would rather slip aside, and chuse / To talk with Wits in dirty shoes'.[87] His only concern as a writer was to expose vice; he had no interest in acquiring power or wealth, although he might have done, had he been less honest with his pen. There is a considerable digression on how Swift left the Court in horror and despair in 1714, and how since then he had lived in peaceable exile in the 'land of slaves and fens', confining himself to a few friends 'of the middling kind' (a phrase he intended as a compliment, distinguishing such companions from the 'mongrel breed' of Ireland's Whiggish new aristocracy).[88] A great many beyond Swift's immediate circle might have contested the truth of these assertions – and detected a movement in the poem from the engaging cynicism and self-deprecation of the opening to more than a touch of self-regarding idealism in the final pages. The obituarist in the tavern sounds like a plant the more he speaks; which of course he is. But Swift could retort that fashioning an occasion for this defender to speak up for him was a necessity. The corruption of the times made it so; as, more essentially, did the formula of human self-interest expounded by La Rochefoucauld. Putting words in the mouth of someone to whom he was nobody was the only way of getting a fair verdict. The 'Verses' comprise an example of what teachers of rhetoric called *prolepsis*, speaking of the future as if it were already present, and also *procatalepsis* – anticipating the objections your opponent will make, permitting them up to a point but then rebutting them.

> Perhaps I may allow, the Dean
> Had too much Satyr in his Vein;
> And seem'd determin'd not to starve it,
> Because no Age could more deserve it.[89]

As part of his general strategy of anticipation, Swift has already admitted that he is bound by La Rochefoucauld's principle as much as anyone else. The veiled egotism of the speech in the tavern is counterbalanced by

the 'proem' of the 'Verses', where Swift reveals his envy at the talents of
his friends – desiring this man's gift and that man's scope. The proud
priest who shuns the attention of dukes will thus always be the wit who
is insecure yet competitive in the same breath.

> Why must I be outdone by Gay,
> In my own hum'rous biting Way?
> Arbuthnot is no more my Friend,
> Who dares to Irony pretend;
> Which I was born to introduce,
> Refin'd it first, and shew'd its use.[90]

The elegiac speech given in the tavern is decidedly unironic; but then so
was Swift himself a great deal of the time. Privately he might tell the
Pilkingtons that he now found Pope's laudatory lines to him in *The
Dunciad* 'very stiff'; but he was furious when he learned that Mr Pilkington had displeased Pope personally. In 1732 Swift persuaded his old friend
and publisher Alderman Barber, who had been elected lord mayor, to take
Matthew Pilkington as his chaplain. Swift recommended the 'little man'
fulsomely to his other choice friends. In time they were all upset by the
behaviour of Swift's candidate. 'I told him,' wrote Mrs Pilkington, 'I was
sure Mr P—n did not deserve the Character Mr Pope had given of him.'
Swift's reaction, if Laetitia Pilkington may be trusted, was almost frenzied.

> Upon this the Dean lost all Patience, and flew into such a Rage, that he
> quite terrified me; he asked me, Why did I not swear that my Husband
> was six Foot high? And, did I think myself a better Judge than Mr
> Pope? Or, did I presume to give him the Lie? And a thousand other
> Extravagancies. As I durst not venture to speak a Word more, my Heart
> swelled so that I burst into Tears, which, he attributing to Pride and
> Resentment, made him, if possible, ten times more angry, and I am not
> sure he would not have beat me; but that, fortunately for me, a Gentle-
> man came to visit him.

Even when his temper cooled, Swift was unmoved by her tears. The next
day, according to Pilkington, he told her to 'shake off the Leavings of
your sex'.[91] Many years earlier, Esther Vanhomrigh had complained of
Swift's remorseless anger. His 'killing, killing words' were made all the
worse by his habitually sombre expression.[92] By the time Laetitia Pilkington knew him, this trait was all the more marked. 'I cannot recollect

that I ever saw the Dean laugh,' she wrote. She was possibly sharper-sighted in observing him, however, than Swift's earlier friend. 'Perhaps he thought it [laughing] beneath him, for when any Pleasantry passed, which might have excited it, he used to suck in his Cheeks, as Folks do when they have a Plug of Tobacco in their Mouths, to avoid risibility.'[93] Pilkington's view suggests that Swift had a firm habit of suppressing laughter, so as not to appear ridiculous. His stony-facedness was a sign of his need to remain in control, to be the one who made jokes but did not participate in or provide an object for them. Pilkington picked up on the sign that he was really amused, in that obsessive sucking in of the cheeks, but that he felt it was shameful to seem so.

Swift was celebrated, then as now, as an ironist; he had, as he claimed, refined and showed the uses irony could serve, and developed it as a language in its own right. Meanwhile his passionate rage, pride and occasional self-pity are perhaps not qualities we might associate now with an ironic personality. Modern-day ironists avoid committing them-selves too heavily to any dogma, or even taking deep offence. The advantage of such a position is that it allows culture to be pluralist and libertarian, and still allow for what Richard Rorty called 'solidarity'.[94] The one great crime against such a culture is to attack the safety in which critical and ironic views are freely expressed. Swift's irony could follow such a principle when making free with the ideas of his enemies. His *Vindication of His Excellency the Lord Carteret* in 1730 is delivered in the voice of a Whig who fantastically displays all the warped prior-ities of the ruling faction: the essay has a flavour of the extravagant excursions in *A Tale of a Tub*. Yet in Swift irony takes another, arguably more dominant form, which found its ultimate expression in the *Modest Proposal*. For Swift there is no contradiction between irony and what we might now take as pure intolerance. He was not at all a tolerant per-son. Swift's irony instead very often expresses the anger of a moral authority who is presented with the standards of a debased majority, and illustrates their corruption by speaking for a moment as if he accepted and shared it. It is a bit much to torture one example among thousands; but a blunt instance of this would be when Swift coldly praises the English fortune-hunting clergymen, given good Irish bene-fices, 'who have condescended to leave their native country and come hither to be Bishops, merely to promote Christianity among us'.[95] Here the ironic stress is on the word 'merely'. Since Swift has in fact already admitted that he is not sure how such men are qualified to be bishops, it's apparent that they have not travelled to Ireland purely in order to advance the Gospel. Ireland is thus implicitly much more Christian without them. The irony in such a sentence is, then, an angry imitation of the air of the degenerate majority. It succeeds in getting a note of contempt to be heard, but is still a contained, outnumbered voice, confident of its superiority but deprived of real power.

Unsurprisingly, when this Swiftian voice could speak in situations where it did have power – or had leave to imagine wielding it – its tone could turn to uncompromisingly destructive anger against everyone and everything that had previously held it in check. It would outline schemes to discipline or even extinguish Presbyterians, Catholic peasants, Yahoos. It would denigrate femininity, emotional softness, laxity in schools. Mrs Pilkington got a taste of the intolerant fury behind Swift's irony the day she dared criticize Pope and then appealed with tears. One of the real questions hanging over Swift's career resurfaces every time one gauges the emotion behind much of his ironic writing. The question is not whether he was tyrannical in such a situation where he had the greater power (since he bullied his poor younger friend, unforgivably, after letting her believe it was safe to voice her thoughts freely), but rather how he might have handled the chance to pursue a political programme of his own. In 1714 he seems to have baulked at the extreme Tory measures advanced opportunistically by Bolingbroke – but how he might have acted, and what policies he might have supported, had his party retained power after the death of Queen Anne, remains a striking question.

A strong talent for irony, then, did not preclude a failure sometimes to count to ten. As for the instance in which he got so angry with Laetitia Pilkington, Swift was very sensitive about the remaining members of Scriblerus. The salute to Gay in the 'Verses' on Swift's death took on added pathos when the playwright died, quite suddenly, in December 1732. Gay was seemingly the first to whom Swift confided the existence of his long poem, and the trouble he was having with it. At that time, late in 1731, Swift didn't question the reasonable assumption that he would die long before his friend, for Gay was almost eighteen years younger. During his alienation from the Walpole regime, a young couple, Catherine and Charles Douglas, the Duchess and Duke of Queensberry, supported Gay at Court. Their backing became all the more necessary when his earlier friend and patron, Richard Boyle, Earl of Burlington, turned cold towards him after the success of *The Beggar's Opera*. Burlington was an easy-going Whig and a 'personality', more interested in his architectural schemes and the arts than hard politics: but Gay's Mr Peacham was more than his loyalty to Walpole could bear. Burlington's coffers, incidentally, weren't quite as full as Gay and others imagined. Fortunately, however, the Queensberrys were ready to catch Gay if he fell.

From 1730, a few of Gay's last efforts for the stage failed to take off. Performance of another opera, a follow-up, *Polly*, was prohibited by government, though with the Queensberrys' spirited encouragement Gay published the script at his own expense and came away with a very rare and respectable profit. The Duchess in particular was not to be thwarted on such a point, and took it as a price worth paying when she was banished from Court for drumming up subscriptions for the work. She was a Hyde by birth, the daughter of the Earl of Rochester, and took exile as one of life's unavoidable hazards. Gay fell ill that summer, and was taken home by the Duke and Duchess. He spent much of what proved to be the remainder of his days on their estate at Amesbury, where he frequently invited Swift to visit him – with his hosts' full approval. In May 1732 Swift commented that from recent accounts of Gay's movements he was 'giddy and volatile as ever'. He also observed, though, how Gay combined a love of moving from place to place, party to party, with a 'rooted laziness' when it came to his physical fitness.[96] Gay was in London, where he delivered one last drama, *Achilles*, to Covent Garden late in November 1732, when a developing intestinal problem flared up. From London he had written to Swift: 'I wish the arguments made use of to draw you here were every way of more consequence.'[97] Forty-seven years old and never much one for the outdoors, he had weakened his health earlier that autumn by answering taunts about his weight and laziness with a long ride to Somerset and back.[98] On 1 December, he collapsed in town with what Arbuthnot immediately saw was a fatal inflammation of the gut and bowel.

Pope and Arbuthnot were with Gay when he died, three days later. From an 'Impulse foreboding some Misfortune,' Swift left their letter unopened for five days.[99] All three of the last Scriblerians mourned deeply, and all had separate troubles magnifying the loss. Pope was in daily pain; Swift reported the deaths of a number of other, younger acquaintances; and Arbuthnot's stoicism was still struggling to withstand the loss of his son Charles a year earlier. In January, Arbuthnot wrote to Swift of how 'almost every body' in London lamented Gay. He was buried in Westminster Abbey, 'as if he had been a peer of the realm', where the Duchess of Queensberry paid for a fine monument above his grave.[100] His famous epitaph still carries its spark of flippancy amid all the grave height and stillness of the Abbey:

> Life is a jest, and all things show it;
> I thought so once, but now I know it.

Samuel Johnson protested against this 'trifling distich', calling for buf-
foonery to be banned from English tombstones.[101]

Writing to Pope later that month, and knowing his words would be
passed on to Arbuthnot, Swift acknowledged their 'account of our losing
Mr Gay; upon which event I shall say nothing'. He was only disturbed,
he said, that his long life had not hardened him to such news.[102] Swift's
friendship with Pope remained firm, although with some tension as Pope
engineered a fourth joint volume of their *Miscellanies* in prose and verse.
Swift had given the poet a free editorial hand with these works in the
late 1720s, then was upset by Pope's choice and arrangement of the
pieces. In the meantime, he had designs for an edition that would prevent – or delay – the woeful posthumous situation he imagined in his
'Verses on the Death of Dr Swift', where the works of the Dean are
nowhere to be found among the dust piles of Duck Lane. The outcome
would be Faulkner's 1735 Irish edition of Swift's *Works*, an event that
Pope was increasingly anxious to forestall by getting the *Miscellanies*
into print well in advance. The contents of both editions would naturally
be duplicated – and Curll still lurked, ready to pilfer; but, unlike Swift,
Pope relied on sales to maintain his comforts at Twickenham.

Despite occasional shows of temper, Swift was still smitten with the
Pilkingtons. He had described them to Pope as 'a little young poetical
parson, who has a littler young poetical wife'. In 1730 he had endorsed
Mr Pilkington's *Poems*, some of which he found 'not unpleasant', and
had reserved for the couple the profits of a 'Dublin Miscellany', full of
satirical writings by various hands that the young parson was entrusted
with collecting and editing.[103] Since then Mr Pilkington had acted in the
role of 'operator' for Swift, and had continued to do so on arriving in
London. Pressing John Barber to award the young clergyman his mayoral chaplaincy, Swift praised Mr Pilkington for possessing 'more wit,
sense, and discretion, than any of your *London-Parsons*'.[104] Barber
accepted him for Swift's sake, and soon reported that 'he comes out a
facetious agreeable fellow.' The chaplain caught the Duchess of Buckingham and Normanby's eye in the park, and Barber answered her inquiry
by telling her he was a present from Dublin. 'She smilingly replied, "He
is no fool then, I am sure."'[105] Arbuthnot also responded positively to
this 'very agreeable ingenious man' and 'valued' him for his musical talent.[106]

Behind his pleasant exterior Mr Pilkington seethed at such condescension even as he sought out higher praise. He seems to have often felt threatened and frustrated, and turned his competitive and revengeful feelings on his talented wife. Quite some time before he embarked for England, his marriage to Laetitia had become a façade. In her *Memoirs* Mrs Pilkington affected puzzlement at her husband's fading love. She could only explain the problem as stemming from envy of her talents, which she took care to deprecate. Mrs Pilkington had been deprived of the education Matthew had received, but was well read in the major English works from Shakespeare on, had a sharp spontaneous wit and an excellent memory. Reading Horace one winter evening, Mr Pilkington announced that he would write an ode in exact imitation of the Augustan's manner. Tranquilly Laetitia sat down to do the same, and when they came to compare their efforts Matthew was grievously angry and upset. Her lines, which had a sweet succinctness, were evidently superior.

> I envy not the Proud their Wealth,
> Their Equipage and State;
> Give me but Innocence and Health,
> I ask not to be great.

Such humility seemed too much like presumption to the cherubic parson. He berated his wife for allowing Swift to turn her mind, and declared that 'a Needle became a Woman's Hand better than a Pen and Ink.' Quoting Swift's 'Verses on the Death of Dr Swift', Mrs Pilkington advised all her women readers not to write better poetry than their husbands. She threw her ode into the fire, which could hardly make Mr Pilkington feel any better.[107] And with the same power of recall that apparently allowed her to memorize Swift's 'Verses' at a single reading, she was able to write the poem out in her autobiography many years afterwards.[108] There were apparently moments when Swift saw a distinction between the two in Mrs Pilkington's favour. 'Pox on you for a Dunce,' he supposedly berated Mr Pilkington on one occasion at the deanery, and told him he would rather give his wife a fellowship than admit him as a lowly scholar-servant.[109] Other mutual acquaintances drew similar contrasts.[110]

However Mrs Pilkington might have exaggerated these incidents with an eye to getting even, there is little doubt that Mr Pilkington treated her with great contempt. Before boarding the viceroyal yacht for England, he told her that he would find her an encumbrance if she accompanied him, and that he 'did not intend to pass there for a married Man'.[111] When she stole away to join him the following year, she found him as good as his word. He was infatuated with a Drury Lane actress, whom he visited every evening. Soon after Mrs Pilkington arrived, Mr Pilkington began urging her to accept the attentions of James Worsdale, a portrait-painter. 'So, it seems, I was to be the Bait, wherewith he was to angle for Gold out of a Rival's Pocket.'[112] Mrs Pilkington took on the part of virtuous heroine in her own dispiriting adventure. Worsdale was generous with gifts of money for as long as it seemed she might accept him as a lover. She insisted that she refused him to the last, pushing furniture against the door of the room at the Windsor Inn where Worsdale had reserved a single bed for their overnight stay. Mr Pilkington was furious with her when she distracted her seducer with another young woman, whose 'Spirit', she commented, 'was far above her Ability'.[113] Mrs Pilkington's spirit, notwithstanding such unpleasantness, remained eager, observant and droll: while supporting her husband in a respectable illusion, for the sake of convenience and lingering love, she seemingly enjoyed London. She left a vivid thumbnail portrait of Swift's old friend and ally Alderman Barber, the Tory printer and now Lord Mayor:

> Who, on account of the resolute Opposition he had given to the Excise
> Act, was the Darling of the People. He was but indifferent as to his
> Person, or rather homely than otherwise, but he had an excellent
> Understanding, and the Liveliness of his Genius shone in his Eyes,
> which were very black and sparkling.[114]

Swift had written stirringly to Barber on his election as the Lord Mayor, addressing him as a comrade – 'We were both followers of the same court and the same cause' – and giving him joy 'of governing the noblest City in the world'.[115] They were both of a rebel hue, both also pillars of the establishment.

At this point Swift was still blind to the irregularities in Mr Pilkington's personal life. Had he been aware of them, he would never have given glowing introductions or entrusted him with arranging a number of delicate publications; except that perhaps, just possibly, unconsciously he recognized that Mr Pilkington was exactly the sort of double-faced trickster who could lay the necessary ruses. Even so, Mr Pilkington's callousness to his wife augured badly for others who placed their trust in him. By July 1733 Swift was expressing his concern to Barber at hearing very seldom from the publisher's chaplain.[116] In November, as his term came to an end, Barber reassured Swift that through gratuities Mr Pilkington had earned more than any of his predecessors in the same post. In addition he mentioned, warningly, that he hardly ever 'had the favour of his company in an evening', and that his chaplain had developed ties to the Prime Minister's son, Edward Walpole, 'from whom he has great dependences'.[117] Laetitia, had she cared to, might have told Swift as much many months before, for she had seen Matthew board the yacht bound for England in the company of the younger Walpole. Mr Pilkington had been recommended to this enemy 'by a Man of Quality since dead'.[118]

In August 1733 Laetitia had sailed with Mary Barber (the poet, and no relation of the outgoing Lord Mayor's). Mrs Barber was carrying a packet of poems to London from Swift that Mr Pilkington would be charged with seeing through the press. It was a parcel full of firecrackers. In November there appeared a long poem Swift had evidently begun during the period of his visits to Market Hill but updated only recently. Published anonymously, yet instantly recognizable, this was his 'Epistle to a Lady', a dialogue in verse with an emanation of Lady Acheson. The poem is occasioned by the lady's request that he address her in the heroic style. Swift declines:

> I, as all the Parish knows,
> Hardly can be grave in Prose:
> Still to lash, and lashing Smile,
> Ill befits a lofty Style.[119]

The poem instead becomes, like the yet unpublished 'Verses', a work of self-portraiture, though with a still greater emphasis on 'lashing' the Hanover kingdoms in their present state. To the delight of Walpole's enemies (and many, doubtless, of the minister's bought-up friends), Swift openly thumbed his nose at the long-lasting – yet, post-Excise bill, much tested – Whig ascendancy.

> When my Muse officious ventures
> On the Nation's Representers;
> Teaching by what *Golden* Rules
> Into Knaves they turn their Fools:
> How the Helm is ruled by — [Walpole]
> At whose Oars, like Slaves, they all pull:
> Let the Vessel split on Shelves,
> With the Freight enrich themselves:

> Safe within my little Wherry,
> All their Madness makes me merry:
> Like the Watermen of Thames,
> I row by, and call them Names.[120]

Here was 'Mr Dean', as the poem repeatedly identifies its main speaker, taunting the chief minister across the water from his vast riverside mansion in Chelsea. With many slights against the entire political hierarchy, the 'Epistle' suggests that the worst insult it might offer is to say 'You are of a lower Class / Than my friend Sir R[obert] Br[as]s' – that is, of course, Walpole himself.[121]

Walpole's patience was to be tested further by a greater poem a few weeks later. On New Year's Eve 1733, a folio pamphlet called *On Poetry: A Rapsody* was issued. This, often rated Swift's finest work in verse, was a long meditation on what being a poet involved. For the majority, it meant living a life of falsification, for 'All Human Race would fain be Wits / And Millions miss, for one that hits.' For the true children of Apollo, meanwhile, it meant coping with a life apart.

> Not Beggar's Brat, on Bulk begot,
> Nor Bastard of a Pedlar Scot,
> Nor Boy brought up to cleaning Shoes,
> The Spawn of Bridewell, or the Stews;
> Nor Infants dropt, the spurious Pledges
> Of Gipsies littering under Hedges,
> Are so disqualified by Fate
> To rise in Church, or Law, or State,
> As he, whom Phoebus in his Ire
> Hath blasted with poetick Fire.[122]

Some of Shakespeare's witches' incantational rhythms seem to influence Swift's tetrameters here. Laetitia Pilkington, as it happened, had learned not long before that the Dean was well acquainted with *Macbeth*.[123] The sentiment was a commonplace, but one still deeply personal to Swift. It reflected his abiding conviction that, despite all he had achieved, officially he was an outcast, and had been so since the beginning. The beggars, changelings and urchins imagined here read like a list of those Swift felt, at an unacknowledged level, were his real equals. The passage evokes his abiding anger at his birth and his fortunes.

Like the 'Epistle', 'On Poetry' gives the impression of having been written in separate stretches, even though great consistency of tone and tempo is maintained. For the rousingly enunciated thoughts and sketches of the poet's lot give way to an invocation of the muse for help in describing a desecrated country. The 'rhapsody' becomes out-and-out battery of the Hanover regime. The empery of the second George is ridiculed in the most sardonic of mock-panegyrics, as is Walpole.[124] Swift lauds the Prime Minister for his service to all the institutions the minister had ruined, and all but pings the great silver star on his silk-coated chest, placed there when Walpole received the Order of the Garter in 1726. And it was true, Walpole's 'breast and sides' *were* 'Herculean', but in terms of pure girth rather than musculature.[125]

Walpole's temper broke: the strain and injury over Excise were still fresh, and there were limits to the provocations he could tolerate. In the New Year the government moved, arresting the printer of the 'Epistle', John Wilford, on 11 January 1734. At this a number of other publishing associates were alarmed. Lawton Gilliver, the bookseller to whom Mr Pilkington had sold the copyright for the 'Epistle' (and another poem, 'On Reading Dr Young's Satires', printed with it), was aware he was next on the authorities' list. He demanded an emergency meeting with the original publisher of Swift's *Travels*, Benjamin Motte. Mr Pilkington had offered Motte the copyright for the 'Epistle' first; but Motte distrusted Mr Pilkington. Earlier, in 1733, Mr Pilkington had tempted Motte with a poem he insisted was Swift's work, 'The Life and Genuine Character of Dr Swift'. Motte, while paying Mr Pilkington the sum of twenty guineas Swift had promised him, decided at first to pass; yet eventually he bought the poem. When it was published, though, Swift denounced it (untruthfully) as a hoax and libel. He convinced Motte; and Motte accordingly felt cheated. It was in fact a deliberately mutilated version of the 'Verses on the Death of Dr Swift' that Swift, on a malicious whim, had then accused Mrs Pilkington of cobbling together.

Suspicion of Mr Pilkington did not, however, affect Motte's sound business instincts when he was offered another set of poems that the bookseller knew could only be by Swift.[126] Thus Motte, in the eyes of government, was a perfectly valid target. Once he felt the authorities closing in, Gilliver was determined to implicate both Motte and his supplier. Motte offered to pay half Gilliver's costs in return for his silence, and waited for him, as agreed, early one morning, at a tavern in Cork Street. After an hour, Gilliver did not appear. Instead, a messenger arrived, and told Motte that Gilliver was already being questioned at Westminster. 'A couple of sharp sluts' – the messenger's daughters, Motte surmised – watched their quick interview closely.[127] Soon he, along with Matthew Pilkington, and indeed Mrs Barber, who was identified as having supplied the manuscript, joined the printer in jail.

Shortly afterwards, a story evidently reached Ireland that Mr Pilkington, breaking down under interrogation – or perhaps yielding to an offer of help from his ally Edward Walpole – had named Swift as the author of the offending poems. The chief minister supposedly ordered a warrant for Swift's arrest. 'As he had full proof that Swift was the author, in his first transport of passion, he determined to get him in to his clutches.' Walpole grudgingly dropped the plan when a friend who knew the Irish situation asked him coolly 'whether he had ten thousand men to spare' – for that was the size of the army the government would need to take Swift from his loyal Dubliners by force. Such, at least, was one of the legends that had grown up about the Dean by the time his friend Sheridan's son came to write Swift's biography.[128] Substantiating the general outline of the story, if not the detail, is ample testimony that Mr Pilkington did betray Swift's name under oath. His reputation was ruined by the time he made his way brokenly back to Ireland. His wife, worn out and disgusted from resisting Worsdale, had returned alone late in 1733. There she was scolded by Mrs Barber for her conduct in London. Mrs Pilkington attributed this cruelty to envy in her childless friend, and mused on 'how cruel all barren Creatures naturally are'.[129]

Stranded, and quite unwanted by all of Swift's associates, Mr Pilkington could pay his fares thanks only to a note that his father-in-law had unwillingly sent him. Elderly Dr Van Lewin would rather have put him on a ship to the West Indies. Laetitia protested against this classic paternal verdict: and, so she claimed, also defended Matthew from the charges of treachery. 'Every day there was a new abuse published on him,' she recalled. Along with slurs against her own character – gossip from London was rarely delayed by the tides – life in Dublin grew distinctly uncomfortable for the couple. At that time, however, Archbishop Hoadly proved much more kindly than his brother Benjamin, and promised that he would protect Mr Pilkington on his return. Swift, though silent, had not yet renounced his ties with the child-like pair. Mr Pilkington had in the meantime supposedly developed a rheumatoid complaint from the stress of imprisonment. On his release, he had nothing to live on but his humble Irish benefice.[130] His prospects in London must have been very dire, however, for him to see no option but to face mass condemnation in Dublin. Using Van Lewin's money, he arrived, ghost-like, 'pale and dejected . . . and the Disregard he met with from every body went very near his Heart'.[131]

Before his arrest and the uproar that followed, Mr Pilkington had supplied Motte's front-man, a retailer called James Roberts, with materials by Swift for one other slim collection.[132] Along with the pamphlets containing 'On Poetry' and 'An Epistle', the small quarto volume that released 'A Beautiful Young Nymph Going to Bed' and two other scandal-provoking works was dated '1734': this was a common publishing tactic used for a number of reasons, one of which was simply to make a volume seem as fresh as possible. The quarto poems belong to a group that has provoked more controversy than any of Swift's works except the fourth part of the *Travels*. In accepting 'A Beautiful Young Nymph', while rejecting Mr Pilkington's other wares that autumn, Motte knew that he was paying for authentic Swift. They were clearly part of the same family as 'The Lady's Dressing Room', a poem Swift had published in 1732. Motte also seems to have thought that 'A Beautiful Young Nymph' might not provoke the same reprisals in official quarters as 'On Poetry' or 'An Epistle'. Instead these poems stirred another kind of outrage, which lasted well into the twentieth century.

With 'A Beautiful Young Nymph Going to Bed' Swift continued work he began with 'The Progress of Beauty' in 1719, the quatrain poem that described the nocturnal rituals of an afflicted prostitute called Celia. Here Swift's goal was again to mortify readers who tried to isolate their lusts from the realities of physical decay. The courtesan this time is called Corinna, 'pride of Drury-Lane', and she returns home at night, climbing the four storeys to her garret, to dismantle her prosthetics.

> Then, seated on a three-legg'd Chair,
> Takes off her artificial Hair:
> Now, picking out a Crystal Eye,
> She wipes it clean, and lays it by.
> Her eyebrows from a Mouse's Hyde,
> Stuck on with Art on either Side,
> Pulls off with Care, and first displays 'em,
> Then in a Play-book smoothly lays 'em.

She removes her 'plumpers', devices placed in the mouth to push out concave cheeks:

> Untwists a Wire; and from her Gums
> A set of Teeth completely comes.
> Pulls out the Rags contriv'd to prop
> Her flabby Dugs and down they drop.[133]

And so the procedure continues. When Corinna wakes, she is in disarray. A rat has run off with her plaster, the glass eye has rolled away, the cat has pissed on her plumpers. Swift declines to describe the reassembly operation, although he praises her 'Arts' in performing it – 'the Anguish, Toil and Pain / Of gath'ring up herself again'. His final line stipulates the response deemed proper to such a scene: 'Who sees, will spew; who smells, be poison'd.'[134]

Comedy at the expense of older women trying to keep their youthful looks was extremely common. Lady Wishfort, frowning 'a little too rashly' in Congreve's *Way of the World*, was one of innumerable women characters punished not so much for vanity as simply growing old: cracks appear in the 'white varnish' on her face, and she cries out, 'I look like an old peel'd wall.'[135] To an undeniable extent, Swift's 'A Beautiful Young Nymph' might be filed under the same class of humour. The 'Verses on the Death of Dr Swift' seem to sanction such a reading, by digressing on Swift's satiric purpose.

> He spar'd a Hump or crooked Nose,
> Whose Owners set not up for Beaux.[136]

That is to say, if ugly people didn't pretend to be beautiful, Swift left them alone. Congreve, in *The Way of the World*, is making fairly simple if unpleasant fun of the way an ageing woman tries to look younger. But in the case of Swift's 'A Beautiful Young Nymph', as with 'The Progress of Beauty', there is a more interesting dynamic at work than in the scene with Lady Wishfort. The view is complicated first by Corinna's social plight: unlike Congreve's lady, she needs to seem desirable in order to survive. No wealth or social status will cushion her as her physical problems increase. Congreve's ageing belle stirs a belly-laugh that is at once chauvinistic and also slightly sympathetic. Swift's Corinna, though her physical condition is truly pitiable, does more than that: she calls the reaction of the reader or viewer into question. Swift is forcing his readers – especially his male ones – to think about the way they define the women they are willing to find beautiful. In effect, he is saying, 'Here is a woman falling physically to pieces, yet she is a being you, her potential customers, are willing to regard in a sexual light. She fails all your definitions of what is beautiful, even though she tricks you into believing she matches those definitions. How much, in fact, are you willing to deceive yourselves for the sake of carnal pleasure?' In one of Swift's very favourite books, Rabelais's rogue for all seasons, Panurge, splurges six thousand florins by paying men of Paris to take a number of 'good old women' to bed – saying, 'By God, I will have their skincoat shaken once more before they die.'[137] Swift preserves Rabelais's robustly and wildly inappropriate comic mode, but reverses the point of the comedy. There is no need, he is saying, to bribe men to fornicate; they will countenance any amount of cosmetic deception. And this indiscriminate concupiscence allows Corinna to survive.

As with Celia in 'The Progress of Beauty', Swift's poem is so caught up in the challenges Corinna deals with in coping with her physical condition that if anything it almost compliments her, as a being, on her versatility and powers of endurance. More than the woman being caricatured, the target instead seems to be the self-deceiving nature of the sexual drive itself. Only human forms matching conventional ideas of grace and beauty may be considered desirable; objects and textures that inspire disgust need to be suppressed altogether. The result, Swift's 'Beautiful Nymph' reveals, is that deprivation and suffering are overlooked for the sake of carnal thrill. This was a trait that Swift evidently found inherently hypocritical – much like morally brutal people of fashion believing that their latest manners and accessories were enough to exempt them from classification as Yahoos. The poems of Swift's booklet essentially form a subsection of his anti-Yahoo argument. They are a criticism not (or not only) of women but of sexuality itself – though how coherently the Dean in his late sixties separated the two is endlessly debatable. He was by this time, presumably, living a celibate existence. The poems indicate how his own sexuality may have troubled him, with memories of his relationships with Stella and Vanessa contributing to his discomfort.

Such criticism, in essence a criticism of a creaturely drive, involved an attack on the way people censored actual perceptions. Swift could claim he was free of such distortions, since he was outwardly at least a priest devoted to a single life. The title of 'A Beautiful Young Nymph Going to Bed' pointedly alludes to Donne's 'To His Mistress Going to Bed'. But the echoes in the main text are clipped: for the speaker is only an observer, not a presence or participant, in the scene of undressing that follows. Another poem in the 1734 booklet was 'Cassinus and

Peter', a Peter-and-Paul story in which one Cambridge undergraduate comforts another, his friend, who is aghast at discovering that his beloved, Celia, also shits.[138] Should this mean that Cassinus, the afflicted lover, should no longer find her beautiful? The joke of the poem seems to be on the youngster's naive and narrow sense of what makes a partner attractive; and no doubt on the traditional Puritanism of Cambridge. The other remaining poem published in this pamphlet explores the implications of an opposite, over-permissive tendency. Here Chloe is adored by Strephon as a model not only because of beauty but cleanliness.

> No Humours gross, or frowsy Steams,
> No noisome Whiffs, or sweaty Streams,
> Before, behind, above, below,
> Could from her taintless Body flow.[139]

As such, Chloe is unreal – and reality erupts on the couple's wedding night. Chloe stuns Strephon by leaving for the chamber pot just after joining him in bed. At first he is appalled, like Cassinus, to realize that his goddess also sometimes needs the lavatory. But then he is liberated – and also goes to relieve himself in front of Chloe. From the early days of their marriage, all inhibitions are lost. For Swift – or his poem's speaker, at least – this is letting things get out of hand. As such he invokes 'Fair Decency, celestial Maid' to descend from heaven 'to beauty's aid' and restore due limits. The last ninety lines of Swift's poem become a homily on this subject, and close with an image of what constitutes true conjugal happiness.

> On Sense and Wit your Passion found,
> By Decency cemented round;
> Let Prudence with good Nature strive,
> To keep Esteem and Love alive.
> Then come old Age whene'er it will,
> Your Friendship shall continue still:
> And thus a mutual gentle Fire,
> Shall never but with Life expire.[140]

Here was the formula that had guided Swift in his long friendship for Esther Johnson – whatever her wishes might originally have been. 'Prudence' in that long relationship, for Swift, meant cancelling the marital and possibly the sexual aspects of their affection altogether. The 'mutual gentle Fire' of friendship similarly recalls the ideal form of association he proposed in *Cadenus and Vanessa*, 'A constant, rational delight ... Which gently warms'.[141] How Swift in fact had lapsed from such principles with either or both of his late women friends remains a secret of history.

Resisting the case for the moderation of friendship, however, in 'Strephon and Chloe', at the end of Swift's story neither of the lovers seems at all disappointed with the other, even though they go to the toilet quite openly together. Chloe's 'beauty' is not at all seen to fade in Strephon's eyes when he gains more complete information on her bodily functions: in fact he seems rather relieved. In consequence, the moral of Swift's closing address isn't really supplied by the story he tells. The narrow-mindedness of Cassinus, who can't get over the idea of Celia needing to defecate, seems overall much worse than the relaxed attitude of Strephon and Chloe. In all three 1734 poems there is a strong correlation between indecency and deceit. To restrict Celia or Chloe to the impossible requirements of sterile goddess is impossible; yet to revel in filth, for Swift, is abhorrent. Equally, it is for him indecent to paint and reconstruct a physically disfigured woman such as Corinna, the 'beautiful nymph', purely in order to treat her as a sexual object. If, gentlemen, that *is* how you wish to use a one-eyed, partially handicapped elderly woman, you should look on her as she is while you do so. Swift's speaker, for one, does look at her, fixedly, and with something like erotic fascination – yet his gaze is just shy of the all-embracing frankness of a Rabelais or a Panurge.

The same issues percolate in a poem Swift published a couple of years earlier. In 'The Lady's Dressing Room', which caused much outrage in 1732, Swift has a Peeping Tom, also called Strephon, sneak into another Celia's room and there gleefully discover she is not as 'sweet and cleanly' as her admirers would believe.[142] Strephon's reward is a perverse pleasure in rummaging through underwear and intimate things, discovering signs of 'Sweat, Dandruff, Powder, Lead and Hair' on her dressing table; her towels are 'beslim'd / With Dirt, and Sweat, and Ear-wax grim'd'.[143] Swift had pity for the domestic servants who had to clean up and empty these leavings. In his *Directions to Servants*, a work he had had in hand for some years, he advised housemaids to shame their negligent mistresses into using the privy by carrying the pot openly through the house and even opening the door to guests while holding it.[144] To the manically hygienic Swift, such slovenliness was inexcusable, and he felt licensed to condemn it personally among his acquaintances. Strephon, moreover, is guilty of an equal if not greater indecency, through his prying, and is punished for it. After creeping into Celia's chamber, 'His foul imagination links / Each Dame he sees with all her Stinks.'[145] Swift is in little doubt that someone entering conjugal life needs to be able to deal with such things. His own, austere course lay open to all who were appalled by them. The position of the Strephon of this poem, condemning dirt while rooting through it, is one to be punished. It is surely impossible, however, not to feel that in part Swift relished taking on the role of this linen-fondling intruder.

Mrs Pilkington, whose home Swift had subjected to a thorough personal hygiene check, said that 'The Lady's Dressing Room' made her mother vomit.[146] When it first appeared in 1732, Swift had defended his poem in an anonymous essay. He was surprised, he claimed, that 'those fatal verses' had 'so inflamed the whole Sex (except a very few of better Judgment)'. Cleanliness, he contended, had been considered 'the chief corporeal Perfection in Women' since ancient times. He continued with a mock-translation from Horace purporting to show that the Latin poet was much more obscene than the modern Irish one.[147]

Undoubtedly cleanliness for Swift was a vital virtue. Dirt and excrement loomed morbidly large in his writing as a result of his fixed desire that they be scrubbed out of existence. He looked for more still. The decent, as the closing lines of 'Strephon and Chloe' indicate, was ultimately a moral category. Swift thought, additionally, that decency came with a classical education. In 1730 he had praised the outgoing viceroy, Lord Carteret, as an incongruously sanitary figure: the ignorant Whig Swift impersonates in his *Vindication* of Carteret urges that the Lord Lieutenant should be excused for his bookish eccentricities and odd choice of companions (gown-men such as Swift, Delany, Sheridan and Stopford). The ignorance that for Swift characterizes the Whiggish side also indicated a moral depravity.[148] It was the opposite characteristic in the seemingly eloquent, learned and modest Matthew Pilkington that first made the young clergyman so enchanting to the Dean.

Through the course of 1734, he finally received reports complaining that Mr Pilkington had fallen far below the standard Swift had once seen in him. Swift hated an informer – and he could not have missed the allegation that Mr Pilkington had betrayed him, though it still remained to be proven. Possibly more galling was a terse aside from Viscount Bolingbroke in the spring: 'Pray Mr Dean be a little more cautious in your Recommendations . . . the fellow wants morals & as I hear Decency sometimes.'[149] The Viscount was still cultivating his 'Retreat' when not making occasional sallies against Walpole. Coming from Bolingbroke, the reprimand about Mr Pilkington was one to sting – since, if he chose, Swift might remember many days such as one in August 1711, when St John met him with a mutual acquaintance on the Mall 'and took a turn or two': 'And then stole away, and we both believed it was to pick up some wench; and tomorrow he will be at the cabinet with the Queen: so goes the world.'[150] Swift had few illusions about many who so often spoke in high moral terms. But he could be dazzled by some who, like Bolingbroke, like Mr Pilkington, cited the classics adeptly: he could, sometimes, pardon a lack of decency.

A thought to worsen the whirlwind, when vertigo and nausea descended, was that by writing so particularly of Corinna the nymph, or of Strephon and Chloe's lurking coprophilia, he might have committed an indecency himself, or, worse, had expressed something of his own latent urges. Was he actually consumed with hatred for women, for physical desire, for the body? This was a thought he resisted, just as, writing as Gulliver, he had denied the charges levelled in much criticism of the *Travels*, 'wherein I see myself accused ... of degrading human Nature (for so they have still the Confidence to style it), and of abusing the Female Sex'.[151]

He could trust only that his true understanders – such as the two other last Scriblerians in England, or Sheridan, Delany and Stopford in Ireland – would see the precedents for his poems in Ovid and Quevedo, his affectionate parody of the Restoration balladeers and the Platonists of the 1630s, and would grasp his real meaning and achievement. The doubt, though, would always remain that there was more to these 'dirty' poems than a blend of all their clever echoes.[152]

# 13. The Last of the Gold

Relentless Dean! To Mischief born
  – *Swift, 'On Cutting Down the Old Thorn at Market Hill'*[1]

## I

Swift was pierced by Pope's complaint, in September 1734, 'about the intervening, officious impertinence of those goers-between us.' Frail and brittle-tempered, though still inexhaustibly prolific, the poet was grumbling not only about Mr Pilkington but other emissaries from Swift who had called on him at Twickenham over the years, a number that included Mrs Barber, Delany and Sheridan. A lot of the trouble surrounding some of these interlopers had nothing to do with Swift. 'I cannot but receive any that call upon your name,' Pope remonstrated, 'and in truth they take it in vain too often.' Protesting as he did, Pope wrote with the delicate nerves of an invalid striving to maintain sociable appearances when unfamiliar company was often anguish. He was also tired from a summer of rambling the Home Counties between his well-off friends' estates, although 'the daemon of verse sticks close to him,' as Bolingbroke informed Swift. A faintly tense silence had consequently stretched, over a number of months, between Twickenham and St Patrick's by autumn 1734, though Pope broke it with characteristically warm professions of friendship. The loss of Gay was biting; he was upset, more than vaguely, about the edition of Swift's works he knew was being prepared in Dublin. On his side, Swift was upset with some lines Pope had written the previous year implying that he was mean. They avoided a squabble. Pope still urged Swift to come to England, and Bolingbroke was among many others who seconded this appeal. In one of his finest small touches, Bolingbroke dismissed Swift's standard plea of ill-health. Did he think that his friends had not suffered the advance of time as well? 'We all go the same road,' he assured Swift, 'and keep much the same Stages. Let this consideration therefore not hinder you from coming among us.'[2]

Swift was contrite about his friends' intrusions on Pope's peace. 'I am sorry at my heart, that you are pestered with People who come in my name,' he replied, as the trees grew bare. He complained of similar impertinent attentions brought by his station in life. He had by this time, it would seem, taken to crossing Mr Pilkington's name out of all letters he received;[3] though his door remained open for the present to Laetitia. He begged only for Pope to make an exception of Sheridan, who spoke frequently of travelling – though he was sure the journey to England was beyond the schoolmaster's finances. In 1733 Swift had relied on Pope's usual hospitality if 'a little staring boy of eleven' presented himself at Twickenham: this was Thomas, Sheridan's third boy (and Swift's fanciful future biographer), sent over for what proved a brief spell at Westminster School.[4] A year later, Swift was suddenly embarrassed for asking such little favours, torn though he was by diverging loyalties, since the few in Dublin he counted real friends were 'fixed to the freehold'.[5]

Despite saying often that his friends were few, he continued to develop new ties. He liked spending time with young people, and took on a grandfatherly role towards the children of his crucial helper, Mrs Whiteway. Her first son, Theophilus Harrison, was a serious and precocious young man, nearing twenty, and seemed set to become a clergyman like his late father. Swift later paid for John, the younger of her boys by her second husband, to be apprenticed to a surgeon.[6] In June 1734 he was extremely impressed by the letter sent with a gift of pork and butter from Sarah, daughter of Archbishop Hoadly. The exchange of compliments indicated the almost genial relations that now existed between the deanery and Hoadly's episcopal palace. Miss Hoadly's letter, Swift cried, was 'written in a fair hand, rightly spelt and good plain sense'. He vowed that he would show it 'to every female scrawler that I meet', though he threatened that doing so would make her seem a much less fashionable young woman of the upper class, since she wrote 'more like a parson than a lady'.[7] All such young people Swift liked to amuse with stories, correct at liberty and boss about. Mrs Pilkington was a special case, but the mixture of fun and terror she describes in Swift's parlour and dining room do seem representative.

Another interesting anomaly in Swift's developing Irish milieu was the son of a Jacobite exile whose name has close associations with the genesis of 'The Battle of the Books'. Charles Boyle, fourth Earl of Orrery, had spent the second half of his life largely in intrigues to bring over the Pretender, the last of which fell flat in 1725. As an undergraduate at Christ Church, though, he had translated the spurious Epistles of Phalaris and was credited with twitting Richard Bentley, who in time proved the epistles were fakes. Without the wit and learning of Francis Atterbury – who, losing patience with his student, presently withdrew them – Boyle had no future in letters, and disdained one in any case because of his social station. A military and public career instead awaited him, without bringing high rank or office, and in which he moved to join the Tories' Jacobite wing. He was among the few known conspirators eventually given freedom to stay in England; he died in London, at his house in Downing Street, in 1731.[8] John, who succeeded him as fifth Earl of Orrery at the age of twenty-four, disliked his father, mainly because of the mistress, Margaret Swordfeger, with whom the old Earl passed his last decade, and who gave him two illegitimate children. John Boyle was prim, scholarly and traditional, and lived much of the time in Ireland: indisputably 'decent', he had cultivated and gained Swift's friendship in 1732. In December that year Swift described the young Lord Orrery to Ford as 'a most deserving Person, a good Scholar, with much wit, manners and modesty'.[9] 'Modesty' was a quality Swift chose to typify men as unalike as taciturn James Stopford and forward Matthew Pilkington; the young Earl, loquacious but meticulously formal, resembled neither, though he absorbed himself quickly into the very heart of Swift's coterie, and Swift grew strongly attached to him. Orrery was to be found not only at the Dean's table but also on his regular outings. He joined Swift and Sheridan on a ride to Tallow Hill, outside Dublin, in mid-May 1733. Climbing 'to take a prospect of the adjacent country', the trio meditated on a fast stream gushing from a huge rock into a natural basin below. They agreed that the waters must be contained in some reservoir within the hill. Swift sent for a two-gallon pail, which the stream filled in a minute; meaning, they computed, that the rock produced more than a million gallons every year – which could only indicate that the hill itself was in danger of bursting, and flooding the city, within the very near future.[10]

Though nearly seventy, physically Swift was close to being as active as ever. Mrs Pilkington had observed him crashing up and down the deanery's separate staircases during bad weather.[11] He had blamed a muscle strained during one such workout for keeping him from England in 1732.[12] When such setbacks cleared, and his giddiness kept away, he remained for several years more the restless walker and rider of old, satisfying his other great obsession, with hygiene, by keeping a basin of clean water handy when he changed his clothes after exercise.[13]

Since they knew that, barring his vertiginous attacks, Swift's health was extremely sound, his English friends continued calling on him to visit. He might have relented, if the indignity of spinning in deafness among polite company had not been too horrible to contemplate: 'I never can hope to leave this country till I leave this World,' he sighed. He was also held from sailing by financial concerns. Though his income was more than sufficient for him to live in perfect comfort and to afford quite extensive beneficial acts, as the years passed the sight of money wasted was a gnawing anguish. In a tender note to Arbuthnot in November 1734 ('You tear my heart with the ill account of your Health') he claimed that the cost of maintaining his state on a long trip to England was more than he could afford. 'I am not in Circumstances to keep horses and Servants in London,' he said; the bottle of French wine he drank each day as a painkiller ('I love it not,' he protested) would be an impossible luxury on the other side of the sea.[14] When the necessary adjustments are made – for his small untruth about wine, for instance – Swift's real point was not a lack of money, but an unwillingness to devote more of it to such comforts and dignities. The alternative shame of living humbly – without his stables, servants to manage the frequent callers or a well-stocked cellar to numb his aches and pains – was intolerable. Delany and Sheridan, both of whom were profligate, would criticize their friend for stinginess. But what seemed avarice to others seemed pure sense to Swift. 'I desire to be represented as a man of thrift onely as it produceth liberty and Independence,' he told Pope, 'without any thoughts of hoarding.'[15] The remark illuminates one of the keywords in the epitaph he wrote for his tomb. Liberty for Swift partly meant the freedom money could procure from debasing necessities – from scrabbling for food, from being dirty, from losing one's dignity in sickness or adversity. Financial independence was necessary to escape the condition of Yahoo-dom.

Irish trade and agriculture were improving, but still stricken. Falling revenues from tithes and rents had lowered his income by £300, he told Arbuthnot in the letter just mentioned.[16] Earlier in 1734 he assured the Earl of Oxford that the state of Ireland was as dire as ever; his stock of rhetoric was as plentiful as always in evoking the irremediable.

Nothing in so wretched and enslaved a Nation as this can be worth entertaining your Lordship with. It is a Mass of Beggars, Thieves, Oppressors, Fools and Knaves. All Employments are in the hands of the Kingdom's greatest Enemies. In this great City nine tenths of the Inhabitants are beggars, the chief Streets half ruinous or desolate. It is dangerous to walk the Streets for fear of Houses falling on our heads, and it is the same in every City and Town through the Island.

Mentioning Pope's allegation about his parsimony in the same letter, Swift said, 'I am sure he had not the least ill intention.'[17] A strong if circumstantial link seems plain, though, between Swift's anxiety about his 'great city' and the kingdom beyond, and his growing compulsion to save funds. In his mind, Ireland grew ever nearer ruin simply by remaining as it was; and such impending desolation threatened the fixed financial habits by which he tried to improve the lives of people around him. Mrs Brent, or 'Sir Robert Walpole', as he was fond of calling the deanery's steadfast housekeeper, gave Laetitia Pilkington a firmly worded account of how Swift divided his income:

I told Mrs Brent, I believed the Dean was extremely charitable. Indeed, Madam, replied she, No body can be more so: his income is not above six hundred Pounds a Year, and every year he gives above the Half of it in Private Pensions to decayed Families; besides this, he keeps five hundred Pounds in the constant Service of the industrious Poor: This he lends out in five Pounds at a Time and takes the Payment back at twelve Pence a Week; this does them more Service, than if he gave it to them entirely, as it obliges them to work, and at the same Time keeps up this charitable Fund for the Assistance of so many.[18]

Swift's deanship may be valued at a good deal more than the £600 per annum Mrs Brent estimated (and Pilkington may have lowered the sum to emphasize Swift's humility); but, as he complained to Arbuthnot, his revenues fluctuated with trade and harvests. The general polity described here, however, tallies with Swift's account books and his earlier claim to have saved many tradespeople's families from ruin.[19] His home economics in fact formed the basis of his final line of political action, in the second half of this decade, when he continued to devote himself to local and municipal campaigns and debates. With the grander struggles lost, he refused to give up the last battles in his neighbourhood. Since 1731, moreover, and possibly earlier, he had been nurturing a plan to fund an important institution to benefit Dublin with the proceeds of his estate.

Swift's budgeting anxieties also accord with the other broad sides of the personality manifest in his writings. The link between tendencies to hoard and a preoccupation with shit bears out a Freudian tenet, an aspect of the 'anal retentive' character, and it must be said Swift did more than his bit in support for that particular theory.[20] In his comical *Examination of Certain Abuses* in 1732, he had conjectured that the heaps of human turds to be found in the streets were surely 'laid there by British Fundaments, to make the World believe, that our Irish Vulgar do daily eat and drink'. A British anus, he continued (as opposed to the Hibernian), produced a distinctively 'copple-crowned', conic stool, and so the fraud was evident. The connection between excrement and nourishment is about as basic as it gets, yet it takes a mind with certain innate priorities to make so much of it as Swift does in his *Examination*.[21]

The erotic subtexts of his scatological fascinations have been extensively explored by critics over the centuries. His urgency over pennies, pounds and the price of butter in his pantry resonates with the critical and incredulous attitude to sexuality that emerges in the 'Beautiful Nymph' poems published in 1733, and elsewhere. The latent question in these writings is 'Why are you so caught up in your lusts – for illusions – when there is a danger of *starving*?' In 'The Lady's Dressing Room', Strephon sets out to expose the secret dirt in Celia's personal effects; and his view of women is blighted when he finds his former impressions of them were as misty and idealistic as those of any man he knows. An instrument of particular horror is the 'magnifying glass' that Celia uses, among other purposes, for de-worming her nose.[22] Though incomparable to Strephon, Gulliver is similarly cured of casual lust by the mass magnification provided for him in Brobdingnag. Nothing he sees there repels him so much as the sight of women's naked breasts, in all imaginable conditions.[23] The psychology of these passages is complex; yet one of their manifest intentions is to ridicule the erotic. Swift does so by exposing objects of supposed desire to relentless, thrill-killing scrutiny: Gulliver is appalled when a young Brobdingnagian, one of the 'handsomest' of the Queen's maids of honour, puts him astride one of her nipples. Swift, in the background, is deriding the fuss people make about carnal excitements in the normal world; even though the particularities of Gulliver's predicament (his powerlessness, her apparent monstrosity) clearly divert him. Swift's own drives seem to have been diverted to the question of keeping flesh alive, of filling intestines with food and then providing the 'liberty' and 'independence' he deemed necessary for civilized life.

At one point Bolingbroke had proposed a swap of livings to Swift: he would move to a very pleasantly situated rectory in Berkshire, half a day's ride from the Viscount's manor at Bucklebury in the same county; while the present Rector of Burghfield would take on Swift's deanery at St Patrick's. The benefice would bring Swift a steady £400 a year – quite a reduction from his handsome Dublin income, but constituting the backbone of a very decent retirement plan. Swift's duties in Berkshire would be a fraction of what the busy cathedral required, and, most importantly of all, he would be no more than a day from almost any of his friends in London or the surrounding shires.[24]

Swift was tempted, but declined. The excuse he made to Bolingbroke was the same as the one he gave Arbuthnot for not travelling: the Burghfield living was just a few hundred per annum short of what he needed to live decently. The move would also, in effect, put him out to grass. The loss of station, he said, would break his heart within a month.[25] When put in the frame of his vast correspondence and hugely busy Dublin life, this reason was clearly shorthand for the multitude of attachments that kept him at St Patrick's. Ireland was the site of his complex libidinous effort to stave off certain catastrophe: it gave him, moreover, the dignity of his deanery; it was also the receptacle of his mixed affections, and the home, perhaps above all, of the set of friends and associates that he said came with the freehold on his deanery, and that in effect constituted his family.

The mid-1730s brought major losses to this support structure. At the end of November 1734, Mary Worrall died. The wife of John, the head of the cathedral choir, she had been Swift's friend almost since the time he returned permanently to Dublin, and Esther Johnson's main nurse.[26] She was 'a cheerful woman with a clear voice' who sent Swift 'vittels'. With her husband she would drop by for tea or supper several times a week, and 'sit the evenings'.[27] The following spring brought an even greater shock to his establishment with the death of Anne Brent: she had kept house for him in Dublin since the time he was first made a prebendary of St Patrick's.[28] His memory of her was bound up indelibly with Esther Johnson's time. She had once unearthed a very large and very old bottle of wine on Johnson's birthday. 'Long buried', it had not aged well, yet Swift celebrated it in one of his annual poems for his greatest friend.[29] Brent's death, a great loss in itself, put Stella at a further remove from living acquaintance. Swift's silence on such blows did not mean they mattered little to him. Years earlier, when a rare and favoured footman had died, a plaque had been set in the cathedral commemorating the 'discretion, fidelity, and diligence' of Alexander McGee (or 'Saunders' to Swift). It was put there, read the tablet, by order of McGee's 'grateful master' ('and friend', as Swift originally wrote). Yet this had been an openly eccentric act of tenderness, which followed a classical subgenre of masters paying tribute to servants.[30] Words could not be found for a monument for the woman who had tended Stella or the one who had ordered his domestic life, and with whom he had dined on every quiet evening for years. Mrs Brent's daughter, Anne Ridgeway, took over her duties, and entered Swift's pantheon of domestic legend.

## 2

Another haemorrhage came with two major departures from the deanery setting. Delany moved out of town late in 1734: the air in Dublin disagreed with his wife, and for the added benefit of saving money they based themselves permanently at Delville – where, Swift complained, 'there is no seeing him or dining with him but by those who keep coaches, and they must return the moment after dinner.'[31] A still more depressing loss was Thomas Sheridan. In the spring of 1735 Swift's 'viceroy Trifler' moved permanently to his home county of Cavan, to take up a headmastership. By July, Swift was lamenting Sheridan as his 'greatest loss', and plans were soon afoot for him to visit, even at the risk of Sheridan's haphazard hospitality. He grumbled to Orrery of the shillings lost in carriage fares to Delville, and the ten guests who came sponging dinner at his house on Sunday evenings.[32] Learned Orrery was something of a stand-by for these emergencies, as was another bright young man and junior relative, Deane Swift. But nothing could equal the intellectual fooleries with which Swift and Sheridan could pass an evening. Luckily for both a good share of the fun survived in their frequent notes. They sustained their old rivalry in writing *nugae*, trifles, and any pair of letters might follow a given form – written largely or entirely, for example, in Latin puns or a mash of baby talk and homophones: 'Dear Day Ann,' began one typical example from Sheridan, 'Eye mash aimed off knott wry tin two yew bee four.' ('Dear Dean, I'm ashamed of not writing to you before.')[33] While reading like an Urtext of *Finnegans Wake*, these notes often give revealing hints on English pronunciation in early-eighteenth-century Dublin. They display, above all, two attributes that Swift shared with Sheridan: a very boyish sense of humour, when occasion allowed, and the verbal double-jointedness of a master crossword-setter.

Swift's immediate social fellowship was fragmenting, but it was also evolving. Over the sea, two years after the death of Gay, another unfill-able space was opening, in the shape of Dr John Arbuthnot's tall figure and ample contours. Swift received advance warning of the affable, polymathic Scot's departure from the patient himself. In the autumn of 1734 Arbuthnot let him know that he did not expect to survive the winter. He was afflicted with a chronic swelling of the tissues, oedema, a 'dropsy'. A recent ride to Hampstead had done him more good than he could have hoped for: an outing on the saddle usually, he coolly reported, put blood in his water. But he expected his symptoms to intensify when he went back to London. What he needed, he knew, was a break from his medical practice. Lacking the means to retire, he was positive from long experience that no man of his age with his complaint could hope for more than a temporary easing. However limited by the medical science of his time, as a diagnostician Arbuthnot was generally unerring, and so it proved in his own case. He died at the end of February 1735. In keeping with the spirit of advance notice that accompanied Arbuthnot's passing, Swift reacted to a premature report of his friend's death. 'What a havoc hath death made among our friends since that of the Queen!' he expostulated, in a letter to John Barber. Arbuthnot, lowering his eyes from the prospect of winter, had approached death with the same resignation and easy-going scepticism he had expressed in the dog-days of 1714.

> I am at present in the case of a man that was almost in harbour & then blown back to Sea; who has a reasonable hope of going to a good place & an absolute certainty of leaving a very bad one – not that I have any particular disgust at the world for I have as great comfort in my own family and from the kindness of my friends as any man, but the world in the main displeaseth me.[34]

As he had been forewarned of the worst, Swift's mourning for Arbuthnot was more resigned in 1735 than it had been for Gay in the winter of 1732/3. And although the death of Queen Anne marked a freezing point for hope in his conscious scheme of things, Swift was not a man to sit staring all day at empty chairs. He stayed tirelessly interested in promising people and their doings, and a full account of all his involvements with all his numerous acquaintance would fill many volumes. The Grat-

tan family and their associates, Delany's friend Dr Helsham, the brothers
John and William Richardson – the first a parson dedicated to propagat-
ing Irish-language bibles and prayer-books, the second a squire whom
Swift befriended – these are only a handful of names from the fair-sized
hosts of tradespeople, surgeons, clerics and landowners with whom
Swift fraternized and collaborated.

Deane Swift, just mentioned, was a grandson of Swift's long-deceased
and little-loved uncle Godwin. 'I have kindred enough,' Swift grumbled
in 1735, 'but not a grain of merit among them': except, he went on, after
a guilty moment, 'one Female, who is the onely Cousin I suffer to see
me'.[35] Here he was referring to Martha Whiteway, whose company and
organizing skills were now indispensable to him. He was also being
untrue to fact and to his own thoughts, for Deane Swift was a cousin
Swift saw regularly, and in whom he manifestly did find a granule or so
of virtue. Since 1726, Swift had been helping this young relative (who
was twenty-eight in 1735) with a tangled dispute over a legacy. The
assistance he gave involved providing Deane with a mortgage on a property near Trim amounting to some £2,000, a further instance of how
Swift's benevolence in action belied his brusqueness in word.[36] After
some study at Trinity, Deane had now moved to Oxford, where a trusted
acquaintance later assured Swift he was a 'modest, sober, ingenious
young man'.[37] The life of the mature student suited him, apparently. At
the end of the decade he married Martha Whiteway's daughter Mary;
and as a sign of his favour Swift gave him a complete set of Faulkner's
edition of his *Works*, which appeared in four volumes in 1735.

In the autumn of 1735, as Parliament gathered, Ireland was still stuck
deep in depression. Though circumstances overall might have improved
somewhat since the late 1720s, Swift's mind was fixed on individual
instances of hardship, the cruel impressions made during his walks and
rides around the city and beyond. The Irish wool trade seemed as hopeless as ever, with the by-products of hunger and destitution evident
wherever he went. 'This Kingdom is now absolutely starving,' he assured
Pope in September, 'by the means of every Oppression that can possibly
be inflicted on mankind.'[38] In disgust he refused to stay in Dublin for the
spectacle of a Parliament. The blow-ins returning from England; the
members of both Houses dominating the social scene and hemming over
their prayers in the cathedral – they sickened him. 'The Club meets in a
week,' he reminded Sheridan, and 'I am not able to live within the Air of
such rascals.'[39] Business delayed him for a month, and then he left for
Cavan. He had very little concern now for whoever took offence at his

opinions or even his manners. Before setting out, he made a sharp remark, at a grand public dinner, about George Dodington, the Walpole aide from whom he had stolen the notebook in which he wrote his 'Holyhead Journal' in 1727.[40] In a similar temper, he insulted the company of Cavan aldermen he had unwillingly invited to dinner. They had met him some weeks before at Sheridan's request, four miles outside the Ulster market town, 'to compliment him on his arrival'. The 'eldest Burgess' of Cavan made a speech in Swift's honour; on being informed that the dignitary was also the town apothecary, Swift replied, 'I thought so . . . for he spoke as if his mouth was full of drugs.' The great citizen had no desire for his hosts' provincial attention and still less for the expense or effort of their company at dinner. He put off feasting them as long into his stay as possible.

> He gave them a shabby dinner at the inn, and called for the bill before the guests had got half enough wine. He disputed several articles, said there were two bottles of wine more charged than were used, flew into a violent passion, and abused his servants grossly for not keeping better count. The servants ran away, and Doctor Sheridan, without speaking a word, went off and left him to himself.[41]

Sheridan's sixteen-year-old son, the author of this account (written much later), found Swift thin, old and peevish. The family trod quietly around their distinguished visitor, and gladly left him largely to Sheridan to entertain. Sheridan's view of Swift was slowly becoming contaminated with resentment at his unwillingness to offer the same sort of financial help the Dean gave to relatives and poor tradesmen's families, and so his son's account, coloured with memories of paternal mutterings, tends to emphasize Swift's avarice and accelerate the onset of old age.[42] But Swift took kindly memories with him from Cavan of young Thomas: 'Did I tell you,' he mentioned in a letter to Sheridan the following year, 'that I much esteem your younger son.' The one thing that he found disconcerting was the sense the boy gave of constantly watching, of being on the alert.[43] A sharp observation of striking characters, and a witty promptness in expressing it, would persist in Sheridan's line through this son, who became an actor and theatre-manager of note, and his grandson Richard Brinsley, author of *The School for Scandal*.

Despite the Sheridans' accusations of meanness, Swift spent his weeks in Cavan as their paying boarder. His letters to Martha Whiteway that autumn do much to clear up how the charges of stinginess arose. With the sense of a kingdom starving all around him, he found it intolerable to throw fancy dinners for strangers or see his friend, who was always stretched financially, fritter his income on entertainment he could not afford. Similarly, Swift growled, 'I do not like to see my money laid out in cleaning curtains, or covering chairs,' he told Whiteway (though he submitted to her judgement that these were necessary expenses). The really big and indisputably generous sums he allotted to help relatives such as Deane Swift or struggling Dublin neighbours made a material difference to their lives. The relatively small amounts of money it increasingly pained him to squander cost him a share of the regard of old friends such as Sheridan.

At Cavan, Swift's temper and melancholy were assuredly tested by a badly bruised shin that left him unable to walk or ride; though by 3 December he could inform Whiteway that he had twice been riding and taken a stroll 'in the town, that is to say, in the dirt, every day'. He was glad of the 'fine frost'; it brought the risk of further slips and injuries but at least tamed the mud.[44] He expressed gratitude for Whiteway's letters, which were full of wit and kindness, and made him think of her as a friend rather than as a relative: 'My love to your brats,' he snapped, in one letter in which he and Sheridan wrote alternate paragraphs. He bristled at news from Dublin that there were plans to lower the value of the Irish guinea and raise the duty further on wine.[45] With his strength regained, in the middle of December he returned to Dublin, and despite his anger at politics was in very good form over Christmas. Sheridan was there – without the wife whom Swift disliked intensely – having travelled ahead of the Dean on a fundraising trip for a new schoolhouse. Delany, he also conceded, might be worth the occasional cab fare to Delville. 'The immortal Dean is come to town in high spirits,' wrote Orrery.[46]

Less than two months into 1736, however, Swift's deanery family was cruelly bereaved when Whiteway's son Theophilus, who had been poorly all autumn, died of spotted fever – 'to my infinite sorrow and disappointment,' wrote Swift, 'and to the near breaking of his Mother's heart.' He reflected sourly on the physician who had missed all the advance symptoms. When the plague-like spots appeared on the young man's skin, the doctor had repeatedly declared that 'He does not lose ground'; until, concluded Swift with a bitter twist, 'he got ground, which was a grave.'[47] Consoling his friend, cousin, domestic helper and unofficial secretary became his work of the moment. He chided her gently for refusing to leave her house while her daughter and friends carried out the necessary preparations for Theophilus's funeral. He gave her the words required of a pastor and also put a 'convenient apartment' at her disposal in the deanery, where she could escape her house, a place that would only keep reminding her of her bereavement.[48] He nursed his own grief too, for Sheridan had observed at Christmas how young Harrison was 'every day growing more and more' to his friend and companion. 'It wounds my heart every time I recollect him,' he told Swift.[49]

A few days later Swift was thrown into further shock when Orrery attended a ball at Dublin Castle and almost died of a fever after dancing all night. The Duke of Dorset, when Swift visited, informed him that he found Orrery in an outer room, his 'body all in a sweat', at half past two in the morning. Swift reprimanded his protégé, 'my dear lord', soundly. 'I should not grieve much if your illness would punish you enough,' he lectured – shortly before collapsing into more than a month of deafness and vertigo.[50] Orrery lacked the constitution and temperament for what his peers considered an evening's entertainment, and borrowed images from Gulliver to describe the pains such revelry had put him through: 'I have been at a Feast. Paper mills, thunder and the King's kitchen are soft music to the noises I have heard. Nonsense and wine have flown in plenty, gigantic saddles of mutton and Brobdingnagian rumps of beef weigh down the table.'[51]

All this time, the Irish Parliament continued debating and, as Swift saw it, legislating for the further subjugation of Ireland. While he lay sick in late March and April, he composed a verse diatribe on what he denounced as 'The Legion Club'. The Commons had just voted to deny the clergy's right to demand tithes on the profit made from the pasturing of cattle ('agistment'). This insult, which established a precedent allowing Parliament to deprive clerics of their divinely ordained and legal property, provoked one last surge of scorn from Swift against the entire political order. On 24 April he tipped off Sheridan that a threepenny book would soon appear with a 'masterly poem', although he admitted that surely the printer 'will be condemn'd to be Hang'd for it'.[52] On this occasion none of Dublin's printers were prepared to risk the gallows or a fatal fever caught in prison, and the poem did not see the press. Manuscripts of 'The Legion Club' soon proliferated, however, and Swift's fellow enemies of government felt free to add verses of their own. Swift was soon complaining to Sheridan of how the text had been 'altered and enlarged' and 'murdered'. He maintained the position, meanwhile, of one who had only *seen* the original, not produced it: for he was receiving personal threats from the 'Puppyes' he had offended, and there was talk of summoning the author before the Privy Council.[53]

'The Legion Club' was Swift's last major work in prose or verse (though not the last to reach the public). The title refers to the demon of the Gadarenes in the Gospels, or rather to the multitude of spirits possessing two men. 'Legion' was a byword for the mad, for Pandemonium, for Bedlam. And Swift saw this force incarnate in Dublin's Parliament House. He could not exorcize it, so he set out to describe it. In the opening lines the poem's speaker jauntily mentions walking the city, across College Green, towards the grand, refined Neoclassical structure, domed and fronted by a great portico, which had by then become an object of great civic pride. If only the devils it contained, Swift's poem reflected, could do justice to the marble carapace.

> As I stroll the City, oft I
> Spy a Building large and lofty,
> Not a Bow-shot from the College,
> Half the Globe from Sense and Knowledge . . .
> Tell us what this Pile Contains?
> Many a Head that holds no Brains.
> These Demoniacs let me dub
> With the Name of *Legion Club*.[54]

The result was a vehement individual effort that invited the additions Swift worried had been made to his poem, turning it into an appropriately multi-vocal work to pit against 'Legion'. Much of the 242-line text is devoted to a roll-call of the demons running riot in the building in the form of all too recognizable leading citizens. It would always be possible to add another villain to Swift's original cast. Even so, the overall spirit of the version that has reached us is Swift's.

> Dear Companions hug and kiss,
> Toast *Old Glorious* [William III] in your Piss.
> Tie them, Keeper, in a Tether;
> Let them stare and stink together.[55]

Glimpses of deranged communities abound in Swift, and the care of lunatics was prominent in his plans for the future of his estate. But these were demons, not madmen. 'The Legion Club' bears out a remark he had made back in 1730. As he had declared of Viscount Allen, he could sympathize with one who was demented but he was obliged to renounce him if he was an agent of the devil. For, as Swift argued,

Madness only operates by inflaming and enlarging the good or evil Dispositions of the Mind: For the Curators of Bedlam assure us, that some Lunaticks are Persons of Honour, Truth, Benevolence, and many other Virtues, which appear in their highest Ravings, although after a wild incoherent Manner; while others, on the contrary, discover in every Word and Action, the utmost Baseness and Depravity of human Minds.[56]

The magnifying power of satire, then, was for Swift an external equivalent of the internal 'enlarging' force of madness: and, like the magnifying mirror Strephon discovers in Celia's room, or the mass of close-ups bodies present to Gulliver in Brobdingnag, insanity only exposes all the more clearly what and who the person at hand really is. Thus 'The Legion Club', for Swift, had still greater merit as a work of basic moral truth.

Nevertheless, in the long run he was defeated, and he knew it all the more as he turned seventy and his strength began to fail. Politically his real legacy lay not with what he did, nor even the institutions and ideas in which he believed. He had a sixteenth-century perspective on society: in 1737 he renewed an earlier call that beggars be made to wear badges showing their parish of origin. Anticipating cries of 'What shall we do with the Foreign Beggars [that is, beggars from other towns],' he declared, 'They must be driven or whipt out of Town; and let the next Country Parish do as they please, or rather after the Practice in *England*, send them from one Parish to another, until they reach their own homes.' At one level Swift's attitude to poverty, one held by many in any age, was condemnatory: for he believed 'there is not a more undeserving vicious Race of human kind than the Bulk of those who are reduced to Beggary, even in this beggarly country.'[57] Such statements, to which Swift had often been prone, brought their sadistic relief; before they are mistaken for his manifesto they should be put alongside the one-man initiatives he paid for and undertook for local beggars and impoverished labourers, and his inveterate tendency, when it came to the crisis, to side with the underdog. The contents of Swift's thinking did not comprise his lasting endowment. This was tied up, rather, in the boundless energy and art with which he exposed the wrongdoing of those in power and gave dignity to the language of protest; setting the first great example in English letters of how those holding office might be held to account for their vices.

His views, meanwhile, on everything from Communion to coinage remained as set as ever. At the end of the parliamentary session in 1736, Dorset left Ireland with a mandate to press for the value of gold coins to be lowered in Ireland. This made good economic sense: there was a terrible shortage of lower-value, silver coinage in Ireland, which disabled small transactions and the payment of wages. It was made worse by people bringing gold from England to spend in Ireland, where it was worth more. Swift was entirely aware of the resulting lack of ready money: 'You have twenty Merchants in London who could each of them purchase our whole Cash,' he wrote in 1734.[58] He disputed passionately, however, the theory that Ireland's inert gold reserves were useless, or that they should be exchanged for English copper and silver. The whole force of his campaign as the Drapier had come from his success in eroding confidence in English-imported small change. It was all a plot, he felt, for robbing the kingdom of its gold. The people who would benefit most were the absentees who took their rents and other revenues out of Ireland. A rent-roll charged in silver would amount to more in guineas than it had before gold was devalued. Sinecures, similarly, which built up an income out of small charges on official services and duties, would enable office-holders to purchase more gold coins than they would have got previously for the same amounts.[59]

On 19 April, when Swift was still too sick to attend, the Lord Mayor – currently Richard Grattan, Swift's friend – met with aldermen and members of the Common Council to prepare an official protest against the impending devaluation. The following year, after a summer of widespread rioting, when the value of gold was lowered in a proclamation dated 29 August, Swift ordered a black flag to be hung from the steeple of St Patrick's, and the bells to be muffled and toll. Dozens ran to the cathedral, to learn what disaster was being signalled, and were told 'the signs of mourning were on account of the lowering of the gold.'[60] This time he had written no paper on the issue – he may have felt there was no need, or just lacked wind for it. Large numbers in the city and the government doubtless shared his views on the subject. Privately, there may have been a sense that he would be repeating old thoughts; and a new satirical form in which to present them did not, evidently, occur to him. Being the Dean was by now more than sufficient. Direct action and open threats had greater appeal. At a mayoral feast on 29 September, Archbishop Boulter 'bluntly taxed' Dean Swift, in front of all the great and good assembled in the hall, 'for endeavouring to raise the mob'. Boulter, needless to say, was still above all a servant of the English ministry; he was also an articulate if unstimulating supporter of the currency reform. As ever, he was more comfortable with covert lobbying, drafting memoranda and sending directions in writing than with a public joust. Swift was at ease with all forms of political combat, and Boulter was mistaken if he thought the presence of the Lord Lieutenant, the Lord Mayor, assorted aldermen and other high officials, and his own authority as Primate of All Ireland might have chastened his enemy.

> The Doctor [Swift] answered that he loved his country, and thought the diminution of the coin was a prejudice to it, that he could by lifting up a finger have influenced the mob to tear him [Boulter] in pieces, but he deferred doing it, because it would make for an odd figure in history that a Primate was destroyed by the people for doing an odd job; he would not at present give it another name.

With this mobster-like utterance, Swift swept out in full state. Wigged, begowned, bristle-browed and strong-limbed, he was unopposable. Boulter was left gaping, his allies glaring, and Swift's supporters looking amusedly down at their plates or exchanging sidelong glances. One younger man present wrote that Swift had made himself 'more mad and absurd than ever'. Yet the Primate, harried now with death threats, demanded an armed guard of six men to stand watch in his house at night.[61]

Swift regarded the city as his fiefdom, and the Kingdom beyond it as 'his country'. Though he still insisted on calling it English – or, more precisely, wishing it might enjoy the same freedoms as England – and though he surveyed it with the proprietorial eye of a demagogue, his great aim for it remained autonomy and self-determination, liberty. In November he turned seventy, and the festivities for his birthday were held in the traditional manner, though on an all but unparalleled scale. The windows of the cathedral were lit and bonfires blazed on the steeple; the air shook with volleys fired in salute, huzzahs and singing that lasted well into the night.[62]

### 3

Two portraits from the 1730s give contrasting images of Swift: one, dating from 1735, was done by Francis Bindon, a Dublin-based artist originally from County Clare, and a student of Sir Godfrey Kneller. It shows Swift as the man behind the Drapier – in full clerical garb but with the face of a burgher. The brow below the long wig is very high, the eyebrows thick and black, the nose large and unsubtle. A sheen on the cheeks and forehead give ungraceful emphasis to Swift's shaven yet still stubborn beard. The familiar jowl has developed little since the sitter was captured by Jervas, but the wry ambivalence of mouth is lost on this painter; or perhaps, in fairness to Bindon, it had faded away. He holds a scroll that, in the original, bore the fourth letter by the Drapier; in a contemporary copy, it displays a reference to Gulliver's final voyage. In the background roll Irish hills and symbolic horses play. Swift groaned at the effort of sitting (or rather standing) for this portrait, and looked on it as a mistake. Lord Howth, who commissioned it, was nevertheless delighted, and took pains to ensure that he was not fobbed off with a copy when it was brought to hang in his castle.[63]

The other study, an almost magical drawing by Isaac Whood, a portraitist based in Lincoln's Inn Fields, shows the friend of Pope and Gay. The stolid militancy of the Howth portrait is entirely absent, and the ineffable creator of the Drapier and Gulliver much more in evidence. Swift is shown in profile. Accordingly, a large soft ear, round-lobed, is central in the composition and appropriately so – as the organ that was the source of much of his invention, and also his worst disorders in health. He wears the soft felt cap and loose gown that were the uniform of public figures in a philosophic or artistic guise. His eyelids droop a little; he looks downward. His mouth is almost pouting – as if an interjection has just occurred to him, or just been withheld. The ball of his jaw is relaxed, relieving the face of the somewhat square, moralistic aspect it took on in the poorer copies of Jervas's canvases. His collar is open, the nape of his neck fleshy and oddly vulnerable. Swift's eyebrows, such a strong feature in other studies, are pronounced yet much lighter here. Maybe Whood was idealizing his sitter; or maybe releasing him from the near-caricature that appears in Bindon's reading of Swift's figure for Howth.

Swift's words and actions, and contemporary responses to him, bear out both representations during this late period, the velvety writer and the titanic patriot. The unintentional roughness of Bindon's picture was arguably the more readily seen as Swift passed his seventieth birthday, evident in the angry chief turning his back on the shocked Primate at the Lord Mayor's dinner. This blunt foe of minced words speaks out very clearly in a denunciation of the Pilkingtons, who divorced messily the following winter. Mr Pilkington had acquired a mistress of independent means, and had caught his wife alone in her bedroom with Robert Adair, a surgeon. 'He proved the falsest Rogue, and she the most profligate Whore in either Kingdom,' was Swift's last word (almost) on the couple. Moreover, he blamed Delany for introducing them to him in the first place.[64]

With almost the same frankness Swift berated his London publisher, Motte, for protesting against his arrangements in Dublin with Faulkner. Motte felt he had the prior claim on Swift's works. But Swift had no sympathy – this was another instance of Englishmen fixing the game yet still claiming foul play. 'You send what Books you please hither,' he chided, 'and the Booksellers here can send nothing to you that is written here.'

> As this is absolute Oppression, if I were a bookseller in this Town
> [Dublin], I would use all the safe Means to reprint London Books, and
> run them to any Town in England that I could, because whoever neither
> offends the Laws of God, or the Country he liveth in, committeth no
> Sin.[65]

Such fighting talk belongs to the stolid figure set forth by Bindon. Without the lasting art and dexterity typified in Whood's image of Swift, however, the stout pugnacity voiced above, as in so many other instances, could have had no rhetorical effect. And a gentler character can be heard very distinctly in Swift's farewell letters to Orrery in 1737. His young friend, who had never been quite well since his near-fatal excess of dancing the year before, was leaving for what looked like being a long period in England. Swift was touched by Orrery's valedictions: with no Sheridan close by, and his friendship with Delany at a low point, he would miss the Earl's learning and refinements.

> You will never be quiet until you have broken my heart ... All your
> Kindnesses and Praises and Acknowledgements, ought to have come
> out of my Mouth and from my Heart to Your Lordship. But as a Friend
> is called a second half, you have been writing your own Character and
> mistook it for mine.[66]

Such casual metaphysics might be dismissed as a courtier's merest formalities; certainly the letter lacks the real and often downright rude easiness that marks out Swift's friendliest letters. Yet the note of tenderness, one Swift generally suppressed, seems authentic.

Swift had entrusted Orrery with a package of manuscripts to carry to England. Not new writing, but two works he had nursed for decades.

One was his long-cherished *History of the Four Last Years of the Queen*, the vindication of the Oxford–Bolingbroke ministry he had been prevented from publishing in 1714. Deane Swift's tutor at St Mary Hall, Oxford, William King, was eager to see the book, and had long awaited the chance to read it. As a Jacobite he was keen to see it in print as a work that would serve as a vessel of truth, truth that would be baneful for the ruling order. The second Earl of Oxford, though, despite his great affection and respect for Swift, was unhappy at the controversy publication would bring both to his family and his father's record. Oxford and a leading survivor of the ministry, Erasmus Lewis, urged Swift to keep his *History* from the press; and shortly even Dr King accepted that all concerned in the endeavour would face ruin.[67] Snorting at William III in a verse libel, as Swift had done, was something like swearing in public – an uncouth act. Advancing an old Tory version of the early century, in the dignified form of a chronicle, was to raise a flag of sedition.

So history repeated itself, and, as in the last months of Tory power, Swift's case for the lost ministry was stifled. Time, he hardly realized, had moved on: his diagnosis of the fall of the Tories was, it seemed, unwanted. Meanwhile, the other book in Orrery's care proved much more congenial. The assiduous Earl handed Mrs Barber in London the manuscript of a set of dialogues entitled *A Compleat Collection of Genteel and Ingenious Conversation*, and the work passed smoothly into print in 1738, to great acclaim. Swift had mentioned redrafting these comic yet highly programmatic scenes to Gay and Pope early in the decade, and stated that he had begun assembling materials for them twenty-eight years earlier. The dialogues were, as he claimed, a 'perfection of folly'.[68] *Polite Conversation*, as the book was always known, reads like a social comedy of the school of Congreve or Wycherley. A reader skipping the long (though very entertaining) introduction would, however, notice that the drama is almost plotless. A group of friendly acquaintances, revolving around Lord and Lady Smart, meet in St James's Park. We are presented to, among others, Lord Sparkish and Mr Neverout, Miss Notable and Lady Answerall. They pass the time of day until invitations to dinner are made. The company reunite at the Smarts' townhouse for the second act-like dialogue; remain together for tea in the third, and then assemble for cards. Play continues, without conversation, into the night. The dialogues are enjoyably bound together by the sheer quality of the lines, which are nevertheless for the most part timeworn and proverbial if not entirely clichéd. But the text sparkles from the way a character always finds an expression, however hackneyed, to answer or expose the absurdity of an old saw uttered by another. The result is a satirical, yet oddly loving compendium of tired jokes refreshed by context and combination.

| | |
|---|---|
| *Colonel Atwit.* | Miss, pray how old are you? |
| *Miss Notable.* | Why I am as old as my Tongue, and a little older than my Teeth. |
| | [. . .] |
| *Colonel Atwit.* | But is it certain that Sir John Blunderbuss is dead at last? |
| *Lord Smart.* | Yes, or he's sadly wrong'd; for they have bury'd him. |
| *Miss Notable.* | Why, if he be dead, he'll eat no more Bread.[69] |

Readers can simply take pleasure in a verbal toy-box, one holding trinkets and play-things collected and modified over decades of social afternoons and evenings in which time had to be passed as agreeably as possible. There is no saying when exactly the above lines were written. Rather than reflecting Swift's art at a particular moment or period, they testify to an ear for natural speech demonstrated over a lifetime – the ear so delicately emphasized in Whood's fine drawing. *Polite Conversation* is, at one level, a shining addition to the genre of phrase-books, word-hoards and collections of proverbs that had been popular in England since Elizabethan times. It is a record of parlour-talk and table-chat. Readers may also sense that overall the joke is on the way that so much of everyday speech consists of stock phrases. This was the comic purpose Swift shared with Gay in August 1731, namely 'to reduce the whole politeness, wit, humour & style of England into a short System for the use of all persons of quality, and particularly the Maids of Honour'.[70] (The ladies in this coveted place at Court had always seemed ideal targets to Swift for a prank-publication of one sort or another.[71]) The uneventful play is framed by another fiction: for the dialogues actually comprise a 'treatise' embodying the life's work of one of Swift's most dedicated, programmatic and self-assured projectors. Simon Wagstaff informs us in the introduction of the many decades he has spent collecting the purest 'Flowers of Wit and Language' that England and the English tongue might supply the modern young person of quality. As such, Wagstaff has equipped all such beginners with a comprehensive resource-book, containing a quip for every possible social eventuality. He is fulsome with compliments about the eloquence of many people and places Swift considered utterly detrimental to the English language, notably Bishop Burnet.[72] The book is not, then, a guide to the garden of rhetoric, but a skit, a bundle of quick, sloppy recipes.

In the abstract, as a satirical device, *Polite Conversation* is almost another product of the Lagado Academy. Wagstaff's scheme is similar in nature to the bizarre and unworkable framework containing all the words of the Laputan language on intersecting wires. The professor who invents this machine claims it will allow the user to write anything on any subject without any study whatsoever.[73] Equally, Wagstaff believes his conversations hold everything his readers might ever find necessary to say in polite company – though he warns that they will need to memorize the entire work and rehearse the mannerisms that go with every particular phrase.[74] Few criticisms of culture could be as stark as the Lagado language contraption; through Wagstaff, Swift commented on the banality and emptiness of thought in supposedly superior dinner and drawing rooms, but with an elaboration of tone and fulness of execution that are far-removed from the brusque descriptions Gulliver leaves of the errant academics. Though with another end in mind, Swift had clearly shared Wagstaff's long project of setting down phrases: a collector's love of his subject, and even a slightly malicious affection, comes through in the care Swift plainly devoted to his assembly, his perfection of folly. The chatter is lively, compulsively readable and, above all, credible as real talk. The conversations read like transcripts, not entries in a treatise, exceeding the handiwork, if not the perseverance, of a Wagstaff. The surface illusion of *Polite Conversation* as a drama, in other words, holds: here Swift salutes the theatre of his youth and shows that, had he cared to, he might have shone by writing for it.

An external point of interest is his decision to dust off the dialogues a year or two after the death of Congreve in 1729. Swift's words and deeds towards the playwright were invariably kindly, despite Congreve's Whiggishness and voluptuous lifestyle. Nevertheless, Swift frequently gave the impression of restraining an urge to put the younger schoolmate in his place. His final written comments on the younger writer maintained this faint ambivalence. Congreve died at the age of fifty-nine, having lived many years with pain and near-blindness. In 1729 Swift had said one could not wish someone so unwell to have suffered longer; then, blending the tones of parson and rival in letters, he also quietly blamed Congreve for his high-risk affairs and a poor concern for his body that had surely ruined a good constitution.[75]

As Swift had once explained to Gay, *Polite Conversation* originally had a companion piece and counterpart. While his dialogues formed a guide-book for those above stairs, *Directions for Servants* purported to be one for the 'lower orders'. Swift claimed that it would cover 'the whole duty of servants'.[76] In fact, the book showed domestic staff how to cope with and exploit the laziness and injustice of their employers. The *Directions* was not, obviously, out to undermine a fixed hierarchy. Its scheme automatically supported the master's part, and also gave employers hints, indirectly, on how servants might trespass on their virtue.

> If your Master or Lady happen once in their Lives to accuse you wrongfully, you are a happy Servant, for you have nothing more to do, than for every Fault you commit, while you are in their Service, to put them in Mind of that false Accusation, and protest yourself equally innocent in the Present Case.[77]

The servants' lot is nonetheless treated with sympathy, and there are shrewd pointers on how those 'in service' might make the best of it. The last dozen bottles to be got from the hogshead, by prudent tilting of the dregs, are the butler's 'perquisite'. When the hay and oats at the inn are good, a groom should say they are bad, and so 'get the name of a diligent servant'.[78] The housemaids' and chambermaids' ordeals with slovenly mistresses are treated sympathetically. The *Directions* show Swift entering into the minutiae of house-management, and predictably two of his priorities are thrift and cleanliness. The butler, he says, should 'clean glasses &c.' in the dark, to save candles. Swift understands what hard work the chambermaid has to do, and so gives advice on how she can observe good hygiene and also conserve her energies. 'Making Beds in hot Weather is a very laborious Work, and you will be apt to sweat; therefore, when you find the Drops running down from your Forehead, wipe them off with a Corner of the Sheet, that they may not be seen on the Bed.'[79] Small wonder that a writer with such an eye for the smallest problems of practical existence never felt inclined to produce an abstract theological work of the kind expected of high-ranking clerics. Like *Polite Conversation*, *Directions to Servants* is filled with direct observation of life in Swift's time. The two works combine satire on folly and foibles with sound advice: *Polite Conversation* supplies good lines, and *Directions to Servants* offers advice that seems sensible. They satirize the 'advice' genre – while still functioning as handbooks.

Swift had admitted to Gay that completing the *Directions* would take a lot of time and strength, and in the end he lacked enough of both.

Some of the entries are mini-fictions, in which Swift really enters into the predicament of the household servant concerned; some are mere notes. The work was published, in questionable form, by Faulkner in 1745 – and rapidly pirated. Despite its unfinished state, Swift was eager to see the draft in print before he died. The manuscript, though, eluded him amid his papers. He was fairly sure that Faulkner had already seen it, and late in 1739 sought his help: 'I wish you could give me some intelligence of it, because, my Memory is quite gone.'[80]

By the turn of the decade Swift was admitting what others had been noticing for some time. Back in 1737, Orrery had confirmed Pope's fears about their friend's memory, and confided his own about the advantage some 'designing people' sought to take of its failing powers.[81] One person in particular drew his suspicions, a breezy-mannered forty-year-old cleric who had ingratiated himself to the point of treating the deanery as his home whenever he came to Dublin. Should someone care to abuse his trust and welcome, the elderly Dean, it appeared, was easy prey. His lapses in memory became more common over the next few years. Swift remained socially vivid when well – lavishing his typically despairing good wishes, for example, on Orrery, when the Earl returned to Ireland to marry a very wealthy heiress. Yet his movements slowed and his spells of puzzlement increased. He knew it, and self-awareness crackled strongly in admissions of muddle. 'You are to suppose,' he informed Pope in May 1739, 'for the little time I shall live, that my memory is entirely gone, and especially of any thing that was told me last night, or this morning.'[82] One sad by-product of age gaining pace on him was that he was unable to regulate disputes among his followers. By the end of 1739 Delany had withdrawn in offence at Swift's stinginess – claiming that the Dean now begrudged old friends a single bottle over dinner – and at the circle of minders Orrery called the 'designing ones'. These included Mrs Whiteway and Deane Swift.

The most singular absence in Swift's house was a man he had expected to predecease by many years. Sheridan died in 1738, claimed by an asthmatic disorder. They had not been perfect friends for some time, and had seen one another only occasionally since Sheridan relocated to Cavan. The letters between them surviving up to the spring of 1738 suggest, nevertheless, that their basic affection was undiminished: two months before Sheridan died, apparently in the home of a former pupil, Swift spoke of him as 'the best scholar in both kingdoms'.[83] He was promising to pass on the recipe for a medicine for asthma John Barber had recommended. In the same letter he wrote defiantly of his own periodic good

health, apart from 'cruel deafness'. He still walked anything from six to
ten miles at a stretch. The hyperbole about Sheridan – for all the schoolmaster's great learning – possibly revealed foreboding on Swift's part: it
reads like a regretful epitaph. For a last glimpse of the spirit that connected the two men it is better to look back at a letter from Cavan in
May 1736. With characteristic openness Sheridan informed Swift of the
agony he was suffering from a bad case of piles, and wrote a merry bit
of doggerel about the goings-on among the chickens in his yard.[84]

# 14. Sanctuary

O spare me a little, that I may recover my strength: before I go hence, and be no more seen.
          – 'Order for the Burial of the Dead' (1662)[1]

I

Just south of the Liffey, and a short way west of the modern city centre, two hospital buildings dating from Swift's lifetime, and one from just after, stand on the fringes of what was once the village of Kilmainham. The district is now best known to tourists for its converted prison. The largest, the Royal Hospital, built in the 1680s, lies to the west of the old village; the other two, Dr Steevens's Hospital and St Patrick's, closer together, are to be found to the east. The Royal was founded as a hostel for old and invalided soldiers of the Irish Army. Its wide granite front, given an open-eyed look by tall round top windows on a projecting portico, is approached down a long formal avenue, which originally ran to the riverside. Founded in 1720, Dr Steevens's Hospital is an imitation in miniature of the closed courtyard plan of the Royal Hospital – much smaller, much less grand, with a pilastered yet oddly slab-like façade, and a more functional bearing. This later institution was established as a general hospital by Grizel Steevens, using money left for the purpose by her physician brother Richard. 'Madam' Steevens, as she was always known, lived in rooms on the left-hand side of the gate. She wore a veil when she left the hospital, to emphasize the retired life she had chosen, although Dubliners preferred the story that she had magically been given the face of a pig when her mother scorned a beggar-woman. Swift knew her; he became a trustee of her hospital in 1721.[2]

St Patrick's Hospital, smaller again, is built from grey granite and has an astylar front – that is, no columns or pilasters. The hospital building began offering refuge and treatment to the mentally ill from the late 1750s. All three establishments aimed at improving the lot of the sick and elderly. More precisely, however, the Royal Hospital was planned as the necessary attribute of an imperial capital, in an effort to match the magnificence of Les Invalides in Paris: the Royal Hospital Chelsea was driven by the same exemplar.[3] Dr Steevens's and St Patrick's hospitals, meanwhile, though striving for architectural kinship with their grander neighbour, sprang up within a more pragmatic and municipally minded effort to bolster Dublin's basic urban facilities. In a converted house on the far side of the river the same incipient trend brought the opening of Britain and Ireland's first maternity hospital, the Rotunda, by Bartholomew Mosse, a physician who died young in 1759.[4]

St Patrick's Hospital was Swift's hospital. The care of the sick, particularly of psychologically unwell people, had long preoccupied him. He had been a governor of Bedlam since 1714. In an essay of 1728, he used the piteous conditions typical of hospitals at the time as a metaphor for the way things were run in Ireland: 'I have known an Hospital, where all the Household-officers grew rich; while the Poor, for whose sake it was built, were almost starving for want of Food and Raiment.' What the well-fed wardens of such an edifice were to their wretched inmates, the chief officers of the kingdom, sent in from England, were to the people 'who have the misfortune to be born here'.[5] A hospital, then, was one of Swift's essential figures for his homeland. A well-run mental hospital was to be a small-scale, long-term act of finite redress, which would stand at the same time as a physical piece of rhetoric. The point was further refined by the specific kind of hospital he wanted to endow: it would be a home for the mentally ill, and thus highlight the disorder he saw as the worst of Ireland's many complaints.

He made no secret of the plan. He most famously expressed his aims for his estate at the end of the 'Verses on the Death of Dr Swift'.

> He gave the little Wealth he had
> To build a House for Fools and Mad:
> And shew'd by one satiric Touch,
> No Nation wanted it so much.
> That Kingdom he hath left his Debtor,
> I wish it soon may have a Better.[6]

Supporting the gesture of that single 'satiric Touch' Swift planned the hospital with all his customary shrewd pragmatism. Mastering the stat-

utes of St Patrick's and the complex operations of the cathedral had long
ago perfected a keen lawyerly and administrative bent, as well as that
'infusion of the alderman' he repeatedly advocated to all officers of state.
A friend of the Scriblerians once described him as dwindling from his
task of 'inflaming kingdoms' to the stature of an 'Irish solicitor': Lord
Bathurst imagined the Dean going about his business in a dirty brown
coat with a little green portmanteau under his arm. Swift's respect for
orderly business was such that he could take this jest as a compliment:
only the thought of dirt on his coat might have troubled him.[7] So, while
declaring that no country needed a good lunatic asylum more than Ireland, he also accounted for the possibility that there might not be enough
suitably deranged people to fill the hospital. In his will, the last version
of which he made in May 1740, he directed that 'if a sufficient Number
of Idiots and Lunaticks cannot readily be found', other chronically ill or
disabled 'incurables' should be admitted. As well as common sense,
Swift's provision on the uses of St Patrick's reflected an older, wider
sense of the purposes a 'hospital' might serve, as a hospice for all kinds
of distressed as well as sick people. At the same time, he was aware of
the growing consensus on sound medical practice, and had surely been
thoroughly advised by the physicians of the adjacent Dr Steevens's Hospital, for he stipulated that infectious cases must by no means be received
into the building.[8]

The organization of St Patrick's illustrates not only Swift's managerial
capacities but also the substantial means he commanded by the end of
his life. Through careful planning in the late 1730s he successfully petitioned the city to grant a plot for the hospital in 1737. He set by a sum
for construction, and the yearly revenue would come from investments
Swift directed his executors to make in further land and property.[9] Thus
he made it relatively easy for the trustees – all municipal officers – to
make the hospital for 'Idiots and Lunaticks' a reality after his death. The
cruelty of the diction here belongs not to Swift but his age, since the very
recent days of sympathetic psychotherapy were quite unimagined. In the
context of his own time, his purpose was still manifestly altruistic – with
just a touch of satire on the national state of mind. Nevertheless, the
definition and numbering of idiots and lunatics was almost as fluid in
the mid-1700s as the diagnosis of pathologies remains in our own time.
It varied as much with social class, age and sex as manifest symptoms.
The inmates Swift imagined for his hospital might be the chained souls
synonymous with Bedlam, or the vociferous captives he describes hurling their excrement in *A Tale of a Tub*. But they might also be 'eccentrics'

who presented no danger but rather a target for scorn to the public, and who lacked a family to look after them. Such residents could look to St Patrick's for a bed and a meal and some basic dignities. Fitting this profile, for example, was a well-known Dublin figure for whom Swift's hospital was too late. Talbot Edgeworth, good-looking, finely dressed, insisted that a certain table in Lucas's coffee-house on Cork Hill be reserved for him as his personal *Stammtisch*. He would set down the name of any man he found sitting there and vow to fight a duel with him when the usurper came of age. He found himself extremely handsome: 'They may look and die,' he said of Dublin's women. Edgeworth was a gentleman, and his family had means. He was the ancestor of two well-known writers: Richard Lovell Edgeworth and, more famously, Maria, the author of *Castle Rackrent*. Yet his background gave him little protection from an unfortunate life and a sad end. 'In short, he was the jest of the men, and the contempt of the women. This unhappy man, being neglected by his relations in his lunacy, was taken into custody during his madness and confined in Bridewell, Dublin, where he died.'[10] The conditions in St Patrick's may have been only a little more comfortable than the city jail. But the hospital offered decencies of the kind Swift deemed essential, and it marked a small step across the wide haunted territory that separated his time from the attitudes and treatments that seem 'decent' today.

## 2

The satirical statement he made for posterity with the hospital depended on a contrast: the distinction between a patron who was sane – or sane enough to see that Ireland's deprivations were crazy – and a deranged majority who accepted things as they were. In his last years, however, and subsequent decades, the view became widespread that it was Swift who belonged in a madhouse.

For almost ten years before the death of Sheridan in 1738, Swift's acquaintance had remarked on the growing strangeness of his ways: and for quite some time quirks such as the blend of suspicion in his hospitality, his scrutiny of servants in the mirror opposite the dinner table or a familiarity with guests crossing the border into rudeness had all been part, as it were, of his act. At some indefinite point Swift stopped merely putting on a show, and such eccentricities became settled character traits – almost as much as his unshakeable concern with cleanliness or fitness.

On Swift's side, these tendencies gained strength as he stopped caring what people thought of them. He had always combined inflexibility on what he saw as points of true principle with a disregard for social fopperies. In his relationship with Esther Johnson, most notably, having satisfied all due proprieties with their respective living arrangements, he was quite prepared to brazen out the gossips of the town. In his late sixties and seventies, this approach simply hardened and grew more elaborate as he became a living myth. As Dean Gulliver, as Dean Drapier, he was untouchable: the supposed refinements of a society he had shown was debased meant little to him. In purely literary terms, the publication of the scatological 'Dressing Room' poems between 1732 and 1734 represents Swift's abandonment (or loss) of a filter. The friends and helpers who lived close to him from day to day, notably Martha Whiteway or Anne Ridgeway, rode out the storms and embarrassments that ensued. Patrick Delany, or even the Earl of Orrery, who felt they outranked such attendants, took Swift's aberrations closer to heart. His tight-fistedness and lapses of decorum were harder to bear. He was getting old, reaching a grand age, even, by any reasonable average of the day; moreover Alzheimer's, or a related form of dementia, seems to have begun its advance. Inevitably, frustrations increased and trusted abilities failed. He was as deaf and giddy as ever, and for longer. The waywardness of memory proved a torment. The elements were all in place for the legend of the lunatic Dean.

An image took root of Swift raving through his final years. The origins in fact of this impression lay in a dramatic episode and an agonizing illness in the course of 1742.

By the beginning of that year, Swift's physical state had weakened considerably. Along with his old symptoms, he now suffered sporadically, and excruciatingly, from the pain of gout. Intellectually, notwithstanding his troubles with memory, he remained alert, although taking an active part in the cathedral's life was gradually proving too much. His opinion was sought on key decisions, and his signature applied to the necessary papers. The year 1740 proved a watershed when, possibly from sheer physical incapacity, he stopped writing long letters. In 1739, however, he was still vigorous to the height of his remaining powers, *strenuum pro virili*, as he put it in his epitaph. He fended off the persecutors of one Reverend Throp, and supported the campaign of Alexander Macaulay to be elected MP for the University of Dublin. Macaulay, a gifted lawyer with a fine career ahead of him at the Bar, was a vocal and compelling critic of British rule. Swift contributed a preface to a pamphlet by Macaulay on the Irish agricultural problem, published by Faulkner, in 1737. The preface consisted of a few lines; no more than a seal of approval.[11] Macaulay requested Swift's further endorsement while fighting for election in 1739. At one point, before a dubious re-count was arranged, it seemed that he had taken one of the prize symbolic seats in the Irish House of Commons. The closeness of the result, at the cost of much work and money from government, was a testimony to Macaulay's quality and also the force of Swift's blessing. He appeared publicly at Macaulay's side, and canvassed influential friends. Swift liked Macaulay's politics and especially his defence of the clergy. He bequeathed Macaulay an appropriate object of controversy, the golden box – the tinder-box, as it proved – in which the Freedom of the City had been presented to him. The story goes that he also gave Macaulay perhaps the most treasured item in his personal museum: the pen-knife Guiscard thrust at Harley in 1711.[12]

The winter of 1739/40 was then extremely hard. On his birthday, Swift graciously received poems in his honour and endured a 21-gun salute. The day before Christmas Eve he assisted Archbishop Hoadly at an ordination ceremony in the cathedral.[13] He may have entered the spacious darkness of St Patrick's only a few further times. Towards New Year, a howling cold came in. The Liffey froze, and snow deepened. The poor of Dublin and the country beyond were pressed to the limits of survival, and countless of them were unable to bear it. The burghers raised what money they could, and Swift gave generously.[14] On 12 January, however, he fretted when a young prebendary, John Lyon, one of his vital assistants, 'worried' him to put some extra shillings in the pot: typically, generosity beat avarice, and he gave twenty.[15] Swift's will mentions a number of thick beaver hats in his wardrobe: they were needed.

Despite a bad cold, Swift suffered less during the freeze than Martha Whiteway, who had developed rheumatism. Later in the year, after returning to her post to help Lyon with the Dean's deep-drifting paperwork, she informed Pope again that Swift's memory was 'much impaired'. A day or so earlier Swift had written that it was 'utterly lost'; and with his old mock-curmudgeonliness told another friend to ignore the 'gasconades' of his beggarly cousin, reporting that she had gone so far as to snatch away his pen. Yet in her private letter to the poet Whiteway made it clear that an hour after reading a new letter from Pope Swift had forgotten all about it. There were spaces in his day that he could not account for. He could no longer manage the correspondence that came in regularly; answering a letter from William Pulteney, the opposition leader, was beyond him. When health and mood permitted, however, he was still sociable: the company of a young attractive clergyman, Francis Wilson, a relatively recent addition to the deanery regulars, was a pleasure to him. And Mrs Whiteway claimed 'his health is as good as can be expected, free from the tortures of old age.'[16] Swift resisted this verdict. In April he was struck acutely with his gout, as he supposed Whiteway would call it (he suspected something much worse); and was laid still lower by another attack in July. 'All I can say is, that I am not in torture,' he wrote in his last preserved personal letter, 'but I daily and hourly expect it.'[17] He made his last will early in May 1740, in a sensible precaution against his memory's growing lacunae: 'of sound mind, though weak in body', he described himself.[18] The legal detail of the hospital scheme was finalized. Solid bequests were made to Whiteway and Anne Ridgeway, other friends and legatees, and also Esther Johnson's old companion, Rebecca Dingley. Symbolic gifts were to be sent to Pope, Oxford and Orrery, the Grattans and other Irish friends, for the most part clergymen. These keepsakes, many of great value, naturally illuminate a trove the deanery had held for many years. Some of them had surely travelled from Goodrich or from Swift's grandfather's period attending Charles I in Wales. A portrait of the sacred King, which Swift was sure was an original Van Dyck, went to steady James Stopford. Amid the inner guard there were no obvious omissions. There was no mention, though, of his sister Jane Fenton, for she had died in 1738. Swift had been paying her an annuity of £15, but with contempt; for he had refused to see her for years. He never got over his displeasure at 'that woman' marrying a tradesman.[19] Arguments were for the most part forestalled since most of Swift's estate was destined for his hospital. His friends had greater fears for his more ephemeral assets, his social standing and literary relics, during whatever time remained to him.

None of Swift's entourage, Whiteway, Worrall, Stopford or Lyon, were what the Earl of Orrery called 'designing people' – none of his trusted aides, that is, bar one.[20] The Reverend Francis Wilson was affable, pleasant-looking and courteous. He was the Rector of Clondalkin, a County Dublin parish about ten miles west of the city, and the Prebendary of Kilmactalway in St Patrick's. He was one of dozens of colleagues and acquaintances who made up the background weather of Swift's professional life in the 1720s and '30s, but he became more prominent in 1737. Much of the property belonging to Swift's deanery lay in the vicinity of Clondalkin, and so Swift entrusted Wilson with the job of collecting his tithes. In return he made a room in the deanery permanently available for Wilson when he visited town.[21] From 1740 on Swift would leave his house only for a few hours at a time, when he would still insist on a good walk. Wilson's visits were evidently frequent, and he must accordingly be reckoned one of the people Swift saw most regularly as his active circuit contracted. 'Dr Wilson and I are both very uneasy to find no better message from you,' Swift wrote to Whiteway during her rheumatic illness in January 1740.[22] Back in 1738, Swift had already referred to him as 'my daily Spunge and inmate'. The rough critical note is of the same tenor as Swift's reference to Whiteway as his 'beggarly cousin'; that is, proof of Swift's affection, not Wilson's villainy. His protégé had prevailed on him to supply Lyon, who managed Swift's alms, with a few more coins, and Swift did so with approving grudging-ness of Wilson's 'pernicious vice and advice'.[23]

His dedicated followers continued to manage his affairs; but in the distribution of trust none had exclusive care of the Dean, nor saw any reason yet to monitor the others. But in the second half of 1740 Mrs Whiteway confided her suspicions to Orrery that some of Swift's papers appeared to be missing. A collection of the Dean's letters was being pre-pared by Faulkner, evidently with Swift's consent. 'There is a time in life when people can hear no reason,' Whiteway said of their ailing friend, 'entre nous.'[24] It was still too soon to say openly that Swift's consent now meant little. Reading somewhat between the lines, Orrery under-stood her as suggesting that someone close to him had purloined materials. That she was incriminating Wilson was still too much to infer, since she told Orrery that she had shared her misgivings with one other, who was 'such a friend to Swift' as the Earl, and that person might well have been Wilson. At a distance, Pope was suggesting Whiteway herself was to blame for irregularities in Swift's escritoire. Orrery, though profi-cient in equivocation, made a show of taking her seriously: 'Do you suspect, madam, any person that is about him for so base a piece of theft as that of stealing papers?'[25]

Her worries, in this instance, were misplaced. Pope was taking advan-tage of Whiteway's strict conscience as part of his effort to screen his involvement in Faulkner's collection. It was one of the webs of white lies a chronically sick man allowed himself for the sake of his only offspring – his writings. Meanwhile the autumn and onset of winter in 1740 was a horrible time for Orrery: he recovered from gout only for his two young sons to catch smallpox, and his anxiety over Whiteway's reports most likely diminished in consequence. In any case, he was part of Pope's machinations. Knowingly or not, Orrery himself had taken the missing letters to England in 1737, with Swift's consent, in order for Pope to make copies. Swift had parted with them reluctantly, but realized they would form the core of a published volume at some point. He and Pope (and Bolingbroke) had always corresponded in a manner that now suggests a public conversation or joint interview between two literary celebrities. Neither, however, wished to seem like the initiator in sending letters to the press. On this occasion, an unauthorized edition suited their intentions very nicely – although Swift was aggrieved to let go of treasured manuscripts, letters from old friends, and Pope was determined to receive his share of the profits.[26]

Exactly how immoral or indeed criminal Wilson's actions were with regard to Swift's archives will always be uncertain. Others besides Wilson were acting surreptitiously. Giving away or mislaying his remaining papers was all too easy for Swift in his worsening confusion, and it was all Whiteway could do to maintain the order she did. Wilson was seen by servants carrying some books from the deanery in a portmanteau that had been empty when he arrived; but these were quite feasibly conscious loans or gifts. Among other bequests to Wilson were his 'best bible', valuable editions of Plato and Clarendon's *History of the Great Rebellion*.[27]

The next year passed, and Swift's decline steepened. For some years now a trusted colleague, John Wynne, had taken over most of the decanal duties as Swift's subdean.[28] At the end of January 1742 Swift drew up an order to Wynne exhorting him to improve standards of discipline within the cathedral choir. Preparations were being made for the premiere of Handel's *Messiah*, and numbers of the Vicars Choral and choirboys had been participating, and also giving impromptu concerts on their own account at indecorous venues around the city. It was alleged that Swift himself had licensed one troupe of players and singers from his chapter to 'assist at a club of Fidlers in Fishamble Street'. In the order, Swift roundly denied such a notion – though perhaps with a qualm that made clarification necessary to forestall any repetition. At risk of expulsion no musicians connected with St Patrick's were to appear as songsters, fiddlers, drummers or 'in any sonal quality'. A second draft of the order moderated the angry tone of the first, which Swift ended with a moving entreaty that his subordinates help him to preserve the dignity of his office as well as the honour of their chapter. The document, the last for the cathedral Swift oversaw, was witnessed by Francis Wilson and one other priest.[29] It offers a parallel with one of Swift's earliest actions as dean, in disciplining the Vicars Choral for their entrepreneurial tendencies towards cathedral property back in 1713.[30] The singers had long

been one of the most volatile groups in the life of the two Dublin cathedrals sharing their services. The Vicars Choral enjoyed the status of
belonging to one of the most prestigious foundations in Britain or Ireland; yet historically doubt had surrounded whether such a vicar even
needed to be ordained.[31] Although based in a clerical realm, they hovered ambiguously close to the secular one. And this was an ambiguity
Swift could never tolerate – even while he smiled at Nonconformist
assertions that music brought popery into a church.[32]

   Rippling through the 1742 document is Swift's instinctive revulsion
at Handel's broader artistic purpose. While always admitting ignorance
and insensitivity in matters of music, partly through temperament, partly
as a result of his impaired hearing, he was unflaggingly diligent in obtaining the best choristers and musicians for the choir that served Dublin's
two cathedrals. As to their role, moreover, and the music it allowed them
to perform, he was inflexible. The aspect of the gathering Germanic tradition that seems most attractive now, the interaction between sacred
themes and secular forms in Handel and Bach, was all but wholly abhorrent to Swift. He had enforced a one-way traffic between holy and
worldly things his entire life. His satire had advanced the ends of the
High Anglican Church, whereas Handel's oratorio was akin to the very
reverse: it was like Swift infiltrating the speculative, 'free-thinking' tendencies of Restoration satire into the province of the work of serious
theology that he had always declined to write. A stand against such
innovations therefore needed to be made, even though ultimately Swift's
embargo on the *Messiah* indicated a loosening grip. For in the end members of the choir did perform in Handel's premiere in the Music Hall at
Fishamble Street.[33]

   Looking back, Francis Wilson's involvement in Swift's life seems sin-
isterly ingratiating. Stifled accusations, of the theft of books and even of
tithes, cling to his career. There were also suspicions that he coveted
Wynne's post as subdean. Yet it is also possible to ask whether he really
extorted anything more than the hospitality extended from a simple
wish for pleasant companionship. If Swift's other Irish friendships are
any measure, Wilson also most likely took a share of ribbing and quite
possibly rage from his host and patron. It seems, though, that Wilson
was conscious of the surveillance he was starting to attract. Some in the
deanery guardroom noticed that until Swift's memory became completely unreliable, Wilson would always conduct business with Mrs
Whiteway present; when Swift's mind failed him, Wilson made and took
payments in private with the Dean. It is just possible that Swift himself

saw a swindle here and there, only for a cloud to return; and that one such lucid moment occurred on the afternoon of 14 June 1742, as he shared a coach with Wilson back to Dublin. That morning Wilson had called at the deanery. Swift expressed, said Wilson afterwards, a wish to take the air, and then dine in Wilson's rectory at Clondalkin. Since Swift's coachman could not be found – or so Wilson claimed – they set off in a hackney cab. Swift's footman Richard Brennan followed them on horseback an hour later. Such a departure was exceptional: Swift now only travelled by a coach he had bought when riding finally became impossible for him, and would never leave the deanery unaccompanied by Mrs Ridgeway. At Newland, Wilson's house, Brennan found the Rector plying the Dean with an extra glass of wine. For almost half a year, Swift had never taken more than two large bumpers, amounting to about half a pint in total. Wilson pooh-poohed a whisper of caution from Brennan; and, although Swift could hardly walk (Brennan said) to the coach after dinner, his friend insisted that he take a heavy glass of brandy at an alehouse on their way home. Swift's friends told Brennan to suppress these alcoholic details in the sworn affidavit he presently gave on what ensued. The coach had not gone much further when Brennan heard shouting – Wilson's voice first, he believed – from inside the cab.

The whole trip, it seemed, had been the prelude to a proposition. As they returned to Dublin, Wilson asked Swift to appoint him subdean of St Patrick's in place of Wynne. There is something a little out of place here: if Wilson was the shrewd con he now appeared to be, he would have known such a tactic was pointless. Almost any promise Swift made now, especially while drunk, would be quickly forgotten. A promise made in front of witnesses would be another matter; but there were none, except for the driver above and a footman following the coach at a varying distance of as much as fifty yards. Wilson, though, was evidently wheedling about something. Another sentence caught by Brennan – 'Sir, I am paying you your money!' – indicated that Swift had put Wilson on the defensive. Within moments the two men, dean and disciple, were evidently struggling. Wilson yelled at the driver – 'villain, rascal' – to stop the coach. The driver stopped his horses, a process long enough to allow the tussle in the coach to continue for a few moments more; upon which Wilson jumped out, cursing wildly, saying that no man would strike him. He would cut the throat of the King himself at such treatment, he declared, shouting now at the window. He called Swift an old blockhead and villain, and stomped off, repeating his imprecations, after ordering the driver to take Swift home.

When Wilson offered his side of the story, he insisted that Swift had treated him in his usual very friendly fashion all day – but then suddenly burst out crying that he was the devil and should go to hell. Swift struck him, scratched him and tore off his wig: Wilson bore the attack until Swift went for his eyes, when he ordered the coach to stop and left the scene, uttering 'natural expressions of resentment and indignation'.[34] The coach had pulled over in the parish of Kilmainham, so pregnant with future meaning for Swift. The coachman got down and Brennan rode up, and further support was soon thick on the ground. Deane Swift informed Orrery: 'The noise of this bustle in the Street, sudden as it was, drew a small handful of the Common people together, who have since declared, that if they had known it was the Dean whom Wilson had abused, they would have torn the Wretch to pieces.' Wilson did well to get away from the 'justice of a gratefull people'. Some of the crowd, it seems, escorted the Dean home. A quarter of an hour later, on reaching the deanery, Swift was heard asking, 'Where is Doctor Wilson? Ought not the Doctor to be here this afternoon?' He had no recollection of what had passed. No time at all was lost in establishing Wilson's iniquity: Brennan's account was clear, Wilson had (after all) run off, and the next morning one of Swift's arms was black and blue.[35]

He may not have been entirely innocent of tampering with the deanery accounts, but Wilson's version of events should not be rejected entirely. It is quite possible that the trip to Clondalkin was not the first of its kind. Wilson, Swift's crony, may have been following the Dean's request by supplying an extra bumper of wine, or sneaking him out – away from the watchful eyes of Ridgeway or Whiteway – on other occasions. An important factor is the diverse nature of what counted as affectionate or friendly exchanges with Swift: a volley of insults on either side was not altogether uncommon. Nor is it unlikely that Swift was indeed the first to rage: the memory of his explosion at Laetitia Pilkington in his 'vineyard' comes suggestively to mind. The anger of a younger man at a similar tirade is hardly unfathomable. A lost story of abusive asides and rejoinders may underlie the words 'blockhead' and 'rascal' that escaped Wilson: they may have been heard more frequently in Swift's closet, under Wilson's breath, than Brennan realized. Wilson, Brennan said, cried that he would cut Swift's throat, and this shocked everyone. But the anomalous point in Brennan's story is Wilson muttering to him and the driver, after the crescendo, that they should take the old blockhead home.[36] In that parting remark can be heard the lasting, unwilling fondness for a master with whom a servant has spectacularly lost patience. Wilson had a roguish aspect; but so did many Swift liked, men as different as Sheridan, Bolingbroke and Faulkner.

An investigation ensued; but Brennan's testimony was deemed insufficient basis for a prosecution. Wilson kept his benefices and avoided prison. The deanery circle, though clearly harbouring few doubts as to Wilson's guilt, was in the meantime anxious to avoid the fuss of a trial, which would only involve further exposure for Swift. A story later circulated that the Dean's servants if not his friends would allow members of the public to come and look at him while he sat in apparent stupor. The record, however, yields nothing but evidence of a united concern, from staff and friends, to keep Swift away from ungenerous leering eyes. The chief consequence of the attack for Swift was his friends' realization that he needed protecting; if Deane Swift may be trusted, his staunch supporters in the city at large also believed that action needed to be taken on behalf of their hero's dignity. 'So absolutely was he then lost to all reason and memory: and indeed it was the talk of the Town, that a Statute of Lunacy ought to be taken out, to guard the Dean against further insults, and wrongs of all kinds.'[37] Swift was soon declared 'incapable of transacting any business . . . or taking care either of his estate or his person'.[38] He was placed in the care of a committee of guardians, a milder fate than many patients of St Patrick's Hospital would meet. He was still resident at his deanery, and remained dean, and retained the attentions of Mrs Whiteway and the rest of his reliable friends and helpers.

The incident with Wilson made Swift's senility public where it was not common knowledge already. A myth of violent insanity was subsequently concocted from a terrible, but purely physical illness that afflicted him later in the year. In November he developed orbital cellulitis, a disease that brought his body out in large boils and caused his left eye to swell as large as an egg.[39] The pain was so great for a week that it took five people to stop him from ripping out his eyes. A month passed in almost sleepless suffering until a sudden calm returned. He responded to Martha Whiteway's presence with kindness and pleasure; and she asked if she might dine with him. 'To be sure,' he said, 'my old friend.' She was the last person his friends could be sure he recognized.[40]

'His madness appears chiefly in most incessant strains of obscenity,' claimed one outsider.[41] Yet there were no further frenzies. All of Swift's vehemence, in fact, drained from his system after his outing with Wilson; or some time before it, if the claim that he attacked Wilson was indeed the pure invention of a swindler. A stroke or, more likely, a series of brain lesions rendered him passive and, by the end of the year, as the symptoms of orbital cellulitis receded, almost entirely silent. A servant shaved his face, but a long beard on his throat was cut periodically with scissors. He was now almost bald, and in the privacy of his house a white mane running down his neck and upper back was deemed harmless. For three years, he sat, lay or wandered the interior of the deanery. His food was cut for him, and he would never touch it till the servant left the room. He would often be found circling it, pacing around the table, regarding the meat on his plate as something very strange. The authorized few were admitted on visits; Whiteway and Ridgeway kept him company each day. He made just a few more celebrated remarks, apparently after a hard search for words on each occasion; notably when he told Mrs Ridgeway that the celebrations for his birthday in 1742 were 'all folly' and that 'they had better let it alone.' By then he had outlived another younger crony: it seems that Francis Wilson died around this time.

To the world beyond, this muted, perplexed, yet peaceable resident was still a force to be reckoned with and one to be grateful for as well. The ablest of a rising generation saw the scale of Swift's contribution to English literature. 'The first polite prose we have was writ by a man who is still alive,' wrote a young David Hume, clarifying in a note that he was referring to 'Dr Swift'. 'Polite' might not be the first word Swift brings to mind, especially in his later works, but Hume was thinking of his 'elegance and propriety of style', the work Swift had done to refine the expressive capacities of the language itself.[42] Swift had civilized English, which for Hume did not mean endowing it with icy formality but rather enriching its tonal possibilities. Another writer, now in his thirties, Samuel Johnson, began making his name partly by sorties in Swiftian irony. His *Debates in the Senate of Lilliput* is only the most obvious of early works bearing a debt to the then silenced master. His *Vindication* of the Whig Licencers of public theatre is a compelling example of how Johnson both profited from a Swift-style persona that reversed his true position, and was frustrated by the form. He developed his own characteristic voice – liberal yet imperial, expansive, meticulous and reliably sincere – by defining it against such early experiments. Johnson was often presumptuously haughty when writing of Swift; but his moments of subsequent dismissiveness may in fact indicate a nagging sense of inadequacy – of dissatisfaction with his early imitations of the Swiftian mode. His intellect and certainly his scholarship might have been the greater, and he was possibly the wiser man, but as a writer overall he trails far behind Swift. Comparing *Rasselas* to the *Travels* is manifestly rigging the contest. With a touch of envious resentment, Johnson was therefore reserved in his appraisal of Swift as a stylist:

> He studied purity: and though perhaps all his structures are not exact, yet it is not often that solecisms can be found ... His sentences are never too much dilated or contracted; and it will not be easy to find any embarrassment in the complication of his clauses ... He always understands himself: and his reader always understands him.

The great critic denied Swift the 'highest praise'; but when set alongside the other writers subjected to Johnsonian scrutiny, this was coming pretty close. Except in *A Tale of a Tub* – a work spoiled, for Johnson, by its display of 'vehemence and rapidity of mind' – Swift avoided the excesses for which Johnson censured Shakespeare among others. Swift's peculiar brand of intensity, meanwhile, the flirtation with mayhem in his writing, not to mention his unequalled capacity to endow a ludicrous line of argument with an air of steadfast reason, was alien to Johnson's temperament and talents.[43]

The control of syntax and diction deserted Swift. But, while his friends may have based their reports on his best days, he seems to have occupied and endured his state calmly. He spoke no 'nonsense' and did nothing antic or self-harmful. His memory had been clouding for years, and he lost the ability to find names, but he trusted those caring for him and seemed to know their purpose instinctively if not intellectually. They responded to him at the same intuitive level. He called a servant a blockhead for breaking up a large coal Swift declared was a stone: but not angrily, and he showed he was dissatisfied with his speech. He seems to have meant to say something about the kind of coal, or the tool being used, or the servant's technique in smashing it. At such moments in his friends' accounts, he is described as shaking his head or shrugging his shoulders or just wandering off. After decades of eloquent labour he was left exploring a limbo close to wordlessness, doing what he could with a communicative minimum: tone, gesture, small changes of expression. He remained alert, and watched intelligently.

'I am what I am, I am what I am,' he said to Anne Ridgeway in March 1744, when she gently prevented him taking up a knife. 'I am a fool,' he told a servant, after a visible struggle to find words or a name, a couple of weeks later.[44] He was heard to say nothing else until he died, on 19 October 1745, just over a month before his seventy-eighth birthday. The cathedral bells were rung muffled for four days. People filed past his body, laid out in the hall of his house, until someone cut a lock of his hair. After that the doors were closed to the crowds.[45]

## 3

Immense care was taken of Swift's dignity during these long, vacant and largely voiceless last years. His reputation suffered regular outrages, though, in the decades that followed his death, largely for political reasons. While Swift was still alive, one Thomas Birch floated tales of his living out his final days in a 'brutality of lust'.[46] There was a particularly determined effort to view one of the most personally ascetic figures in English literature as a rapacious fornicator. The only source for this tradition was a wilfully carnalized reading of *Cadenus and Vanessa*. The possibility that Swift had a physical partnership with two women is hardly proof of the near-bestial prurience for which enemies condemned him. Such inventions said more about the gossips propagating them than about Swift himself, though Dr Johnson was among several biographers who more or less believed them. Moreover, the image of Swift as a misanthropic monster, a hater of the human engulfed in the end by his own psychotic energies, lingered and indeed intensified. Many readers deliberately or unconsciously made connections between aspects of his writing and his final physical state, and responded to him as an innately loathsome being. This was in part due to unsympathetic attitudes to the sick that Swift had shared, but with corrupting doses of Romantic sentimentality on the part of his successors. From the mid-nineteenth century on, great names queued up to abuse him: Thackeray, Lawrence, Huxley and Orwell among the most distinguished. It was Thackeray who perfected the Gothic view of Swift.

> His laugh jars on one's ear . . . He was always alone, alone and gnashing in the darkness, except when Stella's sweet smile came and shone upon him. When that went, silence and utter night closed over him. An immense genius: an awful downfall and ruin.[47]

So wrote Thackeray – affable, relaxed, elegant – embodying a violent contrast with his subject. In this powerful lecture, Swift is depicted as a permanently disenchanted and wilfully bereft figure, albeit the greatest of the 'English Humorists'. Thackeray's facts were limited, and his interpretations openly offhand: Stella's sweet smile, for instance, was sharp rather than saccharine – and Swift seems to have stopped himself laughing at all by the age of fifty.

The work on demonizing Swift began early, however, and the most shocking contemporary denouncer was his cherished friend the Earl of Orrery. His *Remarks on the Life and Writings of Dr Jonathan Swift* (1752) was no straightforward piece of treachery or opportunism. Orrery had always exhibited a desire to belong among the highest critics and judges. He cultivated notions too of being a poet – in the *Remarks*, he printed convoluted lines of praise he had once presented to Swift in a blank commonplace book – and was a competent translator. He equated fastidious classicism with moral probity, in what looks very much like a reaction to his father's eventual loss of face in the controversy over Phalaris.[48] His *Remarks*, then, are best viewed as the outcome of a decision that no doubt cost him great pain, but placed loyalty to Swift below what he convinced himself was a judicious verdict on his old friend's works and character. He seems to have been shaken and repelled by Swift's mental illness, and taken it as a sentence passed by God for earlier sins. The form the *Remarks* took, in a series of letters to his surviving son Hamilton, indicate a further concern for propriety in the long view. Orrery took the opportunity to dissociate himself publicly, while addressing his heir, from the sides of Swift's oeuvre that had long been regarded as degenerate and irreligious – *Cadenus*, the 'Dressing Room' poems and perhaps above all the passages describing the Yahoos.

Orrery's *Remarks* are not entirely critical of Swift; and a cringeworthy egotism is manifest throughout in the Earl's pride at having been Swift's friend. The inclusion of those lines by Orrery mentioned above is manifestly and embarrassingly concerned more with showing off a slender talent for verse than with balancing the account of Swift's career. 'Small is the present, but sincere the friend,' he had written, in 1732.[49] For many points in themselves Swift would surely have been grateful. Orrery explicitly clears him of the hanging charge of Jacobitism, for example, and is categorical about his piety, his achievements as Drapier and his devotion to the Irish cause. But there are many passages that make cruel reading in the light of Orrery's diligent sycophancy towards the Dean in the 1730s. The greatest offence, according to Delany, was taken at Orrery's comments on Swift's supposed affair with Esther Vanhomrigh.[50] From this point in time his account of the close of Swift's life is particularly unfeeling.

Early in the year forty-two, the small remains of his understanding
became entirely confused, and the violence of his rage increased absolutely to a degree of madness. In this miserable state, he seemed to be
appointed as the first proper inhabitant for his own hospital: especially
as from an outragious lunatic, he sunk afterwards into a quiet, speech-
less idiot; and dragged out the remainder of his life in that helpless situation.[51]

The book is saved, possibly, by a few real insights, by some valuable
information and by the Earl's evident belief, for all his unpleasant high-
handedness, that he was doing the right thing by history. 'I will pursue
candour, even with an aching heart,' he says of *A Tale of a Tub*, and the
sentence could stand for the overall attitude of the *Remarks*.[52] Orrery's
supercilious epistles take us to the very heart of what bothered almost
all of Swift's subsequent critics for another two centuries. Swift struck at
the polite idea that lettered society liked to hold of what was essentially
human.

Swift deduces his observations from wrong principles; for in his land of
Houyhnhnms he considers the soul and body in their most degenerate,
and uncultivated state: the former as a slave to the appetites of the latter. He seems insensible of the surprising mechanism, and beauty of
every part of the human composition . . . In painting Yahoos he becomes
one himself.[53]

Shock and revulsion, though, were key to Swift's literary intention. In
countless works, his manifest aim was to disturb, and by doing so to
make readers see themselves differently. He had confronted the same
lofty presumptions in Bolingbroke and Pope in an often quoted letter of
29 September 1725: 'the chief end I propose to my self in all my labours
is to vex the world rather than divert it.'[54] The exchanges between Swift
and his two celebrated friends are so full of self-conscious writing and
learned references that the quite literal and serious import of this line
can be lost. Swift set out in his fictions, as in his provocative pamphlets,
to bother, to raise hackles, to anger and distress. He is in some respects
the satirical cousin of de Sade; and his technique should be classified
above all as the art of upsetting people – people of all persuasions. It is
Swift's determination to *vex* that prevents any political camp from con-
scripting him: his works will alienate left- and right-wingers, agnostics
and dogmatists. Perhaps this is partly why he is culturally so precious.

In life, despite his grumbles, Swift had no wish to segregate himself: yet, while he regarded the high Scriblerians as his closest brethren, he was of another kind to all his classically minded friends, even in the secluded state that most of them professedly sought as a refuge, and in which a few of them died. The deanery of St Patrick's was a genuine stronghold, and ultimately a sanctuary, encircled by the populace of Dublin. Even during the three years of Swift's final invisibility, it remained an emblematic command post, not a private residence – not a place of 'privation', in the literal Roman sense, from the public sphere. Pope's home at Twickenham, by contrast, was a bookend, closing him off from the toxicity of his abusers even as his words redoubled virulence upon their heads. Swift was insensible to news of the 'long disease' of Pope's life, as the poet described his existence, exhausting itself finally in May 1744. Pope was fifty-six years old when he died, having bravely resisted disability for most of them. Meanwhile Bolingbroke's estates, bringing the *otium* he claimed to prize above all, were in reality a source of boredom and at best a screen against lasting frustration. The eventual fall of Walpole in 1742 resulted in anti-climax for the Tory Viscount. Politically his ascent remained frozen at the point it reached in late July 1714, when the Lord Treasurer's staff had fleetingly seemed his. Pre-eminence in office was denied him. Yet he remained in lusty shape until a few months before his death from cancer in 1751, aged seventy-three. A hearty constitution evidently came with the St John line: Bolingbroke's father, whom Swift suspected was immortal, only died a few years before. Marriage, however, brought no children. His titles, which fell short of his ambitions, passed to a nephew. His hopes for posterity rested on the aura he had cultivated as a Tory philosopher of 'the country', but unauthorized publications of compromising works – arranged, to his grief and annoyance, by Pope – renewed the taint of his Jacobite adventures. Among Swift's Irish friends, Delany, having perfected his retreat at Delville, was made the Dean of Down in 1744. His Tory politics, and quite possibly his connection with Swift – though long discontinued – hindered further progress. He died in Bath in 1768. The traitor among Swift's classicists, Orrery, who yearned for his name to rest by that of a Pope or Bolingbroke, ended his days in 1762.

Arguably the greatest disservice this erstwhile admirer did Swift in his *Remarks* was the picture printed at the front of the volume. This was a caricature of Swift in what Orrery called his 'idiotism', bulb-headed and bald, with hugely exaggerated eyes – and eyebrows – and a shrunken tapering chin. The image was the product of perhaps the single true lapse on the part of Swift's protectors at the deanery. A minor portraitist called Rupert Barber was allowed into the house as a favour to his relatives and in particular to his mother, Mary, Swift's friend the poet.[55] Barber's drawing, which looks very much like one made from memory, was copied in further engravings, becoming ever more cartoonish with each rendering. A better and fairer representation of Swift entering the twilight is a head-and-shoulders portrait, apparently by Francis Bindon – a much subtler and more introverted account of a silver-haired, whimsical dean than his earlier full-length study for Lord Howth. At around the same time, Bindon nevertheless updated the Howth portrait on another canvas that displayed still more emblematic attachments around an aggressively postured figure. Such mythification seems very innocent besides Rupert Barber's sketch, which treats Swift as an exhibit at Bedlam or a travelling fair. The impression it leaves can be dispelled, though, by looking at Swift's death-mask, still displayed in a cabinet in his cathedral: a complex, beguiling face, though contracted with age and discomfort, the spare flesh lost. Its features mingle fragility with robustness. The brow seems much less prominent, and much narrower, than Swift's portraits suggest, somewhat pinched at the temples around eyes that are indeed large. The nose is long and broad, but spreading from an oddly delicate bridge. The philtrum of the high upper lip is also wide, flattened by a slight pursing of the mouth. The final thinness of flesh reveals a surprisingly sensitive jawline, almost frail, tense at the chin. This was the face the crowds trooped up to see for one last time in October 1745; and it has the expression of an elderly gentleman doing his best to tolerate their noise.

Seven years later, Orrery's epistles were received with popular outrage. Swift's long-standing printer, one-legged George Faulkner, 'that little hopping fellow', was vilified far and wide for printing the *Remarks*. Dubliners consoled themselves by saying that they had known for a long time that Faulkner's 'understanding' was as wooden as his leg. He made amends only with his famed cheerfulness and profligate hospitality. On his death (in 1775) he donated a bust of Swift to stand by the Dean's cathedral monument.[56] The acrimony over Orrery's *Remarks* was not short-lived, however. Patrick Delany countered with a book of *Observations* on the *Remarks*. With all due respect for difference of rank, he offered some mildly put qualifications of the Earl's most personally critical points. He agreed that Swift had defiled his imagination by creating the Yahoos, but pointed out that Swift himself was 'of a character so very contrary to those hateful animals'.[57] While airing his own repugnance at Swift's dismissal of idealistic humanism, he placed greater emphases on the 'excellencies' in Swift's writing. At the very end Delany reflected the wider estimate of Swift among the enemies of empire: 'He lived a blessing, he died a benefactor, and his name will ever live an honour to Ireland.'[58]

This was a stuffy way of describing how Swift appeared to an apprentice who, let out early from his shop for the traditional fiesta on the Great Patriot's birthday, danced around a bonfire or climbed the steeple of St Patrick's. From that vantage, giving a view of the city, the land sweeping to the coast and the horizon hiding England, Swift was the single true anti-authority figure of his day. He was thrillingly rebellious and self-assured, yet stoutly institutional – a prop of the establishment, but one with a cold-eyed affinity with beggars (if badged, and industrious), incurables and madmen. When the young apprentice was an ageing journeyman, or took over his father-in-law's business, or when the firebrand undergraduate took orders and settled into his fellowship or vicarage, there was no disgrace in toasting Swift's memory. The late Dean's defence of trade and the kingdom's lost freedoms mattered more to such citizens than his assault on the Republic of Letters' fine notions of the human. He was no democrat, and in some ways he fails to match the emancipatory standards of later Irish freedom-fighters: but in his own time, his basic stance made sense. Everyone born in Ireland, for Swift, whether English, Scots or 'mere' Irish, were cast-offs and cattle in the eyes of London. During the harshness of the 1720s, and the very mild improvement that followed for a while, the only option in his mind was for all to pull together. He had suggested the native Irish should sacrifice their language and customs for the sake of employment and survival; but he also contemplated the extinction of the cultural minority to which he belonged. In his will, he bequeathed an inheritance of tithes to his successive vicars of Laracor 'for the time being'. When 'another Form of Christian Religion shall become the Established Faith in this Kingdom', he stipulated that these funds should go directly to the parish poor.[59] He foresaw the end of what he stood for.

So far as his Church was concerned, he had done his best to hold back the rot. The cathedral of St Patrick's, all agreed, was in excellent condition after Swift's tenure as dean, though it is only fair to note that the energies and investments of his predecessor, Stearne, buoyed his efforts in maintaining the fabric. Although so frequently struck deaf, he had taken particular care of the cathedral choir. He repeatedly admitted his shortcomings on the theological side of his profession. He wished, according to Delany, that he might have been a more electrifying preacher. The grandstand sermon was not the ideal form, certainly, for a silent composer, a shaper of public feeling whose medium was the press. Accordingly he did not tolerate bombast, indistinctness or lack of care in young preachers, and his published sermons commanded solid respect as improving models for parsons to follow.[60] In 1774, one 'Mr Broome', an Oxford undergraduate, 'spoke rather saucily' to James Woodforde, then sub-warden at New College. Woodforde, one of the century's most amiable diarists, believed in reserving heavy punishment for much worse transgressions, and so 'I set him one of Swift's sermons to translate,' he wrote, 'for the offence he was guilty of.'[61]

The Church was Swift's passion, his foundation and his last line of defence; but his sympathies and his appeal were broader, albeit almost unwillingly so. In 1763 the weavers of Dublin submitted a petition 'setting forth the great decay of their trade in consequence of the importation of foreign silks'. They could recall the stand the Dean of St Patrick's had urged their forebears to make on the same question forty years earlier.[62] He had expected no improvements without a change of government. Swift calibrated optimism to the lowest conceivable level; at the same time he offered paradoxical hope. He could preach despair while still insisting on action, and, in doing so, inspire. This was true of the Drapier, and true of his greatest creation. For Gulliver has amazing news for all of Europe's readers: the world is much bigger than they thought, and even its smaller, less noticed corners may contain a Lilliput. Equally, Gulliver himself is a phenomenon, a wonder of the world, a thorough shock to the system in every land where he washes up. He is the man-mountain and a mouse, an ignoramus and crypto-Yahoo, a master linguist and a simpleton, an illustration of how one person can be all of those things and more. In a comic tribute to human inhospitality, he is initially mistreated almost everywhere he goes; but invariably inspires admiration, affection and loyalty in all the more likeable foreign citizens he meets. Like Robinson Crusoe he is a font of ingenuity, a model of forbearance and a synonym for intrepidness, but under much more varied (and more interesting) conditions. Above all, perhaps, we see through Gulliver that the world is far from being just what we are told it is on our own bit of earth. All the cultures Gulliver visits are shocked at the proof in his person that things are not as they assumed they were till they saw him. No civilization, Swift shows, has a freehold on 'normality'. Another observer, another culture, is always waiting to unsettle our certainties. At the same time, we see a tendency of ourselves in all the peoples Gulliver spends time among. This is Gulliver's treasure.

At the end of his *Travels*, Gulliver is fighting the reflection of himself he finds in others; the idea that he has something of the Yahoo in his constitution is abhorrent to him. Yet, if we leave him grumbling at visitors and relatives on the last page of his book, is he really so unique from other crotchety, ageing men we might know (or happen to be), taking their retirement badly? Gulliver takes his leave of us with the sourness of the beached adventurer, convinced that his discoveries will be credited to others in the course of time. The smell of people is a torture to him. But this is a distemper that might blow away in the wind if he got the chance to take to sea again, as he has done so promptly and so needlessly after every safe return until his fourth voyage.

Swift's dedicated visitors and attendants did a great deal to ensure that it was possible for later scholars to develop a more accurate vision of Swift. Deane Swift's spirited *Essay* in defence of his relative succumbs here and there to the lure of legend; but his notes on Swift's state in his final years did much to dispel myths of howling mania or psychotic inertia. He lived until 1783, and was two years younger than his great elder relative when he died. Calm clarification can also be found in the letters of Martha Whiteway; John Lyon, the helpful and attentive prebendary, performed a still more extensive duty with the notes he left towards a biography of the Dean.[63] Meanwhile, outside the deanery, for years – indeed, for decades – the population of Dublin retained the sense of Swift that makes him still vital today – as an enlivener, creator and protester.

4

The wider public was therefore indignant, in October 1745, when Swift's executors announced that the Dean would be buried quietly, as his will directed. There was a general desire to give him a state – or anti-state – funeral. Mrs Whiteway, a comfortable rich merchant's widow, said she would pay for the cortège herself.[64] Denying such appeals, the minimalism Swift desired was in the main respected, most conspicuously in the form of his chaste and formidable epitaph. While still alive, he had been somewhat frustrated in his literary arrangements for posterity. The 'Verses on the Death of Dr Swift' were printed in two dreadfully mangled versions. His Latin epitaph was transferred to stone, though, with the precision he requested, on a black marble slab, seven feet from the ground, 'in large Letters, deeply cut, and strongly gilded'.

> Here lies the body
> Of Jonathan Swift, S.T.D.,
> Dean of this cathedral,
> Where wild indignation
> No more
> Can tear his heart.
> Go, traveller
> And be like him, if you can,
> Vigorous to his utmost
> As liberty's avenger.[65]

Despite the strident tone, there is a legalistic formality in the claims Swift makes for himself. The 'utmost' he could offer naturally declined with time: though in the late 1730s merely adding a few words or nothing more than his name to a campaign was enough to bolster it considerably. There is both realism and humility in the idea that everyone should be vigorous *pro virili* – to the limits of their strength. In many ways its wording is clinically exact, showing one last time how Swift, in Johnson's phrase, studied purity; however, as almost always with his work, the implications and paradoxes of the tablet build up in the cavernous chill of St Patrick's the more one stares at it.

The language, first, excluded the non-Latin-reading majority of the public that admired him most, and that truly recognized him as 'liberty's avenger'. The phrase has more often been translated as 'defender', but the strict meaning of the Ecclesiastical Latin term *vindicator*, which has only recently attracted the attention of Claude Rawson among other scholars, better suits Swift's meaning and his general bearing.[66] Liberty in its largest, truest sense for Swift had been murdered generations previously, sometime before the Civil War; but its blood still cried out for retribution. More immediately, though, the phrase has a very local geographical application: Swift was indisputably the champion of *the* liberties of St Patrick's Cathedral, the area beyond the old city walls that was his effective demesne for the best part of three decades.

The wider Swiftian connotations of liberty are troubling. 'Liberating' the Irish peasantry meant suppressing the Irish language. The word's message to the future is regulated by its eighteenth-century senses, a vexed array of meanings that tie it to property, religious tolerance and intolerance, and memories of the Glorious Revolution. Swift was extremely selective as to what constituted real freedom, and even then his personalized sense of the concept is ambiguous. So much of what he wrote, said and did seems, by contrast, to be advocating bondage – submission and adherence to the Established Church, to classical learning, to the old ways of England. Those strictures are moderated, nevertheless, by his overall accomplishment: for by the end Swift had campaigned for more than the rights of those who cherished the Anglican settlement of 1662. His life's work exudes instead an almost Miltonic sense that liberty can be achieved only through labour and adversity. Freedom is only meaningful in a world of restricted options. The strict limits Swift himself abided by were the preconditions of his audacity in literature and politics.

Women travellers visiting the shrine to Swift and Stella – who lie side by side, with two Victorian brass plates above their graves – have another complex position in the liberty he envisaged and defended. Swift's attitude to women is one of the most controversial things about him. His views of the other sex will always ruffle any attempt to take his legacy positively from a 21st-century perspective, since in places his writing evinces fury and loathing towards women and what he understood as femininity. These tendencies need to be set against his conduct towards individuals, for the greatest of male feminists can still treat the women in his life abominably. Swift was far from innocent of cruelty, or at least of cowardice, towards the women he loved – though we perhaps do an injustice to Esther Vanhomrigh's tenacity and free-mindedness if we view her simply as Swift's victim. During the years she insisted on seeing him, he might equally have claimed to be hers. Their long and painful affair, if that is what it was, illustrates a bitter contest between the claims of desire, guilt and public identity; but it also shows them sharing moments of spontaneous delight, as equals in egregiousness. The secrecy of their meetings, a source of such anguish to Swift, illustrates a loss of liberty he could barely accept – a liberty of conscious, rational thought, his beloved 'Reason' – from what looks like pure obsession. Vanhomrigh found words for their state of entanglement much more easily than Swift.

> I know 'tis as impossible for you to burn my letters without reading them as 'tis for me to avoid reproving you when you behave so wrong. Once more I advise you to alter your behaviour quickly for I do assure you I have too much spirit to sit down contented with this treatment. Now, because I love frankness extremely I here tell you that I have

determined to try all manner of human arts to reclaim you and if all those fail I am resolved to have recourse to the black one.[67]

Such feelings were not Vanhomrigh's alone, despite the part she assumed as the pursuer and (here) the sorceress. Both made their threats; both soothed and provoked in their turn. Swift's repeated power-acting, his orders for her to keep her distance, only dissolved into their pattern of mutually yearning, reproving, role-playing and teasing, and finding brief solace in an encounter that would set the whole cycle of pleasurable distress in motion once more. Whatever passed between them in private, Swift was powerless to fight its attractions. Indeed, for all his wariness, he counted on them.

Vanhomrigh's involvement with Swift was a disturbance, an ongoing violation of the quiet order and distance he was otherwise determined to instil in his quasi-domestic life with Johnson. How much offence each took at the other woman's existence might seem self-evident, but they also appear to have accepted, however grudgingly, the singular form of polygamy in which they found themselves. It is tempting to think that Swift used Vanhomrigh as his sexual partner while Johnson served as his living icon of purity; but his letters, poems and the *Journal to Stella* suggest otherwise. In fact he addressed both in similar tones – didactically, comically, warmly and flirtatiously. His poems to Stella might lack some of the breathy passion he expressed in French on occasion to Vanessa; but the letters to Vanessa contain none of his poetry's steady and really quite physical celebration of Stella's beauty. Some of the lines one might expect to have been drawn within the trio aren't there, or at any rate can't be made out now. Both women might have been his lovers; however, the possibility will always remain that for Swift the thrill lay in nothing more than word-play, on paper and in drawing rooms, and that this permitted him to believe it was innocent.

His relationship with Stella is arguably the central puzzle. The early intimacy with eight-year-old Esther Johnson, so far as the record preserves it, is at the same time touching and disquieting. It shows Swift adopting a near-orphaned minor, and encouraging her talent and individuality; but it also hints at a clearer later tendency to demand acquiescence and foster dependency. Something rather like Stockholm syndrome may not be ruled out. Nevertheless, if one sees Johnson as he presents her, as his pupil and chaste soul-mate, or, more precisely, if she wished for the autonomy to read what she wished, converse freely and be spared the constrictions that typically came with conventional marriage, then Swift emerges as the defender of her personal liberty. He can be seen as helping her to lead a more independent life than would otherwise have been possible, sparing her the drudgery and yearly pregnancies that frequently awaited a woman of her original status and limited means. Unlike Vanhomrigh, she left no reliable sign on the record to suggest that she wanted to marry Swift, clear though it is that she disliked her rival. This is not to say such signs might not have been communicated privately; for if she harboured even barely conscious wishes to live otherwise – to have children, for example – then the dual portrait obviously becomes more complicated. The stories that emerged of a secret marriage and unacknowledged children do seem like fantasies of popular sentiment: the concealment of an illegitimate young Swift in Dublin – and there is no trace of a child in any surviving documentation – would definitely have been a masterpiece of suppression, especially given the inability of either parent to perform the necessary cover-up themselves. Swift appears innocent of having neglected any offspring. The periods that by most standards do reflect badly on him came in the last months of both Johnson and Vanhomrigh, when his fear of grief and concern for appearances overcame his desire to comfort and care for them. Even then, in the bolt for home that indirectly produced his 'Holyhead Journal' in 1727, he arguably fought off those selfish preoccupations in order to see Johnson before she died. He might easily enough have remained in England. It was, though, a surge of courage that came too late for Vanhomrigh.

Swift was keen for his two friends to be autonomous financially, to travel freely and to express their thoughts, even though he ticked off both for poor grammar, splenetic tendencies and not taking enough exercise. In the meantime and after both died, he also maintained lengthy and mature friendships with a large number of other women, and supported many of them in their efforts to write, publish and lead meaningful public lives. When it came to women's liberty in general, it must be said that his position was largely restrictive. As on other questions, his progressiveness was largely inadvertent. A great deal of his occasional misogyny was the common property of his age, but even so he tended to leave his personal stamp when reinforcing standard prejudices, notably in his hatred of luxuries in dress. Unlike most men of the time, however, he wavered in the conviction that women were intellectually inferior. He supported women using the light of what he regarded as reason. Typically, he could manage to be both enlightened and cruelly repressive in a single verse or breath. The 'obscene' poems of his later years attack the reigning sexualization of women's bodies and manners, even as they campaign against sexual freedom. While there could be no question for Swift of gender equality, he was keen to liberate women from being regarded as brittle idols or mere social accessories.

It might seem odd as well that Swift should follow the convention of urging the passing traveller – whatever prospective Gulliver might visit the cathedral – to be like him. In so many self-representations in letters and poems, Swift had depicted himself as a man apart, a victim of circumstance, an exile, an outcast, 'disqualified by Fate'[68] – an unfortunate whom no one in their senses would ever try to imitate. He took his stand as a *vindicator* only as a last resort. In bidding those who follow to resist oppression where they find it, his epitaph stimulates people to imitate him if they can – that is, 'if they are capable', but also 'if they are willing', if they can conquer their reservations. Even in cold marble, he makes no pretence to be a figure of easy appeal.

Like most if not all of us, Swift's personality was surely made up of many parts. One of these parts sympathized with the victims of his society; another concealed pain and insecurities in the language and attitudes of an oppressor. The same principle is evident throughout his works. Almost every paragraph Swift wrote is multi-nuanced beyond definition or paraphrase, even though a 'message' is invariably clear. While his epitaph, with its sometimes perplexing phrases, exhorts us to be like Swift, to defend liberty, it still leaves us asking questions. It belongs, in fact, with another striking statement on liberty, funny as well as expostulatory, which occurs in the fourth of his *Drapier's Letters*.

I have done: for those who have used Power to cramp Liberty have gone so far as to resent even the Liberty of Complaining; although a Man upon the Rack was never known to be refused the Liberty of roaring as loud as he thought fit.[69]

Swift's work raises a bowman's two fingers to all those in authority who treat people as vassals or livestock. Few travellers in life will be able to halt an oppressive government in its tracks; but all, Swift's writing demonstrates, have a right to view the conditions of existence alternatively, critically, satirically; to identify their misfortunes and describe them more acutely. His career sceptically highlighted the very moderate and indeed altogether inadequate expectations a moral person might have of life in this world. But simultaneously he proved the existence of other liberties of speech than mere complaining or roaring: a liberty of chiding, deriding, cajoling, bridling, impersonating, inverting, building up and laying bare; a liberty of making the powerful seem less so. By the end of his life he was championing more than the exclusively defined rights that allowed a Protestant of English descent to escape 'slavery'.

Strikingly there is no prayer or any mention of God on Swift's monument. Such an omission doubtless confirmed his enemies and critics in their belief that he was an atheist. The extent and stringency of his devotions will, however, always argue otherwise. More precisely, and strange though it must sound, Swift's religion was the foundation of his materialism. The existence of God was a given; the rites the Almighty required in worship were laid down by tradition. As such, the business of living could and should go on without Puritanical excess or worthless doctrinal speculation. Swift's faith, paradoxically, left him free to partake in the exchanges of stoic apothegms he enjoyed with his learned friends; to observe, for example, to Pope: 'The common saying of life being a Farce is true in every sense but the most important one, for it is a ridiculous tragedy, which is the worst kind of composition.'[70] The remark is, on the surface, blithely un-Christian; Swift's divine maker emerges as a botcher, and we human wretches are trapped in His poor handiwork. But the theatrical metaphor preserves the essence of Swift's very conventional belief. When the ridiculous tragedy, this worst of compositions, ends, we may step out of the theatre into a richer reality; or put the fourpenny book down and pick up the Gospel. So an inquisitor would find no proof of heresy here – certainly not if Swift were to conduct his own defence. Furthermore, his broader attitude to life itself is there, as it is up on the stone in his cathedral, and it is one more of indignation and protest than pious submission. He was, as he said, a vindicator – a fighter and an avenger.

Still, it took a lot to make him turn on England, the kingdom he always claimed as his rightful home. Much as he relished the fray, Swift would always deny that he had turned renegade. The degenerates who had taken over government, Parliament, the Crown – it was they who had left him no option but resistance. This was Swift's line of argument; and this, as well he knew, was the reasoning of a rebel, however reluctant.

# Abbreviations

| | |
|---|---|
| **Deane Swift,** *Essay* | Deane Swift, *An Essay upon the Life, Writings, and Character of Dr Jonathan Swift* (1755) |
| *DNB* | *Oxford Dictionary of National Biography*, updated online edition |
| **Ehrenpreis** | Irvin Ehrenpreis, *Swift: The Man, His Works, and the Age*, 3 vols. (1962–83) |
| **Gilbert,** *History of Dublin* | Sir John Gilbert, *A History of the City of Dublin*, 3 vols. (Dublin, 1859) |
| **Swift,** *Correspondence* | *The Correspondence of Jonathan Swift*, ed. Sir Harold Williams, rev. David Woolley, 5 vols. (Oxford, 1965–72) |
| **Swift,** *Journal* | *Journal to Stella*, ed. Harold Williams, 2 vols. (Oxford, 1948) |
| **Swift,** *Poems* | *The Poems of Jonathan Swift*, ed. Sir Harold Williams, 2nd edn, 3 vols. (Oxford, 1958) |
| **Swift,** *PW* | *The Prose Works of Jonathan Swift*, eds. Herbert Davis et al., 16 vols. (Oxford, 1939–74) |
| **Swift,** *Tale of a Tub* | *A Tale of a Tub*, eds. A. C. Guthkelch and David Nichol Smith, 2nd edn (Oxford, 1958) |
| **Swift,** *Travels* | *Gulliver's Travels*, eds. Ian Higgins, Claude Rawson and Paul Turner (Oxford, 2005) |

# *Notes*

*Book publication is London, unless stated otherwise.*

## INTRODUCTION

1. Gilbert, *History of Dublin*, III, 44; the subsequent account follows that in, ibid., 42–5.
2. The college rules on nocturnal excursions – no student was allowed out after 9 p.m. without written permission – are summarized by John William Stubbs, *The History of the University of Dublin* (Dublin, 1889), 143. On the layout of Trinity in this period, see Stubbs, 188–90, with a very helpful illustration of the college front from a map of Dublin by Charles Brooking (1728) on 189; also Constantia Maxwell, *A History of Trinity College* (Dublin, 1946), 166–7 (Brooking's illustration is reprinted facing 32). The front of the college as Swift knew it was pulled down in the course of the 1750s, after his death; the present front was completed in 1759.
3. The battle took place on 1 July, that is, in the reckoning of the Julian Calendar (Old Style); in the Gregorian Calendar (New Style), adopted in Britain and Ireland in the mid-1700s, the anniversary falls on 11 July. It is commemorated by the Orange Order on the 12th, the date of the Battle of Aughrim, which effectively sealed victory for the Williamites in Ireland in 1691.
4. This description blends a number of sources that will be encountered individually in due course, but the account of Swift's physical appearance derives from the portrait(s) made of him by Charles Jervas in 1710.
5. Swift, *Journal* (21 January 1712), II, 468.
6. In Italian, *presto* means 'swift', and the nickname was conferred on him by Adelaide, Duchess of Shrewsbury, a native of Bologna; see Swift, *Journal* (2 July 1711), I, 325. Swift assumes and plays upon the name throughout the journal.
7. Swift, *The Sentiments of a Church-of-England Man*, PW, II, 25.
8. Swift, *Journal* (2 December 1710), I, 111.
9. Swift, *Journal* (1 December 1710), I, 110–11.
10. The classic summary of the medical evidence is offered by S. L. Shapiro,

'The Medical History of Jonathan Swift', *Eye, Ear, Nose and Throat Monthly*, 48 (1969), 486–9.

11. Swift, *Intelligencer* (No. 3), *PW*, XII, 35.

12. Swift, *Intelligencer* (No. 9), *PW*, XII, 50. Swift referred frequently to White's in the *Journal*. See Aytoun Ellis, *The Penny Universities: A History of the Coffee Houses* (1956), 146.

13. Swift, *Travels* (IV.12), 275; see Claude Rawson's introduction, xxiv.

14. Swift to Charles Ford, 15 April 1721, *Correspondence*, II, 381.

15. James Boswell, *The Life of Samuel Johnson* (2 vols., 1820), I, 397.

16. The Earl of Peterborough to Swift, 29 November 1726, *Correspondence*, III, 191.

17. Swift to Alexander Pope, 29 September 1725, *Correspondence*, III, 102.

18. *The Mirror of Literature, Amusement and Instruction* (23 April 1836), Vol. 27, 258.

19. Swift put Descartes at the front of the 'modern' bowmen, and thus of the upstarts and usurpers, in 'The Battle of the Books' (*Tale of a Tub*, 234); he is slain by Aristotle (towards whom Swift also bore an undergraduate Protestant dislike). See Michael R. G. Spiller, 'The Idol of the Stove: The Background of Swift's Criticism of Descartes', *Review of English Studies*, 25 (1974), 15–24.

20. To be more accurate, since Swift himself was hardly averse to describing the nastiness and brutishness of life, he hated Hobbes the way churchmen down to Eliot have so often hated him: as a hypocritical atheist who refused to see the Established Church and the English constitution as a work of providence. The philosopher features, by way of a minor yet representative example, on Swift's list of leading 'freethinking' offenders in 'The Yahoo's Overthrow' (*Poems*, III, 815, ll. 26–7). On the bearing of Hobbes on Swift, see Alan S. Fisher, 'An End to the Renaissance: Erasmus, Hobbes, and *A Tale of a Tub*', *Huntington Library Quarterly*, 38 (1974), 1–20, and David P. French, 'Swift and Hobbes – A Neglected Parallel', *Boston University Studies in English*, 3 (1957), 243–55. There is also an important *Leviathan* aspect to the Lilliputian section of the *Travels*, and this is explored by John D. Seelye, 'Hobbes's *Leviathan* and the Giantism Complex in the First Book of *Gulliver's Travels*', *Journal of English and Germanic Philology*, 60 (1961), 228–39.

21. Swift, introduction to *Polite Conversation*, *PW*, IV, 123.

22. Swift disliked metaphysical speculations in general as intrusive on the province of the Church – the mixture of geometry and trance with which Descartes approached God in the *Meditations* was abhorrent to him. Yet he spoke only with approval of George Berkeley, whose philosophy he found somewhat farfetched but whose Christian ministry he admired wholeheartedly. See Swift to Lord Carteret, 4 September 1724

(*Correspondence*, III, 31–2), giving an account of Berkeley's 'very curious book' and his 'Romantick' but 'noble and generous' plans for missionary work.

23. Thomas Sheridan, *The Life of the Rev. Dr Jonathan Swift* (2nd edn, Dublin, 1787), 405.

24. ibid., 467.

25. The aptness of *vindicator* and the wording of the epitaph in general have been much debated. In *Swift's Angers* (Cambridge, 2014), 262–6, Claude Rawson discusses the ecclesiastical pedigree of *vindicator* and comments on how odd it was of Swift to use the medieval Latin word in the epitaph he prepared for his monument in St Patrick's Cathedral. In subsequent transcriptions it was amended to the more customary and classical *vindex* (usually 'champion' or 'deliverer'). Contemporaries thought he meant to write *libertatis vindicem*, a more familiar, but also arguably somewhat hackneyed phrase. Recent scholarship (including Rawson's) has suggested that critics of Swift's Latin (such as his friend Orrery) missed his point in this line of the epitaph. Swift's term echoed the standard libertarian expression (found in Livy and Cicero and throughout their imitators), while offering something more idiosyncratic, ecclesiastical and contemporary. For more on the resonance of the term Swift chose, see Péter Dávidházi, 'A Monumental Inscription: The Transcultural Heritage of Swift's Epitaph', in Ladina Bezzola Lambert and Andrea Ochsner, eds., *Moment to Monument: The Making and Unmaking of Cultural Significance* (New Brunswick, NJ, 2009), 51–70 (especially 56–62). A trait to bear in mind in Swift's Latin (and French) is his willingness to use striking, even outlandish and sensational language of an order that he generally spurned in English. His affectionate Latin verses in praise of Thomas Sheridan ('Deliciae Sheridan Musarum', *Poems*, I, 212–14) or the dramatic poem on 'Carberry Rocks' (*Poems*, I, 315–17), written after the death of Esther Vanhomrigh, are cases in point. The letters and epigrams Swift exchanged with Sheridan in 'Anglo-Latin' also give abundant evidence of how Swift treated Latin, perhaps a little unclerically, as a medium for play, for 'Presto'; and, despite the epitaph's outward solemnity, this ludic spirit appears to have infiltrated the ambiguous phrases Swift left for posterity in the cathedral. The key modern appraisal of the epitaph (albeit one reading *vindex* rather than *vindicator*) is Maurice Johnson, 'Swift and "The Greatest Epitaph in History"', *PMLA*, 68, 4 (1953), 814–27. Compelling revaluations offered in the past two decades include Frank Boyle, *Swift as Nemesis: Modernity and Its Satirist* (Stanford, CA, 2000), 4–5, Dustin Griffin, *Swift and Pope* (Cambridge, 2010), 235–40, and Leo Damrosch, *Jonathan Swift: His Life and His World* (New Haven, 2013), 469–72.

26. Swift, 'The Legion Club', *Poems*, III, 831, ll. 47–52.

## I. IRELAND AND THE CIVIL WARS

1. Swift to Thomas Sheridan, 27 March 1733, *Correspondence*, IV, 130.

2. Laetitia Pilkington, *Memoirs* (3 vols., Dublin, 1748), I, 168.

3. The timescale is somewhat elastic even though the basic chronology and magnitude of these early experiences are clear in Swift's record. His brief autobiography asserts that he was 'a year old' when the nurse 'stole him on shipboard' and that he returned two or possibly three years later. He claimed that he was sent to Kilkenny College at the age of six, though in the absence of school records Ehrenpreis plausibly suggests he might have gone earlier ('Family of Swift', *PW*, V, 192; Ehrenpreis, I, 31).

4. Deane Swift, *Essay*, 26.

5. On trends in domestic architecture in Dublin *c.*1660–1720 see Christine Casey, *Dublin: The City within the Grand and Royal Canals and the Circular Road* (New Haven, 2005), 26–7; on the influences from London and beyond, Sir John Summerson, *Architecture in Britain 1530–1830* (1953), 230–31.

6. Edward MacLysaght, *Irish Life in the Seventeenth Century* (3rd edn, Dublin, 1969), 9.

7. ibid., 451.

8. Luke Gernon, 'A Discourse of Ireland, Anno 1620', in C. Litton Falkiner, ed., *Illustrations of Irish History and Topography, Mainly of the Seventeenth Century* (1904), 357.

9. Fynes Moryson, 'Description of Ireland', in Falkiner, *Illustrations of Irish History*, 228, 229, 331.

10. Moryson, 'Description of Ireland', 223.

11. Gernon, 'A Discourse of Ireland, Anno 1620', in Falkiner, *Illustrations*, 349–50.

12. Swift to James Stopford, 26 November 1725, *Correspondence*, III, 116. Swift frequently denounced Ireland in such language. Yet it should be pointed out that in the more specific context of the political events Swift has told Stopford about in this letter, he is levelling a charge of shamefulness not against the Irish but at the way Ireland is being treated and governed by the oppressive English regime.

13. Swift to the Earl of Peterborough, 28 April 1726, *Correspondence*, III, 132.

14. 'The Patriot' was a routine epithet for Swift by the late 1720s; as with 'The Dean' or 'Gulliver' or even 'The Doctor', there was no doubt as to whom it referred. When the Countess of Suffolk invoked him in a letter of September 1731 as 'this Irish Patriot, this Excelent Man at Speech and Pen', she teased him (*Correspondence*, III, 498).

15. One example of this trend in Swift's thinking comes in his overview of recent Irish history in his paper 'On the Bill for the Clergy's Residing on Their Livings', *PW*, XII, 183.

16. Edmund Lloyd, *A Description of the City of Dublin* (1732), 23–4.

17. Swift, *An Answer to a Paper, Called a Memorial*, PW, XII, 18.

18. Eoin Ó Gnímh, 'The Downfall of the Gael' (Samuel Ferguson, trans.), in Padraic Colum, ed., *An Anthology of Irish Verse* (New York, 1922), 261.

19. On the identity of Swift's maternal grandfather, see Ehrenpreis, I, 270–74. Ehrenpreis's evidence has been widely accepted (see Clive Probyn, 'Jonathan Swift', *DNB*), but is contested by Leo Damrosch, *Jonathan Swift: His Life and His World* (New Haven, 2013), 11.

20. Swift, *Tale of a Tub* 155.

21. ibid., (Section VIII), 155.

22. Reprinted in Sir John Temple, *The Irish Rebellion; or, An History of the Attempts of Irish Papists to Extirpate the Protestants in the Kingdom of Ireland; Together with the Barbarous Cruelties and Bloody Massacres which Ensued Thereupon*, Francis Maseres, ed. (1812), 29.

23. Micheál Ó Siochrú, *God's Executioner: Oliver Cromwell and the Conquest of Ireland* (2008), 31.

24. Temple, *The Irish Rebellion*, 84.

25. ibid., 94.

26. Maseres, introduction to Temple, *The Irish Rebellion*, viii.

27. Temple, *The Irish Rebellion*, 85. For a sense of early reaction against Temple's 'partisan work', see Gilbert, *History of Dublin*, II, 316.

28. Temple, *The Irish Rebellion*, 59.

29. William King, *The State of the Protestants in Ireland under the Late King James's Government* (1692), 294.

30. Temple, *The Irish Rebellion*, 25.

31. Account by Anthony à Wood in James Carty, ed., *Ireland from the Flight of the Earls to Grattan's Parliament: A Documentary Record* (Dublin, 1949), 69–70.

32. Swift, 'Family of Swift', PW, V, 191. Ehrenpreis finds 'very private Gentlemen' an odd phrase (I, 4), but Swift surely means it in the core sense of Latin *privatus*, literally one cut off from public life.

33. Swift, 'Family of Swift', PW, I, 188.

34. Julius Caesar, *Commentaries on the Gallic Wars* (V.v); see also Daniel Defoe, *A Tour through the Whole Island of Great Britain*, Pat Rogers, ed. (Harmondsworth, 1971), 172.

35. Bruno Ryves, *Mercurius rusticus; or, The Countries Complaint of the Barbarous Outrages Committed by the Sectaries of This Late Flourishing Kingdom ... to the 25th of March, 1646* (1685), 83.

36. ibid., 85–6.

37. ibid., 87.

38. John Walker, *An Attempt towards Recovering an Account of the Numbers and Sufferings of the Clergy of the Church of England ... in the Late Times of the Grand Rebellion ...* (1714), Part II, 363.

39. Sir Edward Walker, *Historical Discourses, upon Several Occasions* (1705), 132.

40. In fact Thomas Swift's livings were shared between two priests, Giles Rawlins at Goodrich and John Somers at Bridstow. Both were then replaced in 1654, undermining the Dean's later disdainful claim that the 'fanatical saint' was quick to drop his Puritan principles – and cling on to his living – at the Restoration (Walker, *Sufferings of the Clergy*, Part II, 363; Swift, 'Family of Swift', *PW*, V, 190).

41. Ehrenpreis, I, 4; and Swift, 'Family of Swift', *PW*, V, 187.

42. Sir Edward Walker, *A Circumstantial Account of the Preparations for the Coronation of His Majesty King Charles the Second* . . . (1820), 11–12.

43. Swift, 'Family of Swift', *PW*, V, 188.

44. Swift recalled the saying in connection with his own hopes of preferment from his friend the Lord Treasurer in 1713 (*Journal*, II, 627).

45. Swift, 'Family of Swift', *PW*, V, 191.

46. A loose rendering of Éamonn an Dúna, 'Mo lá leóin go deó go n-éagad' (ll. 125–36), in Cecile O'Rahilly, ed., *Five Seventeenth-Century Poems* (Dublin, 1952), 90. Guided by commentary and translation in Lesa Ní Mhunghaile, 'The Legal System in Ireland and the Irish Language 1700–c.1843', in Michael Brown and Seán Patrick Dollan, eds., *The Laws and Other Legalities of Ireland 1689–1850* (Farnham, Surrey, 2011), 325–58 (341); Liam Mac Mathúna (whose translation Ní Mhunghaile quotes), 'Growth of Irish (L1) / English (L2) Literary Code-mixing 1600–1900: Contexts, Genres and Realisations', in Hildegard L. C. Tristram, ed., *The Celtic Languages in Contact: Papers from . . . the XIII International Congress of Celtic Studies, Bonn* . . . (Potsdam, 2007), 217–34 (221); and John Kerrigan, *Archipelagic English: Literature, History and Politics* (Oxford, 2008), 60–61, praising the passage's combination of languages and working with a translation by Meidhbhín Ní Úrdail.

47. Steele [?], *Tatler*, No. 249, Appendix C, *PW*, II, 245.

## 2. UPBRINGING

1. *The Book of Common Prayer* [1662], Brian Cummings, ed. (Oxford, 2011), 458.

2. Swift, *Tale of a Tub*, 48.

3. Sir William Brereton, 'Travels', in C. Litton Falkiner, ed., *Illustrations of Irish History and Topography, Mainly of the Seventeenth Century* (1904), 377.

4. T. K. Moylan, 'Vagabonds and Sturdy Beggars: Poverty, Pigs and Pestilence in Medieval Dublin', in Howard B. Clarke, ed., *Medieval Dublin: The Living City* (Dublin, 1990), 192–9 (193).

5. John Dunton, *Letters on Travels in Ireland*, printed by Edward MacLysaght, *Irish Life in the Seventeenth Century* (3rd edn, Dublin, 1969), Appendix B, 379. Many of these letters were printed by Dunton in *The Dublin Scuffle* (1699).
6. Moylan, 'Vagabonds and Sturdy Beggars', 197; H. S. Crawford, 'The Market Cross of Dublin', in Howard B. Clarke, ed., *Medieval Dublin: The Making of a Metropolis* (Dublin 1990), 252–3.
7. Maurice Craig, *Dublin 1660–1860* (Dublin 1969), 47–8.
8. Dunton, *Letters on Travels in Ireland*, in MacLysaght, , *Irish Life in the Seventeenth Century*, Appendix B, 383.
9. Carole Fabricant, *Swift's Landscape* Appendix B (Baltimore, Maryland, 1982), 28–30.
10. Dunton, *Letters on Travels in Ireland*, in MacLysaght, *Irish Life in the Seventeenth Century*, 388.
11. Falkiner, *Illustrations of Irish History and Topography*, 43.
12. Swift, *An Examination of Certain Abuses, Corruptions and Enormities in the City of Dublin*, PW, XII, 218–19.
13. Swift, *The Humble Petition of the Footmen of Dublin*, PW, XII, 236.
14. Swift, *A Proposal for Correcting, Improving and Ascertaining the English Tongue*, PW, IV, 13.
15. Sir Henry Craik, *The Life of Jonathan Swift* (2 vols., 2nd edn, 1894), I, 11. See also Ehrenpreis, I, 23.
16. Laetitia Pilkington, *Memoirs* (3 vols., Dublin, 1748), I, 67–8.
17. 'The Thanksgiving of Women after Child-birth', *The Book of Common Prayer* [1662], 457.
18. Swift, *Tale of a Tub*, 44.
19. Swift, 'Family of Swift', *PW*, V, 192.
20. Ehrenpreis, I, 4–5.
21. Hannah Wolley, *The Queen-like Cabinet* (1670), 378–9.
22. Thomas Dineley, excerpts from a travel journal in James Carty, ed., *Ireland from the Flight of the Earls to Grattan's Parliament: A Documentary Record* (Dublin, 1949), 20–21.
23. Swift, 'Family of Swift', *PW*, V, 192.
24. Pilkington, *Memoirs*, I, 68.
25. Swift, 'Dedication to Prince Posterity', *Tale of a Tub*, 33.
26. Swift, *Travels* (II.1), 82.
27. Ehrenpreis, I, 31.
28. Daniel Defoe, *A Tour through the Whole Island of Great Britain*, Pat Rogers, ed. (Harmondsworth, 1971), 553.
29. Fynes Moryson, 'The Description of Ireland', in Falkiner, *Illustrations of Irish History and Topography*, 220.
30. Swift, 'Family of Swift', *PW*, V, 192.
31. Swift, *Travels* (II.6), 54.

32. ibid. (II.1), 81.

33. Swift, *Tale of a Tub*, 48.

34. John Dryden, *Annus Mirabilis: The Year of Wonders, MDCLXVI*, stanzas 223, 256, in *The Poems of John Dryden: Vol. I*, Paul Hammond, ed. (Abingdon, 1995), 184, 191.

35. Frederick Joseph Harvey Darton, *Children's Books in England: Five Centuries of Social Life* (Cambridge, 1932; 2011 edn), 45, 47.

36. John Norris, *Spiritual Counsel; or, A Father's Advice to His Children* (1694), 76–7. See Darton, *Children's Books*, 54–8; Ivy Pinchbeck and Margaret Hewitt, *Children in English Society. Vol. I: From Tudor Times to the Eighteenth Century* (1969), 265–75.

37. Swift, *Tale of a Tub*, 78.

38. Luke Gernon, 'A Discourse of Ireland, Anno 1620', in Falkiner, *Illustrations of Irish History and Topography*, 355.

39. Fynes Moryson, 'The Description of Ireland', in Falkiner, *Illustrations of Irish History and Topography*, 221.

40. Anonymous, 'A Discourse of Ireland', in Falkiner, *Illustrations of Irish History and Topography* 354.

41. Thomas Molyneux, in a manuscript quoted in Ehrenpreis, I, 35.

42. MacLysaght, *Irish Life in the Seventeenth Century*, 410.

43. Jorevin de Rocheford, 'Description of England and Ireland after the Restoration', in Falkiner, *Illustrations of Irish History and Topography*, 414–15.

44. Swift, *Tale of a Tub*, 280.

45. The question would appear to rest on a paper in Kilkenny College archives dated '1666', which sets out estimates for the first round of modifications. Irvin Ehrenpreis was inclined to view this as a 'misreading' of '1686'. That theory begs the question, however, of why plans should have been commissioned in 1686 for a building bearing the year 1684 on its entrance. See John Browne, 'Kilkenny College', *Transactions of the Kilkenny Archaeological Society*, I (1849–51), 221–9 (223); Ehrenpreis, I, 35.

46. Browne, 'Kilkenny College', 223–5; also the Kilkenny School Statutes (1684), in Edward Leach, ed., *The History and Antiquities of Kilkenny*, in *Collectanea de Rebus Hibernicus*, IX (1786), 516.

47. Leach, *History and Antiquities of Kilkenny*, 514.

48. Foster Watson, 'The Curriculum and Textbooks of English Schools in the First Half of the Seventeenth Century', *Transactions of the Bibliographical Society* (1900–1901), I.i, 159–260 (160). Still a standard work on the subject, supplemented by *The English Grammar Schools to 1660* (1908).

49. Watson, 'Curriculum and Textbooks of English Schools', 193, 166, 195.

50. Swift to Charles Ford, 12 November 1708, *Correspondence*, I, 109.

51. Swift, *Intelligencer* (No. 9), *PW*, XII, 51. Cf. *Travels* (IV.6), 239.

52. Swift to Bolingbroke and Pope, 5 April 1729, *Correspondence*, III, 329.
53. Richard Allestree, *The Whole Duty of Man: with Devotions for Several Occasions* (1669 edn), 69; see Ehrenpreis, I, 38–40, emphasizing the Puritan tenor of Hammond's preface rather than the really quite positive imperatives (by the standards of the time) of the text itself.
54. See Ehrenpreis, I, 32n., where he suggests that Jane Swift's marriage in Ireland in 1699 indicates her having spent her childhood there.
55. Leslie Stephen, *Swift* (Cambridge, [1882]; 2011 edn), 6–7; Richard Ashe King, *Swift in Ireland* ([1895]; New York, 1971 edn), 14.
56. Watson, 'Curriculum and Textbooks', 195.
57. Leach, *History and Antiquities of Kilkenny*, 512.
58. Browne, 'Kilkenny College', 223. See Ehrenpreis, I, 41n., discounting the story (surely too categorically, since the act itself was unexceptional), but quoting John Lyon's note in support of it.
59. Leach, *History and Antiquities of Kilkenny*, 509.
60. Ehrenpreis, I, 36–7; D. R. Thomas, *The History of the Diocese of St Asaph* (3 vols., 1908–13), I, 137.
61. Browne, 'Kilkenny College', 222.
62. The custom in successive years on Visitation Day; Leach, *History and Antiquities of Kilkenny*, 516.
63. Swift, *Tale of a Tub*, 92. The glimmering donkey skull appears in Section XI, where Jack's fondness for infusions of snapdragon leads him to light up exactly like the macabre lantern (but still stumble in the darkness). 'I cannot well find the author's meaning here, unless it be the hot, untimely, blind Zeal of Enthusiasts,' observed Swift's early commentator, Wotton (*Tale*, 92), but apart from the fact that Jack's herbal tea both heats him up and causes him again to resemble an ass, a kind of self-reversing medicine is at work. Snapdragon, besides being a stimulant (and thus causing Jack metaphorically to glow), was used as a protection against witchcraft. Here snapdragon actually causes Jack to resemble something infernal – the work in truth, though, of 'a roguish boy' and not the devil. The passage is an example of how crowded Swift's writing can be, swiping at both Reformed zeal and old-style superstition, notwithstanding the concrete observation of childish custom it also contains.

## 3. ABUSES OF LEARNING AND RELIGION

1. William Makepeace Thackeray, *English Humorists of the Eighteenth Century*, J. W. Cunliffe and H. A. Watt, eds. (Chicago, 1911), 50.
2. Swift, 'The Mechanical Operation of the Spirit', *Tale of a Tub*, 263. Here Swift's writer is in fact addressing a member of the Academy of Beaux Esprits on the western coast of Australia.

3. Ehrenpreis, I, 51, 83.

4. ibid., Appendix D, 276.

5. ibid., 83–4.

6. ibid., 54.

7. ibid., 84.

8. Swift, *Tale of a Tub*, 277.

9. ibid.

10. W. R. Wilde, 'Memoir of the Dublin Philosophical Society of 1683', *Proceedings of the Royal Irish Academy* (1836–9), 160–76 (166); Gilbert, *History of Dublin*, II, 309.

11. John William Stubbs, *The History of the University of Dublin* (Dublin, 1889), 117. The description of the old college is based on that given by Stubbs on 11–13 and, as stated earlier, 188–90, with the illustration of the college front from Brooking's map of 1728 on 189 and a plan of the college adapted from another, later map by John Rocque (1750) on 191. Constantia Maxwell comments on some of the points of confusion, *A History of Trinity College* (Dublin, 1946), 166–7. She also prints a drawing, made by Thomas Dineley, *c.*1681, of the college in its earlier state – the state in which Swift would first have seen it (facing 17).

12. Jorevin de Rocheford, 'Description of England and Ireland after the Restoration', in C. Litton Falkiner, ed., *Illustrations of Irish History and Topography, Mainly of the Seventeenth Century* (1904), 412.

13. Stubbs, *History of the University of Dublin*, 140–43.

14. Montaigne, 'Our Affections are Transported beyond Our Selves', *Essayes* (1.3), John Florio, trans. (3 vols., 1603; 1910 edn), I, 27. The aside should not be taken as epitomizing Montaigne's own complex attitude to Aristotle, as manifested in the *Essais*.

15. Stubbs, *History of the University of Dublin*, 139–42.

16. R. S. Crane, 'The Houyhnhnms, the Yahoos, and the History of Ideas', in J. A. Mazzeo, ed., *Reason and the Imagination: Studies in the History of Ideas 1600–1800* (New York, 1962), 231–53; Ehrenpreis, I, 49.

17. Ehrenpreis, I, Appendix D, 275.

18. ibid., 277.

19. ibid., 63.

20. Swift, *Travels* (IV.12), 275.

21. Swift to Alexander Pope, 26 November 1725, *Correspondence*, III, 118.

22. Swift, 'Maxims Controlled in Ireland', *PW*, XII, 131.

23. Swift, 'Family of Swift', *PW*, V, 192.

24. Ehrenpreis, I, 62.

25. Swift to Alexander Pope, 29 September 1725, *Correspondence*, III, 104.

26. Swift, 'On Barbarous Denominations in Ireland', *PW*, IV, 282; Ehren-

preis, I, 64, 70; Deane Swift, *Essay*, 36.

27. Ehrenpreis, I, 64.

28. Swift, 'A Character of Primate Marsh', *PW*, V, 211.

29. Ehrenpreis, I, 66.

30. For an introduction to speech the Ancients found 'farfetched' (*alienis*), see Quentin Skinner, *Reason and Rhetoric in the Philosophy of Hobbes* (Cambridge, 1996), 188–90. Philippa Berry writes of an 'Elizabethan cult of the *farfet*' in 'Tudor Laughter on the Verge of Metamorphosis: Ben Jonson and the Comedy of the Far-fet', in *Tudor Theatre 6: For Laughs?* (Berne, 2002), 249–60. See also, more generally, for probably the world's most helpful aide to rhetoric, Gideon Burton's website, *Silva Rhetoricæ*.

31. Swift, *Tale of a Tub*, 40, and introduction, xxviii–xxx.

32. ibid., 149.

33. ibid., 16. There is a double-bluff in this passage, since Swift is attacking his commentator Wotton for wronging a helpless victim by naming him erroneously as the author and suggesting he was dead (see Appendix, 367); when in truth Wotton's attribution was entirely accurate and Swift proved more than capable of defending himself. Despite the very effective robustness of tone, it is Swift who is arguing erroneously (and duplicitously).

34. Gilbert Burnet, *Bishop Burnet's History of His Own Time*, M. J. Routh, ed. (6 vols., Oxford, 1823), I, 459.

35. Swift, *Tale of a Tub*, 20.

36. ibid., 7. Leo Damrosch recently suggested that an anecdote of an encounter between Swift and Dryden, in which the latter told his younger relative, 'Cousin Swift, you will never be a poet', merits consideration (*Jonathan Swift: His Life and His World* (New Haven, 2013), 5). The tale was among those dismissed by Ehrenpreis (I, ix); certainly it would explain the distinctly personal taint of vitriol in Swift's opinion of Dryden.

37. Burnet, *History of His Own Time*, I, 468.

38. *Mercurius Civicus; or, The London Almanack 1674* (1674), C2v.

39. Anngret Simms, 'Medieval Dublin in a European Context: From Prototown to Chartered Town', in Howard B. Clarke, ed., *Medieval Dublin: The Living City* (Dublin, 1990), 37–52 (40–41).

40. James Farewell, *The Irish Hudibras; or, Fingalian Prince* (1689), 35. The work is also attributed in a later edition to a schoolmaster called William Moffet.

41. Swift, *Travels* (I.4), 42.

42. Swift, *Tale of a Tub*, 165.

43. Swift, *Travels* (I.6), 52.

44. Swift, *Tale of a Tub*, 269.

45. Ehrenpreis, I, 68–9, working from Trinity College records.

46. Swift, *Journal* (1 July 1712), II, 544.
47. Burnet, *History of His Own Time*, III, 241.
48. Gilbert, *History of Dublin*, II, 71–2.
49. Burnet, *History of His Own Time*, IV, 2.
50. Burnet, *History of His Own Time*, III, 266–7.
51. G. V. Bennett, *The Tory Crisis in Church and State 1688–1730: The Career of Francis Atterbury, Bishop of Rochester* (Oxford, 1975), 11. Bennett gives an exceptionally lucid and graceful survey of the post-Revolutionary ecclesiastical situation.
52. Swift made this remark to Esther Johnson in March 1713 (*Journal*, II, 637), when the long wait for preferment was beginning to depress him and the fine dinners he attended seemed almost distasteful. Memories of want if not poverty came back. By 'stuffing' it isn't clear whether he referred to sage, onion and breadcrumbs or the act of glutting himself.
53. Maxwell, *A History of Trinity College*, 81.
54. William King, *The State of the Protestants of Ireland under the Late King James's Government* (1692), 298.

## 4. THE TEMPLES AND THE TUB

1. Swift, 'Occasioned by Sir W— T—'s Late Illness', *Poems*, I, 52, ll. 31–2.
2. Gilbert, *History of Dublin*, II, 315–16.
3. William Makepeace Thackeray, *English Humorists of the Eighteenth Century*, J. W. Cunliffe and H. A. Watt, eds. (Chicago, 1911), 14–15.
4. Hugh Noyes, *The Isle of Wight Bedside Anthology* (Newport, 1951), 25–6, 77–8. The stanza quoted is from a local folksong.
5. *Epistolae Ho-elianae: The Familiar Letters of James Howell*, Joseph Jacobs, ed. (1895), 54.
6. Dorothy Osborne, *Letters to Sir William Temple*, Kenneth Parker, ed. (1987), 45, 47.
7. Swift, 'Ode to Sir William Temple', *Poems*, I, 29, ll. 81–6.
8. Sir William Temple, *The Early Essays and Romances of Sir William Temple . . . with the Life and Character of Sir William Temple, by His Sister Lady Giffard*, G. C. Moore Smith, ed. (Oxford, 1930), 149. He is clearly referring here to burliness rather than to physical fitness. In her 'character' of her brother, Lady Giffard insists he was 'lean but extream active' as a young man (27).
9. ibid., 95.
10. Osborne, *Letters*, 126.
11. Samuel Johnson, *The Lives of the Most Eminent English Poets, with Critical Observations on Their Works* (4 vols., rev. edn, 1783), III, 356; Deane Swift, *Essay*, 108.
12. The miniature of Lady Giffard was auctioned at Christie's in June 2013.

13. The note is printed by Moore Smith in Temple, *Early Essays and Romances*, 194.

14. Sir William Temple, 'To My Son', *Works* (2 vols., 1740), I, 108.

15. ibid., 27–31.

16. 'A Description of Mother Ludwell's Cave', Temple, *Early Essays and Romances*, 186–8.

17. ibid., xxviii.

18. Ehrenpreis, I, 104.

19. Swift, 'On the Death of Mrs Johnson', *PW*, V, 227.

20. Swift, *Travels* (II.2), 86, 304n.; Ehrenpreis, III, 457.

21. Swift, 'On the Death of Mrs Johnson', *PW*, V, 228.

22. William Flower to Swift, 18 March 1729, *Correspondence*, III, 318.

23. Swift, 'Family of Swift', *PW*, V, 193.

24. Swift, *Directions to Servants*, *PW*, XIII, 22.

25. Sir William Temple to Sir Robert Southwell, 29 May 1690, *Correspondence*, I, 1–2.

26. Deane Swift, *Essay*, 108; John Boyle, Earl of Cork and Orrery, *Remarks on the Life and Writings of Dr Jonathan Swift* (1752), 20; Ehrenpreis, II, 2.

27. Deane Swift, *Essay*, 99–100.

28. Robert H. Murray, ed., *The Journal of John Stevens* (Oxford, 1912), 123, 133–4.

29. Swift, *Tale of a Tub*, Section III, 94.

30. Swift, 'Ode to the King. On His Irish Expedition', *Poems*, I, 9, ll. 107–10.

31. Murray, *Journal of John Stevens*, 130, 109.

32. James Farewell, *The Irish Hudibras; or, Fingalian Prince (1689)*, 45–7.

33. Swift, 'Family of Swift', *PW*, V, 193.

34. Constantia Maxwell, *Country and Town in Ireland under the Georges* (Dundalk, 1949), 49.

35. Swift to the Reverend John Kendall, 11 February 1692, *Correspondence*, I, 2–5.

36. ibid.

37. Sir William Temple to Sir Robert Southwell, 29 May 1690, in Swift, *Correspondence*, I, 4.

38. Swift to Thomas Swift, 3 May 1692, *Correspondence*, I, 9.

39. Swift, 'Ode to the King', *Poems*, I, 6, ll. 1–4.

40. Swift, 'Ode to the Athenian Society', *Poems*, 14–15.

41. Swift, *Correspondence*, I, 8–9.

42. Swift, 'Ode to Dr William Sancroft', *Poems*, I, 40, ll. 176–9.

43. Swift to Thomas Swift, 3 May 1692, *Correspondence*, I, 10.

44. ibid.

45. ibid., 7.

46. Swift, 'Ode to the Honourable Sir William Temple', *Poems*, I, 27, ll. 39–49.

47. Swift to William Swift, 29 November 1692, *Correspondence*, I, 12.
48. Swift, 'Ode to the Honourable Sir William Temple', *Poems*, I, 32, l. 199.
49. Swift to Mrs Howard, 19 August 1727, *Correspondence*, III, 232.
50. Sir William Temple, 'Upon the Gardens of Epicurus', *Works*, II, 205–6.
51. Swift, 'Occasioned by Sir W—T—'s Late Illness and Recovery', *Poems*, I, 51–5.
52. Swift, 'Family of Swift', *PW*, V, 194.
53. John Dunton, quoted in Gilbert, *History of Dublin*, II, 70; see also Edward MacLysaght, *Irish Life in the Seventeenth Century* (3rd edn, Dublin, 1969), 384–5.
54. C. E. Ward, ed., *The Letters of John Dryden* (Durham, North Carolina, 1942), 63; C. Y. Ferdinand and D. F. McKenzie, 'William Congreve', *DNB*.
55. Swift, 'To Mr Congreve', *Poems*, I, 46–7, ll. 115–20.
56. ibid., 48, ll. 161–2.
57. Swift to Thomas Swift, 6 December 1693, *Correspondence*, I, 13–14.
58. Swift to Deane Swift, sr, 3 June 1694, *Correspondence*, I, 16.
59. George Story, *A True and Impartial History of the Most Material Occurrences in the Kingdom of Ireland during the Two Last Years* (2nd edn, 1693), 72, 160; reprinted along with Story's *Continuation* of his history in the same year.
60. Sir Henry Piers, 'A Chorographical Description of the County of West-meath' [1682], in *Collectanea de Rebus Hibernicis*, No. 1 (Dublin, 1786), 115.
61. Dunton, *Letters on Travels in Ireland*, in MacLysaght, *Irish Life in the Seventeenth Century*, 356.
62. Richard Head, *The Western Wonder* (1674), 29; quoted by MacLysaght, *Irish Life in the Seventeenth Century*, 107.
63. Murray, *Journal of John Stevens*, 139–40; quoted by MacLysaght, *Irish Life in the Seventeenth Century*, 107.
64. Swift, *Tale of a Tub*, 272–3. See note on 272.
65. William Molyneux, *The Case of Ireland's being Bound by Acts of Parliament in England, Stated* ([1698]; 1759 edn), 41–2.
66. Swift to Jane Waring, 29 April 1696, *Correspondence*, I, 18–23.
67. ibid., 22. On a misprint carried over from Ball to Williams's edition of the letters, see Ehrenpreis, I, 167n.
68. Ehrenpreis, I, 169, 257.
69. Swift, 'On Stella's Birth-day', *Poems*, II, 721.
70. Swift, *Tale of a Tub*, 34–5.
71. On Swift's suspected Asperger's syndrome, see, for example, Ioan James, *Asperger's Syndrome and High Achievement: Some Very Remarkable People* (2006), 45–52; John M. Ortiz, *The Myriad Gifts of Asperger's Syndrome* (2008), 158; John Harpur et al., *Succeeding in College with Asperger Syndrome* (2004), 249.

72. For a summary of commentary on Swift's evident strong yet troubled interest in Lucretius, see Marcus Walsh, ed., *The Cambridge Edition of the Works of Jonathan Swift. Volume I*: A Tale of a Tub *and Other Works* (Cambridge, 2010), lxxi. Walsh prints 'Swift's Moor Park Reading List' on 272–3.

73. Lucretius, *The Nature of Things* [*De rerum natura* VI.673–9], *A Philosophical Poem Literally Translated into English Prose by the Rev. John Selby Watson* (1851), 272.

74. Swift, *Travels* (I.4), 43.

75. Swift, a contribution to the *Tatler*, 28 September 1710 (No. 230), *PW*, II, 177. While admiring Persons's style, Swift disliked his ideas and belittled his understanding of history. See the marginalia to his copy of Persons's *A Conference about the Next Succession* (1594), giving particular attention in 1705 to a section that 'savours much of the Jesuit' (*PW*, V, 243).

76. Swift in his 'Apology' of 1709 gave 1696 as the year of composition (*Tale of a Tub*, 4).

77. Swift, *Tale of a Tub*, 73–5.

78. G. V. Bennett, *The Tory Crisis in Church and State 1688–1730: The Career of Francis Atterbury, Bishop of Rochester* (Oxford, 1975), 28–9. In 'An Answer to Some Considerations on the Spirit of Martin Luther', Atterbury was responding to a Papist tract, possibly by Obadiah Walker, that crudely accused Luther of moral indecency and the Anglican Church of basing its creed on his work.

79. Swift, *Journal* (15 March 1712), II, 514.

80. Swift, *Tale of a Tub*, 153.

81. James Boswell, *The Life of Samuel Johnson* (2 vols., 1820), I, 397.

82. Swift, *Tale of a Tub*, 5.

83. ibid., 79.

84. This is by no means to exhaust the meanings Swift drummed up with his title; the tub is, to mention merely a few others, the dwelling-place and pedagogic tool of the caustic philosopher Diogenes; a biblical instrument of spiritual cleansing; and a readily accessible acoustic device!

85. John Evelyn, quoted by Martin C. Battestin in 'The Idea of Order in Nature and the Arts 1660–1750', in *The Providence of Wit: Aspects of Form in Augustan Literature and the Arts* (Oxford, 1974), 34. This paragraph necessarily relies on a taxonomy that, though very useful, is in many ways limited; for another overview of the Augustan mode, see, notably, Howard Erskine-Hill, *The Augustan Idea in English Literature* (1983).

86. Numerous attempts have been made to put Swift's oeuvre in an 'evolutionary' continuum of English prose style. Yet, apart from the marked aversion he displays to anything over-labyrinthine in figure or syntax,

Swift's works generally resist such classifications, since at times he assumed a 'grand' and at others an acutely colloquial style, displaying his marked talent for impersonating labourers and servants. Although no 'Baroque' writer himself, he deeply admired earlier prose-writers differing in style and political allegiance as much as Bacon and Persons. For a sense of broader developments in literary style over the period just before Swift's maturity, see Thomas N. Corns, *A History of Seventeenth-century English Literature* (Oxford, rev. edn 2014). A more compact and idiosyncratic portal into this very large subject, bringing hermetic alchemists into the picture, is provided by Michael Srigley, 'The Lascivious Metaphor: The Evolution of the Plain Style in the Seventeenth Century', *Studia Neophilologica*, 60 (1988), 179–92.

87. George A. Aitken, *The Life and Works of John Arbuthnot* (Oxford, 1892), 23.

88. Bennett, *The Tory Crisis in Church and State*, 38–43.

89. Temple, *Miscellanea*, Part 2, in *Works*, II, 173–4, 142.

90. Temple, quoted in Swift, *PW*, I, xviii.

91. Swift, 'The Bookseller to the Reader', in 'The Battle of the Books', *Tale of a Tub*, 214.

92. Swift, 'Battle of the Books', *Tale of a Tub*, 258.

93. Swift, *Tale of a Tub*, 127–9.

94. ibid., 172.

95. ibid., 50.

96. ibid., 53.

97. ibid., 3.

98. Swift to Benjamin Tooke, 29 June 1710, *Correspondence*, I, 165.

99. Swift to the Reverend John Kendall, 11 February 1692, *Correspondence*, I, 3.

100. Swift, *Tale of a Tub*, 4.

101. The shimmery quality of Swift's personae has long been a subject of discussion; the apparent inconsistencies in Gulliver's character became a major subtopic in literary theory. See, as notable examples in an academic canon full of disagreement, Allan Bloom, 'Giants and Dwarfs: An Outline of *Gulliver's Travels*', in *Giants and Dwarfs: Essays 1960–1990* (New York, 1990), 35–54; Hugh Kenner, *Joyce's Voices* (1978), 3–5, arguing that the random 'objectivity' of Gulliver's viewpoint is integral to Swift's design; Ehrenpreis, III, 442–72 (with particularly crucial remarks, on 459 and 462–3, on Swift's way of responding to topics and 'inculcating' opinions without harmonizing or reconciling them); also, by way of contrast, John Lawlor, 'The Evolution of Gulliver's Character', in *Gulliver's Travels: An Annotated Text with Critical Essays*, Robert A. Greenberg, ed. (New York, 1961), 320–24. Claude Rawson tackles the matter with characteristic precision in his introduction to the *Travels*, xxii–xxiii.

102. Swift, *Tale of a Tub*, 4.

103. Swift, *Works*, John Nichols, ed. (19 vols., 1808), I, 44.

104. Swift, *Miscellaneous Prose Works*, Sir Walter Scott, ed. (3 vols., Edinburgh, 1847), I, 116.

105. Swift, 'Family of Swift', *PW*, V, 195.

106. Swift, 'The Problem', *Poems*, I, 65, ll. 7–12. Williams first suggested Romney rather than Berkeley as the poem's target (see his note, ibid., 64–5).

107. Lucy Aikin, *The Life of Joseph Addison* (2 vols., 1843), II, 154.


## 5. RECOVERING ESTHER

1. Swift, *Poems*, II, 724, ll. 43–4.

2. Ehrenpreis, II, 6.

3. Constantia Maxwell, *A History of Trinity College* (Dublin, 1946), 88.

4. Swift to Jane Waring, 29 April 1696, *Correspondence*, I, 21.

5. Ehrenpreis, II, 34 and n.

6. See the 'small scrap of manuscript' printed by Herbert Davis in *PW*, I, xix.

7. Swift, 'Family of Swift', *PW*, V, 195; Ehrenpreis, II, 6–8; John Forster, *The Life of Jonathan Swift* (1875), 123–5.

8. Swift, 'The Discovery. An. 1699', *Poems*, I, 62.

9. John Macky, *Memoirs of the Secret Services ...* (1733), 97; Temple Scott, *Prose Works of Jonathan Swift* (12 vols., 1897–1908), X, 79.

10. Thomas Sheridan, *The Life of the Rev. Dr Jonathan Swift* (2nd edn, 1787), 381, 30.

11. William King, *The State of the Protestants of Ireland under the Late King James's Government* (1692), 1–2, 293, 301.

12. Swift, 'Family of Swift', *PW*, V, 195.

13. Ehrenpreis, II, 9–11.

14. Swift to Bishop King, 16 July 1700, *Correspondence*, I, 36–7, 37 n. 3.

15. Deane Swift, *Essay*, 112.

16. C. Litton Falkiner, ed., *Illustrations of Irish History and Topography, Mainly of the Seventeenth Century* (1904), on Dublin Castle and the King's House at Chapelizod, 25–7, 53–5, 62–5.

17. Ehrenpreis, II, 14.

18. Forster, *The Life of Jonathan Swift*, 135.

19. Swift to Esther Vanhomrigh, 8 July 1713, *Correspondence*, I, 372–3.

20. Louis A. Landa, *Swift and the Church of Ireland* (Oxford, 1954), 35–41.

21. Swift to John Stearne, 17 April 1710, *Correspondence*, I, 163.

22. Swift, *Journal* (8 January 1712), II, 458.

23. John Savage, *Picturesque Ireland* (New York, 1884), 269. Reprinted in

Leo Damrosch, *Jonathan Swift: His Life and His World* (New Haven, 2013), 96.

24. Swift to Esther Vanhomrigh, 8 July 1713, *Correspondence*, I, 373.

25. Swift, *Journal* (19 March 1711), I, 220.

26. Henry Craik, *The Life of Jonathan Swift* (2 vols., 2nd edn, 1894), I, 100.

27. Ehrenpreis, II, 18–20.

28. Swift, *Journal* (25 September 1711), I, 368; Swift to Benjamin Motte, 25 October 1735, *Correspondence*, IV, 411.

29. Swift to Motte, 25 October 1735, *Correspondence*, IV, 411.

30. Swift to Jane Waring, 29 April 1696, *Correspondence*, I, 22–3.

31. Swift to Jane Waring, 4 May 1700, *Correspondence*, I, 35–6.

32. Swift, 'When I Come to be Old', *PW*, I, xxxvii.

33. *Correspondence*, I, 36 n. 1.

34. Swift, *Journal* (15 February 1711), I, 193.

35. Swift, 'To their Excellencies . . . The Humble Petition of Frances Harris, Who Must Starve, and Die a Maid if It Miscarries', *Poems*, I, 69, ll. 1–11.

36. Craik, *The Life of Jonathan Swift*, I, 101.

37. Swift, 'A Ballad on the Game of Traffick', *Poems*, I, 74–5.

38. Tradition has it that this parliamentary order, which became notorious in Irish nationalist discourse, was made on 27 June 1698: see, for example, Hugh F. Kearney, *Ireland: Contested Ideas of Nationalism and History* (New York, 2007), 245. James G. O'Hara, however, rejects the story as a myth in his recent *DNB* entry on Molyneux ('Reputation and Influence').

39. William Congreve, *Love for Love* (IV.1), in *The Complete Plays*, Herbert Davis, ed. (Chicago, 1967), 289.

40. Daniel Defoe, *A Tour through the Whole Island of Great Britain*, Pat Rogers, ed. (Harmondsworth, 1971), 296–7.

41. *Mercurius Civicus; or, The London Almanack 1674* (1674), C3r.

42. Defoe, *A Tour through the Whole Island of Great Britain*, 302.

43. Swift, 'An Inquiry into the Behaviour of the Queen's Last Ministry', *PW*, VIII, 139.

44. Gulliver mentions that the 'great Oven' in the King of Brobdingnag's palace is just a little smaller than the cupola of St Paul's: Swift, *Travels* (II.4), 103.

45. Swift, 'On the Death of Mrs Johnson', *PW*, V, 227.

46. Swift, 'To Stella, Visiting Me in My Sickness', *Poems*, II, 725, 723, ll. 65–6, 1–6.

47. Macky, *Memoirs*, 133.

48. ibid., 48–9; Swift, 'Marginalia', *PW*, V, 258.

49. Swift, *Tale of a Tub*, 27.

50. *ibid.*, 176.

51. Swift to William Tisdall, 3 February 1704, *Correspondence*, I, 43. One should nevertheless observe the context – here Swift was urging the virtue of delay on a rival for Esther Johnson.

52. Swift, 'On Poetry: A Rapsody', *Poems*, II, 644, ll. 117–26.

53. Swift, *Tale of a Tub*, 34–5.

54. Swift, *A Discourse of the Contests and Dissensions between the Nobles and the Commons in Athens and Rome*, *PW*, I, 232.

55. ibid., *PW*, I, 233.

56. The dedication Swift drafted late in 1719 states that he began his history some sixteen years previously; although the cause he gives for having abandoned the work, his indignation at a prevailing 'faction', presumably refers to the Tory witch-hunt of Somers (*PW*, V, 11). Ehrenpreis places the composition of the 'Historical Sketches' in 1700–1701 (II, Chapter 7).

57. Swift, 'History of England', *PW*, V, 26, 21–22.

58. Sir William Temple, *Works* (2 vols., 1740), IV, 495.

59. Temple, preface to 'Observations upon the United Provinces of the Netherlands', *Works*, I, xxxvii.

60. Swift, 'On the Death of Stella', *PW*, V, 228.

61. ibid.

## 6. DRIFTING WITH WHIGS, 1702–1709

1. Swift to William Tisdall, 3 February 1704, *Correspondence*, I, 43.

2. J. S. Clark, ed., *The Life of James the Second, King of England* (2 vols., 1816), II, 592–604.

3. Swift, *Travels* (IV.8), 247 and 351n.; the reference to Sorrel was proposed by Michael dePorte in 'Avenging Naboth: Swift and Monarchy', *Philological Quarterly*, 69 (1990), 429.

4. Gilbert, *History of Dublin*, III, 41–56.

5. Swift, *The Conduct of the Allies*, *PW*, VI, 17.

6. William Monck Mason, *The History and Antiquities of the Collegiate and Cathedral Church of St Patrick near Dublin* (Dublin, 1820), 44n.; Ehrenpreis, II, 76; Swift's surviving account books begin in November 1702.

7. There are at least two versions of this portrait, from the studio of Sir Godfrey Kneller; one hangs at Kensington Palace, the other at Beningbrough Hall, Yorkshire.

8. Lucy Aikin, *The Life of Joseph Addison* (2 vols., 1843), I, 117.

9. Swift, 'Memoirs, Relating to that Change which Happened in the Queen's Ministry in the Year 1710', *PW*, VIII, 119.

10. John Macky, *Memoirs of the Secret Services ...* (1733), 21–2.

11. Swift, *A Letter from a Member of the House of Commons in Ireland*

. . . *Concerning the Sacramental Test*, *PW*, II, 118; passage quoted in Deane Swift, *Essay*, 129.

12.  Swift, 'Memoirs, Relating to that Change which Happened in the Queen's Ministry in the Year 1710', *PW*, VIII, 120; this remark occurring in the much quoted and debated passage where Swift declares 'I found myself much inclined to be what they called a Whig in politics . . . But, as to religion, I confessed myself to be an High-churchman.'

13.  Swift to William Tisdall, 16 December 1703, *Correspondence*, I, 38–40.

14.  Swift to William Tisdall, 3 February 1704, *Correspondence*, I, 41–4.

15.  Swift to William Tisdall, 20 April 1704, *Correspondence*, I, 44–6.

16.  Swift, entries for 6–16 November 1708, Paul V. Thompson and Dorothy Jay Thompson, eds., *The Account Books of Jonathan Swift* (London and Newark, Delaware, 1984), 62.

17.  Swift to Knightley Chetwode, October 1724, *Correspondence*, III, 36.

18.  Swift, *Travels* (II.1), 80.

19.  Cecile O'Rahilly, *Five Seventeenth-century Poems* (Dublin, 1952), notes on 17, 85, 101.

20.  Swift, *Poems*, I, 96, ll. 1–6.

21.  From Ned Ward's *London Spy*, quoted by Aytoun Ellis, *The Penny Universities: A History of the Coffee Houses* (1956), 44–5. For more recent studies, see Brian William Cowan, *The Social Life of Coffee: The Emergence of the British Coffee-house* (New Haven, 2005), and David Brandon, *Life in a Seventeenth-century Coffee Shop* (2011).

22.  Swift, *Journal* (8 February 1711), I, 183.

23.  Swift, 'Hints Towards an Essay on Conversation', *PW*, IV, 90.

24.  John Boyle, Earl of Cork and Orrery, *Remarks on the Life and Writings of Dr Jonathan Swift* (1752), 105.

25.  Swift to Mrs Vanhomrigh, 6 June 1713, *Correspondence*, I, 366.

26.  Orrery, *Remarks*, 107.

27.  Swift to Anne Long, 18 November 1711, *Correspondence*, I, 278.

28.  Swift, 'On the Death of Stella', *PW*, V, 230.

29.  Joseph Addison, *The Campaign*, in Charles Cowden Clarke, ed., *The Poetical Works* (Edinburgh, 1859), 51, ll. 287–92.

30.  Aikin, *Life of Addison*, I, 177.

31.  Swift, 'A Meditation upon a Broom-Stick, and Somewhat Beside', *PW*, I, 240–41. On the broader connections to Boyle in Swift, see Gregory Lynall, *Swift and Science: The Satire, Politics and Theology of Natural Knowledge 1690–1730* (Basingstoke, 2012), 17–49.

32.  Swift, *Travels* (II.5), 105.

33.  Swift, 'The Battle of the Books', *Tale of a Tub*, 243.

34.  The story is told in Thomas Sheridan, *The Life of the Rev. Dr Jonathan Swift* (2nd edn, 1787), 38–9.

35.  Swift, *Predictions for the Year 1708 . . . by Isaac Bickerstaff Esq.*, *PW*, II, 141.

36. Richard Steele, preface to the octavo edition of 1710, the *Tatler* (repr. 1823), xi.

37. Swift to Benjamin Tooke, 29 June 1710, *Correspondence*, I, 165–6.

38. Swift, *Tale of a Tub*, 9.

39. Patrick Delany, *Some Observations upon Lord Orrery's Remarks on the Life and Writings of Dr Jonathan Swift* (Dublin, 1754), 13–14.

40. Swift, *Baucis and Philemon. Imitated from the Eighth Book of Ovid* (ll. 7, 23–8, 51–88, 173–8), *Poems*, I, 111–16.

41. Swift, *Predictions for the Year 1708*, PW, II, 143.

42. Patrick Curry, 'John Partridge', *DNB*.

43. Swift, 'Memoirs, Relating to that Change which Happened in the Queen's Ministry in the Year 1710', *PW*, VIII, 121.

44. Macky, *Memoirs*, 24.

45. Swift to Archbishop King, 10 June 1708, *Correspondence*, I, 84–6.

46. G. V. Bennett, *The Tory Crisis in Church and State 1688–1730: The Career of Francis Atterbury, Bishop of Rochester* (Oxford, 1975), 81.

47. Swift to William Tisdall, 16 December 1703, *Correspondence*, I, 39.

48. Swift, *A Letter . . . Concerning the Sacramental Test*, PW, II, 114.

49. Sir William Temple, 'Observations upon the United Provinces of the Netherlands', *Works* (2 vols., 1740), I, 108.

50. Swift, *A Letter . . . Concerning the Sacramental Test*, PW, II, 122.

51. Swift to Archbishop King, 15 April 1708, *Correspondence*, I, 79–80.

52. Stephen H. Daniel, *John Toland: His Methods, Manners and Mind* (Quebec, 1983), 5–7. See also Daniel's *DNB* entry on Toland and Robert Rees Evans, *Pantheisticon: The Career of John Toland* (New York, 1991).

53. John Toland, *Christianity Not Mysterious* (2nd edn,1698), x.

54. Swift, 'Remarks upon a Book, intitled, *The Rights of the Christian Church*', *PW*, II, 67–107. Swift's attitude in withholding works from the press is a subject worthy of study in its own right. He was invariably reluctant for a good thought or 'hint' to be lost. His motives in self-censorship evolve fascinatingly over the years, from sensitivity to Whiggish friends in the early 1700s to the possessiveness and wounded pride that made him reluctant to part with letters for Pope to publish towards the end of his life. On Swift's treatment of his manuscripts, see Stephen Karian, *Jonathan Swift in Print and Manuscript* (Cambridge, 2010)

55. Swift, *An Argument against Abolishing Christianity*, PW, II, 36.

56. Swift, *The Sentiments of a Church-of-England Man*, PW, II, 5.

57. Swift to Ambrose Philips, 14 September 1708, *Correspondence*, I, 100.

58. *Tatler*, 21 April 1709 (No. 5), 10.

59. *Tatler*, 18 April 1709 (No. 4), 8.

60. Edward Bottoms, 'Charles Jervas', *DNB*.

61. Swift, *Journal* (11 September 1710), I, 14. Some doubt still exists as to

whether the portrait of 1709–10 (in the National Portrait Gallery) is indeed Jervas's original.

62. Swift to Lady Giffard, 10 November 1709, *Correspondence*, I, 156.
63. Recalling Gulliver's impression of the 'great Oven' in the King of Brobdingnag's palace as being slightly smaller than the cupola of St Paul's: Swift, *Travels* (II.4), 103.
64. Swift, 'A Description of the Morning', *Poems*, I, 124–5.
65. Swift, 'Account of His Mother's Death', *PW*, V, 196.
66. John Lyon, 'Biographical Anecdotes of Dean Swift', in *A Supplement to Dr Swift's Works* (3 vols., 1779), I, xxv–vi.

## 7. RECRUITED BY TORIES, 1710–1714

1. Sir Andrew Fontaine to Swift, 27 June 1710, *Correspondence*, I, 164.
2. V. G. Kiernan, 'George Macartney', *DNB*.
3. Swift, describing Hamilton's death in the *Journal* (15 November, 1712), II, 570–73. For the Duke's prank on Swift and Swift's description of his character, see I, 323; the Duchess's kindnesses to Swift are mentioned at II, 553, 559.
4. Voltaire, *Candide; or, Optimism*, Chapter 3 (New York, 1911), 10.
5. Swift, 'Some Considerations upon the Consequences Hoped and Feared from the Death of the Queen', *PW*, VIII, 103.
6. Swift, *The History of the Four Last Years of the Queen*, *PW*, VII, 68.
7. Swift, *Journal* (30 October 1711), I, 397.
8. Swift, *Journal* (22 January 1712), II, 469.
9. Swift, *Journal* (15 October 1710), I, 59.
10. John Macky, *Memoirs of the Secret Services* ... (1733), 115–16.
11. Swift, *Journal* (30 September 1710), I, 35.
12. Swift, *Journal* (3, 4 October 1710), I, 40–41.
13. Swift, 'Description of a City Shower', *Poems*, I, 137, 139, ll. 17–20, 61–3.
14. Swift, *Journal* (15 October 1710), I, 60.
15. *Tatler*, 10 March 1710 (No. 144), 286.
16. Swift, *Examiner*, 2 November 1710 (No. 13), *PW*, III, 3.
17. Julia G. Longe, ed., *Martha, Lady Giffard: Her Life and Correspondence 1664–1722* (1911), 248.
18. Addison to Ambrose Philips, 23 December 1710, *The Letters of Joseph Addison*, Walter Graham, ed. (Oxford, 1941), 249.
19. Swift, *Journal* (15 January 1711), I, 165.
20. Swift, *Travels* (II.3), 95.
21. Swift, *Journal* (1 March 1713), II, 630.
22. Swift, *Journal* (21 January 1711), I, 171.
23. Swift, *Journal* (1 September 1711), I, 349.

24. Swift, *Journal* (31 October 1710), I, 77.

25. Swift, *Journal* (26–30 January 1711), I, 177.

26. Swift, *Journal* (26–30 June 1711), I, 288.

27. Swift, *Journal* (15 September 1712), II, 556.

28. Swift, *Journal* (15 January 1711), I, 165.

29. David Woolley first pointed out this habit of Swift's in his 'Note to the Corrected Impression' of Swift, *Correspondence*, IV, and incorporated such observations into his later four-volume edition of the letters (Frankfurt, 1999–2004).

30. Swift, *Journal* (13 February and 23 March 1712), II, 487, 522.

31. Alexander Pope, *The Rape of the Lock*, in *The Poems of Alexander Pope*, John Butt, ed. (repr. 1968), 227, Canto III, ll. 10–19.

32. John Wilmot, Earl of Rochester, 'A Ramble in St James's Park', in *Complete Poems*, David M. Vieth, ed. (New Haven, 1967; repr. 2002), 41, ll. 23–32.

33. Swift, *Journal* (25 July 1711), I, 319–20.

34. The Earl of Peterborough to Swift, 18 April 1711, *Correspondence*, I, 218.

35. Swift, *Journal* (31 December 1710), I, 145. 'I pray God he may recover to receive his Reward.'

36. Swift, *Journal* (7–8 February 1711), I, 183.

37. Swift, *Examiner*, 27 February 1711 (No. 27), *PW*, III, 82.

38. Swift, *Journal* (16 October 1711), II, 384.

39. Swift, *Examiner*, 2 November 1710 (No. 13), *PW*, III, 5–6.

40. Swift, *Examiner*, 28 December 1710 (No. 21), *PW*, III, 47.

41. Swift, 'Remarks upon a Book, intitled, *The Rights of the Christian Church*', *PW*, II, 67–8.

42. Francis Hare, *The Allies and the Late Ministry Defended* ... (4 parts, 1711–12), Part I, reprinted in *A Third Collection of Scarce and Valuable Tracts, on the Most Interesting and Entertaining Subjects* (4 vols., 1751), IV, 467. See *PW*, VI, x–xi, and on Hare's (astute) criticism of *The Conduct of the Allies and of the Late Ministry in Beginning and Carrying on the Present War*, Ehrenpreis, II, 494–5.

43. Swift, *Examiner*, 30 November 1710 (No. 17), *PW*, III, 25.

44. Swift, *Examiner*, 24 May 1711 (No. 42), *PW*, III, 157–62.

45. Swift, *Examiner*, 7 December 1710 (No. 18), *PW*, III, 29.

46. Arthur Mainwaring [?], *Medley*, 12 February 1711 (No. 20), in *Swift vs Mainwaring: 'The Examiner' and 'The Medley'*, Frank H. Ellis, ed. (Oxford, 1985), 236. The long introduction to this volume offers an exceptionally clear-sighted overview of the period and its disputes.

47. Swift, *Journal* (17 February 1711), I, 193–4.

48. Gerald Sandford Graham, *The Walker Expedition to Quebec 1711* (2nd edn, New York, 1969), 30. A lower figure of 5,000 troops (a contemporary estimate) is given in many histories (ibid., 127).

49. Swift, *Journal* (12 January 1711), I, 162–3.
50. Swift, *Tale of a Tub*, 165.
51. Swift, *A New Journey to Paris*, PW, III, 213.
52. Swift, *Journal* (21 April 1711), I, 248.
53. Swift, *Journal* (11 September 1711), I, 357–8.
54. Swift, *Journal* (29 May 1711), I, 282.
55. Swift to Archbishop King, 8 March 1711, *Correspondence*, I, 215.
56. ibid., 214–15.
57. Swift, *Journal* (8 March 1711), I, 211–12.
58. Swift, 'To Mr Harlyes Surgeon', *Poems*, I, 140.
59. Swift, *Journal* (7 September 1711), I, 353.
60. Swift, *Journal* (23 October 1711), II, 393.
61. Swift, 'Memoirs, Relating to that Change which Happened in the Queen's Ministry in the Year 1710', PW, VIII, 128.
62. Swift to Archbishop King, 8 January 1712, *Correspondence*, I, 283.
63. Swift, *Some Remarks on the Barrier Treaty*, PW, VI, 87.
64. Swift, *The Conduct of the Allies and of the Late Ministry in Beginning and Carrying on the Present War*, PW, VI, 42.
65. Swift, *Journal* (8 January 1712), II, 460.
66. Swift, *Journal* (6 January 1713), II, 597.
67. Swift, 'The Description of a Salamander', *Poems*, I, 82. Williams tut-tuts on an 'inexcusable' libel in his prefatory note to the poem.
68. Roy A. Sundstrom, 'Sidney, first Earl of Godolphin', *DNB*.
69. Swift, 'Memoirs, Relating to that Change which Happened in the Queen's Ministry in the Year 1710', PW, VIII, 122.
70. Swift, 'A Short Character of His Excellency, Thomas, Earl of Wharton', PW, III, 179.
71. Swift, *Journal* (14 September 1711), I, 360.
72. Swift, *Journal* (6 January 1711), I, 156.
73. G. V. Bennett, *The Tory Crisis in Church and State 1688–1730: The Career of Francis Atterbury, Bishop of Rochester* (Oxford, 1975), 53.
74. Archbishop King to Swift, 1 September 1711, *Correspondence*, I, 254.
75. Swift, *Journal* (12–13 September 1711), I, 358–9.
76. Swift, *A Letter from a Member of the House of Commons in Ireland to a Member of the House of Commons in England Concerning the Sacramental Test*, PW, II, 282. Swift cancelled this passage in 1727.
77. Swift to Archbishop King, 1 October 1711, *Correspondence*, I, 262.
78. Swift, *Journal* (12 March 1713), II, 637.
79. Swift, *Journal* (4 October 1711), II, 376.
80. Padraic Colum, introduction to *Gulliver's Travels, Presented by Willy Pogány* (New York, 1917), xi.
81. *The History of the Four Last Years of the Queen* was published in London and Dublin in 1758.
82. Swift, *Travels*, II.6, 121.

83. Swift, *Journal* (11 November 1710), I, 92; and, making an identical point almost exactly a year later, (3 November 1711), II, 401.

84. Swift, *Journal* (3 April 1711), I, 230: Harold Williams, the *Journal*'s modern editor, points out that the parenthesis might be an interpolation by Deane Swift, who transcribed this portion of the letters.

85. Swift to Archbishop King, 29 March 1712, *Correspondence*, I, 293.

86. Swift, *Journal* (18 March 1712), I, 516.

87. Deane Swift, *Essay*, 26.

88. Swift, *Journal* (12 December 1712), II, 579.

89. Swift, *Journal* (10 November 1711), II, 409.

90. On the early-modern meanings of 'slut', see for example Eugene Hammond, *Jonathan Swift: Irish Blow-in* (Delaware, 2016), 565.

91. Swift to Esther Vanhomrigh, 15 August 1712, *Correspondence*, I, 308.

92. Esther Vanhomrigh to Swift, 2 September 1712, *Correspondence*, I, 310.

93. Swift, *Journal* (2 September 1711), I, 375. Here Swift more than faintly rebukes Johnson for the incident, referring to the porter as '*your* acquaintance'.

94. Swift to Esther Vanhomrigh, 3 September 1712, *Correspondence*, I, 311. It seems that Vanhomrigh did, though, go to Windsor a few weeks later, and that the visit was not a happy one: see Ehrenpreis, II, 645.

95. Esther Vanhomrigh to Swift, 'June London 1713', *Correspondence*, I, 369.

96. Esther Vanhomrigh to Swift, 30 June [?] 1713, and Swift's reply, 8 July, *Correspondence*, I, 372–3.

97. On the dating of the poem, see Sir Harold Williams's long introductory note to his text in *Poems*, II, 684. Early printings of *Cadenus and Vanessa* date the poem 1713; though remarks by Swift, despite his unreliable memory for dates, would place it in 1712.

98. Swift, *Cadenus and Vanessa*, *Poems*, II, 687, l. 29.

99. ibid., 703, ll. 524–7.

100. ibid., 711, ll. 780–85.

101. Swift to Knightley Chetwode, 19 April 1726, *Correspondence*, III, 129–30.

102. Swift, *Cadenus and Vanessa*, *Poems*, II, 687, ll. 36–40.

103. Paul Baines and Pat Rogers, *Edmund Curll, Bookseller* (Oxford, 2007), 47; Swift, *Journal* (14 May 1711), I, 269.

104. Swift, *Journal* (17 October 1710, 28 February 1711), I, 62, 203.

105. Swift, *Journal* (6 April 1713), I, 654. He mentions seeing *Cato* in an unfinished state on 2 April (I, 651); another index of the confidence Addison placed in him.

106. Swift, *Journal* (15 January 1711), I, 165.

107. Swift, *Journal* (13–14 February 1713), I, 617–18.

108. Swift, *Journal* (1 January 1713), II, 593.

109. Swift, *Journal* (18 April 1713), II, 662.
110. Swift, *Journal* (13 April 1713), II, 660.
111. Paul V. Thompson and Dorothy Jay Thompson, eds., *The Account Books of Jonathan Swift* (London and Newark, Delaware, 1984), 154.
112. Swift to Esther Vanhomrigh, 8 July 1713, *Correspondence*, I, 372–3.
113. With his customary shrewdness, Ehrenpreis pieced together Swift's social activities at Laracor this summer from entries in his account books (II, 667–8). For the entries for this stay at Laracor (now edited and published), see Thompson and Thompson, *Account Books of Jonathan Swift*, 157–9.
114. Swift to Archbishop King, 20 October 1713, *Correspondence*, I, 397.
115. Stuart Handley, 'Charles Talbot, Duke of Shrewsbury', *DNB*; J. G. Simms, 'The Establishment of Protestant Ascendancy 1691–1714', in T. W. Moody et al., eds., *A New History of Ireland. Volume IV: Eighteenth-century Ireland* (Oxford, 1986), 29–32; Ehrenpreis, II, 719–22.
116. John Dunton, *Letters on Travels in Ireland*, printed by Edward MacLysaght, *Irish Life in the Seventeenth Century* (3rd edn, Dublin, 1969), 381–3.
117. See in particular *Some Advice Humbly Offer'd to the Members of the October Club in a Letter from a Person of Honour* (January 1712), *PW*, VI, 67–80.
118. Swift, *Tale of a Tub*, 155.
119. Swift, 'The Author upon Himself', *Poems*, I, 196, l. 67 and note.
120. Swift, *The Publick Spirit of the Whigs*, *PW*, VIII, 49.
121. The Duchess of Ormond to Swift, 24 April 1714, *Correspondence*, II, 18.
122. Swift, 'An Inquiry into the Behaviour of the Queen's Last Ministry', *PW*, VIII, 158–9; the comparative remark on Harley's 'Passions' is on 152.
123. Charles Ford to Swift, 31 July 1714, *Correspondence*, II, 93.
124. Swift, 'An Inquiry into the Behaviour of the Queen's Last Ministry', *PW*, VIII, 156.

## 8. THE PHANTOM ACADEMY

1. Swift, 'Thoughts on Various Subjects', *PW*, IV, 247.
2. John Geree to Swift, 24 April 1714, *Correspondence*, II, 19. For Swift's efforts to help 'young Parson Geree' to a better living see also *Journal* (22 December 1712), II, 585–6.
3. Swift to Esther Vanhomrigh, 8 June 1714, *Correspondence*, II, 26.
4. John Barber to Swift, 8 June 1714, *Correspondence*, II, 29.
5. Swift, *Journal* (10 May 1712), II, 533.
6. John Gay to Swift, 16 May 1732, *Correspondence*, IV, 23. Here Gay

echoes an opinion Swift expressed to him on the *Treatise Concerning the Principles of Human Knowledge*.

7. Swift, *Journal* (12, 17 April 1713), II, 659, 662. Swift's somewhat remote but always cordial relationship with Berkeley would merit at least a chapter of its own. At one level it is surprising that Swift should have admired Berkeley's philosophy (on which see, for example, *Correspondence*, III, 31-2), since its best-known premise is that reality is nothing but perception. However, Berkeley's arguments ultimately undermine the validity of any single viewpoint except God's and thus challenge the 'free-thinking' positions so abhorrent to the High Church school.

8. Swift to John Arbuthnot, 3 July 1714, *Correspondence*, II, 46.

9. Swift to John Arbuthnot, 16 June 1714, *Correspondence*, II, 36.

10. Swift to John Arbuthnot, 3 July 1714, *Correspondence*, II, 47-8.

11. George A. Aitken, *The Life and Works of John Arbuthnot* (Oxford, 1892), 70. See also George Sherburn, ed., *The Correspondence of Alexander Pope* (5 vols., Oxford, 1956), I, 234-5; Ehrenpreis, II, 754.

12. Swift to John Gay, 12 June 1714, *Correspondence*, II, 33. He was answering Gay's letter of 8 June 1714, *Correspondence*, II, 27-8.

13. David Nokes, 'John Gay' ('Early Years in London and First Publications'), *DNB*.

14. Swift, *Journal* (24 August 1711), I, 341.

15. Swift to John Arbuthnot, 3 July 1714, *Correspondence*, II, 46.

16. Swift, *Journal* (9 March 1713), II, 635.

17. Alexander Pope, *Windsor-Forest*, *Poems of Alexander Pope*, John Butt, ed. (repr. 1968), 199, ll. 111-14.

18. ibid., 210, ll. 407-12.

19. Swift, 'An Inquiry into the Behaviour of the Queen's Last Ministry', *PW*, VIII, 171.

20. John Arbuthnot to Swift, 17 July 1714, *Correspondence*, II, 69.

21. Charles Ford to Swift, 20 July 1714, *Correspondence*, II, 73.

22. Swift to the Earl of Oxford, 3 July 1714, *Correspondence*, II, 44-5.

23. Swift to John Arbuthnot, 3 July 1714, *Correspondence*, II, 47.

24. John Arbuthnot to Swift, 10 July 1714, *Correspondence*, II, 57.

25. Viscount Bolingbroke, *Letters and Correspondence, Public and Private, of the Right Honourable Henry St John, Lord Viscount Bolingbroke, during the Time He was Secretary of State to Queen Anne* (4 vols., 1798), I, 150.

26. Swift, *Journal* (22 June 1711), I, 295.

27. Swift, *A Proposal for Correcting the English Tongue*, *PW*, IV, 10.

28. A later dean of St Patrick's, J. H. Bernard, offers some fine observations on Swift's craft as a letter-writer in his introduction to the first volume of the *Correspondence*, edited by F. Elrington Ball (1910).

29. John Oldmixon, *Reflections on Dr Swift's Letter to the Earl of Oxford*,

*about the English Tongue* (1712), and Arthur Mainwaring et al., *The British Academy* (1712; repr. Los Angeles, 1948). The argument these men of letters clearly wished to have about the questions Swift raised is distorted by the need to maintain a political barrage against him.

30. Swift, *Journal* (31 May 1712), II, 535. Ehrenpreis's reflections on the issues in the *Proposal* provide a typically sharp and sane overview (II, 547).

31. Richard Steele, *Guardian* (12 May 1713) (1823), 83.

32. Steele to Swift, 19 May 1713 and Swift to Steele, 23 May 1713, *Correspondence*, I, 351, 355.

33. Steele to Swift, 26 May 1713 and Swift to Steele, 27 May 1713, *Correspondence*, I, 358–60.

34. Swift, *Proposal for Correcting the English Tongue*, PW, IV, 16.

35. See Ehrenpreis, II, 547; Williams's note, Swift, *Correspondence*, I, 358; Rae Blanchard, ed. *The Correspondence of Richard Steele* (Oxford, 1941), 76n. Davis in *PW*, IV, preserves the annotation to the passage given in early editions of Swift's works, which supplies Addison's name.

36. Swift, *The Importance of the* Guardian *Considered*, PW, VIII, 5.

37. Swift, *The Publick Spirit of the Whigs*, PW, VIII, 36.

38. Swift, *Journal* (22 June 1711), I, 295.

39. C. Y. Ferdinand and D. F. McKenzie, 'William Congreve', DNB; J. C. Hodges, *William Congreve, the Man: A Biography from New Sources* (New York and London, 1941), 98n.

40. Swift, 'A Libel on Doctor Delany', *Poems*, II, 481, ll. 41–4.

41. Swift, 'Memoirs, Relating to that Change which Happened in the Queen's Ministry in the Year 1710', *PW*, VIII, 119.

42. Swift, 'Marginalia', *PW*, V, 269, 271.

43. Swift, *A Preface to the Right Reverend Dr Burnet Bishop of Sarum's Introduction . . .*, *PW*, IV, 58.

44. ibid.

45. Swift, 'Marginalia', *PW*, V, 269.

46. Swift, 'An Inquiry into the Behaviour of the Queen's Last Ministry', *PW*, VIII, 136.

47. Swift, *A Letter of Thanks from my Lord Wharton to the Lord Bishop of St Asaph, in the Name of the Kit-Cat Club*, *PW*, VI, 152–3.

48. Swift, *Travels* (III.5), 171–3.

49. Swift, *Travels* (III.6), 175.

50. Steele, *Tatler*, 18 June 1709 (No. 30), 70.

51. Swift, *Journal* (13 December 1710), I, 122 and n. 27.

52. Swift, *Tale of a Tub*, 176.

53. Swift, *Journal* (20 November 1711), II, 417; his companions on that occasion were Sir Andrew Fountaine and the Earl of Pembroke.

54. Swift, *Journal* (19 March and 4 April 1713), II, 641, 654.

55. Andrew W. Moore, 'Sir Andrew Fountaine', *DNB*; quoting from W. T. Whitley, *Artists and Their Friends in England 1700–1799* (2 vols., 1928), I, 18.

56. Ehrenpreis, II, 303–4, commenting on the 'fatherly treatment' he finds throughout Swift's relationship with Ford; but noticing that the younger man also provided a stand-in for Swift's now very distant cousin Thomas, and other juniors he felt free to treat generously but condescendingly.

57. Swift, *Journal* (1 July 1712), I, 543.

58. Swift, *Journal* (4 February and 7 March 1711), I, 182, 208.

59. 'Bishop Kennett's Picture of Swift', *Correspondence*, V, 228–9.

60. Swift, 'The Author upon Himself', *Poems*, I, 94, ll. 13–14.

61. Raymond N. MacKenzie, 'Edmund Curll' ('Early Publications'), *DNB*.

62. Ros Ballaster, 'Delarivier Manley' ('Final Publications'), *DNB*. Old Fish Street ran east–west, below Cannon Street, ending near the site of the present Mansion House tube station.

63. Swift, *Journal* (28 January 1712), I, 474.

64. The best starting points for an exploration of Grub Street as a symbolic and physical element of eighteenth-century London remains Pat Rogers's *Hacks and Dunces: Pope, Swift and Grub Street* (1980) and also his earlier and more extensive version of the same book, *Grub Street: Studies in a Subculture* (1972).

65. Swift, *Journal* (7 August and 28 October 1712), I, 553, 568.

66. Swift, 'Corinna', *Poems*, I, 150, ll. 25–8.

67. Paul Baines and Pat Rogers, *Edmund Curll, Bookseller* (Oxford, 2007), 51.

68. The Duke of Ormond to Swift, 3 May 1715, *Correspondence*, II, 166–7.

69. Edmund Curll, *An Impartial History of the Life, Character, Amours, Travels and Transactions of Mr John Barber* (1741), 3. The Gazetteer in question was Dr William King (not to be confused with his namesake the Archbishop of Dublin), Charles Ford's predecessor. Swift claimed that he was also responsible for 'settling' King in the office (one he soon resigned): *Journal* (31 December 1711), II, 452.

70. Archbishop King to Swift, 17 March 1711, *Correspondence*, I, 216–17.

71. Swift, *Journal* (7 April 1711), I, 237.

72. Swift to Archbishop King, 10 April 1711, Archbishop King to Swift, 19 April 1711 and Swift to Archbishop King, 10 May 1711, *Correspondence*, I, 219–21, 223–5, 228.

73. Swift, *Journal* (21 March 1712), I, 518.

74. Swift, *Journal* (17 November 1712), I, 574.

75. Swift, 'A Farther Account of the Duel Fought between His Grace the Duke of Hamilton and the Lord Mohun' (*Post Boy*, 18–20 November 1712), *PW*, VI, 198–9.

76. Swift, *Journal* (11 November 1710), I, 119.

77. Swift, *Journal* (25 December 1711), II, 445.

78. Swift, obituary notice in the *Post Boy*, 25–7 December 1711, *PW*, VI, 196.

79. Paul V. Thompson and Dorothy Jay Thompson, eds., *The Account Books of Jonathan Swift* (London and Newark, Delaware, 1984), entry for 22 December 1711, 117.

80. Swift, 'An Inquiry into the Behaviour of the Queen's Last Ministry', *PW*, VIII, 139. Swift echoed this passage, suggestively, in a letter to Bolingbroke of 19 December 1719 (*Correspondence*, II, 333). See also his 'Thoughts on Various Subjects', *PW*, IV, 251.

81. Swift, *Some Free Thoughts upon the Present State of Affairs*, *PW*, VIII, 77.

82. Swift to Charles Ford, 1 July 1714, *Correspondence*, II, 43–4.

83. Charles Ford to Swift, 6 July 1714, *Correspondence*, II, 50–52.

84. Swift, *Some Free Thoughts upon the Present State of Affairs*, *PW*, VIII, 87.

85. Erasmus Lewis to Swift, 6 July 1714, *Correspondence*, II, 53.

86. Viscount Bolingbroke to Swift, 13 July 1714, *Correspondence*, II, 61.

87. Swift to Charles Ford, 18 July 1714, *Correspondence*, II, 71.

88. Charles Ford to Swift, 20 July 1714, *Correspondence*, II, 73.

89. Swift, *Some Free Thoughts upon the Present State of Affairs*, *PW*, VIII, 97.

90. Abel Boyer, *The Political State of Great Britain* (8 vols., 1711–15), VII, 561; Ehrenpreis, II, 734–5.

91. Swift, 'The Author upon Himself', *Poems*, I, 194, ll. 37–9.

92. Swift to Charles Ford, 25 July 1714, *Correspondence*, II, 83; pointed out by Ehrenpreis, II, 735.

93. Swift to John Arbuthnot, 25 July 1714, *Correspondence* II, 82–3.

94. Ian Higgins, 'Notes', in Swift, *Travels*, 286. In 1758 Benjamin Franklin seems to have visited the same church in search of his (Nonconformist) grandfather's grave.

95. John Arbuthnot to Swift, 26 June 1714, *Correspondence*, II, 41.

96. The Earl of Oxford to Swift, 27 July 1714, *Correspondence*, II, 85.

97. Viscount Bolingbroke to Swift, 3 August 1714, *Correspondence*, II, 101.

98. Swift, 'Some Considerations upon the Consequences Hoped and Feared from the Death of the Queen', *PW*, VIII, 103.

99. John Arbuthnot to Swift, 12 August 1714, *Correspondence*, II, 121.

100. Swift, 'The Author upon Himself', *Poems*, I, 193, 195, ll. 2, 51–2 and notes.

101. Charles Ford to Swift, 17 July 1714, *Correspondence*, II, 65–6.

102. Swift, 'The Author upon Himself', *Poems*, I, 193, l. 1, at least according to Swift's sometime admirer, the Earl of Orrery.

103. Lady Masham to Swift, 29 July 1714, *Correspondence*, II, 87–8.

104. Swift to Charles Ford, 3 August 1714, *Correspondence*, II, 99.

105. Viscount Bolingbroke to Swift, 11 August 1714, *Correspondence*, II, 117. I have altered Bolingbroke's punctuation in the passage quoted (which reads 'to bless. to bless me'), but the repetition is clearly a rare stutter in the Secretary's much vaunted fluency of composition.

106. Swift to Esther Vanhomrigh, 12 August 1714, *Correspondence*, II, 123.

107. Swift, 'Horace, *Lib.* 2. *Sat.* 6 [ll. 1–6]', *Poems*, I, 198. On the poem's date, see Swift to Charles Ford, 3 August 1714, *Correspondence*, II, 99.

## 9. SMALL DOMINIONS

1. Swift, 'An Epistle to a Lady', *Poems*, II, 629, ll. 1–2.

2. Swift to the Earl of Oxford, 19 July 1715, *Correspondence*, II, 182.

3. Jonathan Smedley, 'Verses, Fix'd on the Cathedral Door, the Day of Dean Gulliver's Installment', in *Gulliveriana; or, A Fourth Volume of Miscellanies* (1728), 77, ll. 9–12.

4. Swift to Archdeacon Walls, 22 December 1716, *Correspondence*, II, 234.

5. Swift, 'Dean Smedley Gone to Seek his Fortune', *Poems*, II, 455, ll. 1–12.

6. Swift, 'The Author upon Himself', *Poems*, I, 191–6, ll. 9–10. The key phrase in these lines furnished Maurice Johnson the well-chosen title of his important study, *The Sin of Wit: Jonathan Swift as a Poet* (Syracuse, New York, 1950).

7. Swift to Esther Vanhomrigh, 5 November 1714, *Correspondence*, II, 142 and notes. See also A. Martin Freeman, ed., *Vanessa and Her Correspondence with Jonathan Swift* (1921), 100–101 and notes.

8. On the early history of St Patrick's see the opening chapters by Howard B. Clarke of an excellent and much needed recent volume of essays, John Crawford and Raymond Gillespie, eds., *St Patrick's Cathedral: A History* (Dublin, 2009), 23–95.

9. This description of the cathedral draws on the striking and painstaking account given by Michael O'Neill in his chapters on the architectural history of the cathedral in Crawford and Gillespie, *St Patrick's Cathedral*, 96–119, 219–30, 328–49. On a visit to the cathedral in July 2015, I was also helped greatly by a short summary of the cathedral's development by the same author in the 2015 spring edition of the congregational newsletter *St Patrick's People*, 4–9.

10. John Dunton, *Letters on Travels in Ireland*, printed by Edward MacLysaght, *Irish Life in the Seventeenth Century* (3rd edn, Dublin, 1969), 383–4.

11. Conflict between deans of St Patrick's and archbishops of Dublin was common long before Swift and King's occasional spats: see Howard

B. Clarke, 'External Influences and Relations c.1220 to c.1500', in Crawford and Gillespie, *St Patrick's Cathedral*, 77.

12. Raymond Gillespie, 'Reform and Decay 1500–1598', in Crawford and Gillespie, *St Patrick's Cathedral*, 151–73 (154).

13. This account of the cathedral is also based on the opening chapters of William Monck Mason, *The History and Antiquities of the Collegiate and Cathedral Church of St Patrick, near Dublin* (Dublin, 1820), 1–18, as well as the new history edited by John Crawford and Raymond Gillespie.

14. See Maurice Craig's pages on the early development of Stephen's Green in *Dublin 1660–1860* (Dublin, 1969), 19–21.

15. Swift to John Worrall, 31 December 1713, *Correspondence*, I, 427. See also Ehrenpreis, II, 714–15, and Monck Mason, *Church of St Patrick*, 97–8, n. 1.

16. Kerry Houston, 'Reformation to the Roseingraves: Music 1550–1750', in Crawford and Gillespie, *St Patrick's Cathedral*, 244, 246–7.

17. Swift to Archdeacon Walls, 20 October 1713, *Correspondence*, I, 395.

18. Monck Mason, *Church of St Patrick*, 14.

19. See the map of the Liberty of St Sepulchre's in Monck Mason, *Church of St Patrick*, facing 11. The ground plan is a visual summary of the precincts and obviously cannot record smaller alterations made year by year; but it gives a more than adequate sense, when placed alongside other sources, of the cathedral and its grounds as Swift knew them.

20. Swift to Knightley Chetwode, 27 September 1714, *Correspondence*, II, 133.

21. John Lyon, 'Biographical Anecdotes of Dean Swift', in *A Supplement to Dr Swift's Works* (3 vols., 1779), I, xlv.

22. ibid., xxv–vi.

23. Swift to Knightley Chetwode, 6 October 1714, *Correspondence*, II, 135. On Lyon's 'materials' see A. C. Elias, Jr, 'Swift's Don Quixote, Dunkin's Virgil Travesty, and Other New Intelligence: John Lyon's "Materials for a Life of Dr Swift", 1765', *Swift Studies*, 13 (1998), 27–104.

24. Swift to Alexander Pope, 28 June 1715, *Correspondence*, II, 177.

25. Swift to Knightley Chetwode, 27 September 1714, *Correspondence*, II, 133.

26. Lyon, 'Biographical Anecdotes', in *A Supplement to Dr Swift's Works*, xii, xl, xlv.

27. Craig, *Dublin 1660–1860*, 27. Essex Bridge was replaced by Grattan Bridge; St Mary's Church is now a pub–restaurant.

28. Swift to Esther Vanhomrigh, 8 July 1714, *Correspondence*, II, 56.

29. Swift to Esther Vanhomrigh, [?] November 1714 and 'End of 1714', *Correspondence*, II, 147.

30. Esther Vanhomrigh to Swift, [?] December 1714, Swift to Esther Vanhomrigh, [?] 27 December 1714, *Correspondence*, II, 148–51.

31. Lyon, 'Biographical Anecdotes', in *A Supplement to Dr Swift's Works*, I, xlv.

32. The Duke of Ormond to Swift, 3 May 1715, *Correspondence*, II, 166.

33. Edmund Lloyd, *A Description of the City of Dublin in Ireland* (1732), 18–19.

34. Swift, 'Maxims Controlled in Ireland', *PW*, XII, 134–5.

35. Swift, *An Examination of Certain Abuses, Corruptions, and Enormities in the City of Dublin*, *PW*, XII, 220. Swift was writing here in 1732, but, while his fixation with excrement had strengthened in the interlude, the situation he described with respect to Dublin's poverty and sanitation had changed very little.

36. Swift, 'An Answer to Several Letters Sent Me from Unknown Hands', *PW*, XII, 86.

37. Lyon, 'Biographical Anecdotes', in *A Supplement to Dr Swift's Works*, xlv.

38. Swift to Alexander Pope, 30–31 March 1733, *Correspondence*, IV, 136.

39. Swift to Archdeacon Walls, 27 December 1714, *Correspondence*, II, 151–2 and notes.

40. Swift to Knightley Chetwode, 13 March 1722, *Correspondence*, II, 422; and Patrick Delany, *Some Observations upon Lord Orrery's Remarks on the Life and Writings of Dr Jonathan Swift* (Letter XIV) (Dublin, 1754), 132–3.

41. Swift, 'Dean of St Patrick's Petition to the House of Lords, against Lord Blayney', *PW*, V, 199–200.

42. Swift, 'On the Bill for the Clergy's Residing on Their Livings', *PW*, XII, 182.

43. Swift, *Travels* (III.8), 188.

44. Swift, 'On the Bill for the Clergy's Residing on Their Livings', *PW*, XII, 185.

45. Thomas Sheridan, *The Life of the Rev. Dr Jonathan Swift* (2nd edn, 1787), 356.

46. Sir Jonah Barrington, *Personal Sketches of His Own Times* (2 vols., 1827), I, 2–3.

47. Constantia Maxwell, *Country and Town in Ireland under the Georges* (Dundalk, 1949), 17.

48. Daniel Defoe, *A Tour through the Whole Island of Great Britain*, Pat Rogers, ed. (Harmondsworth, 1971), 223.

49. Louis A. Landa, *Swift and the Church of Ireland* (Oxford, 1954), 77–84.

50. Swift, *Correspondence*, II, 224, n. 2.

51. Swift to Archdeacon Walls, 26 February 1716, *Correspondence*, II, 193.

52. See Ehrenpreis, III, 40–49, on Swift's running duel with King over promotions.

53. Swift to Bishop Atterbury, 24 March 1716, *Correspondence*, II, 194.

54. Swift to Archdeacon Walls, 26 February 1716, *Correspondence*, II, 193.

55. Swift to Archdeacon Walls, 4 October 1716, *Correspondence*, II, 218.

56. Bishop Atterbury to Swift, 6 April 1716, *Correspondence*, II, 195–7, and Swift to Bishop Atterbury, 18 April 1716, 197–9.

57. Swift, *Journal* (26 November 1710), I, 104.

58. Swift, *Journal* (19 March 1711), I, 220.

59. Swift to Archdeacon Walls, 6 May 1716, *Correspondence*, II, 201.

60. Swift to Archbishop King, 17 June 1716, *Correspondence*, II, 205–7, writing from Gallstown in County Louth.

61. Alexander Pope to Swift, 20 June 1716, *Correspondence*, II, 211.

62. Swift to Alexander Pope, 30 August 1716, *Correspondence*, II, 215.

63. Swift to Archdeacon Walls, 13 December 1716, *Correspondence*, II, 229.

64. Swift to Esther Vanhomrigh, [?] December 1716, *Correspondence*, II, 239.

65. Swift to Charles Ford, 22 July 1722, *Correspondence*, II, 431.

66. Swift to Archdeacon Walls, 4 October and 6 December 1716, *Correspondence*, II, 218, 228.

67. Swift to Archdeacon Walls, 3 January 1717, *Correspondence*, II, 243.

68. Swift, '*Bon Mots de* Stella', *PW*, V, 237. The remark was made, Swift says, 'in the late King's time', though possibly of course during a later visit by Jervas.

69. Swift to Archdeacon Walls, 13 January 1717, *Correspondence*, II, 248.

70. Swift to Archdeacon Walls, 27 January 1717, *Correspondence*, II, 251.

71. Swift to Archdeacon Walls, 31 January 1717, *Correspondence*, II, 253.

72. Swift, 'Character of Dr Sheridan', *PW*, V, 216.

73. Swift, 'The History of the Second Solomon', *PW*, V, 222.

74. Thomas Sheridan, 'To the Dean of St Patrick's', in Swift, *Poems*, III, 970, ll. 1–8.

75. Swift, 'The Dean of St Patrick's to Tho: Sheridan', *Poems*, III, 976, ll. 5–8, 9–12, 36.

76. Ehrenpreis, III, 53.

77. Joseph Addison to Swift, 20 March 1718, *Correspondence*, II, 286.

78. Paul V. Thompson and Dorothy Jay Thompson, eds., *The Account Books of Jonathan Swift* (London and Newark, Delaware, 1984), 178.

79. Swift, 'Ad Amicum Eruditum Thomam Sheridan', *Poems*, I, 213. The poem may not be dated precisely, but Faulkner assigned it to 1717; Williams (n. 1) and Ehrenpreis (III, 63) broadly agree.

80. Swift, 'On Dr Rundle', *Poems*, III, 821, l. 61.

81. Swift, 'To Mr Delany', *Poems*, I, 215–19.

82. Swift to Patrick Delany, 10 November 1718, *Correspondence*, II, 301; on the delay in sending, Ehrenpreis, III, 66.

83. Swift and Thomas Sheridan, 'Sheridan, A Goose', in Swift, *Poems*, III, 982, 984, l. 1, and in Sheridan's answer, ll. 31–2.

84. Delany, *Observations* (Letter II), 12–13.

## 10. BURSTING BUBBLES

1. Swift, *A Letter to the Shop-keepers, Tradesmen, Farmers, and Common-people of Ireland, Concerning the Brass Half-pence Coined by Mr Woods*, PW, X, 4.

2. Swift to Charles Ford, 8 December 1719, *Correspondence*, II, 330.

3. D. W. Hayton, 'John Evans, East India Company Chaplin and Church of Ireland Bishop of Meath', *DNB*.

4. Ehrenpreis, III, 52, citing Evans's correspondence with Wake.

5. Swift to Dean Stearne, 17 April 1710, *Correspondence*, I, 163. The make-up of his 'audience' at Laracor seems to have changed little over the years.

6. Patrick Delany, *Some Observations upon Lord Orrery's Remarks on the Life and Writings of Dr Jonathan Swift* (Letter XVI) (Dublin, 1754), 147.

7. Swift to Bishop Evans, 22 May 1719, *Correspondence*, II, 327.

8. Swift to Charles Ford, 8 December 1719, *Correspondence*, II, 329.

9. See Ehrenpreis on Chetwode, III, 60–62: his verdict is that Chetwode was the sort of person one should avoid befriending (62 n. 2).

10. It is dated 1718 by the National Portrait Gallery; though if he didn't paint it earlier, Jervas might have made drawings for it during his trip to Ireland in autumn 1716.

11. Esther Vanhomrigh to Swift, [?] December 1720, *Correspondence*, II, 363.

12. Swift to Esther Vanhomrigh, 12 May 1719, *Correspondence*, II, 325.

13. Swift to Esther Vanhomrigh, 4 August 1720, *Correspondence*, II, 352.

14. Esther Vanhomrigh to Swift, 1720, *Correspondence*, II, 364.

15. Swift to Esther Vanhomrigh, 13 or 20 July 1720; *Correspondence*, II, 350. On Dr Price, later Archbishop of Cashel, see ibid., 351 n. 1.

16. Swift, *Correspondence*, I, 36 n. 1

17. Swift to Esther Vanhomrigh, 4 August 1720, *Correspondence*, II, 352.

18. Swift to Esther Vanhomrigh, 13 August 1720, *Correspondence*, II, 356.

19. Esther Vanhomrigh to Swift, [?] mid-August 1720, *Correspondence*, II, 357.

20. Swift to Esther Vanhomrigh, 15 October 1720, *Correspondence*, II, 359–60.

21. Leo Damrosch, *Jonathan Swift: His Life and His World* (New Haven, 2013), 328.

22. Swift to Esther Vanhomrigh, 15 October 1720, *Correspondence*, II, 361: 'The Governr was with me at six a Clock this morning but did not stay two minutes, and deserves a chiding wch you must give when you drink yr Coffee next.' Damrosch (*Jonathan Swift*, 328) interprets this passage as hinting at an erotic dream, because Swift sometimes referred to Vanhomrigh as 'Governor Huff' (e.g. Swift to Esther Vanhomrigh, 13 August 1720, *Correspondence*, II, 355). This leads one to ask: is

Vanhomrigh indeed the 'Governor' who was fleetingly with Swift in his dream? And why and how is *she* to administer the chiding (to herself, effectively) over her next coffee? It is also not entirely certain that 'Governor Huff' elsewhere in the correspondence *was* in fact a name for Vanhomrigh; it could equally denote the spirit of spleen and depression that Swift urged his friend so often to resist. As such, the sentence from October 1720 quoted above could simply mean, 'I was feeling rather moody at about six this morning, but only for about two minutes, and you must tell off Governor Huff for making me melancholy.'

23. Swift to Esther Vanhomrigh, 4 August 1720, *Correspondence*, II, 353.
24. Esther Vanhomrigh to Swift, 1720, *Correspondence*, II, 354.
25. Swift to Esther Vanhomrigh, 13 August 1720, *Correspondence*, II, 356.
26. Swift, 'To Stella, Visiting Me in My Sickness', *Poems*, III, 726, ll. 93–108.
27. Swift to Esther Vanhomrigh, 27 February 1721, *Correspondence*, II, 377–8.
28. Swift to Esther Vanhomrigh, 5 July 1721, *Correspondence*, II, 392.
29. Swift, 'On Stella's Birth-day [1719]', *Poems*, III, 721–2.
30. Swift, 'Stella's Birth-day [1721]', *Poems*, III, 734, l. 16.
31. Swift, 'The Progress of Beauty', *Poems*, I, 226, ll. 13–16.
32. ibid., 229, ll. 111–16.
33. See the discussion of this question by Louise Barnett in *Jonathan Swift in the Company of Women* (New York, 2007), 125–53. On the group of poems to which 'The Progress of Beauty' belongs, and indeed Swift's work more broadly, see William Ian Miller's brilliant *Anatomy of Disgust* (Cambridge, Massachusetts, 1997), in which Swift features prominently as a 'grand and desperate' witness of the association between disgust and misanthropy (xlv and *passim*).
34. Swift, 'The Progress of Beauty', *Poems*, I, 229, ll. 117–20.
35. Swift to Archbishop King, 31 December 1713, *Correspondence*, I, 425, and to Charles Ford, August 1714, *Correspondence*, II, 127.
36. The Declaratory Act was prompted by the Annesley Case, a complex series of appeals and counter-appeals that crossed between Dublin and Westminster; see Ehrenpreis, III, 29–30.
37. Swift to Charles Ford, 4 April 1720, *Correspondence*, II, 342, n. 2.
38. Swift, *Travels* (I.5), 47.
39. Ehrenpreis, III, 123; the proposal was made in response to the Wool Act of 1699. Cf. J. G. Simms, 'The Establishment of Protestant Ascendancy 1691–1714', in T. W. Moody et al., eds., *A New History of Ireland. Volume IV: Eighteenth-century Ireland* (Oxford, 1986), 13–15.
40. Swift, *A Proposal for the Universal Use of Irish Manufacture*, *PW*, IX, 18.
41. Edmund Lloyd, *A Description of the City of Dublin* (1732), 20–21.

42. Swift to Alexander Pope, 10 January 1721, *Correspondence*, II, 367–8.

43. Swift, 'Marginalia', *PW*, V, 258.

44. Swift to Alexander Pope, 10 January 1721, *Correspondence*, II, 371.

45. Swift to Charles Ford, 15 April 1721, *Correspondence*, II, 380.

46. Swift, *A Proposal for the Universal Use of Irish Manufacture*, PW, IX, 15.

47. Swift, 'Causes of the Wretched Condition of Ireland', *PW*, IX, 201.

48. John Boyle, Earl of Cork and Orrery, *Remarks on the Life and Writings of Dr Jonathan Swift* (1752), 70–71.

49. Swift to Charles Ford, 15 December 1720, *Correspondence*, II, 364–5.

50. Swift, 'The Bubble' ['Upon the South Sea Project'], *Poems*, I, 250–56, ll. 65–9, 9–16, 137–40.

51. Swift, *A Proposal for the Universal Use of Irish Manufacture*, PW, IX, 19.

52. Swift to Alexander Pope, 10 January 1720, *Correspondence*, II, 367.

53. Raymond Gillespie, 'An Age of Modernization 1598–1690', in John Crawford and Raymond Gillespie, eds., *St Patrick's Cathedral: A History* (Dublin, 2009), 178, 193.

54. On the southside of the Liffey; now in the district of Lower Exchange Street. See Maurice Craig, *Dublin 1660–1860* (Dublin, 1969), 80–81.

55. Swift, 'An Epilogue, to be Spoke at the Theatre Royal', *Poems*, I, 273–4, ll. 1–4 and Williams's note.

56. Swift to Charles Ford, 15 April 1721, *Correspondence*, II, 381.

57. Matthew Prior to Swift, 28 February 1721, *Correspondence*, II, 378.

58. Viscount Bolingbroke to Swift, 28 July 1721, *Correspondence*, II, 394–6.

59. Swift, 'Marginalia', *PW*, V, 243.

60. Thomas Herbert, *Travels*, Sir William Foster, ed. (1928), 28.

61. Swift, 'The Bubble', *Poems*, I, 254, ll. 86–9.

62. Swift, 'Marginalia', *PW*, V, 243. See David Harvey, 'Jonathan Swift on Herodotus', *Notes & Queries*, 234 (1989), 50–51.

63. Swift to Charles Ford, 15 April 1721, *Correspondence*, II, 381.

64. Swift to Bishop Evans, 5 June 1721, *Correspondence*, II, 389.

65. Swift to Archbishop King, 28 September 1721, *Correspondence*, II, 404–7, and Matthew Prior to Swift, 28 February 1721, *Correspondence*, II, 378.

66. Swift, 'The Journal', *Poems*, I, 278–83.

67. Swift to the Reverend Daniel Jackson, 6 October 1721, *Correspondence*, II, 407–8; Swift, 'The Journal', *Poems*, I, 283, ll. 121–2.

68. Swift to the Reverend Daniel Jackson, 6 October 1721, *Correspondence*, II, 408.

69. Swift to the Reverend Daniel Jackson, 26 (or 28) March 1722, *Correspondence*, II, 425.

70. Swift to Knightley Chetwode, 30 January 1722 and 13 March 1722, *Correspondence*, II, 417, 421.

71. G. V. Bennett, *The Tory Crisis in Church and State: The Career of Francis Atterbury, Bishop of Rochester* (Oxford, 1975), 242–3.

72. Swift, 'A Satirical Elegy on the Death of a Late Famous General', *Poems*, I, 296–7, ll. 25–32.

73. Swift, 'Upon the Horrid *Plot* Discovered by Harlequin, the Bishop of Rochester's French Dog ... Written in the Year 1722', *Poems*, I, 298, ll. 1–14.

74. Swift 'To Stella, Who Collected and Transcribed His Poems', *Poems*, II, 730, ll. 87–92.

75. Ehrenpreis, III, 325, arguing convincingly that the Talbot's Castle scheme was a 'device' to put some money Johnson's way. At around the same time, Ehrenpreis points out, Swift was making complex investments to benefit the widow of Anthony Raymond (the former Rector of Trim) as well as 'Mrs Johnson'.

76. Swift to Esther Vanhomrigh, 1 June 1722, *Correspondence*, II, 426–7.

77. Viscount Bolingbroke to Swift, 1 January 1722, *Correspondence*, II, 415.

78. Esther Vanhomrigh to Swift, [seemingly after 1] June 1722, *Correspondence*, II, 429.

79. Swift to Charles Ford, 22 July 1722, *Correspondence*, II, 430.

80. Swift to Esther Vanhomrigh, 13 July 1722, *Correspondence*, II, 429.

81. Swift to Charles Ford, 22 July 1722, *Correspondence*, II, 431.

82. Swift to Esther Vanhomrigh, 7 August 1722, *Correspondence*, II, 433.

83. David Nokes, 'John Gay ('The Middle Years')', *DNB*.

84. This and the quotations from Gay in the preceding paragraph are from Gay to Swift, 22 December 1722, *Correspondence*, II, 439–40.

85. Swift, 'To Charles Ford Esquire on His Birthday ... 1722–3', *Poems*, I, 309–15.

86. Swift to John Gay, 8 January 1722, *Correspondence*, II, 444.

87. Swift, 'A Letter to a Young Lady, on Her Marriage', *PW*, IX, 87.

88. ibid., 90–91.

89. ibid., 92–3.

90. ibid.

91. Orrery, *Remarks*, 107.

92. Delany, *Observations* (Letter VI), 45–6.

93. Swift, 'Stella at Wood-Park', *Poems*, II, 750, ll. 14–20.

94. Swift to Robert Cope, 11 May 1722, *Correspondence*, II, 453.

95. Swift to John Gay, 8 January 1722, *Correspondence*, II, 442.

96. Clive Probyn, in his recent *DNB* article on Vanhomrigh, favours the theory that there was a breach; Ehrenpreis believed that they didn't quarrel, but that Swift's fear of loss prevented him from contacting Vanhomrigh (II, 389).

97. Delany, *Observations* (Letter VIII), 84. Delany's text reads 'nothing, which would either do honour to her character' but this is clearly a misprint.

98. Swift to Knightley Chetwode, 'Past twelve at night', 2 June 1723, *Correspondence*, II, 457.

99. Orrery, *Remarks*, 108.

100. Delany, *Observations* (Letter X), 76.

101. Swift, 'Carbery Rocks in the County of Cork, Ireland', William Dunkin, trans., *Poems*, I, 318, ll. 1–6.

102. Delany, *Observations* (Letter XI), 94.

103. Swift to Thomas Sheridan, 3 August 1723, *Correspondence*, II, 463.

104. Swift, 'Stella at Wood-Park', *Poems*, II, 751, ll. 47–56.

105. Delany, *Observations* (Letter V), 40.

106. Swift, *Some Arguments against Enlarging the Power of Bishops in Letting of Leases*, *PW*, IX, 47, 45.

107. Alexander Pope to Swift, August 1723, *Correspondence*, II, 458.

108. Alexander Swift, 'To Charles Ford on his Birthday', *Poems*, I, 313, ll. 35–50.

109. Bennett, *The Tory Crisis in Church and State*, 277.

110. *Tatler*, 10 September 1709 (No. 66), 148.

111. Delany, *Observations* (Letter IV), 28.

112. See Louis A. Landa, introduction to the Sermons, *PW*, IX, 97–8.

113. Delany, *Observations* (Letter XV), 140.

114. Swift, 'On the Trinity', *PW*, IX, 166.

115. Swift to Knightley Chetwode, 14 July 1724, *Correspondence*, III, 22.

## 11. DEAN GULLIVER

1. Swift, 'Horace, Book I, Ode XIV [ll. 9–10, 37–8]', *Poems*, III, 770–71: the 'ship' (and 'floating isle') is Swift's adapted allegory of Ireland.

2. 'Hibernicus', *Dublin Weekly Journal*, 27 August 1726.

3. J. H. Plumb, *Sir Robert Walpole. Vol. II: The King's Minister* (1960), 67–8.

4. John Boyle, Earl of Cork and Orrery, *Remarks on the Life and Writings of Dr Jonathan Swift* (1752), 71–3.

5. Swift, *A Letter to the Whole People of Ireland*, *PW*, X, 53, 62.

6. Swift, *A Letter to the Lord Chancellor Middleton*, *PW*, X, 100–101; 'Whitshed's Motto on His Coach', *Poems*, I, 347, ll. 1–2.

7. Swift and Sir William Fownes, 'Verses Left in a Window of Dublin Castle', *Poems*, II, 368.

8. Lord Carteret to Swift, 4 August 1724, *Correspondence*, III, 26.

9. Swift to Knightley Chetwode, 18 January 1725, *Correspondence*, III, 49.

10. John Dunton, *Letters on Travels in Ireland*, printed by Edward MacLysaght, *Irish Life in the Seventeenth Century* (3rd edn, Dublin, 1969), 385–6.

11. The story of how the King of Laputa crushed the Lindalino rebellion

(*Travels*, III.3) was added to the copy emended by Charles Ford, but still not included in the subsequent authorized edition of 1735 (Vol. III of Faulkner's Dublin edition of Swift's *Works*).

12. Swift, *Travels* (III.3), 155.

13. Viscount Bolingbroke to 'the three Yahoos of Twickenham', 23 July 1726, *Correspondence*, III, 146–7.

14. Swift to Alexander Pope, 6 March 1729, *Correspondence*, III, 315. See also, notably, 'Verses on the Death of Dr Swift', *Poems*, II, 559, ll. 179–83.

15. Swift to John Worrall, 15 July 1726, *Correspondence*, III, 141.

16. Swift to James Stopford, 20 July 1726, *Correspondence*, III, 145.

17. See Ehrenpreis's conjectures on this process, III, 494.

18. 'Richard Sympson' to Benjamin Motte, 8 August 1726, Motte to 'Sympson', 11 August 1726, and 'Sympson' to Motte (a single terse line), 13 August 1726, *Correspondence*, III, 152–5.

19. Swift to Thomas Sheridan, 8 July 1726, *Correspondence*, III, 140.

20. Alexander Pope to Swift, 22 August 1726, *Correspondence*, III, 156.

21. Swift to Alexander Pope, late August 1726, *Correspondence*, III, 158.

22. Patrick Delany, *Some Observations upon Lord Orrery's Remarks on the Life and Writings of Dr Jonathan Swift* (Letter XII) (Dublin, 1754), 100.

23. Dunton, *Letters on Ireland*, in MacLysaght, *Irish Life in the Seventeenth Century*, 387.

24. Gilbert, *History of Dublin*, II, 147–51.

25. 'Hibernicus', *Dublin Weekly Journal*, 10 December 1726; this was in fact one of the very few issues that winter in which Steel's advert did *not* appear. It can be found in the previous issue, on 3 December.

26. John Gay to Swift, 17 November 1726, *Correspondence*, III, 182.

27. John Arbuthnot to Swift, 5 November 1726, *Correspondence*, III, 180.

28. Alexander Pope to Swift, 16 November 1726, *Correspondence*, III, 182.

29. Ehrenpreis, III, 493, summarizing Pope's efforts to persuade Swift that being paid for one's writing might not be entirely immoral.

30. See Ehrenpreis, III, 498, for a summary of the early publication history, working largely from Sir Harold Williams's introduction to Herbert Davis's edition of the *Travels* for *PW*, XI, 22–4. Ehrenpreis's entire chapter '"Gulliver" in Print' (III, 497–508) is mandatory reading. The literature on the text of the *Travels* has of course grown substantially since, but Williams's introduction to *PW*, XI, his own 1926 edition of the *Travels* and the elegant 1950 Sandars Lectures, printed as *The Text of Gulliver's Travels*, surely remain key reference points – not only for Swift's text but bibliographical studies in general.

31. The Earl of Peterborough to Swift, 29 November 1726, *Correspondence*, III, 192.

32. Swift, *Travels* (I.3), 33–4. For an earlier remark, in an unpublished

pamphlet on rope-dancers becoming bishops, see Swift, 'Remarks upon a Book, intitled *The Rights of the Christian Church*', *PW*, II, 5.

33. Swift, *Travels into Several Remote Nations of the World. In Four Parts* (2 vols., 2 Parts in each vol., 1726), Part IV, 92–4; *Travels* (IV.6), 237–8.

34. 'A Letter from Capt. Gulliver to His Cousin Sympson', printed at the front of later editions, complained about an interpolated passage in the first, arranged by Motte, which exonerated Queen Anne from ruling by means of a chief minister. 'Gulliver' names Godolphin and Oxford and categorically rejects the addition for making him say 'the thing which is not' (*Travels*, I, 7). On the unauthorized passage, supposedly by one Andrew Tooke, a clergyman who had died by 1733, see Ehrenpreis, III, 497, and Swift to Charles Ford, 9 October 1733, *Correspondence*, III, 198.

35. Ehrenpreis, III, 502–4.

36. Swift to Viscount Bolingbroke, 19 December 1719, *Correspondence*, II, 332.

37. Swift to James Stopford, 15 October 1726, *Correspondence*, III, 170.

38. Swift, 'Stella's Birthday. March 13. 1726/7', *Poems*, II, 763–6.

39. Hugh Boulter to William Wake, Archbishop of Canterbury, 24 February 1728, in *Letters Written by His Excellency Hugh Boulter, D.D.* (2 vols., Dublin, 1770), I, 178.

40. Swift, *Intelligencer* (No. 19), *PW*, 56.

41. See Claude Rawson's excellent and wide-ranging *God, Gulliver and Genocide: Barbarism and the European Imagination 1492–1945* (Oxford, 2001), 81–4. Rawson's entire section on the early-modern context is profoundly relevant to any student of Swift. As one such student my own sense is that, to borrow a quotation used by Herbert Davis, Swift's character contained the 'bundle of Inconsistencies' Swift recognized in himself as in any thinking person (introduction, *PW*, XII, xlvii). Establishing a sense of his view of the 'native' Irish not only involves appreciating the fluidity of that term, but also the competing instincts in his mind. A deep suspicion of the Irish peasantry, a potential willingness to support even the worst clauses of the penal laws as a necessary last resort, would always vie with the almost irresistible empathy that he fought when confronted with the sight of human suffering. Swift's meaning, on this question, lies with the resolution or lack thereof that a reader finds in the contest Swift's writings exhibit between his aggressive and sympathetic tendencies – both of which are in places restrained, and in others set loose. Rawson's thinking and research on Swift's relationship with Ireland has recently been supplemented by his chapter 'Swift, Ireland and the Paradoxes of Ethnicity' in *Swift's Angers* (Cambridge, 2014), 21–46, with extensive and still more detailed readings on the Irish tracts in the following chapter,

47–82. Other readers nevertheless have found much more evidence of Swift's fellow feeling for the native Catholic majority and opposition to the English colonial presence: see notably Carole Fabricant, *Swift's Landscape* (Baltimore, 1982), 78–9, in a compelling chapter on Swift's 'Antipastoral Vision'.

42. This was especially the case in Ulster, where Protestants formed a majority, and which provided much of Swift's first-hand observation of the crisis during his stays with the Achesons in 1728–9. More generally, one should also consider the extent to which the north informed his view of rural Ireland – ever since his short year as a young priest near Belfast Lough in 1695–6. His letters from the south and west in the early 1720s clearly regard the terrain as almost foreign country. On the complex topic of the demography of the poor, see, as a starting point, Ian McBride's careful questioning of the standard equation of Catholic 'Irishness' with the worst of the island's poverty in his powerful book *Eighteenth-century Ireland: The Isle of Slaves* (Dublin, 2009), 131–5.

43. Ehrenpreis, III, 512.

44. ibid., 518.

45. Davis, introduction, *PW*, V; 'The Appendix' to Deane Swift, *Essay*, 2 (pagination recommences at the end of the main text).

46. Swift, 'A Letter to the Writer of *The Occasional Paper*', *PW*, V, 93–8.

47. Swift to Thomas Sheridan, 13 May 1727, *Correspondence*, III, 206–8.

48. Swift to Thomas Sheridan, 24 June 1727, *Correspondence*, III, 218–19.

49. Swift to Archbishop King, 18 May 1727, *Correspondence*, III, 210. King's purely official reply is on 212. Some doubt exists as to whether Swift actually sent the letter of the 18th, first printed by Deane Swift in 1768; Ehrenpreis, III, 535.

50. Swift to Thomas Sheridan, 12 August 1727, *Correspondence*, III, 228–9; Ehrenpreis, III, 537.

51. Swift to Mrs Howard, 17 August 1727, *Correspondence*, III, 232.

52. Mrs Howard to Swift, 18 August 1727, *Correspondence*, III, 232.

53. Swift to Mrs Howard, 19 August 1727, *Correspondence*, III, 232.

54. Swift, 'Character of Mrs Howard. Written in the Year 1727', *PW*, V, 215. The character was written in June (see Ehrenpreis, III, 590).

55. L'Abbé Desfontaines to Swift, 4 July 1727, *Correspondence*, III, 217.

56. Swift to Thomas Sheridan, 29 August and 2 September 1727, *Correspondence*, III, 234, 236.

57. Swift to John Worrall, 12 September 1727, *Correspondence*, III, 238.

58. George Bubb Dodington, later first Lord Melcumbe, introduction, *PW*, V, xxv.

59. Swift to Alexander Pope, 12 October 1727, *Correspondence*, III, 242 and n. 1; Pope and Gay identified Swift's point of departure by the inn from which the Chester coach set off.

60. Gay and Pope to Swift, 22 October 1727, *Correspondence*, III, 245.

61. 'Ridland' is a mysterious place; there seems to be no trace of it. 'Redland', however, features in some Cheshire addresses, notably a hotel in Chester itself. Geographically the most likely candidate for this stop on Swift's journey is Ruthin in north Wales, the county town of Denbighshire (the name of which partly derives from *rhudd*, Welsh for 'red'). A combination of irregular early-modern spellings and pronunciation and Swift's deficient hearing seems responsible for the ambiguity.

62. Daniel Defoe, *A Tour through the Whole Island of Great Britain*, Pat Rogers, ed. (Harmondsworth, 1971), 385.

63. Swift, 'Holyhead Journal', *PW*, V, 204.

64. ibid., 203.

65. Swift, *An Answer to a Paper, Called a Memorial of the Poor Inhabitants, Tradesmen and Labourers of the Kingdom of Ireland*, *PW*, XII, 20.

66. Swift to Pope, 6 March 1729, *Correspondence*, III, 312.

67. Swift, *Travels* (I.1), 19.

68. Voltaire, *Letters Concerning the English Nation* (Letter 22) (1733), 214–15. Voltaire described Swift primarily as a poet; but the charge of vulgarity Desfontaines feared would be laid against Gulliver was equally sustainable against a great deal of Swift's published verse.

69. Swift, 'Holyhead Journal', *PW*, V, 205.

70. John Wheldon to Swift, September 1727, and Swift to John Wheldon, 27 September 1727, *Correspondence*, III, 239–40. Swift mentions Wheldon's application in the 'Holyhead Journal', *PW*, V, 206.

71. Swift, 'Holyhead Journal', *PW*, V, 207.

72. ibid., 204.

73. idid., 206.

74. ibid., 207.

75. ibid., 204.

76. ibid., 205.

77. Deane Swift, *Essay*, 26.

78. Swift, 'Holyhead Journal', *PW*, V, 208.

79. ibid., 205–6.

80. ibid., 208. Evidently Swift showed the journal to Sheridan, who told Pope about it (see Pope's undated letter, *Correspondence*, III, 261).

81. Gay and Pope to Swift, 22 October 1727, *Correspondence*, III, 246.

82. Swift, 'Prayers for a Sick Person During Her Illness', *PW*, IX, 253–4.

83. Swift, 'On the Death of Mrs Johnson', *PW*, V, 228.

84. Swift to Gay and Pope, 23 November 1727, *Correspondence*, III, 250.

85. Swift to Benjamin Motte, 28 December 1727, *Correspondence*, III, 258.

86. Voltaire to Swift, 14 December 1727, *Correspondence*, III, 256.

87. Swift, 'Holyhead Journal', *PW*, V, 204.

88. Swift, 'On the Death of Mrs Johnson', *PW*, V, 230.

89. ibid., 229.

90. Quoted in Ehrenpreis, III, 571.

91. Boulter to Lord Carteret, 14 December 1728, in *Letters*, I, 215.
92. James Farewell, *The Irish Hudibras; or, Fingalian Prince* (1689), 32–3. The irony (like the verse) is crude but should be registered: Farewell is presenting one of the worst examples of housing in Ireland as a home fit for a hero.
93. Swift, *A Short View of the State of Ireland*, PW, XII, 10.
94. Swift, 'An Answer to Several Letters from Unknown Persons', PW, XII, 78.
95. Quoted in Ehrenpreis, III, 571.
96. Swift, 'An Answer to Several Letters from Unknown Persons', PW, XII, 77.
97. Swift, *Intelligencer* (No. 19), PW, XII, 55.
98. Swift, 'An Answer to Several Letters from Unknown Persons', PW, XII, 77.
99. Swift, *Intelligencer* (No. XIX), PW, XII, 55.
100. Swift, 'An Answer to Several Letters from Unknown Persons', PW, XII, 80.
101. Swift to Mrs Moore, 7 December 1727, *Correspondence*, III, 254.
102. Swift to Martha Blount, 29 February 1728, *Correspondence*, III, 269.
103. Swift, *Intelligencer* (No. 1), PW, XII, 29.
104. Swift to Lord Carteret, 17 April 1725, *Correspondence*, III, 58.
105. Ehrenpreis, III, 361.
106. Swift, 'The History of the Second Solomon', PW, V, 223.
107. Swift to the Earl of Oxford, 1 October 1725, *Correspondence*, III, 106.
108. Swift to Thomas Sheridan, 11 September 1725, *Correspondence*, III, 94.
109. The mix-up with Sheridan's chaise was evidently the outcome of a suggestion that Sheridan should join him at Market Hill and that they would return together (Swift to Sheridan, 2 August 1728, *Correspondence*, III, 296).
110. Swift, 'The History of the Second Solomon', PW, V, 223–5.
111. The word 'beauset' does not occur in the *OED* or *Webster's* but is fairly common in eighteenth- and nineteenth-century English (e.g. 'On receiving it [a key], he opened the beauset, took a silver waiter or salver out of it' in 'A Particular Account of a Singular Sleep-walker', *Weekly Magazine of Original Essays, Fugitive Pieces, and Interesting Intelligence*, Vol. II (Philadelphia, 1798), 250); The Thomas Nugent, *The Grand Tour; or, A Journey through the Netherlands, Germany, Italy and France* (2nd ed., 4 vols., 1756), describes a beauset laden with silver plate 'which takes up one intire side of the room' (II, 189). As Swift suggests here, lights were commonly placed within a beauset, reflecting on the plate displayed inside. Thus the beauset in Sheridan's property at Quilca was evidently a rickety piece of furniture with draughts whistling through chinks in its panelling, troubling the candles. The presence of the wind also indicates the ramshackle state of the house itself.

112. Swift, 'The Blunders, Deficiencies, Distresses, and Misfortunes of Quilca', *PW*, V, 219.
113. Swift, 'The History of the Second Solomon', *PW*, V, 223.
114. Swift, *Intelligencer* (Nos. 5 and 7), *PW*, XII, 41–4.
115. ibid., 44–5.
116. Swift, 'The History of the Second Solomon', *PW*, V, 223–4.
117. John Gay to Swift, 15 February 1728, *Correspondence*, III, 265.
118. Swift to Lord Carteret, 18 January 1728, *Correspondence*, III, 260.
119. David Nokes, 'John Gay ('*The Beggar's Opera*, and after')', *DNB*.
120. John Gay to Swift, 20 March 1728, *Correspondence*, III, 272.
121. Swift to Alexander Pope, 30 August 1716, *Correspondence*, III, 215.
122. Swift to John Gay, 28 March 1728, *Correspondence*, III, 276.
123. Swift, *Travels* (IV.6), 235.
124. Swift, *Intelligencer* (No. 3), *PW*, XII, 33–4.
125. Swift to John Gay, 28 March 1728, *Correspondence*, III, 276.
126. Alexander Pope to Swift, 1 January 1728, *Correspondence*, III, 261.
127. Pope, *The Dunciad Variorum*, in *The Poems of Alexander Pope*, John Butt, ed. (repr. 1968), 351, ll. 19–21.
128. See for example Swift, 'Holyhead Journal', 201.
129. Swift to Alexander Pope, 16 July 1728, *Correspondence*, III, 293.
130. Jonathan Smedley, *Gulliveriana; or, A Fourth Volume of Miscellanies* (1728), xvi.
131. ibid.
132. ibid., 8.
133. ibid., xxix.
134. Anonymous, *Some Memoirs of the Amours and Intrigues of a Certain Irish Dean* (1728), 3.
135. Swift, *Cadenus and Vanessa*, *Poems*, III, 712, ll. 818–23.
136. Smedley, *Gulliveriana*, xxix–xxx.
137. Swift, 'Dean Smedley Gone to Seek His Fortune', *Poems*, II, 455, ll. 15–16.
138. Quoted by Ehrenpreis, III, 601.
139. Swift to John Worrall, 31 August 1725, *Correspondence*, III, 92; see also Swift's letter to the same, 18 January 1729, III, 308 and n. It was common for printers' widows to carry on their business, and Swift evidently retained Mrs Harding as a trusted associate. Publishing his work was of course extremely lucrative by the standards of the trade.
140. William Flower to Swift, 18 March 1729, *Correspondence*, III, 318–19.
141. Swift, 'My Lady's Lamentation and Complaint against the Dean', *Poems*, III, 856, ll. 159–64.
142. Constantia Maxwell, *Country and Town in Ireland under the Georges* (Dundalk, 1949), 211–13.
143. Swift, 'On Cutting down the Old Thorn at Market Hill', *Poems*, III, 849, ll. 1–24.

144. Swift, 'My Lady's Lamentation and Complaint against the Dean, *Poems*, III, 853 and 855, ll. 51–2, 147–8.

145. ibid., 856–7, ll. 169–70, 183–4 and 187–202.

146. Swift, 'Lady Acheson Weary of the Dean', *Poems*, III, 861, ll. 38–9.

147. Swift to Thomas Sheridan, 2 August 1728, *Correspondence*, III, 296.

148. Ehrenpreis, III, 597; Francis Elrington Ball, *The Correspondence of Jonathan Swift* (6 vols., 1910–14), IV, 41 n. 2.

149. Swift to John Worrall, 28 September 1728, *Correspondence*, III, 301–2.

150. Sheridan, 'Ballyspellin', ll. 69–72, and Swift, 'An Answer to the Ballyspellin Ballad', ll. 7–12, *Poems*, II, 440. The 'grisette' is mentioned in l. 54.

151. Ehrenpreis, III, 598.

152. Swift, 'The History of the Second Solomon', *PW*, V, 225.

153. He wrote to Thomas Staunton from his 'deanry house' on 15 December 1728 (*Correspondence*, III, 306).

154. Swift to Alexander Pope, 13 February 1729, *Correspondence*, III, 311.

155. *Dublin Journal*, 627; Ehrenpreis, III, 627.

156. Smedley, *Gulliveriana*, 9.

157. *Dublin Intelligence*, 10 May 1729; Ehrenpreis, III, 619.

158. Maurice Craig, *Dublin 1660–1860* (Dublin, 1969), 124; Gilbert, *History of Dublin*, III, 72–3.

159. Swift to Alexander Pope, 11 August 1729, *Correspondence*, III, 341.

160. Swift, *A Modest Proposal*, *PW*, XII, 109–11.

161. Peter H. Wilson, *Europe's Tragedy: A New History of the Thirty Years War* (2009), 611.

162. Swift, 'An Answer to Several Letters from Unknown Persons', *PW*, XII, 80.

163. Swift, 'An Answer to Several Letters Sent Me from Unknown Hands', *PW*, XII, 89.

164. Conceivably Carolan was a guest of the family at Quilca; Swift mock-mournfully put 'no blind harpers!' on a list of absences awaiting Sheridan at his 'cabin' in his letter of 22 December 1722 (*Correspondence*, III, 441).

165. Swift, *The Description of an Irish Feast*, *Poems*, I, 245, ll. 37–44.

166. For a recent discussion of the *Description* see Joseph McMinn, *Jonathan Swift and the Arts* (Newark, Delaware, 2010), 46–8. McMinn treats the poem as an exception in the apartheid society of eighteenth-century Ireland. In a similar vein Carole Fabricant sees the poem exemplifying Swift's 'Irishness as a writer' in her essay 'Swift the Irishman' for Christopher Fox, ed., *The Cambridge Companion to Jonathan Swift* (Cambridge, 2003), 48–72 (63–4). Gregory A. Schirmer, however, detects condescension on Swift's part even in his choice of a 'thumping' dimeter that entirely ignores the rhythmic subtlety of the original, in *Out of What Began: A History of Irish Poetry in English* (Ithaca, New York, 1998), 15–16.

167. Swift, 'Verses Occasioned by the Sudden Drying Up of St Patrick's Well', *Poems*, II, 789–94.

168. For an overview of broader colonial policy on 'The Conversion of the Natives' in the period, see S. J. Connolly, *Religion, Law and Power: The Making of Protestant Ireland 1660–1760* (Oxford, 1992), 294–307.

169. Swift, *A Modest Proposal*, PW, XII, 112.

170. Swift, 'My Lady's Lamentation and Complaint against the Dean', *Poems*, III, 851, l. 8.

171. John Gay to Swift, 15 February 1728, *Correspondence*, III, 266. Gay mentioned Swift's habit with his knife in a later letter (9 November 1728; *Correspondence*, III, 357).

172. Swift describing his complaint to Pope, 12 October 1728, *Correspondence*, III, 242.

173. Swift, 'The Dean's Reasons for Not Building at Drapier's Hill', *Poems*, III, 901, ll. 65–8, 84–90.

174. Swift to Charles Ford, 9 December 1732, *Correspondence*, IV, 92.


## 12. INDECENCY AND INDIGNATION

1. Patrick Delany, *Some Observations upon Lord Orrery's Remarks on the Life and Writings of Dr Jonathan Swift* (Letter VII) (Dublin 1754), 54.

2. Swift, *Travels* (I.6), 51.

3. Swift, 'A Letter to the Archbishop of Dublin, Concerning the Weavers', *PW*, XII, 65.

4. Swift to Alexander Pope, 19 July 1725, *Correspondence*, III, 78.

5. Swift to Alexander Pope, 29 September 1725, *Correspondence*, III, 102.

6. Swift to James Stopford, 20 July 1726, *Correspondence*, III, 143, 144, 145.

7. Swift, *Considerations upon Two Bills*, PW, XII, 193.

8. Delany, *Observations* (Letter XI), 89.

9. Swift to Alexander Pope, 6 February 1729, *Correspondence*, III, 369. Ehrenpreis (III, 637) supports a later dating of this letter.

10. Gilbert, *History of Dublin*, II, 158.

11. Delany, *Observations* (Letter XIV), 124–5; Swift, *Poems*, I, 260–62.

12. While keeping his sister at a personal distance he was meticulous in paying her an annuity: see *Correspondence*, III, 511n.

13. Delany, *Observations* (Letter XIV), 122.

14. Laetitia Pilkington, *Memoirs* (3 vols., Dublin, 1748), I, 52. Swift described Mrs Barber as such to Pope, 6 February 1729, *Correspondence*, III, 369. On the date of this first encounter, see Ehrenpreis, III, 639.

15. e.g., Swift, 'The Lady's Dressing Room', l. 12, 'Strephon and Chloe', l. 22, *Poems*, II, 526, 584.

16. Pilkington, *Memoirs*, I, 52–3.

17. Delany, *Observations* (Letter XI), 90–91.

18. Swift to Thomas Sheridan, 27 March 1733, *Correspondence*, IV, 130.

19. Swift, 'To Betty the Grizette. Written in the Year 1730', *Poems*, II, 523, ll. 7–10.

20. Pilkington, *Memoirs*, I, 54.

21. ibid., 66.

22. See Charles Ford to Swift, 3 June 1736, and Swift's reply, 22 June 1736, *Correspondence*, IV, 498–501 and 504–6.

23. Ehrenpreis, III, 654.

24. Swift to Alexander Pope, 26 February 1730, *Correspondence*, III, 374–5.

25. Delany, *Observations* (Letter XVI), 149.

26. Swift, *A Vindication of His Excellency the Lord Carteret*, PW, XII, 157.

27. Swift, 'A Libel on D— D—. and a Certain Great Lord', *Poems*, II, 479–86.

28. Patrick Delany, 'An Epistle to His Excellency John, Lord Carteret', in Swift, *Poems*, II, 471–4.

29. Swift, 'An Epistle upon an Epistle from a Certain Doctor to a Certain Great Lord', *Poems*, II, 475–9, ll. 3–6.

30. Ehrenpreis, III, 656.

31. James Arbuckle, 'A Panegyric on then Reverend D—n S—t in Answer to the Libel on Dr D—y', in Swift, *Poems*, II, 491–9; on the uncertain date of the lampoon and the evidence establishing Arbuckle's authorship, see Ehrenpreis, III, 653, n. 4.

32. As Swift reported to Pope on 26 February 1730, *Correspondence*, III, 374. On the truth of this report, see Ehrenpreis, III, 653.

33. Maurice Craig, *Dublin 1660–1860* (Dublin, 1969), 22–3.

34. Swift, 'The Substance of What was Said by the Dean of St Patrick's to the Lord Mayor and Some of the Aldermen', PW, XII, 145–8.

35. Swift to Lord Bathurst, October 1730, *Correspondence*, III, 409.

36. Lord Bathurst to Swift, 9 September 1730, *Correspondence*, III, 407.

37. Delany, *Observations* (Letter XII), 99.

38. Illustrating this discrepancy is one of the documentary preoccupations of Irvin Ehrenpreis's vast biography: indeed it is the subject of the opening sentence of his first volume (I, 3).

39. Swift to Mrs Whiteway, 28 December 1730, *Correspondence*, III, 431.

40. *Dublin Intelligence*, 14 April 1731.

41. Swift to the Countess of Holderness, 22 May 1729, *Correspondence*, III, 336–7. The Countess was Frederica, daughter of Meinhardt, the third Duke of Schomberg, younger son of the revolution hero. Her first

marriage was to Robert Darcy, third Earl of Holderness; in 1724 she had married Benjamin Mildmay, later Earl FitzWalter.

42. 'Decanus et Capitulum maximopere etiam atque etiam petierunt, ut haeredes Ducis monumentum in memoriam parentis erigendum curarent . . . Plus potuit fama virtutis apud alienos quam sanguinis proximitas apud suos.' The monument can still be seen in the cathedral; the stone and lettering may have inspired Swift for the arrangements for his own nearby epitaph. The epitaph is placed lucidly in the context of Swift's other texts for inscriptions in the cathedral and also of his capacities for vengeance by Claude Rawson, *Swift's Angers* (Cambridge, 2014), 264; see also T. C. Barnard, 'St Patrick's Cathedral in the Age of Swift', in John Crawford and Raymond Gillespie, eds., *St Patrick's Cathedral: A History* (Dublin, 2009), 211-12

43. Swift, *Correspondence*, III, 336n., Williams quoting Lady Mary Wortley Montagu.

44. Swift to Alexander Pope, 20 April 1731, *Correspondence*, III, 457.

45. Swift to the Reverend Philip Chamberlain, 24 May 1731, *Correspondence*, III, 468-9.

46. Swift to Alexander Pope, 20 July 1731, *Correspondence*, III, 480.

47. For the counterfeit letter, obtained for Swift by Pope, see *Correspondence*, V, 259-60. Pope and the Countess of Suffolk (formerly Mrs Howard) vouched for Swift. Swift responded like a Brobdingnagian: to thank Pope or the Countess, he wrote to her on 26 October 1731, would be 'an injury . . . because to think me guilty would disgrace your understandings' (*Correspondence*, III, 499).

48. Kerry Houston, 'Reformation to the Roseingraves: Music 1550-1750', in Crawford and Gillespie, *St Patrick's Cathedral*, 252.

49. Swift, 'The Dean to Himself on St Cecilia's Day', *Poems*, II, 522, ll. 1-4. The poem, first published in 1765, may equally be connected with another major, if slightly less elaborate, celebration of the feast-day the previous year.

50. Swift, *Considerations upon Two Bills*, PW, XII, 194.

51. ibid., 191-2.

52. Swift, *Journal* (27 December 1712), II, 589.

53. Boulter to the Duke of Newcastle, 12 October 1725, in *Letters Written by His Excellency Hugh Boulter, D.D.* (2 vols., Dublin, 1770), I, 40.

54. Boulter to the Duke of Newcastle, 10 February 1726, in *Letters*, I, 51.

55. Swift, 'Advice to the Freemen of Dublin', *PW*, XIII, 80. Here (in 1733) Swift himself adopted the colonial manner: rather than stressing the autonomy of Ireland as the kingdom of a monarch based in England, he commends the original English for subduing the Irish nation to the English Crown.

56. Boulter to the Duke of Newcastle, 4 March 1725, in *Letters*, I, 12.

57. Boulter to Lord Carteret, 24 August 1727, in *Letters*, I, 154.

58. Boulter to the Duke of Newcastle, 31 August 1727, in *Letters*, I, 158.

59. Boulter to the Duke of Newcastle, 26 August 1727, in *Letters*, I, 157.

60. Swift, *An Answer to a Paper, Called a Memorial of the Poor Inhabitants, Tradesmen and Labourers of the Kingdom of Ireland*, PW, XII, 23–4.

61. See Boulter, *Letters*, I, 168–78 and *passim*.

62. Swift, 'Advice to the Freemen of Dublin', *PW*, XIII, 83.

63. ibid., 81–2.

64. Swift, *Queries Relating to the Sacramental Test*, PW, XII, 258–9.

65. Swift, *The Presbyterians' Plea of Merit, in Order to Take Off the Test*, PW, XII, 263.

66. Boulter to the Duke of Newcastle, 18 December 1733, in *Letters*, II, 86–7.

67. Swift, 'On the Words – Brother Protestants, and Fellow Christians', *Poems*, III, 811–12, ll. 3–6, 11–14, 29–32.

68. Swift to the Duke of Dorset, January 1734, *Correspondence*, IV, 219–21; Swift, 'On the Words – Brother Protestants, and Fellow Christians', *Poems*, III, 811, ll. 25–6.

69. *Dublin Journal*, 8 January 1734.

70. Swift [?], Appendix D, *PW*, V, 341–3. The declaration was surely prepared for these champions, if not by Swift himself then by one of his stalwarts.

71. Swift, 'The Yahoo's Overthrow', *Poems*, III, 816, ll. 51–4. Swift's conflict with Bettesworth did not rest here. In 1736 the Serjeant-at-Law was inflamed by another aside, and had two of Swift's printers – Waters (yet again) and Faulkner – thrown into prison. Swift reacted with some pithy lines 'On a Printer's being Sent to Newgate, by —' (*Poems*, III, 822–4 and introductory note on 822).

72. Swift, 'The Yahoo's Overthrow', *Poems*, III, 816, l. 4.

73. *Dublin Journal*, 21 April 1733.

74. Pilkington, *Memoirs*, I, 78–80.

75. ibid., 83.

76. ibid., 86.

77. Swift, 'Verses on the Death of Dr Swift', *Poems*, II, 555, ll. 47–52.

78. Pilkington, *Memoirs*, I, 88.

79. Swift to John Gay, 1 December 1731, *Correspondence*, III, 506.

80. Swift, 'Verses on the Death of Dr Swift', *Poems*, II, 553, ll. 7–8.

81. ibid., 555, ll. 67–70.

82. ibid., 556, ll. 83, 81, 89–92.

83. ibid., 557, ll. 115–16.

84. ibid., ll. 135–42.

85. ibid., 561, ll. 209–12.

86. ibid., 563, ll. 255–6. The inquirer, notably, is a country squire, unbrilliant, yet a representative of the landed interest Swift saw as the basis of the common good.

87. ibid., 565, ll. 311–12.
88. ibid., 568 and 570, ll. 396, 436.
89. ibid., 571, ll. 465–8.
90. ibid., 555, ll. 53–8.
91. Pilkington, *Memoirs*, I, 75, 130–32.
92. Esther Vanhomrigh to Swift, December 1714, *Correspondence*, II, 150–51.
93. Pilkington, *Memoirs*, I, 91.
94. Richard Rorty, *Contingency, Irony and Solidarity* (Cambridge, 1989); see especially, in this context, the chapter 'Private Irony and Liberal Hope', 73–95. A companion volume to Rorty's wonderful book might be Kundera's *Art of the Novel* (1988): I'm grateful to Miran Možina for showing me the connection. Perhaps the great paradox in Swift's psyche was his ability in fiction to appreciate the contingency of almost every aspect of human existence, long before the invention of anthropology, while resisting such a principle with all his strength in his social and political activities. To a more limited extent the same duality of mind was present in More and Milton. The Church could never be for Swift a 'contingent' (that is temporary, dependent, historically limited) institution. Yet an institution that was permanent and morally definitive was evidently the best solution he found, at a formative age, to the baffling relativity of all other things in life. His deep pessimism found an outlet in the expectation, expressed ultimately in his will, that the Church as he knew and desired it would eventually cease to be.
95. Swift, 'On the Bill for the Clergy's Residing on Their Livings', *PW*, XII, 181.
96. Swift to John Gay, 4 May 1732, *Correspondence*, IV, 15.
97. John Gay to Swift, 16 November 1732, *Correspondence*, IV, 86.
98. David Nokes attributed Gay's determination to ride from Amesbury to the home of Sir William Wyndham to goads from Swift (*John Gay: A Profession of Friendship* (Oxford, 1995), 521).
99. Alexander Pope and John Arbuthnot to Swift, 5 December 1732, *Correspondence*, IV, 87 and n. 2, giving Swift's endorsement of the letter 'on my dear Friend Mr Gay's death'.
100. John Arbuthnot to Swift, 13 January 1733, *Correspondence*, IV, 101.
101. Samuel Johnson, 'On Gay's Epitaph', in Donald Greene, ed., *Samuel Johnson: The Major Works* (Oxford, 2000), 51–3.
102. Swift to Alexander Pope, January 1733, *Correspondence*, IV, 103.
103. Swift to Lord Bathurst, October 1730, *Correspondence*, III, 411–12.
104. Swift to John Barber, 22 July 1732, *Correspondence*, IV, 47. He repeated his entreaty on 10 August (*Correspondence*, IV, 57).
105. John Barber to Swift, 6 February 1733, *Correspondence*, IV, 110. The Duchess of Buckingham and Normanby was Catherine Sheffield, illegitimate daughter of James II.

106. Arbuthnot to Swift, 13 January 1733, *Correspondence*, IV, 101.

107. Pilkington, *Memoirs*, I, 120–23.

108. ibid., 134. Swift (rather deceitfully) accused her of having made a copy of the poem, and used it as the basis of an unauthorized edition (see ibid., 133–7).

109. ibid., 119.

110. Notably when Mrs Pilkington wrote an impromptu poem in praise of a harpsichord player who excelled her husband on the keyboard (ibid., 116–17).

111. ibid., 123.

112. ibid., 158–9.

113. ibid., 161.

114. ibid., 159.

115. Swift to John Barber, 11 September and 14 December 1732, *Correspondence*, IV, 71 and 93.

116. Swift to John Barber, July 1733, *Correspondence*, IV, 175.

117. John Barber to Swift, 17 November 1733, *Correspondence*, IV, 208.

118. Pilkington, *Memoirs*, I, 124.

119. Swift, 'An Epistle to a Lady', *Poems*, II, 634, ll. 137–40.

120. ibid., ll. 155–66.

121. ibid., 637, ll. 245–6.

122. Swift, 'On Poetry: A Rapsody', *Poems*, II, 641, ll. 33–42.

123. Accepting her challenge to put her memory to the test, Swift picked a line from Act III, Scene 1, 'Put rancours in the Vessel of my Peace', and asked her to recite the rest of the speech. She did so perfectly: the line itself, though, is misprinted in her *Memoirs* (I, 135).

124. Swift, 'On Poetry: A Rapsody', *Poems*, II, 654–7.

125. ibid., 656, l. 463.

126. Ehrenpreis, III, 756. See Benjamin Motte to Swift, 31 July 1735, *Correspondence*, IV, 371.

127. Benjamin Motte to Swift, 31 July 1735, *Correspondence*, IV, 371–2.

128. Thomas Sheridan, *The Life of the Rev. Dr Jonathan Swift* (2nd edn, 1787), 239–40.

129. Pilkington, *Memoirs*, I, 168.

130. He had been appointed the Rector of St Mark's, Dublin, in July 1733: *Dublin Journal*, 10 July 1733.

131. Pilkington, *Memoirs*, I, 171–3.

132. Ehrenpreis, III, 356, explaining Roberts's function as a 'screen' for Motte.

133. Swift, 'A Beautiful Young Nymph Going to Bed', *Poems*, II, 581–2, ll. 9–22.

134. ibid., 583, ll. 69–70, 74.

135. Congreve, *The Way of the World* (3.1.144–8), *Complete Plays*, Herbert Davis, ed. (Chicago, 1967), 429.

136. Swift, 'Verses on the Death of Dr Swift', *Poems*, II, 572, ll. 467–8.

137. Sir Thomas Urquhart and Peter Motteux, trans., *The Complete Works of Doctor François Rabelais* (2 vols., 1927), I, 340–41.

138. Swift, 'Cassinus and Peter', *Poems*, II, 597, l. 118.

139. Swift, 'Strephon and Chloe', *Poems*, II, 584, ll. 11–14.

140. ibid., 593, ll. 307–14.

141. Swift, *Cadenus and Vanessa*, *Poems*, II, 711, ll. 781–4.

142. On the voyeuristic tendency here and more generally in Swift's poetic speakers and characters, see Louise K. Barnett, 'Voyeurism in Swift's Poetry', *Studies in the Literary Imagination*, 17, 1 (1984), 17–26.

143. Swift, 'The Lady's Dressing Room', *Poems*, II, 527, ll. 24, 45–6.

144. Swift, *Directions to Servants*, PW, XIII, 60.

145. Swift, 'The Lady's Dressing Room', *Poems*, II, 529, ll. 121–2.

146. Pilkington, *Memoirs*, III, 161. Louise Barnett points out how an experience with a 'dirty landlady' later convinced Pilkington (whose rooms Swift found very cleanly kept) that there was 'some realistic basis for the poem' (*Jonathan Swift in the Company of Women* (New York, 2007), 101).

147. Swift, *A Modest Defence of a Late Poem by an Unknown Author, Called 'The Lady's Dressing Room'*, PW, V, 338.

148. Swift, *A Vindication of His Excellency the Lord Carteret*, PW, XII, 160–62.

149. Viscount Bolingbroke to Swift, 12 April 1734, *Correspondence*, IV, 232.

150. Swift, *Journal* (24 August 1711), I, 339.

151. Swift, 'A Letter from Capt. Gulliver to His Cousin Sympson', *Travels* (I.8).

152. On the patterns of allusion in the 'Nymph' quarto, see the section 'Obscenity' in Ehrenpreis, III, 688–95; Peter J. Schakel, 'Swift's Remedy for Love: The Scatological Poems', *Papers on Language and Literature*, 14, 2 (1978), 147–52, and Schakel's *The Poetry of Jonathan Swift* (Madison, Wisconsin, 1978) (esp., on the 1734 quarto, 106–15); and, for a more recent argument, summarizing debate by women critics of Swift, see Barnett, *Jonathan Swift in the Company of Women*, 154–70.


## 13. THE LAST OF THE GOLD

1. Swift, 'On Cutting Down the Old Thorn at Market Hill', *Poems*, III, 850, l. 58.

2. Pope (and Viscount Bolingbroke) to Swift, 15 September 1734, and Bolingbroke to Swift, 27 June to 6 July 1734, *Correspondence*, IV, 253, 242–3. The lines Swift found offensive were in Pope's imitation of Horace, *Satires* II.ii (*Poems of Alexander Pope*, John Butt, ed. (repr. 1968), 624, ll. 161–4), published 1734. In his poem, Pope has Swift

tick him off for wasting money on his property that can benefit no heir or some posthumous purpose. Swift, who saw the lines before they were printed, had evasively communicated his bruised feelings to Pope on 1 May 1733, *Correspondence*, IV, 154.

3. John Arbuthnot to Swift, 13 January 1734, *Correspondence*, IV, 101n.

4. Swift to Alexander Pope, 1 May 1733, *Correspondence*, IV, 155.

5. Swift to Alexander Pope, 1 November 1734, *Correspondence*, IV, 263.

6. Swift to Mrs Whiteway, 15 May 1736, *Correspondence*, IV, 489.

7. Swift to Miss Hoadly, 4 June 1734, *Correspondence*, IV, 235.

8. Lawrence B. Smith, 'Charles Boyle, fourth Earl of Orrery', *DNB*.

9. Swift to Charles Ford, 9 December 1732, *Correspondence*, IV, 91.

10. Walter Scott, ed., *The Works of Jonathan Swift* (19 vols., 2nd edn, Edinburgh, 1824), XVIII, 130n.

11. Laetitia Pilkington, *Memoirs* (3 vols., Dublin, 1748), I, 81.

12. 'I declare that a corporeal false Step is worse than a thousand political ones,' he complained in writing to Gay on 4 May 1732; *Correspondence*, IV, 14.

13. Patrick Delany, *Some Observations upon Lord Orrery's Remarks on the Life and Writings of Dr Jonathan Swift* (Letter XIII) (Dublin, 1754), 119.

14. Swift to John Arbuthnot, November 1734, *Correspondence*, IV, 267–8.

15. Swift to Alexander Pope, 1 May 1733, *Correspondence*, IV, 154.

16. Swift to John Arbuthnot, November 1734, *Correspondence*, IV, 268.

17. Swift to the Earl of Oxford, 30 August 1734, *Correspondence*, IV, 249.

18. Pilkington, *Memoirs*, I, 81–2. For a contemporary view of Swift's charitable activities, see also (for example) Delany, *Observations* (Letter VI), 43–4.

19. 'The Substance of What was Said by the Dean of St Patrick's to the Lord Mayor and Some of the Aldermen', *PW*, XII, 147.

20. The Freudian 'anal retentive' is pathologically caught at a stage of development that maximizes a 'voluptuous feeling' in the act of defecating yet also obsessively regulates bowel movements. Elements of sadism and meanness are also traditionally part of this pathology, in which the libido remains centred on the anus rather than on the genitals: see (for starters) *Introductory Lectures on Psychoanalysis*, James Strachey, trans. (rev. edn, 1990), 123–46 and *passim*. A vigorous early Freudian response to Swift is Norman O. Brown, 'The Excremental Vision', in *Life against Death* (2nd edn, Middletown, Connecticut, 1989), 179–201. Swiftians have repeatedly returned to Brown's ideas, which offered a valuable way out of simply being appalled, the 'modern sensibility's' stock reaction to Swift: for one example of a nuanced development, see Frank Boyle, 'Gulliverian Narcissism', in *Swift as Nemesis: Modernity and Its Satirist* (Stanford, California, 2000), 26–51. Ehrenpreis's character analyses of Swift are often Freudian (his assessment of Swift's fear of physical contact with women (III, 690) is

movingly persuasive). For a manageable starting point in a very large critical bibliography on specific works, see Thomas B. Gilmore, Jr, 'Freud and Swift: A Psychological Reading of "Strephon and Chloe" ', *Papers on Language and Literature*, 14, 2 (1978), 147–52. A key idea to hold in mind amid the psychoanalytical detail is that Swift's writing expresses (unconscious) excitement and mirth about the very things it treats as disgusting (poo, detritus, (women's) unclean personal effects and belongings, physical deformity and affliction).

21. Swift, *An Examination of Certain Abuses, Corruptions and Enormities in the City of Dublin*, PW, XII, 220.

22. Swift, 'The Lady's Dressing Room', *Poems*, II, 527, ll. 59–68.

23. Swift, *Travels* (II.1, II.4 and II.5), 82, 101, 107–8. See Louise Barnett, *Jonathan Swift in the Company of Women* (New York, 2007), 111–13.

24. Viscount Bolingbroke to Swift, 18 July 1732, *Correspondence*, IV, 43.

25. Swift to Gay, 12 August 1732 and 3 October 1732, *Correspondence*, IV, 58, 73.

26. Reported solemnly by Faulkner in the *Dublin Journal*, 30 November 1734.

27. Swift to Charles Ford, 20 November 1733, *Correspondence*, IV, 753.

28. Swift to Lady Elizabeth Germain, 5 May 1735, *Correspondence*, IV, 328.

29. Swift to Alexander Pope, 6 March 1729, *Correspondence*, III, 314. See also Swift, 'Stella's Birthday. A Great Bottle of Wine, Long Buried, being that Day Dug Up', *Poems*, II, 740–43.

30. Delany, *Observations* (Letter XIV), 132–3, on the monument for 'Magee' and reactions to it.

31. Swift to Mary Pendarves, 22 February 1735, *Correspondence*, IV, 298. Swift's correspondent is Delany's future wife, a noted writer in her day. They married in 1743.

32. Swift to Lord Orrery, 17 July 1735, *Correspondence*, IV, 367.

33. Thomas Sheridan to Swift, 16 August 1734, *Correspondence*, IV, 246.

34. John Arbuthnot to Swift, 4 October 1734, and Swift to John Barber, 1 March 1735, *Correspondence*, IV, 256, 300.

35. Swift to Lady Elizabeth Germain, 5 May 1735, *Correspondence*, IV, 328.

36. Ehrenpreis, III, 754.

37. William King to Swift, 24 June 1737, *Correspondence*, V, 54. Ehrenpreis (III, 859) points out that the only source for this letter is Deane Swift himself; but whether or not it received a tweak from his editorial hand, the reference evidently satisfied Swift enough for him to recommend his cousin to Pope (who still had his suspicions about 'goers-between').

38. Swift to Alexander Pope, 3 September 1735, *Correspondence*, IV, 385.

39. Swift to Thomas Sheridan, 30 September 1735, *Correspondence*, IV, 398.

40. See Ehrenpreis, III, 822.

41. Thomas Sheridan, *The Life of the Rev. Dr Jonathan Swift* (2nd edn, 1787), 333-4.

42. See Ehrenpreis, III, 823-4.

43. Swift to Thomas Sheridan, 2 March 1735, *Correspondence*, IV, 466.

44. Swift to Martha Whiteway, 6 December 1735, *Correspondence*, IV, 446.

45. Swift (and Thomas Sheridan) to Martha Whiteway, 28 November 1735, *Correspondence*, IV, 442.

46. Emily Charlotte Boyle, Countess of Cork and Orrery, ed., *The Orrery Papers* (2 vols., 1903), I, 144.

47. Swift to Thomas Sheridan, 2 March 1733, *Correspondence*, IV, 466.

48. Swift to Martha Whiteway, 25 February 1736, *Correspondence*, IV, 464.

49. Thomas Sheridan to Swift, 29 February 1736, *Correspondence*, IV, 464.

50. Swift to Lord Orrery, 9 March 1736, *Correspondence*, IV, 467.

51. Quoted by Constantia Maxwell, *Country and Town in Ireland under the Georges* (Dundalk, 1949), 25.

52. Swift and Martha Whiteway to Thomas Sheridan, 24 April 1736, *Correspondence*, IV, 478-80.

53. Swift to Thomas Sheridan, 22 May 1736, *Correspondence*, IV, 492.

54. Swift, 'The Legion Club', *Poems*, III, 829, ll. 1-12.

55. ibid., 835, ll. 150-54.

56. Swift, *A Vindication of His Excellency the Lord Carteret*, PW, XII, 158.

57. Swift, *A Proposal for Giving Badges to the Beggars in All the Parishes of Dublin*, PW, XIII, 133, 135.

58. Swift to the Earl of Oxford, 30 August 1734, *Correspondence*, IV, 249.

59. Swift explained his reasoning to Sheridan in a letter of 15 May 1736, *Correspondence*, IV, 487. He also comments on the continuing saga surrounding 'The Legion Club'.

60. Ehrenpreis, III, 860; Francis Elrington Ball, *The Correspondence of Jonathan Swift* (6 vols., 1910-14), VI, 47, n. 3.

61. Ball, ed., *The Correspondence of Jonathan Swift*, VI, 206-7.

62. *Dublin Journal*, 3 December 1737.

63. Swift to Thomas Sheridan, 15 and 16 June 1735, protesting that 'I have just sate 2 hours and a half', and Lord Howth to Swift, 6 July 1735, *Correspondence*, IV, 352, 358.

64. Swift to John Barber, 9 March 1738, *Correspondence*, V, 95.

65. Swift to Benjamin Motte, 25 May 1736, *Correspondence*, IV, 493.

66. Swift to the Earl of Orrery, 11 June 1737, *Correspondence*, V, 43-4.

67. William King to Deane Swift, 25 April 1738, *Correspondence*, V, 107-8.

68. Swift to Alexander Pope, 12 June 1732, *Correspondence*, IV, 31.

69. Swift, *A Compleat Collection of Genteel and Ingenious Conversation*, *PW*, IV, 143.

70. Swift to John Gay and the Duchess of Queensberry, 28 August 1731, *Correspondence*, III, 493.

71. Many years earlier, at Windsor, Swift and Arbuthnot had tried arranging a hoax at the expense of Queen Anne's choice attendants: Swift, *Journal* (19 September 1711), I, 363.

72. Swift, 'An Introduction to the Following Treatise', *PW*, IV, 107.

73. Swift, *Travels* (III.5), 171–2.

74. Swift, 'An Introduction to the Following Treatise', *PW*, IV, 103.

75. Swift to Alexander Pope, 13 February 1729, *Correspondence*, III, 311.

76. Swift to John Gay and the Duchess of Queensberry, 28 August 1731, *Correspondence*, III, 493.

77. Swift, *Directions to Servants*, *PW*, XIII, 13.

78. ibid., 22, 50.

79. ibid., 27, 55.

80. Swift to George Faulkner, 4 December 1739, *Correspondence*, V, 172.

81. Orrery to Pope, quoted by Ehrenpreis, III, 850.

82. Swift to Alexander Pope, 10 May 1739, 'at a conjecture', *Correspondence*, IV, 151.

83. Swift to John Barber, 8 August 1738, *Correspondence*, IV, 118.

84. Thomas Sheridan to Swift, May 1736, *Correspondence*, IV, 495. On the final state of relations between Swift, Sheridan and Delany, see Ehrenpreis, III, 871–2; Delany, *Observations* (Letter I), 2–3; Sheridan, *The Life of the Rev. Dr Jonathan Swift*, 337–40.

## 14. SANCTUARY

1. *The Book of Common Prayer* [1662], Brian Cummings, ed. (Oxford, 2011), 452.

2. Maurice Craig, *Dublin 1660–1860* (Dublin, 1969), 96–7.

3. Craig, *Dublin 1660–1860*, 60. The Royal Hospital now gives a spacious home to the Irish Museum of Modern Art, while St Patrick's University Hospital still provides publicly available mental health care and Steevens' hospital is used by the Irish health service for administrative purposes.

4. Craig, *Dublin*, 139–40.

5. Swift, *A Short View of the State of Ireland*, *PW*, XII, 12, 9.

6. Swift, 'Verses on the Death of Dr Swift', *Poems*, II, 572, ll. 479–80.

7. Lord Bathurst to Swift, 29 March 1733, *Correspondence*, IV, 132.

8. Swift, 'Dr Swift's Will', *PW*, XIII.

9. For more detail on these arrangements see Ehrenpreis, III, 818–19, 878–9.

10. Gilbert, *History of Dublin*, I, 9–10.

11. Swift, 'A Letter to the Printer of *Some Thoughts on the Tillage of Ireland*', *PW*, XIII, 143.

12. Ehrenpreis, III, 880–81; Lawrence Dundas Campbell, *The Miscellaneous Works of Hugh Boyd, the Author of the Letters to Junius* (2 vols., 1800), I, 2–3; Swift, 'Dr Swift's Will', 155.

13. Paul V. Thompson and Dorothy Jay Thompson, eds., *The Account Books of Jonathan Swift* (London and Newark, Delaware, 1984), 297.

14. *Dublin Journal*, 22 January 1740.

15. Thompson and Thompson, *Account Books*, 293.

16. Martha Whiteway to Alexander Pope, 16 May 1740, Martha Whiteway and Swift to William Richardson, 13 May 1740, and William Pulteney to Swift, 3 June 1740, *Correspondence*, V, 185–7, 189–91, 187–89.

17. Swift to Martha Whiteway, 26 July 1740, *Correspondence*, V, 192.

18. Swift, 'Dr Swift's Will', *PW*, XIII, 149.

19. Swift to John Gay, 19 March 1730, and to Benjamin Motte, 25 October 1735, *Correspondence*, III, 380, and IV, 411; Ehrenpreis (III, 870) and Williams concur in believing the '15ll. Per Ann: in Surrey' went to Swift's sister.

20. Orrery to Pope, quoted by Ehrenpreis, III, 850.

21. Ehrenpreis, III, 910–11; Swift, *Correspondence*, V, 176, n. 1.

22. Swift to Martha Whiteway, 18 January 1740, *Correspondence*, V, 176.

23. Thompson and Thompson, *Account Books*, 291.

24. Martha Whiteway to the Earl of Orrery, 7 October 1740, *Correspondence*, V, 193.

25. The Earl of Orrery to Martha Whiteway, 24 December 1740, *Correspondence*, V, 196.

26. On Pope's artfulness in the culmination of the *Letters* project, see Ehrenpreis, III, 894–7 (and the entire chapter, 883–98, in which puzzles remain).

27. Ehrenpreis, III, 913; Swift, 'Dr Swift's Will', *PW*, XIII, 155.

28. Swift, *Correspondence*, V, 210 n. 2.

29. ibid., 266–8.

30. Swift to John Worrall, 31 December 1713, *Correspondence*, I, 427.

31. Kerry Houston, 'Reformation to the Roseingraves: Music 1550–1750', in John Crawford and Raymond Gillespie, eds., *St Patrick's Cathedral: A History* (Dublin, 2009), 242–3, and Raymond Gillespie, 'An Age of Modernization 1598–1690', in ibid., 182.

32. Swift, 'The Dean to Himself on St Cecilia's Day', *Poems*, II, 522.

33. Harry White, 'Handel in Dublin: A Note', *Eighteenth-century Ireland*, 2 (1987), 182–6; Harry White and Barra Boydell, eds., *The Encyclopaedia of Music in Ireland* (2 vols., Dublin, 2013), I, 573–4; Joseph McMinn, *Jonathan Swift and the Arts* (Newark, Delaware, 2010),

30–33. Ehrenpreis's analysis of the 'exhortation' (III, 912) typically preserves the ambiguity of the document itself.

34. The sources for what happened on the road from Clondalkin may be found in Francis Elrington Ball, *The Correspondence of Jonathan Swift* (6 vols., 1910–14), VI, 179–81; Swift, *Correspondence*, V, 209–12; and Maxwell B. Gold, 'The Brennan Affidavit', *The Times Literary Supplement*, 17 May 1934, 360.

35. Deane Swift to the Earl of Orrery, 19 December 1742, *Correspondence*, V, 211.

36. Brennan's reliability as a witness is meanwhile questionable: he was fond of a good story. He told another one, entirely specious, about a son of Swift and Esther Johnson (see Donald M. Berwick, *The Reputation of Jonathan Swift 1781–1882* (New York, 1965), 26).

37. Deane Swift to the Earl of Orrery, 19 December 1742, *Correspondence*, V, 211.

38. Ball, *The Correspondence of Jonathan Swift*, VI, 183–4.

39. Ehrenpreis, III, 916–17.

40. Mrs Whiteway to the Earl of Orrery, 22 November 1742, *Correspondence*, V, 207.

41. Ehrenpreis, III, 919.

42. David Hume, 'Of Civil Liberty' [1741], in *Essays and Treatises on Several Subjects* (2 vols., Edinburgh, 1825), I, 85.

43. Samuel Johnson, *Lives of the Most Eminent English Poets*, Roger Lonsdale, ed. (2 vols., Oxford, 2006), 406–8.

44. Deane Swift to the Earl of Orrery, 4 April 1744, *Correspondence*, V, 214–15.

45. William Monck Mason, *The History and Antiquities of the Collegiate and Cathedral Church of St Patrick, near Dublin* (Dublin, 1820), 412–13.

46. Ehrenpreis, III, 919.

47. William Makepeace Thackeray, *English Humorists of the Eighteenth Century,* J. W. Cunliffe and H. A. Watt, eds. (Chicago, 1911), 64.

48. John Boyle, Earl of Cork and Orrery, *Remarks on the Life and Writings of Dr Jonathan Swift* (1752), 321–5.

49. ibid., 203; the verses are printed in Swift, *Poems*, II, 609–10.

50. Patrick Delany, *Some Observations upon Lord Orrery's Remarks on the Life and Writings of Dr Jonathan Swift* (Letter X) (Dublin, 1754), 75.

51. Orrery, *Remarks*, 265.

52. ibid., 301.

53. ibid., 189.

54. Swift to Alexander Pope, 29 September 1725, *Correspondence*, III, 102.

55. See Robert Folkenflik, 'The Rupert Barber Portraits of Jonathan Swift', in Brian A. Connery, ed., *Representations of Swift* (Newark, Delaware, 2002), 117–49 (123).

56. Gilbert, *History of Dublin*, II, 32, 39–40, 52.

57. Delany, *Observations* (Letter XIII), 118.

58. ibid. (Letter XX), 197.

59. Swift, 'The Will of Dr Swift', *PW*, XIII, 152–3. Swift had purchased the 'Inheritance of the Tythes of the Parish of Effernock' and these were thus his private property to bestow as he saw fit.

60. See Delany, *Observations* (Letter IV), 28, on Swift's self-criticism as a preacher; (Letter XIV), 129, on his dedication to the cathedral choir; and (Letter XV), 140, on the training of preachers.

61. James Woodforde, *The Diary of a Country Parson*, selected passages, John Beresford, ed. (Oxford, 1935) (7 July 1774), 97.

62. Gilbert, *History of Dublin*, II, 27.

63. On Lyon's archival activities, see A. C. Elias, 'Swift's *Don Quixote* . . . John Lyon's "Materials for a Life of Dr Swift", 1765', *Swift Studies*, 13 (1998), 27–104, and also T. C. Barnard, 'St Patrick's Cathedral in the Age of Swift', in Crawford and Gillespie, *St Patrick's Cathedral*, 212–13.

64. Martha Whiteway to one of Swift's executors, 22 October 1745, *Correspondence*, V, 215.

65. Translated from Swift, 'The Will of Dr Swift', *PW*, XIII, 149. It is very difficult to catch the text's simultaneous notes of magnificent defiance, irony and clerical humility. The first is of course amplified very impressively by Yeats; for the more reserved undertone, see Clive Probyn's simple prose rendering at the end of his *DNB* entry on Swift.

66. On the meaning of *vindicator* in the Latin original, and a possible mistake in transcription, see Rawson, *Swift's Angers* (Cambridge, 2014), 262–4, in a compelling discussion of the epitaph's variants and ambiguities, and the other commentaries suggested earlier on p. 645, n. 25.

67. Esther Vanhomrigh to Swift, [?] 1719–20, *Correspondence*, II, 335.

68. Swift, 'On Poetry: A Rapsody', *Poems*, II, 641, l. 38.

69. Swift, *A Letter to the Whole People of Ireland*, PW, X, 63.

70. Swift to Alexander Pope, 20 April 1731, *Correspondence*, III, 456.

# Further Reading and Reference

*Place of publication is London unless stated otherwise.*

## EDITIONS OF SWIFT'S WORKS AND LETTERS

Ball, Francis Elrington, ed., *The Correspondence of Jonathan Swift*, 6 vols. (1910–14)

Davis, Herbert, general ed., *The Prose Works of Jonathan Swift*, 16 vols. (Oxford, 1939–74)

Ellis, Frank H., ed., *Swift vs Mainwaring: 'The Examiner' and 'The Medley'* (Oxford, 1985)

Faulkner, George, ed., *The Works of J. S., D.D., D.S.P.D.*, 20 vols. (extended and revised several times) (Dublin, 1735–68)

Freeman, A. Martin, ed., *Vanessa and Her Correspondence with Jonathan Swift* (1921)

Guthkelch, A. C., and David Nichol Smith, eds., *A Tale of a Tub*, 2nd edn (Oxford, 1958)

Hawkesworth, John, ed., *The Works of Jonathan Swift*, 6 vols. (quarto; 12 vols., octavo; reissued, extended and revised several times; for a period more widely used than Faulkner's generally more authoritative text) (Edinburgh, 1755–75)

—, and Deane Swift, eds., *Letters of Jonathan Swift*, 6 vols. (1768–9)

Higgins, Ian, Claude Rawson and David Womersley, general eds., *The Cambridge Edition of the Works of Jonathan Swift*, 17 vols. (Cambridge, 2008–), five volumes published to date

—, Claude Rawson and Paul Turner, eds., *Gulliver's Travels* (Oxford, 2005)

Partridge, Eric, ed., *Swift's Polite Conversation* (1963)

Pope, Alexander, and Jonathan Swift, *Miscellanies in Prose and Verse*, 3 vols. (1727)

Rogers, Pat, ed., *Complete Poems of Jonathan Swift* (Harmondsworth, 1983)

Scott, Sir Walter, *The Works of Jonathan Swift*, 2nd edn, 19 vols. (Edinburgh, 1824)

Smith, David Nichol, ed., *The Letters of Jonathan Swift to Charles Ford* (Oxford, 1935)

Williams, Sir Harold, *Journal to Stella*, 2 vols. (Oxford, 1948); subsequently reprinted as Vols. XV–XVI of Davis's edition of the *Prose Works*

—, *The Poems of Jonathan Swift*, 2nd edn, 3 vols. (Oxford, 1958)

—, and David Woolley, eds., *The Correspondence of Jonathan Swift*, 5 vols. (Oxford, 1965–72)

Woolley, David, ed., *The Correspondence of Jonathan Swift, D.D.* 4 vols. (Frankfurt, 1999–2007)

Woolley, James, ed., *Jonathan Swift and Thomas Sheridan: The Intelligencer* (Oxford, 1992)

## BIOGRAPHICAL WORKS ON SWIFT

Boyle, John, Earl of Cork and Orrery, *Remarks on the Life and Writings of Dr Jonathan Swift* (1752)

Craik, Sir Henry, *The Life of Jonathan Swift*, 2nd edn, 2 vols. (1894)

Delany, Patrick, *Some Observations upon Lord Orrery's Remarks on the Life and Writings of Dr Jonathan Swift* (Dublin, 1754)

Ehrenpreis, Irvin, *Swift: The Man, His Works, and the Age*, 3 vols. (1962–83)

Elias, A. C., Jr, *Swift at Moor Park: Problems in Biography and Criticism* (Philadelphia, 1982)

Forster, John, *The Life of Jonathan Swift* (1875)

Glendinning, Victoria, *Jonathan Swift: A Portrait* (1999)

Gwynn, Stephen, *The Life and Friendships of Dean Swift* (1933)

Hawkesworth, John, *An Account of the Life of Dr Swift*, in Hawkesworth, ed., *The Works of Jonathan Swift*, Vol. I, (Edinburgh, 1755)

Jackson, R. W., *Swift and His Circle* (Dublin, 1945)

Johnston, Denis, *In Search of Swift* (Dublin, 1959)

Lyon, John, 'Biographical Anecdotes of Dean Swift', in *A Supplement to Dr Swift's Works*, Vol. I (1779)

Middleton Murry, John, *Jonathan Swift: A Critical Biography* (1954)

Nokes, David, *Jonathan Swift, A Hypocrite Reversed: A Critical Biography* (Oxford, 1985)

Scott, Sir Walter, *Memoirs of Jonathan Swift*, in Scott, ed., *The Works of Jonathan Swift*, Vol. I, 2nd edn (Edinburgh, 1824)

Sheridan, Thomas, *The Life of the Rev. Dr Jonathan Swift*, 2nd edn (1787)

Stephen, Leslie, *Swift* (1882)

Swift, Deane, *An Essay upon the Life, Writings, and Character of Dr Jonathan Swift* (1755)

Wilde, Sir William, *The Closing Years of Dean Swift's Life* (Dublin, 1849)

## WORKS BY CONTEMPORARIES ASSOCIATED WITH SWIFT

Addison, Joseph, *Cato, A Tragedy, and Selected Essays*, eds. Christine Dunn Henderson and Mark E. Yellin (Indianapolis, 2004)

—, *Poetical Works*, ed. Charles Cowden Clarke (Edinburgh, 1859)

—, and Richard Steele, *The Tatler*, ed. Donald F. Bond, 2 vols. (Oxford, 1987)

—, and Richard Steele, *The Spectator*, ed. Donald F. Bond, 5 vols. (Oxford, 1965)

Burnet, Gilbert, Bishop of Salisbury, *Bishop Burnet's History of His Own Time*, ed. M. J. Routh, 6 vols. (Oxford, 1823)

Congreve, William, *Complete Plays*, ed. Herbert Davis (Chicago, 1967)

Gay, John, *Dramatic Works*, ed. John Fuller, 2 vols. (Oxford, 1983)

—, *Poetical Works*, ed. G. C. Faber (1926)

Kerby-Miller, Charles, ed., *Memoirs of the Extraordinary Life, Works, and Discoveries of Martinus Scriblerus* (Oxford, 1988)

King, William, Archbishop of Dublin, *Original Works*, 3 vols. (1776)

Parnell, Thomas, *Collected Poems*, eds. Claude Rawson and F. P. Lock (Newark, Delaware, 1989)

Philips, Ambrose, *The Poems*, ed. M. G. Segar (Oxford, 1936; repr. 1969)

Pope, Alexander, *The Poems: A One-volume Edition of the Twickenham Text*, ed. John Butt, rev. edn (1968)

—, *The Prose Works*, eds. Norman Ault and Rosemary Cowler, 2 vols. (New York, 1986)

Prior, Matthew, *The Literary Works*, eds. H. B. Wright and M. K. Spears, 2nd edn, 2 vols. (Oxford, 1971)

St John, Henry, Viscount Bolingbroke, *Political Writings*, ed. David Armitage (Cambridge, 1997)

Steele, Richard, *The Plays*, ed. Shirley Strum Kenny (Oxford, 1971)

Temple, Sir William, *Works*, 2 vols. (1740)

—, *Early Essays and Romances*, ed. G. C. Moore Smith (Oxford, 1930)

## MISCELLANEOUS BIOGRAPHICAL SOURCES

Addison, Joseph, *Letters*, ed. W. Graham (Oxford, 1941)

Aikin, Lucy, *The Life of Joseph Addison*, 2 vols. (1843)

Aitken, George A., *The Life of Richard Steele*, 2 vols. (1889)

—, *The Life and Works of John Arbuthnot* (Oxford, 1892)

Boyle, Emily Charlotte, Countess of Cork and Orrery, ed., *The Orrery Papers*, 2 vols. (1903)

Cartwright, J. J., ed., *The Wentworth Papers 1705–1739* (1883)

Cotton, Henry, *Fasti ecclesiae Hibernicae: The Succession of the Prelates and Members of the Cathedral Bodies of Ireland*, 4 vols. (Dublin, 1848–51)

Gay, John, *The Letters*, ed. C. F. Burgess (Oxford, 1966)

Johnson, Samuel, *The Lives of the Most Eminent English Poets*, ed. Roger Lonsdale, 4 vols. (Oxford, 2006)

LeFanu, William, *A Catalogue of Books Belonging to Dr Jonathan Swift* (Cambridge, 1988)

Macky, John, *Memoirs of the Secret Services . . .* (1733)

Oldmixon, John [?], *Memoirs of the Life of the Most Noble Thomas, Late Marquess of Wharton* (1715)

Osborne, Dorothy, *Letters to Sir William Temple*, ed. Kenneth Parker (Harmondsworth, 1987)

Pilkington, Laetitia, *Memoirs*, 3 vols. (Dublin, 1748)

Pope, Alexander, *Correspondence*, ed., George Sherburn, 5 vols. (Oxford, 1956)

Snyder, H. L., ed., *The Marlborough–Godolphin Correspondence*, 3 vols. (Oxford, 1975)

Spence, Joseph, *Observations, Anecdotes and Characters of Books and Men*, ed. James M. Osborn, 2 vols. (1966)

Steele, Sir Richard, *Correspondence*, ed. Rae Blanchard (Oxford, 1941)

Swift, Jonathan, *Miscellaneous and Autobiographical Pieces, Fragments and Marginalia*, ed. Herbert Davis (Vol. V of Davis's edition of Swift's *Prose Works*) (1962)

Thompson Paul V., and Dorothy Jay Thompson, eds., *The Account Books of Jonathan Swift* (London and Newark, Delaware, 1984)

Williams, Sir Harold, *Dean Swift's Library* (Cambridge, 1932)

## MODERN STUDIES OF CONTEMPORARIES
## ASSOCIATED WITH SWIFT

Baines, Paul, and Pat Rogers, *Edmund Curll, Bookseller* (Oxford, 2007)

Barnard, Toby, and Jane Fenlon, eds., *The Dukes of Ormonde 1610–1745* (Woodbridge, 2000)

Beattie, L. M., *John Arbuthnot: Mathematician and Satirist* (Cambridge, Massachusetts, 1935)

Bennett, G. V., *The Tory Crisis in Church and State 1688–1730: The Career of Francis Atterbury, Bishop of Rochester* (Oxford, 1975)

Biddle, Sheila, *Bolingbroke and Harley* (1975)

Churchill, Winston S., *Marlborough: His Life and Times*, rev. edn, 2 vols. (1947)

Dickinson, H. T., *Bolingbroke* (1970)

Dickinson, William Calvin, *Sidney Godolphin, Lord Treasurer, 1702–1710* (Lewiston, New York, 1990)

Green, David, *Sarah, Duchess of Marlborough* (1967)

Gregg, E., *Queen Anne* (1980)

Haley, K. H. D., *An English Diplomat in the Low Countries: Sir William Temple and John De Witt 1665–1672* (Oxford, 1986)

Hammond, B. S., *Pope and Bolingbroke: A Study of Friendship and Influence* (Columbia, Missouri, 1984)

Hill, Brian W., *Robert Harley: Speaker, Secretary of State and Premier Minister* (New Haven, 1988)

Hodges, J. C., *William Congreve, the Man: A Biography from New Sources* (1941)

Longe, Julia G., ed., *Martha, Lady Giffard: Her Life and Correspondence 1664–1722* (1911)

Mack, Maynard, *Alexander Pope: A Life* (New York, 1985)

O'Regan, Philip, *Archbishop William King of Dublin (1650–1729) and the Constitution in Church and State* (Dublin, 2000)

Petrie, Sir Charles, *Bolingbroke* (1937)

Plumb, J. H., *Sir Robert Walpole*, 2 vols. (1956–60)

Sherburn, George, *The Early Career of Alexander Pope* (Oxford, 1934)

Simms, J. G., *William Molyneux of Dublin 1656–1698*, ed. P. H. Kelly (Dublin, 1982)

Sundstrom, R. A., *Sidney Godolphin, Servant of the State* (Newark, Delaware, 1992)

Varey, Simon, *Henry St John, Viscount Bolingbroke* (Boston, 1984)

Winton, Calhoun, *Captain Steele: The Early Career of Richard Steele* (Baltimore, Maryland, 1964)

Woodbridge, Homer Edwards, *Sir William Temple: The Man and His Work* (New York, 1940)

## LITERARY BACKGROUND

Armstrong, Isobel, and Virginia Blaine, eds., *Women's Poetry in the Enlightenment: The Making of a Canon 1730–1820* (Basingstoke, 1998)

Battestin, Martin C., *The Providence of Wit: Aspects of Form in Augustan Literature and the Arts* (Oxford, 1974)

DePorte, Michael V., *Nightmares and Hobbyhorses: Swift, Sterne, and Augustan Ideas of Madness* (San Marino, California, 1974)

Donaldson, Ian, 'The Satirists' London', *Essays in Criticism*, 25 (1975), 101–22

Downie, J. A., *To Settle the Succession of the State: Literature and Politics 1678–1750* (Basingstoke, 1994)

Ehrenpreis, Irvin, *Literary Meaning and Augustan Values* (Charlottesville, Virginia, 1974)

Elliott, Robert C., *The Power of Satire: Magic, Ritual, Art* (Princeton, New Jersey, 1960)

Engell, James, *Forming the Critical Mind: Dryden to Coleridge* (Cambridge, Mass., 1989)

Erskine-Hill, Howard, *The Augustan Idea in English Literature* (1983)

Goldgar, Bertrand A., *Walpole and the Wits: The Relation of Politics to Literature 1722–1742* (Lincoln, Nebraska, 1976)

Landa, Louis A., *Essays in Eighteenth-century Literature* (Princeton, New Jersey, 1980)

Paulson, Ronald, *The Fictions of Satire* (Baltimore, 1967)

Rawson, Claude, *Order from Confusion Sprung: Studies in Eighteenth-century Literature from Swift to Cowper* (1985)

—, *Satire and Sentiment 1660–1830* (Cambridge, 1994)

Rogers, Pat, *Hacks and Dunces: Pope, Swift and Grub Street* (1980)

Speck, W. A., *Society and Literature in England 1700–1760* (Dublin, 1983)

## SOCIAL, CULTURAL AND POLITICAL BACKGROUND

Black, Jeremy, and Jeremy Gregory, eds., *Culture, Politics and Society in Britain 1660–1800* (Manchester, 1991)

Blanning, Tim, *The Pursuit of Glory: Europe 1648–1815* (2007)

Connolly, S. J., *Religion, Law and Power: The Making of Protestant Ireland 1660–1760* (Oxford, 1992)

Craig, Maurice, *Dublin 1660–1860* (Dublin, 1969)

Crawford, John, and Raymond Gillespie, eds., *St Patrick's Cathedral: A History* (Dublin, 2009)

Cruickshanks, Eveline, and Jeremy Black, eds., *The Jacobite Challenge* (Edinburgh, 1988)

Cullen, L. M., *An Economic History of Ireland since 1660*, 2nd edn (1993)

Dickinson, H. T., *Liberty and Property: Political Ideology in Eighteenth-century Britain* (1977)

Dickson, David, *New Foundations: Ireland 1660–1800* (Dublin, 1987)

Dickson, P. G. M., *The Financial Revolution in England: A Study in the Development of Public Credit 1688–1756* (1967)

Doherty, Richard, *The Williamite War in Ireland 1688–1691* (Dublin, 1998)

Ford, Alan, *The Protestant Reformation in Ireland 1590–1641* (Dublin, 1997)

Gentles, Ian, *The English Revolution and the Wars of the Three Kingdoms 1638–1652* (2007)

Goodwin, A., 'Wood's Halfpence', *English Historical Review*, 51 (1936), 647–74

Harris, Tim, *Restoration: Charles II and His Kingdoms* (2005)

—, *Revolution: The Great Crisis of the British Monarchy 1685–1720* (2006)

Hay, Douglas, et al., *Albion's Fatal Tree: Crime and Society in Eighteenth-century England*, rev. edn (2011)

Herlihy, Kevin, ed., *The Politics of Irish Dissent 1650–1800* (Dublin, 1997)

Holmes, G. S., *British Politics in the Age of Anne*, rev. edn (1987)

Kelly, James, *Poynings' Law and the Making of Law in Ireland 1660–1800* (Dublin, 2007)

McBride, Ian, *Eighteenth-century Ireland: The Isle of Slaves* (Dublin, 2009)

MacCulloch, Diarmaid, *Reformation: Europe's House Divided 1490–1700* (2003)

McLynn, Frank, *The Jacobites* (1985)

Milne, Kenneth, *Christ Church Cathedral, Dublin: A History* (Dublin, 2000)

Ó Siochrú, Micheál, *God's Executioner: Oliver Cromwell and the Conquest of Ireland* (2008)

Ohlmeyer, Jane H., ed., *Political Thought in Seventeenth-century Ireland* (Cambridge, 2000)

Phillips, Walter Alison, ed., *History of the Church of Ireland from the Earliest Times to the Present Day*, 3 vols. (1933–4)

Porter, Roy, *English Society in the Eighteenth Century* (1982)

Power, T. P., and Kevin Whelan, eds., *Endurance and Emergence: Catholics in Ireland in the Eighteenth Century* (Dublin, 1990)

Rose, Craig, *England in the 1690s: Revolution, Religion and War* (Oxford, 1999)

Roseveare, H., *The Financial Revolution 1660–1760* (1991)

Szechi, Daniel, *Jacobitism and Tory Politics 1710–1714* (Edinburgh, 1984)

Trevelyan, George Macaulay, *England under Queen Anne*, 3 vols. (1930–38)

York, N. L., *Neither Kingdom nor Nation: The Irish Quest for Constitutional Rights 1698–1800* (Washington, D.C., 1994)

## OTHER WORKS ON (OR INCLUDING DISCUSSION OF) SWIFT

Barnett, Louise, *Jonathan Swift in the Company of Women* (New York, 2007)

Boyle, Frank, *Swift as Nemesis: Modernity and Its Satirist* (Stanford, 2000)

Brown, Norman O., *Life against Death* (Middletown, Connecticut, 1989)

Carnochan, W. B., *Lemuel Gulliver's Mirror for Man* (Berkeley, California, 1968)

Connery, Brian A., ed., *Representations of Swift* (Newark, Delaware, 2002)

Cook, Richard I., *Jonathan Swift as a Tory Pamphleteer* (Seattle, 1967)

Craven, Kenneth, *Jonathan Swift and the Millennium of Madness* (Leiden, 1992)

Donoghue, Denis, *Jonathan Swift: A Critical Introduction* (Cambridge, 1969)

—, ed., *Swift Revisited* (Cork, 1968)

Douglas, Aileen, Patrick Kelly and Ian Campbell Ross, eds., *Locating Swift: Essays from Dublin on the 250th Anniversary of the Death of Jonathan Swift 1667–1745* (Dublin, 1998)

Downie, J. A., *Jonathan Swift, Political Writer* (1984)

Ehrenpreis, Irvin, *The Personality of Jonathan Swift* (1958)

Erskine-Hill, Howard, *Swift: Gulliver's Travels* (Cambridge, 1993)

Ewald, William Bragg, *The Masks of Jonathan Swift* (Oxford, 1954)

Fauske, Christopher J., *Jonathan Swift and the Church of Ireland 1710–1724* (Dublin, 2002)

Ferguson, Oliver W., *Jonathan Swift and Ireland* (Urbana, Illinois, 1962)

Fox, Christopher, ed., *The Cambridge Companion to Jonathan Swift* (Cambridge, 2003)

Goldgar, Bertrand A., *The Curse of Party: Swift's Relations with Addison and Steele* (Lincoln, Nebraska, 1961)

Greenberg, Robert A., Gulliver's Travels: *An Annotated Text with Critical Essays* (New York, 1961)

Harth, Phillip, *Swift and Anglican Rationalism: The Religious Background of* A Tale of a Tub (Chicago, 1961)

Higgins, Ian, *Swift's Politics: A Study in Disaffection* (Cambridge, 1994)

James, Ioan, *Asperger's Syndrome and High Achievement: Some Very Remarkable People* (2006)

Jeffares, A. Norman, ed., *Fair Liberty Was All His Cry: A Tercentenary Tribute to Jonathan Swift* (1967)

Johnson, Maurice, *The Sin of Wit: Jonathan Swift as a Poet* (Syracuse, New York, 1950)

Landa, Louis A., *Swift and the Church of Ireland* (Oxford, 1954)

Le Brocquy, Sybil, *Cadenus: A Reassessment in the Light of New Evidence of the Relationships between Swift, Stella and Vanessa*, rev. edn (Dublin and London, 1967)

—, *Swift's Most Valuable Friend* (Dublin, 1968)

Levine, Joseph M., *The Battle of the Books: History and Literature in the Augustan Age* (Ithaca, New York, 1991)

Lock, F. P., *The Politics of* Gulliver's Travels (Oxford, 1980)

—, *Swift's Tory Politics* (1983)

McMinn, Joseph, *Jonathan Swift and the Arts* (Newark, Delaware, 2010)

Mahony, Robert, *Jonathan Swift: The Irish Identity* (New Haven, 1995)

Miller, William Ian, *The Anatomy of Disgust* (Cambridge, Massachusetts, 1997)

Orwell, George, *Shooting an Elephant* (1950)

Paulson, Ronald, *Theme and Structure in Swift's* Tale of a Tub (New Haven, 1960)

Price, Martin, *Swift's Rhetorical Art: A Study in Structure and Meaning* (New Haven, 1953)

Quintana, Ricardo, *The Mind and Art of Jonathan Swift* (Gloucester, Massachusetts, 1936)

—, *Swift: An Introduction* (1962)

Rawson, Claude, *God, Gulliver, and Genocide: Barbarism and the European Imagination 1492–1945* (Oxford, 2001)

—, *Swift's Angers* (Cambridge, 2014)

Reilly, Patrick, *Jonathan Swift: the Brave Desponder* (Manchester, 1982)

Rosenheim, Edward W., *Swift and the Satirist's Art* (Chicago, 1963)

Schakel, Peter J., *The Poetry of Jonathan Swift: Allusion and the Development of a Poetic Style* (Madison, Wisconsin, 1978)

Sneidern, Maja-Lisa von, *Savage Indignation: Colonial Discourse from Milton to Swift* (Newark, Delaware, 2005)

Steele, Peter, *Jonathan Swift: Preacher and Jester* (Oxford, 1978)

Thackeray, William Makepeace, *The English Humorists of the Eighteenth Century* (1851)

Vickers, Brian, ed., *The World of Jonathan Swift: Essays for the Tercentenary* (Oxford, 1968)

Williams, Kathleen, *Jonathan Swift and the Age of Compromise* (Lawrence, Kansas, 1958)

## BIBLIOGRAPHICAL SOURCES

Berwick, Donald M., *The Reputation of Jonathan Swift 1781–1882* (New York, 1941; repr. 1975)

Landa, Louis A., and James Edward Tobin, *Jonathan Swift: A List of Critical Studies Published from 1895 to 1945* (New York, 1945; repr. 1975)

Rodino, Richard H., *Swift Studies 1965–1980: An Annotated Bibliography* (New York, 1984)

'A Bibliography of Critical Studies in the Ehrenpreis Centre for Swift Studies, Münster', updated in 2011, can be found online at http://www.uni-muenster.de/

Those interested in following the latest discussion and scholarship on Swift are encouraged to consult journals such as *Eighteenth-century Studies*, the official quarterly publication of the American Society for Eighteenth-century Studies, and *Swift Studies*, published annually by the Friends of the Ehrenpreis Centre for Swift Studies in Münster

# Acknowledgements

I would like to thank Mary Mount, my wonderful editor at Viking, who first suggested Swift as a subject almost ten years ago, and Toby Eady, my literary agent, friend and mentor. The project could not have gone ahead without the intervention of Jill Bialosky at Norton. I'm very thankful to her for her trust and great goodwill. In the closing stages I became profoundly grateful to Donna Poppy for the incredible care with which she checked facts and quotations and copy-edited the text, for the fog-dispelling human sense she used to challenge some of my interpretations and for the learning and wit she brought to the whole process. It goes without saying that all remaining errors, inaccuracies and short-comings are entirely mine. My thanks as well to all at Penguin and Norton who helped see the book into print, especially Isabel Wall and Keith Taylor. The index was prepared by Douglas Matthews.

I've been helped by members of staff, and often fellow visitors and readers, at many libraries, museums and monuments around Britain and Ireland – at more obvious ports of call such as Cambridge University Library, the British Museum and the Victoria and Albert Museum, but also in local libraries, archives, manor houses and churches. More often than not, these were fleeting encounters, but insight can often survive even a moment of awkwardness – as with one elderly gentleman who struck up a conversation one day in the Cambridge UL, and kindly told me a great deal about engraving in the early 1700s. However he stalked off, understandably peeved, when we established that I was not, as he'd thought, a librarian, and so couldn't aid his search for one particular framed print.

As with all studies of Swift written today, this one is hugely indebted to the scholarship of three centuries, in particular to the lifetimes of work by Francis Elrington Ball, Herbert Davis, Louis A. Landa, Pat Rogers and Sir Harold Williams, David Woolley, among Swift's foremost editors, and to the biographical research of John Forster, Sir Henry Craik and, perhaps above all, Irvin Ehrenpreis. Victoria Glendinning's beautiful *Portrait* of Swift is superlative in dealing with among other things the personalities of Vanessa and Stella. Leo Damrosch's recent biography brought out Swift's urbanity and underlying gentleness, and offered a stimulating challenge to many of Ehrenpreis's findings and assertions: I only regret that my attempt to write about Swift was at such a late stage when I read Professor Damrosch's book. By the same principle Ehrenpreis's account of Swift's life and work will always need balancing against those of Louise Barnett, Pat Rogers, Ian Higgins, David Nokes, Clive Probyn, Ricardo Quintana and Claude Rawson, to name just a few of the most illuminating and illustrious of Swiftians. All these writers and many others have guided me, and I hope my notes and suggestions for further reading do at least some justice to the debt I owe them. I have tended to use the texts of Davis and Williams as standard reference points for readers seeking to consult specific passages, for the simple reason that their volumes still seem to be the most widely available, and the lasting value of the scholarship behind them is surely indisputable. This is by no means to deny, though, how the work of these editors has been enriched and refined by, for example, the experts preparing the ongoing new Cambridge edition of Swift's works or by Woolley's new volumes of the letters. New editions of the poems, of the *Travels* and *A Tale of a Tub* continue to reflect the changing constitution of Swift's readership, and journals abound with more insights than a single life would probably be long enough to synthesize. More is understood now about the 'spectrum' of Asperger's syndrome, elements of which Swift's personality seems to have displayed. A vast amount of work has been done on Swift's neglected women contemporaries, on early-modern society, politics and landscape; a new edition of the *Oxford Dictionary of National Biography* has enhanced the detail on famous and much lesser-known figures in Swift's lifetime. These sources and more have directed my steps at every turn.

As always, I felt the constant influence of excellent teachers. Many problems were eased by comments remembered from tutorials with John Fuller, Susan Hitch, David Norbrook and Frank Romany. I approached Swift via the late Tudor and earlier Stuart periods, and have thus felt the advantage throughout of being supervised and advised as a postgraduate student by Gavin Alexander, Colin Burrow and John Kerrigan. I was also guided by conversations on aspects of Swift's period, some many years ago, with Christopher Burlinson, David Colclough, Freya Johnston, Richard Lodge, Raphael Lyne and Nick Seddon. I was extremely lucky to meet William Ian Miller and to hear him discuss Swift in a lecture on his book *The Anatomy of Disgust*, here in

Ljubljana; this really broadened my view of the social and psychological aspects of the Dean's approach to revulsion. On techniques of writing biography and history, I learned a great deal in a very short time some years ago through talks with Anna Beer, Dominic Hibberd, Simon Schama and John Worthen. Going right back, I must also say that the understanding of British history I gained from David Dunton and Alan Monger, my two A-level teachers, established by their humour, learning and practicality, is still foundational for me.

Many friends have tolerantly listened to or read through stories and arguments from the book, discussed Swift's character, work and time with me and contributed either their specialist knowledge or common sense or both: I send my thanks to Matej Accetto, Noah Charney, Oliver Currie, Jožica Demšar, Matjaž Jager, Iggy McGovern, Richard Major, Miran Možina, Aleš Novak, Dan O'Brien, Martina Ožbot, Miha Pintarič, Renata Salecl and Katja Škrubej.

Research and writing has had to go on alongside my job as a schoolteacher here in Slovenia, and quite often extra copy-editing and translating work. Many people were supportive and patient, especially colleagues at Bežigrad Gimnazija and International School, as I tried to strike a balance.

There is no way of footnoting affection or moral support. But here I can at least record how Christopher Burlinson and Patricia Boulhosa, the Mountford family, Nicky and Christopher Padfield, Steve White and Anne Considine, Tanja Gostinčar and Jure Smole, Borut Šantej and Barbara Vrečko, and my brother Daniel Stubbs and his wife Isobel Ramsay have all been wonderfully kind over the years with their welcome and hospitality. For their backup I cannot fail to mention my parents, Mary and Christopher Stubbs, my sister Ciara and her husband Paul Ferrier, my (other) brother Conal, and my parents-in-law Rajko Šugman and Elizabeta Šugman Kancler. My great friend Robert Macfarlane has helped me in a combination of almost all the ways I have tried to acknowledge in others here – inspiring, advising, encouraging.

I was born in England, but on both sides my family comes from Ireland. I spent a lot of time there when I was younger. Knowing a country from the 1980s on is obviously not automatically an aid to understanding it in the seventeenth and eighteenth centuries; but prior acquaintance and a sense of attachment have helped me, I think. In this personal context I am especially grateful to my excellent aunt and uncle, Denise and Robin Gallagher, for always making me at home. Robin was brilliantly kind in driving and accompanying me to Swift's haunts in Dublin and beyond, helped me to make sense of many locations, and turned the journeys into great fun.

Above all, my thanks go to the three people who live with me, who have tolerated my absence, absent-mindedness and often lack of good humour during these years with Swift, and at the same time given me all that is best in life: Katja, Lana and Martin.

*Ljubljana, July 2016*

# Index